The Random House Basic Dictionary

Spanish-English
English-Spanish

From the Ballantine Reference Library
Published by Ballantine Books:

NEW WORDS DICTIONARY
Harold LeMay, Sid Lerner, and Marian Taylor

1000 MOST CHALLENGING WORDS
Norman W. Schur

1000 MOST IMPORTANT WORDS
Norman W. Schur

PRACTICAL ENGLISH: 1,000 MOST EFFECTIVE
WORDS
Norman W. Schur

THE RANDOM HOUSE BASIC DICTIONARY
French-English-French
Edited by Francesca L. V. Langbaum

THE RANDOM HOUSE BASIC DICTIONARY
German-English-German
Edited by Jenni Karding Moulton

THE RANDOM HOUSE BASIC DICTIONARY
Italian-English-Italian
Edited by Robert A. Hall, Jr.

THE RANDOM HOUSE BASIC DICTIONARY
Spanish-English-Spanish
Edited by Donald F. Sola

THE RANDOM HOUSE BASIC DICTIONARY OF
SYNONYMS AND ANTONYMS
Edited by Laurence Urdang

THE RANDOM HOUSE DICTIONARY
Edited by Jess Stein

TEST YOUR WORD POWER
Jerome B. Agel

THE WORD-A-DAY VOCABULARY BUILDER
Berger Evans

The Random House Basic Dictionary

Spanish-English
English-Spanish

Edited by
Donald F. Solá
Cornell University

Under the General Editorship of
Professor Frederick B. Agard
Cornell University

The Ballantine Reference Library
Ballantine Books · New York

Library of Congress Catalog Card Number: 67-20648

ISBN 0-345-33711-5

This edition published by arrangement with Random House, Inc.

Previously published as *The Spanish Vest Pocket Dictionary* and *The Random House Spanish Dictionary*.

Manufactured in the United States of America

First Ballantine Books Edition: August 1981
Twelfth Printing: August 1988

First Special Edition: August 1981
Second Special Edition: October 1981

Concise Pronunciation Guide

Spanish Letter	Pronunciation
a	Like English *a* in *father*.
b, v	At beginning of word group and after *m* or *n* like English *b*. Elsewhere, like English *v*, but pronounced with both lips instead of upper teeth and lower lip.
c	Before *e* or *i*, like English *th* in *thin* (in Northern Spain); like Spanish *s* (in Southern Spain and the Americas); elsewhere, like English *k* in *key*.
ch	Like English *ch* in *child*.
d	At beginning of word group and after *n* or *l*, like English *d*. Elsewhere, like English *th* in *either*.
e	Like English *e* in *bet*.
f	As in English.
g	Before *e* or *i*, the same as Spanish *j*. Elsewhere, like English *g* in *get*.
gu	Before *e* or *i*, like English *g* in *get*. Elsewhere, like English *gw* in *Gwynn*.
gü	Like English *gw* in *Gwynn*.
h	Silent.
i	Like English *i* in *machine*, but more clipped. Before or after another vowel, like English *y* (except when accented.)
j	Like English *h*, but more rasping.
k	Like English *k*.
l	Like English *l* in *like*, but with the tongue behind the upper front teeth.
ll	Like English *lli* in *million* (in Northern Spain); like Spanish *y* (in Southern Spain and the Americas).
m	As in English.
n	As in English.
ñ	Like English *ny* in *canyon*.
o	Approximately like English *o* in *vote*, but more clipped.
p	As in English.
qu	Like English *k*.
r	Not at all like American English *r*; a quick flap of the tongue-tip on the roof of the mouth.
rr	A strongly "rolled" or trilled version of Spanish *r*.
s	Like English *s* in *lease*.
t	As in English.
u	Like English *oo* in *boot*, but more clipped. Before *e* or after another vowel, like English *w* (except when accented).
v	See *b* above.
x	Like English *x*; although before consonants many speakers pronounce it like Spanish *s*; like Spanish *j* (in Mexican Indian words).
y	Approximately like English *y* in *yes*.
z	Like English *th* in *thin* (in Northern Spain); like English *s* in *lease* (in Southern Spain and the Americas).

Spanish Accentuation

In a number of words spoken stress is marked by an accent (´): *nación, país, médico, día*.

Words which are not so marked are, generally speaking, stressed on the next-to-the-last syllable if they end in a vowel, *n*, or *s*; and on the last syllable if they end in a consonant other than *n* or *s*.

Note: An accent is placed over some words to distinguish them from others having the same spelling and pronunciation but differing in meaning.

Irregular Verbs

Infinitive	Present	Future	Preterit	Past Part.
andar	ando	andaré	anduve	andado
caber	quepo	cabré	cupe	cabido
caer	caigo	caeré	caí	caído
conducir	conduzco	conduciré	conduje	conducido
dar	doy	daré	dí	dado
decir	digo	diré	dije	dicho
estar	estoy	estaré	estuve	estado
haber	he	habré	hube	habido
hacer	hago	haré	hice	hecho
ir	voy	iré	fuí	ido
jugar	juego	jugaré	jugué	jugado
morir	muero	moriré	morí	muerto
oír	oigo	oiré	oí	oído
poder	puedo	podré	pude	podido
poner	pongo	pondré	puse	puesto
querer	quiero	querré	quise	querido
saber	sé	sabré	supe	sabido
salir	salgo	saldré	salí	salido
ser	soy	seré	fuí	sido
tener	tengo	tendré	tuve	tenido
traer	traigo	traeré	traje	traído
valer	valgo	valdré	valí	valido
venir	vengo	vendré	vine	venido
ver	veo	veré	ví	visto

Abbreviations

a.	adjective
abbr.	abbreviation
adv.	adverb
aero.	aeronautical
agr.	agriculture
anat.	anatomy
art.	article
bot.	botany
chem.	chemistry
coll.	colloquial
com.	commercial
conj.	conjunction
dem.	demonstrative
f.	feminine
fin.	finance
geog.	geography
govt.	government
gram.	grammar
interj.	interjection
interrog.	interrogative
leg.	legal
m.	masculine
mech.	mechanics
med.	medicine
Mex.	Mexico
mus.	musical
n.	noun
naut.	nautical
pl.	plural
prep.	preposition
pron.	pronoun
punct.	punctuation
rel.	relative, religion
S.A.	Spanish American
v.	verb

Useful Phrases

Good day, Good morning.   Buenos días.
Good afternoon.   Buenas tardes.
Good night, Good evening.   Buenas noches.
Hello.   ¡Hola!
See you later.   Hasta luego.
Goodbye.   ¡Adiós!
How are you?   ¿Cómo está usted?
I am fine, thank you.   Estoy bien, gracias.
I am pleased to meet you.   Mucho gusto en conocerle.
Thank you very much.   Muchas gracias.
You're welcome.   De nada.
Please.   Por favor.
Good luck.   ¡Buena suerte!
To your health.   ¡Salud!

Please help me.   Ayúdeme, por favor.
I don't know.   No sé.
I don't understand.   No entiendo.
Do you understand?   ¿Entiende usted?
I don't speak Spanish.   No hablo español.
Do you speak English?   ¿Habla usted inglés?
How do you say...in Spanish?   ¿Cómo se dice...en español?
Speak slowly, please.   Hable despacio, por favor.
Please repeat.   Repita, por favor.
I don't like it.   No me gusta.

What is your name?   ¿Cómo se llama usted?
My name is...   Me llamo...
I am an American.   Soy norteamericano.

How is the weather?   ¿Qué tiempo hace?
It's cold (hot) today.   Hace frío (calor) hoy.
What time is it?   ¿Qué hora es?

How much is it?   ¿Cuánto es?
It is too much.   Es demasiado.
What do you wish?   ¿Qué desea usted?
I want to buy...   Quiero comprar...

I am hungry. Tengo hambre.

I am thirsty. Tengo sed.

Where is there a restaurant? ¿Dónde hay un restaurante?

The bill, please. La cuenta, por favor.

Where is there a hotel? ¿Donde hay un hotel?

Where is the post office? ¿Dónde está el correo?

Take me to… Lléveme a…

I believe I am ill. Creo que estoy enfermo.

Please call a doctor. Por favor, llame al médico.

I want to send a telegram. Quiero poner un telegrama.

As soon as possible. Cuanto antes.

Round trip Ida y vuelta.

Where can I change my money? ¿Dónde puedo cambiar mi dinero?

Can you accept my check? ¿Puede aceptar usted mi cheque?

What is the postage? ¿Cuánto es el franqueo?

Right away. ¡Pronto!

Help. ¡Socorro!

Come in. ¡Pase usted!

Pardon me. Dispense usted.

Stop. ¡Pare!

Look out. ¡Cuidado!

Hurry. ¡De prisa!

Go on. ¡Siga!

To (on, at) the right A la derecha.

To (on, at) the left A la izquierda.

Straight ahead Adelante.

Signs

Caution Precaución

Danger Peligro

Exit Salida

Entrance Entrada

Stop Alto

Closed Cerrado

Open Abierto

Slow Despacio

No smoking Prohibido fumar

No admittance Prohibida la entrada

One way una vía

Women Señoras, Mujeres, Damas

Men Señores, Hombres, Caballeros

Ladies' Room El cuarto de damas

Men's Room El servicio

Weights and Measures

The Spanish use the *Metric System* of weights and measures, which is a decimal system in which multiples are shown by the prefixes: deci- (one tenth); centi- (one hundredth); mili- (one thousandth); deca- (ten); hecto (hundred); kilo- (thousand).

1 centímetro	=	.3937 inches
1 metro	=	39.37 inches
1 kilómetro	=	.621 mile
1 centigramo	=	.1543 grain
1 gramo	=	15.432 grains
1 kilogramo	=	2.2046 pounds
1 tonelada	=	2,204 pounds
1 centilitro	=	.338 ounces
1 litro	=	1.0567 quart (liquid); .908 quart (dry)
1 kilolitro	=	264.18 gallons

Money

	Monetary Unit		Monetary Unit
Spain	peseta	**El Salvador**	colón
Argentina	peso	**Guatemala**	quetzal
Bolivia	peso	**Haiti**	gourde
Brazil	cruzeiro	**Honduras**	lempira
Chile	escudo	**Mexico**	peso
Colombia	peso	**Nicaragua**	córdoba
Costa Rica	colón	**Panama**	balboa
Cuba	peso	**Paraguay**	guaraní
Dominican		**Peru**	sol
Republic	peso	**Uruguay**	peso
Ecuador	sucre	**Venezuela**	bolívar

Numerals

Cardinal

1	uno, una	30	treinta
2	dos	31	treinta y uno
3	tres	32	treinta y dos
4	cuatro	40	cuarenta
5	cinco	50	cincuenta
6	seis	60	sesenta
7	siete	70	setenta
8	ocho	80	ochenta
9	nueve	90	noventa
10	diez	100	cien
11	once	101	ciento uno
12	doce	102	ciento dos
13	trece	200	doscientos, -as
14	catorce	300	trescientos, -as
15	quince	400	cuatrocientos, -as
16	dieciséis	500	quinientos, -as
17	diecisiete	600	seiscientos, -as
18	dieciocho	700	setecientos, -as
19	diecinueve	800	ochocientos, -as
20	veinte	900	novecientos, -as
21	veinte y uno (or veintiuno)	1,000	mil
		2,000	dos mil
22	veinte y dos (or veintidos)	100,000	cien mil
		1,000,000	un millón
		2,000,000	dos millones

Ordinal

1st	primero	6th	sexto
2nd	segundo	7th	séptimo
3rd	tercero	8th	octavo
4th	cuarto	9th	noveno
5th	quinto	10th	décimo

Days of the Week

Sunday	domingo
Monday	lunes
Tuesday	martes
Wednesday	miércoles
Thursday	jueves
Friday	viernes
Saturday	sábado

Months

January	enero	July	julio
February	febrero	August	agosto
March	marzo	September	septiembre
April	abril	October	octubre
May	mayo	November	noviembre
June	junio	December	diciembre

Spanish-English

A

a, *prep.* to; at.
abacero, *m.* grocer.
abad, *m.* abbot.
abadía, *f.* abbey.
abajo, *adv.* down; downstairs.
abandonar, *v.* abandon.
abanico, *m.* fan. —abanicar, *v.*
abaratar, *v.* cheapen.
abarcar, *v.* comprise; clasp.
abastecer, *v.* supply, provision.
abatido, *a.* dejected, despondent.
abatir, *v.* depress, dishearten.
abdicar, *v.* abdicate.
abdomen, *m.* abdomen.
abeja, *f.* bee.
abejarrón, *m.* bumblebee.
abertura, *f.* opening, aperture, slit.
abeto, *m.* fir.
abierto, *a.* open; overt.
abismo, *m.* abyss, chasm.
ablandar, *v.* soften.
abochornar, *v.* embarrass.
abogado, *m.* lawyer, attorney.
abolengo, *m.* ancestry.
abolición, *f.* abolition.
abolladura, *f.* dent. —abollar, *v.*
abominable, *a.* abominable.
abominar, *v.* abhor.
abonar, *v.* pay; fertilize.
abonarse, *v.* subscribe.
abono, *m.* fertilizer; subscription.
aborrecer, *v.* hate, loathe, abhor.
aborto, *m.* abortion.
abovedar, *v.* vault.
abrasar, *v.* burn.
abrazar, *v.* embrace; clasp.
abrazo, *m.* embrace.
abreviar, *v.* abbreviate, abridge, shorten.
abreviatura, *f.* abbreviation.
abrigar, *v.* harbor, shelter.
abrigarse, *v.* bundle up.
abrigo, *m.* overcoat; shelter; (*pl.*) wraps.
abril, *m.* April.
abrir, *v.* open; (med.) lance.
abrochar, *v.* clasp.
abrojo, *m.* thorn.
abrumar, *v.* overwhelm, crush, swamp.
absceso, *m.* abscess.
absolución, *f.* absolution; acquittal.
absoluto, *a.* absolute; downright.
absolver, *v.* absolve, pardon.
absorbente, *a.* absorbent.
absorber, *v.* absorb.
absorción, *f.* absorption.
abstenerse, *v.* abstain; refrain.
abstinencia, *f.* abstinence.
abstracción, *f.* abstraction.
abstraer, *v.* abstract.
absurdo, 1. *a.* absurd. 2. *m.* absurdity.

abuela, *f.* grandmother.
abuelo, *m.* grandfather; (*pl.*) grandparents.
abultado, *a.* bulky.
abultamiento, *m.* bulge. —abultar, *v.*
abundancia, *f.* abundance, plenty.
abundante, *a.* abundant, plentiful.
abundar, *v.* abound.
aburrido, *a.* boring, tedious.
aburrimiento, *m.* boredom.
aburrir, *v.* bore.
abusar, *v.* abuse, misuse.
abusivo, *a.* abusive.
abuso, *m.* abuse.
abyecto, *a.* abject, low.
acá, *adv.* here.
acabar, *v.* finish. **a. de . .**, to have just . . . .
academia, *f.* academy.
académico, *a.* academic.
acaecer, *v.* happen.
acanalar, *v.* groove.
acaparar, *v.* hoard; monopolize.
acariciar, *v.* caress, stroke.
acaso, *m.* chance. **por si a.**, just in case.
acceder, *v.* accede.
accesible, *a.* accessible.
acceso, *m.* access, approach.
accesorio, *m.* accessory.
accidental, *a.* accidental.
accidente, *m.* accident, wreck.
acción, *f.* action, act; (com.) share of stock.
acechar, *v.* ambush, spy on.
aceite, *m.* oil.
aceitoso, *a.* oily.
aceituna, *f.* olive.
aceleración, *f.* acceleration.
acelerar, *v.* accelerate, speed up.
acento, *m.* accent.
acentuar, *v.* accent, accentuate, stress.
acepillar, *v.* brush; plane (wood).
aceptable, *a.* acceptable.
aceptación, *f.* acceptance.
aceptar, *v.* accept.
acequia, *f.* ditch.
acera, *f.* sidewalk.
acerca de, *prep.* about, concerning.
acercar, *v.* bring near.
acercarse, *v.* approach, come near, go near.
acero, *m.* steel.
acertar, *v.* guess right. **a. en**, hit (a mark).
acertijo, *m.* puzzle, riddle.
acidez, *f.* acidity.
ácido, 1. *a.* sour. 2. *m.* acid.
aclamación, *f.* acclamation.
aclamar, *v.* acclaim.
aclarar, *v.* brighten; clarify, clear up.
acoger, *v.* welcome, receive.
acogida, *f.* welcome, reception.
acometer, *v.* attack.

acomodador, *m.* usher.
acomodar, *v.* accommodate, fix up.
acompañamiento, *m.* accompaniment; following.
acompañar, *v.* accompany.
acondicionar, *v.* condition.
aconsejable, *a.* advisable.
aconsejar, *v.* advise.
acontecer, *v.* happen.
acontecimiento, *m.* event, happening.
acorazado, *m.* battleship.
acordarse, *v.* remember, recollect.
acortar, *v.* shorten.
acosar, *v.* beset, harry.
acostar, *v.* lay down; put to bed.
acostarse, *v.* lie down; go to bed.
acostumbrado, *a.* accustomed, customary.
acostumbrar, *v.* accustom.
acrecentar, *v.* increase.
acreditar, *v.* accredit.
acreedor -ra, *n.* creditor.
acróbata, *m.* acrobat.
actitud, *f.* attitude.
actividad, *f.* activity.
activista, *a. & n.* activist.
activo, *a.* active.
acto, *m.* act.
actor, *m.* actor.
actriz, *f.* actress.
actual, *a.* present.
actuar, *v.* act.
acuarela, *f.* watercolor.
acuario, *m.* aquarium.
acuático, *a.* aquatic.
acuchillar, *v.* slash, knife.
acudir, *v.* rally; hasten; be present.
acuerdo, *m.* accord, agreement; settlement. **de a.**, in agreement, agreed.
acumulación, *f.* accumulation.
acumular, *v.* accumulate.
acuñar, *v.* coin, mint.
acupuntura, *f.* acupuncture.
acusación, *f.* accusation, charge.
acusado -da, *a. & n.* accused; defendant.
acusador -ra, *n.* accuser.
acusar, *v.* accuse; acknowledge.
acústica, *f.* acoustics.
achicar, *v.* diminish, dwarf; humble.
adaptación, *f.* adaptation.
adaptar, *v.* adapt.
adecuado, *a.* adequate.
adelantado, *a.* advanced; fast (clock).
adelantamiento, *m.* advancement, promotion.
adelantar, *v.* advance.
adelante, *adv.* ahead, forward, onward, on.
adelanto, *m.* advancement, progress, improvement.
adelgazar, *v.* make thin.

ademán, *m.* attitude; gesture.

además, *adv.* in addition, besides, also.

adentro, *adv.* in, inside.

adepto, *a.* adept.

aderezar, *v.* prepare; trim.

adherirse, *v.* adhere, stick.

adhesivo, *a.* adhesive.

adición, *f.* addition.

adicional, *a.* additional, extra.

adicto, *a. & m.* addicted; addict.

adiós, *m. & interj.* good-bye, farewell.

adivinar, *v.* guess.

adjetivo, *m.* adjective.

adjunto, *a.* enclosed.

administración, *f.* administration.

administrador, *m.* administrator.

administrar, *v.* administer; manage.

administrativo, *a.* administrative.

admirable, *a.* admirable.

admiración. *f.* admiration; wonder.

admirar, *v.* admire.

admisión, *f.* admission.

admitir, *v.* admit, acknowledge.

adolescencia, *f.* adolescence, youth.

adolescente, *a.* adolescent.

adónde, *adv.* where.

adondequiera, *conj.* wherever.

adopción, *f.* adoption.

adoptar, *v.* adopt.

adoración, *f.* worship, love, adoration. —**adorar,** *v.*

adormecer, *v.* drowse.

adornar, *v.* adorn; decorate.

adorno, *m.* adornment, trimming.

adquirir, *v.* acquire, obtain.

adquisición, *f.* acquisition, attainment.

aduana, *f.* custom house, customs.

aducto. *m.* input.

adujada, *f.* (naut.) coil of rope.

adulación, *f.* flattery.

adular, *v.* flatter.

adulterar, *v.* adulterate.

adulterio, *m.* adultery.

adulto, *a. & m.* adult.

adusto, *a.* gloomy; austere.

adverbio, *m.* adverb.

adversario, *m.* adversary.

adversidad, *f.* adversity.

adverso, *a.* adverse.

advertencia, *f.* warning.

advertir, *v.* warn; notice.

adyacente, *a.* adjacent.

aéreo, *a.* aerial; air.

aeromoza, *f.* stewardess, flight attendant.

aeroplano, *m.* airplane.

aeropuerto, *m.* airport.

aerosol, *m.* aerosol, spray.

afable, *a.* affable, pleasant.

afanarse, *v.* toil.

afear, *v.* deface, mar, deform.

afectación, *f.* affectation.

afectar, *v.* affect.

afecto, *m.* affection, attachment.

afeitada, *f.* shave. —**afeitarse,** *v.*

afeminado, *a.* effeminate.

afición, *f.* fondness, liking; hobby.

aficionado, *a.* fond.

aficionado -da, *n.* fan, devotee; amateur.

aficionarse a, *v.* become fond of.

afilado, *a.* sharp.

afilar, *v.* sharpen.

afiliación, *f.* affiliation.

afiliado, *m.* affiliate. —**afiliar,** *v.*

afinar, *v.* polish, tune up.

afinidad, *f.* relationship.

afirmación, *f.* affirmation, statement.

afirmar, *v.* affirm, assert.

afirmativa, *f.* affirmative. — **afirmativo,** *a.*

aflicción, *f.* affliction; sorrow, grief.

afligido, *a.* sorrowful, grieved.

afligir, *v.* grieve, distress.

aflojar, *v.* loosen.

afortunado, *a.* fortunate, successful, lucky.

afrenta, *f.* insult, outrage, affront. —**afrentar,** *v.*

afrentoso, *a.* shameful.

africano -na, *a. & n.* African.

afuera, *adv.* out, outside.

afueras, *f.pl.* suburbs.

agacharse, *v.* squat, crouch; cower.

agarrar, *v.* seize, grasp, clutch.

agarro, *m.* clutch, grasp.

agencia, *f.* agency.

agente, *m.* agent, representative.

ágil, *a.* agile, spry.

agitación, *f.* agitation, ferment.

agitado, *a.* agitated; excited.

agitador, *m.* agitator.

agitar, *v.* shake, agitate, excite.

agobiar, *v.* oppress, burden.

agosto, *m.* August.

agotamiento, *m.* exhaustion.

agotar, *v.* exhaust, use up, sap.

agradable, *a.* agreeable, pleasant.

agradar, *v.* please.

agradecer, *v.* thank; appreciate, be grateful for.

agradecido, *a.* grateful, thankful.

agradecimiento, *m.* gratitude, thanks.

agravar, *v.* aggravate, make worse.

agravio, *m.* wrong. —**agraviar,** *v.*

agregado, *a. & m.* aggregate.

agregar, *v.* add; gather.

agresión, *f.* aggression; (leg.) battery.

agresivo, *a.* aggressive.

agresor, *m.* aggressor.

agrícola, *a.* agricultural.

agricultor, *m.* farmer.

agricultura, *f.* agriculture, farming.

agrio, *a.* sour.

agrupar, *v.* group.

agua, *f.* water. —**aguar,** *v.*

aguacate, *m.* avocado, alligator pear.

aguantar, *v.* endure, stand, put up with.

aguardar, *v.* await; expect.

aguardiente, *m.* brandy.

agudo, *a.* sharp, keen, shrill, acute.

agüero, *m.* omen.

águila, *f.* eagle.

aguja, *f.* needle.

agujero, *m.* hole.

aguzar, *v.* sharpen.

ahí, *adv.* there.

ahogar, *v.* drown; choke; suffocate.

ahondar, *v.* deepen.

ahora, *adv.* now.

ahorcar, *v.* hang (execute).

ahorrar, *v.* save, save up; spare.

ahorros, *m.pl.* savings.

ahumar, *v.* smoke.

airado, *a.* angry, indignant.

aire, *m.* air. —**airear,** *v.*

aislamiento, *m.* isolation.

aislar, *v.* isolate.

ajedrez, *m.* chess.

ajeno, *a.* alien; someone else's.

ají, *m.* chili.

ajo, *m.* garlic.

ajustado, *a.* adjusted; trim; exact.

ajustar, *v.* adjust.

ajuste, *m.* adjustment, settlement.

al, *contr.* of a + el.

ala, *f.* wing; brim (of hat).

alabanza, *f.* praise. —**alabar,** *v.*

alabear, *v.* warp.

alambique, *m.* still.

alambre, *m.* wire. **a. de púas,** barbed wire.

alarde, *m.* boasting, ostentation.

alargar, *v.* lengthen; stretch out.

alarma, *f.* alarm. —**alarmar,** *v.*

alba, *f.* daybreak, dawn.

albanega, *f.* hair net.

albañil, *m.* bricklayer; mason.

albaricoque, *m.* apricot.

albergue, *m.* shelter. —**albergar,** *v.*

alborotar, *v.* disturb, make noise, brawl, riot.

alboroto, *m.* brawl, disturbance, din, tumult.

álbum, *m.* album.

alcachofa, *f.* artichoke.

alcalde, *m.* mayor.

alcance, *m.* reach; range; scope.

alcanfor, *m.* camphor.

alcanzar, *v.* reach, overtake, catch.

alcayata, *f.* spike.

alce, *m.* elk.

alcoba, *f.* bedroom; alcove.

alcohol, *m.* alcohol.

alcohólico, a. alcoholic.
aldaba, f. latch.
aldea, f. village.
alegación, f. allegation.
alegar, v. allege.
alegrar, v. make happy, brighten.
alegrarse, v. be glad.
alegre, a. gay, cheerful, merry.
alegría, f. gaiety, cheer.
alejarse, v. move away, off.
alemán -ana, a. & n. German.
Alemania, f. Germany.
alentar, v. cheer up, encourage.
alergía, f. allergy.
alerta, adv. on the alert.
aleve, alevoso, a. treacherous.
alfabeto, m. alphabet.
alfalfa, f. alfalfa.
alfarería, f. pottery.
alférez, m. (naval) ensign.
alfil, m. (chess) bishop.
alfiler, m. pin.
alfombra, f. carpet, rug.
alforja, f. knapsack; saddle-bag.
algarabía, f. jargon; din.
álgebra, f. algebra.
algo, pron. & adv. something, somewhat; anything.
algodón, m. cotton.
alguien, pron. somebody, someone; anybody, anyone.
algún -no -na, a. & pron. some; any.
alhaja, f. jewel.
aliado, a. & m. allied; ally. —aliar, v.
alianza, f. alliance.
alicates, m.pl. pliers.
aliento, m. breath. dar a., encourage.
aligerar, v. lighten.
alimentar, v. feed, nourish.
alimento, m. nourishment, food.
alinear, v. line up; (pol.) align.
alisar, v. smooth.
alistamiento, m. enlistment.
alistar, v. make ready, prime.
alistarse, v. get ready; (mil.) enlist.
aliviar, v. alleviate, relieve, ease.
alivio, m. relief.
alma, f. soul.
almacén, m. department store; storehouse.
almacenaje, m. storage.
almacenar, v. store.
almanaque, m. almanac.
almeja, f. clam.
almendra, f. almond.
almíbar, m. syrup.
almidón, m. starch. —almidonar, v.
almirante, m. admiral.
almohada, f. pillow.
almuerzo, m. lunch. —almorzar, v.
alojamiento, m. lodging, accommodations.
alojar, v. lodge, house.
alojarse, v. stay, room.

alquiler, m. rent. —alquilar, v.
alrededor, adv. around.
alrededores, m.pl. environs.
altanero, a. haughty.
altar, m. altar.
altavoz, m. loudspeaker.
alteración, f. alteration.
alterar, v. alter.
alternativa, f. alternative. —alternativo, a.
alterno, a. alternate. —alternar, v.
alteza, f. highness.
altivo, a. proud, haughty; lofty.
alto, 1. a. high, tall; loud. 2. m. height, story (house).
altura, f. height, altitude.
alud, m. avalanche.
aludir, v. allude.
alumbrado, m. lighting.
alumbrar, v. light.
aluminio, m. aluminum.
alumno -na, m. student, pupil.
alusión, f. allusion.
alza, f. rise; boost.
alzar, v. raise, lift.
allá, adv. there. más a., beyond, farther on.
allanar, v. flatten, smooth, plane.
allí, adv. there. por a., that way.
ama, f. housewife, mistress (of house). a. de llaves, housekeeper.
amable, a. kind; pleasant, sweet.
amalgamar, v. amalgamate.
amamantar, v. suckle, nurse.
amanecer, 1. m. dawn, daybreak. 2. v. dawn; awaken.
amante, m. lover.
amar, v. love.
amargo, a. bitter.
amargón, m. dandelion.
amargura, f. bitterness.
amarillo, a. yellow.
amarradero, m. mooring.
amarrar, v. hitch, moor, tie up.
amartillar, v. hammer; cock (a gun).
amasar, v. knead, mold.
ámbar, m. amber.
ambarino, a. amber.
ambición, f. ambition.
ambicionar, v. aspire to.
ambicioso, a. ambitious.
ambiente, m. environment, atmosphere.
ambigüedad, f. ambiguity.
ambiguo, a. ambiguous.
ambos, a. & pron. both.
ambulancia, f. ambulance.
amenaza, f. threat, menace.
amenazar, v. threaten, menace.
ameno, a. pleasant.
americana, f. suit coat.
americano -na, a. & n. American.
ametralladora, f. machine gun.
amigable, a. amicable, friendly.
amígdala, f. tonsil.
amigo -ga, n. friend.

amistad, f. friendship.
amistoso, a. friendly.
amniocéntesis, m. amniocentesis.
amo, m. master.
amonestación, f.pl. banns.
amonestar, v. admonish.
amoníaco, m. ammonia.
amontonar, v. amass, pile up.
amor, m. love. a. propio, self-esteem.
amorío, m. romance, love affair.
amoroso, a. amorous; loving.
amortecer, v. deaden.
amparar, v. aid, befriend; protect, shield.
amparo, m. protection.
ampliar, v. enlarge; elaborate.
amplificar, v. amplify.
amplio, a. ample, roomy.
ampolla, f. bubble; bulb; blister.
amputar, v. amputate.
amueblar, v. furnish.
analfabeto, a. & m. illiterate.
análisis, m. or f. analysis.
analizar, v. analyze.
analogía, f. analogy.
análogo, a. similar, analogous.
anarquía, f. anarchy.
anatomía, f. anatomy.
ancho, a. wide, broad.
anchoa, f. anchovy.
anchura, f. width, breadth.
anciano -na, a. & m. old, aged (person).
ancla, f. anchor. —anclar, v.
anclaje, m. anchorage.
andamio, m. scaffold.
andar, v. walk; move, go.
andén, m. (railroad) platform.
andrajoso, a. ragged, uneven.
anécdota, f. anecdote.
anegar, v. flood, drown.
anestesia, f. anesthetic.
anexar, v. annex.
anexión, f. annexation.
anfitrión, m. host.
ángel, m. angel.
angosto, a. narrow.
anguila, f. eel.
angular, a. angular.
ángulo, m. angle.
angustia, f. anguish, agony.
angustiar, v. distress.
anhelar, v. long for.
anidar, v. nest, nestle.
anillo, m. ring; circle.
animación, f. animation; bustle.
animado, a. animated, lively; animate.
animal, a. & m. animal.
ánimo, m. state of mind, spirits; courage.
aniquilar, v. annihilate, destroy.
aniversario, m. anniversary.
anoche, adv. last night.
anochecer, 1. m. twilight, nightfall. 2. v. get dark.
anónimo, a. anonymous.
anormal, a. abnormal.
anotación, f. annotation.

anotar, *v.* annotate.
ansia, ansiedad, *f.* anxiety.
ansioso, *a.* anxious.
antagonismo, *m.* antagonism.
antagonista, *m. & f.* antagonist, opponent.
anteayer, *adv.* day before yesterday.
antebrazo, *m.* forearm.
antecedente, *a. & m.* antecedent.
anteceder, *v.* precede.
antecesor, *m.* ancestor.
antemano, de a., in advance.
antena, *f.* antenna.
anteojos, *m.pl.* eyeglasses.
antepasado, *m.* ancestor, forefather.
anterior, *a.* previous, former.
antes, *adv.* before; formerly.
anticipación, *f.* anticipation.
anticipar, *v.* anticipate; advance.
anticuado, *a.* antiquated, obsolete.
antídoto, *m.* antidote.
antigüedad, *f.* antiquity; antique.
antiguo, *a.* former; old; ancient, antique.
antílope, *m.* antelope.
antinuclear, *a.* antinuclear.
antipatía, *f.* antipathy.
antipático, *a.* disagreeable, nasty.
antiséptico, *a. & m.* antiseptic.
antojarse, *v.* **se me antoja . . .** etc., I desire . . ., take a fancy to . . ., etc.
antojo, *m.* whim, fancy.
antorcha, *f.* torch.
antracita, *f.* anthracite.
anual, *a.* annual, yearly.
anudar, *v.* knot; tie.
anular, *v.* annul, void.
anunciar, *v.* announce; proclaim, advertise.
anuncio, *m.* announcement; advertisement.
añadir, *v.* add.
añil, *m.* bluing.
año, *m.* year.
apacible, *a.* peaceful, peaceable.
apaciguamiento, *m.* appeasement.
apaciguar, *v.* appease; placate.
apagado, *a.* dull.
apagar, *v.* extinguish, quench, put out.
aparador, *m.* buffet, cupboard.
aparato, *m.* apparatus; machine; appliance, set.
aparecer, *v.* appear, show up.
aparejo, *m.* rig. **—aparejar**, *v.*
aparentar, *v.* pretend; profess.
aparente, *a.* apparent.
apariencia, aparición, *f.* appearance.
apartado, 1. *a.* aloof; separate. **2.** *m.* post-office box.
apartamento, *m.* apartment. **a. en propiedad**, condominium.
apartar, *v.* separate; remove.
aparte, *adv.* apart; aside.

apartheid, *m.* apartheid.
apasionado, *a.* passionate.
apatía, *f.* apathy.
apearse, *v.* get off, alight.
apedrear, *v.* stone.
apelación, *f.* appeal. **—apelar**, *v.*
apellido, *m.* family name.
apenas, *adv.* scarcely, hardly.
apéndice, *m.* appendix.
apercibir, *v.* prepare, warn.
aperitivo, *m.* appetizer.
aperos, *m.pl.* implements.
apetecer, *v.* desire, have appetite for.
apetito, *m.* appetite.
ápice, *m.* apex.
apilar, *v.* stack.
apio, *m.* celery.
aplacar, *v.* appease; placate.
aplastar, *v.* crush, flatten.
aplaudir, *v.* applaud, cheer.
aplauso, *m.* applause.
aplazar, *v.* postpone, put off.
aplicable, *a.* applicable.
aplicado, *a.* industrious, diligent.
aplicar, *v.* apply.
aplomo, *m.* aplomb, poise.
apoderado, *m.* attorney.
apoderarse de, *v.* get hold of, seize.
apodo, *m.* nickname. **—apodar**, *v.*
apologético, *a.* apologetic.
apoplejía, *f.* apoplexy.
aposento, *m.* room, flat.
apostar, *v.* bet, wager.
apóstol, *m.* apostle.
apoyar, *v.* support, prop; lean.
apoyo, *m.* support; prop; aid; approval.
apreciable, *a.* appreciable.
apreciar, *v.* appreciate, prize.
aprecio, *m.* appreciation, regard.
apremio, *m.* pressure, compulsion.
aprender, *v.* learn.
aprendiz, *m.* apprentice.
aprensión, *f.* apprehension.
aprensivo, *a.* apprehensive.
apresurado, *a.* hasty, fast.
apresurar, *v.* hurry, speed up.
apretado, *a.* tight.
apretar, *v.* squeeze; press; tighten.
apretón, *m.* squeeze.
aprieto, *m.* plight, predicament.
aprobación, *f.* approbation, approval.
aprobar, *v.* approve.
apropiación, *f.* appropriation.
apropiado, *a.* appropriate. **—apropiar**, *v.*
aprovechar, *v.* profit by.
aprovecharse, *v.* take advantage.
aproximado, *a.* approximate.
aproximarse a, *v.* approach.
aptitud, *f.* aptitude.
apto, *a.* apt.
apuesta, *f.* bet, wager, stake.

apuntar, *v.* point, aim; prompt; write down.
apunte, *m.* annotation, note; promptings, cue.
apuñalar, *v.* stab.
apurar, *v.* hurry; worry.
apuro, *m.* predicament, scrape, trouble.
aquel, aquella, *dem. a.* that.
aquél, aquélla, *dem. pron.* that (one); the former.
aquello, *dem. pron.* that.
aquí, *adv.* here. **por a.**, this way.
aquietar, *v.* allay; lull, pacify.
ara, *f.* altar.
árabe, *a. & n.* Arab, Arabic.
arado, *m.* plow. **—arar**, *v.*
arándano, *m.* cranberry.
araña, *f.* spider. **a. de luces**, chandelier.
arbitración, *f.* arbitration.
arbitrador -ra, *n.* arbitrator.
arbitraje, *m.* arbitration.
arbitrar, *v.* arbitrate.
arbitrario, *a.* arbitrary.
árbitro, *m.* arbiter, umpire, referee.
árbol, *m.* tree; mast.
arbusto, *m.* bush, shrub.
arca, *f.* chest; ark.
arcada, *f.* arcade.
arcaico, *a.* archaic.
arce, *m.* maple.
arcilla, *f.* clay.
arco, *m.* arc; arch; (archer's) bow. **a. iris**, rainbow.
archipiélago, *m.* archipelago.
archivo, *m.* archive; file. **—archivar**, *v.*
arder, *v.* burn.
ardid, *m.* stratagem, cunning.
ardiente, *a.* ardent, burning, fiery.
ardilla, *f.* squirrel.
ardor, *m.* ardor, fervor.
arduo, *a.* arduous.
área, *f.* area.
arena, *f.* sand; arena.
arenoso, *a.* sandy.
arenque, *m.* herring.
arete, *n.* earring.
argentino -na, *a. & n.* Argentine.
argüir, *v.* dispute, argue.
árido, *a.* arid.
aristocracia, *f.* aristocracy.
aristócrata, *f.* aristocrat.
aristocrático, *a.* aristocratic.
aritmética, *f.* arithmetic.
arma, *f.* weapon, arm.
armadura, *f.* armor; reinforcement; framework.
armamento, *m.* armament.
armar, *v.* arm.
armario, *m.* cabinet, bureau, wardrobe.
armazón, *m.* framework, frame.
armería, *f.* armory.
armisticio, *m.* armistice.
armonía, *f.* harmony.
armonioso, *a.* harmonious.
armonizar, *v.* harmonize.
arnés, *m.* harness.

aroma, f. aroma, fragrance.
aromático, a. aromatic.
arpa, f. harp.
arquear, v. arch.
arquitecto, m. architect.
arquitectura, f. architecture.
arquitectural, a. architectural.
arrabal, m. suburb.
arraigar, v. take root, settle.
arrancar, v. pull out, tear out; start up.
arranque, m. dash, sudden start; fit of anger.
arrastrar, v. drag.
arrebatar, v. snatch, grab.
arrebato, m. sudden attack, fit of anger.
arrecife, m. reef.
arreglar, v. arrange; repair, fix; adjust, settle.
arreglárselas, v. manage, shift for oneself.
arreglo, m. arrangement, settlement.
arremeter, v. attack.
arrendar, v. rent.
arrepentimiento, m. repentance.
arrepentirse, v. repent.
arrestar, v. arrest.
arriba, adv. up; upstairs.
arriendo, m. lease.
arriero, m. muleteer.
arriesgar, v. risk.
arrimarse, v. lean.
arrodillarse, v. kneel.
arrogancia, f. arrogance.
arrogante, a. arrogant.
arrojar, v. throw, hurl; shed.
arrollar, v. roll, coil.
arroyo, m. brook; gully; gutter.
arroz, m. rice.
arruga, f. ridge; wrinkle.
arrugar, v. wrinkle, crumple.
arruinar, v. ruin, destroy, wreck.
arsenal, m. arsenal; armory.
arsénico, m. arsenic.
arte, m. (f. in pl.) art, craft; wiliness.
arteria, f. artery.
artesa, f. trough.
artesano, m. artisan, craftsman.
ártico, a. arctic.
articulación, f. articulation; joint.
articular, v. articulate.
artículo, m. article.
artífice, m. & f. artisan.
artificial, a. artificial.
artificio, m. artifice, device.
artificioso, a. affected.
artillería, f. artillery.
artista, m. & f. artist.
artístico, a. artistic.
arzobispo, m. archbishop.
as, m. ace.
asado, m. roast.
asaltador, m. assailant.
asaltar, v. assail, attack.
asalto, m. assault. —**asaltar,** v.
asamblea, f. assembly.

asar, v. roast; broil, cook (meat).
asaz, adv. enough; quite.
ascender, v. ascend, go up; amount.
ascenso, m. ascent.
ascensor, m. elevator.
ascensorista, m. & f. (elevator) operator.
asco, m. nausea; disgusting thing. **qué a.,** how disgusting.
aseado, a. tidy. —**asear,** v.
asediar, v. besiege.
asedio, m. siege.
asegurar, v. assure; secure.
asegurarse, v. make sure.
asemejarse a, v. resemble.
asentar, v. settle; seat.
asentimiento, m. assent. —**asentir,** v.
aseo, m. neatness, tidiness.
aserción, f. assertion.
aserrar, v. saw.
asesinar, v. assassinate; murder, slay.
asesinato, m. assassination, murder.
asesino -na, n. murderer, assassin.
aseveración, f. assertion.
aseverar, v. assert.
asfalto, m. asphalt.
así, adv. so, thus, this way, that way. **a como,** as well as. **a. que,** as soon as.
asiático -ca, a. & n. Asiatic.
asiduo, a. assiduous.
asiento, m. seat; chair; site.
asignar, v. assign; allot.
asilo, m. asylum, sanctuary.
asimilar, v. assimilate.
asir, v. grasp.
asistencia, f. attendance, presence.
asistir, v. be present, attend.
asno, m. donkey.
asociación, f. association.
asociado, m. associate, partner.
asociar, v. associate.
asolar, v. desolate; burn, parch.
asoleado, a. sunny.
asomar, v. appear, loom up, show up.
asombrar, v. astonish, amaze.
asombro, m. amazement, astonishment.
aspa, f. reel. —**aspar,** v.
aspecto, m. aspect.
aspereza, f. harshness.
áspero, a. rough, harsh.
aspiración, f. aspiration.
aspirador, m. vacuum cleaner.
aspirar, v. aspire.
aspirina, f. aspirin.
asqueroso, a. dirty, nasty, filthy.
asta, f. shaft.
asterisco, m. asterisk.
astilla, f. splinter, chip. —**astillar,** v.
astillero, m. dry dock.
astro, m. star.
astronauta, m. astronaut.

astronomía, f. astronomy.
astucia, f. cunning.
astuto, a. astute, sly, shrewd.
asumir, v. assume.
asunto, m. matter, affair, business; subject.
asustar, v. frighten, scare, startle.
atacar, v. attack, charge.
atajo, m. shortcut.
ataque, m. attack, charge; spell, stroke.
atar, v. tie, bind, fasten.
atareado, a. busy.
atascar, v. stall, stop, obstruct.
ataúd, m. casket, coffin.
atavío, m. dress; gear, equipment.
atemorizar, v. frighten.
atención, f. attention.
atender, v. heed; attend to, wait on.
atenerse a, v. count on, depend on.
atentado, m. crime, offense.
atento, a. attentive, courteous.
ateo, a. atheist.
aterrizar, v. land.
atesorar, v. hoard.
atestar, v. witness.
atestiguar, v. attest, testify.
atinar, v. hit upon.
atisbar, v. scrutinize, pry.
Atlántico, m. Atlantic.
atlántico, a. Atlantic.
atlas, m. atlas.
atleta, m. athlete.
atlético, a. athletic.
atletismo, m. athletics.
atmósfera, f. atmosphere.
atmosférico, a. atmospheric.
atómico, a. atomic.
átomo, m. atom.
atormentar, v. torment, plague.
atornillar, v. screw.
atracción, f. attraction.
atractivo, 1. a. attractive. **2.** m. attraction.
atraer, v. attract; lure.
atrapar, v. trap, catch.
atrás, adv. back; behind.
atrasado, a. belated; backward; slow (clock).
atrasar, v. delay, retard; be slow.
atraso, m. delay; backwardness; (pl.) arrears.
atravesar, v. cross.
atreverse, v. dare.
atrevido, a. daring, bold.
atrevimiento, m. boldness.
atribuir, v. attribute, ascribe.
atributo, m. attribute.
atrincherar, v. entrench.
atrocidad, f. atrocity, outrage.
atronar, v. deafen.
atropellar, v. trample; fell.
atroz, a. atrocious.
aturdir, v. daze, stun, bewilder.
audacia, f. audacity.
audaz, a. audacious, bold.
audible, a. audible.
audiovisual, a. audiovisual.
auditorio, m. audience.
aula, f. classroom, hall.

aullar, v. howl, bay.

aullido, m. howl.

aumentar, v. augment; increase, swell.

aun, aún, adv. still; even. **a. cuando**, even though, even if.

aunque, conj. although, though.

áureo, a. golden.

aureola, f. halo.

aurora, f. dawn.

ausencia, f. absence.

ausentarse, v. stay away.

ausente, a. absent.

auspicio, m. auspice.

austeridad, f. austerity.

austero, a. austere.

austriaco -ca, a. & n. Austrian.

auténtico, a. authentic.

auto, automóvil, m. auto, automobile.

autobús, m. bus.

automático, a. automatic.

autonomía, f. autonomy.

autor, m. author.

autoridad, f. authority.

autoritario, a. authoritative.

autorizar, v. authorize.

auxiliar, **1**. a. auxiliary. **2**. v. assist, aid.

auxilio, m. aid, assistance.

avaluar, v. evaluate, appraise.

avance, m. advance. —**avanzar**, v.

avaricia, f. avarice.

avariento, a. miserly, greedy.

avaro -ra, a. & m. miser; miserly.

ave, f. bird.

avena, f. oat.

avenida, f. avenue; flood.

avenirse, v. compromise; agree.

aventajar, v. surpass, get ahead of.

aventar, v. fan; scatter.

aventura, f. adventure.

aventurar, v. venture, risk, gamble.

aventurero, a. & m. adventurous; adventurer.

avergonzado, a. ashamed, abashed.

avergonzar, v. shame, abash.

avería, f. damage. —**averiar**, v.

averiguar, v. ascertain, find out.

aversión, f. aversion.

avestruz, m. ostrich.

aviación, f. aviation.

aviador -ra, n. aviator.

ávido, a. avid; eager.

avión, m. airplane.

avisar, v. notify, let know; warn, advise.

aviso, m. notice, announcement; advertisement; warning.

avispa, f. wasp.

avivar, v. enliven, revive.

aya, f. governess.

ayatola, m. ayatollah.

ayer, adv. yesterday.

ayuda, f. help, aid. —**ayudar**, v.

ayudante, a. assistant, helper; adjutant.

ayuno, m. fast. —**ayunar**, v.

ayuntamiento, m. city hall.

azada, azadón, m. hoe.

azafata, f. stewardess, flight attendant.

azar, m. hazard, chance. **al a.**, at random.

azotar, v. whip, flog; belabor.

azote, m. scourge, lash.

azúcar, m. sugar.

azul, a. blue.

azulado, a. azure.

azulejo, m. tile; bluebird.

B

baba, f. drivel, —**babear**, v.

babador, m. bib.

babucha, f. slipper.

bacalao, m. codfish.

bacía, f. washbasin.

bacterias, f.pl. bacteria.

bacteriología, f. bacteriology.

bachiller -ra, n. bachelor (degree).

bahía, f. bay.

bailador -ra, n. dancer.

bailar, v. dance.

bailarín -ina, n. dancer.

baile, m. dancing, dance.

baja, f. fall (in price); (mil.) casualty.

bajar, v. lower; descend.

bajeza, f. baseness.

bajo, **1**. prep. under, below. **2**. a. low; short; base.

bala, f. bullet; ball; bale.

balada, f. ballad.

balancear, v. balance; roll, swing, sway.

balanza, f. balance; scales.

balbuceo, m. stammer; babble. —**balbucear**, v.

balcón, m. balcony.

balde, m. bucket, pail. **de b.**, gratis. **en b.**, in vain.

balística, f. ballistics.

balompié, m. football.

balón, m. football; (auto.) balloon tire.

baloncesto, m. basketball.

balota, f. ballot, vote, —**balotar**, v.

balsa, f. raft.

bálsamo, m. balm.

baluarte, m. bulwark.

ballena, f. whale.

bambolearse, v. sway.

bambú, m. bamboo.

banal, a. banal, trite.

banana, f. banana.

banano, m. banana tree.

bancarrota, f. bankruptcy.

banco, m. bank; bench; school of fish.

banda, f. band.

bandada, f. covey; flock.

bandeja, f. tray.

bandera, f. flag; banner; ensign.

bandido, m. bandit.

bando, m. faction.

bandolero, m. bandit, robber.

banquero, m. banker.

banqueta, f. stool; (Mex.) sidewalk.

banquete, m. feast, banquet.

banquillo, m. stool.

bañera, f. bathtub.

baño, m. bath; bathroom.

bañar, v. bathe.

baraja, f. pack of cards; game of cards.

baranda, f. railing, banister.

barato, a. cheap.

barba, f. beard; chin.

barbacoa, f. barbecue; stretcher.

barbaridad, f. barbarity; (Am.) excess (in anything).

bárbaro, a. barbarous; crude.

barbería, f. barbershop.

barbero, m. barber.

barca, f. (small) boat.

barcaza, f. barge.

barco, m. ship, boat.

barniz, m. varnish. —**barnizar**, v.

barómetro, m. barometer.

barón, m. baron.

barquilla, f. (naut.) log.

barra, f. bar.

barraca, f. hut, shed.

barrear, v. bar, barricade.

barreno, m. blast, blasting, —**barrenar**, v.

barrer, v. sweep.

barrera, f. barrier.

barricada, f. barricade.

barriga, f. belly.

barril, m. barrel; cask.

barrio, m. district, ward, quarter.

barro, m. clay, mud.

base, f. base; basis. —**basar**, v.

bastante, **1**. a. enough, plenty of. **2**. adv. enough; rather, quite.

bastar, v. suffice, be enough.

bastardo -a, a. & n. bastard.

bastear, v. baste.

bastidor, m. wing (in theater).

bastón, m. (walking) cane.

bastos, m.pl. clubs (cards).

basura, f. refuse, dirt; garbage; junk.

basurero, m. scavenger.

batalla, f. battle. —**batallar**, v.

batallón, m. battalion.

batata, f. sweet potato.

bate, m. bat. —**batear**, v.

batería, f. battery.

batido, m. (cooking) batter.

batir, v. beat; demolish; conquer.

baúl, m. trunk.

bautisomo, m. baptism.

bautista, m. & f. Baptist.

bautizar, v. Christen, baptize.

bautizo, m. baptism.

baya, f. berry.

bayoneta, f. bayonet.

beato, a. blessed.

bebé, m. baby.

beber, v. drink.

bebible, a. drinkable.

bebida, f. drink, beverage.

beca, f. grant, scholarship.
becado -da, n. scholar.
becerro, m. calf; calfskin.
beldad, f. beauty.
belga, a. & n. Belgian.
Bélgica, f. Belgium.
belicoso, a. warlike.
beligerante, a. & n. belligerent.
bellaco, 1. a. sly, roguish. 2. m. rogue.
belleza, f. beauty.
bello, a. beautiful.
bellota, f. acorn.
bendecir, v. bless.
bendición, f. blessing, benediction.
bendito, a. blessed.
beneficio, m. benefit. —**beneficiar**, v.
beneficioso, a. beneficial.
benevolencia, f. benevolence.
benévolo, a. benevolent.
benigno, a. benign.
beodo, a. drunk.
berenjena, f. eggplant.
beso, m. kiss. —**besar**, v.
bestia, f. beast, brute.
betabel, m. beet.
Biblia, f. Bible.
bíblico, a. Biblical.
biblioteca, f. library.
bicarbonato, m. bicarbonate.
bicicleta, f. bicycle.
bien, 1. adv. well. 2. n. good; (pl.) possessions.
bienestar, m. well-being, welfare.
bienhechor -ra, n. benefactor.
bienvenida, f. welcome.
bienvenido, a. welcome.
biftec, m. steak.
bifurcación, f. fork. —**bifurcar**, v.
bigamía, f. bigamy.
bígamo -a, n. bigamist.
bigotes, m.pl. mustache.
bilis, f. bile.
billar, m. billiards.
billete, m. ticket; bank note, bill.
billón, m. billion.
biodegradable, a. biodegradable.
biografía, f. biography.
biología, f. biology.
biombo, m. screen.
bisel, m. bevel. —**biselar**, v.
bisonte, m. bison.
bisté, bistec, m. steak.
bizarro, a. brave; generous; smart.
bizcocho, m. biscuit, cake.
blanco, 1. a. white; blank. 2. m. white; target.
blandir, v. brandish, flourish.
blando, a. soft.
blanquear, v. whiten; bleach.
blasfemar, v. blaspheme, curse.
blasfemia, f. blasphemy.
blindado, a. armored.
blindaje, m. armor.
bloque, m. block. —**bloquear**, v.
bloqueo, m. blockade. —**bloquear**, v.

blusa, f. blouse.
bobo -ba, a. & n. fool; foolish.
boca, f. mouth.
bocado, m. bit; bite, mouthful, morsel.
bocanada, f. puff (of smoke); mouthful (of liquor).
bocina, f. horn.
bochorno, m. sultry weather; embarrassment.
boda, f. wedding.
bodega, f. wine cellar; (naut.) hold; grocery store.
bofetada, f. **bofetón**, m. slap.
boga, f. vogue; fad.
bogar, v. row (a boat).
bohemio -a, a. & n. Bohemian.
boicoteo, m. boycott. —**boicotear**, v.
boina, f. beret.
bola, f. ball.
bolera, f. bowling alley.
boletín, m. bulletin.
boleto, m. ticket.
boliche, m. bowling alley.
boliviano -a, a. & n. Bolivian.
bolos, m.pl. bowling.
bolsa, f. purse; stock exchange.
bolsillo, m. pocket.
bollo, m. bun, loaf.
bomba, f. pump; bomb; gas station.
bombardear, v. bomb; bombard, shell.
bombear, v. pump.
bombero, m. fireman.
bombilla, f. (light) bulb.
bonanza, f. prosperity; fair weather.
bondad, f. kindness; goodness.
bondadoso, a. kind, kindly.
bonito, a. pretty.
bono, m. bonus; (fin.) bond.
boqueada, f. gasp; gape. —**boquear**, v.
boquilla, f. cigarette holder.
bordado, m., **bordadura**, f. embroidery.
bordar, v. embroider.
borde, m. border, rim, edge, brink, ledge.
borla, f. tassel.
borracho, a. drunk.
borrachón, m. drunkard.
borrador, m. eraser.
borradura, f. erasure.
borrar, v. erase, rub out.
borrasca, f. squall, storm.
borrico, m. donkey.
bosque, m. forest, wood.
bostezo, m. yawn. —**bostezar**, v.
bota, f. boot.
botalón, m. (naut.) boom.
botánica, f. botany.
botar, v. throw out, throw away.
bote, m. boat; can, box.
botica, f. pharmacy, drugstore.
boticario, m. pharmacist, druggist.
botín, m. booty, plunder, spoils.
boto, a. dull, stupid.

botón, m. button.
botones, m. bellboy (in a hotel).
bóveda, f. vault.
boxeador, m. boxer.
boxeo, m. boxing. —**boxear**, v.
boya, f. buoy.
boyante, a. buoyant.
bozal, m. muzzle.
bramido, m. roar, bellow. —**bramar**, v.
brasileño -ña, a. & n. Brazilian.
bravata, f. bravado.
bravear, v. bully.
braza, f. fathom.
brazada, f. (swimming) stroke.
brazalete, m. bracelet.
brazo, m. arm.
brea, f. tar, pitch.
brecha, f. gap, breach.
bregar, v. scramble.
breña, f. rough country with brambly shrubs.
Bretaña, f. Britain.
breve, a. brief, short. **en b.**, shortly, soon.
brevedad, f. brevity.
bribón, m. rogue, rascal.
brida, f. bridle.
brigada, f. brigade.
brillante, 1. a. brilliant, shiny. 2. m. diamond.
brillo, m. shine, glitter. —**brillar**, v.
brinco, m. jump; bounce, skip. —**brincar**, v.
brindis, m. toast. —**brindar**, v.
brío, m. vigor.
brioso, a. vigorous, spirited.
brisa, f. breeze.
británico, a. British.
brocado, m. brocade.
brocha, f. brush.
broche, m. brooch, clasp, pin.
broma, f. joke. —**bromear**, v.
bronce, m. bronze; brass.
bronquitis, f. bronchitis.
brotar, v. gush; sprout; bud.
brote, m. bud, shoot.
bruja, f. witch.
brújula, f. compass.
bruma, f. mist.
brumoso, a. misty.
brusco, a. brusque; abrupt, curt.
brutal, a. savage, brutal.
brutalidad, f. brutality.
bruto, 1. a. brutish; ignorant. 2. m. blockhead.
bucear, v. dive.
bueno, a. good, fair; well (in health).
buey, m. ox, steer.
búfalo, m. buffalo.
bufanda, f. scarf.
bufón -ona, n. fool, buffoon, clown.
buho, m. owl.
buhonero, m. peddler, vender.
bujía, f. spark plug.
bulevar, m. boulevard.
bulto, m. bundle; lump.
bullicio, m. bustle, noise.
bullicioso, a. boisterous, noisy.
buñuelo, m. bun.

buque, *m.* ship.
burdo, *a.* coarse.
burgués -esa, *a. & n.* bourgeois.
burla, *f.* mockery; fun.
burlador, *m.* trickster, jokester.
burlar, *v.* mock, deride.
burlarse de, *v.* scoff at; make fun of.
burro, *m.* donkey.
busca, *f.* search, pursuit, quest.
buscar, *v.* seek, look for; look up.
busto, *m.* bust.
butaca, *f.* armchair; (theat.) orchestra seat.
buzo, *m.* diver.
buzón, *m.* mailbox.

C

cabal, *a.* exact; thorough.
cabalgar, *v.* ride horseback.
caballeresco, *a.* gentlemanly, chivalrous.
caballería, *f.* cavalry; chivalry.
caballeriza, *f.* stable.
caballero, *m.* gentleman; knight.
caballete, *m.* sawhorse; easel; ridge (of roof).
caballo, *m.* horse.
cabaña, *f.* cabin; booth.
cabecear, *v.* pitch (as a ship).
cabecera, *f.* head (of bed; table).
cabello, *m.* hair.
caber, *v.* fit into; be contained in. **no cabe duda**, there is no doubt.
cabeza, *f.* head; warhead.
cabildo, *m.* city hall.
cabizbajo, *a.* downcast.
cablegrama, *m.* cablegram.
cabo, *m.* end; (geog.) cape; (mil.) corporal. **llevar a c.**, carry out, accomplish.
cabra, *f.* goat.
cacahuete, *m.* peanut.
cacao, *m.* cocoa; chocolate.
cacerola, *f.* pan, casserole.
cachorro, *m.* cub; puppy.
cada, *a.* each, every.
cadáver, *m.* corpse.
cadena, *f.* chain.
cadera, *f.* hip.
cadete, *m.* cadet.
caer, *v.* fall.
café, *m.* coffee; café.
cafetal, *m.* coffee plantation.
cafetera, *f.* coffee pot.
caída, *f.* fall, drop; collapse.
caimán, *m.* alligator.
caja, *f.* box, case.
cajero -ra, *n.* cashier.
cajón, *m.* drawer.
cal, *f.* lime.
calabaza, *f.* calabash, pumpkin.
calabozo, *m.* jail, cell.
calambre, *m.* cramp.
calamidad, *f.* calamity, disaster.
calcetín, *m.* sock.
calcio, *m.* calcium.

calcular, *v.* calculate, figure.
cálculo, *m.* calculation, estimate.
caldera, *f.* kettle, caldron; boiler.
caldo, *m.* broth.
calefacción, *f.* heat, heating.
calendario, *m.* calendar.
calentar, *v.* heat, warm.
calidad, *f.* quality, grade.
caliente, *a.* hot, warm.
calificar, *v.* qualify.
calma, *f.* calm, quiet.
calmado, *a.* calm.
calmante, *a.* soothing, calming.
calmar, *v.* calm, quiet, lull, soothe.
calor, *n.* heat, warmth. **tener c.**, to be hot, warm; feel hot, warm. **hacer c.**, to be hot, warm (weather).
calorífero, *m.* radiator.
calumnia, *f.* slander. —**calumniar**, *v.*
caluroso, *a.* warm, hot.
calvario, *m.* Calvary.
calvo, *a.* bald.
calzado, *m.* footwear.
calzar, *v.* wear (as shoes).
calzoncillos, *m.pl.* shorts.
calzones, *m.pl.* trousers.
callado, *a.* silent, quiet.
callarse, *v.* quiet down; keep still; stop talking.
calle, *f.* street.
callejón, *m.* alley.
callo, *m.* callus, corn.
cama, *f.* bed.
cámara, *f.* chamber; camera.
camarada, *m. & f.* comrade.
camarera, *f.* chambermaid; waitress.
camarero, *m.* steward; waiter.
camarón, *m.* shrimp.
camarote, *m.* stateroom, berth.
cambiar, *v.* exchange, change, trade; cash.
cambio, *m.* change, exchange. **en c.**, on the other hand.
cambista, *m.* banker, broker.
cambur, *m.* banana.
camello, *m.* camel.
camilla, *f.* stretcher.
caminar, *v.* walk.
caminata, *f.* tramp, hike.
camino, *m.* road; way.
camión, *m.* truck.
camisa, *f.* shirt.
camisería, *f.* haberdashery.
camiseta, *f.* undershirt; T-shirt.
campamento, *m.* camp.
campana, *f.* bell.
campanario, *m.* bell tower, steeple.
campaneo, *m.* chime.
campaña, *f.* campaign.
campeón, *m.* champion.
campeonato, *m.* championship.
campesino -na, *n.* peasant.
campestre, *a.* country, rural.
campo, *m.* field; (the) country.
Canadá, *m.* Canada.

canadiense, *a. & n.* Canadian.
canal, *m.* canal; channel.
canalla, *f.* rabble.
canario, *m.* canary.
canasta, *f.* basket.
cáncer, *m.* cancer.
canciller, *m.* chancellor.
canción, *f.* song.
candado, *m.* padlock.
candela, *f.* fire; light; candle.
candelero, *m.* candlestick.
candidato -ta, *n.* candidate; applicant.
candidatura, *f.* candidacy.
canela, *f.* cinnamon.
cangrejo, *m.* crab.
caníbal, *m.* cannibal.
canje, *m.* exchange, trade. — **canjear**, *v.*
cano, *a.* gray.
canoa, *f.* canoe.
cansado, *a.* tired, weary.
cansancio, *m.* fatigue.
cansar, *v.* tire, fatigue, wear out.
cantante, *m. & f.* singer.
cantar, 1. *m.* song. 2. *v.* sing.
cántaro, *m.* pitcher.
cantera, *f.* (stone) quarry.
cantidad, *f.* quantity, amount.
cantina, *f.* bar, tavern; restaurant.
canto, *m.* chant, song, singing; edge.
caña, *f.* cane, reed; sugar cane.
cañón, *m.* canyon; cannon; gun barrel.
caoba, *f.* mahogany.
caos, *m.* chaos.
caótico, *a.* chaotic.
capa, *f.* cape, cloak; coat (of paint).
capacidad, *f.* capacity; capability.
capacitar, *v.* enable.
capataz, *m.* foreman.
capaz, *a.* capable, able.
capellán, *m.* chaplain.
caperuza, *f.* hood.
capilla, *f.* chapel.
capital, *m.* capital. *f.* capital (city).
capitalista, *a. & n.* capitalist.
capitán, *m.* captain.
capitular, *v.* yield.
capítulo, *m.* chapter.
capota, *f.* hood.
capricho, *m.* caprice; fancy, whim.
caprichoso, *a.* capricious.
cápsula, *f.* capsule.
capturar, *v.* capture.
capucha, *f.* hood.
capullo, *m.* cocoon.
cara, *f.* face.
caracol, *m.* snail.
carácter, *m.* character.
característica, *f.* characteristic.
característico, *a.* characteristic.
caramba, mild exclamation.
caramelo, *m.* caramel; candy.
carátula, *f.* dial.
caravana, *f.* caravan.
carbón, *m.* carbon; coal.

carbonizar, v. char.
carburador, m. carburetor.
carcajada, f. burst of laughter.
cárcel, f. prison, jail.
carcelero, m. jailer.
carcinogénico, a. carcinogenic.
cardenal, m. cardinal.
carecer, v. lack.
carestía, f. scarcity; famine.
carga, f. cargo; load, burden; freight.
cargar, v. carry; load; charge.
cargo, m. load; charge, office.
caricia, f. caress.
caridad, f. charity.
cariño, m. affection, fondness.
cariñoso, a. affectionate, fond.
carisma, m. charisma.
caritativo, a. charitable.
carmesí, a. & m. crimson.
carnaval, m. carnival.
carne, f. meat, flesh; pulp.
carnero, m. ram; mutton.
carnicería, f. meat market; massacre.
carnicero, m. butcher.
carnívoro, a. carnivorous.
caro, a. dear, costly, expensive.
carpa, f. tent.
carpeta, f. folder; briefcase.
carpintero, m. carpenter.
carrera, f. race; career.
carreta, f. wagon, cart.
carrete, m. reel, spool.
carretera, f. road, highway.
carril, m. rail.
carrillo, m. cart (for baggage or shopping).
carro, m. car, automobile; cart.
carroza, f. chariot.
carruaje, m. carriage.
carta, f. letter; (pl.) cards.
cartel, m. placard, poster; cartel.
cartera, f. pocketbook, handbag, wallet; portfolio.
cartero, m. mailman, postman.
cartón, m. cardboard.
cartucho, m. cartridge; cassette.
casa, f. house, dwelling; home.
casaca, f. dress coat.
casado, a. married.
casamiento, m. marriage.
casar, v. marry, marry off.
casarse, v. get married. **c. con,** marry.
cascabel, m. jingle bell.
cascada, f. waterfall, cascade.
cascajo, m. gravel.
cascanueces, m. nutcracker.
cascar, v. crack, break, burst.
cáscara, f. shell, rind, husk.
casco, m. helmet; hull.
casera, f. landlady; housekeeper.
caserío, m. settlement.
casero, 1. a. homemade. **2.** m. landlord, superintendent.
caseta, f. cottage, hut.
casi, adv. almost, nearly.
casilla, f. booth; ticket office; pigeonhole.
casino, m. club; clubhouse.

caso, m. case. **hacer c. a,** pay attention to.
casorio, m. informal wedding.
caspa, f. dandruff.
casta, f. caste.
castaña, f. chestnut.
castaño, 1. a. brown. **2.** m. chestnut tree.
castañuela, f. castanet.
castellano, a. & m. Castillian.
castidad, f. chastity.
castigar, v. punish.
castigo, m. punishment.
castillo, m. castle.
castizo, a. pure, genuine; noble.
casto, a. chaste.
castor, m. beaver.
casual, adj. accidental, coincidental.
casualidad, f. coincidence. **por c.,** by chance.
casuca, f. hut, shanty, hovel.
catadura, f. act of tasting; appearance.
catalán, a. & m. Catalonian.
catálogo, m. catalogue. —**catalogar,** v.
catar, v. taste; examine, try; bear in mind.
catarata, f. cataract, waterfall.
catarro, m. head cold.
catástrofe, m. catastrophe.
catecismo, m. catechism.
cátedra, f. professorship.
catedral, f. cathedral.
catedrático, m. professor.
categoría, f. category.
categórico, a. categorical.
catequizar, v. catechize.
catolicismo, m. Catholicism.
católico -ca, a. & n. Catholic.
catorce, a. & pron. fourteen.
catre, m. cot.
cauce, m. riverbed; ditch.
caución, f. precaution; security, guarantee.
cauchal, m. rubber plantation.
caucho, m. rubber.
caudal, m. means, fortune; (pl.) holdings.
caudaloso, a. prosperous, rich.
caudillaje, m. leadership; tyranny.
caudillo, m. leader, chief.
causa, f. cause. —**causar,** v.
cautela, f. caution.
cauteloso, a. cautious.
cautivar, v. captivate.
cautiverio, m. captivity.
cautividad, f. captivity.
cautivo -va, a. & n. captive.
cauto, a. cautious.
cavar, v. dig.
caverna, f. cavern, cave.
cavernoso, a. cavernous.
cavidad, f. cavity, hollow.
cavilar, v. criticize, cavil.
cayado, m. shepherd's staff.
cayo, m. small rocky islet, key.
caza, f. hunting, pursuit, game.
cazador, m. hunter.
cazar, v. hunt.
cazatorpedero, m. destroyer.
cazo, m. ladle, dipper; pot.

cazuela, f. crock.
cebada, f. barley.
cebo, m. bait. —**cebar,** v.
cebolla, f. onion.
ceceo, m. lisp. —**cecear,** v.
cecina, f. dried beef.
cedazo, m. sieve, sifter.
ceder, v. cede; transfer; yield.
cedro, m. cedar.
cédula, 1. f. decree. **c. personal,** identification card.
céfiro, m. zephyr.
cegar, v. blind.
ceguedad, ceguera, f. blindness.
ceja, f. eyebrow.
cejar, v. go backwards; yield, retreat.
celada, f. trap; ambush.
celaje, m. appearance of the sky.
celar, v. watch carefully, guard.
celda, f. cell.
celebración, f. celebration.
celebrante, m. officiating priest.
celebrar, v. celebrate, observe.
célebre, a. celebrated, noted, famous.
celebridad, f. fame; celebrity; pageant.
celeridad, f. speed, rapidity.
celeste, a. celestial.
celestial, a. heavenly.
célibe, 1. a. unmarried. **2.** m. & f. unmarried person.
celo, m. zeal; (pl.) jealousy.
celosía, f. Venetian blind.
celoso, a. jealous; zealous.
céltico, a. Celtic.
célula, f. (biol.) cell.
celuloide, m. celluloid.
cellisca, f. sleet. —**cellisquear,** v.
cementar, v. cement.
cementerio, m. cemetery.
cemento, m. cement.
cena, f. supper.
cenagal, m. swamp, marsh.
cenagoso, a. swampy, marshy, muddy.
cenar, v. dine, eat.
cencerro, m. cowbell.
cendal, m. thin, light cloth; gauze.
cenicero, m. ashtray.
ceniciento, a. ashen.
cenit, m. zenith.
ceniza, f. ash, ashes.
censo, m. census.
censor, m. critic.
censura, f. reproof, censure; censorship.
censurable, a. objectionable.
censurar, v. censure, criticize.
centavo, m. cent.
centella, f. thunderbolt, lightning.
centellear, v. twinkle, sparkle.
centelleo, m. sparkle.
centenar, m. (a) hundred.
centenario, m. centennial, centenary.
centeno, m. rye.

centigrado, *a.* centigrade.
centimetro, *m.* centimeter.
céntimo, *m.* cent.
centinela, *m.* sentry, guard.
central, *a.* central.
centrar, *v.* center.
céntrico, *a.* central.
centro, *m.* center.
centroamericano -na, *a. & n.* Central American.
ceñidor, *m.* belt, sash; girdle.
ceñir, *v.* gird.
ceño, *m.* frown.
ceñudo, *a.* frowning, grim.
cepa, *f.* stump.
cepillo, *m.* brush; plane. —**cepillar**, *v.*
cera, *f.* wax.
cerámica, *m.* ceramics.
cerca, 1. *adv.* near. 2. *f.* fence, hedge.
cercado, *m.* enclosure; garden.
cercamiento, *m.* enclosure.
cercanía, *f.* proximity.
cercano, *a.* near, nearby.
cercar, *v.* surround.
cercenar, *v.* clip; lessen, reduce.
cerciorar, *v.* make sure; affirm.
cerco, *m.* hoop; siege.
cerda, *f.* bristle.
cerdo, *m.* hog.
cerdoso, *a.* bristly.
cereal, *a. & m.* cereal.
cerebro, *m.* brain.
ceremonia, *f.* ceremony.
ceremonial, *a. & m.* ceremonial, ritual.
ceremonioso, *a.* ceremonious.
cereza, *f.* cherry.
cerilla, *f.*, **cerillo**, *m.* match.
cerner, *v.* sift.
cero, *m.* zero.
cerrado, *a.* cloudy; obscure; stupid.
cerradura, *f.* lock.
cerrajero, *m.* locksmith.
cerrar, *v.* close, shut.
cerro, *m.* hill.
cerrojo, *m.* latch, bolt.
certamen, *m.* contest; competition.
certero, *a.* accurate, exact; certain, sure.
certeza, *f.* certainty.
certidumbre, *f.* certainty.
certificado, *m.* certificate.
certificar, *v.* certify; register (a letter).
cerúleo, *a.* cerulean, sky-blue.
cervecería, *f.* brewery; beer saloon.
cervecero, *m.* brewer.
cerveza, *f.* beer.
cesante, *a.* unemployed.
cesar, *v.* cease.
césped, *m.* sod, lawn.
cesta, *f.*, **cesto**, *m.* basket.
cetrino, *a.* yellow, lemon-colored.
cetro, *m.* scepter.
cicatero, *a.* stingy.
cicatriz, *f.* scar.
cicatrizar, *v.* heal.
ciclamato, *m.* cyclamate.

ciclo, *m.* cycle.
ciclón, *m.* cyclone.
ciego -ga, 1. *a.* blind. 2. *n.* blind person.
cielo, *m.* heaven; sky, heavens; ceiling.
ciempiés, *m.* centipede.
cien, **ciento**, *a. & pron.* hundred. **por c.**, per cent.
ciénaga, *f.* swamp, marsh.
ciencia, *f.* science.
cieno, *m.* mud.
científico, 1. *a.* scientific. 2. *n.* scientist.
cierre, *m.* fastener, snap, clasp.
cierto, *a.* certain, sure, true.
ciervo, *m.* deer.
cierzo, *m.* northerly wind.
cifra, *f.* cipher, number. —**cifrar**, *v.*
cigarra, *f.* locust.
cigarrera, **cigarrillera**, *f.* cigarette case.
cigarrillo, *m.* cigarette.
cigarro, *m.* cigar; cigarette.
cilíndrico, *a.* cylindrical.
cilindro, *m.* cylinder.
cima, *f.* summit, peak.
cimarrón, 1. *a.* wild, untamed. 2. *m.* runaway slave.
címbalo, *m.* cymbal.
cimbrar, *v.* shake, brandish.
cimientos, *m.pl.* foundation.
cinc, *m.* zinc.
cincel, *m.* chisel. —**cincelar**, *v.*
cinco, *a. & pron.* five.
cincuenta, *a. & pron.* fifty.
cincha, *f.* (harness) cinch. —**cinchar**, *v.*
cine, *m.* movies; movie theater.
cíngulo, *m.* girdle.
cínico, *a. & n.* cynical; cynic.
cinta, *f.* ribbon, tape; (movie) film.
cintilar, *v.* glitter, sparkle.
cinto, *m.* belt; girdle.
cintura, *f.* waist.
cinturón, *m.* belt.
ciprés, *m.* cypress.
circo, *m.* circus.
circuito, *m.* circuit.
circulación, *f.* circulation.
circular, 1. *a. & m.* circular. 2. *v.* circulate.
círculo, *m.* circle, club.
circundante, *a.* surrounding.
circundar, *v.* encircle, surround.
circunferencia, *f.* circumference.
circunlocución, *n.* circumlocution.
circunscribir, *v.* circumscribe.
circunspección, *n.* decorum, propriety.
circunspecto, *a.* circumspect.
circunstancia, *f.* circumstance.
circunstante, *m.* bystander.
circunvecino, *a.* neighboring, adjacent.
cirio, *m.* candle.
ciruela, *f.* plum; prune.
cirugía, *f.* surgery.
cirujano, *m.* surgeon.

cisne, *m.* swan.
cisterna, *f.* cistern.
cita, *f.* citation; appointment, date.
citación, *f.* citation; (legal) summons.
citar, *v.* cite, quote; summon; make an appointment with.
ciudad, *f.* city.
ciudadanía, *f.* citizenship.
ciudadano -na, *n.* citizen.
ciudadela, *f.* fortress, citadel.
cívico, *a.* civic.
civil, *a. & n.* civil; civilian.
civilidad, *f.* politeness, civility.
civilización, *f.* civilization.
civilizador, *a.* civilizing.
civilizar, *v.* civilize.
cizallas, *f.pl.* shears. —**cizallar**, *v.*
cizaña, *f.* weed; vice.
clamar, *v.* clamor.
clamor, *m.* clamor.
clamoreo, *m.* persistent clamor.
clamoroso, *a.* clamorous.
clandestino, *a.* secret, clandestine.
clara, *f.* white (of egg).
claraboya, *m.* skylight; bull's-eye.
clarear, *v.* clarify; become light, dawn.
claridad, *f.* clarity.
clarificar, *v.* clarify.
clarín, *m.* bugle, trumpet.
clarinete, *m.* clarinet.
clarividencia, *f.* clairvoyance.
claro, *a.* clear; bright; light (in color); of course.
clase, *f.* class; classroom; kind, sort.
clásico, *a.* classic, classical.
clasificar, *v.* classify, rank.
claustro, *m.* cloister.
cláusula, *f.* clause.
clausura, *f.* cloister; inner sanctum.
clavado, *m.* dive.
clavar, *v.* nail, peg, pin.
clave, *f.* code; (mus.) key.
clavel, *m.* carnation.
clavetear, *v.* nail.
clavija, *f.* pin, peg.
clavijero, *m.* hatrack.
clavo, *m.* nail, spike.
clemencia, *f.* clemency.
clemente, *a.* merciful.
clerecía, *f.* clergy.
clerical, *a.* clerical.
clérigo, *m.* clergyman.
clero, *m.* clergy.
cliente, *m. & f.* customer, client.
clientela, *f.* clientele, practice.
clima, *m.* climate.
clímax, *m.* climax.
clínica, *f.* clinic.
clíper, *m.* clipper ship.
cloaca, *f.* sewer.
cloquear, *v.* cluck, cackle.
cloqueo, *m.* cluck.
cloro, *m.* chlorine.
club, *m.* club, association.
clueca, *f.* brooding hen.

coacción, n. compulsion.
coagular, v. coagulate, clot.
coágulo, m. clot.
coalición, f. coalition.
coartar, v. limit.
cobarde, a. & n. cowardly; coward.
cobardía, f. cowardice.
cobertizo, m. shed.
cobertor, m., **cobija,** f. blanket.
cobertura, f. cover, wrapping.
cobijar, v. cover; protect.
cobrador, m. collector.
cobranza, f. collection or recovery of money.
cobrar, v. collect; charge; cash.
cobre, m. copper.
cobrizo, a. coppery.
cobro, m. collection or recovery of money.
coca, f. coca leaves.
cocaína, f. cocaine.
cocal, m. coconut plantation.
cocear, v. kick; resist.
cocer, v. cook, boil, bake.
cocido, m. stew.
cociente, m. quotient.
cocimiento, m. cooking.
cocina, f. kitchen.
cocinar, v. cook.
cocinero -ra, m. cook.
coco, m. coconut; coconut tree.
cocodrilo, m. crocodile.
coctel, m. cocktail.
coche, m. coach; car, automobile.
cochera, f. garage.
cochero, m. coachman; cab driver.
cochinada, f. filth; herd of swine.
cochino, m. pig, swine.
codazo, m. nudge with the elbow.
codicia, f. avarice, greed; lust.
codiciar, v. covet.
codicioso, a. covetous; greedy.
código, m. (law) code.
codo, m. elbow.
codorniz, f. quail.
coetáneo, a. contemporary.
cofrade, m. fellow member of a club, etc.
cofre, m. coffer; chest; trunk.
coger, v. catch; pick; take.
cogote, m. nape.
cohecho, m. bribe. —**cohechar,** v.
coheredero, m. co-heir.
coherente, a. coherent.
cohesión, f. cohesion.
cohete, m. fire cracker, rocket.
cohibición, n. restraint; repression.
cohibir, v. restrain; repress.
coincidencia, f. coincidence.
coincidir, v. coincide.
cojear, v. limp.
cojera, m. limp.
cojín, m. cushion.
cojinete, m. small cushion, pad.
cojo, a. lame.
col, f. cabbage.

cola, f. tail; glue; line, queue.
hacer c., stand in line.
colaboración, f. collaboration.
colaborar, v. collaborate.
coladera, f. strainer.
colador, m. colander, strainer.
colapso, m. collapse, prostration.
colar, v. strain; drain.
colateral, a. collateral.
colcha, f. bedspread, quilt.
colchón, m. mattress.
colear, v. wag the tail.
colección, f. collection, set.
coleccionar, v. collect.
colecta, f. collection (a prayer).
colectivo, a. collective.
colector, m. collector.
colega, m. & f. colleague.
colegial, m. college student.
colegiatura, f. college scholarship.
colegio, m. (private) school, college.
colegir, v. infer, deduce.
cólera, f. rage, wrath.
colérico, adj. angry, irritated.
coleto, m. leather jacket.
colgador, m. rack, hanger.
colgaduras, f.,pl. drapery.
colgante, a. hanging.
colgar, v. hang up, suspend.
colibrí, m. hummingbird.
coliflor, m. cauliflower.
coligarse, v. band together, unite.
colilla, f. butt of a cigar or cigarette.
colina, f. hill, hillock.
colinabo, m. turnip.
colindante, a. neighboring, adjacent.
colindar, v. neighbor, abut.
coliseo, m. theater; coliseum.
colisión, f. collision.
colmar, v. heap up, fill liberally.
colmena, f. hive.
colmillo, m. eyetooth; tusk; fang.
colmo, m. height, peak, extreme.
colocación, f. place, position; employment, job; arrangement.
colocar, v. place, locate, put, set.
colombiano -na, a. & n. Colombian.
colon, m. colon (of intestines).
colonia, f. colony.
colonial, a. colonial.
colonización, f. colonization.
colonizador, m. colonizer.
colonizar, v. colonize.
colono, m. colonist; tenant farmer.
coloquio, m. conversation, talk.
color, m. color. —**colorar,** v.
coloración, f. coloring.
colorado, a. red, ruddy.
colorar, v. color, paint; dye.
colorete, m. rouge.

colorido, m. color, coloring. —**colorir,** v.
colosal, a. colossal.
columbrar, v. discern.
columna, f. column, pillar, shaft.
columpiar, v. swing.
columpio, m. swing.
collado, m. hillock.
collar, m. necklace; collar.
coma, f. coma; comma.
comadre, f. midwife; gossip; close friend.
comadreja, m. weasel.
comandancia, m. command; command post.
comandante, m. commandant; commander; major.
comandar, v. command.
comandita, f. silent partnership.
comanditario, m. silent partner.
comando, m. command.
comarca, f. region; border, boundary.
comba, f. bulge.
combar, v. bend; bulge.
combate, m. combat. —**combatir,** v.
combatiente, a. & m. combatant.
combinación, f. combination; (lady's) slip.
combinar, v. combine.
combustible, 1. a. combustible. **2.** m. fuel.
combustión, f. combustion.
comedero, m. trough.
comedia, f. comedy; play.
comediante, m. actor; comedian.
comedido, a. polite, courteous; obliging.
comedirse, v. to be polite or obliging.
comedor, m. dining room. **coche c.,** dining car.
comendador, m. commander.
comensal, m. member of a household.
comentador, m. commentator.
comentario, m. commentary.
comento, m. comment. —**comentar,** v.
comenzar, v. begin, start, commence.
comer, v. eat, dine.
comercial, a. commercial.
comerciante, m. merchant, trader, businessman.
comerciar, v. trade, deal, do business.
comercio, m. commerce, trade, business.
comestible, 1. a. edible. **2.** m. (pl.) groceries, provisions.
cometa, m. comet. f. kite.
cometer, v. commit.
cometido, m. commission; duty; task.
comezón, f. itch.
comicios, m.pl. primary elections.

cómico -ca, a. & n. comic, comical; comedian.
comida, f. food; dinner; meal.
comidilla, f. light meal; gossip.
comienzo, m. beginning.
comilitona, f. banquet.
comilón, m. glutton; heavy eater.
comillas, f.pl. quotation marks.
comisario, m. commissary.
comisión, f. commission. — **comisionar,** v.
comisionado, m. agent, commissioner.
comisionar, v. commission.
comiso, m. (law) confiscation of illegal goods.
comistrajo, m. mess, hodgepodge.
comité, m. committee.
comitiva, f. retinue.
como, conj. & adv. like, as.
como, adv. how.
cómoda, f. bureau, chest (of drawers).
cómodamente, adv. conveniently.
comodatario, m. pawnbroker.
comodato, m. loan.
comodidad, f. convenience, comfort; commodity.
cómodo, a. comfortable; convenient.
comodoro, m. commodore.
compacto, a. compact.
compadecer, v. be sorry for, pity.
compadraje, m. clique.
compadre, m. close friend.
compaginar, v. put in order; arrange.
companage, m. cold lunch.
compañerismo, m. companionship.
compañero -ra, n. companion, partner.
compañía, f. company.
comparable, a. comparable.
comparación, f. comparison.
comparar, v. compare.
comparativamente, adv. comparatively.
comparativo, a. comparative.
comparecer, v. appear.
comparendo, m. summons.
comparsa, f. carnival masquerade; retinue.
compartimiento, m. compartment.
compartir, v. share.
compás, m. compass; beat, rhythm.
compasar, v. measure exactly.
compasible, a. compassionate.
compasión, f. compassion.
compasivo, a. compassionate.
compatibilidad, f. compatibility.
compatible, a. compatible.
compatriota, m. & f. compatriot.
compeler, v. compel.
compendiar, v. summarize; abridge.

compendiariamente, adv. briefly.
compendio, m. summary; abridgment.
compendiosamente, adv. briefly.
compensación, f. compensation.
compensar, v. compensate.
competencia, f. competence; competition.
competente, a. competent.
competentemente, adv. competently.
competición, f. competition.
competidor, a. & n. competitive; competitor.
competir, v. compete.
compilación, f. compilation.
compilar, v. compile.
compinche, m. pal.
complacencia, f. complacency.
complacer, v. please, oblige, humor.
complaciente, a. pleasing, obliging.
complejidad, f. complexity.
complejo, a. & n. complex.
complemento, m. complement; (gram.) object.
completamente, adv. completely.
completamiento, m. completion, finish.
completar, v. complete.
completo, a. complete, full, perfect.
complexidad, f. complexity.
complexión, f. nature, temperament.
complexo, a. complex, intricate.
complicación, f. complication.
complicado, a. complicated.
complicar, v. complicate.
cómplice, m. & f. accomplice, accessory.
complicidad, f. complicity.
complot, m. conspiracy.
componedor, m. typesetter.
componenda, f. compromise; settlement.
componente, a. & m. component.
componer, v. compose; fix, repair.
componible, a. reparable.
comportable, a. endurable.
comportamiento, m. behavior.
comportarse, v. behave.
comporte, m. behavior.
composición, f. composition.
compositivo, a. synthetic; composite.
compositor -ra, n. composer.
compostura, f. composure; repair; neatness.
compota, f. (fruit) sauce.
compra, f. purchase. **ir de compras,** to go shopping.
comprador -ra, n. buyer, purchaser.
comprar, v. buy, purchase.
comprehensivo, a. comprehensive.

comprender, v. comprehend, understand; include, comprise.
comprensibilidad, f. comprehensibility.
comprensible, a. understandable.
comprensión, f. comprehension, understanding.
comprensivo, m. comprehensive.
compresa, f. medical compress.
compresión, f. compression.
comprimir, v. compress.
comprobación, f. proof.
comprobante, 1. a. proving. **2.** m. proof.
comprobar, v. prove; verify, check.
comprometer, v. compromise.
comprometerse, v. become engaged.
compromiso, m. compromise; engagement.
compropietario, m. co-owner.
compuerta, f. floodgate.
compuesto, m. composition; compound.
compulsión, f. compulsion.
compulsivo, a. compulsive.
compunción, f. compunction.
compungirse, v. regret, feel remorse.
computación, f. computation.
computador, m. computer.
computar, v. compute.
cómputo, m. computation.
comulación, f. cumulation.
comulgar, v. take communion.
comulgatorio, m. communion altar.
común, a. common, usual.
comunal, m. common people.
comunero, m. commoner.
comunicable, a. communicable.
comunicación, f. communication.
comunicante, m. & f. communicant.
comunicar, v. communicate; convey.
comunicativo, a. communicative.
comunidad, f. community.
comunión, f. communion.
comunismo, m. communism.
comunista, a. & n. communistic; communist.
comúnmente, adv. commonly; usually; often.
con, prep. with.
concavidad, f. concavity.
cóncavo, 1. a. concave. **2.** m. concavity.
concebible, a. conceivable.
concebir, v. conceive.
conceder, v. concede.
concejal, m. councilman.
concejo, m. city council.
concento, m. harmony.
concentración, f. concentration.
concentrar, v. concentrate.

concepción, f. conception.
conceptible, a. conceivable.
concepto, m. concept; opinion.
concerniente, a. concerning.
concernir, v. concern.
concertar, v. arrange.
concertina, f. concertina.
concesión, f. concession.
conciencia, f. conscience; consciousness; conscientiousness.
concienzudo, a. conscientious.
concierto, m. concert.
conciliación, f. conciliation.
conciliador, m. conciliator.
conciliar, v. conciliate.
concilio, m. council.
concisión, f. conciseness.
conciso, a. concise.
concitar, v. instigate, stir up.
conciudadano, m. fellow citizen.
concluir, v. conclude.
conclusión, f. conclusion.
conclusivo, a. conclusive.
concluso, a. concluded; closed.
concluyentemente, adv. conclusively.
concomitante, a. concomitant, attendant.
concordador, m. moderator; conciliator.
concordancia, f. agreement, concord.
concordar, v. agree; put or be in accord.
concordia, f. concord, agreement.
concretamente, adv. concretely.
concretar, v. summarize.
concretarse, v. limit oneself to.
concreto, a. & m. concrete.
concubina, f. concubine, mistress.
concupiscente, a. lustful.
concurrencia, f. assembly; attendance; competition.
concurrente, a. concurrent.
concurrido, a. heavily attended or patronized.
concurrir, v. concur; attend.
concurso, m. contest, competition; meeting.
concha, f. (sea) shell.
conde, m. (title) count.
condecente, a. appropriate, proper.
condecoración, f. decoration; medal; badge.
condecorar, v. decorate with a medal.
condena, f. prison sentence.
condenación, f. condemnation.
condenar, v. condemn; damn; sentence.
condensación, f. condensation.
condensar, v. condense.
condesa, f. countess.
condescendencia, f. condescension.
condescender, v. condescend, deign.
condescendiente, a. condescending.

condición, f. condition.
condicional, a. conditional.
condicionalmente, adv. conditionally.
condimentar, v. season, flavor.
condimento, m. condiment, seasoning, dressing.
condiscípulo, m. schoolmate.
condolencia, f. condolence, sympathy.
condolerse de, v. sympathize with.
condómino, m. co-owner.
condonar, v. condone.
cóndor, m. condor (bird).
conducción, f. conveyance.
conducente, a. conducive.
conducir, v. conduct, escort, lead; drive.
conducta, f. conduct, behavior.
conducto, m. pipe, conduit; sewer.
conductor, m. driver; conductor.
conectar, v. connect.
conejera, f. rabbit warren; place of ill repute.
conejo, m. rabbit.
conexión, f. connection; coupling.
conexivo, a. connective.
conexo, a. connected, united.
confalón, m. ensign, standard.
confección, f. workmanship; ready-made article; concoction.
confeccionar, v. concoct.
confederación, f. confederation.
confederado, a. & m. confederate.
confederar, v. confederate, unite, ally.
conferencia, f. lecture; conference.
conferenciante, m. & f. lecturer, speaker.
conferenciar, v. confer.
conferencista, m. & f. lecturer, speaker.
conferir, v. confer.
confesar, v. confess.
confesión, f. confession.
confesionario, m. confessional.
confesor, m. confessor.
confetti, m.pl. confetti.
confiable, a. dependable.
confiado, a. confident; trusting.
confianza, f. confidence, trust, faith.
confiar, v. entrust; trust, rely.
confidencia, f. confidence, secret.
confidencial, a. confidential.
confidente, m. & f. confidant.
confidentemente, adv. confidently.
confín, m. confine.
confinamiento, m. confinement.
confinar, v. confine, imprison; border on.
confirmación, f. confirmation.
confirmar, v. confirm.

confiscación, f. confiscation.
confiscar, v. confiscate.
confitar, v. sweeten; make into candy or jam.
confite, m. candy.
confitería, f. confectionery; candy store.
confitura, f. confection.
conflagración, f. conflagration.
conflicto, m. conflict.
confluencia, f. confluence, junction.
confluir, v. flow into each other.
conformación, f. conformation.
conformar, v. conform.
conforme, 1. a. acceptable, right, as agreed; in accordance, in agreement. **2.** conj. according as.
conformidad, f. conformity; agreement.
conformismo, m. conformism.
conformista, m. conformist.
confortar, v. comfort.
confraternidad, m. brotherhood, fraternity.
confricar, v. rub.
confrontación, f. confrontation.
confrontar, v. confront.
confucianismo, m. Confucianism.
confundir, v. confuse; puzzle, mix up.
confusamente, adv. confusedly.
confusión, f. confusion, mix-up; clutter.
confuso, a. confused; confusing.
confutación, n. disproof.
confutar, v. refute, disprove.
congelable, a. congealable.
congelación, f. congealment; deep freeze.
congelado, a. frozen, congealed.
congelar, v. congeal, freeze.
congenial, a. congenial; analogous.
congeniar, v. be congenial.
congestión, f. congestion.
conglomeración, f. conglomeration.
congoja, f. grief, anguish.
congraciamiento, m. flattery; ingratiation.
congraciar, v. flatter; ingratiate oneself.
congratulación, f. congratulation.
congratular, v. congratulate.
congregación, f. congregation.
congregar, v. congregate.
congresista, m. & f. congressional representative.
congreso, m. congress; conference.
conjetura, f. conjecture. —**conjeturar,** v.
conjetural, a. conjectural.
conjugación, f. conjugation.
conjugar, v. conjugate.

conjunción, *f.* union; conjunction.

conjuntamente, *adv.* together, jointly.

conjunto. 1. *a.* joint, unified. 2. *m.* whole.

conjuración, *f.* conspiracy, plot.

conjurado, *m.* conspirator, plotter.

conjurar, *v.* conjure.

conllevador, *m.* helper, aide.

conmemoración, *f.* commemoration; remembrance.

conmemorar, *v.* commemorate.

conmemorativo, *a.* commemorative, memorial.

conmensal, *m.* messmate.

conmigo, *adv.* with me.

conmilitón, *m.* fellow soldier.

conminación, *f.* threat, warning.

conminar, *v.* threaten.

conminatorio, *a.* threatening, warning.

conmiseración, *f.* sympathy.

conmoción, *f.* commotion, stir.

conmovedor, *a.* moving, touching.

conmover, *v.* move, affect, touch.

conmutación, *f.* commutation.

conmutador, *m.* electric switch.

conmutar, *v.* exchange.

connotación, *f.* connotation.

connotar, *v.* connote.

connubial, *a.* connubial.

connubio, *m.* matrimony.

cono, *m.* cone.

conocedor -ra, *n.* expert, connoisseur.

conocer, *v.* know, be acquainted with; meet, make the acquaintance of.

conocible, *a.* knowable.

conocido -da, 1. *a.* familiar, well known. 2. *n.* acquaintance, person known.

conocimiento, *m.* knowledge, acquaintance; consciousness.

conque, *conj.* so then; and so.

conquista, *f.* conquest.

conquistador, *m.* conqueror.

conquistar, *v.* conquer.

consabido, *a.* aforesaid.

consagración, *f.* consecration.

consagrado, *a.* consecrated.

consagrar, *v.* consecrate, dedicate, devote.

consanguinidad, *f.* consanguinity.

consciente, *a.* conscious, aware.

conscientemente, *adv.* consciously.

conscripción, *f.* conscription for military service.

consecución, *f.* attainment.

consecuencia, *f.* consequence.

consecuente, *a.* consequent; consistent.

consecuentemente, *adv.* consequently.

consecutivamente, *adv.* consecutively.

consecutivo, *a.* consecutive.

conseguir, *v.* obtain, get, secure; succeed in, manage to.

conseja, *n.* fable.

consejero -ra, *n.* adviser, counselor.

consejo, *m.* council; counsel (piece of) advice.

consenso, *m.* consensus.

consentido, *a.* spoiled, bratty.

consentimiento, *m.* consent.

consentir, *v.* allow, permit.

conserje, *m.* superintendent, keeper.

conserva, *f.* conserve, preserve.

conservación, *f.* conservation.

conservador, *a. & m.* conservative.

conservar, *v.* conserve.

conservativo, *a.* conservative, preservative.

conservatorio, *m.* conservatory.

considerable, *a.* considerable, substantial.

considerablemente, *adv.* considerably.

consideración, *f.* consideration.

consideradamente, *adv.* considerably.

considerado, *a.* considerate.

considerando, *conj.* whereas.

considerar, *v.* consider.

consigna, *f.* watchword.

consignación, *f.* consignment.

consignar, *v.* consign.

consignatorio, *m.* consignee; trustee.

consigo, *adv.* with herself, with himself, with oneself, with themselves, with yourself, with yourselves.

consiguiente, 1. *a.* consequent. 2. *m.* consequence.

consiguientemente, *adv.* consequently.

consistencia, *f.* consistency.

consistente, *a.* consistent.

consistir, *v.* consist.

consistorio, *m.* consistory.

consocio, *m.* associate; partner; comrade.

consola, *f.* console.

consolación, *f.* consolation.

consolar, *v.* console.

consolatorio, *a.* consolatory.

consolidación, *n.* consolidation.

consolidado, *a.* consolidated.

consolidar, *v.* consolidate.

consonancia, *f.* agreement, accord, harmony.

consonante, *a. & n.* consonant.

consonar, *v.* rhyme.

consorte, *m. & f.* consort, mate.

conspicuo, *a.* conspicuous.

conspiración, *f.* conspiracy, plot.

conspirador -ra, *n.* conspirator.

conspirar, *v.* conspire, plot.

constancia, *f.* perseverance; record.

constante, *a.* constant.

constantemente, *adv.* constantly.

constar, *v.* consist; be clear, b on record.

constelación, *f.* constellation.

consternación, *f.* consterna tion.

consternar, *v.* dismay.

constipación, *f.* head cold.

constipado, *a.* having a hea cold.

constitución, *f.* constitution.

constitucional, *a.* constitu tional.

constitucionalidad, *f.* constitu tionality.

constituir, *v.* constitute.

constitutivo, *m.* constituent.

constituyente, *a.* constituent.

constreñidamente, *adv.* com pulsively; with constraint.

constreñimiento, *m.* compu sion; constraint.

constreñir, *v.* constrain.

constricción, *f.* constriction.

construcción, *f.* construction.

constructivo, *a.* constructive.

constructor, *m.* builder.

construir, *v.* construct, build.

consuelo, *m.* consolation.

cónsul, *m.* consul.

consulado, *m.* consulate.

consular, *a.* consular.

consulta, *f.* consultation.

consultación, *f.* consultation.

consultante, *m. & f.* consul tant.

consultar, *v.* consult.

consultivo, *a.* consultative.

consultor, *m.* adviser.

consumación, *f.* consumm tion; end.

consumado, *a.* consummat downright.

consumar, *v.* consummate.

consumidor, *m.* consumer.

consumir, *v.* consume.

consumo, *m.* consumption.

consunción, *f.* consumptio tuberculosis.

contabilidad, *f.* accountin bookkeeping.

contabilista, **contable**, *m. &* accountant.

contacto, *m.* contact.

contado, *m.* al c., (for) cash.

contador -ra, *n.* accountar bookkeeper.

contagiar, *v.* infect.

contagio, *m.* contagion.

contagioso, *a.* contagious.

contaminación, *f.* contamin tion, pollution.

contaminar, *v.* contamina pollute.

contar, *v.* count; relate, r count, tell. **c. con**, count o

contemperar, *v.* moderate.

contemplación, *f.* contempl tion.

contemplador -ra, *n.* thinker

contemplar, *v.* contemplate.

contemplativamente, *a* thoughtfully.

contemplativo, *a.* contemplative.

contemporáneo -nea, *a. & n.* contemporary.

contención, *f.* contention.

contencioso, *a.* quarrelsome; argumentative.

contender, *v.* cope, contend; conflict.

contendiente, *m. & f.* contender.

contenedor -ra, *n.* tenant.

contener, *v.* contain; curb, control.

contenido, *m.* contents.

contenta, *f.* endorsement.

contentamiento, *m.* contentment.

contentar, *v.* content, satisfy.

contentible, *a.* contemptible.

contento, 1. *a.* contented, happy. 2. *m.* contentment, satisfaction, pleasure.

contérmino, *a.* adjacent, abutting.

contestable, *a.* disputable.

contestación, *f.* answer. —**contestar**, *v.*

contextura, *f.* texture.

contienda, *f.* combat; match; strife.

contigo, *adv.* with you.

contiguamente, *adv.* closely.

contiguo, *a.* adjoining, next.

continencia, *f.* continence, moderation.

continental, *a.* continental.

continente, *m.* continent; mainland.

continentemente, *adv.* in moderation.

contingencia, *f.* contingency.

contingente, *a.* contingent; incidental.

continuación, *f.* continuation. —**a c.**, thereupon, hereupon.

continuamente, *adv.* continuously.

continuar, *v.* continue, keep on.

continuidad, *f.* continuity.

continuo, *a.* continual; continuous.

contorcerse, *v.* writhe, twist.

contorción, *f.* contortion.

contorno, *m.* contour; profile; outline; neighborhood.

contra, *prep.* against.

contraalmirante, *m.* rear admiral.

contraataque, *m.* counterattack.

contrabalancear, *v.* counterbalance.

contrabandear, *v.* smuggle.

contrabandista, *m.* smuggler.

contrabando, *m.* contraband, smuggling.

contracción, *f.* contraction.

contracepción, *f.* contraception, birth control.

contractual, *a.* contractual.

contradecir, *v.* contradict.

contradicción, *f.* contradiction.

contradictorio, *adj.* contradictory.

contraer, *v.* contract; shrink.

contrahacedor -ra, *n.* imitator.

contrahacer, *v.* forge.

contralor, *m.* comptroller.

contramandar, *v.* countermand.

contraorden, *f.* countermand.

contraparte, *f.* counterpart.

contrapesar, *v.* counterbalance, offset.

contrapeso, *m.* counterweight.

contrapunto, *m.* counterpoint.

contrariamente, *adv.* contrarily.

contrariar, *v.* contradict; vex; antagonize; counteract.

contrariedad, *f.* contrariness; opposition; contradiction; disappointment; trouble.

contrario, *a. & m.* contrary, opposite.

contrarrestar, *v.* resist; counteract.

contrasol, *m.* sunshade.

contraste, *m.* contrast. —**contrastar**, *v.*

contratar, *v.* engage, contract.

contratiempo, *m.* accident; misfortune.

contratista, *m.* contractor.

contrato, *m.* contract.

contribución, *f.* contribution; tax.

contribuir, *v.* contribute.

contribuyente, *m.* contributor; taxpayer.

contrición, *f.* contrition.

contristar, *v.* afflict.

contrito, *a.* contrite, remorseful.

control, *m.* control. —**controlar**, *v.*

controversia, *f.* controversy.

controversista, *m.* disputant.

controvertir, *v.* dispute.

contumacia, *f.* stubbornness.

contumaz, *adj.* stubborn.

contumelia, *f.* contumely; abuse.

conturbar, *v.* trouble, disturb.

contusión, *f.* contusion; bruise.

convalecencia, *f.* convalescence.

convalecer, *v.* convalesce.

convaleciente, *a.* convalescent.

convecino, *adj.* near, close.

convencedor, *adj.* convincing.

convencer, *v.* convince.

convencimiento, *m.* conviction, firm belief.

convención, *f.* convention.

convencional, *a.* conventional.

conveniencia, *f.* suitability; advantage, interest.

conveniente, *a.* suitable; advantageous, opportune.

convenio, *m.* pact, treaty; agreement.

convenir, *v.* assent, agree, concur; be suitable, fitting, convenient.

convento, *m.* convent.

convergencia, *f.* convergence.

convergir, *v.* converge.

conversación, *f.* conversation.

conversar, *v.* converse.

conversión, *f.* conversion.

convertible, *a.* convertible.

convertir, *v.* convert.

convexidad, *f.* convexity.

convexo, *a.* convex.

convicción, *f.* conviction.

convicto, *adj.* guilty.

convidado -da, *n.* guest.

convidar, *v.* invite.

convincente, *a.* convincing.

convite, *m.* invitation, treat.

convocación, *f.* convocation.

convocar, *v.* convoke, assemble.

convoy, *m.* convoy, escort.

convoyar, *v.* convey; escort.

convulsión, *f.* convulsion.

convulsivo, *adj.* convulsive.

conyugal, *adj.* conjugal.

cónyuge, *n.* spouse, mate.

coñac, *m.* cognac, brandy.

cooperación, *f.* cooperation.

cooperador, *adj.* cooperative.

cooperar, *v.* cooperate.

cooperativo, *a.* cooperative.

coordinación, *f.* coordination.

coordinar, *v.* coordinate.

copa, *f.* goblet.

copartícipe, *m.* partner.

copete, *m.* tuft; toupee.

copia, *f.* copy. —**copiar**, *v.*

copiadora, *f.* copier.

copioso, *a.* copious.

copista, *m.* copyist.

copla, *f.* popular song.

coplero, *m.* poetaster.

cópula, *f.* connection.

coqueta, *f.* flirt. —**coquetear**, *v.*

coraje, *m.* courage, bravery; anger.

coral, 1. *a.* choral. 2. *m.* coral.

coralino, *a.* coral.

corazón, *m.* heart.

corazonada, *f.* foreboding.

corbata, *f.* necktie.

corbeta, *f.* corvette.

corcova, *f.* hump, hunch.

corcovado, *m.* hunchback.

corcho, *m.* cork.

cordaje, *m.* rigging.

cordel, *m.* string, cord.

cordero, *m.* lamb.

cordial, *a.* cordial, hearty.

cordialidad, *f.* cordiality.

cordillera, *f.* mountain range.

cordón, *m.* cord; (shoe) lace.

cordura, *f.* sanity.

coreografía, *f.* choreography.

corista, *f.* chorus girl.

corneja, *f.* crow.

córneo, *a.* horny.

corneta, *f.* bugle, horn, cornet.

corniforme, *a.* horn-shaped.

cornisa, *f.* cornice.

cornucopia, *f.* cornucopia.

coro, *m.* chorus; choir.

corola, *f.* corolla.

corolario, *m.* corollary.

corona, *f.* crown, halo, wreath.

coronación, *f.* coronation.

coronamiento, *f.* completion of a task.

coronar, v. crown.
coronel, m. colonel.
coronilla, f. small crown.
corporación, f. corporation.
corporal, adj. corporeal, bodily.
corpóreo, a. corporeal.
corpulencia, f. corpulence.
corpulento, a. corpulent, stout.
corpuscular, a. corpuscular.
corpúsculo, m. corpuscle.
corral, m. corral, pen, yard.
correa, f. belt, strap.
corrección, f. correction.
correcto, a. correct, proper, right.
corrector, m. corrector, proofreader.
corredera, f. race course.
corredizo, a. easily untied.
corredor, m. corridor; runner.
corregible, a. corrigible.
corregidor, m. corrector; magistrate, mayor.
corregir, v. correct.
correlación, f. correlation.
correlacionar, v. correlate.
correlativo, a. correlative.
correo, m. mail.
correoso, a. leathery.
correr, v. run.
correría, f. raid; escapade.
correspondencia, f. correspondence.
corresponder, v. correspond.
correspondiente, a. & m. corresponding; correspondent.
corresponsal, m. correspondent.
corretaje, m. brokerage.
correvedile, m. tale bearer; gossip.
corrida, f. race. **c. (de toros),** bullfight.
corrido, a. abashed; expert.
corriente, 1. a. current, standard. **2.** f. current, stream. **m. al c.,** informed, up to date.
corroboración, f. corroboration.
corroborar, v. corroborate.
corroer, v. corrode.
corromper, v. corrupt.
corrompido, adj. corrupt.
corrupción, f. corruption.
corruptela, f. corruption, vice.
corruptibilidad, f. corruptibility.
corruptor, m. corrupter.
corsario, m. corsair.
corsé, m. corset.
corso, m. piracy.
cortadillo, m. small glass.
cortado, a. cut.
cortadura, f. cut.
cortante, a. cutting, sharp, keen.
cortapisa, f. obstacle.
cortaplumas, m. penknife.
cortar, v. cut, cut off, cut out.
corte, f. court, m. cut.
cortedad, f. smallness; shyness.
cortejar, v. pay court to, woo.
cortejo, m. court, courtship; sweetheart.

cortés, a. civil, courteous, polite.
cortesana, f. courtesan.
cortesano. 1. a. courtly, courteous. **2.** m. courtier.
cortesía, f. courtesy.
corteza, f. bark; rind; crust.
cortijo, m. farmhouse.
cortina, f. curtain.
corto, a. short.
corva, a. bend of the knee.
cosa, f. thing. **c. de,** a matter of, roughly.
cosecha, f. crop, harvest. **—cosechar,** v.
coser, v. sew, stitch.
cosmético, a. & m. cosmetic.
cosmopolita, a. & n. cosmopolitan.
coso, m. arena for bull fights.
cosquilla, f. tickle. **—cosquillar,** v.
cosquilloso, a. ticklish.
costa, f. coast; cost, expense.
costado, m. side.
costal, m. sack, bag.
costanero, a. coastal.
costar, v. cost.
costarricense, a. & n. Costa Rican.
coste, m. cost, price.
costear, v. defray, sponsor; sail along the coast of.
costilla, f. rib; chop.
costo, m. cost, price.
costoso, a. costly.
costra, f. crust.
costumbre, f. custom, practice, habit.
costura, f. sewing; seam.
costurera, f. seamstress, dressmaker.
cota de malla, coat of mail.
cotejar, v. compare.
coteleta, f. cutlet.
cotidiano, a. daily; everyday.
cotillón, m. cotillion.
cotización, f. quotation.
cotizar, v. quote (a price).
coto, m. enclosure; boundary.
cotón, m. printed cotton cloth.
cotufa, f. Jerusalem artichoke.
coturno, m. buskin.
covacha, f. small cave.
coxal, a. of the hip.
coy, m. hammock.
coyote, m. coyote.
coyuntura, f. joint; juncture.
coz, f. kick.
crac, m. failure.
cráneo, m. skull.
craniano, a. cranial.
crapuloso, a. drunken.
crasiento, a. greasy, oily.
craso, a. fat; gross.
cráter, m. crater.
craza, f. crucible.
creación, f. creation.
creador -ra, a. & n. creative; creator.
crear, v. create.
creativo, a. creative.
crébol, m. holly tree.
crecer, v. grow, grow up; increase.

creces, f.pl. increase, addition.
crecidamente, adv. abundantly.
crecido, a. increased, enlarged; swollen.
creciente, 1. a. growing. **2.** f. crescent.
crecimiento, m. growth.
credenciales, f.pl. credentials.
credibilidad, f. credibility.
crédito, m. credit.
credo, m. creed, belief.
crédulamente, adv. credulously, gullibly.
credulidad, f. credulity.
crédulo, a. credulous.
creedero, a. credible.
creedor, a. credulous, believing.
creencia, f. belief.
creer, v. believe; think.
creíble, a. credible, believable.
crema, f. cream.
cremación, f. cremation.
cremar, v. cremate.
crémor tártaro, cream of tartar.
creosota, f. creosote.
crepitar, v. crackle.
crepuscular, a. of or like the dawn or dusk.
crepúsculo, m. dusk, twilight.
crescendo, m. crescendo.
crespo, a. crisp; curly.
crespón, m. crepe.
cresta, f. crest.
crestado, a. crested.
creta, f. chalk.
cretáceo, a. chalky.
cretinismo, m. cretinism.
cretino, n. & a. cretin.
cretona, f. cretonne.
creyente, 1. a. believing. **2.** n. believer.
creyón, m. crayon.
cría, f. (stock) breeding; young (of an animal), litter.
criada, f. girl servant, maid.
criadero, m. (agr.) nursery.
criado -da, m. servant.
criador, a. fruitful, prolific.
crianza, f. breeding; upbringing.
criar, v. raise, rear, bring up; breed.
criatura, f. creature; infant.
criba, f. sieve; crib.
cribado, a. sifted.
cribar, v. sift.
crimen, m. crime.
criminal, a. & m. criminal.
criminalidad, f. criminality.
criminalmente, adv. criminally.
criminoso, a. criminal.
crin, f. mane of a horse.
crinolina, f. crinoline.
criocirugía, f. cryosurgery.
criollo -lla, a. & n. native; creole.
cripta, f. crypt.
criptografía, f. cryptography.
crisantemo, m. chrysanthemum.
crisis, f. crisis.
crisma, m. chrism.

crisol, m. crucible.

crispamiento, m. twitch, contraction.

crispar, v. contract (the muscles); twitch.

crista, f. heraldic crest.

cristal, m. crystal; lens.

cristalería, f. glassware.

cristalino, a. crystalline.

cristalización, f. crystallization.

cristalizar, v. crystallize.

cristianar, v. baptize.

cristiandad, f. Christendom.

cristianismo, m. Christianity.

cristiano -na, a. & n. Christian.

Cristo, m. Christ.

criterio, m. criterion; judgment.

crítica, f. criticism; critique.

criticable, a. blameworthy.

criticador, a. critical.

criticar, v. criticize.

crítico, a. & m. critical; critic.

croar, v. croak.

crocante, m. peanut brittle.

crocidar, v. crow.

crocodilo, m. crocodile.

cromático, a. chromatic.

cromo, m. chromium.

cromotipia, f. color printing.

crónica, f. chronicle.

crónico, a. chronic.

cronicón, m. concise chronicle.

cronista, m. chronicler.

cronología, f. chronology.

cronológicamente, adv. chronologically.

cronológico, a. chronologic.

cronometro, m. chronometer.

croqueta, f. croquette.

croquis, m. sketch; rough outline.

crótalo, m. rattlesnake; castanet.

cruce, m. crossing, crossroads, junction.

crucero, m. cruiser.

crucífero, a. cross-shaped.

crucificado, a. crucified.

crucificar, v. crucify.

crucifijo, m. crucifix.

crucifixión, f. crucifixion.

crudamente, adv. crudely.

crudeza, f. crudeness.

crudo, a. crude, raw.

cruel, a. cruel.

crueldad, f. cruelty.

cruelmente, adv. cruelly.

cruentamente, adv. bloodily.

cruento, a. bloody.

crujía, f. corridor.

crujido, m. creak.

crujir, v. crackle, creak; rustle.

cruórico, a. bloody.

crup, m. croup.

crustáceo, m. & a. crustacean.

cruz, f. cross.

cruzada, f. crusade.

cruzado -da, n. crusader.

cruzamiento, m. crossing.

cruzar, v. cross.

cruzarse con, v. to (meet and) pass.

cuaderno, m. notebook.

cuadra, f. block; (hospital) ward.

cuadradamente, adv. exactly, precisely; completely, in full.

cuadradillo, m. lump of sugar.

cuadrado, a. & m. square.

cuadrafónico, a. quadraphonic.

cuadragésima, f. Lent.

cuadragesimal, a. Lenten.

cuadrángulo, m. quadrangle.

cuadrante, m. quadrant; dial.

cuadrar, v. square; suit.

cuadricular, a. in squares.

cuadrilátero, a. quadrilateral.

cuadrilla, f. band, troop, gang.

cuadrinieto, n. great-grandchild.

cuadro, m. picture; painting; frame. a cuadros, checked, plaid.

cuadro de servicio, timetable.

cuadrupedal, a. quadruped.

cuádruplo, a. a fourfold.

cuajada, f. curd.

cuajamiento, m. coagulation.

cuajar, v. coagulate; overdecorate.

cuajo, m. rennet; coagulation.

cuakerismo, m. Quakerism.

cuákero, n. & a. Quaker.

cual, rel. pron. which.

cuál, a. & pron. what, which.

cualidad, f. quality.

cualitativo, a. qualitative.

cualquiera, a. & pron. whatever, any; anyone.

cuando, conj. when.

cuando, adv. when. de cuando en cuando, from time to time.

cuantía, f. quantity; amount.

cuantiar, v. estimate.

cuantidad, f. quantity.

cuantiosamente, adv. abundantly.

cuantioso, a. abundant.

cuantitativo, a. quantitative.

cuanto, a., adv. & pron. as much as, as many as; all that which. en c., as soon as. en c. a, as for. c. antes, as soon as possible. c. más . . . tanto más, the more . . . the more. unos cuantos, a few.

cuánto, a. & adv. how much, how many.

cuaquerismo, m. Quakerism.

cuáquero, n. & a. Quaker.

cuarenta, a. & pron. forty.

cuarentena, f. quarantine.

cuaresma, f. Lent.

cuaresmal, a. Lenten.

cuarta, f. quarter; quadrant; quart.

cuartana, f. ague.

cuartear, v. divide into quarters.

cuartel, m. (mil.) quarters; barracks; (naut.) hatch. c. general, headquarters. sin c., giving no quarter.

cuartelada, f. military uprising.

cuarterón, n. & a. quadroon.

cuarteto, m. quartet.

cuartillo, m. pint.

cuarto, 1. a. fourth. 2. m. quarter; room.

cuarto de baño, bathroom.

cuarto de dormir, bedroom.

cuarzo, m. quartz.

cuasi, adv. almost, nearly.

cuate, a. & n. twin.

cuatrero, m. cattle rustler.

cuatrillón, m. quadrillion.

cuatro, a. & pron. four.

cuatrocientos, a. & pron. four hundred.

cuba, f. cask, tub, vat.

cubano -na, a. & n. Cuban.

cubero, m. cooper.

cubertura, f. cover.

cubeta, f. small barrel, keg.

cúbico, a. cubic.

cubierta, f. cover; envelope; wrapping; tread (of a tire); deck.

cubiertamente, adv. secretly, stealthily.

cubierto, m. place (at table).

cubil, m. lair.

cubo, m. cube; bucket.

cubrecama, f. bedspread.

cubrir, v. cover.

cubrirse, v. put on one's hat.

cucaracha, f. cockroach.

cuclillo, m. cuckoo.

cuco, a. sly.

cuculla, f. hood, cowl.

cuchara, f. spoon, tablespoon.

cucharada, f. spoonful.

cucharita, cucharilla, f. teaspoon.

cucharón, m. dipper, ladle.

cuchicheo, m. whisper. —cuchichear, v.

cuchilla, f. cleaver.

cuchillada, f. slash.

cuchillería, f. cutlery.

cuchillo, m. knife.

cucho, m. fertilizer.

cuchufleta, f. jest.

cuelga, f. cluster, bunch.

cuelgacapas, m. coat rack.

cuello, m. neck; collar.

cuenca, f. socket; (river) basin; wooden bowl.

cuenco, m. earthen bowl.

cuenta, f. account; bill. darse c., to realize. tener en c., to keep in mind.

cuentagotas, m. dropper (for medicine).

cuentista, m. informer.

cuento, m. story, tale.

cuerda, f. cord; chord; rope; string; spring (of clock). dar c. a, to wind (clock).

cuerdamente, adv. sanely; prudently.

cuerdo, a. sane; prudent.

cuerno, m. horn.

cuero, m. leather; hide.

cuerpo, m. body; corps.

cuervo, m. crow, raven.

cuesco, m. pit, stone (of fruit).

cuesta, f. hill, slope. a cuestas, to carry on one's back.

cuestación, f. solicitation for charity.

cuestión, f. question; affair; argument.
cuestionable, a. questionable.
cuestionar, v. question; discuss; argue.
cuestionario, m. questionnaire.
cuete, m. firecracker.
cuetzale, m. quetzal.
cueva, f. cave; cellar.
cugujada, f. lark.
cuidado, m. care, caution, worry. **tener c.,** to be careful.
cuidadosamente, adv. carefully.
cuidadoso, a. careful, painstaking.
cuidante, n. caretaker, custodian.
cuidar, v. take care of.
cuita, f. trouble, care, grief.
cuitado, a. unfortunate; shy, timid.
cuitamiento, m. timidity.
culata, f. haunch, buttock; butt of a gun.
culatada, f. recoil.
culatazo, m. blow with the butt of a gun; recoil.
culebra, f. snake.
culero, a. lazy, indolent.
culinario, a. culinary.
culminación, f. culmination.
culminar, v. culminate.
culpa, f. fault, guilt, blame. **tener la c.,** to be at fault. **echar la culpa a,** to blame.
culpabilidad, f. guilt, fault, blame.
culpable, a. at fault, guilty, to blame.
culpar, v. blame, accuse.
cultamente, adv. politely, elegantly.
cultivable, a. arable.
cultivación, f. cultivation.
cultivador, m. cultivator.
cultivar, v. cultivate.
cultivo, m. cultivation; (growing) crop.
culto, 1. a. cultured, cultivated. **2.** m. cult; worship.
cultura, f. culture; refinement.
cultural, a. cultural.
culturar, v. cultivate.
cumbre, m. summit, peak.
cumpleaños, m.pl. birthday.
cumplidamente, adv. completely.
cumplido, a. polite, polished.
cumplimentar, v. compliment.
cumplimiento, m. fulfillment; compliment.
cumplir, v. comply; carry out, fulfill; reach (years of age).
cumular, v. accumulate.
cumulativo, a. cumulative.
cúmulo, m. heap, pile.
cuna, f. cradle.
cundir, v. spread; expand; propagate.
cuneiforme, a. cuneiform, wedge-shaped.
cuneo, m. rocking.
cuña, f. wedge.
cuñada, f. sister-in-law.

cuñado, m. brother-in-law.
cuñete, m. keg.
cuociente, m. quotient.
cuota, f. quota; dues.
cuotidiano, a. daily.
cupé, m. coupé.
cupido, m. lover.
cupo, m. share; assigned quota.
cupón, m. coupon.
cúpula, f. dome.
cura, m. priest. f. treatment, (medical) care. **c. de urgencia,** first aid.
curable, a. curable.
curación, f. healing; cure; (surgical) dressing.
curado, a. cured, healed.
curador, m. custodian; curator.
curandero, m. healer, medicine man.
curar, v. cure, heal, treat.
curativo, a. curative, healing.
curia, f. ecclesiastical court.
curiosear, v. snoop, pry, meddle.
curiosidad, f. curiosity.
curioso, a. curious.
curro, a. showy, loud, flashy.
cursante, n. student.
cursar, v. frequent; attend to.
cursi, a. vulgar, shoddy, in bad taste.
curso, m. course.
curtidor, m. tanner.
curtir, v. tan.
curva, f. curve; bend.
curvatura, f. curvature.
cúspide, f. top, peak.
custodia, f. custody.
custodiar, v. guard, watch.
custodio, m. custodian.
cutáneo, a. cutaneous.
cutícula, f. cuticle.
cutis, m. or f. skin, complexion.
cuyo, a. whose.

CH

chabancano, a. clumsy.
chacal, m. jackal.
chacó, m. shako.
chacona, f. chaconne.
chacota, f. fun, mirth.
chacotear, v. joke.
chacra, f. small farm.
chafallar, v. mend badly.
chagra, m. rustic; rural person.
chal, m. shawl.
chalán, m. horse trader.
chaleco, m. vest.
chalet, m. chalet.
challí, m. challis.
chamada, f. brushwood.
chamarillero, m. gambler.
chamarra, f. coarse linen jacket.
chambelán, m. chamberlain.
champaña, m. champagne.
champú, m. shampoo.
chamuscar, v. scorch.
chancaco, a. brown.

chancear, v. jest, joke.
chanciller, m. chancellor.
chancillería, f. chancery.
chancla, f. old shoe.
chancleta, f. slipper.
chanclos, m.pl. galoshes.
chancro, m. chancre.
changador, m. porter, handyman.
chantaje, m. blackmail.
chantajista, n. blackmailer.
chanto, m. flagstone.
chantre, m. precentor.
chanza, f. joke, jest. —**chancear,** v.
chanzoneta, f. chansonette.
chapa, f. (metal) sheet, plate; lock.
chaparrada, f. shower.
chaparral, m. chaparral.
chaparreras, f.pl. chaps.
chaparrón, m. downpour.
chapear, v. veneer.
chapeo, m. hat.
chapitel, m. spire, steeple; (architecture) capital.
chapodar, v. lop.
chapón, m. inkblot.
chapotear, v. paddle or splash in the water.
chapoteo, m. splash.
chapucear, v. fumble, bungle.
chapucero, a. sloppy, bungling.
chapurrear, v. speak (a language) brokenly.
chapuz, m. dive; ducking.
chapuzar, v. dive, duck.
chaqueta, f. jacket, coat.
charada, f. charade.
charamusca, f. twisted candy stick.
charanga, f. military band.
charanguero, m. peddler.
charca, f. pool, pond.
charco, m. pool, puddle.
charla, f. chat; chatter, prattle. —**charlar,** v.
charladuría, f. chatter.
charlatán, m. charlatan.
charlatanismo, m. charlatanism.
charol, m. varnish.
charolar, v. varnish; polish.
charquear, v. jerk (beef).
charquí, m. jerked beef.
charrán, a. roguish.
chascarillo, m. risqué story.
chasco, m. disappointment, blow; practical joke.
chasis, m. chassis.
chasquear, v. fool, trick; disappoint; crack (a whip).
chasquido, m. crack (sound).
chata, f. bedpan.
chato, a. flat-nosed, pug-nosed.
chauvinismo, m. chauvinism.
chauvinista, n. & a. chauvinist.
chelín, m. shilling.
cheque, m. (bank) check.
chica, f. girl.
chicana, f. chicanery.
chicle, m. chewing gum.
chico, 1. a. little. **2.** m. boy.

chicote, *m.* cigar; cigar butt.
chicotear, *v.* whip, flog.
chicha, *f.* an alcoholic drink.
chícharo, *f.* pea.
chicharra, *f.* cicada; talkative person.
chicharrón, *m.* crisp fried scrap of meat.
chichear, *v.* hiss in disapproval.
chichón, *m.* bump, bruise, lump.
chifladura, *f.* mania; whim; jest.
chiflar, *v.* whistle; become insane.
chiflido, *m.* shrill whistle.
chile, *m.* chili.
chileno -na, *a. & n.* Chilean.
chillido, *m.* shriek, scream, screech. —**chillar,** *v.*
chillón, *a.* shrill.
chimenea, *f.* chimney, smokestack; fireplace.
china, *f.* pebble; maid; Chinese woman.
chinarro, *m.* large pebble, stone.
chinche, *f.* bedbug; thumbtack.
chinchilla, *f.* chinchilla.
chinchorro, *m.* fishing net.
chinela, *f.* slipper.
chinero, *m.* china closet.
chino -na, *a. & n.* Chinese.
chiquero, *m.* pen for pigs, goats, etc.
chiquito, 1. *a.* small, tiny. **2.** *n.* small child.
chiribitil, *m.* small room, den.
chirimía, *f.* flageolet.
chiripa, *f.* stroke of good luck.
chirla, *f.* mussel.
chirle, *a.* insipid.
chirona, *f.* prison, jail.
chirrido, *m.* squeak, chirp. —**chirriar,** *v.*
chis, *interj.* hush!
chisgarabís, *n.* meddler; unimportant person.
chisguete, *m.* squirt, splash.
chisme, *m.* gossip. —**chismear,** *v.*
chismero, *m.* gossiper.
chismoso, *adj.* gossiping.
chispa, *f.* spark.
chispeante, *a.* sparkling.
chispear, *v.* sparkle.
chisporrotear, *v.* emit sparks.
chistar, *v.* mumble.
chiste, *m.* joke, gag; witty saying.
chistera, *f.* fish basket; top hat.
chistoso, *a.* funny, comic, amusing.
chito, *interj.* hush!
chiva, *f.* female goat.
chivato, *m.* kid, young goat.
chivo, *m.* male goat.
chocante, *a.* striking; shocking; unpleasant.
chocar, *v.* collide, clash, crash; shock.
chocarrear, *v.* joke, jest.

choclo, *m.* clog; overshoe; ear of corn.
chocolate, *m.* chocolate.
chocolatería, *f.* chocolate shop.
chochear, *v.* be in one's dotage.
chochera, *f.* dotage, senility.
chofer, chófer, *m.* chauffeur, driver.
chofeta, *f.* chafing dish.
cholo, *m.* half-breed.
chopo, *m.* black poplar.
choque, *m.* collision, clash, crash; shock.
chorizo, *m.* sausage.
chorrear, *v.* spout; drip.
chorro, *m.* spout; spurt, jet. **llover a chorros,** to pour (rain).
choto, *m.* calf, kid.
choza, *f.* hut, cabin.
chozno, *m.* great-grandson.
chubasco, *m.* shower, squall.
chubascoso, *a.* squally.
chuchería, *f.* trinket, knickknack.
chulería, *f.* pleasant manner.
chuleta, *f.* chop, cutlet.
chulo, *m.* rascal, rogue; joker.
chupa, *f.* jacket.
chupada, *f.* suction.
chupado, *a.* very thin.
chupaflor, *m.* hummingbird.
chupar, *v.* suck.
churrasco, *m.* roasted meat.
chuscada, *f.* joke, jest.
chusco, *a.* funny, humorous.
chusma, *f.* mob, rabble.
chuzo, *m.* pike.

D

dable, *a.* possible.
dactilógrafo, *m.* typewriter.
dádiva, *f.* gift.
dadivosamente, *adv.* generously.
dadivoso, *a.* generous, bountiful.
dador, *m.* giver.
dados, *m.pl.* dice.
daga, *f.* dagger.
dalia, *f.* dahlia.
daltonismo, *m.* color blindness.
dallador, *m.* lawn mower.
dallar, *v.* mow.
dama, *f.* lady.
damasco, *m.* apricot.
damisela, *f.* young lady, girl.
danés -esa, *a. & n.* Danish, Dane.
danza, *f.* (the) dance. —**danzar,** *v.*
danzante, *m.* dancer.
dañable, *a.* condemnable.
dañar, *v.* hurt, harm; damage.
dañino, dañoso, *a.* harmful.
daño, *m.* damage; harm.
dañoso, *a.* harmful.
dar, *v.* give; strike (clock). **d. a,** face, open on. **d. con,** find, locate.
dardo, *m.* dart.
dársena, *f.* dock.
datar, *v.* date.

dátil, *m.* date (fruit).
dativo, *m. & a.* dative.
datos, *m.pl.* data.
de, *prep.* of; from; than.
debajo, *adv.* underneath. **d. de,** under.
debate, *m.* debate.
debatir, *v.* debate, argue.
debe, *m.* debit.
debelación, *f.* conquest.
debelar, *v.* conquer.
deber, 1. *v.* owe; must; be to, be supposed to. **2.** *m.* obligation.
debido, *a.* due.
débil, *a.* weak, faint.
debilidad, *f.* weakness.
debilitación, *f.* weakness.
debilitar, *v.* weaken.
débito, *m.* debit.
debutante, *f.* debutante.
debutar, *v.* make a debut.
década, *f.* decade.
decadencia, *f.* decadence, decline, decay.
decadente, *a.* decadent, declining, decaying.
decaer, *v.* decay, decline.
decalitro, *m.* decaliter.
decálogo, *m.* decalogue.
decámetro, *m.* decameter.
decano, *m.* dean.
decantado, *a.* much discussed; overexalted.
decapitación, *f.* beheading.
decapitar, *v.* behead.
decencia, *f.* decency.
decenio, *m.* decade.
decente, *a.* decent.
decentemente, *adv.* decently.
decepción, *f.* disappointment; delusion.
decepcionar, *v.* disappoint, disillusion.
decibelio, *m.* decibel.
decididamente, *adv.* decidedly.
decidir, *v.* decide.
decigramo, *m.* decigram.
decilitro, *m.* deciliter.
décima, *f.* ten-line stanza.
decimal, *a.* decimal.
décimo, *a.* tenth.
decir, *v.* tell, say. **es d.,** that is (to say).
decisión, *f.* decision.
decisivamente, *adv.* decisively.
decisivo, *a.* decisive.
declamación, *f.* declamation, speech.
declamar, *v.* declaim.
declaración, *f.* declaration; statement; plea.
declarar, *v.* declare, state.
declarativo, *a.* declarative.
declinación, *f.* descent; decay; decline; declension.
declinar, *v.* decline.
declive, *m.* declivity, slope.
decocción, *f.* decoction.
decomiso, *m.* seizure, confiscation.
decoración, *f.* decoration, trimming.
decorado, *m.* (theat.) scenery, set.

20

decorar, v. decorate, trim.
decorativo, a. decorative, ornamental.
decoro, m. decorum; decency.
decoroso, a. decorous.
decrecer, v. decrease.
decrépito, a. decrepit.
decreto, m. decree. —**decretar**, v.
dechado, m. model; sample; pattern; example.
dedal, m. thimble.
dédalo, m. labyrinth.
dedicación, f. dedication.
dedicar, v. devote; dedicate.
dedicatoria, f. dedication, inscription.
dedo, m. finger, toe.
deducción, f. deduction.
deducir, v. deduce; subtract.
defectivo, a. defective.
defecto, m. defect, flaw.
defectuoso, a. defective, faulty.
defender, v. defend.
defensa, f. defense.
defensivo, a. defensive.
defensor, m. defender.
deferencia, f. deference.
deferir, v. defer.
deficiente, a. deficient.
déficit, m. deficit.
definición, f. definition.
definido, a. definite.
definir, v. define; establish.
definitivamente, adv. definitely.
definitivo, a. definite; definitive.
deformación, f. deformation.
deformar, v. deform.
deforme, a. deformed; ugly.
deformidad, f. deformity.
defraudar, v. defraud.
defunción, f. death.
degeneración, f. degeneration.
degenerado, a. degenerate. —**degenerar**, v.
deglutir, v. swallow.
degollar, v. behead.
degradación, f. degradation.
degradar, v. degrade, debase.
deidad, f. deity.
deificación, f. deification.
deificar, v. deify.
deifico, a. divine, deific.
deismo, m. deism.
dejadez, f. neglect, untidiness; laziness.
dejado, a. untidy; lazy.
dejar, v. let, allow; leave. **d. de,** stop, leave off. **no d. de,** not fail to.
dejo, m. abandonment; negligence; aftertaste; accent.
del, contr. of **de** + **el**.
delantal, m. apron.
delante, adv. ahead, forward; in front.
delantero, a. forward, front, first.
delator, m. informer; accuser.
delegación, f. delegation.
delegado -da, n. delegate. —**delegar**, v.

deleite, m. delight. —**deleitar**, v.
deleitoso, a. delightful.
deletrear, v. spell; decipher.
delfín, m. dolphin; dauphin.
delgadez, f. thinness, slenderness.
delgado, a. thin, slender, slim, slight.
deliberación, f. deliberation.
deliberadamente, adv. deliberately.
deliberar, v. deliberate.
deliberativo, a. deliberative.
delicadamente, adv. delicately.
delicadeza, f. delicacy.
delicado, a. delicate, dainty.
delicia, f. delight; deliciousness.
delicioso, a. delicious.
delincuencia, f. delinquency.
delincuente, a. & m. delinquent; culprit, offender.
delineación, f. delineation, sketch.
delinear, v. delineate, sketch.
delirante, a. delirious.
delirar, v. rave, be delirious.
delirio, m. delirium; rapture, bliss.
delito, m. crime, offense.
delta, m. delta (of river).
demagogia, f. demagogy.
demagogo, m. demagogue.
demanda, f. demand, claim.
demandador -ra, n. plaintiff.
demandar, v. sue; demand.
demarcación, f. demarcation.
demarcar, v. demarcate, limit.
demás, a. & n. other; (the) rest (of). **por d.,** too much.
demasía, f. excess; audacity; iniquity.
demasiado, a. & adv. too; too much; too many.
demencia, f. dementia; insanity.
demente, a. demented.
democracia, f. democracy.
demócrata, m. & f. democrat.
democrático, a. democratic.
demoler, v. demolish, tear down.
demolición, f. demolition.
demonio, m. demon, devil.
demontre, m. devil.
demora, f. delay, —**demorar**, v.
demostración, f. demonstration.
demostrador, m. demonstrator.
demostrar, v. demonstrate, show.
demostrativo, a. demonstrative.
demudar, v. change; disguise; conceal.
denegación, f. denial, refusal.
denegar, v. deny, refuse.
dengue, m. prudishness; dengue.
denigración, f. defamation, disgrace.
denigrar, v. defame, disgrace.
denodado, a. brave, dauntless.

denominación, f. denomination.
denominar, v. name, call.
denotación, f. denotation.
denotar, v. denote, betoken, express.
densidad, f. density.
denso, a. dense.
dentado, a. toothed; serrated; cogged.
dentadura, f. set of teeth.
dental, a. dental.
dentífrico, m. dentifrice.
dentista, m. dentist.
dentistería, f. dentistry.
dentro, adv. within, inside. **d. de poco,** in a short while.
denuedo, m. bravery, courage.
denuesto, m. insult, offense.
denuncia, f. denunciation; declaration.
denunciación, f. denunciation.
denunciar, v. denounce.
deparar, v. offer; grant.
departamento, m. department, section.
departir, v. talk, chat.
dependencia, f. dependence; branch office.
depender, v. depend.
dependiente, a. & m. dependent; clerk.
depilatorio, a. depilatory.
deplorable, a. deplorable, wretched.
deplorablemente, adv. deplorably.
deplorar, v. deplore.
deponer, v. depose.
deportación, f. deportation; exile.
deportar, v. deport.
deporte, m. sport. —**deportivo**, a.
deposición, f. assertion, deposition; removal; movement.
depositante, m. & f. depositor.
depósito, m. deposit. —**depositar**, v.
depravación, f. depravation; depravity.
depravado, a. depraved, wicked.
depravar, v. deprave, corrupt, pervert.
depreciación, f. depreciation.
depreciar, v. depreciate.
depredación, f. depredation.
depredar, v. pillage, depredate.
depresión, f. depression.
depresivo, a. depressive.
deprimir, v. depress.
depurar, v. purify.
derecha, f. right (hand, side).
derechera, f. shortcut.
derecho, **1.** a. right; straight. **2.** m. right; (the) law. **derechos,** (com.) duty.
derechura, f. straightness.
derelicto, a. abandoned, derelict.
deriva, f. (naut.) drift.
derivación, f. derivation.
derivar, v. derive.

derogar, v. derogate; repeal; abrogate.

derramamiento, m. overflow.

derramar, v. spill, pour, scatter.

derrame, m. overflow; discharge.

derretir, v. melt, dissolve.

derribar, v. demolish, knock down; bowl over, floor, fell.

derrocamiento, m. overthrow.

derrocar, v. overthrow; oust; demolish.

derrochar, v. waste.

derroche, m. waste.

derrota, f. rout, defeat. —**derrotar**, v.

derrumbamiento, derrumbe, m. collapse; landslide.

derrumbarse, v. collapse, tumble.

derviche, m. dervish.

desabotonar, v. unbutton.

desabrido, a. insipid, tasteless.

desabrigar, v. uncover.

desabrochar, v. unbutton, unclasp.

desacierto, m. error.

desacobardar, v. remove fear; embolden.

desacomodadamente, adv. inconveniently.

desacomodado, a. unemployed.

desacomodar, v. molest; inconvenience; dismiss.

desacomodo, m. loss of employment.

desconsejado, a. imprudent, ill advised, rash.

desaconsejar, v. dissuade.

desacordadamente, adv. unadvisedly.

desacordar, v. differ, disagree; be forgetful.

desacorde, a. discordant.

desacostumbradamente, adv. unusually.

desacostumbrado, a. unusual, unaccustomed.

desacostumbrar, v. give up a habit or custom.

desacreditar, v. discredit.

desacuerdo, m. disagreement.

desadeudar, v. pay one's debts.

desadormecer, v. waken, rouse.

desadornar, v. divest of ornament.

desadvertidamente, adv. inadvertently.

desadvertido, a. imprudent.

desadvertimiento, m. imprudence, rashness.

desadvertir, v. act imprudently.

desafección, f. disaffection.

desafecto, a. disaffected.

desafiar, v. defy; challenge.

desafinar, v. be out of tune.

desafío, m. defiance; challenge.

desaforar, v. infringe one's rights; be outrageous.

desafortunado, a. unfortunate.

desafuero, m. violation of the law; outrage.

desagraciado, a. graceless.

desagradable, a. disagreeable, unpleasant.

desagradablemente, adv. disagreeably.

desagradecido, a. ungrateful.

desagradecimiento, m. ingratitude.

desagrado, m. displeasure.

desagraviar, v. make amends.

desagregar, v. separate, disintegrate.

desagriar, v. mollify, appease.

desaguadero, m. drain, outlet; cesspool; sink.

desaguador, m. water pipe.

desaguar, v. drain.

desaguisado, m. offense; injury.

desahogadamente, adv. impudently; brazenly.

desahogado, a. impudent, brazen; cheeky.

desahogar, v. relieve.

desahogo, m. relief; nerve, cheek.

desahuciar, v. give up hope for; despair of.

desairado, a. graceless.

desaire, m. slight; scorn. —**desairar**, v.

desajustar, v. mismatch, misfit; make unfit.

desalar, v. hurry, hasten.

desalentar, v. make out of breath; discourage.

desaliento, m. discouragement.

desaliñar, v. disarrange; make untidy.

desaliño, m. slovenliness, untidiness.

desalivar, v. salivate.

desalmadamente, adv. mercilessly.

desalmado, a. merciless.

desalojamiento, m. displacement; dislodging.

desalojar, v. dislodge.

desalquilado, a. vacant, unrented.

desamar, v. cease loving.

desamasado, a. dissolve, undo.

desamistarse, v. quarrel, disagree.

desamor, m. disaffection, dislike; hatred.

desamorado, a. cruel; harsh; rude.

desamparador, m. deserter.

desamparar, v. desert, abandon.

desamparo, m. desertion, abandonment.

desamueblar, v. dismantle.

desandrajado, a. shabby, ragged.

desanimadamente, adv. in a discouraged manner; spiritlessly.

desanimar, v. dishearten, discourage.

desánimo, m. discouragement.

desanudar, v. untie; loosen; disentangle.

desapacible, a. rough, harsh; unpleasant.

desaparecer, v. disappear.

desaparición, f. disappearance.

desapasionadamente, adv. dispassionately.

desapasionado, a. dispassionate.

desapego, m. impartiality.

desapercibido, adj. unprepared.

desapiadado, a. merciless, cruel.

desaplicación, f. indolence, laziness; negligence.

desaplicado, a. indolent, lazy; negligent.

desaposesionar, v. dispossess.

desapreciar, v. depreciate.

desapretador, m. screwdriver.

desapretar, v. loosen; relieve, ease.

desaprisionar, v. set free, release.

desaprobación, f. disapproval.

desaprobar, v. disapprove.

desaprovechado, a. useless, profitless; backward.

desaprovechar, v. waste; be backward.

desarbolar, v. unmast.

desarmado, a. disarmed, defenseless.

desarmar, v. disarm.

desarme, m. disarmament.

desarraigar, v. uproot; eradicate; expel.

desarreglar, v. disarrange, mess up.

desarrollar, v. develop.

desarrollo, m. development.

desarropar, v. undress; uncover.

desarrugar, v. remove wrinkles from.

desaseado, a. dirty; disorderly.

desasear, v. make dirty or disorderly.

desaseo, m. dirtiness; disorder.

desasir, v. loosen; disengage.

desasociable, a. unsociable.

desasosegar, v. disturb.

desasosiego, m. uneasiness.

desastrado, a. ragged, wretched.

desastre, m. disaster.

desastroso, a. disastrous.

desatar, v. untie, undo.

desatención, f. inattention; disrespect; rudeness.

desatender, v. ignore; disregard.

desatentado, a. inconsiderate; imprudent.

desatinado, a. foolish; insane, wild.

desatino, m. blunder. —**desatinar**, v.

desautorizado, a. unauthorized.

desautorizar, v. deprive of authority.

desavenencia, *f.* disagreement, discord.

desaventajado, *a.* disadvantageous.

desayuno, *m.* breakfast. —**desayunarse,** *v.*

desazón, *f.* insipidity; uneasiness.

desazonado, *a.* insipid; uneasy.

desbandada, *f.* disbanding.

desbandarse, *v.* disband.

desbarajuste, *m.* disorder, confusion.

desbaratar, *v.* destroy.

desbastar, *v.* plane, smoothen.

desbocado, *a.* foul-spoken, indecent.

desbocarse, *v.* use obscene language.

desbordamiento, *m.* overflow; flood.

desbordar, *v.* overflow.

desbrozar, *v.* clear away rubbish.

descabal, *a.* incomplete.

descabalar, *v.* render incomplete; impair.

descabellado, *a.* absurd, preposterous.

descabezar, *v.* behead.

descaecimiento, *m.* weakness; dejection.

descafeinado, *a.* decaffeinated.

descalabrar, *v.* injure, wound (esp. the head).

descalabro, *m.* accident, misfortune.

descalzarse, *v.* take off one's shoes.

descalzo, *a.* shoeless; barefoot.

descaminado, *a.* wrong, misguided.

descaminar, *v.* mislead; lead into error.

descamisado, *a.* shirtless; shabby.

descanso, *m.* rest. —**descansar,** *v.*

descarado, *a.* saucy, fresh.

descarga, *f.* discharge.

descargar, *v.* discharge, unload, dump.

descargo, *m.* acquittal.

descarnar, *v.* skin.

descaro, *m.* gall, effrontery.

descarriar, *v.* lead or go astray.

descarrilamiento, *m.* derailment.

descarrilar, *v.* derail.

descartar, *v.* discard.

descascarar, *v.* peel; boast, brag.

descendencia, *f.* descent, origin; progeny.

descender, *v.* descend.

descendiente, *m.& f.* descendant.

descendimiento, *m.* descent.

descenso, *m.* descent.

descentralización, *f.* decentralizing.

descifrar, *v.* decipher, puzzle out.

descoco, *m.* boldness, brazenness.

descolgar, *v.* take down.

descolorar, *v.* discolor.

descolorido, *a.* pale, faded.

descollar, *v.* stand out; excel.

descomedido, *a.* disproportionate; rude.

descomedirse, *v.* be rude.

descomponer, *v.* decompose; break down, get out of order.

descomposición, *f.* discomposure; disorder, confusion.

descompuesto, *a.* impudent, rude.

descomulgar, *v.* excommunicate.

descomunal, *a.* extraordinary, huge.

desconcertar, *v.* disconcert, baffle.

desconcierto, *m.* confusion, disarray.

desconectar, *v.* disconnect.

desconfiado, *a.* distrustful.

desconfianza, *f.* distrust.

desconfiar, *v.* distrust, mistrust; suspect.

descongestionante, *m.* decongestant.

desconocer, *v.* ignore, fail to recognize.

desconocido -da, *n.* stranger.

desconocimiento, *m.* ingratitude; ignorance.

desconsolado, *a.* disconsolate, wretched.

desconsuelo, *m.* grief.

descontar, *v.* discount, subtract.

descontentar, *v.* dissatisfy.

descontento, *m.* discontent.

descontinuar, *v.* discontinue.

desconvenir, *v.* disagree.

descorazonar, *v.* dishearten.

descorchar, *v.* uncork.

descortés, *a.* discourteous, impolite, rude.

descortesía, *f.* discourtesy, rudeness.

descortezar, *v.* peel.

descoyuntar, *v.* dislocate.

descrédito, *m.* discredit.

describir, *v.* describe.

descripción, *f.* description.

descriptivo, *a.* descriptive.

descuartizar, *v.* dismember, disjoint.

descubridor, *m.* discoverer.

descubrimiento, *m.* discovery.

descubrir, *v.* discover; uncover; disclose.

descubrirse, *v.* take off one's hat.

descuento, *m.* discount.

descuidado, *a.* reckless, careless; slack.

descuido, *m.* neglect. —**descuidar,** *v.*

desde, *prep.* since; from. **d. luego,** of course.

desdén, *m.* disdain. —**desdeñar,** *v.*

desdeñoso, *a.* contemptuous, disdainful, scornful.

desdicha, *f.* misfortune.

deseable, *a.* desirable.

desear, *v.* desire, wish.

desecar, *v.* dry, desiccate.

desechar, *v.* scrap, reject.

desecho, *m.* remainder, residue; (*pl*) waste.

desembalar, *v.* unpack.

desembarazado, *a.* free; unrestrained.

desembarazar, *v.* free; extricate; unburden.

desembarcar, *v.* disembark, go ashore.

desembocar, *v.* flow into.

desembolsar, *v.* disburse; expend.

desembolso, *m.* disbursement.

desemejante, *a.* unlike, dissimilar.

desempacar, *v.* unpack.

desempeñar, *v.* carry out; redeem.

desempeño, *m.* fulfillment.

desencajar, *v.* disjoint; disturb.

desencantar, *v.* disillusion.

desencanto, *m.* disillusion.

desencarcelar, *v.* set free; release.

desenfadado, *a.* free; unembarrassed; spacious.

desenfado, *m.* freedom; ease; calmness.

desengaño, *m.* disillusion. —**desengañar,** *v.*

desenlace, *m.* outcome, conclusion.

desenredar, *v.* disentangle.

desensartar, *v.* unthread.

desentenderse, *v.* overlook; avoid noticing.

desenterrar, *v.* disinter, exhume.

desenvainar, *v.* unsheath.

desenvoltura, *f.* impudence, boldness.

desenvolver, *v.* evolve, unfold.

deseo, *m.* wish, desire, urge.

deseoso, *a.* desirous.

deserción, *f.* desertion.

desertar, *v.* desert.

desertor, *m.* deserter.

desesperación, *f.* despair, desperation.

desesperado, *a.* desperate; hopeless.

desesperar, *v.* despair.

desfalcar, *v.* embezzle.

desfavorable, *a.* unfavorable.

desfigurar, *v.* disfigure, mar.

desfiladero, *m.* defile.

desfile, *m.* parade. —**desfilar,** *v.*

desgaire, *m.* slovenly appearance.

desgana, *f.* lack of appetite; repugnance.

desgarrar, *v.* tear, lacerate.

desgastar, *v.* wear away, waste, erode.

desgaste, *m.* wear; erosion.

desgracia, *f.* misfortune.

desgraciado, *a.* unfortunate.

desgranar, *v.* shell.

desgreñar, *v.* dishevel.

deshacer, *v.* undo, take apart, destroy.

deshacerse de, v. get rid of, dispose of.
deshecho, a. undone; wasted.
deshelar, v. thaw; melt.
desheredamiento, m. disinheriting.
desheredar, v. disinherit.
deshielo, m. thaw, melting.
deshinchar, v. reduce a swelling.
deshojarse, v. shed (leaves).
deshonestidad, f. dishonesty.
deshonesto, a. dishonest.
deshonra, f. dishonor.
deshonrar, v. disgrace; dishonor.
deshonroso, a. dishonorable.
desierto, m. desert, wilderness.
designar, v. appoint, name.
designio, m. purpose, intent.
desigual, a. uneven, unequal.
desigualdad, f. inequality.
desilusión, f. disappointment.
desinfección, f. disinfection.
desinfectar, v. disinfect.
desintegrar, v. disintegrate, zap.
desinterés, m. indifference.
desinteresado, a. disinterested, unselfish.
desistir, v. desist, stop.
desleal, a. disloyal.
deslealtad, f. disloyalty.
desleir, v. dilute, dissolve.
desligar, v. untie, loosen; free, release.
deslindar, v. make the boundaries of.
deslinde, m. demarcation.
desliz, m. slip; false step; weakness.
deslizarse, v. slide; slip; glide; coast.
deslumbramiento, m. dazzling glare; confusion.
deslumbrar, v. dazzle; glare.
deslustre, m. tarnish. **—deslustrar,** v.
desmán, m. mishap; misbehavior; excess.
desmantelar, v. dismantle.
desmañado, a. awkward, clumsy.
desmayar, v. dismay, appall.
desmayo, m. faint. **—desmayarse,** v.
desmejorar, v. make worse; decline.
desmembrar, v. dismember.
desmemoria, f. forgetfulness.
desmemoriado, a. forgetful.
desmentir, v. contradict, disprove.
desmenuzable, a. crisp, crumbly.
desmenuzar, v. crumble, break into bits.
desmesurado, a. excessive.
desmonetización, f. demonetization.
desmonetizar, v. demonetize.
desmontado, a. dismounted.
desmoralización, f. demoralization.
desmoralizar, v. demoralize.

desmoronar, v. crumble, decay.
desmovilizar, v. demobilize.
desnatar, v. skim.
desnaturalización, f. denaturalization.
desnaturalizar, v. denaturalize.
desnegamiento, m. denial, contradiction.
desnervar, v. enervate.
desnivel, m. unevenness or difference in elevation.
desnudamente, adv. nakedly.
desnudar, v. undress.
desnudez, f. bareness, nudity.
desnudo, a. bare, naked.
desnutrición, f. malnutrition.
desobedecer, v. disobey.
desobediencia, f. disobedience.
desobediente, a. disobedient.
desobedientemente, adv. disobediently.
desobligar, v. release from obligation; offend.
desocupado, a. idle, not busy; vacant.
desocupar, v. vacate.
desolación, f. desolation; ruin.
desolado, a. desolate. **—desolar,** v.
desollar, v. skin.
desorden, m. disorder.
desordenar, v. disarrange.
desorganización, f. disorganization.
desorganizar, v. disorganize.
despabilado, a. vigilant, watchful; lively.
despacio, adv. slowly.
despachar, v. dispatch, ship, send.
despacho, m. shipment; dispatch, promptness; office.
desparpajo, m. glibness; fluency of speech.
desparramar, v. scatter.
despavorido, a. terrified.
despecho, m. spite.
despedazar, v. tear up.
despedida, f. farewell; leave-taking; discharge.
despedir, v. dismiss, discharge; see off.
despedirse de, v. say good-bye to, take leave of.
despegar, v. unglue; separate.
despego, m. indifference; disinterest.
despejar, v. clear, clear up.
despejo, m. sprightly; clear; unobstructed.
despensa, f. pantry.
despensero, m. butler.
despeñar, v. throw down.
desperdicio, m. waste. **—desperdiciar,** v.
despertador, m. alarm clock.
despertar, v. wake, wake up.
despesar, m. dislike.
despicar, v. satisfy.
despidida, f. gutter.
despierto, a. awake; alert, wide-awake.
despilfarrado, a. wasteful, extravagant.

despilfarrar, v. waste, squander.
despilfarro, m. waste, extravagance.
despique, m. revenge.
desplazamiento, m. displacement.
desplegar, v. display; unfold.
desplome, m. collapse. **—desplomarse,** v.
desplumar, v. defeather, pluck.
despoblar, v. depopulate.
despojar, v. strip; despoil, plunder.
despojo, m. plunder, spoils; (pl.) remains, debris.
desposado, a. newly married.
desposar, v. marry.
desposeer, v. dispossess.
déspota, m. & f. despot.
despótico, a. despotic.
despotismo, m. despotism, tyranny.
despreciable, a. contemptible.
despreciar, v. spurn, despise, scorn.
desprecio, m. scorn, contempt.
desprender, v. detach, unfasten.
desprenderse, v. loosen, come apart. **d. de,** part with.
desprendido, a. disinterested.
despreocupado, a. unprejudiced.
desprevenido, a. unprepared, unready.
desproporción, f. disproportion.
despropósito, m. nonsense.
desprovisto, a. devoid.
después, adv. afterwards, later; then, next. **d. de, d. que,** after.
despuntar, v. blunt; remove the point of.
desquiciar, v. unhinge; disturb, unsettle.
desquitar, v. get revenge, retaliate.
desquite, m. revenge, retaliation.
destacamento, m. (mil.) detachment.
destacarse, v. stand out, be prominent.
destapar, v. uncover.
destello, m. sparkle, gleam.
destemplar, v. change; soften.
desteñir, v. fade, discolor.
desterrado -da, n. exile.
desterrar, v. banish, exile.
destierro, m. banishment, exile.
destilación, f. distillation.
destilar, v. distill.
destilería, f. distillery.
destinación, f. destination.
destinar, v. destine, intend.
destinatorio -ria, n. addressee.
destino, m. destiny, fate; destination.
destitución, f. dismissal; abandonment.
destituido, a. destitute.
destorcer, v. undo, straighten out.

destornillado, a. reckless, careless.

destornillador, m. screwdriver.

destraillar, v. unleash; set loose.

destral, m. hatchet.

destreza, f. cleverness, dexterity, skill.

destripar, v. eviscerate, disembowel.

destrísimo, a. extremely dexterous.

destronamiento, m. dethronement.

destronar, v. dethrone.

destrozador, m. destroyer, wrecker.

destrozar, v. destroy, wreck.

destrozo, m. destruction, ruin.

destrucción, f. destruction.

destructibilidad, f. destructibility.

destructible, a. destructible.

destructivamente, adv. destructively.

destructivo, a. destructive.

destruir, v. destroy; wipe out.

desuello, m. impudence.

desunión, f. disunion; discord; separation.

desunir, v. disconnect, sever.

desusadamente, adv. unusually.

desusado, a. archaic; obsolete.

desuso, m. disuse.

desvalido, a. helpless, destitute.

desvalijador, m. highwayman.

desván, m. attic.

desvanecerse, v. vanish; faint.

desvariado, a. delirious; disorderly.

desvarío, m. raving. —**desvariar,** v.

desvedado, a. free; unrestrained.

desveladamente, adv. watchfully, alertly.

desvelado, a. watchful; alert.

desvelar, v. be watchful; keep awake.

desvelo, m. vigilance; uneasiness.

desventaja, f. disadvantage.

desventar, v. let air out of.

desventura, f. misfortune.

desventurado, a. unhappy; unlucky.

desvergonzado, a. shameless, brazen.

desvergüenza, f. shamelessness.

desvestir, v. undress.

desviación, f. deviation.

desviado, a. devious.

desviar, v. divert; deviate.

desvío, m. detour; side track; indifference.

desvirtuar, v. decrease the value of.

deszumar, v. remove the juice from.

detalle, m. detail. —**detallar,** v.

detective, m. detective.

detención, f. detention, arrest.

detenedor, m. stopper; catch.

detener, v. detain, stop; arrest.

detenidamente, adv. carefully, slowly.

detenido, adv. stingy; thorough.

détente, f. detente.

detergente, a. detergent.

deterioración, f. deterioration.

deteriorar, v. deteriorate.

determinable, a. determinable.

determinación, f. determination.

determinar, v. determine.

determinismo, m. determinism.

determinista, n. & a. determinist.

detestable, a. detestable, hateful.

detestablemente, adv. detestably, hatefully, abhorrently.

detestación, f. detestation, hatefulness.

detestar, v. detest.

detonación, f. detonation.

detonar, v. detonate, explode.

detracción, f. detraction, defamation.

detractar, v. detract, defame, vilify.

detraer, v. detract.

detrás, adv. behind; in back.

detrimento, m. detriment, damage.

deuda, f. debt.

deudo -da, n. relative, kin.

deudor -ra, n. debtor.

Deuteronomio, m. Deuteronomy.

devalar, v. drift.

devanar, v. to wind, as on a spool.

devanear, v. talk deliriously, rave.

devaneo, m. frivolity; idle pursuit; delirium.

devantal, m. apron.

devastación, f. devastation, ruin, havoc.

devastador, m. devastator.

devastar, v. devastate.

devenir, v. happen, occur; become.

devoción, f. devotion.

devocionario, m. prayer book.

devocionero, a. devotional.

devolver, v. return, give back.

devorar, v. devour.

devotamente, adv. devotedly, devoutly, piously.

devoto, a. devout; devoted.

deyección, f. depression, dejection.

día, m. day. **buenos días,** good morning.

diabetes, f. diabetes.

diabético, a. diabetic.

diablear, v. play pranks.

diablo, m. devil.

diablura, f. mischief.

diabólicamente, adv. diabolically.

diabólico, a. diabolic, devilish.

diaconado, m. deaconship.

diaconía, f. deaconry.

diácono, m. deacon.

diacrítico, a. diacritic.

diadema, f. diadem, crown.

diáfano, a. transparent.

diafragma, m. diaphragm.

diagnosticar, v. diagnose.

diagonal, f. diagonal.

diagonalmente, adv. diagonally.

diagrama, m. diagram.

dialectal, a. dialectal.

dialéctico, a. dialectic.

dialecto, m. dialect.

diálogo, m. dialogue.

diamante, m. diamond.

diamantista, m. diamond cutter; jeweler.

diametral, a. diametric.

diametralmente, adv. diametrically.

diámetro, m. diameter.

diana, f. reveille.

diapasón, m. pitch; tuning fork.

diaplejía, f. paralysis.

diariamente, adv. daily.

diario, a. & m. daily; daily paper; diary; journal.

diarrea, f. diarrhea.

diatriba, f. diatribe, harangue.

dibujo, m. drawing, sketch. —**dibujar,** v.

dicción, f. diction.

diccionario, m. dictionary.

diccionarista, n. lexicographer.

diciembre, m. December.

dicotomía, f. dichotomy.

dictado, m. dictation.

dictador, m. dictator.

dictadura, f. dictatorship.

dictamen, m. dictate.

dictar, v. dictate; direct.

dictatoria, a. dictatorial; tyrannic.

dicha, f. happiness.

dicho, m. saying.

dichoso, a. happy; fortunate.

didáctico, a. didactic.

diecinueve, a. & pron. nineteen.

dieciocho, a. & pron. eighteen.

dieciséis, a. & pron. sixteen.

diecisiete, a. & pron. seventeen.

diente, m. tooth.

diestramente, adv. skillfully, ably; ingeniously.

diestro, a. dexterous, skillful; clever.

dieta, f. diet; allowance.

dietética, f. dietetic.

diez, a. & pron. ten.

diezmal, a. decimal.

diezmar, v. decimate.

difamación, f. defamation, smear.

difamar, v. defame, smear, libel.

difamatorio, a. defamatory.

diferencia, f. difference.

diferencial, a. & f. differential.

diferenciar, v. differentiate, distinguish.
diferente, a. different.
diferentemente, adv. differently.
diferir, v. differ; defer, put off.
difícil, a. difficult, hard.
difícilmente, adv. with difficulty or hardship.
dificultad, f. difficulty.
dificultar, v. make difficult.
dificultoso, a. difficult, hard.
difidencia, f. diffidence.
difidente, a. diffident.
difteria, f. diphtheria.
difundir, v. diffuse, spread.
difunto, a. deceased, dead, late.
difusamente, adv. diffusely.
difusión, f. diffusion, spread.
digerible, a. digestible.
digerir, v. digest.
digestible, a. digestible.
digestión, f. digestion.
digestivo, a. digestive.
digesto, m. digest or code of laws.
digitado, a. digitate.
digital, 1. a. digital. **2.** f. foxglove.
dignación, f. condescension; deigning.
dignamente, adv. with dignity.
dignarse, v. condescend, deign.
dignidad, f. dignity.
dignificar, v. dignify.
dignatario, m. dignitary.
digno, a. worthy; dignified.
digresión, f. digression.
digresivo, a. digressive.
dij, dije, m. trinket, piece of jewelry.
dilación, f. delay.
dilapidación, f. dilapidation.
dilatación, f. dilatation, enlargement.
dilatar, v. dilate; delay; expand.
dilatoria, f. delay.
dilecto, a. loved.
dilema, m. dilemma.
diligencia, f. diligence, industriousness.
diligente, a. diligent, industrious.
diligentemente, adv. diligently.
dilogía, f. ambiguous meaning.
dilución, f. dilution.
diluir, v. dilute.
diluvial, a. diluvial.
diluvio, m. flood, deluge.
dimensión, f. dimension; measurement.
diminución, f. diminution.
diminuto, diminutivo, a. diminutive, little.
dimisión, f. resignation.
dimitir, v. resign.
Dinamarca, f. Denmark.
dinamarqués -esa, a. & n. Danish, Dane.
dinámico, a. dynamic.
dinamita, f. dynamite.
dinamitero, m. dynamiter.
dínamo, m. dynamo.

dinasta, m. dynast, king, monarch.
dinastía, f. dynasty.
dinástico, a. dynastic.
dinero, m. money, currency.
dinosauro, m. dinosaur.
diócesi, f. diocese.
Dios, m. God.
dios -sa, m. god, goddess.
diploma, m. diploma.
diplomacia, f. diplomacy.
diplomado -da, m. graduate.
diplomarse, v. graduate (from a school).
diplomática, f. diplomacy.
diplomático, a. & m. diplomat; diplomatic.
dipsomanía, f. dipsomania.
diptongo, m. diphthong.
diputación, f. deputation, delegation.
diputado, m. deputy.
diputar, v. depute, delegate; empower.
dique, m. dike; dam.
dirección, f. direction; address; guidance; (com.) management.
directamente, adv. directly.
directo, a. direct.
director, m. director; manager.
dirigente, a. directing, controlling, managing.
dirigible, m. dirigible.
dirigir, v. direct; lead; manage.
dirigirse a, v. address; approach, turn to; head for.
dirruir, v. destroy, devastate.
disanto, m. holy day.
discantar, v. sing (esp. in counterpoint); discuss.
disceptación, f. argument, quarrel.
disceptar, v. argue, quarrel.
discernimiento, m. discernment.
discernir, v. discern.
disciplina, f. discipline.
disciplinable, a. disciplinable.
disciplinar, v. discipline, train, teach.
discípulo -la, n. disciple, follower; pupil.
disco, m. disk; (phonograph) record.
discontinuación, f. discontinuation.
discontinuar, v. discontinue, break off, cease.
discordancia, f. discordance.
discordar, v. disagree, conflict.
discordia, f. discord.
discoteca, f. disco, discotheque.
discreción, f. discretion.
discrecional, a. optional.
discrecionalmente, adv. optionally.
discrepancia, f. discrepancy.
discretamente, adv. discreetly.
discreto, a. discreet.
discrimen, m. risk, hazard.
discriminación, f. discrimination.
discriminar, v. discriminate.

disculpa, f. excuse; apology.
disculpar, v. excuse; exonerate.
disculparse, v. apologize.
discurrir, v. roam; flow; think; plan.
discursante, n. lecturer, speaker.
discursivo, a. discursive.
discurso, m. speech, talk.
discusión, f. discussion.
discutible, a. debatable.
discutir, v. discuss; debate; contest.
disecación, f. dissection.
disecar, v. dissect.
disección, f. dissection.
diseminación, f. dissemination.
diseminar, v. disseminate, spread.
disensión, f. dissension; dissent.
disenso, m. dissent.
disentería, f. dysentery.
disentir, v. disagree, dissent.
diseñador -ra, n. designer.
diseño, m. design. —**diseñar,** v.
disertación, f. dissertation.
disfamación, f. defamation.
disforme, a. deformed, monstrous, ugly.
disformidad, f. deformity.
disfraz, m. disguise. —**disfrazar,** v.
disfrutar, v. enjoy.
disfrute, m. enjoyment.
disgustar, v. displease; disappoint.
disgusto, m. displeasure; disappointment.
disidencia, f. dissidence.
disidente, a. & n. dissident.
disímil, a. unlike.
disimilitud, f. dissimilarity.
disimulación, f. dissimulation.
disimulado, a. dissembling, feigning; sly.
disimular, v. hide, dissemble.
disímulo, m. pretense.
disipación, f. dissipation.
disipado, a. dissipated; wasted; scattered.
disipar, v. waste; scatter.
dislexia, f. dyslexia.
dislocación, f. dislocation.
dislocar, v. dislocate; displace.
disminuir, v. diminish, lessen, reduce.
disociación, f. dissociation.
disociar, v. dissociate.
disolubilidad, f. dissolubility.
disoluble, a. dissoluble.
disolución, f. dissolution.
disolutemente, adv. dissolutely.
disoluto, a. dissolute.
disolver, v. dissolve.
disonancia, f. dissonance; discord.
disonante, a. dissonant; discordant.
disonar, v. be discordant; clash in sound.
dísono, a. dissonant.
dispar, a. unlike.

disparadamente, *adv.* hastily, hurriedly.
disparar, *v.* shoot, fire (a weapon).
disparatado, *a.* nonsensical.
disparatar, *v.* talk nonsense.
disparate, *m.* nonsense, tall tale.
disparejo, *a.* uneven, unequal.
disparidad, *f.* disparity.
disparo, *m.* shot.
dispendio, *m.* extravagance.
dispendioso, *a.* expensive; extravagant.
dispensa, dispensación, *f.* dispensation.
dispensable, *a.* dispensable; excusable.
dispensar, *v.* dispense, excuse; grant.
dispensario, *m.* dispensary.
dispepsia, *f.* dyspepsia.
dispéptico, *a.* dyspeptic.
dispersar, *v.* scatter; dispel; disband.
dispersión, *f.* dispersion, dispersal.
disperso, *a.* dispersed.
displicente, *a.* unpleasant.
disponer, *v.* dispose. **d. de,** have at one's disposal.
disponible, *a.* available.
disposición, *f.* disposition; disposal.
dispuesto, *a.* disposed, inclined; attractive.
disputa, *f.* dispute, argument.
disputable, *a.* disputable.
disputador, *m.* disputant.
disputar, *v.* argue; dispute.
disquisición, *f.* disquisition.
distancia, *f.* distance.
distante, *a.* distant.
distantemente, *adv.* distantly.
distar, *v.* be distant, be far.
distención, *f.* distension, swelling.
distender, *v.* distend, swell, enlarge.
dístico, *m.* couplet.
distinción, *f.* distinction, difference.
distingo, *m.* restriction.
distinguible, *a.* distinguishable.
distinguido, *a.* distinguished, prominent.
distinguir, *v.* distinguish; make out, spot.
distintamente, *adv.* distinctly, clearly; differently.
distintivo, *a.* distinctive.
distinto, *a.* distinct, different.
distracción, *f.* distraction, pastime; absent-mindedness.
distraer, *v.* distract.
distraídamente, *adv.* absent-mindedly, distractedly.
distraído, *a.* absent-minded; distracted.
distribución, *f.* distribution.
distribuidor -ra, *n.* distributor.
distribuir, *v.* distribute.
distributivo, *a.* distributive.
distribuidor, *m.* distributor.
distrito, *m.* district.

disturbar, *v.* disturb, trouble.
disturbio, *m.* disturbance, outbreak; turmoil.
disuadir, *v.* dissuade.
disuasión, *f.* dissuasion; deterrence.
disuasivo, *a.* dissuasive.
disyunción, *f.* disjunction.
ditirambo, *m.* dithyramb.
diurno, *a.* diurnal.
diva, *f.* singer.
divagación, *f.* digression.
divagar, *v.* digress, ramble.
diván, *m.* couch.
divergencia, *f.* divergence.
divergente, *a.* divergent, differing.
divergir, *v.* diverge.
diversamente, *adv.* diversely.
diversidad, *f.* diversity.
diversificar, *v.* diversify, vary.
diversión, *f.* diversion, pastime.
diverso, *a.* diverse, different; (*pl.*) various, several.
divertido, *a.* humorous, amusing.
divertimiento, *m.* diversion; amusement.
divertir, *v.* entertain, amuse.
divertirse, *v.* enjoy oneself, have a good time.
dividendo, *m.* dividend.
dividirse, *v.* (med.) boil.
dividir, *v.* divide, separate.
divieso, *m.* (med.) boil.
divinamente, *adv.* divinely.
divinidad, *f.* divinity.
divinizar, *v.* deify.
divino, *a.* divine; heavenly.
divisa, *f.* badge, emblem.
divisar, *v.* sight, make out.
divisibilidad, *f.* divisibility.
divisible, *a.* divisible.
división, *f.* division.
divisivo, *a.* divisive.
diviso, *a.* divided.
divo, *m.* god.
divorcio, *m.* divorce. **—divorciar,** *v.*
divulgable, *a.* divulgable.
divulgación, *f.* divulgation.
divulgar, *v.* divulge, reveal.
dobladamente, *adv.* doubly.
dobladillo, *m.* hem of a skirt or dress.
dobladura, *f.* fold, bend.
doblar, *v.* fold; bend.
doble, *a.* double.
doblegable, *a.* flexible, foldable.
doblegar, *v.* fold, bend; yield.
doblez, *m.* fold; duplicity.
doblón, *m.* doubloon.
doce, *a.* & *pron.* twelve.
docena, *f.* dozen.
docente, *a.* educational.
dócil, *a.* docile.
docilidad, *f.* docility, tractableness.
dócilmente, *adv.* docilely, meekly.
doctamente, *adv.* learnedly, profoundly.
docto, *a.* learned, expert.

doctor, *m.* doctor.
doctorado, *m.* doctorate.
doctoral, *a.* doctoral.
doctrina, *f.* doctrine.
doctrinador, *m.* teacher.
doctrinal, *m.* catechism.
doctrinar, *v.* teach.
documentación, *f.* documentation.
documental, *a.* documentary.
documento, *m.* document.
dogal, *m.* noose.
dogma, *m.* dogma.
dogmáticamente, *adv.* dogmatically.
dogmático, *m.* dogmatic.
dogmatismo, *m.* dogmatism.
dogmatista, *m.* dogmatist.
dogo, *m.* bulldog.
dolar, *v.* cut, chop, hew.
dólar, *m.* dollar.
dolencia, *f.* pain; disease.
doler, *v.* ache, hurt, be sore.
doliente, *a.* ill; aching.
dolor, *m.* pain; grief, sorrow, woe.
dolorido, *a.* painful, sorrowful.
dolorosamente, *adv.* painfully, sorrowfully.
doloroso, *a.* painful, sorrowful.
dolosamente, *adv.* deceitfully.
doloso, *a.* deceitful.
domable, *a.* that can be tamed or managed.
domar, *v.* tame; subdue.
dombo, *m.* dome.
domesticable, *a.* that can be domesticated.
domesticación, *f.* domestication.
domésticamente, *adv.* domestically.
domesticar, *v.* tame.
domesticidad, *f.* domesticity.
doméstico, *a.* domestic.
domicilio, *m.* dwelling, home, residence.
dominación, *f.* domination.
dominador, *a.* dominating.
dominante, *a.* dominant.
dominar, *v.* rule, dominate; master.
dómine, *m.* teacher.
domingo, *m.* Sunday.
dominio, *m.* domain; rule; power.
dominó, *m.* domino.
domo, *m.* dome.
Don, *title used before a man's first name.*
don, *m.* gift.
dona, *f.* woman.
donación, *f.* donation.
donador -ra, *n.* giver, donor.
donaire, *m.* grace.
donairosamente, *adv.* gracefully.
donairoso, *a.* graceful.
donante, *n.* giver, donor.
donar, *v.* donate.
donativo, *m.* donation, contribution; gift.
doncella, *f.* lass; maid.
donde, dónde, *conj.* & *adv.* where.

dondequiera, *adv.* wherever, anywhere.
donosamente, *adv.* gracefully; wittily.
donoso, *a.* graceful; witty.
donosura, *f.* gracefulness; wittiness.
Doña, *title used before a lady's first name.*
dorado, *a.* gilded.
dorador, *m.* gilder.
dorar, *v.* gild.
dórico, *a.* Doric.
dormidero, *a.* sleep-inducing; soporific.
dormido, *a.* asleep.
dormir, *v.* sleep.
dormirse, *v.* fall asleep, go to sleep.
dormitar, *v.* doze.
dormitorio, *m.* dormitory; bedroom.
dorsal, *a.* dorsal.
dorso, *m.* spine.
dos, *a. & pron.* two. **los d.,** both.
dosañal, *a.* biennial.
doscientos, *a. & pron.* two hundred.
dosel, *m.* canopy; platform; dais.
dosificación, *f.* dosage.
dosis, *f.* dose.
dotación, *f.* endowment; (naut.) crew.
dotador, *m.* donor.
dotar, *v.* endow; give a dowry to.
dote, *m.* dowry; (*pl.*) talents.
dragaminas, *m.* mine sweeper.
dragar, *v.* dredge; sweep.
dragón, *m.* dragon; dragoon.
dragonear, *v.* pretend to be.
drama, *m.* drama; play.
dramática, *f.* dramatics.
dramáticamente, *adv.* dramatically.
dramático, *a.* dramatic.
dramatizar, *v.* dramatize.
dramaturgo, *m.* playwright, dramatist.
drástico, *a.* drastic.
drenaje, *m.* drainage.
dríada, *f.* dryad.
driza, *f.* halyard.
droga, *f.* drug.
droguería, *f.* drugstore.
droguero, *m.* druggist.
dromedario, *m.* dromedary.
druida, *m.* Druid.
dualidad, *f.* duality.
dubitable, *a.* doubtful.
dubitación, *f.* doubt.
ducado, *m.* duchy.
ducal, *a.* ducal.
dúctil, *a.* ductile.
ductilidad, *f.* ductility.
ducha, *f.* shower (bath).
duda, *f.* doubt.
dudable, *a.* doubtful.
dudar, *v.* doubt; hesitate; question.
dudosamente, *adv.* doubtfully.
dudoso, *a.* dubious; doubtful.
duela, *f.* stave.

duelista, *m.* duelist.
duelo, *m.* duel; grief; mourning.
duende, *m.* elf, hobgoblin.
dueño -ña, *n.* owner; landlord, -lady; master, mistress.
dulce, 1. *a.* sweet. **agua d.,** fresh water. **2.** *m.* piece of candy; (*pl.*) candy.
dulcedumbre, *f.* sweetness.
dulcemente, *adv.* sweetly.
dulcería, *f.* confectionery; candy shop.
dulcificar, *v.* sweeten.
dulzura, *f.* sweetness; mildness.
duna, *f.* dune.
dúo, *m.* duet.
duodenal, *a.* duodenal.
duplicación, *f.* duplication; doubling.
duplicadamente, *adv.* doubly.
duplicado, *a. & m.* duplicate.
duplicar, *v.* double, duplicate, repeat.
duplicidad, *f.* duplicity.
duplo, *a.* double.
duque, *m.* duke.
duquesa, *f.* duchess.
durabilidad, *f.* durability.
durable, *a.* durable.
duración, *f.* duration.
duradero, *a.* lasting, durable.
duramente, *adv.* harshly, roughly.
durante, *prep.* during.
durar, *v.* last.
durazno, *m.* peach.
dureza, *f.* hardness.
durmiente, *a.* dormant.
duro, *a.* hard; stiff; stern; stale.
dux, *m.* doge.

E

e, *conj.* and.
ebanista, *m.* cabinetmaker.
ebanizar, *v.* give an ebony finish to.
ébano, *m.* ebony.
ebonita, *f.* ebonite.
ebrio, *a.* drunken, inebriated.
ebullición, *f.* boiling.
eclecticismo, *m.* eclecticism.
ecléctico, *n. & a.* eclectic.
eclesiástico, *a. & m.* ecclesiastic.
eclipse, *m.* eclipse. —**eclipsar,** *v.*
eclipsis, *f.* ellipsis.
écloga, *f.* eclogue.
eco, *m.* echo.
ecología, *f.* ecology.
ecológico, *a.* ecological.
ecologista, *m. & f.* ecologist.
economía, *f.* economy; thrift. **e. política,** economics.
económicamente, *adv.* economically.
económico, *a.* economic; economical, thrifty.
economista, *f.* economist.

economizar, *v.* save, economize.
ecuación, *f.* equation.
ecuador, *m.* equator.
ecuanimidad, *f.* equanimity.
ecuatorial, *a.* equatorial.
ecuatoriano -na, *a. & n.* Ecuadorian.
ecuestre, *a.* equestrian.
ecuménico, *a.* ecumenical.
echada, *f.* throw.
echadillo, *m.* foundling; orphan.
echar, *v.* throw, toss; pour. **e. a,** start to. **e. a perder,** spoil, ruin. **e. de menos,** miss.
echarse, *v.* lie down.
edad, *f.* age.
edecán, *m.* aide-de-camp.
Edén, *m.* Eden.
edición, *f.* edition; issue.
edicto, *m.* edict, decree.
edificación, *f.* construction.
edificador, *n.* constructor; builder.
edificar, *v.* build.
edificio, *m.* edifice, building.
editar, *v.* publish, issue.
editor, *m.* publisher.
editorial, *a.* editorial.
edredón, *m.* quilt.
educación, *f.* upbringing; breeding; education.
educador, *m.* educator.
educar, *v.* educate, bring up; train.
educativo, *a.* educational.
educción, *f.* deduction.
educir, *v.* educe.
educto, *m.* output.
efectivamente, *adv.* actually, really.
efectivo, *a.* effective; actual, real. **en e.,** (com.) in cash.
efecto, *m.* effect.
efectuar, *v.* effect; cash.
eferente, *a.* efferent.
efervescencia, *f.* effervescence; zeal.
eficacia, *f.* efficacy.
eficaz, *a.* efficient, effective.
eficazmente, *adv.* efficaciously.
eficiencia, *f.* efficiency.
eficiente, *a.* efficient.
efigie, *f.* effigy.
efímera, *f.* May fly.
efímero, *a.* ephemeral, passing.
efulvio, *m.* effluvium.
efundir, *v.* effuse; pour out.
efusión, *f.* effusion.
egipcio -cia, *a. & n.* Egyptian.
Egipto, *m.* Egypt.
égira, *f.* hegira.
egoísmo, *m.* egoism, egotism, selfishness.
egoísta, *a. & n.* selfish, egoistic; egoist.
egotismo, *m.* egotism.
egotista, *m.* egotist.
egreso, *m.* expense, outlay.
eje, *m.* axis; axle.
ejecución, *f.* execution; performance; enforcement.
ejecutar, *v.* execute; enforce; carry out.

ejecutivo, a. & m. executive.

ejecutor, m. executor.

ejemplar, 1. a. exemplary. 2. m. copy.

ejemplificación, f. exemplification.

ejemplificar, v. illustrate.

ejemplo, m. example.

ejercer, v. exert; practice.

ejercicio, m. exercise, drill. —ejercitar, v.

ejercitación, f. exercise, training, drill.

ejercitar, v. exercise, train, drill.

ejército, m. army.

ejotes, m.pl. string beans.

el, art. & pron. the; the one.

él, pron. he, him; it.

elaboración, f. elaboration; working up.

elaborado, a. elaborate.

elaborador, m. manufacturer, maker.

elaborar, v. elaborate; manufacture; brew.

elación, f. elation; magnanimity; turgid style.

elasticidad, f. elasticity.

elástico, m. elastic.

elección, f. election; option, choice.

electivo, a. elective.

electo, a. elected, chosen, appointed.

electorado, m. electorate.

electoral, a. electoral.

electricidad, f. electricity.

electricista, m. electrician.

eléctrico, a. electric.

electrización, f. electrification.

electrocardiograma, m. electrocardiogram.

electrocución, f. electrocution.

electrocutar, v. electrocute.

electrodo, m. electrode.

electroimán, m. electromagnet.

electrólisis, f. electrolysis.

electrólito, m. electrolyte.

electrón, m. electron.

elefante, m. elephant.

elegancia, f. elegance.

elegante, a. elegant, smart, stylish, fine.

elegantemente, adv. elegantly.

elegía, f. elegy.

elegibilidad, f. eligibility.

elegible, a. eligible.

elegir, v. select, choose; elect.

elemental, a. elementary.

elementalmente, adv. elementally; fundamentally.

elementar, a. elementary.

elemento, m. element.

elevación, f. elevation; height.

elevador, m. elevator.

elevamiento, m. elevation.

elevar, v. elevate; erect, raise.

elidir, v. elide.

eliminación, f. elimination.

eliminar, v. eliminate.

elipse, f. ellipse.

elipsis, f. ellipsis.

elíptico, a. elliptic.

elocuencia, f. eloquence.

elocuente, a. eloquent.

elocuentemente, adv. eloquently.

elogio, m. praise, compliment. —elogiar, v.

elucidación, f. elucidation.

elucidar, v. elucidate.

eludir, v. elude.

ella, pron. she, her; it.

ello, pron. it.

ellos -as, pron. pl. they, them.

emaciación, f. emaciation.

emanar, v. emanate, stem.

emancipación, f. emancipation, freeing.

emancipador, n. emancipator.

emancipar, v. emancipate, free.

embajada, f. embassy; legation; (coll.) errand.

embajador, m. ambassador.

embalar, v. pack, bale.

embaldosado, m. tile floor.

embalsamador, m. embalmer.

embalsamar, v. embalm.

embarazada, a. pregnant.

embarazadamente, adv. embarrassedly.

embarazar, v. embarrass.

embarazo, m. embarrassment; pregnancy.

embarbascado, a. difficult; complicated.

embarcación, f. boat, ship; embarkation.

embarcadero, m. wharf, pier, dock.

embarcador, m. shipper, loader, stevedore.

embarcar, v. ship.

embarcarse, v. embark; sail.

embargador, m. one who impedes; one who orders an embargo.

embargante, a. impeding, hindering.

embargar, v. impede, restrain; (leg.) seize, embargo.

embargo, m. seizure, embargo. sin e., however, nevertheless.

embarnizar, v. varnish.

embarque, m. shipment.

embarrador, m. plasterer.

embarrancar, v. get stuck in mud.

embarrar, v. plaster; besmear with mud.

embasamiento, m. foundation of a building.

embastecer, v. get fat.

embaucador, m. imposter.

embaucar, v. deceive, trick, hoax.

embaular, v. pack in a trunk.

embausamiento, m. amazement.

embebecer, v. amaze, astonish; entertain.

embeber, v. absorb; incorporate; saturate.

embelecador, m. imposter.

embeleco, m. fraud, perpetration.

embeleñar, v. fascinate, charm.

embelesamiento, m. rapture.

embelesar, v. fascinate, charm.

embeleso, m. rapture, bliss.

embellecer, v. beautify, embellish.

embestida, f. violent assault; attack.

emblandecer, v. soften; moisten; move to pity.

emblema, m. emblem.

emblemático, a. emblematic.

embocadura, f. narrow entrance; mouth of a river.

embocar, v. eat hastily; gorge.

embolia, f. embolism.

embolsar, v. pocket.

embonar, v. improve, fix, repair.

emborrachador, a. intoxicating.

emborrachar, v. get drunk.

emboscada, f. ambush.

emboscar, v. put or lie in ambush.

embotado, a. blunt, dull (edged). —embotar, v.

embotadura, f. bluntness; dullness.

embotellar, v. put in bottles.

embozado, v. muzzled; muffled.

embozar, v. muzzle; muffle.

embozo, m. muffler.

embrague, m. (auto.) clutch.

embravecer, v. be or make angry.

embriagado, a. drunken, intoxicated.

embriagar, v. intoxicate.

embriaguez, f. drunkenness.

embrión, m. embryo.

embrionario, a. embryonic.

embrochado, a. embroidered.

embrollo, m. muddle. —embrollar, v.

embromar, v. tease; joke.

embuchado, m. pork sausage.

embudo, m. funnel.

embuste, m. lie, fib.

embustear, v. lie, fib.

embustero -ra, n. liar.

embutir, v. stuff, cram.

emendación, f. emendation, change, correction.

emergencia, f. emergency.

emérito, a. emeritus.

emético, m. & a. emetic.

emigración, f. emigration.

emigrante, a. & n. emigrant.

emigrar, v. emigrate.

eminencia, f. eminence, height.

eminente, a. eminent.

emisario, m. emissary, spy; outlet.

emisión, f. issue; emission.

emisor, m. radio transmitter.

emitir, v. emit.

emoción, f. feeling, emotion, thrill.

emocional, a. emotional.

emocionante, a. exciting.

emocionar, v. touch, move, excite.

emolumento, m. emolument; perquisite.

empacar, v. pack.

mpacho, m. shyness, timidity; embarrassment.

mpadronamiento, m. census; list of taxpayers.

mpalizada, f. palisade, stockade.

mpanada, f. meat pie.

mpañar, v. blur; soil, sully.

mpapar, v. soak.

mpapelado, m. wallpaper.

mpaque, m. packing; appearance, mien.

mpaquetar, v. pack, package.

mparejarse, v. match, pair off; level, even off.

mparentado, a. related by marriage.

mparrado, m. arbor.

mpastadura, f. (dental) filling.

mpastar, v. fill (a tooth).

mpate, m. tie, draw. —empatarse, v.

mpecer, v. hurt, harm, injure; prevent.

mpedernir, v. harden.

mpeine, m. groin; instep; hoof.

mpellar, v. shove, jostle.

mpellón, m. hard push, shove.

mpeñar, v. pledge; pawn.

mpeñarse en, v. persist in, be bent on.

mpeño, m. persistence; pledge; pawning.

mpeoramiento, m. deterioration.

mpeorar, v. get worse.

mperador, m. emperor.

mperatriz, f. empress.

mpernar, v. nail.

mpero, conj. however.

mperramiento, m. stubbornness.

mpezar, v. begin, start.

mpinado, a. steep.

mpinar, v. raise; exalt.

mpíreo, a. celestial, heavenly; divine.

mpíricamente, adv. empirically.

mpírico, a. empirical.

mpirismo, m. empiricism.

mplastarse, v. get smeared.

mplasto, m. salve.

mplazamiento, m. court summons.

mplazar, v. summon to court.

mpleado -da, n. employee.

mplear, v. employ; use.

mpleo, m. employment; job; use.

mpobrecer, v. make or become impoverished.

mpobrecimiento, m. impoverishment.

mpolvado, a. dusty.

mpolvar, v. powder.

mpollador, m. incubator.

mpollar, v. hatch.

mporcar, v. soil, make dirty.

mporio, m. emporium.

mprendedor, a. enterprising.

mprender, v. undertake.

mpreñar, v. make pregnant; beget.

empresa, f. enterprise, undertaking.

empresario, m. impresario.

empréstito, m. loan.

empujón, m. push; shove. —empujar, v.

empuñar, v. grasp, seize; wield.

emulación, f. emulation; envy, rivalry.

emulador, m. emulator; rival.

émulo, a. rival. —emular, v.

emulsión, f. emulsion.

emulsionar, v. emulsify.

en, prep. in, on, at.

enaguas, f.pl. petticoat; skirt.

enajenable, a. alienable.

enajenación, f. alienation; derangement, insanity.

enajenar, v. alienate.

enamoradamente, adv. lovingly.

enamorado, a. in love.

enamorador, m. wooer; suitor; lover.

enamorarse, v. fall in love.

enano -na, n. midget; dwarf.

enardecer, v. inflame.

enastado, a. horned.

encabestrar, v. halter.

encabezado, m. headline.

encabezador, m. reaping machine.

encabezamiento, m. title; census; tax roll.

encabezar, v. head.

encachar, v. hide.

encadenamiento, m. connection, linkage.

encadenar, v. chain; link, connect.

encajar, v. fit in, insert.

encaje, m. lace.

encalar, v. whitewash.

encalvecer, v. lose one's hair.

encallarse, v. be stranded.

encallecido, a. hardened; calloused.

encaminar, v. guide; direct; be on the way to.

encandilar, v. dazzle; daze.

encantación, f. incantation.

encantado, a. charmed, fascinated, enchanted.

encantador, a. charming, delightful.

encante, m. public auction.

encanto, m. charm, delight. —encantar, v.

encapillado, m. clothes one is wearing.

encapotar, v. cover, cloak; muffle.

encaramarse, v. perch; climb.

encararse con, v. face.

encarcelación, f. imprisonment.

encarcelar, v. jail, imprison.

encarecer, v. recommend; extol.

encarecidamente, adv. extremely; ardently.

encargado, m. agent; attorney; representative.

encargar, v. entrust.

encargarse, v. take charge, be in charge.

encargo, m. errand; assignment; (com.) order.

encarnación, f. incarnation.

encarnado, a. red.

encarnar, v. embody.

encarnecer, v. grow fat or heavy.

encarnizado, a. bloody, fierce.

encarrilar, v. set right; put on the track.

encartar, v. ban, outlaw; summon.

encastar, v. improve by crossbreeding.

encastillar, v. be obstinate or unyielding.

encatarrado, a. suffering from a cold.

encausar, v. prosecute; take legal action against.

encauzar, v. channel; direct.

encefalitis, f. encephalitis.

encelamiento, m. envy, jealousy.

encenagar, v. wallow in mud.

encendedor, m. lighter.

encender, v. light; set fire to, kindle; turn on.

encendido, m. ignition.

encerado, m. oilcloth; tarpaulin.

encerar, v. wax.

encerrar, v. enclose; confine, shut in.

encía, f. gum.

encíclico, 1. a. encyclic. 2. f. encyclical.

enciclopedia, f. encyclopedia.

enciclopédico, a. encyclopedic.

encierro, m. confinement; enclosure.

encima, adv. on top. e. de, on. por e. de, above.

encina, f. oak.

encinta, a. pregnant.

enclavar, v. nail.

enclenque, a. frail, weak, sickly.

encogerse, v. shrink. e. de hombros, shrug the shoulders.

encogido, a. shy, bashful, timid.

encojar, v. make or become lame; cripple.

encolar, v. glue, paste, stick.

encolerizar, v. make or become angry.

encomendar, v. commend; recommend.

encomiar, v. praise, laud, extol.

encomienda, f. commission, charge; (postal) package.

encomio, m. encomium, eulogy.

enconar, v. irritate, annoy, anger.

encono, m. rancor, resentment.

enconoso, a. rancorous, resentful.

encontrado, a. opposite.

encontrar, v. find; meet.

encorajar, v. encourage; incite.

encorralar, v. corral.

encorvadura, f. bend, curvature.

encorvar, v. arch, bend.

encorvarse, v. stoop.

encrucijada, f. crossroads.

encuadrar, v. frame.

encubierta, a. secret, fraudulent.

encubrir, v. hide, conceal.

encuentro, m. encounter; match, bout.

encurtido, m. pickle.

enchapado, m. veneer.

enchufe, m. (elec.) plug, socket.

endeble, a. rail, weak, sickly.

enderezar, v. straighten; redress.

endiablado, a. devilish.

endibia, f. endive.

endiosar, v. deify.

endorso, endoso, m. endorsement.

endosador, m. endorser.

endosar, v. endorse.

endosatario, m. endorsee.

endulzar, v. sweeten; soothe.

endurar, v. harden; endure.

endurecer, v. harden.

enemigo -ga, n. foe, enemy.

enemistad, f. enmity.

éneo, a. brass.

energía, f. energy.

enérgicamente, adv. energetically.

enérgico, a. forceful; energetic.

enero, m. January.

enervación, f. enervation.

enfadado, a. angry.

enfadar, v. anger, vex.

enfado, m. anger, vexation.

énfasis, m. or f. emphasis, stress.

enfáticamente, adv. emphatically.

enfático, a. emphatic.

enfermar, v. make ill; fall ill.

enfermedad, f. illness, sickness, disease.

enfermera, f. nurse.

enfermería, f. sanitorium.

enfermo -ma, a. & n. ill, sick; sickly; patient.

enfilar, v. line up; put in a row.

enflaquecer, v. make thin; grow thin.

enfoque, m. focus. —**enfocar**, v.

enfrascamiento, m. entanglement.

enfrascar, v. entangle oneself.

enfrenar, v. bridle, curb; restrain.

enfrente, adv. across, opposite; in front.

enfriadera, f. icebox; cooler.

enfriar, v. chill, cool.

enfurecer, v. infuriate, enrage.

engalanar, v. adorn, trim.

enganchar, v. hook, hitch, attach.

engañar, v. deceive, cheat.

engaño, m. deceit; delusion.

engañoso, a. deceitful.

engarce, m. connection, link.

engastar, v. to put (gems) in a setting.

engaste, m. setting.

engatusar, v. deceive, trick.

engendrar, v. engender, beget, produce.

engendro, m. fetus, embryo.

engolfar, v. be deeply absorbed.

engolosinar, v. allure, charm, entice.

engomar, v. gum.

engordador, a. fattening.

engordar, v. fatten; grow fat.

engranaje, m. (mech.) gear.

engranar, v. gear; mesh together.

engrandecer, v. increase, enlarge; exalt; exaggerate.

engrasación, f. lubrication.

engrasar, v. grease, lubricate.

engreído, a. conceited.

engreimiento, m. conceit.

engullidor, m. devourer.

engullir, v. devour.

enhebrar, v. thread.

enhestadura, f. raising.

enhestar, v. raise, erect, set up.

enhiesto, a. erect, upright.

enhorabuena, f. congratulations.

enigma, m. enigma, puzzle.

enigmáticamente, adv. enigmatically.

enigmático, a. enigmatic.

enjabonar, v. soap, lather.

enjalbegar, v. whitewash.

enjambradera, f. queen bee.

enjambre, m. swarm. —**enjambrar**, v.

enjaular, v. cage, coop up.

enjebe, m. lye.

enjuagar, v. rinse.

enjugar, v. wipe, dry off.

enjutez, f. dryness.

enjuto, a. dried; lean, thin.

enlace, m. attachment; involvement; connection.

enladrillador, m. bricklayer.

enlardar, v. baste.

enlazar, v. lace; join, connect; wed.

enlodar, v. cover with mud.

enloquecer, v. go insane; drive crazy.

enloquecimiento, m. insanity.

enlustrecer, v. polish, brighten.

enmarañar, v. entangle.

enmendación, f. emendation.

enmendador, m. emender, reviser.

enmendar, v. amend, correct.

enmienda, f. amendment; correction.

enmohecer, v. rust; mold.

enmohecido, a. rusty; moldy.

enmudecer, v. silence; become silent.

ennegrecer, v. blacken.

ennoblecer, v. ennoble.

enodio, m. young deer.

enojado, a. angry, cross.

enojarse, v. get angry.

enojo, m. anger. —**enojar**, v.

enojosamente, adv. angrily.

enorme, a. enormous, huge.

enormemente, adv. enormously; hugely.

enormidad, f. enormity; hugeness.

enraizar, v. take root, sprout.

enramada, f. bower.

enredado, a. entangled, snarled.

enredar, v. entangle, snarl; mess up.

enredo, m. tangle, entanglement.

enriquecer, v. enrich.

enrojecerse, v. color; blush.

enrollar, v. wind, coil, roll up.

enromar, v. make dull, blunt.

enronquecimiento, m. hoarseness.

enroscar, v. twist, curl, wind.

ensacar, v. put in a bag.

ensalada, f. salad.

ensaladera, f. salad bowl.

ensalmo, m. charm, enchantment.

ensalzamiento, m. praise.

ensalzar, v. praise, laud, extol.

ensamblar, v. join; unite; connect.

ensanchamiento, m. widening, expansion, extension.

ensanchar, v. widen, expand, extend.

ensangrentado, a. bloody; bloodshot.

ensañar, v. enrage, infuriate, rage.

ensayar, v. try out; rehearse.

ensayista, n. essayist.

ensayo, m. attempt; trial; rehearsal.

ensenada, f. cove.

enseña, f. ensign, standard.

enseñador, m. teacher.

enseñanza, f. education; teaching.

enseñar, v. teach, train; show.

enseres, m.pl. household goods.

ensilaje, m. ensilage.

ensillar, v. saddle.

ensordecer, v. deafen.

ensordecimiento, m. deafness.

ensuciar, v. dirty, muddy, soil.

ensueño, m. illusion, dream.

entablar, v. board up; initiate, begin.

entallador, m. sculptor, carver.

entapizar, v. upholster.

ente, m. being.

entenada, f. stepdaughter.

entenado, m. stepson.

entender, v. understand.

entendimiento, m. understanding.

entenebrecer, v. darken.

enterado, a. aware, informed.

enteramente, adv. entirely, completely.

enterar, v. inform.

enterarse, v. find out.

entereza, f. entirety; integrity; firmness.

entero, a. entire, whole, total.
enterramiento, m. burial, interment.
enterrar, v. bury.
entestado, a. stubborn, willful.
entibiar, v. to cool; moderate.
entidad, f. entity.
entierro, m. interment, burial.
entonación, f. intonation.
entonamiento, m. intonation.
entonar, v. chant; harmonize.
entonces, adv. then.
entono, m. arrogance; affectation.
entortadura, f. crookedness.
entortar, v. make crooked; bend.
entrada, f. entrance; admission, admittance.
entrambos, a. & pron. both.
entrante, a. coming, next.
entrañable, a. affectionate.
entrañas, f.pl. entrails, bowels; womb.
entrar, v. enter, go in, come in.
entre, prep. among; between.
entreabierto, a. ajar, half-open.
entreabrir, v. set ajar.
entreacto, m. intermission.
entrecejo, a. frowning.
entrecuesto, m. spine, backbone.
entredicho, m. prohibition.
entrega, f. delivery.
entregar, v. deliver, hand; hand over.
entrelazar, v. intertwine, entwine.
entremedias, adv. meanwhile; halfway.
entremés, m. side dish.
entremeterse, v. meddle, intrude.
entremetido, m. meddler; intermediary.
entrenador, m. coach. —entrenar, v.
entrenarse, v. train.
entrepalado, a. variegated; spotted.
entrerenglonar, v. interline.
entresacar, v. select, choose; sift.
entretanto, adv. meanwhile.
entretenedor, m. entertainer.
entretener, v. entertain, amuse; delay.
entretenimiento, m. entertainment, amusement.
entrevista, f. interview. —entrevistar, v.
entristecedor, a. sad.
entristecer, v. sadden.
entronar, v. enthrone.
entroncar, v. be related or connected.
entronización, f. enthronement.
entronque, m. relationship; connection.
entumecer, v. become or be numb; swell.
entusiasmado, a. enthusiastic.
entusiasmo, m. enthusiasm.

entusiasta, m. & f. enthusiast.
entusiástico, a. enthusiastic.
enumeración, f. enumeration.
enumerar, v. enumerate.
enunciación, f. enunciation; statement.
enunciar, v. enunciate.
envainar, v. sheathe.
envalentonar, v. encourage, embolden.
envanecimiento, m. conceit, vanity.
envasar, v. put in a container; bottle.
envase, m. container.
envejecer, v. age, grow old.
envejecimiento, m. oldness, age.
envenenar, v. poison.
envés, m. wrong side; back.
envestir, v. put in office; invest.
enviada, f. shipment.
enviado, m. envoy.
enviar, v. send; ship.
envidia, f. envy. —envidiar, v.
envidiable, a. enviable.
envidioso, a. envious.
envilecer, v. vilify, debase, disgrace.
envío, m. shipment.
envión, m. shove.
envoltura, f. wrapping.
envolver, v. wrap, wrap up.
enyesar, v. plaster.
enyugar, v. yoke.
eperlano, m. smelt (fish).
épica, f. epic writing.
épico, a. epic.
epicureísmo, m. Epicureanism.
epicúreo, n. & a. epicurean.
epidemia, f. epidemic.
epidémico, a. epidemic.
epidermis, f. epidermis.
epigrama, m. epigram.
epigramático, a. epigrammatic.
epilepsia, f. epilepsy.
epiléptico, n. & a. epileptic.
epílogo, m. epilogue.
episcopado, m. bishopric; episcopate.
episcopal, a. episcopal.
episódico, a. episodic.
episodio, m. episode.
epístola, f. epistle, letter.
epitafio, m. epitaph.
epitomadamente, adv. concisely.
epitomar, v. epitomize, summarize.
época, f. epoch, age.
epopeya, f. epic.
epsomita, f. Epsom salts.
equidad, f. equity.
equilibrado, a. stable.
equilibrio, m. equilibrium, balance.
equinoccio, m. equinox.
equipaje, m. luggage, baggage.
equipar, v. equip.
equiparar, v. compare.
equipo, m. equipment; team.
equitación, f. horsemanship.
equitativo, a. fair, equitable.
equivalencia, f. equivalence.

equivalente, a. equivalent.
equivaler, v. equal, be equivalent.
equivocación, f. mistake.
equivocado, a. wrong, mistaken.
equivocarse, v. make a mistake, be wrong.
equívoco, a. equivocal, ambiguous.
era, f. era, age.
erario, m. exchequer.
erección, f. erection; elevation.
eremita, m. hermit.
erguir, v. erect; straighten up.
erigir, v. erect, build.
erisipela, f. erysipelas.
erizado, a. bristly.
erizarse, v. bristle.
erizo, m. hedgehog; sea urchin.
ermita, f. hermitage.
ermitaño, m. hermit.
erogación, f. expenditure. —erogar, v.
erosión, f. erosion.
erótico, a. erotic.
erradicación, f. eradication.
erradicar, v. eradicate.
errado, a. mistaken, erroneous.
errante, a. wandering, roving.
errar, v. be mistaken.
errata, f. erratum.
errático, a. erratic.
erróneamente, adv. erroneously.
erróneo, a. erroneous.
error, m. error, mistake.
eructo, m. belch. —eructar, v.
erudición, f. scholarship, learning.
eruditamente, adv. learnedly.
erudito, m. scholar.
erupción, f. eruption; rash.
eruptivo, a. eruptive.
esbozo, m. outline, sketch. —esbozar, v.
escabechar, v. pickle; preserve.
escabel, m. small stool or bench.
escabroso, a. rough, irregular; craggy; rude.
escabullirse, v. steal away, sneak away.
escala, f. scale; ladder. hacer e., to make a stop.
escalada, f. escalation.
escalador, m. climber.
escalar, v. climb; scale.
escaldar, v. scald.
escalera, f. stairs, staircase; ladder.
escalfado, a. poached.
escalofriado, a. chilled.
escalofrío, m. chill.
escalón, m. step.
escaloña, f. scallion.
escalpar, v. scalp.
escalpelo, m. scalpel.
escama, f. (fish) scale. —escamar, v.
escamondar, v. trim; cut; prune.
escampada, f. stampede.

escandalizar, v. shock, scandalize.

escandalizativo, a. scandalous.

escándalo, m. scandal.

escandaloso, a. scandalous; disgraceful.

escandinavo, n. & a. Scandinavian.

escandir, v. scan.

escanilla, f. cradle.

escañuelo, m. small footstool.

escapada, f. escapade.

escapar, v. escape.

escape, m. escape; (auto.) exhaust.

escápula, f. scapula.

escarabajo, m. black beetle; scarab.

escaramucear, v. skirmish; dispute.

escarbadientes, m. toothpick.

escarbar, v. scratch; poke.

escardar, v. weed.

escarcha, f. frost.

escarlata, f. scarlet.

escarmentar, v. correct severely.

escarnecedor, m. scoffer; mocker.

escarnecer, v. mock, make fun of.

escarola, f. endive.

escarpado, 1. a. steep. 2. m. bluff.

escarpe, m. escarpment.

escasamente, adv. scarcely; sparingly; barely.

escasear, v. be scarce.

escasez, f. shortage, scarcity.

escaso, a. scant; scarce.

escatimoso, a. malicious; sly, cunning.

escena, f. scene; stage.

escenario, m. stage (of theater); scenario.

escénico, a. scenic.

escépticamente, adv. skeptically.

escepticismo, m. skepticism.

escéptico -ca, a. & n. skeptic; skeptical.

esclarecer, v. clear up.

esclavitud, f. slavery; bondage.

esclavizar, v. enslave.

esclavo -va, n. slave.

escoba, f. broom.

escocés, a. & n. Scotch, Scottish; Scot.

Escocia, f. Scotland.

escofinar, v. rasp.

escoger, v. choose, select.

escogido, a. choice, select.

escogimiento, m. choice.

escolar, 1. a. scholastic, (of) school. 2. m. student.

escolasticismo, m. scholasticism.

escolta, f. escort. —escoltar, v.

escollo, m. reef.

escombro, m. mackerel.

escombros, m.pl. debris, rubbish.

esconce, m. corner.

escondedero, m. hiding place.

esconder, v. hide, conceal.

escondidamente, adv. secretly.

escondimiento, m. concealment.

escopeta, f. shotgun.

escopetazo, m. gunshot.

escoplo, m. chisel.

escorbuto, m. scurvy.

escorpena, f. grouper.

escorpión, m. scorpion.

escorzón, m. toad.

escribiente, m. & f. clerk.

escribir, v. write.

escritor -ra, n. writer, author.

escritorio, m. desk.

escritura, f. writing, handwriting.

escrófula, f. scrofula.

escroto, m. scrotum.

escrúpulo, m. scruple.

escrupuloso, a. scrupulous.

escrutinio, m. scrutiny; examination.

escuadra, f. squad; fleet.

escuadrón, m. squadron.

escualidez, f. squalor; poverty.

escuálido, a. squalid.

escualo, m. shark.

escuchar, v. listen; listen to.

escudero, m. squire.

escudo, m. shield; protection; coin of certain countries.

escuela, f. school.

escuerzo, m. toad.

esculpir, v. carve, sculpture.

escultor, m. sculptor.

escultura, f. sculpture.

escupidera, f. cuspidor.

escupir, v. spit.

escurridor, m. colander, strainer.

escurrir, v. drain off; wring out.

escurrirse, v. slip; sneak away.

ese, esa, dem. a. that.

ése, ésa, dem. pron. that (one).

esencia, f. essence; perfume.

esencial, a. essential.

esencialmente, adv. essentially.

esfera, f. sphere.

esfinge, f. sphinx.

esforzar, v. strengthen.

esforzarse, v. strive, exert oneself.

esfuerzo, m. effort, attempt; vigor.

esgrima, f. fencing.

eslabón, m. link (of a chain).

eslabonar, v. link, join, connect.

eslavo, a. & n. Slavic; Slav.

esmalte, m. enamel. —esmaltar, v.

esmerado, a. careful, thorough.

esmeralda, f. emerald.

esmerarse, v. take pains, do one's best.

esmeril, m. emery.

eso, dem. pron. that.

esófago, m. esophagus.

esotérico, a. esoteric.

espacial, a. spatial.

espacio, m. space. —espaciar, v.

espaciosidad, f. spaciousness.

espacioso, a. spacious.

espada, f. sword; spade (in cards).

espadarte, m. swordfish.

espalda, f. back.

espaldera, f. espalier.

espantar, v. frighten, scare; scare away.

espanto, m. fright.

espantoso, a. frightening, frightful.

España, f. Spain.

español -ola, a. & n. Spanish; Spaniard.

esparcir, v. scatter, disperse.

espárrago, m. asparagus.

espartano, n. & a. Spartan.

espasmo, m. spasm.

espasmódico, a. spasmodic.

espata, f. spathe.

espato, m. spar (mineral).

espátula, f. spatula.

especia, f. spice. —especiar, v.

especial, a. special, especial.

especialidad, f. specialty.

especialista, m. & f. specialist.

especialización, f. specialization.

especialmente, adv. especially.

especie, f. species; sort.

especiería, f. grocery store.

especiero, m. grocer.

especificar, v. specify.

específico, a. specific.

espécimen, m. specimen.

especioso, a. neat; polished; specious.

espectáculo, m. spectacle, show.

espectador -ra, n. spectator.

espectro, m. specter, ghost.

especulación, f. speculation.

especulador, m. speculator.

especular, v. speculate.

especulativo, a. speculative.

espejo, m. mirror.

espelunca, f. dark cave, cavern.

espera, f. wait.

esperanza, f. hope, expectation.

esperar, v. hope; expect; wait; wait for, watch for.

espesar, v. thicken.

espeso, a. thick, dense, bushy.

espesor, m. thickness, density.

espía, m. & f. spy. —espiar, v.

espigón, m. bee sting.

espina, f. thorn.

espinaca, f. spinach.

espinal, a. spinal.

espinazo, m. spine.

espineta, f. spinet.

espino, m. briar.

espinoso, a. spiny, thorny.

espión, m. spy.

espionaje, m. espionage.

espiración, f. expiration.

espiral, a. & m. spiral.

espirar, v. expire; breathe, exhale.

espíritu, m. spirit.

espiritual, a. spiritual.

espiritualidad, f. spirituality.

espiritualmente, adv. spiritually.

espita, f. faucet, spigot.
espléndido, a. splendid.
esplendor, m. splendor.
espolear, v. incite, urge on.
espoleta, f. wishbone.
esponja, f. sponge.
esponjoso, a. spongy.
esponsales, m.pl. engagement, betrothal.
esponsalicio, a. nuptial.
espontáneamente, adv. spontaneously.
espontaneidad, f. spontaneity.
espontáneo, a. spontaneous.
espora, f. spore.
esporádico, a. sporadic.
esposa, f. wife.
esposar, v. shackle.
esposo, m. husband.
espuela, f. spur. —espolear, v.
espuma, f. foam. —espumar, v.
espumadera, f. colander.
espumajear, v. foam at the mouth.
espumajo, m. foam.
espumar, v. foam, froth; skim.
espumoso, a. foamy; sparkling (wine).
espurio, a. spurious.
esputar, v. spit, expectorate.
esputo, m. spit, saliva.
esquela, f. note.
esqueleto, m. skeleton.
esquema, m. scheme; diagram.
esquero, m. leather sack or pouch.
esquiciar, v. outline, sketch roughly.
esquicio, m. rough sketch or outline.
esquife, m. skiff.
esquilar, v. fleece, shear.
esquilmo, m. harvest.
esquimal, n. & a. Eskimo.
esquina, f. corner.
esquivar, v. evade, shun.
estabilidad, f. stability.
estable, a. stable.
establecedor, m. founder, originator.
establecer, v. establish, set up.
establecimiento, m. establishment.
establero, m. groom.
establo, m. stable.
estaca, f. stake.
estación, f. station; season.
estacionar, v. station; park (a vehicle).
estacionario, a. stationary.
estadista, m. statesman.
estadística, f. statistics.
estadístico, a. statistical.
estado, m. state; condition; status.
estafa, f. swindle, fake. —estafar, v.
estafeta, f. post office.
estagnación, f. stagnation.
estallar, v. explode; burst; break out.
estallido, m. crash; crack; explosion.
estampa, f. stamp. —estampar, v.

estampado, m. printed cotton cloth.
estampida, f. stampede.
estampilla, f. (postage) stamp.
estancado, a. stagnant.
estancar, v. stanch, stop, check.
estancia, f. stay; (S.A.) small farm.
estanciero -ra, n. small farmer.
estandarte, m. banner.
estanque, m. pool; pond.
estante, m. shelf.
estaño, m. tin. —estañar, v.
estar, v. be; stand; look.
estática, f. static.
estático, a. static.
estatua, f. statue.
estatura, f. stature.
estatuto, m. statute, law.
este, m. east.
este, esta, dem. a. this.
éste, ésta, dem. pron. this (one); the latter.
estelar, a. stellar.
estenografía, f. stenography.
estenógrafo -fa, n. stenographer.
estera, f. mat, matting.
estereofónico, a. stereophonic.
estéril, a. barren; sterile.
esterilidad, f. sterility, fruitlessness.
esterilizar, v. sterilize.
estética, f. esthetics.
estético, a. esthetic.
estetoscopio, m. stethoscope.
estibador, m. stevedore.
estiércol, m. dung, manure.
estigma, m. stigma; disgrace.
estilo, m. style; sort.
estilográfica, f. (fountain) pen.
estima, f. esteem.
estimable, a. estimable, worthy.
estimación, f. estimation.
estimar, v. esteem; value; estimate; gauge.
estimular, v. stimulate.
estímulo, m. stimulus.
estío, m. summer.
estipulación, f. stipulation.
estipular, v. stipulate.
estirar, v. stretch.
estirpe, m. stock, lineage.
esto, dem. pron. this.
estocada, f. stab, thrust.
estofado, m. stew. —estofar, v.
estoicismo, m. stoicism.
estoico, n. & a. stoic.
estómago, m. stomach.
estorbar, v. bother, hinder, interfere with.
estorbo, m. hindrance.
estornudo, m. sneeze. —estornudar, v.
estrabismo, m. strabismus.
estrago, m. devastation, havoc.
estrangulación, f. strangulation.
estrangular, v. strangle.
estratagema, f. stratagem.
estrategia, f. strategy.
estratégico, a. strategic.
estrato, m. stratum.

estrechar, v. tighten; narrow.
estrechez, f. narrowness; tightness.
estrecho, 1. a. narrow, tight. 2. m. strait.
estregar, v. scour, scrub.
estrella, f. star.
estrellamar, f. starfish.
estrellar, v. shatter, smash.
estremecimiento, m. shudder. —estremecerse, v.
estrenar, v. wear for the first time; open (a play).
estreno, m. debut, first performance.
estrenuo, a. strenuous.
estreptococo, m. streptococcus.
estría, f. groove.
estribillo, m. refrain.
estribo, m. stirrup.
estribor, m. starboard.
estrictamente, adv. strictly.
estrictez, f. strictness.
estricto, a. strict.
estrofa, f. stanza.
estropajo, m. mop.
estropear, v. cripple, damage, spoil.
estructura, f. structure.
estructural, a. structural.
estruendo, m. din, clatter.
estuario, m. estuary.
estuco, m. stucco.
estudiante -ta, n. student.
estudiar, v. study.
estudio, m. study; studio.
estudioso, a. studious.
estufa, f. stove.
estulto, a. foolish.
estupendo, a. wonderful, grand, fine.
estupidez, f. stupidity.
estúpido, a. stupid.
estupor, m. stupor.
estuque, m. stucco.
esturión, m. sturgeon.
etapa, f. stage.
éter, m. ether.
etéreo, a. ethereal.
eternal, a. eternal.
eternidad, f. eternity.
eterno, a. eternal.
ética, f. ethics.
ético, a. ethical.
etimología, f. etymology.
etiqueta, f. etiquette; tag, label.
étnico, a. ethnic.
etrusco, n. & a. Etruscan.
eufemismo, m. euphemism.
eufonía, f. euphony.
Europa, f. Europe.
europeo -pea, a. & n. European.
eutanasia, f. euthanasia.
evacuación, f. evacuation.
evacuar, v. evacuate.
evadir, v. evade.
evangélico, a. evangelical.
evangelio, m. gospel.
evangelista, m. evangelist.
evaporación, f. evaporation.
evaporarse, v. evaporate.

evasión, f. evasion.
evasivamente, adv. evasively.
evasivo, a. evasive.
evento, m. event, occurrence.
eventual, a. eventual.
eventualidad, f. eventuality.
evicción, f. eviction.
evidencia, f. evidence.
evidenciar, v. prove, show.
evidente, a. evident.
evitación, f. avoidance.
evitar, v. avoid, shun.
evocación, f. evocation.
evocar, v. evoke.
evolución, f. evolution.
exacerbar, v. irritate deeply.
exactamente, adv. exactly.
exactitud, f. precision, accuracy.
exacto, a. exact, accurate.
exageración, f. exaggeration.
exagerar, v. exaggerate.
exagonal, a. hexagonal.
exaltación, f. exaltation.
exaltamiento, m. exaltation.
exaltar, v. exalt.
examen, m. test, examination.
examinar, v. test, examine.
exánime, a. spiritless, weak.
exasperación, f. exasperation.
exasperar, v. exasperate.
excavación, f. excavation.
excavar, v. excavate.
exceder, v. exceed, surpass; outrun.
excelencia, f. excellence.
excelente, a. excellent.
excéntrico, a. eccentric.
excepción, f. exception.
excepcional, a. exceptional.
excepto, prep. except, except for.
exceptuar, v. except.
excesivamente, adv. excessively.
excesivo, a. excessive.
exceso, m. excess.
excitabilidad, f. excitability.
excitación, f. excitement.
excitar, v. excite.
exclamación, f. exclamation.
exclamar, v. exclaim.
excluir, v. exclude, bar, shut out.
exclusión, f. exclusion.
exclusivamente, adv. exclusively.
exclusivo, a. exclusive.
excomulgar, v. excommunicate.
excomunión, f. excommunication.
excreción, f. excretion.
excremento, m. excrement.
excretar, v. excrete.
exculpar, v. exonerate.
excursión, f. excursion.
excursionista, n. excursionist.
excusa, f. excuse. —**excusar,** v.
excusado, m. toilet.
excusarse, v. apologize.
exención, f. exemption.
exento, a. exempt. —**exentar,** v.
exhalación, f. exhalation.

exhalar, v. exhale, breathe out.
exhausto, a. exhausted.
exhibición, f. exhibit, exhibition.
exhibir, v. exhibit, display.
exhortación, f. exhortation.
exhortar, v. exhort, admonish.
exhumacion, f. exhumation.
exhumar, v. exhume.
exigencia, f. requirement, demand.
exigente, a. exacting, demanding.
exigir, v. require, exact, demand.
eximir, v. exempt.
existencia, f. existence; (econ.) supply.
existente, a. existent.
existir, v. exist.
éxito, m. success.
éxodo, m. exodus.
exoneración, f. exoneration.
exonerar, v. exonerate, acquit.
exorar, v. beg, implore.
exorbitancia, f. exorbitance.
exorbitante, a. exorbitant.
exorcismo, m. exorcism.
exornar, v. adorn, decorate.
exótico, a. exotic.
expansibilidad, f. expansibility.
expansión, f. expansion.
expansivo, a. expansive; effusive.
expatriación, f. expatriation.
expatriar, v. expatriate.
expectación, f. expectation.
expectorar, v. expectorate.
expedición, f. expedition.
expediente, m. expedient, means.
expedir, v. send off, ship; expedite.
expeditivo, a. speedy, prompt.
expedito, a. speedy, prompt.
expeler, v. expel, eject.
expendedor, m. dealer.
expender, v. expend.
expensas, f.pl. expenses, costs.
experiencia, f. experience.
experimentado, a. experienced.
experimental, a. experimental.
experimentar, v. experience.
experimento, m. experiment.
expertamente, adv. expertly.
experto, a. & m. expert.
expiación, f. atonement.
expiar, v. atone for.
expiración, f. expiration.
expirar, v. expire.
explanación, f. explanation.
explanar, v. make level.
expletivo, n. & a. expletive.
explicable, a. explicable.
explicación, f. explanation.
explicar, v. explain.
explicativo, a. explanatory.
explícitamente, adv. explicitly.
explícito, adj. explicit.
exploración, f. exploration.
explorador, m. explorer; scout.
explorar, v. explore; scout.
exploratorio, a. exploratory.

explosión, f. explosion; outburst.
explosivo, a. explosive.
explotación, f. exploitation.
explotar, v. exploit.
exponer, v. expose; set forth.
exportación, f. exportation; export.
exportador, m. exporter.
exportar, v. export.
exposición, f. exhibit; exposition; exposure.
expósito, n. foundling; orphan.
expresado, a. aforesaid.
expresamente, adv. clearly, explicitly.
expresar, v. express.
expresión, f. expression.
expresivo, a. expressive; affectionate.
expreso, a. & m. express.
exprimir, v. squeeze.
expropiación, f. expropriation.
expropiar, v. expropriate.
expulsar, v. expel, eject; evict.
expulsión, f. expulsion.
expurgación, f. expurgation.
expurgar, v. expurgate.
exquisitamente, adv. exquisitely.
exquisito, a. exquisite.
éxtasi, m. ecstasy.
extemporáneo, a. extemporaneous, impromptu.
extender, v. extend; spread; widen; stretch.
extensamente, adv. extensively.
extensión, f. extension, spread, expanse.
extenso, a. extensive, widespread.
extenuación, f. weakening; emaciation.
extenuar, v. extenuate.
exterior, a. & m. exterior; foreign.
exterminar, v. exterminate.
exterminio, m. extermination, ruin.
extinción, f. extinction.
extinguir, v. extinguish.
extinto, a. extinct.
extintor, m. fire extinguisher.
extirpar, v. eradicate.
extorsión, f. extortion.
extra, n. extra.
extracción, f. extraction.
extractar, v. summarize.
extracto, m. extract; summary.
extradición, f. extradition.
extraer, v. extract.
extranjero -ra, 1. a. foreign. **2.** n. foreigner; stranger.
extrañar, v. surprise; miss.
extraño, a. strange, queer.
extraordinariamente, adv. extraordinarily.
extraordinario, a. extraordinary.
extravagancia, f. extravagance.
extravagante, a. extravagant.
extraviado, a. lost, misplaced.
extraviarse, v. stray, get lost.

extravío, *m.* aberration, deviation.
extremadamente, *adv.* extremely.
extremado, *a.* extreme.
extremaunción, *f.* extreme unction.
extremidad, *f.* extremity.
extremista, *n. & a.* extremist.
extremo, *a. & m.* extreme, end.
extrínseco, *a.* extrinsic.
exuberancia, *f.* exuberance.
exuberante, *a.* exuberant.
exudación, *f.* exudation.
exudar, *v.* exude, ooze.
exultación, *f.* exultation.

F

fábrica, *f.* factory.
fabricación, *f.* manufacture, manufacturing.
fabricante, *m.* manufacturer, maker.
fabricar, *v.* manufacture, make.
fabril, *a.* making, building.
fábula, *f.* fable, myth.
fabuloso, *a.* fabulous.
facción, *f.* faction, party; (*pl.*) features.
faccioso, *a.* factious.
fácil, *a.* easy.
facilidad, *f.* facility, ease.
facilitar, *v.* facilitate, make easy.
fácilmente, *adv.* easily.
facsímil, *m.* facsimile.
factible, *a.* feasible.
factor, *m.* factor.
factótum, *m.* factotum; jack of all trades.
factura, *f.* invoice, bill.
facurar, *v.* check (baggage).
facultad, *f.* faculty; ability.
facultativo, *a.* optional.
fachada, *f.* façade, front.
faena, *f.* task; work.
falacia, *f.* fallacy; deceitfulness.
falda, *f.* skirt; lap.
falibilidad, *f.* fallibility.
falsear, *v.* falsify, counterfeit, forge.
falsedad, *f.* falsehood; lie; falseness.
falsificación, *f.* falsification; forgery.
falsificar, *v.* falsify, counterfeit, forge.
falso, *a.* false; wrong.
falta, *f.* error, mistake; fault; lack. **hacer f.,** to be lacking, to be necessary. **sin f.,** without fail.
faltar, *v.* be lacking, be missing; be absent.
faltriquera, *f.* pocket.
falla, *f.* failure, fault.
fallar, *v.* fail.
fallecer, *v.* pass away, die.
fallo, *m.* verdict.

fama, *f.* fame; reputation; glory.
familia, *f.* family; household.
familiar, *a.* familiar; domestic; (of) family.
familiaridad, *f.* familiarity, intimacy.
familiarizar, *v.* familiarize, acquaint.
famoso, *a.* famous.
fanal, *m.* lighthouse; lantern, lamp.
fanático -ca, *a. & n.* fanatic.
fanatismo, *m.* fanaticism.
fanfarria, *f.* bluster. **—fanfarrear,** *v.*
fango, *m.* mud.
fantasía, *f.* fantasy; fancy, whim.
fantasma, *m.* phantom; ghost.
fantástico, *a.* fantastic.
faquín, *m.* porter.
faquir, *m.* fakir.
farallón, *m.* cliff.
Faraón, *m.* Pharaoh.
fardel, *m.* bag; package.
fardo, *m.* bundle.
farináceo, *a.* farinaceous.
faringe, *f.* pharynx.
fariseo, *m.* pharisee, hypocrite.
farmacéutico, *m.* pharmacist.
farmacia, *f.* pharmacy.
faro, *m.* beacon; lighthouse; headlight.
farol, *m.* lantern; (street) light.
farra, *f.* spree.
fárrago, *m.* medley; hodge-podge.
farsa, *f.* farce.
fascinación, *f.* fascination.
fascinar, *v.* fascinate, bewitch.
fase, *f.* phase.
fastidiar, *v.* disgust; irk, annoy.
fastidio, *m.* disgust; annoyance.
fastidioso, *a.* annoying; tedious.
fatal, *a.* fatal.
fatalidad, *f.* fate; calamity; bad luck.
fatalismo, *m.* fatalism.
fatalista, *n. & a.* fatalist.
fatiga, *f.* fatigue. **—fatigar,** *v.*
fauno, *m.* faun.
favor, *m.* favor; behalf. **por f.,** please.
favorable, *a.* favorable.
favorablemente, *adv.* favorably.
favorecer, *v.* favor; flatter.
favoritismo, *m.* favoritism.
favorito -ta, *a. & n.* favorite.
faz, *f.* face.
fe, *f.* faith.
fealdad, *f.* ugliness, homeliness.
febrero, *m.* February.
febril, *a.* feverish.
fécula, *f.* starch.
fecundar, *v.* fertilize.
fecundidad, *f.* fecundity, fertility.
fecundo, *a.* fecund, fertile.
fecha, *f.* date. **—fechar,** *v.*
federación, *f.* confederacy.

federal, *a.* federal.
felicidad, *f.* happiness; bliss.
felicitación, *f.* congratulation.
felicitar, *v.* congratulate; compliment.
feligrés -esa, *n.* parishioner.
feliz, *a.* happy; fortunate.
felón, *m.* felon.
felonía, *f.* felony.
felpa, *f.* plush.
felpudo, *m.* doormat.
femenino, *a.* feminine.
feminismo, *m.* feminism.
feminista, *n.* feminist.
fenecer, *v.* conclude; die.
fénix, *m.* phoenix; model.
fenomenal, *a.* phenomenal.
fenómeno, *m.* phenomenon.
feo, *a.* ugly, homely.
feracidad, *f.* feracity, fertility.
feraz, *a.* fertile, fruitful; copious.
feria, *f.* fair; market.
feriado, *a.* **día f.,** holiday.
fermentación, *f.* fermentation.
fermento, *m.* ferment. **—fermentar,** *v.*
ferocidad, *f.* ferocity, fierceness.
feroz, *a.* ferocious, fierce.
férreo, *a.* of iron.
ferrería, *f.* ironworks.
ferretería, *f.* hardware; hardware store.
ferrocarril, *m.* railroad.
fértil, *a.* fertile.
fertilidad, *f.* fertility.
fertilizar, *v.* fertilize.
férvido, *a.* fervid, ardent.
ferviente, *a.* fervent.
fervor, *m.* fervor, zeal.
fervoroso, *a.* zealous, eager.
festejar, *v.* entertain, fete.
festejo, *m.* feast.
festín, *m.* feast.
festividad, *f.* festivity.
festivo, *a.* festive.
fétido, *adj.* fetid.
feudal, *a.* feudal.
feudo, *m.* feud.
fiado, *adj.* on trust, on credit.
fianza, *f.* bail.
fiar, *v.* trust, sell on credit; give credit.
fiarse de, *v.* trust (in), rely on.
fiasco, *m.* fiasco.
fibra, *f.* fiber; vigor.
fibroso, *a.* fibrous.
ficción, *f.* fiction.
ficticio, *a.* fictitious.
ficha, *f.* slip, card; chip.
fidedigno, *a.* trustworthy.
fideicomisario, *m.* trustee.
fideicomiso, *m.* trust.
fidelidad, *f.* fidelity.
fideo, *m.* noodle.
fiebre, *f.* fever.
fiel, *a.* faithful.
fieltro, *m.* felt.
fiera, *f.* wild animal.
fiereza, *f.* fierceness, wildness.
fiero, *a.* fierce; wild.
fiesta, *f.* festival, feast; party.
figura, *f.* figure. **—figurar,** *v.*
figurarse, *v.* imagine.

figurón, *m.* dummy.

fijar, *v.* fix; set, establish; post.

fijarse en, *v.* notice.

fijeza, *f.* firmness.

fijo, *a.* fixed, stationary, permanent, set.

fila, *f.* row, rank, file, line.

filantropía, *f.* philanthropy.

filete, *m.* fillet.

film, *m.* film. **—filmar,** *v.*

filo, *m.* (cutting) edge.

filón, *m.* vein (of ore).

filosofía, *f.* philosophy.

filosófico, *a.* philosophical.

filósofo, *m.* philosopher.

filtro, *m.* filter. **—filtrar,** *v.*

fin, *m.* end, purpose, goal. a f. **de que,** in order that. **en f.,** in short. **por f.,** finally, at last.

final, 1. *a.* final. **2.** *m.* end.

finalidad, *f.* finality.

finalmente, *adv.* at last.

financiero, 1. *a.* financial. **2.** *m.* financier.

finca, *f.* real estate; estate; farm.

finés, *a.* Finnish.

fineza, *f.* courtesy, politeness; fineness.

fingimiento, *m.* pretense.

fingir, *v.* feign, pretend.

fino, *a.* fine; polite, courteous.

firma, *f.* signature; (com.) firm.

firmamento, *m.* firmament, heavens.

firmar, *v.* sign.

firme, *a.* firm, fast, steady, sound.

firmemente, *adv.* firmly.

firmeza, *f.* firmness.

fisco, *m.* exchequer, treasury.

física, *f.* physics.

físico, *a. & n.* physical; physicist.

fisiología, *f.* physiology.

fláccido, *a.* flaccid, soft.

flaco, *a.* thin, gaunt.

flagelación, *f.* flagellation.

flagelar, *v.* flagellate, whip.

flagrancia, *f.* flagrancy.

flagrante, *a.* flagrant.

flama, *f.* flame; ardor, zeal.

flamante, *a.* flaming.

flamenco, *m.* flamingo.

flan, *m.* custard.

flanco, *m.* side; (mil.) flank.

flanquear, *v.* flank.

flaqueza, *f.* thinness; weakness.

flauta, *f.* flute.

flautín, *m.* piccolo.

flautista, *m. & f.* flutist, piper.

fleco, *m.* fringe; flounce.

flecha, *f.* arrow.

flechero, *m.* archer.

flema, *f.* phlegm.

flete, *m.* freight. **—fletar,** *v.*

flexibilidad, *f.* flexibility.

flexible, *a.* flexible, pliable.

flirtear, *v.* flirt.

flojo, *a.* limp; loose, flabby, slack.

flor, *f.* flower; compliment.

flora, *f.* flora.

floral, *a.* floral.

florecer, *v.* flower, bloom; flourish.

floreo, *m.* flourish.

florero, *m.* flower pot; vase.

floresta, *f.* forest.

florido, *a.* flowery; flowering.

florista, *m. & f.* florist.

flota, *f.* fleet.

flotante, *a.* floating.

flotar, *v.* float.

flotilla, *f.* flotilla, fleet.

fluctuación, *f.* fluctuation.

fluctuar, *v.* fluctuate.

fluente, *a.* fluent.

fluidez, *f.* fluency.

flúido, *a. & m.* fluid, liquid.

fluir, *v.* flow.

flujo, *m.* flow, flux.

flúor, *m.* fluorine.

fluorescencia, *f.* fluorescence.

fluorescente, *a.* fluorescent.

fobia, *f.* phobia.

foca, *f.* seal.

foco, *m.* focus, center.

fogata, *f.* bonfire.

fogón, *m.* hearth, fireplace.

fogosidad, *f.* vehemence, ardor.

fogoso, *a.* vehement, ardent.

folklore, *m.* folklore.

follaje, *m.* foliage.

folleto, *m.* pamphlet, booklet.

fomentar, *v.* develop, promote, further, foster.

fomento, *m.* fomentation.

fonda, *f.* eating house, inn.

fondo, *m.* bottom; back (part); background; (pl.) funds; finances. **a f.,** thoroughly.

fonética, *f.* phonetics.

fonético, *a.* phonetic.

fonógrafo, *m.* phonograph.

forastero -ra, 1. *a.* foreign, exotic. **2.** *n.* stranger.

forjar, *v.* forge.

forma, *f.* form, shape. **—formar,** *v.*

formación, *f.* formation.

formal, *a.* formal.

formaldehído, *m.* formaldehyde.

formalidad, *f.* formality.

formalizar, *v.* finalize; formulate.

formidable, *a.* formidable.

formidablemente, *adv.* formidably.

formón, *m.* chisel.

fórmula, *f.* formula.

formular, *v.* formulate, draw up.

formulario, *m.* form.

foro, *m.* forum.

forraje, *m.* forage, fodder.

forrar, *v.* line.

forro, *m.* lining.

fortalecer, *v.* fortify.

fortaleza, *f.* fort, fortress; fortitude.

fortificación, *f.* fortification.

fortitud, *f.* fortitude.

fortuitamente, *adv.* fortuitously.

fortuito, *a.* fortuitous.

fortuna, *f.* fortune; luck.

forúnculo, *m.* boil.

forzar, *v.* force, compel, coerce.

forzosamente, *adv.* compulsorily; forcibly.

forzoso, *a.* compulsory; necessary. **paro f.,** unemployment.

forzudo, *a.* powerful, vigorous.

fosa, *f.* grave.

fósforo, *m.* match; phosphorus.

fósil, *m.* fossil.

foso, *m.* ditch, trench; moat.

fotocopiadora, *f.* photocopier.

fotografía, *f.* photograph. **—fotografiar,** *v.*

frac, *m.* dress coat.

fracasar, *v.* fail.

fracaso, *m.* failure.

fracción, *f.* fraction.

fractura, *f.* fracture, break.

fragancia, *f.* fragrance; perfume; aroma.

fragante, *a.* fragrant.

frágil, *a.* fragile, breakable.

fragilidad, *f.* fragility.

fragmentario, *a.* fragmentary.

fragmento, *m.* fragment, bit.

fragor, *m.* noise, clamor.

fragoso, *a.* noisy.

fragua, *f.* forge. **—fraguar,** *v.*

fraile, *m.* monk.

frambuesa, *f.* raspberry.

francamente, *adv.* frankly, candidly.

francés, -esa, *a. & n.* French; Frenchman.

Francia, *f.* France.

franco, *a.* frank.

franela, *f.* flannel.

frangible, *a.* breakable.

franqueo, *m.* postage.

franqueza, *f.* frankness.

franquicia, *f.* franchise.

frasco, *m.* flask, bottle.

frase, *f.* phrase; sentence.

fraseología, *f.* phraseology; style.

fraternal, *a.* fraternal, brotherly.

fraternidad, *f.* fraternity, brotherhood.

fraude, *m.* fraud.

fraudulento, *a.* fraudulent.

frazada, *f.* blanket.

frecuencia, *f.* frequency.

frecuente, *a.* frequent.

frecuentemente, *adv.* frequently, often.

fregadero, *m.* sink.

fregadura, *f.* scouring, scrubbing.

fregar, *v.* scour, scrub, mop.

freír, *v.* fry.

fréjol, *m.* kidney bean.

frenesí, *m.* frenzy.

frenéticamente, *adv.* frantically.

frenético, *a.* frantic, frenzied.

freno, *m.* brake. **—frenar,** *v.*

frente, 1. *m.* forehead. **2.** *m.* front. **en f., al f.,** opposite, across. **f. a,** in front of.

fresa, *f.* strawberry.

fresca, *f.* fresh, cool air.

fresco, *a.* fresh; cool; crisp.
frescura, *f.* coolness, freshness.
fresno, *m.* ash tree.
fresquería, *f.* soda fountain.
friabilidad, *f.* brittleness.
friable, *a.* brittle.
frialdad, *f.* coldness.
fríamente, *adv.* coldly; coolly.
fricandó, *m.* fricandeau.
fricar, *v.* rub together.
fricción, *f.* friction.
friccionar, *v.* rub.
friega, *f.* friction.
frigidez, *f.* frigidity.
frígido, *a.* frigid.
frijol, *m.* bean.
frío, *a. & n.* cold. **tener f.,** to be cold, feel cold. **hacer f.,** to be cold (weather).
friolento, friolero, *a.* chilly; sensitive to cold.
friolera, *f.* trifle, trinket.
friso, *m.* frieze.
fritillas, *f.pl.* fritters.
frito, *a.* fried.
fritura, *f.* fritter.
frívolamente, *adv.* frivolously.
frivolidad, *f.* frivolity.
frívolo, *a.* frivolous.
frondoso, *a.* leafy.
frontera, *f.* frontier; border.
frotar, *v.* rub.
fructífero, *a.* fruitful.
fructificar, *v.* bear fruit.
fructuoso, *a.* fruitful.
frugal, *a.* frugal, thrifty.
frugalidad, *f.* frugality; thrift.
frugalmente, *adv.* frugally, thriftily.
fruncir, *v.* gather, contract. **f. el entrecejo,** frown.
frusleria, *f.* trinket.
frustrar, *v.* frustrate, thwart.
fruta, *f.* fruit.
fruto, *m.* fruit; product; profit.
fucsia, *f.* fuchsia.
fuego, *m.* fire.
fuelle, *m.* bellows.
fuente, *f.* fountain; source; platter.
fuera, *adv.* without, outside.
fuero, *m.* statute.
fuerte, 1. *a.* strong; loud. **2.** *m.* fort.
fuertemente, *adv.* strongly; loudly.
fuerza, *f.* force, strength.
fuga, *f.* flight, escape.
fugarse, *v.* flee, escape.
fugaz, *a.* fugitive, passing.
fugitivo -va, *a. & n.* fugitive.
fulcro, *m.* fulcrum.
fulgor, *m.* gleam, glow. **—fulgurar,** *v.*
fulminante, *a.* explosive.
fumador, *m.* smoker.
fumar, *v.* smoke.
fumigación, *f.* fumigation.
fumigador, *m.* fumigator.
fumigar, *v.* fumigate.
fumoso, *a.* smoky.
función, *f.* function; performance, show.

funcionar, *v.* function, work, run.
funcionario, *m.* official, functionary.
funda, *f.* case, sheath, slip-cover.
fundación, *f.* foundation.
fundador -ra, *n.* founder.
fundamental, *a.* fundamental, basic.
fundamentalmente, *adv.* fundamentally.
fundamento, *m.* base, basis, foundation.
fundar, *v.* found, establish.
fundición, *f.* foundry; melting, meltdown.
fundir, *v.* fuse; smelt.
fúnebre, *a.* dismal.
funeral, *a.* funeral.
funestamente, *adv.* sadly.
fungo, *m.* fungus.
furente, *a.* furious, enraged.
furia, *f.* fury.
furiosamente, *adv.* furiously.
furioso, *a.* furious.
furor, *m.* furor; fury.
furtivamente, *adv.* furtively.
furtivo, *a.* furtive, sly.
furúnculo, *m.* boil.
fusibilidad, *f.* fusibility.
fusible, *a.* fuse.
fusil, *m.* rifle, gun.
fusilar, *v.* shoot.
fusión, *f.* fusion; merger.
fusionar, *v.* unite, fuse, merge.
fútbol, *m.* football, soccer.
fútil, *a.* trivial.
futilidad, *f.* triviality.
futuro, *a. & m.* future.
futurología, *f.* futurology.

G

gabán, *m.* overcoat.
gabinete, *m.* closet; cabinet; study.
gacela, *f.* gazelle.
gaceta, *f.* gazette, newspaper.
gacetilla, *f.* personal news section of a newspaper.
gaélico, *a.* Gaelic.
gafas, *f.pl.* eyeglasses.
gaguear, *v.* stutter, stammer.
gaita, *f.* bagpipe.
gaje, *m.* salary; fee.
gala, *f.* gala, ceremony; (*pl.*) regalia. **tener a g.,** to be proud of.
galán, *m.* gallant.
galano, *a.* stylishly dressed; elegant.
galante, *a.* gallant.
galantería, *f.* gallantry, compliment.
galápago, *m.* fresh-water turtle.
galardón, *m.* prize; reward.
gáleo, *m.* swordfish.
galera, *f.* wagon; shed.
galería, *f.* gallery, (theat.) balcony.
galés, *n. & a.* Welsh.
galgo, *m.* greyhound.

galillo, *m.* uvula.
galocha, *f.* galosh.
galón, *m.* gallon; (mil.) stripe.
galope, *m.* gallop. **—galopar,** *v.*
gallardete, *m.* pennant.
galleta, *f.* cracker.
gallina, *f.* hen.
gallinero, *m.* chicken coop.
gallo, *m.* rooster.
gambito, *m.* gambit.
gamuza, *f.* chamois.
gana, *f.* desire, wish, mind (to). **de buena g.,** willingly. **tener ganas de,** to feel like.
ganado, *m.* cattle.
ganador -ra, *n.* winner.
ganancia, *f.* gain, profit; (*pl.*) earnings.
ganapán, *m.* drudge.
ganar, *v.* earn; win; beat.
gancho, *m.* hook, hanger, clip, hairpin.
gandul -la, *n.* idler, tramp, hobo.
ganga, *f.* bargain.
gangrena, *f.* gangrene.
gansarón, *m.* gosling.
ganso, *m.* goose.
garabato, *m.* hook; scrawl, scribble.
garaje, *m.* garage.
garantía, *f.* guarantee; collateral, security.
garantizar, *v.* guarantee, secure, pledge.
garbanzo, *m.* chickpea.
garbo, *m.* grace.
garboso, *a.* graceful, sprightly.
gardenia, *f.* gardenia.
garfa, *f.* claw, talon.
garganta, *f.* throat.
gárgara, *f.* gargle. **—gargarizar,** *v.*
garita, *f.* sentry box.
garito, *m.* gambling house.
garlopa, *f.* carpenter's plane.
garra, *f.* claw.
garrafa, *f.* decanter, carafe.
garrideza, *f.* elegance, handsomeness.
garrido, *a.* elegant, handsome.
garrote, *m.* club, cudgel.
garrotillo, *m.* croup.
garrudo, *a.* powerful, brawny.
garza, *f.* heron.
gas, *m.* gas.
gasa, *f.* gauze.
gaseosa, *f.* carbonated water.
gaseoso, *a.* gaseous.
gasolina, *f.* gasoline.
gastar, *v.* spend; use up, wear out; waste.
gastritis, *f.* gastritis.
gastrómano, *m.* glutton.
gastrónomo -ma, *n.* gourmet, epicure.
gatear, *v.* creep.
gatillo, *m.* trigger.
gato -ta, *n.* cat.
gaucho, *m.* Argentine cowboy.
gaveta, *f.* drawer.
gavilla, *f.* sheaf.
gaviota, *f.* sea gull.
gayo, *a.* merry, gay.
gazapera, *f.* rabbit warren.

gazapo, *m.* rabbit.

gazmonado, *f.* prudishness.

gazmoño, *m.* prude.

gaznate, *m.* windpipe.

gelatina, *f.* gelatine.

gemelo -la, *n.* twin.

gemelos, *m.pl.* cuff links; opera glasses.

gemido, *m.* moan, groan, wail. **—gemir,** *v.*

genciana, *f.* gentian.

genealogía, *f.* genealogy, pedigree.

generación, *f.* generation.

generador, *m.* generator.

general, *a. & m.* general.

generalidad, *f.* generality.

generalización, *f.* generalization.

generalizar, *v.* generalize.

generalmente, *adv.* generally.

género, *m.* gender; kind; *(pl.)* goods, material.

generosidad, *f.* generosity.

generoso, *a.* generous.

génesis, *m.* genesis.

genial, *a.* genial; brilliant.

genio, *m.* genius; temper; disposition.

genitivo, *m.* genitive.

gente, *f.* people, folk.

gentil, *a.* gracious; graceful.

gentileza, *f.* grace, graciousness.

gentío, *m.* mob, crowd.

genuino, *a.* genuine.

geografía, *f.* geography.

geográfico, *a.* geographical.

geométrico, *a.* geometric.

geranio, *m.* geranium.

gerencia, *f.* management.

gerente, *m.* manager, director.

germen, *m.* germ.

germinar, *v.* germinate.

gerundio, *m.* gerund.

gesticulación, *f.* gesticulation.

gesticular, *v.* gesticulate, gesture.

gestión, *f.* conduct; effort.

gesto, *m.* gesture, facial expression.

gigante, *a. & m.* gigantic, giant.

gigantesco, *a.* gigantic, huge.

gimnasio, *m.* gymnasium.

gimnástica, *f.* gymnastics.

gimotear, *v.* whine.

ginebra, *f.* gin.

girado, *m.* (com.) drawee.

girador, *m.* (com.) drawer.

girar, *v.* revolve, turn, spin, whirl.

giratorio, *a.* rotary, revolving.

giro, *m.* whirl, turn, spin; (com.) draft. **g. postal,** money order.

gitano -na, *a. & n.* Gypsy.

glacial, *a.* glacial, icy.

gladiador, *m.* gladiator.

glándula, *f.* gland.

glasé, *m.* glacé.

glicerina, *f.* glycerine.

globo, *m.* globe; balloon.

gloria, *f.* glory.

glorieta, *f.* bower.

glorificación, *f.* glorification.

glorificar, *v.* glorify.

glorioso, *a.* glorious.

glosa, *f.* gloss. **—glosar,** *v.*

glosario, *m.* glossary.

glotón -ona, *a. & n.* gluttonous; glutton.

glutin, *m.* gluten; glue.

gobernación, *f.* government.

gobernador, *m.* governor.

gobernalle, *m.* rudder, tiller, helm.

gobernante, *m.* ruler.

gobernar, *v.* govern.

gobierno, *m.* government.

goce, *m.* enjoyment.

gola, *f.* throat.

golfo, *m.* gulf.

golondrina, *f.* swallow.

golosina, *f.* delicacy.

golpe, *m.* blow, stroke. **de g.,** suddenly.

golpear, *v.* strike, beat, pound.

gollete, *m.* upper portion of one's throat.

goma, *f.* rubber; gum; glue; eraser.

gonce, *m.* hinge.

góndola, *f.* gondola.

gordo, *a.* fat.

gordura, *f.* fatness.

gorila, *m.* gorilla.

gorja, *f.* gorge.

gorjeo, *m.* warble, chirp. **—gorjear,** *v.*

gorrión, *m.* sparrow.

gorro, *m.* cap.

gota, *f.* drop (of liquid).

gotear, *v.* drip, leak.

goteo, *m.* leak.

gotera, *f.* leak; gutter.

gótico, *a.* Gothic.

gozar, *v.* enjoy.

gozne, *m.* hinge.

gozo, *m.* enjoyment, delight, joy.

gozoso, *a.* joyful, joyous.

grabado, *m.* engraving, cut, print.

grabador, *m.* engraver.

grabar, *v.* engrave; record.

gracia, *f.* grace; wit, charm. **hacer g.,** to amuse, strike as funny. **tener g.,** to be funny, to be witty.

gracias, *f.pl.* thanks, thank you.

gracioso, *a.* witty, funny.

grada, *f.* step.

gradación, *f.* gradation.

grado, *m.* grade; rank; degree.

graduado -da, *n.* graduate.

gradual, *a.* gradual.

graduar, *v.* grade, graduate.

gráfico, *a.* graphic, vivid.

grafito, *m.* graphite.

grajo, *m.* jackdaw.

gramática, *f.* grammar.

gramo, *m.* gram.

gran, grande, *a.* big; large; great.

granada, *f.* grenade; pomegranate.

granar, *v.* seed.

grandeza, *f.* greatness.

grandiosidad, *f.* grandeur.

grandioso, *a.* grand, magnificent.

grandor, *m.* size.

granero, *m.* barn; granary.

granito, *m.* granite.

granizada, *f.* hailstorm.

granizo, *m.* hail. **—granizar,** *v.*

granja, *f.* grange; farm; farmhouse.

granjear, *v.* earn, gain; get.

granjero, *m.* farmer.

grano, *m.* grain; kernel.

granuja, *m.* waif, urchin.

grapa, *f.* clamp, clip.

grasa, *f.* grease, fat.

grasiento, *a.* greasy.

gratificación, *f.* gratification; reward; tip.

gratificar, *v.* gratify; reward; tip.

gratis, *adv.* gratis, free.

gratitud, *f.* gratitude.

grato, *a.* grateful; pleasant.

gratuito, *a.* gratuitous.

gravamen, *m.* tax; burden; obligation.

grave, *a.* grave, serious, severe.

gravedad, *f.* gravity, seriousness.

gravitación, *f.* gravitation.

gravitar, *v.* gravitate.

gravoso, *a.* burdensome.

graznido, *m.* croak. **—graznar,** *v.*

Grecia, *f.* Greece.

greco, *a. & n.* Greek.

greda, *f.* clay.

gresca, *f.* revelry; quarrel.

griego -ga, *a. & n.* Greek.

grieta, *f.* opening; crevice, crack.

grifo, *m.* faucet.

grillo, *m.* cricket.

grima, *f.* fright.

gringo -ga, *n.* foreigner (usually North American).

gripa, gripe, *f.* grippe.

gris, *a.* gray.

grito, *m.* shout, scream, cry. **—gritar,** *v.*

grosella, *f.* currant.

grosería, *f.* grossness; coarseness.

grosero, *a.* coarse, vulgar, discourteous.

grotesco, *a.* grotesque.

grúa, *f.* crane.

gruesa, *f.* gross.

grueso, 1. *a.* bulky; stout; coarse, thick. **2.** *m.* bulk.

grulla, *f.* crane.

gruñido, *m.* growl, snarl, mutter. **—gruñir,** *v.*

grupo, *m.* group, party.

gruta, *f.* cavern.

guadaña, *f.* scythe. **—guadañar,** *v.*

guagua, *f.* (S.A.) baby; (Carib.) bus.

gualdo, *m.* yellow, golden.

guano, *m.* guano (fertilizer).

guante, *m.* glove.

guapo, *a.* handsome.

guarda, *m. or f.* guard.

guardabarros, *m.* fender.

guardacostas, *m.* revenue ship.

guardar, *v.* keep, store, put away; guard.

guardarropa, *f.* coat room.

guardarse de, *v.* beware of, avoid.

guardia, 1. *f.* guard; watch. **2.** *m.* policeman.

guardián, *m.* guardian, keeper, watchman.

guardilla, *f.* attic.

guarida, *f.* den.

guarismo, *m.* number, figure.

guarnecer, *v.* adorn.

guarnición, *f.* garrison; trimming.

guasa, *f.* joke, jest.

guayaba, *f.* guava.

gubernativo, *a.* governmental.

guerra, *f.* war.

guerrero, *m.* warrior.

guía, 1. *m. & f.* guide. **2.** *f.* guidebook, directory.

guiar, *v.* guide; steer, drive.

guija, *f.* pebble.

guillotina, *f.* guillotine.

guindar, *v.* hang.

guinga, *f.* gingham.

guiñada, *f.*, **guiño,** *m.* wink. — **guiñar,** *v.*

guión, *m.* dash, hyphen.

guirnalda, *f.* garland, wreath.

guisa, *f.* guise, manner.

guisado, *m.* stew.

guisante, *m.* pea.

guisar, *v.* cook.

guita, *f.* twine.

guitarra, *f.* guitar.

guitarrista, *n.* guitarist.

gula, *f.* gluttony.

gurú, *m.* guru.

gusano, *m.* worm, caterpillar.

gustar, *v.* please; taste.

gusto, *m.* pleasure; taste; liking.

gustoso, *a.* pleasant, tasteful.

gutural, *a.* guttural.

H

haba, *f.* bean.

habanera, *f.* Cuban dance melody.

haber, *v.* have. **h. de,** be to be, be supposed to.

haberes, *m.pl.* property; worldly goods.

habichuela, *f.* bean.

hábil, *a.* skillful; capable; clever.

habilidad, *f.* ability; skill; talent.

habilidoso, *a.* able, skillful, talented.

habilitado, *m.* paymaster.

habilitar, *v.* qualify; supply, equip.

hábilmente, *adv.* ably.

habitación, *f.* dwelling; room.

habitante, *m. & f.* inhabitant.

habitar, *v.* inhabit; dwell.

hábito, *m.* habit; custom.

habitual, *a.* habitual.

habituar, *v.* accustom, habituate.

habla, *f.* speech.

hablador, *a.* talkative.

hablar, *v.* talk, speak.

haca, *f.* pony.

hacedor, *m.* maker.

hacendado, *m.* hacienda owner; farmer.

hacendoso, *a.* industrious.

hacer, *v.* do; make. **hace dos años,** etc., two years ago, etc.

hacerse, *v.* become, get to be.

hacia, *prep.* toward.

hacienda, *f.* property; estate; ranch; farm; (govt.) treasury.

hacha, *f.* ax, hatchet.

hada, *f.* fairy.

hado, *m.* fate.

halagar, *v.* flatter.

halar, *v.* haul, pull.

halcón, *m.* hawk, falcon.

haleche, *m.* anchovy.

hallado, *a.* found. **bien h.,** welcome. **mal h.,** uneasy.

hallar, *v.* find, locate.

hallarse, *v.* be located; happen to be.

hallazgo, *m.* find, thing found.

hamaca, *f.* hammock.

hambre, *f.* hunger. **tener h., estar con h.,** to be hungry.

hambrear, *v.* hunger; starve.

hambriento, *a.* starving, hungry.

haragán, *m.* idler, lazy person.

haraganear, *v.* loiter.

harapo, *m.* rag, tatter.

haraposo, *a.* ragged, shabby.

harem, *m.* harem.

harina, *f.* flour, meal.

harnero, *m.* sieve.

hartar, *v.* satiate.

harto, *a.* stuffed; fed up.

hartura, *f.* superabundance, glut.

hasta, 1. *prep.* until, till; as far as, up to. **h. luego,** good-bye, so long. **2.** *adv.* even.

hastío, *m.* distaste, loathing.

hato, *m.* herd.

hay, *v.* there is, there are. **h. que,** it is necessary to. **no h. de qué,** you're welcome, don't mention it.

haya, *f.* beech tree.

haz, *f.* bundle, sheaf; face.

hazaña, *f.* deed; exploit, feat.

hebdomadario, *a.* weekly.

hebilla, *f.* buckle.

hebra, *f.* thread, string.

hebreo -rea, *a. & n.* Hebrew.

hechicero -ra, *n.* wizard, witch.

hechizar, *v.* bewitch.

hechizo, *m.* spell.

hecho, *m.* fact; act; deed.

hechura, *f.* workmanship, make.

hediondez, *f.* stench.

helada, *f.* frost.

helado, *m.* ice cream.

helar, *v.* freeze.

helecho, *m.* fern.

hélice, *f.* propeller.

helicóptero, *m.* helicopter.

helio, *m.* helium.

hembra, *f.* female.

hemisferio, *m.* hemisphere.

hemoglobina, *f.* hemoglobin.

henchir, *v.* stuff.

hendedura, *f.* crevice, crack.

heno, *m.* hay.

hepática, *f.* liverwort.

heraldo, *m.* herald.

herbáceo, *a.* herbaceous.

herbívoro, *a.* herbivorous.

heredar, *v.* inherit.

heredero -ra, *n.* heir; successor.

hereditario, *a.* hereditary.

hereje, *m. & f.* heretic.

herejía, *f.* heresy.

herencia, *f.* inheritance; heritage.

herético, *a.* heretical.

herida, *f.* wound, injury.

herir, *v.* wound, injure.

hermafrodita, *a. & m.* hermaphrodite.

hermana, *f.* sister.

hermano, *m.* brother.

hermético, *a.* airtight.

hermoso, *a.* beautiful, handsome.

hermosura, *f.* beauty.

hernia, *f.* hernia, rupture.

héroe, *m.* hero.

heroico, *a.* heroic.

heroína, *f.* heroine.

heroísmo, *m.* heroism.

herradura, *f.* horseshoe.

herramienta, *f.* tool; implement.

herrería, *f.* blacksmith's shop.

herrero, *m.* blacksmith.

herrumbre, *f.* rust.

hertzio, *m.* hertz.

hervir, *v.* boil.

hesitación, *f.* hesitation.

heterogéneo, *a.* heterogeneous.

heterosexual, *a.* heterosexual.

hexágono, *m.* hexagon.

hez, *f.* dregs, sediment.

híbrido, *n. & a.* hybrid.

hidalgo -ga, *m.* noble.

hidalguía, *f.* nobility; generosity.

hidráulico, *a.* hydraulic.

hidrofobia, *f.* rabies.

hidrógeno, *m.* hydrogen.

hidropesía, *f.* dropsy.

hiedra, *f.* ivy.

hiel, *f.* gall.

hielo, *m.* ice.

hiena, *f.* hyena.

hierba, *f.* grass; herb; marijuana.

hierbabuena, *f.* mint.

hierro, *m.* iron.

hígado, *m.* liver.

higiene, *f.* hygiene.

higiénico, *a.* sanitary, hygienic.

higo, *m.* fig.

higuera, *f.* fig tree.

hija, *f.* daughter.

hijastro, *m.* stepchild.

hijo, *m.* son.

hila, *f.* line.

hilandero, *m.* spinner.

hilar, *v.* spin.

hilera, f. row, line, tier.

hilo, m. thread; string; wire; linen.

himno, m. hymn.

hincar, v. drive, thrust, sink.

hincarse, v. kneel down.

hinchar, v. swell.

hindú, n. & a. Hindu.

hinojo, m. knee.

hipnótico, a. hypnotic.

hipnotismo, m. hypnotism.

hipnotizar, v. hypnotize.

hipo, m. hiccough.

hipocresía, f. hypocrisy.

hipócrita, a. & n. hypocritical; hypocrite.

hipódromo, m. race track.

hipoteca, f. mortgage. —**hipotecar,** v.

hipótesis, f. hypothesis.

hirsuto, a. hairy, hirsute.

hispano, a. Hispanic, Spanish American.

Hispanoamérica, f. Spanish America.

hispanoamericano -na, a. & n. Spanish American.

histerectomía, f. hysterectomy.

histeria, f. hysteria.

histérico, a. hysterical.

historia, f. history; story.

historiador, m. historian.

histórico, a. historic, historical.

histrión, m. actor.

hocico, m. snout, muzzle.

hogar, m. hearth; home.

hoguera, f. bonfire, blaze.

hoja, f. leaf; sheet (of paper); pane; blade.

hajalata, f. tin.

hojalatero, m. tinsmith.

hojear, v. scan, skim through.

hola, interj. hello.

Holanda, f. Holland, Netherlands.

holandés -esa, a. & n. Dutch; Hollander.

holganza, f. leisure; diversion.

holgazán, 1. a. idle, lazy. **2.** m. idler, loiterer, tramp.

holgazanear, v. idle, loiter.

holografía, f. holography.

holograma, m. hologram.

hollín, m. soot.

hombre, m. man.

hombría, f. manliness.

hombro, m. shoulder.

homenaje, m. homage.

homeópata, m. homeopath.

homicidio, m. homicide.

homilía, f. homily.

homosexual, a. homosexual, gay.

honda, f. sling.

hondo, a. deep.

hondonada, f. ravine.

hondura, f. depth.

honestidad, f. modesty, unpretentiousness.

honesto, a. honest; pure; just.

hongo, m. fungus; mushroom.

honor, m. honor.

honorable, a. honorable.

honorario, 1. a. honorary. **2.** m. honorarium, fee.

honorífico, a. honorary.

honra, f. honor. —**honrar,** v.

honradez, f. honesty.

honrado, a. honest, honorable.

hora, f. hour, time (of day).

horadar, v. perforate.

horario, m. timetable, schedule.

horca, f. gallows; pitchfork.

horda, f. horde.

horizontal, a. horizontal.

horizonte, m. horizon.

hormiga, f. ant.

hormiguear, v. itch.

hormiguero, m. ant hill.

hornero -ra, f. baker.

hornillo, m. stove.

horno, m. oven; kiln.

horóscopo, m. horoscope.

horrendo, a. dreadful, horrendous.

horrible, a. horrible, hideous, awful.

horrido, a. horrid.

horror, m. horror.

horrorizar, v. horrify.

horroroso, a. horrible, frightful.

hortelano, m. horticulturist.

hospedaje, m. lodging.

hospedar, v. give or take lodgings.

hospital, m. hospital.

hospitalario, a. hospitable.

hospitalidad, f. hospitality.

hospitalmente, adv. hospitably.

hostia, f. host.

hostil, a. hostile.

hostilidad, f. hostility.

hotel, m. hotel.

hoy, adv. today. **h. día, h. en día,** nowadays.

hoya, f. dale, valley.

hoyo, m. pit, hole.

hoyuelo, m. dimple.

hoz, f. sickle.

hucha, f. chest, money box; savings.

hueco, 1. a. hollow, empty. **2.** m. hole, hollow.

huelga, f. strike.

huella, f. track, trace; footprint.

huérfano -na, a. & n. orphan.

huero, a. empty.

huerta, f. (vegetable) garden.

huerto, m. orchard.

hueso, m. bone; fruit pit.

huésped, m. & f. guest.

huesudo, a. bony.

huevo, m. egg.

huida, f. flight, escape.

huir, v. flee.

hule, m. oilcloth.

humanidad, f. humanity, mankind; humaneness.

humanista, m. humanist.

humanitario, a. humane.

humano, a. human; humane.

humareda, f. dense cloud of smoke.

humedad, f. humidity, moisture, dampness.

humedecer, v. moisten, dampen.

húmedo, a. humid, moist, damp.

humildad, f. humility, meekness.

humilde, a. humble, meek.

humillación, f. humiliation.

humillar, v. humiliate.

humo, m. smoke; (pl.) airs, affectation.

humor, m. humor, mood.

humorista, m. humorist.

hundimiento, m. collapse.

hundir, v. sink; collapse.

húngaro -ra, a. & n. Hungarian.

Hungría, f. Hungary.

huracán, m. hurricane.

huraño, a. shy, bashful.

hurgar, v. stir.

hurón, m. ferret.

hurraca, f. magpie.

hurtadillas, a h., f.pl. on the sly.

hurtador, m. thief.

hurtar, v. steal, rob of; hide.

hurtarse, v. hide; withdraw.

husmear, v. scent, smell.

huso, m. spindle; bobbin.

I

ibérico, a. Iberian.

iberoamericano -na, a. & n. Latin American.

ida, f. departure; trip out. **i. y vuelta,** round trip.

idea, f. idea.

ideal, a. & m. ideal.

idealismo, m. idealism.

idealista, m. & f. idealist.

idear, v. plan, conceive.

idéntico, a. identical.

identidad, f. identity; identification.

identificar, v. identify.

idilio, m. idyll.

idioma, m. language.

idiota, a. & n. idiotic; idiot.

idiotismo, m. idiom; idiocy.

idolatrar, v. idolize, adore.

ídolo, m. idol.

idóneo, a. suitable, fit, apt.

iglesia, f. church.

ignición, f. ignition.

ignominia, f. ignominy, shame.

ignominioso, a. ignominious, shameful.

ignorancia, f. ignorance.

ignorante, a. ignorant.

ignorar, v. be ignorant of, not know.

ignoto, a. unknown.

igual, 1. a. equal; the same; (pl.) alike. **2.** m. equal.

igualar, v. equal; equalize; match.

igualdad, f. equality.

ijada, f. flank (of an animal).

ilegal, a. illegal.

ilegítimo, a. illegitimate.

ileso, a. unharmed.

ilícito, a. illicit, unlawful.

iluminación, f. illumination.

iluminar, v. illuminate.

ilusión, f. illusion.
ilusorio, a. illusive.
ilustración, f. illustration; learning.
ilustrador, m. illustrator.
ilustrar, v. illustrate.
ilustre, a. illustrious, honorable, distinguished.
imagen, f. image.
imaginación, f. imagination.
imaginar, v. imagine.
imaginario, a. imaginary.
imaginativo, a. imaginative.
imán, m. magnet; imam.
imbécil, a. & n. imbecile; stupid, foolish; fool.
imbuir, v. imbue, instil.
imitación, f. imitation.
imitador, m. imitator.
imitar, v. imitate.
impaciencia, f. impatience.
impaciente, a. impatient.
impar, a. unequal, uneven, odd.
imparcial, a. impartial.
impasible, a. impassive, unmoved.
impávido, adj. fearless, intrepid.
impedimento, m. impediment, obstacle.
impedir, v. impede, hinder, stop, obstruct.
impeler, v. impel; incite.
impensado, a. unexpected.
imperar, v. reign; prevail.
imperativo, a. imperative.
imperceptible, a. imperceptible.
imperdible, n. safety pin.
imperecedero, a. imperishable.
imperfecto, a. imperfect, faulty.
imperial, a. imperial.
imperialismo, m. imperialism.
impericia, f. inexperience.
imperio, m. empire.
imperioso, a. imperious, domineering.
impermeable, 1. a. waterproof. **2.** m. raincoat.
impersonal, a. impersonal.
impertinencia, f. impertinence.
ímpetu, m. impulse; impetus.
impetuoso, a. impetuous.
impiedad, f. impiety.
impío, a. impious.
implacable, a. implacable, unrelenting.
implicar, v. implicate, involve.
implorar, v. implore.
imponente, a. impressive.
imponer, v. impose.
importación, f. import, importing.
importancia, f. importance.
importador, m. importer.
importante, a. important.
importar, v. be important, matter; import.
importe, m. value, amount.
importunar, v. beg, importune.
imposibilidad, f. impossibility.
imposibilitado, a. helpless.
imposible, a. impossible.

imposición, f. imposition.
impostor, m. imposter, faker.
impotencia, f. impotence.
impotente, a. impotent.
imprecar, v. curse.
impreciso, adj. inexact.
impregnar, v. impregnate.
imprenta, f. press; printing house.
imprescindible, a. essential.
impresión, f. impression.
impresionable, a. emotional.
impresionar, v. impress.
impresor, m. printer.
imprevisión, f. oversight, thoughtlessness.
imprevisto, a. unexpected, unforeseen.
imprimir, v. print; imprint.
improbable, a. improbable.
improbo, a. dishonest.
improductivo, a. unproductive.
improperio, m. insult.
impropio, a. improper.
improvisación, f. improvisation.
improvisar, v. improvise.
improviso, a. unforeseen.
imprudencia, f. imprudence.
imprudente, a. imprudent, reckless.
impuesto, m. tax.
impulsar, v. prompt, impel.
impulsivo, a. impulsive.
impulso, m. impulse.
impureza, f. impurity.
impuro, a. impure.
imputación, f. imputation.
imputar, v. impute, attribute.
inaccesible, a. inaccessible.
inacción, f. inaction; inactivity.
inaceptable, a. unacceptable.
inactivo, a. inactive; sluggish.
inadecuado, a. inadequate.
inadvertencia, f. oversight.
inadvertido, a. inadvertent, careless; unnoticed.
inagotable, a. inexhaustible.
inalterado, a. unchanged.
inanición, f. starvation.
inanimado, adj. inanimate.
inapetencia, f. lack of appetite.
inaplicable, a. inapplicable; unfit.
inaudito, a. unheard of.
inauguración, f. inauguration.
inaugurar, v. inaugurate, open.
incandescente, a. incandescent.
incansable, a. tireless.
incapacidad, f. incapacity.
incapacitar, v. incapacitate.
incapaz, a. incapable.
incauto, a. unwary.
incendiar, v. set on fire.
incendio, m. fire, conflagration.
incertidumbre, f. uncertainty, suspense.
incesante, a. continual, incessant.
incidente, m. incident, event.
incienso, m. incense.

incierto, a. uncertain, doubtful.
incisión, f. incision, cut.
incitamiento, m. incitement, motivation.
incitar, v. incite, instigate.
incivil, a. impolite, rude.
inclemencia, f. inclemency.
inclemente, a. inclement, merciless.
inclinación, f. inclination, bent; slope.
inclinar, v. incline; influence.
inclinarse, v. slope; lean, bend over; bow.
incluir, v. include; enclose.
inclusivo, a. inclusive.
incluso, prep. including.
incógnito, a. unknown.
incoherente, a. incoherent.
incombustible, a. fireproof.
incomodar, v. disturb, bother, inconvenience.
incomodidad, f. inconvenience.
incómodo, m. uncomfortable; cumbersome; inconvenient.
incomparable, a. incomparable.
incompatible, a. incompatible.
incompetencia, f. incompetence.
incompetente, a. incompetent.
incompleto, a. incomplete.
incondicional, a. unconditional.
inconexo, a. incoherent; unconnected.
incongruente, a. not suitable.
inconsciencia, f. unconsciousness.
inconsciente, a. unconscious.
inconsecuencia, f. inconsistency.
inconsecuente, a. inconsistent.
inconsiderado, a. inconsiderate.
inconstancia, f. changeableness.
inconstante, a. changeable.
inconveniencia, f. unsuitability.
inconveniente, 1. a. unsuitable. **2.** m. disadvantage; objection.
incorporar, v. incorporate, embody.
incorporarse, v. sit up.
incorrecto, a. incorrect, wrong.
incredulidad, f. incredulity.
incrédulo, a. incredulous.
increíble, a. incredible.
incremento, m. increase.
incubar, v. hatch.
inculto, a. uncultivated.
incurable, a. incurable.
incurrir, v. incur.
indagación, f. investigation, inquiry.
indagador, m. investigator.
indagar, v. investigate, inquire into.
indebido, a. undue.
indecencia, f. indecency.
indecente, a. indecent.
indeciso, a. undecided.

indefenso, *a.* defenseless.
indefinido, *a.* indefinite.
indeleble, *a.* indelible.
indemnizar, *v.* indemnify.
independencia, *f.* independence.
independiente, *a.* independent.
India, *f.* India.
indicación, *f.* indication.
indicar, *v.* indicate, point out.
indicativo, *a. & m.* indicative.
índice, *m.* index; forefinger.
indicio, *m.* hint, clue.
indiferencia, *f.* indifference.
indiferente, *a.* indifferent.
indígena, *a. & n.* native.
indigente, *a.* indigent, poor.
indignación, *f.* indignation.
indignado, *a.* indignant, incensed.
indignar, *v.* incense.
indigno, *a.* unworthy.
indio -dia, *a. & n.* Indian.
indirecto, *a.* indirect.
indiscreción, *f.* indiscretion.
indiscreto, *a.* indiscreet.
indiscutible, *a.* unquestionable.
indispensable, *a.* indispensable.
indisposición, *f.* indisposition, ailment; reluctance.
indistinto, *a.* indistinct, unclear.
individual, *a.* individual.
individualidad, *f.* individuality.
individuo, *a. & m.* individual.
indócil, *a.* headstrong, unruly.
índole, *f.* nature, character, disposition.
indolencia, *f.* indolence.
indolente, *a.* indolent.
indómito, *a.* untamed, wild; unruly.
inducir, *v.* induce, persuade.
indudable, *a.* certain, indubitable.
indulgencia, *f.* indulgence.
indulgente, *a.* indulgent.
indultar, *v.* free; pardon.
industria, *f.* industry.
industrial, *a.* industrial.
industrioso, *a.* industrious.
inédito, *a.* unpublished.
ineficaz, *a.* inefficient.
inepto, *a.* incompetent.
inequívoco, *a.* unmistakable.
inercia, *f.* inertia.
inerte, *a.* inert.
inesperado, *a.* unexpected.
inestable, *a.* unstable.
inevitable, *a.* inevitable.
inexacto, *a.* inexact.
inexperto, *a.* unskilled.
inexplicable, *a.* inexplicable, unexplainable.
infalible, *a.* infallible.
infame, *a.* infamous, bad.
infamia, *f.* infamy.
infancia, *f.* infancy; childhood.
infante, *m.* infant.
infantería, *f.* infantry.
infantil, *a.* infantile, childish.
infatigable, *a.* untiring.
infausto, *a.* unlucky.

infección, *f.* infection.
infeccioso, *a.* infectious.
infectar, *v.* infect.
infeliz, *a.* unhappy, miserable.
inferior, *a.* inferior; lower.
inferir, *v.* infer; inflict.
infernal, *a.* infernal.
infestar, *v.* infest.
infiel, *a.* unfaithful.
infierno, *m.* hell.
infiltrar, *v.* infiltrate.
infinidad, *f.* infinity.
infinito, *a.* infinite.
inflación, *f.* inflation.
inflamación, *f.* inflammation.
inflamar, *v.* inflame, set on fire.
inflar, *v.* inflate, pump up, puff up.
inflexible, *a.* inflexible, rigid.
inflexión, *f.* inflection.
infligir, *v.* inflict.
influencia, *f.* influence.
influenza, *f.* influenza, flu.
influir, *v.* influence, sway.
influyente, *a.* influential.
información, *f.* information.
informal, *a.* informal.
informar, *v.* inform; report.
informe, *m.* report; (*pl.*) information, data.
infortunio, *m.* misfortune.
infracción, *f.* violation.
infrascrito, *m.* signer, undersigned.
infringir, *v.* infringe, violate.
infructuoso, *a.* fruitless.
infundir, *v.* instil, inspire with.
ingeniería, *f.* engineering.
ingeniero, *m.* engineer.
ingenio, *m.* wit; talent.
ingeniosidad, *f.* ingenuity.
ingenioso, *a.* witty, ingenious.
ingenuidad, *f.* candor; naïveté.
ingenuo, *a.* ingenuous, naïve, candid.
Inglaterra, *f.* England.
ingle, *f.* groin.
inglés -esa, *a. & n.* English; Englishman.
ingratitud, *f.* ingratitude.
ingrato, *a.* ungrateful.
ingrediente, *m.* ingredient.
ingresar en, *v.* enter; join.
ingreso, *m.* entrance; (*pl.*) earnings, income.
inhábil, *a.* unskilled, incapable.
inhabilitar, *v.* disqualify.
inherente, *a.* inherent.
inhibir, *v.* inhibit.
inhumano, *a.* cruel, inhuman.
iniciador, *m.* initiator.
inicial, *a.* initial.
iniciar, *v.* initiate, begin.
iniciativa, *f.* initiative.
inicuo, *a.* wicked.
iniquidad, *f.* iniquity; sin.
injuria, *f.* insult. **—injuriar,** *v.*
injusticia, *f.* injustice.
injusto, *a.* unjust, unfair.
inmaculado, *a.* immaculate; pure.
inmediato, *a.* immediate.
inmensidad, *f.* immensity.

inmenso, *a.* immense.
inmersión, *f.* immersion.
inmigración, *f.* immigration.
inmigrante, *a. & n.* immigrant.
inmigrar, *v.* immigrate.
inminente, *a.* imminent.
inmoderado, *a.* immoderate.
inmodesto, *a.* immodest.
inmoral, *a.* immoral.
inmoralidad, *f.* immorality.
inmortal, *a.* immortal.
inmortalidad, *f.* immortality.
inmóvil, *a.* immobile, motionless.
inmundicia, *f.* dirt, filth.
inmune, *a.* immune.
inmunidad, *f.* immunity.
innato, *a.* innate, inborn.
innecesario, *a.* unnecessary, needless.
innoble, *a.* ignoble.
innocuo, *a.* innocuous.
innovación, *f.* innovation.
innumerable, *a.* innumerable, countless.
inocencia, *f.* innocence.
inocente, *a.* innocent.
inocular, *v.* inoculate.
inodoro, *m.* toilet.
inofensivo, *a.* inoffensive, harmless.
inolvidable, *a.* unforgettable.
inoportuno, *a.* inopportune.
inquietar, *v.* disturb, worry, trouble.
inquieto, *a.* anxious, uneasy, worried; restless.
inquietud, *f.* concern, anxiety, worry; restlessness.
inquilino -na, *n.* occupant, tenant.
inquirir, *v.* inquire into, investigate.
inquisición, *f.* inquisition, investigation.
insaciable, *a.* insatiable.
insalubre, *a.* unhealthy.
insano, *a.* insane.
inscribir, *v.* inscribe; record.
inscribirse, *v.* register, enroll.
inscripción, *f.* inscription; registration.
insecto, *m.* insect.
inseguro, *a.* unsure, uncertain; insecure, unsafe.
insensato, *a.* stupid, senseless.
insensible, *a.* unfeeling, heartless.
inseparable, *a.* inseparable.
inserción, *f.* insertion.
insertar, *v.* insert.
insidioso, *a.* insidious, crafty.
insigne, *a.* famous, noted.
insignia, *f.* insignia, badge.
insignificante, *a.* insignificant, negligible.
insincero, *a.* insincere.
insinuación, *f.* insinuation; hint.
insinuar, *v.* insinuate, suggest, hint.
insipidez, *f.* insipidity.
insípido, *a.* insipid.
insistencia, *f.* insistence.
insistente, *a.* insistent.

insistir, v. insist.
insolación, f. sunstroke.
insolencia, f. insolence.
insolente, a. insolent.
insólito, a. unusual.
insolvente, a. insolvent.
insomnio, m. insomnia.
insoportable, a. unbearable.
inspección, f. inspection.
inspeccionar, v. inspect, examine.
inspector, m. inspector.
inspiración, f. inspiration.
inspirar, v. inspire.
instalación, f. installation, fixture.
instalar, v. install, set up.
instantánea, f. snapshot.
instantáneo, a. instantaneous.
instante, a. & m. instant. al i., at once.
instar, v. coax, urge.
instigar, v. instigate, urge.
instintivo, a. instinctive.
instinto, m. instinct.
institución, f. institution.
instituto, m. institute. —instituir, v.
institutriz, f. governess.
instrucción, f. instruction; education.
instructivo, a. instructive.
instructor, m. instructor.
instruir, v. instruct, teach.
instrumento, m. instrument.
insuficiente, a. insufficient.
insufrible, a. intolerable.
insular, a. island, insular.
insulto, m. insult. —insultar, v.
insuperable, a. insuperable.
insurgente, n. & a. insurgent, rebel.
insurrección, f. insurrection, revolt.
insurrecto, a. & m. insurgent.
intacto, a. intact.
integral, a. integral.
integridad, f. integrity; entirety.
íntegro, a. entire; upright.
intelecto, m. intellect.
intelectual, a. & n. intellectual.
inteligencia, f. intelligence.
inteligente, a. intelligent.
inteligible, a. intelligible.
intemperie, f. bad weather.
intención, f. intention.
intendente, m. manager.
intensidad, f. intensity.
intensificar, v. intensify.
intensivo, a. intensive.
intenso, a. intense.
intentar, v. attempt, try.
intento, m. intent.
interceptar, v. intercept.
intercesión, f. intercession.
interés, m. interest; concern; appeal.
interesante, a. interesting.
interesar, v. interest, appeal to.
interferencia, f. interference.
interino, a. temporary.
interior, 1. a. interior, inner; 2. m. interior.
interjección, f. interjection.

intermedio, 1. a. intermediate. 2. m. intermediary; intermission.
interminable, a. interminable, endless.
intermisión, f. intermission.
intermitente, a. intermittent.
internacional, a. international.
internarse en, v. enter into, go into.
interno, a. internal.
interpelar, v. ask questions; quiz.
interponer, v. interpose.
interpretación, f. interpretation.
interpretar, v. interpret; construe.
intérprete, m. & f. interpreter.
interrogación, f. interrogation.
interrogar, v. question, interrogate.
interrogativo, a. interrogative.
interrumpir, v. interrupt.
interrupción, f. interruption.
intersección, f. intersection.
intervalo, m. interval.
intervención, f. intervention.
intervenir, v. intervene, interfere.
intestino, m. intestine.
intimación, f. intimation, hint.
intimar, v. suggest, hint.
intimidad, f. intimacy.
intimidar, v. intimidate.
íntimo -ma, a. & n. intimate.
intolerable, a. intolerable.
intolerancia, f. intolerance, bigotry.
intolerante, a. intolerant.
intranquilo, a. uneasy.
intravenoso, a. intravenous.
intrepidez, f. daring.
intrépido, a. intrepid.
intriga, f. intrigue, plot, scheme. —intrigar, v.
intrincado, a. intricate, involved.
introducción, f. introduction.
introducir, v. introduce.
intruso -sa, m. intruder.
intuición, f. intuition.
inundación, f. flood. —inundar, v.
inútil, a. useless.
invadir, v. invade.
inválido -da, a. & n. invalid.
invariable, a. constant.
invasión, f. invasion.
invasor, m. invader.
invencible, a. invincible.
invención, f. invention.
inventar, v. invent; devise.
inventario, m. inventory.
inventivo, a. inventive.
invento, m. invention.
inventor, m. inventor.
invernáculo, m. greenhouse.
invernal, a. wintry.
inverosímil, a. improbable, unlikely.
inversión, f. inversion; (com.) investment.
inverso, a. inverse, reverse.

invertir, v. invert; reverse; (com.) invest.
investigación, f. investigation.
investigador, m. investigator.
investigar, v. investigate.
invierno, m. winter.
invisible, a. invisible.
invitación, f. invitation.
invitar, v. invite.
invocar, v. invoke.
involuntario, a. involuntary.
inyección, f. injection.
inyectar, v. inject.
ir, v. go. irse, go away, leave.
ira, f. anger, ire.
iracundo, a. wrathful, irate.
iris, m. iris. arco i., rainbow.
Irlanda, f. Ireland.
irlandés -esa, a. & n. Irish; Irishman.
ironía, f. irony.
irónico, a. ironical.
irracional, a. irrational; insane.
irradiación, f. radiation.
irradiar, v. radiate.
irrazonable, a. unreasonable.
irregular, a. irregular.
irreligioso, a. irreligious.
irremediable, a. irremediable, hopeless.
irresistible, a. irresistible.
irresoluto, a. irresolute, wavering.
irrespetuoso, a. disrespectful.
irreverencia, f. irreverence.
irreverente, adj. irreverent.
irrigación, f. irrigation.
irrigar, v. irrigate.
irritación, f. irritation.
irritar, v. irritate.
irrupción, f. raid, attack.
isla, f. island.
isleño -ña, n. islander.
israelita, n. & a. Israelite.
Italia, f. Italy.
italiano -na, a. & n. Italian.
itinerario, m. itinerary; timetable.
izar, v. hoist.
izquierda, f. left (hand, side).
izquierdista, n. & a. leftist.
izquierdo, a. left.

J

jabalí, m. wild boar.
jabón, m. soap.
jabonar, v. soap.
jaca, f. nag.
jacinto, m. hyacinth.
jactancia, f. boast. —jactarse, v.
jactancioso, a. boastful.
jadear, v. pant, puff.
jaez, m. harness; kind.
jalar, v. haul, pull.
jalea, f. jelly.
jaletina, f. gelatin.
jamás, adv. never, ever.
jamón, m. ham.
Japón, m. Japan.
japonés -esa, a. & n. Japanese.
jaqueca, f. headache.

jarabe, *m.* syrup.
jaranear, *v.* jest; carouse.
jardín, *m.* garden.
jardinero -ra, *n.* gardener.
jarra, *f.* jar; pitcher.
jarro, *m.* jug, pitcher.
jaspe, *m.* jasper.
jaula, *f.* cage; coop.
jauría, *f.* pack of hounds.
jazmín, *m.* jasmine.
jefatura, *f.* headquarters.
jefe, *m.* chief, boss.
Jehová, *m.* Jehovah.
jengibre, *m.* ginger.
jerez, *m.* sherry.
jerga, *f.* slang.
jergón, *m.* straw bed.
jerigonza, *f.* jargon.
jeringa, *f.* syringe.
jeringar, *v.* inject; annoy.
jeroglífico, *m.* hieroglyph.
jesuita, *m.* Jesuit.
Jesús, *m.* Jesus.
jeta, *f.* snout.
jícara, *f.* cup.
jinete, *m.* horseman.
jingoísmo, *m.* jingoism.
jingoísta, *n. & a.* jingoist.
jira, *f.* tour, picnic, outing.
jirafa, *f.* giraffe.
jocundo, *a.* jovial.
jornada, *f.* journey; day's work.
jornal, *m.* day's wage.
jornalero, *m.* day laborer, workman.
joroba, *f.* hump.
jorobado, *a.* humpbacked.
joven, **1.** *a.* young. **2.** *m. & f.* young person.
jovial, *a.* jovial, jolly.
jovilidad, *f.* joviality.
joya, *f.* jewel, gem.
joyelero, *m.* jewel box.
joyería, *f.* jewelry; jewelry store.
joyero, *m.* jeweler.
juanete, *m.* bunion.
jubilación, *f.* retirement; pension.
jubilar, *v.* retire, pension.
jubileo, *m.* jubilee, public festivity.
júbilo, *m.* glee, rejoicing.
jubiloso, *a.* joyful, gay.
judaico, *a.* Jewish.
judaísmo, *m.* Judaism.
judía, *f.* bean, string bean.
judicial, *a.* judicial.
judío -día, *a. & n.* Jewish; Jew.
juego, *m.* game; play; gambling; set. **j. de damas**, checkers.
juerga, *f.* spree.
jueves, *m.* Thursday.
juez, *m.* judge.
jugador -ra, *n.* player.
jugar, *v.* play; gamble.
juglar, *m.* minstrel.
jugo, *m.* juice.
jugoso, *a.* juicy.
juguete, *m.* toy, plaything.
juguetear, *v.* trifle.
juguetón, *a.* playful.

juicio, *m.* sense, wisdom, judgment.
juicioso, *a.* wise, judicious.
julio, *m.* July.
jumento, *m.* donkey.
junco, *m.* reed, rush.
junio, *m.* June.
junípero, *m.* juniper.
junquillo, *m.* jonquil.
junta, *f.* board, council; joint, coupling.
juntamente, *adv.* jointly.
juntar, *v.* join; connect; assemble.
junto, *a.* together. **j. a**, next to.
juntura, *f.* joint, juncture.
jurado, *m.* jury.
juramento, *m.* oath.
jurar, *v.* swear.
jurisconsulto, *m.* jurist.
jurisdicción, *f.* jurisdiction; territory.
jurisprudencia, *f.* jurisprudence.
justa, *f.* joust. **—justar**, *v.*
justicia, *f.* justice, equity.
justiciero, *a.* just.
justificación, *f.* justification.
justificadamente, *adv.* justifiably.
justificar, *v.* justify, warrant.
justo, *a.* right; exact; just; righteous.
juvenil, *a.* youthful.
juventud, *f.* youth.
juzgado, *m.* court.
juzgar, *v.* judge, estimate.

K, L, LL

káiser, *m.* kaiser.
karate, *m.* karate.
kepis, *m.* military cap.
kerosena, *f.* kerosene.
kilo, kilogramo, *m.* kilogram.
kilohertzio, *m.* kilohertz.
kilolitro, *m.* kiloliter.
kilómetro, *m.* kilometer.
kiosco, *m.* newsstand; pavilion.
la, **1.** *art. & pron.* the; the one. **2.** *pron.* her, it, you; (*pl.*) them, you.
laberinto, *m.* labyrinth, maze.
labia, *f.* eloquence, fluency.
labio, *m.* lip.
labor, *f.* labor, work.
laborar, *v.* work; till.
laboratorio, *m.* laboratory.
laborioso, *a.* industrious.
labrador, *m.* farmer.
labranza, *f.* farming; farmland.
labrar, *v.* work, till.
labriego -ga, *n.* peasant.
laca, *f.* shellac.
lacio, *a.* withered; limp; straight.
lactar, *v.* nurse, suckle.
lácteo, *a.* milky.
ladear, *v.* tilt, tip; sway.
ladera, *f.* slope.
ladino, *a.* cunning, crafty.
lado, *m.* side. **al l. de**, beside. **de l.**, sideways.

ladra, *f.* barking. **—ladrar**, *v.*
ladrillo, *m.* brisk.
ladrón -ona, *n.* thief, robber.
lagarto, *m.* lizard; (Mex.) alligator.
lago, *m.* lake.
lágrima, *f.* tear.
lagrimear, *v.* weep, cry.
laguna, *f.* lagoon; gap.
laico, *a.* lay.
laja, *f.* stone slab.
lamentable, *a.* lamentable.
lamentación, *f.* lamentation.
lamentar, *v.* lament; wail; regret, be sorry.
lamento, *m.* lament, wail.
lamer, *v.* lick; lap.
lámina, *f.* print, illustration.
lámpara, *f.* lamp.
lampiño, *a.* beardless.
lana, *f.* wool.
lanar, *a.* woolen.
lance, *m.* throw; episode; quarrel.
lancha, *f.* launch; small boat.
lanchón, *m.* barge.
langosta, *f.* lobster; locust.
languidecer, *v.* languish, pine.
languidez, *f.* languidness.
lánguido, *a.* languid.
lanza, *f.* lance, spear.
lanzada, *f.* thrust, throw.
lanzar, *v.* throw, hurl; launch.
lañar, *v.* cramp; clamp.
lapicero, *m.* mechanical pencil.
lápida, *f.* stone; tombstone.
lápiz, *m.* pencil; crayon.
lapso, *m.* lapse.
lardo, *m.* lard.
largar, *v.* loosen; free.
largo, **1.** *a.* long. **a lo l. de**, along. **2.** *m.* length.
largor, *m.* length.
largueza, *f.* generosity; length.
largura, *f.* length.
laringe, *f.* larynx.
larva, *f.* larva.
lascivia, *f.* lasciviousness.
lascivo, *a.* lascivious.
láser, *m.* laser.
laso, *a.* weary.
lástima, *f.* pity. **ser l.**, to be a pity, to be too bad.
lastimar, *v.* hurt, injure.
lastimoso, *a.* pitiful.
lastre, *m.* ballast. **—lastrar**, *v.*
lata, *f.* tin can; tin (plate); (coll.) annoyance, bore.
latente, *a.* latent.
lateral, *a.* lateral, side.
latigazo, *m.* lash, whipping.
látigo, *m.* whip.
latín, *m.* Latin (language).
latino, *a.* Latin.
latir, *v.* bet, pulsate.
latitud, *f.* latitude.
latón, *m.* brass.
laúd, *m.* lute.
laudable, *a.* laudable.
láudano, *m.* laudanum.
laurel, *m.* laurel.
lava, *f.* lava.
lavabo, lavamanos, *m.* washroom, lavatory.

avandera, f. washerwoman, laundress.
avandería, f. laundry.
avar, v. wash.
avatorio, m. lavatory.
aya, f. spade. —layar, v.
azar, v. lasso.
azareto, m. hospital; quarantine.
azo, m. tie, knot; bow; loop.
e, pron. him, her, you; (pl.) them, you.
eal, a. loyal.
ealtad, f. loyalty, allegiance.
ebrel, m. greyhound.
ección, f. lesson.
ecito, m. yolk.
ector -ra, n. reader.
ectura, f. reading.
eche, f. milk.
echería, f. dairy.
echero, m. milkman.
echo, m. bed, couch.
echoso, a. milky.
echuga, f. lettuce.
echuza, f. owl.
eer, v. read.
egación, f. legation.
egado, m. bequest.
egal, a. legal, lawful.
egalizar, v. legalize.
egar, v. bequeath, leave, will.
egible, a. legible.
egión, f. legion.
egislación, f. legislation.
egislador, m. legislator.
egislar, v. legislate.
egislativo, a. legislative.
egislatura, f. legislature.
egítimo, a. legitimate.
ego, m. layman.
egua, f. league (measure).
egumbres, f.pl. vegetables.
ejano, a. distant, far-off.
ejía, f. lye.
ejos, adv. far. a lo l., in the distance.
elo, a. stupid, foolish.
ema, m. theme; slogan.
engua, f. tongue; language.
enguado, m. sole, flounder.
enguaje, m. speech, language.
enguaraz, a. talkative.
ente, m. or f. lens. m.pl. eyeglasses.
enteja, f. lentil.
entitud, f. slowness.
ento, a. slow.
eña, f. wood, firewood.
eón, m. lion.
eopardo, m. leopard.
erdo, a. dull-witted.
esbiana, f. lesbian.
esión, f. wound; damage.
etanía, f. litany.
etárgico, a. lethargic.
etargo, m. lethargy.
etra, f. letter (of alphabet); print; words (of a song).
etrado, 1. a. learned. 2. m. lawyer.
etrero, m. sign, poster.
eva, f. (mil.) draft.

levadura, f. yeast, leavening, baking powder.
levantador, m. lifter; rebel, mutineer.
levantar, v. raise, lift.
levantarse, v. rise, get up; stand up.
levar, v. weigh (anchor).
leve, a. slight, light.
levita, f. frock coat.
léxico, m. lexicon, dictionary.
ley, f. law, statute.
leyenda, f. legend.
lezna, f. awl.
libación, f. libation.
libelo, m. libel.
libélula, f. dragonfly.
liberación, f. liberation, release.
liberal, a. liberal.
libertad, f. liberty, freedom.
libertador, m. liberator.
libertar, v. free, liberate.
libertinaje, m. licentiousness.
libertino, m. libertine.
libidine, f. licentiousness; lust.
libidinoso, a. libidinous; lustful.
libra, f. pound.
libranza, f. draft, bill of exchange.
librar, v. free, rid.
libre, a. free, unoccupied.
librería, f. bookstore.
librero, m. bookseller.
libreta, f. notebook; booklet.
libreto, m. libretto.
libro, m. book.
licencia, f. permission, license, leave; furlough.
licenciado -da, n. graduate.
licencioso, a. licentious.
lícito, a. lawful.
licor, m. liquor.
lid, f. fight. —lidiar, v.
líder, m. leader.
liebre, f. hare.
lienzo, m. linen.
liga, f. league, confederacy; garter.
ligadura, f. ligature.
ligar, v. tie, bind, join.
ligero, a. light; fast, nimble.
ligustro, m. privet.
lija, f. sandpaper.
lijar, v. sandpaper.
lima, f. file; lime.
limbo, m. limbo.
limitación, f. limitation.
límite, m. limit. —limitar, v.
limo, m. slime.
limón, m. lemon.
limonada, f. lemonade.
limonero, m. lemon tree.
limosna, f. alms.
limosnero -ra, n. beggar.
limpiabotas, m. bootblack.
limpiadientes, m. toothpick.
limpiar, v. clean, wash, wipe.
límpido, a. limpid, clear.
limpieza, f. cleanliness.
limpio, m. clean.
linaje, m. lineage, ancestry.
linaza, f. linseed.

lince, a. sharp-sighted, observing.
linchamiento, m. lynching.
linchar, v. lynch.
lindar, v. border, bound.
linde, m. boundary; landmark.
lindero, m. boundary.
lindo, a. pretty, lovely, nice.
línea, f. line.
lineal, a. lineal.
linfa, f. lymph.
lingüista, m. & f. linguist.
lingüístico, a. linguistic.
linimento, m. liniment.
lino, m. linen; flax.
linóleo, m. linoleum.
linterna, f. lantern; flashlight.
lío, m. pack, bundle; mess, scrape; hassle.
liquidación, f. liquidation.
liquidar, v. liquidate; settle up.
líquido, a. & m. liquid.
lira, f. lyre.
lírico, a. lyric.
lirio, m. lily.
lirismo, m. lyricism.
lis, f. lily.
lisiar, v. cripple, lame.
liso, a. smooth, even.
lisonja, f. flattery.
lisonjear, v. flatter.
lisonjero -ra, n. flatterer.
lista, f. list; stripe; menu.
listar, v. list; put on a list.
listo, a. ready; smart, clever.
listón, m. ribbon.
litera, f. litter, bunk, berth.
literal, a. literal.
literario, a. literary.
literato, m. literary person, writer.
literatura, f. literature.
litigación, f. litigation.
litigio, m. litigation; lawsuit.
litoral, m. coast.
litro, m. liter.
liturgia, f. liturgy.
liviano, a. light (in weight).
lívido, a. livid.
lo, pron. the; him, it, you; (pl.) them, you.
loar, v. praise, laud.
lobina, f. striped bass.
lobo, m. wolf.
lóbrego, a. murky; dismal.
local, 1. a. local. 2. m. site.
localidad, f. locality, location; seat (in theater).
localizar, v. localize.
loción, f. lotion.
loco -ca, 1. a. crazy, insane, mad. 2. n. lunatic.
locomotora, f. locomotive.
locuaz, a. loquacious.
locución, f. locution, expression.
locura, f. folly; madness, insanity.
lodo, m. mud.
lodoso, a. muddy.
lógica, f. logic.
lógico, a. logical.
lograr, v. achieve; succeed in.
logro, m. accomplishment.
lombriz, f. earthworm.

lomo, *m.* loin; back (of an animal).

lona, *f.* canvas.

longevidad, *f.* longevity.

longitud, *f.* longitude; length.

lonja, *f.* shop; market.

lontananza, *f.* distance.

loro, *m.* parrot.

losa, *f.* slab.

lote, *m.* lot, share.

lotería, *f.* lottery.

loza, *f.* china, crockery.

lozanía, *f.* freshness, vigor.

lozano, *a.* fresh, spirited.

lubricación, *f.* lubrication.

lubricar, *v.* lubricate.

lucero, *m.* (bright) star.

lúcido, *a.* lucid, clear.

luciente, *a.* shining, bright.

luciérnaga, *f.* firefly.

lucimiento, *m.* success; splendor.

lucir, *v.* shine, sparkle; show off.

lucrativo, *a.* lucrative, profitable.

lucha, *f.* fight, struggle; wrestling. **—luchar,** *v.*

luchador, *m.* fighter, wrestler.

luego, *adv.* right away; afterwards, next. **l. que,** as soon as. **desde l.,** of course. **hasta l.,** good-bye, so long.

lugar, *m.* place, spot; space, room.

lúgubre, *a.* gloomy; dismal.

lujo, *m.* luxury. **de l.,** de luxe.

lujoso, *a.* luxurious.

lumbre, *f.* fire; light.

luminoso, *a.* luminous.

luna, *f.* moon.

lunar, *m.* beauty mark, mole; polka dot.

lunático, *a. & n.* lunatic.

lunes, *m.* Monday.

luneta, *f.* (theat.) orchestra seat.

lustre, *m.* polish, shine. **—lustrar,** *v.*

lustroso, *a.* shiny.

luto, *m.* mourning.

luz, *f.* light. **dar a l.,** give birth to.

llaga, *f.* sore.

llama, *f.* flame; llama.

llamada, *f.* call; knock. **—llamar,** *v.*

llamarse, *v.* be called, be named. **se llama . . .** etc., his name is . . . etc.

llamativo, *a.* gaudy, showy.

llamear, *v.* blaze.

llaneza, *f.* simplicity.

llano, 1. *a.* flat, level; plain. **2.** *m.* plain.

llanta, *f.* tire.

llanto, *m.* crying, weeping.

llanura, *f.* prairie, plain.

llave, *f.* key; wrench; faucet; (elec.) switch. **ll. inglesa,** monkey wrench.

llegada, *f.* arrival.

llegar, *v.* arrive; reach. **ll. a ser,** become, come to be.

llenar, *v.* fill.

lleno, *a.* full.

llenura, *f.* abundance.

llevadero, *a.* tolerable.

llevar, *v.* take, carry, bear; wear (clothes). **ll. a cabo,** carry out.

llevarse, *v.* take away, run away with. **ll. bien,** get along well.

llorar, *v.* cry, weep.

lloroso, *a.* sorrowful, tearful.

llover, *v.* rain.

llovido, *m.* stowaway.

llovizna, *f.* drizzle, sprinkle. **—lloviznar,** *v.*

lluvia, *f.* rain.

lluvioso, *a.* rainy.

M

maca, *f.* blemish, flaw.

macaco, *a.* ugly, horrid.

macareno, *a.* boasting.

macarrones, *m.pl.* macaroni.

macear, *v.* molest, push around.

maceta, *f.* vase; mallet.

macizo, 1. *a.* solid. **2.** *m.* bulk; flower bed.

macular, *v.* stain.

machacar, *v.* pound; crush.

machina, *f.* derrick.

machista, *a.* macho.

macho, *m.* male.

machucho, *a.* mature, wise.

madera, *f.* lumber; wood.

madero, *m.* beam, timber.

madrastra, *f.* stepmother.

madre, *f.* mother. **m. política,** mother-in-law.

madreperla, *f.* mother-of-pearl.

madriguera, *f.* burrow; lair, den.

madrina, *f.* godmother.

madroncillo, *m.* strawberry.

madrugada, *f.* daybreak.

madrugar, *v.* get up early.

madurar, *v.* ripen.

madurez, *f.* maturity.

maduro, *a.* ripe; mature.

maestría, *f.* mastery.

maestro, *m.* master; teacher.

mafia, *f.* mafia.

maganto, *a.* lethargic, dull.

magia, *f.* magic.

mágico, *a. & m.* magic; magician.

magistrado, *m.* magistrate.

magnánimo, *a.* magnanimous.

magnético, *a.* magnetic.

magnetismo, *m.* magnetism.

magnetófono, *m.* tape recorder.

magnificar, *v.* magnify.

magnificencia, *f.* magnificence.

magnífico, *a.* magnificent.

magnitud, *f.* magnitude.

magno, *a.* great, grand.

magnolia, *f.* magnolia.

mago, *m.* magician; wizard.

magosto, *m.* picnic, outing.

magro, *a.* meager; thin.

magullar, *v.* bruise.

mahometano, *n. & a.* Mohammedan.

mahometismo, *m.* Mohammedanism.

maíz, *m.* corn.

majadero, *a. & m.* foolish; fool.

majar, *v.* mash.

majestad, *f.* majesty.

majestuoso, *a.* majestic.

mal, 1. *adv.* badly; wrong. **2.** *m.* evil, ill; illness.

mala, *f.* mail.

malacate, *m.* hoist.

malandanza, *f.* misfortune.

malaventura, *f.* misfortune.

malcomido, *a.* underfed; malnourished.

malcontento, *a.* disssatisfied.

maldad, *f.* badness; wickedness.

maldecir, *v.* curse, damn.

maldición, *f.* curse.

maldito, *a.* accursed, damned.

malecón, *m.* embankment.

maledicencia, *f.* slander.

maleficio, *m.* spell, charm.

malestar, *m.* indisposition.

maleta, *f.* suitcase, valise.

malévolo, *a.* malevolent.

maleza, *f.* weeds; underbrush.

malgastar, *v.* squander.

malhechor, *m.* malefactor, evildoer.

malhumorado, *a.* morose, ill-humored.

malicia, *f.* malice.

maliciar, *v.* suspect.

malicioso, *a.* malicious.

maligno, *a.* malignant, evil.

malo, *a.* bad; evil, wicked; naughty; ill.

malograr, *v.* miss, lose.

malparto, *m.* abortion, miscarriage.

malquerencia, *f.* hatred.

malquerer, *v.* dislike; bear ill will.

malsano, *a.* unhealthy; unwholesome.

malsín, *m.* malicious gossip.

malta, *f.* malt.

maltratar, *v.* mistreat.

malvado, 1. *a.* wicked. **2.** *m.* villain.

malviz, *m.* redwing.

malla, *f.* mesh, net.

mallete, *m.* mallet.

mamá, *f.* mama, mother.

mamar, *v.* suckle; suck.

mamífero, *m.* mammal.

mampara, *f.* screen.

mampostería, *f.* masonry.

mamut, *m.* mammoth.

manada, *f.* flock, herd, drove.

manantial, *m.* spring (of water).

manar, *v.* gush, flow out.

mancebo, *m.* young man.

mancilla, *f.* stain; blemish.

manco, *a.* armless; one-armed.

mancha, *f.* stain, smear, blemish, spot. **—manchar,** *v.*

mandadero, *m.* messenger.

mandado, *m.* order, command.

mandamiento, *m.* commandment; command.

mandar, v. send; order, command.

mandatario, m. attorney; representative.

mandato, m. mandate, command.

mandíbula, f. jaw; jawbone.

mando, m. command, order; leadership.

mandón, a. domineering.

mandril, m. baboon.

manejar, v. handle, manage; drive (a car).

manejo, m. management; horsemanship.

manera, f. way, manner, means. **de m. que,** so, as a result.

manga, f. sleeve.

mangana, f. lariat, lasso.

manganeso, m. manganese.

mango, m. handle; mango (fruit).

mangosta, f. mongoose.

manguera, f. hose.

manguito, m. muff.

maní, m. peanut.

manía, f. mania, madness; hobby.

maníaco, maniático, a. & m. maniac.

manicomio, m. insane asylum.

manicura, f. manicure.

manifactura, f. manufacture.

manifestación, f. manifestation.

manifestar, v. manifest, show.

manifiesto, a. & m. manifest.

manija, f. handle; crank.

maniobra, f. maneuver. —**maniobrar,** v.

manipulación, f. manipulation.

manipular, v. manipulate.

maniquí, m. mannequin.

manivela, f. (mech.) crank.

manjar, m. food, dish.

manlieve, m. swindle.

mano, f. hand.

manojo, m. handful; bunch.

manómetro, m. gauge.

manopla, f. gauntlet.

manosear, v. handle, feel, touch.

manotada, f. slap, smack. —**manotear,** v.

mansedumbre, f. meekness, tameness.

mansión, f. mansion; abode.

manso, a. tame, gentle.

manta, f. blanket.

manteca, f. fat, lard; butter.

mantecado, m. ice cream.

mantecoso, a. buttery.

mantel, m. tablecloth.

mantener, v. maintain, keep; sustain; support.

mantenimiento, m. maintenance.

mantequera, f. butter dish; churn.

mantequilla, f. butter.

mantilla, f. mantilla; baby clothes.

mantillo, m. humus; manure.

manto, m. mantle, cloak.

manual, a. & m. manual.

manubrio, m. handle; crank.

manufacturar, v. manufacture; make.

manuscrito, m. manuscript.

manzana, f. apple; block (of street).

manzano, m. apple tree.

maña, f. skill; cunning; trick.

mañana, 1. adv. tomorrow. **2.** f. morning.

mañanear, v. rise early in the morning.

mañero, a. clever; skillful; lazy.

mapa, m. map, chart.

mapache, m. raccoon.

mapurito, m. skunk.

máquina, f. machine.

maquinación, f. machination; plot.

maquinador, m. plotter, schemer.

maquinal, a. mechanical.

maquinar, v. scheme, plot.

maquinaria, f. machinery.

maquinista, m. machinist; engineer.

mar, m. or f. sea.

marabú, m. marabou.

maraña, f. tangle; maze; snarl; plot.

maravilla, f. marvel, wonder. —**maravillarse,** v.

maravilloso, a. marvelous, wonderful.

marbete, m. tag, label; check.

marca, f. mark, sign; brand, make.

marcar, v. mark; observe, note.

marcial, a. martial.

marco, m. frame.

marcha, f. march, progress. —**marchar,** v.

marchante, m. merchant; customer.

marcharse, v. go away, depart.

marchitable, a. perishable.

marchitar, v. fade, wilt, wither.

marchito, a. faded, withered.

marea, f. tide.

mareado, a. seasick.

marearse, v. get dizzy; be seasick.

mareo, m. dizziness, seasickness.

marfil, m. ivory.

margarita, f. pearl; daisy.

margen, m. or f. margin, edge, rim.

marido, m. husband.

marijuana, f. marijuana, pot, grass.

marimba, f. marimba.

marina, f. navy; seascape.

marinero, m. sailor, seaman.

marino, a. & m. marine, (of) sea; mariner, seaman.

marión, m. sturgeon.

mariposa, f. butterfly.

mariquita, f. ladybird.

mariscal, m. marshal.

marisco, m. shellfish; mollusk.

marital, a. marital.

marítimo, a. maritime.

marmita, f. pot, kettle.

mármol, m. marble.

marmóreo, a. marble.

maroma, f. rope.

marqués, m. marquis.

marquesa, f. marquise.

Marte, m. Mars.

martes, m. Tuesday.

martillo, m. hammer. —**martillar,** v.

mártir, m. & f. martyr.

martirio, m. martyrdom.

martirizar, v. martyrize.

marzo, m. March.

mas, conj. but.

más, a. & adv. more, most; plus. **no m.,** only.

masa, f. mass; dough.

masaje, m. massage.

mascar, v. chew.

máscara, f. mask.

mascarada, f. masquerade.

mascota, f. mascot; good-luck charm.

masculino, a. masculine.

mascullar, v. mumble.

masón, m. Freemason.

masticar, v. chew.

mástil, m. mast; post.

mastín, m. mastiff.

mastuerzo, m. fool, ninny.

mata, f. plant; bush.

matadero, m. slaughterhouse.

matador, m. matador.

matanza, f. killing, bloodshed, slaughter.

matar, v. kill, slay; slaughter.

matasanos, m. quack.

mate, m. checkmate; Paraguayan tea.

matemáticas, f.pl. mathematics.

matemático, a. mathematical.

materia, f. material; subject (matter).

material, a. & m. material.

materialismo, m. materialism.

materializar, v. materialize.

maternal, materno, a. maternal.

maternidad, f. maternity.

matiné, m. matinee.

matiz, m. hue, shade.

matizar, v. blend; tint.

matón, m. bully.

matorral, m. thicket.

matoso, a. weedy.

matraca, f. rattle. —**matraquear,** v.

matrícula, f. registration; tuition.

matricularse, v. enroll, register.

matrimonio, m. matrimony, marriage, married couple.

matriz, f. womb; (mech.) die, mold.

matrona, f. matron.

maullar, v. mew.

máxima, f. maxim.

máxime, a. principally.

máximo, a. & m. maximum.

maya, f. daisy.

mayo, m. May.

mayonesa, f. mayonnaise.

mayor, 1. a. larger, largest;

greater, greatest; elder, eldest, senior. **m. de edad,** major, of age. **al por m.,** at wholesale. 2. *m.* major.

mayoral, *m.* head shepherd; boss; foreman.

mayordomo, *m.* manager; butler, steward.

mayoría, *f.* majority, bulk.

mazmorra, *f.* dungeon.

mazorca, *f.* ear of corn.

me, *pron.* me; myself.

mecánico, *a. & m.* mechanical; mechanic.

mecanismo, *m.* mechanism.

mecanizar, *v.* mechanize.

mecanografía, *f.* typewriting.

mecanógrafo -fa, *n.* typist.

mecedor, *m.* swing.

mecedora, *f.* rocking chair.

mecer, *v.* rock; swing, sway.

mecha, *f.* wick; fuse.

mechón, *m.* lock (of hair).

medalla, *f.* medal.

médano, *m.* sand dune.

media, *f.* stocking.

mediación, *f.* mediation.

mediador, *m.* mediator.

mediados, *m.pl.* **a m. de,** about the middle of (a period of time).

medianero, *m.* mediator.

medianía, *f.* mediocrity.

mediano, *a.* medium; moderate; mediocre.

medianoche, *f.* midnight.

mediante, *prep.* by means of.

mediar, *v.* mediate.

medicamento, *m.* medicine, drug.

medicastro, *m.* quack.

medicina, *f.* medicine.

medicinar, *v.* treat (as a doctor).

médico, 1. *a.* medical. 2. *m.* doctor, physician.

medida, *f.* measure, step.

medidor, *m.* meter.

medio, 1. *a.* half; mid; middle of. 2. *m.* middle; means.

mediocre, *a.* mediocre.

mediocridad, *f.* mediocrity.

mediodía, *m.* midday, noon.

medioeval, *a.* medieval.

medir, *v.* measure, gauge.

meditación, *f.* meditation.

meditar, *v.* meditate.

mediterráneo, *a.* Mediterranean.

medrar, *v.* thrive.

medroso, *a.* fearful, cowardly.

megáfono, *m.* megaphone.

megahertzio, *f.* megahertz.

mejicano, *a. & m.* Mexican.

mejilla, *f.* cheek.

mejor, *a. & adv.* better; best. **a lo m.,** perhaps.

mejora, *f.,* **mejoramiento,** *m.* improvement.

mejorar, *v.* improve, better.

mejoría, *f.* improvement; superiority.

melancolía, *f.* melancholy.

melancólico, *a.* melancholy.

melaza, *f.* molasses.

melena, *f.* mane; long or loose hair.

melindroso, *a.* fussy.

melocotón, *m.* peach.

melodía, *f.* melody.

melodioso, *a.* melodious.

melón, *m.* melon.

meloso, *a.* like honey.

mella, *f.* notch; dent. —**mellar,** *v.*

mellizo -za, *n. & a.* twin.

membrana, *f.* membrane.

membrete, *m.* memorandum; letterhead.

membrillo, *m.* quince.

membrudo, *a.* strong, muscular.

memorable, *a.* memorable.

memorándum, *m.* memorandum; notebook.

memoria, *f.* memory; memoir; memorandum.

mención, *f.* mention. —**mencionar,** *v.*

mendigar, *v.* beg (for alms).

mendigo -a, *n.* beggar.

mendrugo, *m.* crumb, bit.

menear, *v.* shake, wag; stir.

menester, *m.* need, want; duty, task. **ser m.,** to be necessary.

menesteroso, *a.* needy.

mengua, *f.* decrease; lack; poverty.

menguar, *v.* abate, decrease.

menor, *a.* smaller, smallest; lesser, least; younger, youngest, junior. **m. de edad,** minor, under age. **al por m.,** at retail.

menos, *a. & adv.* less; least; minus. **a m. que,** unless. **echar de m.,** to miss.

menospreciar, *v.* cheapen; despise; slight.

mensaje, *m.* message.

mensajero -ra, *n.* messenger.

menstruar, *v.* menstruate.

mensual, *a.* monthly.

mensualidad, *f.* monthly income or allowance; monthly payment.

menta, *f.* mint, peppermint.

mentado, *a.* famous.

mental, *a.* mental.

mentalidad, *f.* mentality.

mente, *f.* mind.

mentecato, *a.* foolish, stupid.

mentir, *v.* lie, tell a lie.

mentira, *f.* lie, falsehood. **parece m.,** it seems impossible.

mentiroso, *a.* lying, untruthful.

mentol, *m.* menthol.

menú, *m.* menu.

menudeo, *m.* retail.

menudo, *a.* small, minute. **a m.,** often.

meñique, *a.* tiny.

meple, *m.* maple.

merca, *f.* purchase.

mercader, *m.* merchant.

mercaderías, *f.pl.* merchandise, commodities.

mercado, *m.* market.

mercancía, *f.* merchandise (*pl.*) wares.

mercante, *a.* merchant.

mercantil, *a.* mercantile.

merced, *f.* mercy, grace.

mercenario -ria, *a. & m.* mercenary.

mercurio, *m.* mercury.

merecedor, *a.* worthy.

merecer, *v.* merit, deserve.

merecimiento, *m.* merit.

merendar, *v.* eat lunch.

merendero, *m.* lunchroom.

meridional, *a.* southern.

merienda, *f.* midday meal, lunch.

mérito, *m.* merit, worth.

meritorio, *a.* meritorious.

merla, *f.* blackbird.

merluza, *f.* haddock.

mermelada, *f.* marmalade.

mero, *a.* mere.

mes, *m.* month.

mesa, *f.* table.

meseta, *f.* plateau.

mesón, *m.* inn.

mesonero, *m.* innkeeper.

mestizo -za, *a. & n.* half-caste.

meta, *f.* goal, objective.

metabolismo, *m.* metabolism.

metafísica, *f.* metaphysics.

metáfora, *f.* metaphor.

metal, *m.* metal.

metálico, *a.* metallic.

metalurgia, *f.* metallurgy.

meteoro, *m.* meteor.

meteorología, *f.* meteorology.

meter, *v.* put (in).

meterse, *v.* interfere, meddle.

metódico, *a.* methodic.

método, *m.* method, approach.

metralla, *f.* shrapnel.

métrico, *a.* metric.

metro, *m.* meter (measure); subway.

metrópoli, *f.* metropolis.

mexicano -na, *a. & n.* Mexican.

mezcla, *f.* mixture; blend.

mezclar, *v.* mix; blend.

mezcolanza, *f.* mixture; hodgepodge.

mezquino, *a.* stingy; petty.

mi, *a.* my.

mí, *pron.* me; myself.

microbio, *m.* microbe, germ.

microficha, *f.* microfiche.

micrófono, *m.* microphone.

microforma, *f.* microform.

microscópico, *a.* microscopic.

microscopio, *m.* microscope.

miedo, *m.* fear. **tener m.,** fear, be afraid.

miedoso, *a.* fearful.

miel, *f.* honey.

miembro, *m.* member; limb.

mientras, *conj.* while. **m. tanto,** meanwhile. **m. más . . . más,** the more . . . the more.

miércoles, *m.* Wednesday.

miga, migaja, *f.* scrap, crumb.

migración, *f.* migration.

migratorio, *a.* migratory.

mil, *a. & pron.* thousand.

milagro, *m.* miracle.

milagroso, *a.* miraculous.

milicia, *f.* militia.

militante, *a.* militant.

militar, 1. a. military. 2. m. military man.

militarismo, m. militarism.

milla, f. mile.

millar, m. (a) thousand.

millón, m. million.

millonario -ria, n. millionaire.

mimar, v. pamper, spoil (a child).

mimbre, m. willow; wicker.

mímico, a. mimic.

mimo, m. mime, mimic.

mina, f. mine. —minar, v.

mineral, a. & m. mineral.

minero, m. miner.

miniatura, f. miniature.

miniaturizar, v. miniaturize.

mínimo, a. & m. minimum.

ministerio, m. ministry; cabinet.

ministro, m. (govt.) minister, secretary.

minoría, f. minority.

minoridad, f. minority; nonage.

minucioso, a. minute; thorough.

minué, m. minuet.

minuta, f. minute; draft.

mío, a. mine.

miopía, f. myopia.

mira, f. gunsight.

mirada, f. look; gaze, glance.

miramiento, m. consideration; respect.

mirar, v. look, look at; watch. m. a, face.

miríada, f. myriad.

mirlo, m. blackbird.

mirón, m. bystander, observer.

mirra, f. myrrh.

mirto, m. myrtle.

misa, f. mass, church service.

misceláneo, a. miscellaneous.

miserable, a. miserable, wretched.

miseria, f. misery.

misericordia, f. mercy.

misericordioso, a. merciful.

misión, f. assignment; mission.

misionario -ria, misionero -ra, n. missionary.

mismo, 1. a. & pron. same; -self, -selves. 2. adv. right, exactly.

misterio, m. mystery.

misterioso, a. mysterious, weird.

místico, a. & m. mystical, mystic.

mitad, f. half.

mítico, a. mythical.

mitigar, v. mitigate.

mitin, m. meeting.

mito, m. myth.

mitón, m. mitten.

mitra, f. miter (bishop's).

mixto, a. mixed.

mixtura, f. mixture.

mobiliario, m. household goods.

mocasín, m. moccasin.

mocedad, f. youthfulness.

moción, f. motion.

mocoso -sa, n. brat.

mochila, f. knapsack, backpack.

mocho, a. cropped, trimmed, shorn.

moda, f. mode, fashion, style.

modales, m.pl. manners.

modelo, m. model, pattern.

moderación, f. moderation.

moderado, a. moderate. —moderar, v.

modernizar, v. modernize.

moderno, a. modern.

modestia, f. modesty.

modesto, a. modest.

módico, a. reasonable, moderate.

modificación, f. modification.

modificar, v. modify.

modismo, m. (gram.) idiom.

modista, f. dressmaker; milliner.

modo, m. way, means.

modular, v. modulate.

mofarse, v. scoff, sneer.

mofletudo, a. fat-cheeked.

mohín, m. grimace.

moho, m. mold, mildew.

mohoso, a. moldy.

mojar, v. wet.

mojón, m. landmark; heap.

molde, m. mold, form.

molécula, f. molecule.

moler, v. grind, mill.

molestar, v. molest, bother, disturb, annoy, trouble.

molestia, f. bother, annoyance, trouble; hassle.

molesto, a. bothersome; annoyed; uncomfortable.

molicie, f. softness.

molinero, m. miller.

molino, m. mill.

molusco, m. mollusk.

mollera, f. top of the head.

momentáneo, a. momentary.

momento, m. moment.

mona, f. female monkey.

monarca, m. monarch.

monarquía, f. monarchy.

monarquista, n. & a. monarchist.

monasterio, m. monastery.

mondadientes, m. toothpick.

moneda, f. coin; money.

monetario, a. monetary.

monición, m. warning.

monigote, m. puppet.

monja, f. nun.

monje, m. monk.

mono -na, 1. a. (coll.) cute. 2. m. & f. monkey.

monólogo, m. monologue.

monopatín, m. skateboard.

monopolio, m. monopoly.

monopolizar, v. monopolize.

monosílabo, m. monosyllable.

monotonía, f. monotony.

monótono, a. monotonous, dreary.

monstruo, m. monster.

monstruosidad, f. monstrosity.

monstruoso, a. monstrous.

monta, f. amount; price.

montaña, f. mountain.

montañoso, a. mountainous.

montar, v. mount, climb; amount; (mech.) assemble. m. a caballo, ride horseback.

montaraz, a. wild, barbaric.

monte, m. mountain, forest.

montón, m. heap, pile.

montuoso, a. mountainous.

montura, f. riding horse, mount.

monumental, a. monumental.

monumento, m. monument.

mora, f. blackberry.

morada, f. residence, dwelling.

morado, a. purple.

moral, 1. a. moral. 2. f. morale.

moraleja, f. moral.

moralidad, f. morality, morals.

moralista, m. & f. moralist.

morar, v. dwell, live, reside.

mórbido, a. morbid.

mordaz, a. caustic; sarcastic.

mordedura, f. bite.

morder, v. bite.

moreno -na, a. & n. brown; dark-skinned; dark-haired; brunette.

morfina, f. morphine.

moribundo, a. dying.

morir, v. die.

morisco -ca, moro -ra, a. & n. Moorish; Moor.

morriña, f. sadness.

morro, m. bluff.

mortaja, f. shroud.

mortal, a. & m. mortal.

mortalidad, f. mortality.

mortero, m. mortar.

mortífero, a. fatal, mortal.

mortificar, v. mortify.

mortuario, a. funereal.

mosaico, a. & m. mosaic.

mosca, f. fly.

mosquito, m. mosquito.

mostacho, m. mustache.

mostaza, f. mustard.

mostrador, m. counter; showcase.

mostrar, v. show, display.

mote, m. nickname; alias.

motín, m. mutiny; riot.

motivo, m. motive, reason.

motocicleta, f. motorcycle.

motor, m. motor.

motorista, n. motorist.

movedizo, a. movable; shaky.

mover, v. move; stir.

movible, a. movable.

móvil, a. mobile.

movilización, f. mobilization.

movilizar, v. mobilize.

movimiento, m. movement, motion.

mozo, m. boy; servant, waiter, porter.

muaré, m. moiré.

mucoso, a. mucous.

muchacha, f. girl; maid (servant).

muchachez, m. boyhood, girlhood.

muchacho, m. boy.

muchedumbre, f. crowd, mob.

mucho, 1. a. much, many. 2. adv. much.

muda, f. change.

N, Ñ

mudanza, f. change; change of residence.
mudar, v. change, shift.
mudarse, v. change residence, move.
mudo -da, a. & n. mute.
mueble, m. piece of furniture; (pl.) furniture.
mueca, f. grimace.
muela, f. (back) tooth.
muelle, m. pier, wharf; (mech.) spring.
muerte, f. death.
muerto -ta, 1. a. dead. **2.** n. dead person.
muesca, f. notch; groove.
muestra, f. sample, specimen, sign.
mugido, m. lowing; mooing.
mugir, v. low, moo.
mugre, f. filth, dirt.
mugriento, a. dirty.
mujer, f. woman; wife.
mujeril, a. womanly, feminine.
mula, f. mule.
mulato, a. & m. mulatto.
muleta, f. crutch; prop.
mulo, m. mule.
multa, f. fine, penalty.
multicolor, a. many-colored.
multinacional, a. multinational.
múltiple, a. multiple.
multiplicación, f. multiplication.
multiplicar, v. multiply.
multiplicidad, f. multiplicity.
multitud, f. multitude, crowd.
mundanal, a. worldly.
mundano, a. worldly, mundane.
mundial, a. worldwide; (of the) world.
mundo, m. world.
munición, f. ammunition.
municipal, a. municipal.
muñeca, f. doll; wrist.
muñeco, m. doll; puppet.
mural, a. & m. mural.
muralla, f. wall.
murciélago, m. bat.
murga, f. musical band.
murmullo, m. murmur; rustle.
murmurar, v. murmur; rustle; grumble.
murta, f. myrtle.
musa, f. muse.
muscular, a. muscular.
músculo, m. muscle.
muselina, f. muslin.
museo, m. museum.
música, f. music.
musical, a. musical.
músico, a. & m. musical; musician.
muslo, m. thigh.
mustio, a. sad.
muta, f. pack of hounds.
mutabilidad, f. mutability.
mutación, f. mutation.
mutilación, f. mutilation.
mutilar, v. mutilate; mangle.
mutuo, a. mutual.
muy, adv. very.

nabo, m. turnip.
nacar, m. mother-of-pearl.
nacarado, a. pearly.
nacer, v. be born.
naciente, a. rising.
nacimiento, m. birth.
nación, f. nation.
nacional, a. national.
nacionalidad, f. nationality.
nacionalismo, m. nationalism.
nacionalista, n. & a. nationalist.
nacionalización, f. nationalization.
nacionalizar, v. nationalize.
nada, 1. pron. nothing; anything. **de n.,** you're welcome. **2.** adv. at all.
nadador, m. swimmer.
nadar, v. swim.
nadie, pron. no one, nobody; anyone, anybody.
nafta, f. naphtha.
naipe, m. (playing) card.
naranja, f. orange.
naranjada, f. orangeade.
naranjo, m. orange tree.
narciso, m. daffodil; narcissus.
narcótico, a. & m. narcotic.
nardo, m. spikenard.
nariz, f. nose; (pl.) nostrils.
narración, f. account.
narrador, m. narrator.
narrar, v. narrate.
narrativo, a. narrative.
nata, f. cream.
natal, a. native, natal.
natalicio, m. birthplace.
natalidad, f. birth rate.
natilla, f. custard.
nativo, a. native; innate.
natural, 1. a. natural. **2.** m. & f. native. m. nature, disposition.
naturaleza, f. nature.
naturalidad, f. naturalness; nationality.
naturalista, a. & m. naturalistic; naturalist.
naturalización, f. naturalization.
naturalizar, v. naturalize, accustom.
naufragar, v. be shipwrecked; fail.
naufragio, m. shipwreck; disaster.
náufrago -ga, a. & n. shipwrecked (person).
náusea, f. nausea.
nausear, v. feel nauseous.
náutico, a. nautical.
navaja, f. razor; pen knife.
naval, a. naval.
nave, f. ship.
navegable, a. navigable.
navegación, f. navigation.
navegador, m. navigator.
navegante, m. navigator.
navegar, v. sail; navigate.
Navidad, f. Christmas.
navío, m. ship.

neblina, f. mist, fog.
nebuloso, a. misty; nebulous.
necedad, f. stupidity; nonsense.
necesario, a. necessary.
necesidad, f. necessity, need, want.
necesitado, a. needy, poor.
necesitar, v. need.
necio -cía, 1. a. stupid, silly. **2.** n. fool.
néctar, m. nectar.
nefando, a. nefarious.
negable, a. deniable.
negación, f. denial, negation.
negar, v. deny.
negarse, v. refuse, decline.
negativa, f. negative, refusal.
negativamente, adv. negatively.
negativo, a. negative.
negligencia, f. negligence, neglect.
negligente, a. negligent.
negociación, f. negotiation, deal.
negociador, m. negotiator.
negociante, m. businessman.
negociar, v. negotiate, trade.
negocio, m. trade; business.
negro -gra, 1. a. black. **2.** n. Black.
nene -na, n. baby.
neo, neón, m. neon.
nervio, m. nerve.
nervioso, a. nervous.
nerviosamente, adv. nervously.
nesciencia, f. ignorance.
nesciente, a. ignorant.
neto, a. net.
neumático, 1. a. pneumatic. **2.** m. (pneumatic) tire.
neumonía, f. pneumonia.
neurótico, a. neurotic.
neutral, a. neutral.
neutralidad, f. neutrality.
neutro, a. neuter; neutral.
neutrón, m. neutron.
nevada, f. snowfall.
nevado, a. snow-white; snow-capped.
nevar, v. snow.
nevera, f. icebox.
nevoso, a. snowy.
ni, 1. conj. nor. **ni . . . ni,** neither . . . nor. **2.** adv. not even.
nicho, m. recess.
nido, m. nest.
niebla, f. fog; mist.
nieto -ta, n. grandchild.
nieve, f. snow.
nilón, m. nylon.
nimio, adj. stingy.
ninfa, f. nymph.
ningún -no -na, a. & pron. no, none, neither (one); any, either (one).
niñera, f. nursemaid.
niñez, f. childhood.
niño -ña 1. a. young; childish; childlike. **2.** n. child.
níquel, m. nickel.
niquelado, a. nickel-plated.
nítido, a. neat, clean, bright.
nitrato, m. nitrate.
nitro, m. niter.

nitrógeno, *m.* nitrogen.
nivel, *m.* level; grade. **—nivelar,** *v.*
no, 1. *adv.* not. **no más,** only. **2.** *interj.* no.
noble, *a.* & *n.* noble; nobleman.
nobleza, *f.* nobility; nobleness.
noción, *f.* notion, idea.
nocivo, *a.* harmful.
noctiluca, *f.* glowworm.
nocturno, *a.* nocturnal.
noche, *f.* night; evening.
Nochebuena, *f.* Christmas Eve.
nodriza, *f.* wet nurse.
nogal, *m.* walnut.
nombradía, *f.* fame.
nombramiento, *m.* appointment, nomination.
nombrar, *v.* name, appoint, nominate; mention.
nombre, *m.* name; noun.
nómina, *f.* list; payroll.
nominación, *f.* nomination.
nominal, *a.* nominal.
nominar, *v.* name.
non, *a.* uneven, odd.
nonada, *f.* trifle.
nordeste, *m.* northeast.
nórdico, *a.* Nordic.
norma, *f.* norm, standard.
normal, *a.* normal, standard.
normalidad, *f.* normality.
normalizar, *v.* normalize; standardize.
noroeste, *m.* northwest.
norte, *m.* north.
norteamericano -na, *a.* & *n.* North American.
Noruega, *f.* Norway.
noruego -ga, *a.* & *n.* Norwegian.
nos, *pron.* us; ourselves.
nosotros -as, *pron.* we, us; ourselves.
nostalgia, *f.* nostalgia, homesickness.
nostálgico, *a.* nostalgic.
nota, *f.* note; grade, mark.
notable, *a.* notable, remarkable.
notación, *f.* notation; note.
notar, *v.* note, notice.
notario, *m.* notary.
noticia, *f.* notice; piece of news; (*pl.*) news.
notificación, *f.* notification.
notificar, *v.* notify.
notorio, *a.* well-known.
novato -ta, *m.* novice.
novecientos, *a.* & *pron.* nine hundred.
novedad, *f.* novelty; piece of news.
novel, *a.* new, inexperienced.
novela, *f.* novel.
novelista, *m.* & *f.* novelist.
novena, *f.* novena.
noveno, *a.* ninth.
noventa, *a.* & *pron.* ninety.
novia, *f.* bride; sweetheart, fiancée.
noviazgo, *m.* engagement, match.

novicio -cia, *n.* novice, beginner.
noviembre, *m.* November.
novilla, *f.* heifer.
novio, *m.* bridegroom; sweetheart, fiancé.
nube, *f.* cloud.
nubile, *a.* marriageable.
nublado, *a.* cloudy.
nuclear, *a.* nuclear.
núcleo, *m.* nucleus.
nudo, *m.* knot.
nuera, *f.* daughter-in-law.
nuestro, *a.* our, ours.
nueva, *f.* news.
nueve, *a.* & *pron.* nine.
nuevo, *a.* new. **de n.,** again, anew.
nuez, *f.* nut; walnut.
nulidad, *f.* nonentity.
nulo, *a.* null, void.
numeración, *f.* numeration.
numerar, *v.* number.
numérico, *a.* numerical.
número, *m.* number; size (of shoe, etc.)
numeroso, *a.* numerous.
numismática, *f.* numismatics.
nunca, *adv.* never; ever.
nupcial, *a.* nuptial.
nupcias, *f.pl.* nuptials, wedding.
nutrición, *f.* nutrition.
nutrimiento, *m.* nourishment.
nutrir, *v.* nourish.
nutritivo, *a.* nutritious.
ñame, *m.* yam.
ñapa, *f.* something extra.
ñoñería, *f.* dotage.
ñoño, *a.* feeble-minded, senile.

O

o, *conj.* or. **o . . . o,** either . . . or.
oasis, *m.* oasis.
obedecer, *v.* obey, mind.
obediencia, *f.* obedience.
obediente, *a.* obedient.
obelisco, *m.* obelisk.
obertura, *f.* overture.
obeso, *a.* obese.
obispo, *m.* bishop.
obituario, *m.* obituary.
objeción, *f.* objection.
objetivo, *a.* & *m.* objective.
objeto, *m.* object. **—objetar,** *v.*
oblicuo, *a.* oblique.
obligación, *f.* obligation, duty.
obligar, *v.* oblige, require, compel; obligate.
obligatorio, *a.* obligatory, compulsory.
oblongo, *a.* oblong.
oboe, *m.* oboe.
obra, *f.* work. **—obrar,** *v.*
obrero -ra, *n.* worker, laborer.
obscenidad, *f.* obscenity.
obsceno, *a.* obscene.
obscurecer, *v.* obscure; darken.
obscuridad, *f.* obscurity; darkness.
obscuro, *a.* obscure; dark.

obsequiar, *v.* court; make presents to, fete.
obsequio, *m.* obsequiousness; gift; attention.
observación, *f.* observation.
observador, *m.* observer.
observancia, *f.* observance.
observar, *v.* observe, watch.
observatorio, *m.* observatory.
obsesión, *f.* obsession.
obstáculo, *m.* obstacle.
obstante, *adv.* **no o.,** however, yet, nevertheless.
obstar, *v.* hinder, obstruct.
obstetricia, *f.* obstetrics.
obstinación, *f.* obstinacy.
obstinado, *a.* obstinate, stubborn.
obstinarse, *v.* persist, insist.
obstrucción, *f.* obstruction.
obstruir, *v.* obstruct, clog, block.
obtener, *v.* obtain, get, secure.
obtuso, *a.* obtuse.
obvio, *a.* obvious.
ocasión, *f.* occasion; opportunity, chance. **de o.,** secondhand.
ocasional, *a.* occasional.
ocasionalmente, *adv.* occasionally.
ocasionar, *v.* cause, occasion.
occidental, *a.* western.
occidente, *m.* west.
océano, *m.* ocean.
ocelote, *m.* ocelot.
ocio, *m.* idleness, leisure.
ociosidad, *f.* idleness, laziness.
ocioso, *a.* idle, lazy.
ocre, *m.* ochre.
octava, *f.* octave.
octavo, *a.* eighth.
octogonal, *a.* octagonal.
octubre, *m.* October.
oculista, *m.* oculist.
ocultación, *f.* concealment.
ocultar, *v.* hide, conceal.
oculto, *a.* hidden.
ocupación, *f.* occupation.
ocupado, *a.* occupied; busy.
ocupante, *m.* occupant.
ocupar, *v.* occupy.
ocuparse de, *v.* take care of, take charge of.
ocurrencia, *f.* occurrence; witticism.
ocurrir, *v.* occur, happen.
ochenta, *a.* & *pron.* eighty.
ocho, *a.* & *pron.* eight.
ochocientos, *a.* & *pron.* eight hundred.
oda, *f.* ode.
odio, *m.* hate. **—odiar,** *v.*
odiosidad, *f.* odiousness; hatred.
odioso, *a.* obnoxious, odious.
odisea, *f.* odyssey.
oeste, *m.* west.
ofender, *v.* offend, wrong.
ofenderse, *v.* be offended, take offense.
ofensa, *f.* offense.
ofensiva, *f.* offensive.
ofensivo, *a.* offensive.
ofensor -ra, *n.* offender.

oferta, f. offer, proposal.
ofertorio, m. offertory.
oficial, a. & m. official; officer.
oficialmente, adv. officially.
oficiar, v. officiate.
oficina, f. office.
oficio, m. office; trade; church service.
oficioso, a. officious.
ofrecer, v. offer.
ofrecimiento, m. offer, offering.
ofrenda, f. offering.
oftalmía, f. ophthalmia.
ofuscamiento, m. obfuscation; bewilderment.
ofuscar, v. obfuscate; bewilder.
ogro, m. ogre.
oído, m. ear; hearing.
oír, v. hear; listen.
ojal, m. buttonhole.
ojalá, interj. expressing wish or hope. **o. que** . . . would that . . .
ojeada, f. glance; peep; look.
ojear, v. eye, look at, glance at, stare at.
ojeriza, f. spite; grudge.
ojiva, f. pointed arch; ogive.
ojo, m. eye. **¡Ojo!** Look out!
ola, f. wave.
olaje, m. surge of waves.
oleada, f. swell.
oleo, m. oil; holy oil; extreme unction.
oleomargarina, f. oleomargarine.
oleoso, a. oily.
oler, v. smell.
olfatear, v. smell.
olfato, m. scent, smell.
oliva, f. olive.
olivar, m. olive grove.
olivo, m. olive tree.
olmo, m. elm.
olor, m. odor, smell, scent.
oloroso, a. fragrant, scented.
olvidadizo, a. forgetful.
olvidar, v. forget.
olvido, m. omission; forgetfulness.
olla, f. pot, kettle. **o. podrida,** stew.
ombligo, m. navel.
ominar, v. foretell.
ominoso, a. ominous.
omisión, f. omission.
omitir, v. omit, leave out.
ómnibus, m. bus.
omnipotencia, f. omnipotence.
omnipotente, a. almighty.
omnipresencia, f. omnipresence.
omnisciencia, f. omniscience.
omnívoro, a. omnivorous.
once, a. & pron. eleven.
onda, f. wave, ripple.
ondear, v. ripple.
ondulación, f. wave, undulation.
ondular, v. undulate, ripple.
onza, f. ounce.
opaco, a. opaque.
ópalo, m. opal.
opción, f. option.

ópera, f. opera.
operación, f. operation.
operar, v. operate; operate on.
operario -ria, n. operator; (skilled) worker.
operarse, v. have an operation.
operativo, a. operative.
opereta, f. operetta.
opiato, m. opiate.
opinar, v. opine.
opinión, f. opinion, view.
opio, m. opium.
oponer, v. oppose.
oporto, m. port (wine).
oportunidad, f. opportunity.
oportunismo, m. opportunism.
oportunista, n. & a. opportunist.
oportuno, a. opportune, expedient.
oposición, f. opposition.
opresión, f. oppression.
opresivo, a. oppressive.
oprimir, v. oppress.
oprobio, m. infamy.
optar, v. select, choose.
óptica, f. optics.
óptico, a. optic.
optimismo, m. optimism.
optimista, a. & n. optimistic; optimist.
óptimo, a. best.
opuesto, a. opposite; opposed.
opugnar, v. attack.
opulencia, f. opulence, wealth.
opulento, a. opulent, wealthy.
oración, f. sentence; prayer; oration.
oráculo, m. oracle.
orador, m. orator, speaker.
oral, a. oral.
orangután, m. orangutan.
orar, v. pray.
oratoria, f. oratory.
oratorio, a. oratorical.
orbe, m. orb; globe.
órbita, f. orbit.
orden, m. or f. order.
ordenador, m. computer; regulator.
ordenanza, f. ordinance.
ordenar, v. order; put in order; ordain.
ordeñar, v. milk.
ordinal, n. & a. ordinal.
ordinario, a. ordinary; common, usual.
oreja, f. ear.
orejera, f. earmuff.
orfanato, m. orphanage.
organdí, m. organdy.
orgánico, a. organic.
organismo, m. organism.
organista, m. & f. organist.
organización, f. organization.
organizar, v. organize.
órgano, m. organ.
orgía, f. orgy, revel.
orgullo, m. pride.
orgulloso, a. proud.
orientación, f. orientation.
oriental, a. Oriental; eastern.
orientar, v. orient.
oriente, m. orient, east.

orificación, f. gold filling (for tooth).
origen, m. origin; parentage; descent.
original, a. original.
originalidad, f. originality.
originalmente, adv. originally.
originar, v. originate.
orilla, f. shore; bank; edge.
orín, m. rust.
orina, f. urine.
orinar, v. urinate.
orines, n.pl. urine.
oriol, m. oriole.
orla, f. border; edging.
ornado, a. ornate.
ornamentación, f. ornamentation.
ornamento, m. ornament. — **ornamentar,** v.
ornar, v. ornament, adorn.
oro, m. gold.
oropel, m. tinsel.
orquesta, f. orchestra.
ortiga, f. nettle.
ortodoxo, a. orthodox.
ortografía, f. orthography, spelling.
ortóptero, a. orthopterous.
oruga, f. caterpillar.
orzuelo, m. sty.
os, pron. you (pl.); yourselves.
osadía, f. daring.
osar, v. dare.
oscilación, f. oscillation.
oscilar, v. oscillate, rock.
ósculo, m. kiss.
oscurecer, oscuridad, oscuro = obscur-.
oso, osa, n. bear.
ostentación, f. ostentation, showiness.
ostentar, v. show off.
ostentoso, a. ostentatious, flashy.
ostra, f. oyster.
ostracismo, m. ostracism.
otalgia, f. earache.
otero, m. hill, knoll.
otoño, m. autumn, fall.
otorgar, v. grant, award.
otro, a. & pron. other, another. **o. vez,** again. **el uno al o.,** one another, each other.
ovación, f. ovation.
oval, ovalado, a. oval.
óvalo, m. oval.
ovario, m. ovary.
oveja, f. sheep.
ovejero, m. shepherd.
ovillo, m. ball of yarn.
oxidación, f. oxidation.
oxidar, v. oxidize; rust.
óxido, m. oxide.
oxígeno, m. oxygen.
oyente, m. hearer; (pl.) audience.
ozono, m. ozone.

P

pabellón, m. pavilion.
pabilo, m. wick.
paciencia, f. patience.

paciente, a. & n. patient.
pacificar, v. pacify.
pacífico, a. pacific.
pacifismo, m. pacifism.
pacifista, n. & a. pacifist.
pacto, m. pact, treaty.
padecer, v. suffer.
padrastro, m. stepfather.
padre, m. father; priest; (pl.) parents.
padrenuestro, m. paternoster.
padrino, m. godfather; sponsor.
paella, f. dish of rice with meat or chicken.
paga, f. pay, wages.
pagadero, a. payable.
pagador, m. payer.
paganismo, m. paganism.
pagano -na, a. & n. heathen, pagan.
pagar, v. pay, pay for.
página, f. page.
pago, m. pay, payment.
país, m. country, nation.
paisaje, m. landscape, scenery, countryside.
paisano -na, n. countryman; compatriot; civilian.
paja, f. straw.
pajar, m. barn.
pájaro, m. bird.
paje, m. page (person).
pala, f. shovel, spade.
palabra, f. word.
palabrero, a. talkative.
palabrista, m. talkative person.
palacio, m. palace.
paladar, m. palate.
paladear, v. taste; relish.
palanca, f. lever.
palangana, f. washbasin.
palco, m. theater box.
palenque, m. palisade.
palidecer, v. turn pale.
palidez, f. paleness.
pálido, a. pale.
paliza, f. beating.
palizada, m. palisade.
palma, palmera, f. palm (tree).
palmada, f. slap, clap.
palmear, v. applaud.
palo, m. pole, stick; suit (in cards); (naut.) mast.
paloma, f. dove, pigeon.
palpar, v. touch, feel.
palpitación, f. palpitation.
palpitar, v. palpitate.
paludismo, m. malaria.
palleta, f. mat, pallet.
pampa, f. (South America) prairie, plain.
pan, m. bread; loaf.
pana, f. corduroy.
pánacea, f. panacea.
panadería, f. bakery.
panadero -ra, m. baker.
panameño -ña, a. & n. Panamanian, of Panama.
panamericano, a. Pan-American.
páncreas, m. pancreas.
pandeo, m. bulge.
pandilla, f. band, gang.
panecillo, m. roll, muffin.

panegírico, m. panegyric.
pánico, m. panic.
panocha, f. ear of corn.
panorámico, a. panoramic.
pantalones, m.pl. trousers, pants.
pantalla, f. (movie) screen; lamp shade.
pantano, m. bog, marsh, swamp.
pantanoso, a. swampy, marshy.
pantera, f. panther.
pantomima, f. pantomime.
panza, f. belly, paunch.
pañal, m. diaper.
paño, m. piece of cloth.
pañuelo, m. handkerchief.
Papa, m. Pope.
papa, f. potato.
papá, m. papa, father.
papado, m. papacy.
papagayo, m. parrot.
papal, a. papal.
papel, m. paper; role, part.
papelera, f. file or folder for papers.
papelería, f. stationery store.
papera, f. mumps.
paquete, m. package.
par, 1. a. even, equal. 2. m. pair; equal, peer. abierto de p. en p., wide open.
para, prep. for; in order to. p. que, in order that. estar p., to be about to.
parabién, m. greeting; congratulation.
parabrisa, m. windshield.
paracaídas, m. parachute.
parachoques, m. (auto.) bumper.
parada, f. stop, halt; parade.
paradero, m. whereabouts; stopping place.
paradigma, m. paradigm.
paradoja, f. paradox.
parafina, f. paraffin.
parafrasear, v. paraphrase.
paraguas, m. umbrella.
paraguayano -na, n. & a. Paraguayan.
paraíso, m. paradise.
paralelo, a. & m. parallel.
parálisis, f. paralysis.
paralizar, v. paralyze.
paramédico, m. paramedic.
parámetro, m. parameter.
parapeto, m. parapet.
parar, v. stop, stem, ward off; stay.
pararse, v. stop; stand up.
parasismo, m. paroxysm.
parasítico, a. parasitic.
parásito, m. parasite.
parcela, f. plot of ground.
parcial, a. partial.
parcialidad, f. partiality; bias.
parcialmente, adv. partially.
pardo, a. brown.
parear, v. pair, match, mate.
parecer, 1. m. opinion. 2. v. seem, appear, look.
parecerse, v. look alike. p. a, look like.

parecido, a. similar.
pared, f. wall.
pareja, f. pair, couple; (dancing) partner.
parentela, f. kinfolk.
parentesco, m. parentage, lineage; kin.
paréntesis, m. parenthesis.
paria, m. outcast.
paridad, f. parity.
pariente, m. & f. relative.
parir, v. give birth to young.
parisiense, n. & a. Parisian.
parlamentario, a. parliamentary.
parlamento, m. parliament.
paro, m. stoppage; strike. p. forzoso, unemployment.
parodia, f. parody.
parodista, m. parodist.
paroxismo, m. paroxysm.
párpado, m. eyelid.
parque, m. park.
parra, f. grapevine.
párrafo, m. paragraph.
parranda, f. spree.
parrandear, v. carouse.
parrilla, f. grill.
párroco, m. parish priest.
parroquia, f. parish.
parroquial, a. parochial.
parsimonia, f. economy, thrift.
parsimonioso, a. economical, thrifty.
parte, f. part. de p. de, on behalf of. alguna p., somewhere. por otra p., on the other hand. dar p. a., to notify.
partera, f. midwife.
partición, f. distribution.
participación, f. participation.
participante, m. & f. participant.
participar, v. participate; announce.
participio, m. participle.
partícula, f. particle.
particular, 1. a. particular; private. 2. m. particular; detail; individual.
particularmente, adv. particularly.
partida, f. departure; (mil.) party; (sport) game.
partidario -ria, n. partisan.
partido, m. side, party, faction; game, match.
partir, v. leave, depart; part, cleave, split.
parto, m. delivery, childbirth.
pasa, f. raisin.
pasado, 1. a. past; last. 2. m. past.
pasaje, m. passage, fare.
pasajero -ra, 1. a. passing, transient. 2. n. passenger.
pasamano, m. banister.
pasaporte, m. passport.
pasar, v. pass; happen; spend (time). p. por alto, overlook. p. lista, call the roll. p. sin, do without.
pasatiempo, m. pastime, hobby.
pascua, f. religious holiday;

(*pl.*) Christmas (season). **P. Florida,** Easter.

paseo, *m.* walk, stroll; drive. **—pasear,** *v.*

pasillo, *m.* aisle; hallway.

pasión, *f.* passion.

pasivo, *a.* passive.

pasmar, *v.* astonish, astound, stun.

pasmo, *m.* spasm; wonder.

paso, 1. *a.* dried (fruit). **2.** *m.* pace, step; (mountain) pass.

pasta, *f.* paste; batter; plastic.

pastar, *v.* graze.

pastel, *m.* pastry; pie.

pastelería, *f.* pastry; pastry shop.

pasteurización, *f.* pasteurization.

pasteurizar, *v.* pasteurize.

pastilla, *f.* tablet, lozenge, drop.

pasto, *m.* pasture; grass.

pastor, *m.* pastor, shepherd.

pastorear, *v.* pasture, tend (a flock).

pastura, *f.* pasture.

pata, *f.* foot (of animal).

patada, *f.* kick.

patán, *m.* boor.

patanada, *f.* rudeness.

patata, *f.* potato.

patear, *v.* stamp, tramp, kick.

patente, *a. & m.* patent. **—patentar,** *v.*

paternal, paterno, *a.* paternal.

paternidad, *f.* paternity, fatherhood.

patético, *a.* pathetic.

patíbulo, *m.* scaffold, gallows.

patín, *m.* skate. **—patinar,** *v.*

patio, *m.* yard, court, patio.

pato, *m.* duck.

patria, *f.* native land.

patriarca, *m.* patriarch.

patrimonio, *m.* inheritance.

patriota, *m. & f.* patriot.

patriótico, *a.* patriotic.

patriotismo, *m.* patriotism.

patrocinar, *v.* patronize, sponsor.

patrón, *m.* patron; boss; (dress) pattern.

patrulla, *f.* patrol. **—patrullar,** *v.*

pausa, *f.* pause. **—pausar,** *v.*

pavesa, *f.* embers.

pavimentar, *v.* pave.

pavimento, *m.* pavement.

pavo, *m.* turkey. **p. real,** peacock.

payaso, *m.* clown.

paz, *f.* peace.

peatón -na, *m.* pedestrian.

peca, *f.* freckle.

pecado, *m.* sin. **—pecar,** *v.*

pecador -ra, *a. & n.* sinful; sinner.

pecera, *f.* aquarium, fishbowl.

peculiar, *a.* peculiar.

peculiaridad, *f.* peculiarity.

pechera, *f.* shirt front.

pecho, *m.* chest; breast; bosom.

pedagogía, *f.* pedagogy.

pedagogo, *m.* pedagogue; teacher.

pedal, *m.* pedal.

pedantesco, *a.* pedantic.

pedazo, *m.* piece.

pedernal, *m.* flint.

pedestal, *m.* pedestal.

pediatría, *f.* pediatrics.

pedicuro, *m.* chiropodist.

pedir, *v.* ask, ask for; request; apply for; order.

pedregoso, *a.* rocky.

pegajoso, *a.* sticky.

pegar, *v.* beat, strike; adhere, fasten, stick.

peinado, *m.* coiffure, hairdo.

peine, *m.* comb. **—peinar,** *v.*

peineta, *f.* (ornamental) comb.

pelagra, *f.* pellagra.

pelar, *v.* skin, pare, peel.

pelea, *f.* fight, row. **—pelearse,** *v.*

pelícano, *m.* pelican.

película, *f.* movie, motion picture, film.

peligrar, *v.* be in danger.

peligro, *m.* peril, danger.

peligroso, *a.* perilous, dangerous.

pelo, *m.* hair.

pelota, *f.* ball.

peltre, *m.* pewter.

peluca, *f.* wig.

peludo, *a.* hairy.

peluquería, *f.* hairdresser's shop, beauty parlor.

peluquero, *m.* hairdresser.

pellejo, *m.* skin, peel (of fruit).

pellizco, *m.* pinch. **—pellizcar,** *v.*

pena, *f.* pain, grief, trouble, woe; penalty. **valer la p.,** to be worthwhile.

penacho, *m.* plume.

penalidad, *f.* trouble; penalty.

pender, *v.* hang, dangle; be pending.

pendiente, 1. *a.* hanging; pending. **2.** *m.* incline, slope; earring, pendant.

pendón, *m.* pennant, flag.

penetración, *f.* penetration.

penetrar, *v.* penetrate, pierce.

penicilina, *f.* penicillin.

península, *f.* peninsula.

penitencia, *f.* penitence, penance.

penitenciaría, *f.* penitentiary.

penoso, *a.* painful, troublesome, grievous.

pensador -ra, *m.* thinker.

pensamiento, *m.* thought.

pensar, *v.* think; intend, plan.

pensativo, *a.* pensive, thoughtful.

pensión, *f.* pension; boardinghouse.

pensionista, *m. & f.* boarder.

pentagonal, *a.* pentagonal.

penuria, *f.* penury, poverty.

peña, *f.* rock.

peñascoso, *a.* rocky.

peón, *m.* unskilled laborer; infantryman.

peonada, *f.* group of laborers.

peonía, *f.* peony.

peor, *a.* worse, worst.

pepino, *m.* cucumber.

pepita, *f.* seed (in fruit).

pequeñez, *f.* smallness; trifle.

pequeño -ña, 1. *a.* small, little, short, slight. **2.** *n.* child.

pera, *f.* pear.

peral, *m.* pear tree.

perca, *f.* perch (fish).

percal, *m.* calico, percale.

percentaje, *m.* percentage.

percepción, *f.* perception.

perceptivo, *a.* perceptive

percibir, *v.* perceive, sense; collect.

percha, *f.* perch; clothes hanger, rack.

perder, *v.* lose; miss; waste. **echar a p.,** spoil.

perdición, *f.* perdition, downfall.

pérdida, *f.* loss.

perdiz, *f.* partridge.

perdón, *m.* pardon, forgiveness.

perdonar, *v.* forgive, pardon; spare.

perdurable, *a.* enduring, everlasting.

perdurar, *v.* endure, last.

perecedero, *a.* perishable.

perecer, *v.* perish.

peregrinación, *f.* peregrination; pilgrimage.

peregrino -na, *n.* pilgrim.

perejil, *m.* parsley.

perenne, *a.* perennial.

pereza, *f.* laziness.

perezoso, *a.* lazy, sluggish.

perfección, *f.* perfection.

perfeccionar, *v.* perfect.

perfectamente, *adv.* perfectly.

perfecto, *a.* perfect.

perfidia, *f.* falseness, perfidy.

pérfido, *a.* perfidious.

perfil, *m.* profile.

perforación, *f.* perforation.

perforar, *v.* pierce, perforate.

perfume, *m.* perfume, scent. **—perfumar,** *v.*

pergamino, *m.* parchment.

pericia, *f.* skill, expertness.

perico, *m.* parakeet.

perímetro, *m.* perimeter.

periódico, 1. *a.* periodic. **2.** *m.* newspaper.

periodista, *m.* journalist.

período, *m.* period.

periscopio, *m.* periscope.

perito -ta, *a. & n.* experienced; expert, connoisseur.

perjudicar, *v.* damage, hurt; impair.

perjudicial, *a.* harmful, injurious.

perjuicio, *m.* injury, damage.

perjurar, *v.* commit perjury.

perjurio, *m.* perjury.

perla, *f.* pearl.

permanecer, *v.* remain, stay.

permanencia, *f.* permanence; stay.

permanente, *a.* permanent.

permiso, *m.* permission; permit; furlough.

permitir, *v.* permit, enable, let, allow.

permuta, *f.* exchange; barter.

pernicioso, *a.* pernicious.

perno, *m.* bolt.

pero, *conj.* but.

peróxido, *m.* peroxide.

perpendicular, *m. & a.* perpendicular.

perpetración, *f.* perpetration.

perpetrar, *v.* perpetrate.

perpetuar, *v.* perpetuate.

perpetuidad, *f.* perpetuity.

perpetuo, *a.* perpetual.

perplejo, *a.* perplexed, puzzled.

perro -rra, *n.* dog.

persecución, *f.* persecution.

perseguir, *v.* pursue; persecute.

perseverancia, *f.* perseverance.

perseverar, *v.* persevere.

persiana, *f.* shutter, Venetian blind.

persistente, *a.* persistent.

persistir, *v.* persist.

persona, *f.* person.

personaje, *m.* personage; (theat.) character.

personal, 1. *a.* personal. **2.** *m.* personnel, staff.

personalidad, *f.* personality.

personalmente, *adv.* personally.

perspectiva, *f.* perspective; prospect.

perspicaz, *a.* perspicacious, acute.

persuadir, *v.* persuade.

persuasión, *f.* persuasion.

persuasivo, *a.* persuasive.

pertenecer, *v.* pertain, belong.

pertinencia, *f.* pertinence.

pertinente, *a.* pertinent; relevant.

perturbar, *v.* perturb, disturb.

peruano -na, *a. & n.* Peruvian.

perversidad, *f.* perversity.

perverso, *a.* perverse.

pesadez, *f.* dullness, importunity.

pesadilla, *f.* nightmare.

pesado, *a.* heavy; dull, dreary, boring.

pésame, *m.* condolence.

pesar, 1. *m.* sorrow; regret. **a p. de,** in spite of. **2.** *v.* weigh.

pesca, *f.* fishing; catch (of fish).

pescado, *m.* fish. —**pescar,** *v.*

pescador, *m.* fisherman.

pesebre, *m.* stall, manger, crib.

peseta, *f.* monetary unit of Spain.

pesimismo, *m.* pessimism.

pesimista, *a. & n.* pessimistic; pessimist.

peso, *m.* weight; load; peso (monetary unit).

pesquera, *f.* fishery.

pesquisa, *f.* investigation.

pestaña, *f.* eyelash.

pestañeo, *m.* wink, blink. —**pestañear,** *v.*

peste, *f.* plague.

pestilencia, *f.* pestilence.

pétalo, *m.* petal.

petición, *f.* petition.

petirrojo, *m.* robin.

petrel, *m.* petrel.

pétreo, *a.* rocky.

petrificar, *v.* petrify.

petróleo, *m.* petroleum.

petunia, *f.* petunia.

pez, *m.* fish (in the water). *f.* pitch, tar.

pezuña, *f.* hoof.

piadoso, *a.* pious.

pianista, *m. & f.* pianist.

piano, *m.* piano.

picadura, *f.* sting, bite, prick.

picamaderos, *m.* woodpecker.

picante, *a.* hot, spicy.

picaporte, *m.* latch.

picar, *v.* sting, bite, prick; itch; chop up, grind up.

pícaro -ra, *a.* knavish, mischievous. **2.** *n.* rogue, rascal.

picarse, *v.* be offended, piqued.

picazón, *f.* itch.

picea, *f.* spruce.

pico, *m.* peak; pick; beak; spout; small amount.

picotazo, *m.* peck. —**picotear,** *v.*

pictórico, *a.* pictorial.

pichón, *m.* pigeon, squab.

pie, *m.* foot. **al p. de la letra,** literally; thoroughly.

piedad, *f.* piety; pity, mercy.

piedra, *f.* stone.

piel, *f.* skin, hide; fur.

pierna, *f.* leg.

pieza, *f.* piece; room; (theat.) play.

pijamas, *m. or f.pl.* pajamas.

pila, *f.* pile, stack; battery; sink.

pilar, *m.* pillar, column.

píldora, *f.* pill.

piloto, *m.* pilot.

pillo, *m.* thief; rascal.

pimienta, *f.* pepper (spice).

pimiento, *m.* pepper (vegetable).

pináculo, *m.* pinnacle.

pincel, *m.* (artist's) brush.

pinchazo, *m.* puncture. —**pinchar,** *v.*

pingajo, *m.* rag, tatter.

pino, *m.* pine.

pinta, *f.* pint.

pintar, *v.* paint; portray, depict.

pintor -ra, *n.* painter.

pintoresco, *a.* picturesque.

pintura, *f.* paint; painting.

pinzas, *f.pl.* pincers, tweezers; claws.

piña, *f.* pineapple.

pío, *a.* pious; merciful.

piojo, *m.* louse.

pionero -ra, *n.* pioneer.

pipa, *f.* tobacco pipe.

pique, *m.* resentment, pique. **echar a p.,** sink (ship).

pira, *f.* pyre.

pirámide, *f.* pyramid.

pirata, *m.* pirate. **p. de aviones,** hijacker.

pisada, *f.* tread, step. —**pisar,** *v.*

piscina, *f.* fishpond; swimming pool.

piso, *m.* floor.

pista, *f.* trace, clue, track; racetrack.

pistola, *f.* pistol.

pistón, *m.* piston.

pitillo, *m.* cigarette.

pito, *m.* whistle. —**pitar,** *v.*

pizarra, *f.* slate; blackboard.

pizca, *f.* bit, speck; pinch.

pizza, *f.* pizza.

placentero, *a.* pleasant.

placer, 1. *m.* pleasure. **2.** *v.* please.

plácido, *a.* placid.

plaga, *f.* plague, scourge.

plagio, *m.* plagiarism; (S.A.) kidnapping.

plan, *m.* plan. —**planear,** *v.*

plancha, *f.* plate, slab, flatiron.

planchar, *v.* iron, press.

planeta, *m.* planet.

plano, 1. *a.* level, flat. **2.** *m.* plan; plane.

planta, *f.* plant; sole (of foot).

plantación, *f.* plantation.

plantar, *v.* plant.

plantear, *v.* pose, present.

plantel, *m.* educational institution; (agr.) nursery.

plasma, *m.* plasma.

plástico, *a. & m.* plastic.

plata, *f.* silver; (coll.) money.

plataforma, *f.* platform.

plátano, *m.* plantain, cooking banana.

platel, *m.* platter.

plática, *f.* chat, talk. —**platicar,** *v.*

platillo, *m.* saucer.

plato, *m.* plate, dish.

playa, *f.* beach, shore.

plaza, *f.* square. **p. de toros,** bullring.

plazo, *m.* term, deadline; installment.

plebe, *f.* common people; masses.

plebiscito, *m.* plebiscite.

plegadura, *f.* fold, pleat. —**plegar,** *v.*

pleito, *m.* lawsuit; dispute.

plenitud, *f.* fullness; abundance.

pleno, *a.* full. **en pleno . . .** in the middle of . . .

pliego, *m.* sheet of paper.

pliegue, *m.* fold, pleat, crease.

plomería, *f.* plumbing.

plomero, *m.* plumber.

plomizo, *a.* leaden.

plomo, *m.* lead; fuse.

pluma, *f.* feather; (writing) pen.

plumafuente, *f.* fountain pen.

plumaje, *m.* plumage.

plumero, *m.* feather duster; plume.

plumoso, *a.* feathery.

plural, *a. & m.* plural.

población, f. population; town.
poblador -ra, n. settler.
poblar, v. populate; settle.
pobre, a. & n. poor; poor person.
pobreza, f. poverty, need.
pocilga, f. pigpen.
poción, f. drink; potion.
poco, **1.** a. & adv. little, not much, (pl.) few. **por p.**, almost, nearly. **2.** m. **un p. (de)**, a little, a bit (of).
poder, **1.** m. power. **2.** v. be able to, can; be possible, may, might. **no p. menos de**, not be able to help.
poderío, m. power, might.
poderoso, a. powerful, mighty, potent.
podrido, a. rotten.
poema, m. poem.
poesía, f. poetry; poem.
poeta, m. poet.
poético, a. poetic.
polaco -ca, a. & n. Polish; Pole.
polar, a. polar.
polaridad, f. polarity.
polea, f. pulley.
polen, m. pollen.
policía, f. police. m. policeman.
poligamia, f. polygamy.
polígloto -ta, n. polyglot.
polilla, f. moth.
política, f. politics; policy.
político, a. & m. politic; political; politician.
póliza, f. (insurance) policy; permit, ticket.
polizonte, m. policeman.
polo, m. pole; polo.
polonés, a. Polish.
Polonia, f. Poland.
polvera, f. powder box; powder puff.
polvo, m. powder; dust.
pólvora, f. powder, gunpowder.
pollada, f. brood.
pollería, f. poultry shop.
pollino, m. donkey.
pollo, m. chicken.
pompa, f. pomp.
pomposo, a. pompous.
ponche, m. punch (beverage).
ponchera, f. punch bowl.
ponderar, v. ponder.
ponderoso, a. ponderous.
poner, v. put, set, lay, place.
ponerse, v. put on; become, get; set (sun). **p. a**, start to.
poniente, m. west.
pontífice, m. pontiff.
popa, f. stern.
popular, a. popular.
popularidad, f. popularity.
populazo, m. populace; masses.
por, prep. by, through, because of; via; for. **p. qué?** why?
porcelana, f. porcelain, chinaware.
porcentaje, m. percentage.
porción, f. portion, lot.
porche, m. porch; portico.

porfiar, v. persist; argue.
pormenor, m. detail.
pornografía, f. pornography.
poro, m. pore.
poroso, a. porous.
porque, conj. because.
porqué, m. reason, motive.
porra, f. stick, club.
porrazo, m. blow.
portaaviones, m. aircraft carrier.
portador -ra, n. bearer.
portal, m. portal.
portar, v. carry.
portarse, v. behave, act.
portátil, a. portable.
portavoz, m. megaphone.
porte, m. bearing; behavior; postage.
portero, m. porter; janitor.
pórtico, m. porch.
portorriqueño -ña, n. & a. Puerto Rican.
portugués -esa, a. & n. Portuguese.
posada, f. lodge, inn.
posar, v. pose.
posdata, f. postscript.
poseer, v. possess, own.
posesión, f. possession.
posibilidad, f. possibility.
posible, a. possible.
posiblemente, adv. possibly.
posición, f. position, stand.
positivo, a. positive.
posponer, v. postpone.
postal, a. postal.
poste, m. post, pillar.
posteridad, f. posterity.
posterior, a. posterior, rear.
postizo, a. false, artificial.
postrado, a. prostrate. —**postrar**, v.
postre, m. dessert.
póstumo, a. posthumous.
postura, f. posture, pose; bet.
potable, a. drinkable.
potaje, m. porridge; pot stew.
potasa, f. potash.
potasio, m. potassium.
pote, m. pot, jar.
potencia, f. potency, power.
potencial, a. & f. potential.
potentado, m. potentate.
potente, a. potent, powerful.
potestad, f. power.
potro, m. colt.
pozo, m. well.
práctica, f. practice. —**practicar**, v.
práctico, a. practical.
pradera, f. prairie, meadow.
prado, m. meadow; lawn.
pragmatismo, m. pragmatism.
preámbulo, m. preamble.
precario, a. precarious.
precaución, f. precaution.
precaverse, v. beware.
precavido, a. cautious, guarded, wary.
precedencia, f. precedence, priority.
precedente, a. & m. preceding; precedent.
preceder, v. precede.

precepto, m. precept.
preciar, v. value, prize.
preciarse de, v. take pride in.
precio, m. price.
precioso, a. precious; beautiful, gorgeous.
precipicio, m. precipice, cliff.
precipitación, f. precipitation.
precipitar, v. precipitate, rush; throw headlong.
precipitoso, a. precipitous, rash.
precisar, v. fix, specify; be necessary.
precisión, f. precision; necessity.
preciso, a. precise; necessary.
precocidad, f. precocity.
precoz, a. precocious.
precursor -ra 1. a. preceding. **2.** n. precursor, forerunner.
predecesor, -ra, a. & n. predecessor.
predecir, v. predict, foretell.
predicación, f. sermon.
predicador, m. preacher.
predicar, v. preach; publish.
predicción, f. prediction.
predilecto, a. favorite, preferred.
predisponer, v. predispose.
predisposición, f. predisposition; bias.
predominante, a. prevailing, prevalent, predominant.
predominar, v. prevail, predominate.
predominio, m. predominance, sway.
prefacio, m. preface.
preferencia, f. preference.
preferentemente, adv. preferably.
preferible, a. preferable.
preferir, v. prefer.
prefijo, m. prefix; area code. —**prefijar**, v.
pregón, m. proclamation, cry.
pregonar, v. proclaim, cry out.
pregunta, f. question, inquiry. **hacer una p.**, to ask a question.
preguntar, v. ask, inquire.
preguntarse, v. wonder.
prehistórico, a. prehistoric.
prejuicio, m. prejudice.
prelacía, f. prelacy.
preliminar, a. & m. preliminary.
preludio, m. prelude.
prematuro, a. premature.
premeditación, f. premeditation.
premeditar, v. premeditate.
premiar, v. reward; award a prize to.
premio, m. prize, award; reward.
premisa, f. premise.
premura, f. pressure; urgency.
prenda, f. jewel; (personal) quality. **p. de vestir**, garment.
prender, v. seize, arrest, catch; attack, pin, clip. **p. fuego a**, set fire to.

prensa, f. printing press; (the) press.

prensar, v. press, compress.

preñado, a. pregnant.

preocupación, f. worry, preoccupation.

preocupar, v. worry, preoccupy.

preparación, f. preparation.

preparar, v. prepare.

preparativo, m. preparation.

preparatorio, m. preparatory.

preponderante, a. preponderant.

preposición, f. preposition.

prerrogativa, f. prerogative, privilege.

presa, f. capture; prey; (water) dam.

presagiar, v. presage, forebode.

presbiteriano -na, n. & a. Presbyterian.

presbítero, m. priest.

prescindir de, v. dispense with; omit.

prescribir, v. prescribe.

prescripción, f. prescription.

presencia, f. presence.

presenciar, v. witness, be present at.

presentable, a. presentable.

presentación, f. presentation; introduction.

presentar, v. present; introduce.

presente, a. & m. present.

preservación, f. preservation.

preservar, v. preserve, keep.

preservativo, a. & m. preservative.

presidencia, f. presidency.

presidencial, a. presidential.

presidente -ta, n. president.

presidio, m. prison; garrison.

presidir, v. preside.

presión, f. pressure.

preso, m. prisoner.

presta, f. mint (plant).

prestador, m. lender.

prestamista, m. & f. money lender.

préstamo, m. loan.

prestar, v. lend.

presteza, f. haste, promptness.

prestidigitación, f. sleight of hand.

prestigio, m. prestige.

presto, 1. a. quick, prompt; ready. **2.** adv. quickly; at once.

presumido, a. conceited, presumptuous.

presumir, v. presume; boast; claim; be conceited.

presunción, f. presumption; conceit.

presunto, a. presumed; prospective.

presuntuoso, a. presumptuous.

presupuesto, m. motive, pretext; budget.

pretender, v. pretend; intend; aspire.

pretendiente, m. suitor; pretender (to throne).

pretensión, f. pretension; claim.

pretérito, a. & m. preterit, past (tense).

pretexto, m. pretext.

prevalecer, v. prevail.

prevención, f. prevention.

prevenir, v. prevent; forewarn; prearrange.

preventivo, a. preventive.

prever, v. foresee.

previamente, adv. previously.

previo, a. previous.

previsión, f. foresight. **p. social,** social security.

prieto, a. blackish, very dark.

primacía, f. primacy.

primario, a. primary.

primavera, f. spring (season).

primero, a. & adv. first.

primitivo, a. primitive.

primo -ma, n. cousin.

primor, m. beauty; excellence; lovely thing.

primoroso, a. exquisite, elegant; graceful.

princesa, f. princess.

principal, 1. a. principal, main. **2.** m. chief, head, principal.

principalmente, adv. principally.

príncipe, m. prince.

principiar, v. begin, initiate.

principio, m. beginning, start; principle.

prioridad, f. priority.

prisa, f. hurry, haste. **darse p.,** hurry, hasten. **tener p.,** be in a hurry.

prisión, f. prison; imprisonment.

prisionero -ra, n. captive, prisoner.

prisma, m. prism.

prismático, a. prismatic.

privación, f. privation, want.

privado, a. private, secret; deprived.

privar, v. deprive.

privilegio, m. privilege.

pro, m. or f. benefit, advantage. **en p. de,** in behalf of. **en p. y en contra,** pro and con.

proa, f. prow, bow.

probabilidad, f. probability.

probable, a. probable, likely.

probablemente, adv. probably.

probar, v. try, sample; taste; test; prove.

probarse, v. try on.

probidad, f. honesty, integrity.

problema, m. problem.

probo, a. honest.

procaz, a. impudent, saucy.

proceder, v. proceed.

procedimiento, m. procedure.

procesar, v. prosecute; sue; process.

procesión, f. procession.

proceso, m. process; (court) trial.

proclama, proclamación, f. proclamation.

proclamar, v. proclaim.

procreación, f. procreation.

procrear, v. procreate.

procurar, v. try; see to it; get; procure.

prodigalidad, f. prodigality.

prodigar, v. lavish, squander, waste.

prodigio, m. prodigy.

pródigo, a. prodigal, profuse, lavish.

producción, f. production.

producir, v. produce.

productivo, a. productive.

producto, m. product.

proeza, f. prowess.

profanación, f. profanation.

profanar, v. defile, desecrate.

profanidad, f. profanity.

profano, a. profane.

profecía, f. prophecy.

proferir, v. utter, express.

profesar, v. profess.

profesión, f. profession.

profesional, a. professional.

profesor -ra, n. professor, teacher.

profeta, m. prophet.

profético, a. prophetic.

profetizar, v. prophesy.

proficiente, a. proficient.

profundamente, adv. profoundly, deeply.

profundidad, f. profundity, depth.

profundizar, v. deepen.

profundo, a. profound, deep.

profuso, a. profuse.

progenie, f. progeny, offspring.

programa, m. program; schedule.

progresar, v. progress, advance.

progresión, f. progression.

progresista, progresivo, a. progressive.

progreso, m. progress.

prohibición, f. prohibition.

prohibir, v. prohibit, forbid.

prohibitivo, a. prohibitive.

prole, f. progeny.

proletariado, m. proletariat.

proliferación, f. proliferation.

prolijo, a. prolix, tedious; long-winded.

prólogo, m. prologue; preface.

prolongar, v. prolong.

promedio, m. average.

promesa, f. promise.

prometer, v. promise.

prometido, a. promised; engaged (to marry).

prominencia, f. prominence.

promiscuamente, adv. promiscuously.

promiscuo, a. promiscuous.

promisorio, a. promissory.

promoción, f. promotion.

promover, v. promote, further.

promulgación, f. promulgation.

promulgar, v. promulgate.

pronombre, m. pronoun.

pronosticación, f. prediction, forecast.

pronosticar, v. predict, forecast.

pronóstico, m. prediction.

prontamente, *adv.* promptly.
prontitud, *f.* promptness.
pronto, 1. *a.* prompt; ready. **2.** *adv.* soon; quickly. **de p.,** abruptly.
pronunciación, *f.* pronunciation.
pronunciar, *v.* pronounce.
propagación, *f.* propagation.
propaganda, *f.* propaganda.
propagandista, *n.* propagandist.
propagar, *v.* propagate.
propicio, *a.* propitious, auspicious, favorable.
propiedad, *f.* property.
propietario -ria, *n.* proprietor; owner; landlord, landlady.
propina, *f.* gratuity, tip.
propio, *a.* proper, suitable; typical; (one's) own; -self.
proponer, *v.* propose.
proporción, *f.* proportion.
proporcionado, *a.* proportionate.
proporcionar, *v.* provide with, supply, afford.
proposición, *f.* proposition, offer; proposal.
propósito, *m.* purpose; plan; **a p.,** by the way, apropos; on purpose.
propuesta, *f.* proposal, motion.
prorrata, *f.* quota.
prórroga, *f.* renewal, extension.
prorrogar, *v.* renew, extend.
prosa, *f.* prose.
prosaico, *a.* prosaic.
proscribir, *v.* prohibit, proscribe, ban.
prosecución, *f.* prosecution.
proseguir, *v.* pursue; proceed, go on.
prosélito, *m.* proselyte.
prospecto, *m.* prospectus.
prosperar, *v.* prosper, thrive, flourish.
prosperidad, *f.* prosperity.
próspero, *a.* prosperous, successful.
prosternado, *a.* prostrate.
prostitución, *f.* prostitution.
prostituir, *v.* prostitute; debase.
prostituta, *f.* prostitute.
protagonista, *m. & f.* protagonist, hero, heroine.
protección, *f.* protection.
protector -ra, *a. & n.* protective; protector.
proteger, *v.* protect, safeguard.
protegido -da, *n.* protégé.
proteína, *f.* protein.
protesta, *f.* protest. **—protestar**, *v.*
protestante, *a. & n.* Protestant.
protocolo, *m.* protocol.
protuberancia, *f.* protuberance, lump.
provecho, *m.* profit, gain, benefit. **¡Buen provecho!** May you enjoy your meal!
provechoso, *a.* beneficial, advantageous, profitable.
proveer, *v.* provide, furnish.

provenir de, *v.* originate in, be due to, come from.
proverbial, *a.* proverbial.
proverbio, *m.* proverb.
providencia, *f.* providence.
providente, *a.* provident.
provincia, *f.* province.
provincial, *a.* provincial.
provinciano -na, *a. & n.* provincial.
provisión, *f.* provision, supply, stock.
provisional, *a.* provisional.
provocación, *f.* provocation.
provocador, *m.* provoker.
provocar, *v.* provoke, excite.
provocativo, *a.* provocative.
proximidad, *f.* proximity, vicinity.
próximo, *a.* next; near.
proyección, *f.* projection.
proyectar, *v.* plan, project.
proyectil, *m.* projectile, missile, shell.
proyecto, *m.* plan, project, scheme.
proyector, *m.* projector.
prudencia, *f.* prudence.
prudente, *a.* prudent.
prueba, *f.* proof; trial; test.
psicoanálisis, *m. or f.* psychoanalysis.
psicología, *f.* psychology.
psicológico, *a.* psychological.
psicólogo, *m.* psychologist.
psiquedélico, *a.* psychedelic.
psiquiatra, *m.* psychiatrist.
psiquiatría, *f.* psychiatry.
publicación, *f.* publication.
publicar, *v.* publish.
publicidad, *f.* publicity.
público, *a. & m.* public.
puchero, *m.* pot.
pudiente, *a.* powerful; wealthy.
pudín, *m.* pudding.
pudor, *m.* modesty.
pudoroso, *a.* modest.
pudrirse, *v.* rot.
pueblo, *m.* town, village; (the) people.
puente, *m.* bridge.
puerco -ca, *n.* pig.
pueril, *a.* childish.
puerilidad, *f.* puerility.
puerta, *f.* door; gate.
puerto, *m.* port, harbor.
puertorriqueño -ña, *a. & n.* Puerto Rican.
pues, 1. *adv.* well . . . **2.** *conj.* as, since, for.
puesto, *m.* appointment, post, job; place; stand. **p. que,** since.
pugilato, *m.* boxing.
pugna, *f.* conflict.
pugnacidad, *f.* pugnacity.
pugnar, *v.* fight; oppose.
pulcritud, *f.* beauty.
pulga, *f.* flea.
pulgada, *f.* inch.
pulgar, *m.* thumb.
pulir, *v.* polish; beautify.
pulmón, *m.* lung.
pulmonía, *f.* pneumonia.
pulpa, *f.* pulp.

púlpito, *m.* pulpit.
pulque, *m.* pulque (fermented maguey juice).
pulsación, *f.* pulsation, beat.
pulsar, *v.* pulsate, beat.
pulsera, *f.* wristband; bracelet; wristwatch.
pulso, *m.* pulse.
pulverizar, *v.* pulverize.
puma, *m.* puma.
pundonor, *m.* point of honor.
punta, *f.* point, tip, end.
puntada, *f.* stitch.
puntapié, *m.* kick.
puntería, *f.* (marksman's) aim.
puntiagudo, *a.* sharp-pointed.
puntillas, *f.pl.* **de p., en p.,** on tiptoe.
punto, *m.* point; period; spot, dot. **dos puntos,** (punct.) colon. **a p. de,** about to. **al p.,** instantly.
puntuación, *f.* punctuation.
puntual, *a.* punctual, prompt.
puntuar, *v.* punctuate.
puñada, *f.* fist, blow.
puñado, *m.* handful.
puñal, *m.* dagger.
puñalada, *f.* stab.
puñetazo, *m.* punch, fist blow.
puño, *m.* fist; cuff; handle.
pupila, *f.* pupil (of eye).
pupitre, *m.* writing desk, school desk.
pureza, *f.* purity; chastity.
purgante, *m.* laxative.
purgar, *v.* purge, cleanse.
purgatorio, *m.* purgatory.
puridad, *f.* purity.
purificación, *f.* purification.
purificar, *v.* purify.
purismo, *m.* purism.
purista, *n.* purist.
puritanismo, *m.* puritanism.
puro, 1. *a.* pure. **2.** *m.* cigar.
púrpura, *f.* purple.
purpúreo, *a.* purple.
purulencia, *f.* purulence.
purulento, *a.* purulent.
pus, *m.* pus.
pusilánime, *a.* pusillanimous.
puta, *f.* prostitute.
putrefacción, *f.* putrefaction, rot.
putrefacto, *a.* putrid, rotten.
pútrido, *a.* putrid.
puya, *f.* goad.

Q

que, 1. *rel. pron.* who, whom; that, which. **2.** *conj.* than.
qué, 1. *a. & pron.* what. **por q., para q.,** why? **2.** *adv.* how.
quebrada, *f.* ravine, gully, gulch; stream.
quebradizo, *a.* fragile, brittle.
quebrar, *v.* break.
queda, *f.* curfew.
quedar, *v.* remain, be located; be left. **q. bien a,** be becoming to.
quedarse, *v.* stay, remain. **q. con,** keep, hold on to.

quedo, *a.* quiet; gentle.
quehacer, *m.* task; chore.
queja, *f.* complaint.
quejarse, *v.* complain, grumble.
quejido, *m.* moan.
quejoso, *a.* complaining.
quema, *f.* burning.
quemadura, *f.* burn.
quemar, *v.* burn.
querella, *f.* quarrel; complaint.
querencia, *f.* affection, liking.
querer, *v.* want, wish; will; love (a person). **q. decir,** mean. **sin q.,** without meaning to; unwillingly.
querido, *a.* dear, loved, beloved.
quesería, *f.* dairy.
queso, *m.* cheese.
quiebra, *f.* break, fracture; damage; bankruptcy.
quien, *rel. pron.* who, whom.
quién, *interrog. pron.* who, whom.
quienquiera, *pron.* whoever, whomever.
quietamente, *adv.* quietly.
quieto, *a.* quiet, still.
quietud, *f.* quiet, quietude.
quijada, *f.* jaw.
quijotesco, *a.* quixotic.
quilate, *m.* carat.
quilla, *f.* keel.
quimera, *f.* chimera, vision; quarrel.
química, *f.* chemistry.
químico, *a. & m.* chemical; chemist.
quimoterapia, *f.* chemotherapy.
quincallería, *f.* hardware store.
quince, *a. & pron.* fifteen.
quinientos, *a. & pron.* five hundred.
quinina, *f.* quinine.
quintana, *f.* country home.
quinto, *a.* fifth.
quirúrgico, *m.* surgeon.
quiste, *m.* cyst.
quitamanchas, *m.* stain remover.
quitanieve, *m.* snowplow.
quitar, *v.* take away, remove.
quitarse, *v.* take off; get rid of.
quitasol, *m.* parasol, umbrella.
quizá, quizás, *adv.* perhaps, maybe.
quórum, *m.* quorum.

R

rábano, *m.* radish.
rabí, rabino, *m.* rabbi.
rabia, *f.* rage; grudge; rabies.
rabiar, *v.* rage, be furious.
rabieta, *f.* tantrum.
rabioso, *a.* furious; rabid.
rabo, *m.* tail.
racimo, *m.* bunch, cluster.
ración, *f.* ration. —**racionar,** *v.*
racionabilidad, *f.* rationality.
racional, *a.* rational.
racionalismo, *m.* rationalism.

racionalmente, *adv.* rationally.
racha, *f.* streak.
radar, *m.* radar.
radiación, *f.* radiation.
radiador, *m.* radiator.
radiante, *a.* radiant.
radical, *a. & m.* radical.
radicalismo, *m.* radicalism.
radicoso, *a.* radical.
radio, *m. or f.* radio.
radioactividad, *f.* radioactivity.
radioactivo, *a.* radioactive.
radiodifundir, *v.* broadcast.
radiodifusión, *f.* (radio) broadcasting.
ráfaga, *f.* gust (of wind).
raíz, *f.* root.
raja, *f.* rip; split, crack. —**rajar,** *v.*
ralea, *f.* stock, breed.
ralo, *a.* thin, scattered.
rama, *f.* branch, bough.
ramillete, *m.* bouquet.
ramo, *m.* branch, bough.
ramonear, *v.* browse.
rampa, *f.* ramp.
rana, *f.* frog.
rancidez, *f.* rancidity.
rancio, *a.* rancid, rank, stale, sour.
ranchero -ra, *n.* small farmer.
rancho, *m.* ranch.
rango, *m.* rank.
ranúnculo, *m.* ranunculus; buttercup.
ranura, *f.* slot.
rapacidad, *f.* rapacity.
rapaz, **1.** *a.* rapacious. **2.** *m.* young boy.
rapé, *m.* snuff.
rápidamente, *adv.* rapidly.
rapidez, *f.* rapidity, speed.
rápido, **1.** *a.* rapid, fast, speedy. **2.** *m.* express (train).
rapiña, *f.* robbery, plundering.
rapsodia, *f.* rhapsody.
raqueta, *f.* (tennis) racket.
rareza, *f.* rarity, freak.
raridad, *f.* rarity.
raro, *a.* rare, strange, unusual, odd, queer.
rasar, *v.* skim.
rascar, *v.* scrape; scratch.
rasgadura, *f.* tear, rip. —**rasgar,** *v.*
rasgo, *m.* trait.
rasgón, *m.* tear.
rasguño, *m.* scratch. —**rasguñar,** *v.*
raso, **1.** *a.* plain. **soldado r.,** (mil.) private. **2.** *m.* satin.
raspar, *v.* scrape; erase.
rastra, *f.* trail, track. —**rastrear,** *v.*
rastrillar, *v.* rake.
rastro, *m.* track, trail, trace; rake.
rata, *f.* rat.
ratificación, *f.* ratification.
ratificar, *v.* ratify.
rato, *m.* while, spell, short time.
ratón, *m.* mouse.
ratonera, *f.* mousetrap.

raya, *f.* dash, line, streak, stripe.
rayar, *v.* rule, stripe; scratch; cross out.
rayo, *m.* lightning bolt; ray; flash.
rayón, *m.* rayon.
raza, *f.* race; breed, stock.
razón, *f.* reason; ratio. **a r. de,** at the rate of. **tener r.,** to be right.
razonable, *a.* reasonable, sensible.
razonamiento, *m.* argument.
razonar, *v.* reason.
reacción, *f.* reaction.
reaccionar, *v.* react.
reaccionario, *m.* reactionary.
reacondicionar, *v.* recondition.
reactivo, *a. & m.* reactive; (chem.) reagent.
reactor, *m.* reactor.
real, *a.* royal, regal; real, actual.
realdad, *f.* royal authority.
realeza, *f.* royalty.
realidad, *f.* reality.
realista, *a. & n.* realistic; realist.
realización, *f.* achievement, accomplishment.
realizar, *v.* accomplish; fulfill; effect; (com.) realize.
realmente, *adv.* in reality.
realzar, *v.* enhance.
reata, *f.* rope; lasso, lariat.
rebaja, *f.* reduction.
rebajar, *v.* cheapen; reduce (in price); lower.
rebanada, *f.* slice. —**rebanar,** *v.*
rebaño, *m.* flock, herd.
rebato, *m.* alarm; sudden attack.
rebelarse, *v.* rebel, revolt.
rebelde, *a. & n.* rebellious; rebel.
rebelión, *f.* rebellion, revolt.
reborde, *m.* border.
rebotar, *v.* rebound.
rebozo, *m.* shawl.
rebuscar, *v.* search thoroughly.
rebuznar, *v.* bray.
recado, *m.* message; errand.
recaída, *f.* relapse. —**recaer,** *v.*
recalcar, *v.* stress, emphasize.
recámara, *f.* (Mex.) bedroom.
recapitulación, *f.* recapitulation.
recapitular, *v.* recapitulate.
recatado, *m.* coy; prudent.
recelar, *v.* fear, distrust.
receloso, *a.* distrustful.
recepción, *f.* reception.
receptáculo, *m.* receptacle.
receptividad, *f.* receptivity.
receptivo, *a.* receptive.
receptor, *m.* receiver.
receta, *f.* recipe; prescription.
recetar, *v.* prescribe.
recibimiento, *m.* reception; cordiality.
recibir, *v.* receive.
recibo, *m.* receipt.
reciclar, *v.* recycle.
recidiva, *f.* relapse.

recién, *adv.* recently, newly, just.

reciente, *a.* recent.

recinto, *m.* enclosure.

recipiente, *m.* recipient.

reciprocación, *f.* reciprocation.

recíprocamente, *adv.* reciprocally.

reciprocar, *v.* reciprocate.

reciprocidad, *f.* reciprocity.

recitación, *f.* recitation.

recitar, *v.* recite.

reclamación, *f.* claim; complaint.

reclamar, *v.* claim; complain.

reclamo, *m.* claim; advertisement, advertising; decoy.

reclinar, *v.* recline, repose, lean.

recluta, *m.* recruit.

reclutar, *v.* recruit, draft.

recobrar, *v.* recover, salvage, regain.

recobro, *m.* recovery.

recoger, *v.* gather; collect; pick up.

recogerse, *v.* retire (for night).

recolectar, *v.* gather, assemble; harvest.

recomendación, *f.* recommendation; commendation.

recomendar, *v.* recommend; commend.

recompensa, *f.* recompense; compensation.

recompensar, *v.* reward; compensate.

reconciliación, *f.* reconciliation.

reconciliar, *v.* reconcile.

reconocer, *v.* recognize; acknowledge; inspect, examine; (mil.) reconnoiter.

reconocimiento, *m.* recognition; appreciation, gratitude.

reconstituir, *v.* reconstitute.

reconstruir, *v.* reconstruct, rebuild.

record, *m.* (sports) record.

recordar, *v.* recall, recollect; remind.

recorrer, *v.* go over; read over; cover (distance).

recorte, *m.* clipping, cutting.

recostarse, *v.* recline, lean back, rest.

recreación, *f.* recreation.

recreo, *m.* recreation.

recriminación, *f.* recrimination.

rectangular, *a.* rectangular.

rectángulo, *m.* rectangle.

rectificación, *f.* rectification.

rectificar, *v.* rectify.

recto, *a.* straight; just, fair. ángulo r., right angle.

recuento, *m.* recount.

recuerdo, *m.* memory, souvenir, remembrance; (*pl.*) regards.

reculada, *f.* recoil. —recular, *v.*

recuperación, *f.* recuperation.

recuperar, *v.* recuperate.

recurrir, *v.* revert; resort, have recourse.

recurso, *m.* resource; recourse.

rechazar, *v.* reject, spurn, discard.

rechinar, *v.* chatter.

red, *f.* net; trap.

redacción, *f.* (editorial) staff; composition (of written material).

redactar, *v.* draft, draw up; edit.

redactor, *m.* editor.

redada, *f.* netful, catch, haul.

redargución, *f.* retort. —redargüir, *v.*

redención, *f.* redemption, salvation.

redentor, *m.* redeemer.

redimir, *v.* redeem.

redoblante, *m.* drummer.

redonda, *f.* neighborhood, vicinity.

redondo, *a.* round, circular.

reducción, *f.* reduction.

reducir, *v.* reduce.

reembolso, *m.* refund. —reembolsar, *v.*

reemplazar, *v.* replace, supersede.

reencarnación, *f.* reincarnation.

reexaminar, *v.* reexamine.

reexpedir, *v.* forward (mail).

referencia, *f.* reference.

referéndum, *m.* referendum.

referir, *v.* relate, report on.

referirse, *v.* refer.

refinamiento, *m.* refinement.

refinar, *v.* refine.

refinería, *f.* refinery.

reflejar, *v.* reflect; think, ponder.

reflejo, *m.* reflection; glare.

reflexión, *f.* reflection, thought.

reflexionar, *v.* reflect, think.

reflujo, *m.* ebb; ebb tide.

reforma, *f.* reform. —reformar, *v.*

reformación, *f.* reformation.

reformador, *m.* reformer.

reforzar, *v.* reinforce, strengthen; encourage.

refractario, *a.* refractory.

refrán, *m.* proverb, saying.

refrenar, *v.* curb, rein; restrain.

refrescar, *v.* refresh, freshen, cool.

refresco, *m.* refreshment; cold drink.

refrigeración, *f.* refrigeration.

refrigerador, *m.* refrigerator.

refrigerar, *v.* refrigerate.

refuerzo, *m.* reinforcement.

refugiado -da, *m.f.* refugee.

refugiarse, *v.* take refuge.

refugio, *m.* refuge, asylum, shelter.

refulgencia, *f.* refulgence.

refulgente, *a.* refulgent.

refulgir, *v.* shine.

refunfuñar, *v.* mutter, grumble, growl.

refutación, *f.* refutation; rebuttal.

refutar, *v.* refute.

regadizo, *a.* irrigable.

regadura, *f.* irrigation.

regalar, *v.* give (a gift), give away.

regalo, *m.* gift, present, con r., in luxury.

regañar, *v.* reprove; scold.

regaño, *m.* reprimand, scolding.

regar, *v.* water, irrigate.

regatear, *v.* haggle.

regateo, *m.* bargaining, haggling.

regazo, *m.* lap.

regencia, *f.* regency.

regeneración, *f.* regeneration.

regenerar, *v.* regenerate.

regente, *m.* regent.

régimen, *m.* regime; diet.

regimentar, *v.* regiment.

regimiento, *m.* regiment.

región, *f.* region.

regional, *a.* regional, sectional.

regir, *v.* rule; be in effect.

registrar, *v.* register; record; search.

registro, *m.* register; record; search.

regla, *f.* rule, regulation. en r., in order.

reglamento, *m.* code of regulations.

regocijarse, *v.* rejoice, exult.

regocijo, *f.* rejoicing; merriment, joy.

regordete, *a.* chubby, plump.

regresar, *v.* go back, return.

regresión, *f.* regression.

regresivo, *a.* regressive.

regreso, *m.* return.

regulación, *f.* regulation.

regular, 1. *a.* regular; fair, middling. 2. *v.* regulate.

regularidad, *f.* regularity.

regularmente, *adv.* regularly.

rehabilitación, *f.* rehabilitation.

rehabilitar, *v.* rehabilitate.

rehén, *m.* hostage.

rehusar, *v.* refuse; decline.

reina, *f.* queen.

reinado, *m.* reign. —reinar, *v.*

reino, *m.* kingdom; realm; reign.

reír, *v.* laugh.

reiteración, *f.* reiteration.

reiterar, *v.* reiterate.

reja, *f.* grating, grillwork.

relación, *f.* relation; account, report.

relacionar, *v.* relate, connect.

relajamiento, *m.* laxity, laxness.

relajar, *v.* relax, slacken.

relámpago, *m.* lightning; flash (of lightning).

relatador, *m.* teller.

relatar, *v.* relate, recount.

relativamente, *adv.* relatively.

relatividad, *f.* relativity.

relativo, *a.* relative.

relato, *m.* account, story.

relegación, *f.* relegation.

relegar, *v.* relegate.

relevar, *v.* relieve.

relicario, m. reliquary; locket.
relieve, m. (sculpture) relief.
religión, f. religion.
religiosidad, f. religiosity.
religioso -sa, 1. a. religious. 2. m. member of a religious order.
reliquia, f. relic.
reloj, m. clock; watch.
relojería, f. watchmaker's shop.
relojero, m. watchmaker.
relucir, v. glow, shine; excel.
relumbrar, v. glitter, sparkle.
rellenar, v. refill; fill up, stuff.
relleno, m. filling; stuffing.
remache, m. rivet. —remachar, v.
remar, v. row (a boat).
rematado, a. finished; sold.
remate, m. end, finish; auction. de r., utterly.
remedador, m. imitator.
remedar, v. imitate.
remedio, m. remedy. —remediar, v.
remendar, v. mend, patch.
remesa, f. shipment; remittance.
remiendo, m. patch.
remilgado, a. prudish; affected.
reminiscencia, f. reminiscence.
remitir, v. remit.
remo, m. oar.
remolacha, f. beet.
remolcador, m. tug (boat).
remolino, m. whirl; whirlpool; whirlwind.
remolque, m. tow. —remolcar, v.
remontar, v. ascend, go up.
remontarse, v. get excited; soar. r. a, date from; go back to (in time).
remordimiento, m. remorse.
remotamente, adv. remotely.
remoto, a. remote.
remover, v. remove; stir; shake; loosen.
rempujar, v. jostle.
remuneración, f. remuneration.
remunerar, v. remunerate.
renacido, a. reborn, born-again.
renacimiento, m. rebirth; renaissance.
rencor, m. rancor, bitterness, animosity; grudge.
rencoroso, a. rancorous, bitter.
rendición, f. surrender.
rendido, a. weary, worn out.
rendir, v. yield; surrender, give up; win over.
renegado, m. renegade.
renglón, m. line; (com.) item.
reno, m. reindeer.
renombre, m. renown.
renovación, f. renovation, renewal.
renovar, v. renew; renovate.
renta, f. income; rent.
rentar, v. yield; rent for.
renuencia, f. reluctance.

renuente, a. reluctant.
renuncia, f. resignation; renunciation.
renunciar, v. resign; renounce, give up.
reñir, v. scold, berate; quarrel; wrangle.
reo, a. & n. criminal; convict.
reorganizar, v. reorganize.
reparación, f. reparation, atonement; repair.
reparar, v. repair; mend; stop, stay over. r. en, notice; consider.
reparo, m. repair; remark; difficulty; objection.
repartición, f., repartimiento, reparto, m. division, distribution.
repartir, v. divide, apportion, distribute; (theat.) cast.
repaso, m. review. —repasar, v.
repatriación, f. repatriation.
repatriar, v. repatriate.
repeler, v. repel.
repente, m. de r., suddenly; unexpectedly.
repentinamente, adv. suddenly.
repentino, a. sudden.
repercusión, f. repercussion.
repertorio, m. repertoire.
repetición, f. repetition.
repetidamente, adv. repeatedly.
repetir, v. repeat.
repisa, f. shelf.
réplica, f. reply; objection.
replicar, v. reply; answer back.
repollo, m. cabbage.
reponer, v. replace; repair.
reponerse, v. recover, get well.
reporte, m. report; news.
repórter, reportero, m. reporter.
reposado, a. tranquil, peaceful, quiet.
reposo, m. repose, rest. —reposar, v.
reposte, f. pantry.
represalia, f. reprisal.
representación, f. representation; (theat.) performance.
representante, m. representative, agent.
representar, v. represent, depict; (theat.) perform.
representativo, a. representative.
represión, f. repression.
represivo, a. repressive.
reprimenda, f. reprimand.
reprimir, v. repress, quell.
reproche, m. reproach. —reprochar, v.
reproducción, f. reproduction.
reproducir, v. reproduce.
reptil, m. reptile.
república, f. republic.
republicano -na, a. & n. republican.
repudiación, f. repudiation.
repudiar, v. repudiate; disown.
repuesto, m. spare part. de r., spare.
repugnancia, f. repugnance.

repugnante, a. repugnant, repulsive.
repugnar, v. disgust.
repulsa, f. refusal; repulse.
repulsivo, a. repulsive.
reputación, f. reputation.
reputar, v. repute; appreciate.
requerir, v. require.
requesón, m. cottage cheese.
requisición, f. requisition.
requisito, m. requisite, requirement.
res, f. head of cattle.
resbalar, v. slide; slip.
resbaloso, a. slippery.
rescate, m. rescue, ransom. —rescatar, v.
rescindir, v. rescind.
resentimiento, m. resentment.
resentirse, v. resent.
reserva, f. reserve. —reservar, v.
reservación, f. reservation.
resfriado, m. (med.) cold.
resfriarse, v. catch cold.
resguardar, v. guard, protect.
residencia, f. residence, seat.
residente, a. & n. resident.
residir, v. reside.
residuo, m. remainder.
resignación, f. resignation.
resignar, v. resign.
resina, f. resin; rosin.
resistencia, f. resistance.
resistir, v. resist; endure.
resolución, f. resolution.
resolutivamente, adv. resolutely.
resolver, v. resolve; solve.
resonante, a. resonant.
resonar, v. resound.
resorte, m. (mech.) spring.
respaldar, v. endorse; back.
respaldo, m. back (of a seat).
respectivo, a. respective.
respecto, m. relation, proportion; r. a, concerning, regarding.
respetabilidad, f. respectability.
respetable, a. respectable.
respeto, m. respect. —respetar, v.
respetuosamente, adv. respectfully.
respetuoso, a. respectful.
respiración, f. respiration, breath.
respirar, v. breathe.
resplandeciente, a. resplendent.
resplandor, m. brightness, glitter.
responder, v. respond, answer.
responsabilidad, f. responsibility.
responsable, a. responsible.
respuesta, f. answer, response, reply.
resquicio, m. crack, slit.
resta, f. subtraction, remainder.
restablecer, v. restore, reestablish.

restablecerse, v. recover, get well.
restar, v. remain; subtract.
restauración, f. restoration.
restaurante, m. restaurant.
restaurar, v. restore.
restitución, f. restitution.
restituir, v. restore, give back.
resto, m. remainder, rest; (pl.) remains.
restorán, m. restaurant.
restregar, v. scrape.
restricción, f. restriction.
restrictivo, a. restrictive.
restringir, v. restrict, curtail.
resucitar, v. resuscitate; resurrect.
resuelto, a. resolute.
resultado, m. result.
resultar, v. result; turn out; ensue.
resumen, m. résumé, summary, **en r.**, in brief.
resumir, v. sum up.
resurgir, v. resurge, reappear.
resurrección, f. resurrection.
retaguardia, f. rear guard.
retal, m. remnant.
retardar, v. retard, show.
retardo, m. delay.
retención, f. retention.
retener, v. retain, keep, withhold.
reticencia, f. reticence.
reticente, a. reticent.
retirada, f. retreat, retirement.
retirar, v. retire, retreat, withdraw.
retiro, m. retirement.
retorcer, v. wring.
retórica, f. rhetoric.
retórico, a. rhetorical.
retorno, m. return.
retozo, m. frolic, romp. —**retozar**, v.
retozón, a. frisky.
retracción, f. retraction.
retractor, v. retract.
retrasar, v. delay, set back; be slow.
retraso, m. delay, lag, slowness.
retratar, v. portray; photograph.
retrato, m. portrait, picture; photograph.
retreta, f. (mil.) retreat.
retrete, m. alcove; toilet.
retribución, f. retribution.
retroactivo, a. retroactive.
retroalimentación, f. feedback.
retroceder, v. recede, go back, draw back, back up.
retumbar, v. resound, rumble.
reumático, a. rheumatic.
reumatismo, m. rheumatism.
reunión, f. gathering, meeting, party; reunion.
reunir, v. gather, collect, bring together.
reunirse, v. meet, assemble, get together.
revelación, f. revelation.
revelar, v. reveal, betray; (phot.) develop.

reventa, f. resale.
reventar, v. burst; split apart.
reventón, m. blowout (of tire).
reverencia, f. reverence.
reverendo, a. reverend.
reverente, a. reverent.
revertir, v. revert.
revés, m. reverse; back, wrong side. **al r.**, just the opposite; inside out.
revisar, v. revise; review.
revisión, f. revision.
revista, f. magazine, periodical; review.
revivir, v. revive.
revocación, f. revocation.
revocar, v. revoke, reverse.
revolotear, v. hover.
revolución, f. revolution.
revolucionario -ria, a. & n. revolutionary.
revolver, v. revolve; stir, agitate.
revólver, m. revolver, pistol.
revuelta, f. revolt; turn.
rey, m. king.
reyerta, f. quarrel, wrangle.
rezar, v. pray.
rezongar, v. grumble; mutter.
ría, f. estuary.
riachuelo, m. creek.
riba, f. embankment.
rico, a. rich, wealthy; delicious.
ridículamente, adv. ridiculously.
ridiculizar, v. ridicule.
ridículo, a. & m. ridiculous; ridicule.
riego, m. irrigation.
rienda, f. rein.
riesgo, m. risk, gamble.
rifa, f. raffle; lottery; scuffle.
rifle, m. rifle.
rígidamente, adv. rigidly.
rigidez, f. rigidity.
rígido, a. rigid, stiff.
rigor, m. rigor.
riguroso, a. rigorous, strict.
rima, f. rhyme. —**rimar**, v.
rincón, m. corner, nook.
rinoceronte, m. rhinoceros.
riña, f. quarrel, feud.
riñón, m. kidney.
río, m. river.
ripio, m. debris.
riqueza, f. wealth.
risa, f. laugh; laughter.
risco, m. cliff.
risibilidad, f. risibility.
risotada, f. peal of laughter.
risueño, a. cheerful, smiling.
rítmico, a. rhythmical.
ritmo, m. rhythm.
rito, m. rite.
ritual, a. & m. ritual.
rivalidad, f. rivalry.
rivera, f. brook.
rizado, a. curly.
rizo, m. curl. —**rizar**, v.
robar, v. rob, steal.
roble, m. oak.
roblón, m. rivet. —**roblar**, v.
robo, m. robbery, theft.
robustamente, adv. robustly.

robusto, a. robust.
roca, f. rock; cliff.
rociada, f. spray, sprinkle. —**rociar**, v.
rocío, m. dew.
rodar, v. roll; roam.
rodear, v. surround, encircle.
rodeo, m. turn, winding; roundup.
rodilla, f. knee.
rodillo, m. roller.
rodio, m. rhodium.
rododendro, m. rhododendron.
roedor, m. rodent.
roer, v. gnaw.
rogación, f. request, entreaty.
rogar, v. beg, plead with, supplicate.
rojizo, a. reddish.
rojo, a. red.
rollo, m. roll; coil.
romadizo, m. head cold.
romance, m. romance, ballad.
románico, a. Romance.
romano -na, a. & n. Roman.
romántico, a. romantic.
romería, f. pilgrimage; picnic.
romero -ra, n. pilgrim.
rompecabezas, m. puzzle (pastime).
romper, v. break, smash, shatter; sever; tear.
rompible, a. breakable.
ron, m. rum.
roncar, v. snore.
ronco, a. hoarse.
ronda, f. round.
rondar, v. prowl.
ronquido, m. snore.
ronzal, m. halter.
roña, f. scab; filth.
ropa, f. clothes, clothing. **r. blanca**, linen. **r. interior**, underwear.
ropero, m. closet.
rosa, f. rose. **r. náutica**, compass.
rosado, a. pink, rosy.
rosal, m. rose bush.
rosario, m. rosary.
rosbif, m. roast beef.
rosca, f. thread (of screw).
róseo, a. rosy.
rostro, m. face, countenance.
rota, f. defeat; (naut.) course.
rotación, f. rotation.
rotatorio, a. rotary.
rótulo, m. label. —**rotular**, v.
rotundo, a. round; sonorous.
rotura, f. break, fracture, rupture.
rozar, v. rub against; chafe; graze.
rubí, m. ruby.
rubio -bia, a. & n. blond.
rubor, m. blush; bashfulness.
rúbrica, f. caption; scroll.
rucho, m. donkey.
rudeza, f. rudeness; roughness.
rudimento, m. rudiment.
rudo, a. rude, rough.
rueda, f. wheel.
ruego, m. plea; entreaty.
rufián, m. ruffian.
rufo, a. sandy (colored).

rugir, *v.* bellow, roar.
rugoso, *a.* wrinkled.
ruibarbo, *m.* rhubarb.
ruido, *m.* noise.
ruidoso, *a.* noisy.
ruina, *f.* ruin, wreck.
ruinar, *v.* ruin, destroy.
ruinoso, *a.* ruinous.
ruiseñor, *m.* nightingale.
ruleta, *f.* roulette.
rumba, *f.* rumba (dance or music).
rumbo, *m.* course, direction.
rumor, *m.* rumor; murmur.
runrún, *m.* rumor.
ruptura, *f.* rupture, break.
rural, *a.* rural.
Rusia, *f.* Russia.
ruso -sa, *a. & n.* Russian.
rústico -ca, *a. & n.* rustic. **en r.,** paperback *f.*
ruta, *f.* route.
rutina, *f.* routine.
rutinario, *a.* routine.

S

sábado, *m.* Saturday.
sábalo, *m.* shad.
sábana, *f.* sheet.
sabañón, *m.* chilblain.
saber, 1. *m.* knowledge. **2.** *v.* know; learn, find out; know how to; taste. **a s.,** namely, to wit.
sabiduría, *f.* wisdom; learning.
sabio, 1. *a.* wise; scholarly. **2.** *m.* sage; scholar.
sable, *m.* saber.
sabor, *m.* flavor, taste, savor.
saborear, *v.* savor, relish.
sabotaje, *m.* sabotage.
sabroso, *a.* savory, tasty.
sabueso, *m.* hound.
sacacorchos, *m.* corkscrew.
sacar, *v.* draw out; take out; take.
sacerdocio, *m.* priesthood.
sacerdote, *m.* priest.
saciar, *v.* satiate.
saco, *m.* sack, bag, pouch; suit coat, jacket.
sacramento, *m.* sacrament.
sacrificio, *m.* sacrifice. **—sacrificar,** *v.*
sacrilegio, *m.* sacrilege.
sacristán, *m.* sexton.
sacro, *a.* sacred, holy.
sacrosanto, *a.* sacrosanct.
sacudir, *v.* shake, jerk, jolt.
sádico, *a.* sadistic.
sadismo, *m.* sadism.
sagacidad, *f.* sagacity.
sagaz, *a.* sagacious, sage.
sagrado, *a.* sacred, holy.
sal, *f.* salt; (coll.) wit.
sala, *f.* room; living room, parlor; hall, auditorium.
salado, *a.* salted, salty; (coll.) witty.
salar, *v.* salt; steep in brine.
salario, *m.* salary, wages.
salchicha, *f.* sausage.

saldo, *m.* remainder, balance; (bargain) sale.
salero, *m.* salt shaker.
salida, *f.* exit, outlet; departure.
salir, *v.* go out, come out; set out, leave, start; turn out, result.
salirse de, *v.* get out of. **s. con la suya,** have one's own way.
salitre, *m.* saltpeter.
saliva, *f.* saliva.
salmo, *m.* psalm.
salmón, *m.* salmon.
salmuera, *f.* pickle; brine.
salobre, *a.* salty.
salón, *m.* parlor, living room; hall.
salpicar, *v.* spatter, splash.
salpullido, *m.* rash.
salsa, *f.* sauce; gravy.
saltamontes, *m.* grasshopper.
salteador, *m.* highwayman.
salto, *m.* jump, leap, spring. **—saltar,** *v.*
saltón, *m.* grasshopper.
salubre, *a.* salubrious, healthful.
salubridad, *f.* health.
salud, *f.* health.
saludable, *a.* healthful, wholesome.
saludar, *v.* greet; salute.
saludo, *m.* greeting; salutation; salute.
salutación, *f.* salutation.
salva, *f.* salvo.
salvación, *f.* salvation; deliverance.
salvador -ra, *n.* savior; rescuer.
salvaguardia, *m.* safeguard.
salvaje, *a. & m.* savage, wild (man).
salvamento, *m.* salvation; rescue.
salvar, *v.* save; salvage; rescue; jump over.
salvavidas, *m.* life preserver.
salvia, *f.* sage (plant).
salvo, 1. *a.* safe. **2.** *prep.* except, save (for). **s. que,** unless.
San, *title.* Saint.
sanar, *v.* heal, cure.
sanatorio, *m.* sanatorium.
sanción, *f.* sanction. **—sancionar,** *v.*
sandalia, *f.* sandal.
sandez, *f.* stupidity.
sandía, *f.* watermelon.
saneamiento, *m.* sanitation.
sangrar, *v.* bleed.
sangre, *f.* blood.
sangriento, *a.* bloody.
sanguinario, *a.* bloodthirsty.
sanidad, *f.* health.
sanitario, *a.* sanitary.
sano, *a.* healthy, sound, sane; healthful, wholesome.
santidad, *f.* sanctity, holiness.
santificar, *v.* sanctify.
santo -ta, 1. *a.* holy, saintly. **2.** *m.* saint.
Santo -ta, *title.* Saint.
santuario, *m.* sanctuary, shrine.

saña, *f.* rage, anger.
sapiente, *a.* wise.
sapo, *m.* toad.
saquear, *v.* sack, ransack, plunder.
sarampión, *m.* measles.
sarape, *m.* (Mex.) woven blanket; shawl.
sarcasmo, *m.* sarcasm.
sarcástico, *a.* sarcastic.
sardina, *f.* sardine.
sargento, *m.* sergeant.
sarna, *f.* itch.
sartén, *m.* frying pan.
sastre, *m.* tailor.
satánico, *a.* satanic.
satélite, *m.* satellite.
sátira, *f.* satire.
satírico, *a. & m.* satirical; satirist.
satirizar, *v.* satirize.
sátiro, *m.* satyr.
satisfacción, *f.* satisfaction.
satisfacer, *v.* satisfy.
satisfactorio, *a.* satisfactory.
saturación, *f.* saturation.
saturar, *v.* saturate.
sauce, *m.* willow.
savia, *f.* sap.
saxófono, *m.* saxophone.
saya, *f.* skirt.
sazón, *f.* season; seasoning. **a la s.,** at that time.
sazonar, *v.* flavor, season.
se, *pron.* -self, -selves.
seca, *f.* drought.
secante, *a.* **papel s.,** blotting paper.
secar, *v.* dry.
sección, *f.* section.
seco, *a.* dry; curt.
secreción, *f.* secretion.
secretar, *v.* secrete.
secretaría, *f.* secretary's office; secretariat.
secretario -ra, *n.* secretary.
secreto, *a. & m.* secret.
secta, *f.* denomination, sect.
secuela, *f.* result; sequel.
secuestrar, *v.* abduct, kidnap; hijack.
secuestro, *m.* abduction, kidnapping.
secular, *a.* secular.
secundario, *a.* secondary.
sed, *f.* thirst. **tener s., estar con s.,** to be thirsty.
seda, *f.* silk.
sedar, *v.* quiet, allay.
sedativo, *a. & m.* sedative.
sede, *f.* seat, headquarters.
sedentario, *a.* sedentary.
sedición, *f.* sedition.
sedicioso, *a.* seditious.
sediento, *a.* thirsty.
sedimento, *m.* sediment.
sedoso, *a.* silky.
seducir, *v.* seduce.
seductivo, *a.* seductive, alluring.
segar, *v.* reap, harvest; mow.
seglar, *m.* layman.
segmento, *m.* segment.
segregar, *v.* segregate.

seguida, *f.* succession. **en s.**, right away, at once.

seguido, *a.* consecutive.

seguir, *v.* follow; continue, keep on, go on.

según, **1.** *prep.* according to, **2.** *conj.* as.

segundo, *a.* & *m.* second. **—segundar**, *v.*

seguridad, *f.* safety; security; assurance.

seguro, **1.** *a.* safe, secure; sure, certain. **2.** *m.* insurance.

seis, *a.* & *pron.* six.

seiscientos, *a.* & *pron.* six hundred.

selección, *f.* selection, choice.

seleccionar, *v.* select, choose.

selecto, *a.* select, choice, elite.

selva, *f.* forest; jungle.

selvoso, *a.* sylvan.

sello, *m.* seal; stamp. **—sellar**, *v.*

semáforo, *m.* semaphore.

semana, *f.* week.

semanal, *a.* weekly.

semántica, *f.* semantics.

semblante, *m.* look, expression.

sembrado, *m.* sown field.

sembrar, *v.* sow, seed.

semejante, **1.** *a.* like, similar; such (a). **2.** *m.* fellowman.

semejanza, *f.* similarity, likeness.

semejar, *v.* resemble.

semilla, *f.* seed.

seminario, *m.* seminary.

senado, *m.* senate.

senador -ra, *n.* senator.

sencillez, *f.* simplicity; naturalness.

sencillo, *a.* simple, natural; single.

senda, *f.* **sendero**, *m.* path.

senectud, *f.* old age.

senil, *a.* senile.

seno, *m.* breast, bosom.

sensación, *f.* sensation.

sensacional, *a.* sensational.

sensato, *a.* sensible, wise.

sensibilidad, *f.* sensibility; sensitiveness.

sensible, *a.* sensitive; emotional.

sensitivo, *a.* sensitive.

sensual, *a.* sensual.

sensualidad, *f.* sensuality.

sentar, *v.* seat. **s. bien**, fit well, be becoming.

sentarse, *v.* sit, sit down.

sentencia, *f.* (court) sentence.

sentidamente, *adv.* feelingly.

sentido, *m.* meaning, sense; consciousness.

sentimental, *a.* sentimental.

sentimiento, *m.* sentiment, feeling.

sentir, *v.* feel, sense; hear; regret, be sorry.

seña, *f.* sign, indication; (*pl.*) address.

señal, *f.* sign, signal; mark.

señalar, *v.* designate, point out; mark.

señor, *m.* gentleman; lord; (title) Mr., Sir.

señora, *f.* lady; wife; (title) Mrs., Madam.

señorita, *f.* young lady; (title) Miss.

sépalo, *m.* sepal.

separación, *f.* separation, parting.

separadamente, *adv.* separately.

separado, *a.* separate. **—separar**, *v.*

septentrional, *a.* northern.

septiembre, *m.* September.

séptimo, *a.* seventh.

sepulcro, *m.* sepulcher.

sepultar, *v.* bury, entomb.

sepultura, *f.* grave.

sequedad, *f.* dryness.

sequía, *f.* drought.

ser, *v.* be.

serenata, *f.* serenade.

serenidad, *f.* serenity.

sereno, **1.** *a.* serene, calm. **2.** *m.* dew; watchman.

serie, *f.* series, sequence.

seriedad, *f.* seriousness.

serio, *a.* serious. **en s.**, seriously.

sermón, *m.* sermon.

seroso, *a.* watery.

serpiente, *f.* serpent, snake.

serrano, *m.* mountaineer.

serrar, *v.* saw.

serrín, *m.* sawdust.

servicial, *a.* helpful, of service.

servicio, *m.* service; toilet.

servidor -ra, *n.* servant.

servidumbre, *f.* bondage; staff of servants.

servil, *a.* servile, menial.

servilleta, *f.* napkin.

servir, *v.* serve. **s. para**, be good for.

servirse, *v.* help oneself.

sesenta, *a.* & *pron.* sixty.

sesgo, *m.* slant. **—sesgar**, *v.*

sesión, *f.* session; sitting.

seso, *m.* brain.

seta, *f.* mushroom.

setecientos, *a.* & *pron.* seven hundred.

setenta, *a.* & *pron.* seventy.

seto, *m.* hedge.

severamente, *adv.* severely.

severidad, *f.* severity.

severo, *a.* severe, strict, stern.

sexismo, *m.* sexism.

sexista, *m.* & *a.* sexist.

sexo, *m.* sex.

sexto, *a.* sixth.

sexual, *a.* sexual.

si, *conj.* if; whether.

sí, **1.** *pron.* -self, -selves. **2.** *interj.* yes.

sicómoro, *m.* sycamore.

sidra, *f.* cider.

siempre, *adv.* always. **para s.**, forever. **s. que**, whenever; provided that.

sierra, *f.* saw; mountain range.

siervo, *m.* slave; serf.

siesta, *f.* (afternoon) nap.

siete, *a.* & *pron.* seven.

sifón, *m.* siphon; siphon bottle.

siglo, *m.* century.

signatura, *f.* signature.

significación, *f.* significance.

significado, *m.* meaning.

significante, *a.* significant.

significar, *v.* signify, mean.

significativo, *a.* significant.

signo, *m.* sign, symbol; mark.

siguiente, *a.* following, next.

sílaba, *f.* syllable.

silbar, *v.* whistle; hiss, boo.

silbato, **silbido**, *m.* whistle.

silencio, *m.* silence, stillness.

silenciosamente, *adv.* silently.

silencioso, *a.* silent, still.

silicato, *m.* silicate.

silicio, *m.* silicon.

silueta, *f.* silhouette.

silvestre, *a.* wild, uncultivated. **fauna s.**, wildlife.

silla, *f.* chair; saddle.

sillón, *m.* armchair.

sima, *f.* chasm; cavern.

simbólico, *a.* symbolic.

símbolo, *m.* symbol.

simetría, *f.* symmetry.

simétrico, *a.* symmetrical.

símil, **similar**, *a.* similar, alike.

similitud, *f.* similarity.

simpatía, *f.* congeniality; friendly feeling.

simpático, *a.* likeable, nice, congenial.

simple, *a.* simple.

simpleza, *f.* silliness; trifle.

simplicidad, *f.* simplicity.

simplificación, *f.* simplification.

simplificar, *v.* simplify.

simular, *v.* simulate.

simultáneo, *a.* simultaneous.

sin, *prep.* without.

sinagoga, *f.* synagogue.

sinceridad, *f.* sincerity.

sincero, *a.* sincere.

sincronizar, *v.* synchronize.

sindicato, *m.* syndicate; labor union.

sindroma, *m.* syndrome.

sinfonía, *f.* symphony.

sinfónico, *a.* symphonic.

singular, *a.* & *m.* singular.

siniestro, *a.* sinister, ominous.

sino, *conj.* but.

sinónimo, *m.* synonym.

sinrazón, *f.* wrong, injustice.

sinsabor, *m.* displeasure, distaste.

sintaxis, *f.* syntax.

síntesis, *f.* synthesis.

sintético, *a.* synthetic.

síntoma, *m.* symptom.

siquiera, *adv.* **ni s.**, not even.

sirena, *f.* siren.

sirviente -ta, *n.* servant.

sistema, *m.* system.

sistemático, *a.* systematic.

sistematizar, *v.* systematize.

sitiar, *v.* besiege.

sitio, *m.* site, location, place, spot.

situación, *f.* situation; location.

situar, v. situate; locate.

smoking, m. tuxedo, dinner jacket.

so, prep. under.

soba, f. massage. —sobar, v.

sobaco, m. armpit.

sobaquero, f. armhole.

soberano -na, a. & m. sovereign.

soberbia, f. arrogance.

soberbio, a. superb; arrogant.

soborno, m. bribe. —sobornar, v.

sobra, f. excess, surplus. de sobra, to spare.

sobrado, m. attic.

sobrante, a. & m. surplus.

sobre, 1. prep. about; above, over. 2. m. envelope.

sobrecama, f. bedspread.

sobrecargo, m. supercargo.

sobredicho, a. aforesaid.

sobrehumano, a. superhuman.

sobrenatural, a. supernatural, weird.

sobrepasar, v. surpass.

sobresalir, v. excel.

sobretodo, m. overcoat.

sobrevivir, v. survive, outlive.

sobriedad, f. sobriety; moderation.

sobrina, f. niece.

sobrino, m. nephew.

sobrio, a. sober, temperate.

socarrén, m. eaves.

sociable, a. sociable.

social, a. social.

socialismo, m. socialism.

socialista, a. & m. socialistic; socialist.

sociedad, f. society; association.

socio -cia, n. associate, partner; member.

sociología, f. sociology.

socorro, m. help, aid. —socorrer, v.

soda, f. soda.

sodio, m. sodium.

sofá, m. sofa, couch.

sofisma, m. sophism.

sofista, m. sophist.

sofocación, f. suffocation.

sofocar, v. smother, suffocate, stifle, choke.

soga, f. rope.

soja, f. soybean.

sol, m. sun.

solada, f. dregs.

solanera, f. sunbath.

solapa, f. lapel.

solar. 1. a. solar. 2. m. building lot.

solaz, m. solace, comfort. —solazar, v.

soldado, m. soldier.

soldar, v. solder, weld.

soledad, f. solitude, privacy.

solemne, a. solemn.

solemnemente, adv. solemnly.

solemnidad, f. solemnity.

soler, v. be in the habit of.

solicitador, m. solicitor.

solicitar, v. solicit; apply for.

solícito, a. solicitous.

solicitud, f. solicitude; application.

sólidamente, adv. solidly.

solidaridad, f. solidarity.

solidez, f. solidity.

solidificar, v. solidify.

sólido, a. & m. solid.

soliloquio, m. soliloquy.

solitario, a. solitary, lone.

solo, 1. a. only; single; alone; lonely. a solas, alone. 2. m. solo.

sólo, adv. only, just.

soltar, v. release; loosen.

soltero -ra, a. & n. single, unmarried (person).

soltura, f. poise, ease, facility.

solubilidad, f. solubility.

solución, f. solution.

solucionar, v. solve, settle.

solvente, m. solvent.

sollozo, m. sob. —sollozar, v.

sombra, f. shade; shadow. —sombrear, v.

sombrero, m. hat.

sombrilla, f. parasol.

sombrío, a. somber, bleak, gloomy.

sombroso, a. shady.

someter, v. subject; submit.

somnolencia, f. drowsiness.

son, m. sound. —sonar, v.

sonata, f. sonata.

sondar, v. sound, fathom.

sonido, m. sound.

sonoridad, f. sonority.

sonoro, a. sonorous.

sonrisa, f. smile. —sonreír, v.

sonrojo, m. flush, blush. —sonrojarse, v.

soñador -ra, a. & n. dreamy; dreamer.

soñar, v. dream.

soñoliento, a. sleepy.

sopa, f. soup.

soplar, v. blow.

soplete, m. blowtorch.

soplo, m. breath; puff, gust.

soportar, v. abide, bear, stand.

soprano, m. & f. soprano.

sorbete, m. sherbet.

sorbo, m. sip. —sorber, v.

sordera, f. deafness.

sórdidamente, adv. sordidly.

sordidez, f. sordidness.

sórdido, a. sordid.

sordo, a. deaf; muffled, dull.

sordomudo -da, a. & n. deaf-mute.

sorpresa, f. surprise. —sorprender, v.

sorteo, m. drawing lots; raffle.

sortija, f. ring.

sosa, f. (chem.) soda.

soso, a. dull, insipid, tasteless.

sospecha, f. suspicion.

sospechar, v. suspect.

sospechoso, a. suspicious.

sostén, m. support; brassiere.

sostener, v. hold; support; maintain.

sostenimiento, m. sustenance.

sota, f. jack (in cards).

sótano, m. basement, cellar.

soto, m. grove.

soviet, m. soviet.

soya, f. soybean.

su, a. his, her, its, their, your.

suave, a. smooth; gentle, soft, mild.

suavidad, f. smoothness; gentleness, softness, mildness.

suavizar, v. soften.

subalterno, a. & m. subordinate.

subasta, f. auction.

subconsciencia, f. subconscious.

súbdito -ta, n. subject.

subida, f. ascent, rise.

subilla, f. awl.

subir, v. rise, climb, ascend, mount. s. a, amount to.

súbito, a. sudden.

subjetivo, a. subjective.

subjuntivo, a. & m. subjunctive.

sublimación, f. sublimation.

sublimar, v. elevate; sublimate.

sublime, a. sublime.

submarino, a. & m. submarine.

subordinación, f. subordination.

subordinado, a. & m. subordinate. —subordinar, v.

subrayar, v. underline.

subscribirse, v. subscribe; sign one's name.

subscripción, f. subscription.

subsecuente, a. subsequent.

subsidiario, a. subsidiary.

subsiguiente, a. subsequent.

substancia, f. substance.

substancial, a. substantial.

substantivo, m. substantive, noun.

substitución, f. substitution.

substituir, v. replace; substitute.

substitutivo, a. substitute.

substituto -ta, n. substitute.

substraer, v. subtract.

subterfugio, m. subterfuge.

subterráneo, 1. a. subterranean, underground. 2. m. place underground; subway.

suburbio, m. suburb.

subvención, f. subsidy, grant.

subversión, f. subversion.

subversivo, a. subversive.

subvertir, v. subvert.

subyugación, f. subjugation.

subyugar, v. subjugate, quell.

succión, f. suction.

suceder, v. happen, occur, befall. s. a, succeed, follow.

sucesión, f. succession.

sucesivo, a. successive. en lo s., in the future.

suceso, m. event.

sucesor -ra, n. successor.

suciedad, f. filth, dirt.

sucio, a. filthy, dirty.

suculento, a. succulent.

sucumbir, v. succumb.

sud, m. south.

sudamericano -na, a. & n. South American.

sudar, v. perspire, sweat.

sudeste, m. southeast.

sudoeste, m. southwest.
sudor, m. perspiration, sweat.
Suecia, f. Sweden.
sueco -ca, a. & n. Swedish; Swede.
suegra, f. mother-in-law.
suegro, m. father-in-law.
suela, f. sole.
sueldo, m. salary, wages.
suelo, m. soil; floor; ground.
suelto, a. loose; free; odd, separate.
sueño, m. sleep; sleepiness; dream. **tener s.,** to be sleepy.
suero, m. serum.
suerte, f. luck; chance; lot.
suéter, m. sweater.
suficiente, a. sufficient.
sufragio, m. suffrage.
sufrimiento, m. suffering, agony.
sufrir, v. suffer; undergo; endure.
sugerencia, f. suggestion.
sugerir, v. suggest.
sugestión, f. suggestion.
sugestionar, v. influence; hypnotize.
suicida, m. & f. suicide (person).
suicidarse, v. commit suicide.
suicidio, m. (act of) suicide.
Suiza, f. Switzerland.
suizo -za, a. & n. Swiss.
sujeción, f. subjection.
sujetar, v. hold, fasten, clip.
sujeto, 1. a. subject, liable. **2.** m. (gram.) subject.
sulfato, m. sulfate.
sulfuro, m. sulfide.
sultán, m. sultan.
suma, f. sum, amount. **en s.,** in short.
sumar, v. add up.
sumaria, f. indictment.
sumario, m. & a. summary.
sumergir, v. submerge.
sumersión, f. submersion.
sumisión, f. submission.
sumiso, a. submissive.
sumo, a. great, high, utmost.
suntuoso, a. sumptuous.
superar, v. overcome, surpass.
superficial, a. superficial, shallow.
superficie, f. surface.
superfluo, a. superfluous.
superhombre, m. superman.
superintendente, m. superintendent.
superior, 1. a. superior; upper, higher. **2.** m. superior.
superioridad, f. superiority.
superlativo, m. & a. superlative.
superstición, f. superstition.
supersticioso, a. superstitious.
supervisar, v. supervise.
supervivencia, f. survival.
suplantar, v. supplant.
suplementario, a. supplementary.
suplemento, m. supplement. — **suplementar,** v.
suplente, a. & m. substitute.

súplica, f. request, entreaty, plea.
suplicación, f. supplication; request, entreaty.
suplicar, v. request, entreat; implore.
suplicio, m. torture, ordeal.
suplir, v. supply.
suponer, v. suppose, pressume, assume.
suposición, f. supposition, assumption.
supremacía, f. supremacy.
supremo, a. supreme.
supresión, f. suppression.
suprimir, v. suppress; abolish.
supuesto, a. supposed. **por s.,** of course.
sur, m. south.
surco, m. furrow. — **surcar,** v.
surgir, v. arise; appear suddenly.
surtido, m. assortment; supply, stock.
surtir, v. furnish, supply.
susceptibilidad, f. susceptibility.
susceptible, a. susceptible.
suscitar, v. stir up.
suscri- = subscri-
suspender, v. withhold; suspend; fail (in a course).
suspensión, f. suspension.
suspenso, m. failing grade. **en s.,** in suspense.
suspicacia, f. suspicion, distrust.
suspicaz, a. suspicious.
suspicazmente, adv. suspiciously.
suspiro, m. sigh. — **suspirar,** v.
sustan- = substan-
sustentar, v. sustain, support.
sustento, m. sustenance, support, living.
susti- = substi-
susto, m. fright, scare.
sustraer = substraer.
susurro, m. rustle; whisper. — **susurrar,** v.
sutil, a. subtle.
sutileza, sutilidad, f. subtlety.
sutura, f. suture.
suyo, a. his, hers, theirs, yours.

T

tabaco, m. tobacco.
tábano, m. horsefly.
taberna, f. tavern, bar.
tabernáculo, m. tabernacle.
tabique, m. dividing wall, partition.
tabla, f. board, plank; table, list.
tablado, m. stage, platform.
tablero, m. panel.
tableta, f. tablet.
tablilla, f. bulletin board.
tabú, m. taboo.
tabular, a. tabular.
tacaño, a. stingy.
tácitamente, adv. tacitly.
tácito, a. tacit.

taciturno, a. taciturn.
taco, m. heel (of shoe); billiard cue.
tacón, m. heel (of shoe).
táctico, a. tactical.
tacto, m. (sense of) touch; tact.
tacha, f. fault, defect.
tachar, v. find fault with; cross out.
tachuela, f. tack.
tafetán, m. taffeta.
taimado, a. sly.
tajada, n. cut, slice, chop. — **tajar,** v.
tajea, f. channel.
tal, a. such. **con t. que.,** provided that. **t. vez,** perhaps.
taladrar, v. drill.
taladro, m. (mech.) drill.
talante, m. humor, disposition.
talco, m. talc.
talega, f. bag, sack.
talento, m. talent.
talón, m. heel (of foot); (baggage) check, stub.
talla, f. engraving; stature; size (of suit).
tallador -ra, n. engraver; dealer (at cards).
talle, m. figure; waist; fit.
taller, m. workshop, factory.
tallo, m. stem, stalk.
tamal, m. tamale.
tamaño, m. size.
tambalear, v. stagger, totter.
también, adv. also, too.
tambor, m. drum.
tamiz, m. sieve, sifter.
tampoco, adv. neither, either.
tan, adv. so.
tanda, f. turn, relay.
tándem, m. tandem bicycle.
tangencia, f. tangency.
tangible, a. tangible.
tango, m. tango (dance or music).
tanque, m. tank.
tanteo, m. estimate. — **tantear,** v.
tanto, 1. a. & pron. so much, so many; as much, as many. **entre t., mientras t.,** meanwhile. **por lo t.,** therefore. **un t.,** somewhat, a bit. **2.** m. point (in games); (pl.) score. **estar al t.,** to be up to date.
tañer, v. play (an instrument); ring (bells).
tapa, f. cap, cover. — **tapar,** v.
tapadero, m. stopper, lid.
tápara, f. caper.
tapete, m. small rug, mat, cover.
tapia, f. wall.
tapicería, f. tapestry.
tapioca, f. tapioca.
tapiz, m. tapestry; carpet.
tapizado (de pared), m. (wall) covering.
tapón, m. plug; cork.
taquigrafía, f. shorthand.
taquilla, f. ticket office; ticket window.
tara, f. hang-up.
tarántula, f. tarantula.

tararear, v. hum.

tardanza, f. delay; lateness.

tardar, v. delay; be late; take (of time). a más t., at the latest.

tarde, 1. adv. late. 2. f. afternoon; early evening.

tardío, a. late, belated.

tarea, f. task, assignment.

tarifa, f. rate; tariff; price list.

tarjeta, f. card.

tarta, f. tart.

tartamudear, v. stammer, falter.

tasa, f. rate.

tasación, f. valuation.

tasar, v. assess, appraise.

tasugo, m. badger.

tautología, f. tautology.

taxi, taxímetro, m. taxi.

taxonomía, f. taxonomy.

taza, f. cup.

te, pron. you; yourself.

té, m. tea.

teátrico, a. theatrical.

teatro, m. theater.

tecla, f. key (of a piano, etc.).

técnica, f. technique.

técnicamente, adv. technically.

técnico, a. technical.

tecnología, f. technology.

techo, m. roof. —techar, v.

tedio, m. tedium, boredom.

tedioso, a. tedious.

teísmo, m. theism.

teja, f. tile.

tejado, m. roof.

tejer, v. weave; knit.

tejido, m. fabric; weaving.

tejón, m. badger.

tela, f. cloth, fabric, web. t. metálica, screen; screening.

telar, m. loom.

telaraña, f. cobweb.

telefonista, m. & f. (telephone) operator.

teléfono, m. telephone. —telefonear, v.

telégrafo, m. telegraph. —telegrafear, v.

telegrama, m. telegram.

telescopio, m. telescope.

televisión, f. television.

telón, m. (theat.) curtain.

telurio, m. tellurium.

tema, m. theme, subject.

temblar, v. tremble, quake; shake, shiver.

temblor, m. tremor; shiver.

temer, v. fear, be afraid of, dread.

temerario, a. rash.

temeridad, f. temerity.

temerosamente, adv. timorously.

temeroso, a. fearful.

temor, m. fear.

témpano, m. kettledrum; iceberg.

temperamento, m. temperament.

temperancia, f. temperance.

temperatura, f. temperature.

tempestad, f. tempest, storm.

tempestuoso, a. tempestuous, stormy.

templado, a. temperate, mild, moderate.

templanza, f. temperance; mildness.

templar, v. temper; tune (an instrument).

templo, m. temple.

temporada, f. season, time, spell.

temporal, temporáneo, a. temporary.

temprano, a. & adv. early.

tenacidad, f. tenacity.

tenaz, a. tenacious, stubborn.

tenazmente, adv. tenaciously.

tendencia, f. tendency, trend.

tender, v. stretch, stretch out.

tendero -ra, n. shopkeeper, storekeeper.

tendón, m. tendon, sinew.

tenebrosidad, f. gloom.

tenebroso, a. dark, gloomy.

tenedor, m. keeper; holder; fork.

tener, v. have; own; hold. t. que, have to, must.

teniente, m. lieutenant.

tenis, m. tennis.

tenor, m. tenor.

tensión, f. tension, stress, strain.

tenso, a. tense.

tentación, f. temptation.

tentáculo, m. tentacle.

tentador, a. alluring, tempting.

tentar, v. tempt, lure; grope, probe.

tentativa, f. attempt.

tentativo, a. tentative.

teñir, v. tint, dye.

teología, f. theology.

teológico, a. theological.

teoría, f. theory.

teórico, a. theoretical.

terapéutico, a. therapeutic.

tercero, a. third.

tercio, m. third.

terciopelo, m. velvet.

terco, a. obstinate, stubborn.

termal, a. thermal.

terminación, f. termination; completion.

terminar, v. terminate, finish.

término, m. term; end.

terminología, f. terminology.

termómetro, m. thermometer.

termos, m. thermos.

ternero -ra, n. calf.

ternura, f. tenderness.

terquedad, f. stubbornness.

terraza, f. terrace.

terremoto, m. earthquake.

terreno, m. 1. a. earthly, terrestrial. 2. m. ground, terrain; lot, plot.

terrible, a. terrible, awful.

terrífico, a. terrific.

territorio, m. territory.

terrón, m. clod, lump; mound.

terror, m. terror.

terso, a. smooth, glossy; terse.

tertulia, f. social gathering, party.

tesis, f. thesis.

tesorería, f. treasury.

tesorero -ra, n. treasurer.

tesoro, m. treasure.

testamento, m. will, testament.

testarudo, a. stubborn.

testificar, v. testify.

testigo, m. witness; testimony.

testimonial, a. testimonal.

testimonio, m. testimony.

teta, f. teat.

tetera, f. teapot.

tétrico, a. sad; gloomy.

texto, m. text.

textura, f. texture.

tez, f. complexion.

ti, pron. you; yourself.

tía, f. aunt.

tibio, a. lukewarm.

tiburón, m. shark.

tiemblo, m. aspen.

tiempo, m. time; weather; (gram.) tense.

tienda, f. shop, store; tent.

tientas, f.pl. andar a t., to grope (in the dark).

tierno, a. tender.

tierra, f. land; ground; earth, dirt, soil.

tieso, a. taut, stiff, hard, strong.

tiesto, m. flower pot.

tiesura, f. stiffness; harshness.

tifo, m. typhus.

tifoideo, f. typhoid fever.

tigre, m. tiger.

tijeras, f.pl. scissors.

tila, f. linden.

timbre, m. seal, stamp; tone; (electric) bell.

tímidamente, adv. timidly.

timidez, f. timidity.

tímido, a. timid, shy.

timón, m. rudder, helm.

tímpano, m. kettledrum; eardrum.

tina, f. tub, vat.

tinaja, f. jar.

tinta, f. ink.

tinte, m. tint, shade.

tintero, m. inkwell.

tinto, a. wine-colored; red (of wine).

tintorería, f. dry cleaning shop.

tintorero -ra, n. dyer; dry cleaner.

tintura, f. tincture; dye.

tiñoso, a. scabby; stingy.

tío, m. uncle.

tiovivo, m. merry-go-round.

típico, a. typical.

tipo, m. type, sort; (interest) rate; (coll.) guy, fellow.

tira, f. strip.

tirabuzón, m. corkscrew.

tirada, f. edition.

tiranía, f. tyranny.

tiránico, a. tyrannical; domineering.

tirano, m. tyrant.

tirante, 1. a. tight, taut; tense. 2. m. (pl.) suspenders.

tirar, v. throw; draw; pull; fire (a weapon).

tiritar, v. shiver.

tiro, m. throw; shot.
tirón, m. pull. **de un t.,** at a stretch, at one stroke.
tísico, n. & a. consumptive.
tisis, f. consumption, tuberculosis.
titania, m. titanium.
títere, m. puppet.
titilación, f. twinkle.
titubear, v. stagger; totter; waver.
titulado, a. entitled; so-called.
titular, 1. a. titular. **2.** v. entitle.
título, m. title, headline.
tiza, f. chalk.
tiznar, v. smudge; stain.
toalla, f. towel.
toalleta, f. small towel.
tobillo, m. ankle.
tocadiscos, m. record player.
tocado, m. hairdo.
tocador, m. boudoir; dressing table.
tocante, a. touching. **t. a,** concerning, relative to.
tocar, v. touch; play (an instrument). **t. a uno,** be one's turn; be up to one.
tocayo, m. namesake.
tocino, m. bacon.
todavía, adv. yet, still.
todo, 1. a. all, whole. **todos los,** every. **2.** pron. all, everything. **con t.,** still, however. **del t.,** wholly; at all.
todopoderoso, a. almighty.
toldo, m. awning.
tolerancia, f. tolerance.
tolerante, a. tolerant.
tolerar, v. tolerate.
toma, f. taking, capture, seizure.
tomaína, f. ptomaine.
tomar, v. take; drink.
tomate, m. tomato.
tomillo, m. thyme.
tomo, m. volume.
tonada, f. tune.
tonel, m. barrel, cask.
tonelada, f. ton.
tonelaje, m. tonnage.
tónico, a. & m. tonic.
tono, m. tone, pitch, shade. **darse t.,** to put on airs.
tonsila, f. tonsil.
tonsilitis, f. tonsilitis.
tontería, f. nonsense, foolishness.
tonto -ta, a. & n. foolish, silly; fool.
topacio, m. topaz.
topar, v. run into. **t. con,** come upon.
tópico, 1. a. topical. **2.** m. topic.
topo, m. mole (animal).
toque, m. touch.
tórax, m. thorax.
torbellino, m. whirlwind.
torcer, v. twist; wind; distort.
toreador, m. toreador.
torero, m. bullfighter.
torio, m. thorium.
tormenta, f. storm.
tormento, m. torment.

tornado, m. tornado.
tornar, v. return; turn.
tornarse en, v. turn into, become.
torneo, m. tournament.
tornillo, m. screw.
toro, m. bull.
toronja, f. grapefruit.
torpe, a. awkward, clumsy; sluggish.
torpedero, m. torpedo boat.
torpedo, m. torpedo.
torre, f. tower.
torrente, m. torrent.
tórrido, a. torrid.
torta, f. cake; loaf.
tortilla, f. omelet; (Mex.) tortilla, pancake.
tórtola, f. dove.
tortuga, f. turtle.
tortuoso, a. tortuous.
tortura, f. torture. **—torturar,** v.
tos, m. cough. **—toser,** v.
tosco, a. coarse, rough, uncouth.
tosquedad, f. coarseness, roughness.
tostar, v. toast; tan.
total, a. & m. total.
totalidad, f. totality, entirety, whole.
totalitario, a. totalitarian.
totalmente, adv. totally; entirely.
tótem, m. totem.
tóxico, a. toxic.
trabajador -ra, 1. a. hardworking. **2.** n. worker.
trabajo, m. work; labor. **—trabajar,** v.
trabar, v. fasten, shackle; grasp; strike up.
tracción, f. traction.
tracto, m. tract.
tractor, m. tractor.
tradición, f. tradition.
tradicional, a. traditional.
traducción, f. translation.
traducir, v. translate.
traductor, m. translator.
traer, v. bring; carry; wear.
tráfico, m. traffic. **—traficar,** v.
tragar, v. swallow.
tragedia, f. tragedy.
trágicamente, adv. tragically.
trágico -ca, 1. a. tragic. **2.** n. tragedian.
trago, m. swallow; drink.
traición, f. treason, betrayal.
traicionar, v. betray.
traidor -ra, a. & n. traitorous; traitor.
traje, m. suit; dress; garb, apparel.
trama, v. plot (of a story).
tramador, m. weaver; plotter.
tramar, v. weave; plot, scheme.
trámite, m. (business) deal, transaction.
tramo, m. span, stretch, section.
trampa, f. trap, snare.
trampista, m. cheater; swindler.

trance, m. critical moment or stage. **a todo t.,** at any cost.
tranco, m. stride.
tranquilidad, f. tranquility, calm, quiet.
tranquilizar, v. quiet, calm down.
tranquilo, a. tranquil, calm, quiet.
transacción, f. transaction.
transbordador, m. ferry.
transcribir, v. transcribe.
transcripción, f. transcription.
transcurrir, v. elapse.
transeúnte, a. & n. transient; passerby.
transexual, a. transsexual.
transferencia, f. transference.
transferir, v. transfer.
transformación, f. transformation.
transformar, v. transform.
transfusión, f. transfusion.
transgresión, f. transgression.
transgresor, m. transgressor.
transición, f. transition.
transigir, v. compromise, settle; agree.
transitivo, a. transitive.
tránsito, m. transit, passage.
transitorio, a. transitory.
transmisión, f. transmission; broadcast.
transmisora, f. broadcasting station.
transmitir, v. transmit; broadcast.
transparencia, f. transparency.
transparente, 1. a. transparent. **2.** m. (window) shade.
transportación, f. transportation.
transportar, v. transport, convey.
transporte, m. transportation; transport.
tranvía, m. streetcar, trolley.
trapacero, n. cheat; swindler.
trapo, m. rag.
tráquea, f. trachea.
tras, prep. after; behind.
trasegar, v. upset, overturn.
trasero, a. rear, back.
traslado, m. transfer. **—trasladar,** v.
traslapo, m. overlap. **—traslapar,** v.
trasnochar, v. sit up all night.
traspalar, v. shovel.
traspasar, v. go beyond; cross; violate; pierce.
trasquilar, v. shear; clip.
trastornar, v. overturn, overthrow, upset.
trastorno, m. overthrow; upheaval.
tratado, m. treaty; treatise.
tratamiento, m. treatment.
tratar, v. treat, handle. **t. de,** deal with; try to; call (a name).
tratarse de, v. be a question of.
trato, m. treatment; manners; (com.) deal.

través, *adv.* **a t. de,** through, across. **de t.,** sideways.
travesía, *f.* crossing; voyage.
travesti, *m.* transvestite.
travestido, *a.* disguised.
travesura, *f.* prank; mischief.
travieso, *a.* naughty, mischievous.
trayectoria, *f.* trajectory.
trazar, *v.* plan, devise; trace; draw.
trazo, *n.* plan, outline; line, stroke.
trébol, *m.* clover.
trece, *a. & pron.* thirteen.
trecho, *m.* space, distance, stretch.
tregua, *f.* truce, respite, lull.
treinta, *a. & pron.* thirty.
tremendo, *a.* tremendous.
tremer, *v.* tremble.
tren, *m.* train.
trenza, *f.* braid. —**trenzar,** *v.*
trepar, *v.* climb, mount.
trepidación, *f.* trepidation.
tres, *a. & pron.* three.
trescientos, *a. & pron.* three hundred.
triángulo, *m.* triangle.
tribu, *f.* tribe.
tribulación, *f.* tribulation.
tribuna, *f.* rostrum, stand; (*pl.*) grandstand.
tribunal, *m.* court, tribunal.
tributario, *a. & m.* tributary.
tributo, *m.* tribute.
triciclo, *m.* tricycle.
trigo, *m.* wheat.
trigonometría, *f.* trigonometry.
trigueño, *a.* swarthy, dark.
trilogía, *f.* trilogy.
trimestral, *a.* quarterly.
trinchar, *v.* carve (meat).
trinchera, *f.* trench, ditch.
trineo, *m.* sled; sleigh.
trinidad, *f.* trinity.
tripa, *f.* tripe, entrails.
triple, *a.* triple. —**triplicar,** *v.*
tripulación, *f.* (ship's) crew.
triste, *a.* sad, sorrowful; dreary.
tristemente, *adv.* sadly.
tristeza, *f.* sadness; gloom.
triunfal, *a.* triumphal.
triunfante, *a.* triumphant.
triunfo, *m.* triumph, trump. —**triunfar,** *v.*
trivial, *a.* trivial, commonplace.
trivialidad, *f.* triviality.
trocar, *v.* exchange, switch; barter.
trofeo, *m.* trophy.
trombón, *m.* trombone.
trompa, trompeta, *f.* trumpet, horn.
tronada, *f.* thunderstorm.
tronar, *v.* thunder.
tronco, *m.* trunk, stump.
trono, *m.* throne.
tropa, *f.* troop.
tropel, *m.* crowd, throng.
tropezar, *v.* trip, stumble. **t. con,** come upon, run into.

trópico, *a. & m.* tropical; tropics.
tropiezo, *m.* stumble; obstacle; slip, error.
trote, *m.* trot. —**trotar,** *v.*
trovador, *m.* troubadour.
trozo, *m.* piece, portion, fragment, selection, passage.
trucha, *f.* trout.
trueco, trueque, *m.* exchange, barter.
trueno, *m.* thunder.
tu, *a.* your.
tú, *pron.* you.
tuberculosis, *f.* tuberculosis.
tubo, *m.* tube, pipe.
tuerca, *f.* (mech.) nut.
tulipán, *m.* tulip.
tumba, *f.* tomb, grave.
tumbar, *v.* knock down.
tumbarse, *v.* tumble.
tumbo, *m.* tumble; somersault.
tumor, *m.* tumor; growth.
tumulto, *m.* tumult, commotion.
tumultuoso, *a.* tumultuous, boisterous.
tunante, *m.* rascal, rogue.
tunda, *f.* spanking, whipping.
túnel, *m.* tunnel.
tungsteno, *m.* tungsten.
túnica, *f.* tunic, robe.
tupir, *v.* pack tight, stuff; stop up.
turbación, *f.* confusion, turmoil.
turbamulta, *f.* mob; crowd.
turbar, *v.* disturb, upset; embarrass.
turbina, *f.* turbine.
turbio, *a.* turbid; muddy.
turco -ca, *a. & n.* Turkish; Turk.
turismo, *m.* touring, (foreign) travel.
turista, *m. & f.* tourist.
turno, *m.* turn; (work) shift.
turquesa, *f.* turquoise.
Turquía, *f.* Turkey.
turrón, *m.* nougat.
tusa, *f.* corncob; corn.
tutear, *v.* use the pronoun **tú,** etc., in addressing a person.
tutela, *f.* guardianship; aegis.
tutor, *m.* tutor; guardian.
tuyo, *a.* your, yours.

U

u, *conj.* or.
ubre, *f.* udder.
ufano, *a.* proud, haughty.
úlcera, *f.* ulcer.
ulterior, *a.* ulterior.
último, *a.* last, final; ultimate; latest. **por ú.,** finally.
ultraje, *m.* outrage. —**ultrajar,** *v.*
umbral, *m.* threshold.
umbroso, *a.* shady.
un, una, *art. & a.* a, an; one; (*pl.*) some.
unánime, *a.* unanimous.
unanimidad, *f.* unanimity.

unción, *f.* unction.
ungüento, *m.* ointment, salve.
único, *a.* only, sole; unique.
unicornio, *m.* unicorn.
unidad, *f.* unit; unity.
unificar, *v.* unify.
uniforme, *a. & m.* uniform.
uniformidad, *f.* uniformity.
unión, *f.* union; joining.
unir, *v.* unite, join.
universal, *a.* universal.
universalidad, *f.* universality.
universidad, *f.* university; college.
universo, *m.* universe.
uno, una, *pron.* one; (*pl.*) some.
untar, *v.* spread; grease; anoint.
uña, *f.* fingernail.
urbanidad, *f.* urbanity; good breeding.
urbano, *a.* urban; urbane; well-bred.
urbe, *f.* large city.
urgencia, *f.* urgency.
urgente, *a.* urgent, pressing. **entrega u.,** special delivery.
urgir, *v.* be urgent.
urna, *f.* urn; ballot box; (*pl.*) polls.
usanza, *f.* usage, custom.
usar, *v.* use; wear.
uso, *m.* use; usage; wear.
usted, *pron.* you.
usual, *a.* usual.
usualmente, *adv.* usually.
usura, *f.* usury.
usurero, *m.* usurer.
usurpación, *f.* usurpation.
usurpar, *v.* usurp.
utensilio, *m.* utensil.
útero, *m.* uterus.
útil, *a.* useful, handy.
utilidad, *f.* utility, usefulness.
utilizar, *v.* use, utilize.
útilmente, *adv.* usefully.
utópico, *a.* utopian.
uva, *f.* grape.

V

vaca, *f.* cow; beef.
vacaciones, *f.pl.* vacation, holidays.
vacancia, *f.* vacancy.
vacante, 1. *a.* vacant. **2.** *f.* vacancy.
vaciar, *v.* empty; pour out.
vacilación, *f.* vacillation, hesitation.
vacilante, *a.* vacillating.
vacilar, *v.* falter, hesitate; waver; stagger.
vacío, 1. *a.* empty. **2.** *m.* void, empty space.
vacuna, *f.* vaccine.
vacunación, *f.* vaccination.
vacunar, *v.* vaccinate.
vacuo, 1. *a.* empty, vacant. **2.** *m.* vacuum.
vadear, *v.* wade through, ford.
vado, *m.* ford.
vagabundo, *a. & m.* vagabond.

vagar, v. wander, rove, roam; loiter.

vago -ga, 1. a. vague, hazy; wandering, vagrant. **2.** n. vagrant, tramp.

vagón, m. railroad car.

vahído, m. dizziness.

vaina, f. sheath; pod.

vainilla, f. vanilla.

vaivén, m. vibration, sway.

vajilla, f. (dinner) dishes.

valentía, f. valor, courage.

valer, 1. m. worth. **2.** v. be worth.

valerse de, v. make use of, avail oneself of.

valía, f. value.

validez, f. validity.

válido, a. valid.

valiente, a. valiant, brave, courageous.

valija, f. valise.

valioso, a. valuable.

valor, m. value, worth; bravery, valor; (pl., com.) securities.

valoración, f. appraisal.

valorar, v. value, appraise.

vals, m. waltz.

valsar, v. waltz.

valuación, f. valuation.

valuar, v. value; rate.

válvula, f. valve.

valla, f. fence, barrier.

valle, m. valley.

vándalo, m. vandal.

vanidad, f. vanity.

vanidoso, a. vain, conceited.

vano, a. vain; inane.

vapor, m. vapor; steam; steamer, steamship.

vaquero, m. cowboy.

vara, f. wand, stick, switch.

varadero, m. shipyard.

varar, v. launch; be stranded; run aground.

variable, a. variable.

variación, f. variation.

variar, v. vary.

variedad, f. variety.

varios, a. & pron. pl. various; several.

varón, m. man; male.

varonil, a. manly, virile.

vasallo, m. vassal.

vasectomía, f. vasectomy.

vasija, f. bowl, container (for liquids).

vaso, m. water glass; vase.

vástago, m. bud, shoot; twig; offspring.

vasto, a. vast.

vecindad, f. **vecindario,** m. neighborhood, vicinity.

vecino -na, a. & n. neighboring; neighbor.

vedar, v. forbid; impede.

vega, f. meadow.

vegetación, f. vegetation.

vegetal, m. vegetable.

vehemente, a. vehement.

vehículo, m. vehicle; conveyance.

veinte, a. & pron. twenty.

vejez, f. old age.

vejiga, f. bladder.

vela, f. vigil, watch; candle; sail.

velar, v. stay up, sit up; watch over.

velo, m. veil.

velocidad, f. velocity, speed; rate.

velomotor, m. motorbike, moped.

veloz, a. speedy, fast, swift.

vellón, m. fleece.

velloso, a. hairy; fuzzy.

velludo, a. downy.

vena, f. vein.

venado, m. deer.

vencedor -ra, n. victor.

vencer, v. defeat, overcome, conquer; (com.) become due, expire.

vencimiento, m. defeat.

venda, f. **vendaje,** m. bandage. —**vendar,** v.

vendedor -ra, n. seller, trader; sales clerk.

vender, v. sell.

vendimia, f. vintage.

veneno, m. poison.

venenoso, a. poisonous.

veneración, f. veneration.

venerar, v. venerate, revere.

venero, m. spring, origin.

véneto, a. Venetian.

venezolano, a. & n. Venezuelan.

vengador, m. avenger.

venganza, f. vengeance, revenge.

vengar, v. avenge.

venida, f. arrival, advent, coming.

venidero, a. future; coming.

venir, v. come.

venta, f. sale; sales.

ventaja, f. advantage; profit.

ventajoso, a. advantageous; profitable.

ventana, f. window.

ventero, m. innkeeper.

ventilación, f. ventilation.

ventilador, m. ventilator, fan.

ventilar, v. ventilate, air.

ventoso, a. windy.

ventura, f. venture; happiness; luck.

ver, v. see. **tener que v. con,** have to do with.

vera, f. edge.

veracidad, f. truthfulness, veracity.

verano, m. summer. —**veranear,** v.

veras, f.pl. **de v.,** really, truly.

veraz, a. truthful.

verbigracia, adv. for example.

verbo, m. verb.

verboso, a. verbose.

verdad, f. truth. **ser v.,** to be true.

verdadero, a. true, real.

verde, a. green; risqué, off-color.

verdor, m. greenness, verdure.

verdugo, m. hangman.

verdura, f. verdure, vegetation; (pl.) vegetables.

vereda, f. path.

veredicto, m. verdict.

vergonzoso, a. shameful, embarrassing; shy, bashful.

vergüenza, f. shame; disgrace; embarrassment.

verificar, v. verify, check.

verja, f. grating, railing.

verosímil, a. likely, plausible.

verraco, m. boar.

verruga, f. wart.

versátil, a. versatile.

verse, v. look, appear.

versión, f. version.

verso, m. verse, stanza; line (of poetry).

verter, v. pour, spill; shed; empty.

vertical, a. vertical.

vertiente, f. slope; watershed.

vertiginoso, a. dizzy.

vértigo, m. vertigo, dizziness.

vestíbulo, m. vestibule, lobby.

vestido, m. dress; clothing.

vestigio, m. vestige, trace.

vestir, v. dress, clothe.

veterano -na, a. & n. veteran.

veterinario, m. veterinary.

veto, m. veto.

vetusto, a. ancient, very old.

vez, f. time; turn. **tal v.,** perhaps. **a la v.,** at the same time. **en v. de,** instead of. **una v.,** once. **otra v.,** again.

vía, f. track; route, way.

viaducto, m. viaduct.

viajante, a. & n. traveling; traveler.

viajar, v. travel; journey, tour.

viaje, m. trip, journey, voyage; (pl.) travels.

viajero -ra, n. traveler; passenger.

viandas, f.pl. victuals, food.

víbora, f. viper.

vibración, f. vibration.

vibrar, v. vibrate.

vicepresidente, m. vice president.

vicio, m. vice.

vicioso, a. vicious; licentious.

víctima, f. victim.

victoria, f. victory.

victorioso, a. victorious.

vid, f. grapevine.

vida, f. life; living.

vídeo, m. videotape.

videodisco, m. videodisc.

vidrio, m. glass.

viejo -ja, a. & n. old; old person.

viento, m. wind. **hacer v.,** to be windy.

vientre, m. belly.

viernes, m. Friday.

viga, f. beam, rafter.

vigente, a. in effect (prices, etc.).

vigilante, a. & m. vigilant, watchful; watchman.

vigilar, v. guard, watch over.

vigilia, f. vigil, watchfulness; (rel.) fast.

vigor, *m.* vigor. **en v.,** in effect, in force.

vil, *a.* vile, low, contemptible.

vileza, *f.* baseness; vileness.

villa, *f.* town; country house.

villancico, *m.* Christmas carol.

villanía, *f.* villainy.

villano, *m.* boor.

vinagre, *m.* vinegar.

vínculo, *m.* link. **—vincular,** *v.*

vindicar, *v.* vindicate.

vino, *m.* wine.

viña, *f.* vineyard.

violación, *f.* violation.

violar, *v.* violate.

violencia, *f.* violence.

violento, *a.* violent; impulsive.

violeta, *f.* violet.

violín, *m.* violin.

violón, *m.* bass viol.

virar, *v.* veer, change course.

virgen, *f.* virgin.

viril, *a.* virile, manly.

virilidad, *f.* virility; manhood.

virtual, *a.* virtual.

virtud, *f.* virtue; efficacy, power.

virtuoso, *a.* virtuous.

viruela, *f.* smallpox.

visa, *f.* visa.

visaje, *m.* grimace.

visera, *f.* visor.

visible, *a.* visible.

visión, *f.* vision.

visionario -ria, *a. & n.* visionary.

visita, *f.* visit; visitor, caller.

visitación, *f.* visitation.

visitante, *a. & n.* visiting; visitor.

visitar, *v.* visit; inspect, examine.

vislumbre, *m.* glimpse.

viso, *m.* looks; outlook.

víspera, *f.* eve, day before.

vista, *f.* view; scene; sight.

vistazo, *m.* glance, glimpse.

vistoso, *a.* beautiful; showy.

visual, *a.* visual.

vital, *a.* vital.

vitalidad, *f.* vitality.

vitamina, *f.* vitamin.

vitando, *a.* hateful.

vituperar, *v.* vituperate; revile.

viuda, *f.* widow.

viudo, *m.* widower.

vivaz, *a.* vivacious, buoyant; clever.

víveres, *m.pl.* provisions.

viveza, *f.* animation, liveliness.

vívido, *a.* vivid, bright.

vivienda, *f.* (living) quarters, dwelling.

vivificar, *v.* vivify, enliven.

vivir, *v.* live.

vivo, *a.* live, alive, living; vivid; animated, brisk.

vocablo, *m.* word.

vocabulario, *m.* vocabulary.

vocación, *f.* vocation, calling.

vocal, 1. *a.* vocal. **2.** *f.* vowel.

vocear, *v.* vociferate.

vodevil, *m.* vaudeville.

volante, 1. *a.* flying. **2.** *m.* memorandum; (steering) wheel.

volar, *v.* fly; explode.

volcán, *m.* volcano.

volcar, *v.* upset, capsize.

voltear, *v.* turn, whirl; overturn.

voltio, *m.* volt.

volumen, *m.* volume.

voluminoso, *a.* voluminous.

voluntad, *f.* will.

voluntario -ria, *a. & n.* voluntary; volunteer.

voluntarioso, *a.* willful.

volver, *v.* turn; return, go back, come back. **v. a hacer** (etc.), do (etc.) again.

volverse, *v.* turn around; turn, become.

vómito, *m.* vomit. **—vomitar,** *v.*

voracidad, *f.* voracity; greed.

voraz, *a.* greedy, ravenous.

vórtice, *m.* whirlpool.

vosotros -as, *pron.pl.* you; yourselves.

votación, *f.* voting, vote.

voto, *m.* vote; vow. **—votar,** *v.*

voz, *f.* voice; word. **a voces,** by shouting. **en v. alta,** aloud.

vuelco, *m.* upset.

vuelo, *m.* flight. **v. libre,** hang gliding.

vuelta, *f.* turn, bend; return. **a la v. de,** around. **dar una v.,** to take a walk.

vuestro, *a.* your, yours.

vulgar, *a.* vulgar, common.

vulgaridad, *f.* vulgarity.

vulgo, *m.* (the) masses, (the) common people.

vulnerable, *a.* vulnerable.

Y, Z

y, *conj.* and.

ya, *adv.* already; now; at once. **y. no,** no longer, any more. **y. que,** since.

yacer, *v.* lie.

yanqui, *a. & n.* North American.

yate, *m.* yacht.

yegua, *f.* mare.

yelmo, *m.* helmet.

yema, *f.* yolk (of an egg).

yerba, *f.* grass; herb.

yerno, *m.* son-in-law.

yerro, *m.* error, mistake.

yeso, *m.* plaster.

yo, *pron.* I.

yodo, *m.* iodine.

yoduro, *m.* iodide.

yugo, *m.* yoke.

yunque, *m.* anvil.

yunta, *f.* team (of animals).

zafarse, *v.* run away, escape. **z. de,** get rid of.

zafio, *a.* coarse, uncivil.

zafiro, *m.* sapphire.

zaguán, *m.* vestibule, hall.

zalamero -ra, *n.* flatterer, wheedler.

zambullir, *v.* plunge, dive.

zanahoria, *f.* carrot.

zanja, *f.* ditch, trench.

zapatería, *f.* shoe store; shoemaker's shop.

zapatero, *m.* shoemaker.

zapato, *m.* shoe.

zar, *m.* czar.

zaraza, *f.* calico; chintz.

zarza, *f.* bramble.

zarzuela, *f.* musical comedy.

zodíaco, *m.* zodiac.

zona, *f.* zone.

zoología, *f.* zoology.

zoológico, *a.* zoological.

zorro -rra, *n.* fox.

zozobra, *f.* worry, anxiety; capsizing.

zozobrar, *v.* capsize.

zumba, *f.* spanking.

zumbido, *m.* buzz, hum. **—zumbar,** *v.*

zumo, *m.* juice, sap.

zurcir, *v.* darn, mend.

zurdo, *a.* left-handed.

zurrar, *v.* flog, drub.

English-Spanish

A

a, *art.* un, una.
abacus, *n.* ábaco *m.*
abandon, 1. *n.* desenfreno, abandono *m.* 2. *v.* abandonar, desamparar.
abandoned, *a.* abandonado.
abandonment, *n.* abandono, desamparo *m.*
abase, *v.* degradar, humillar.
abasement, *n.* degradación, humillación *f.*
abash, *v.* avergonzar.
abate, *v.* menguar, moderarse.
abatement, *n.* disminución *f.*
abbess, *n.* abadesa *f.*
abbey, *n.* abadía *f.*
abbot, *n.* abad *m.*
abbreviate, *v.* abreviar.
abbreviation, *n.* abreviatura *f.*
abdicate, *v.* abdicar.
abdication, *n.* abdicación *f.*
abdomen, *n.* abdomen *m.*
abdominal, *a.* abdominal.
abduct, *v.* secuestrar.
abduction, *n.* secuestración *f.*
abductor, *n.* secuestrador *m.*
aberrant, *a.* extraviado.
aberration, *n.* error, extravío *m.*
abet, *v.* apoyar, favorecer.
abetment, *n.* apoyo *m.*
abettor, *n.* cómplice *m. & f.*
abeyance, *n.* suspensión *f.*
abhor, *v.* abominar, odiar.
abhorrence, *n.* detestación *f.;* aborrecimiento *m.*
abhorrent, *a.* detestable, aborrecible.
abide, *v.* soportar. **to a. by,** cumplir con.
abiding, *a.* perdurable.
ability, *n.* habilidad *f.*
abject, *a.* abyecto; desanimado.
abjuration, *n.* renuncia *f.*
abjure, *v.* renunciar.
ablative, *a. & n.* (gram.) ablativo *m.*
ablaze, *a.* en llamas.
able, *a.* capaz; competente. **to be a.,** poder.
able-bodied, *a.* robusto.
ablution, *n.* ablución *f.*
ably, *adv.* hábilmente.
abnegate, *v.* repudiar; negar.
abnegation, *n.* abnegación; repudiación *f.*
abnormal, *a.* anormal.
abnormality, *n.* anormalidad, deformidad *f.*
abnormally, *adv.* anormalmente.
aboard, *adv.* a bordo.
abode, *n.* residencia *f.*
abolish, *v.* suprimir.
abolishment, *n.* abolición *f.*
abolition, *n.* abolición *f.*
abominable, *a.* abominable.
abominate, *v.* abominar, detestar.

abomination, *n.* abominación; enormidad *f.*
aboriginal, *a.* primitivo.
abortion, *n.* aborto *m.*
abortive, *a.* abortivo.
abound, *v.* abundar.
about, 1. *adv.* como. **about to,** para; a punto de. 2. *prep.* de, sobre, acerca de.
about-face, *n.* (mil.) media vuelta.
above, 1. *adv.* arriba. 2. *prep.* sobre; por encima de.
aboveboard, *a. & adv.* sincero, franco.
abrasion, *n.* raspadura *f.;* (med.) abrasión *f.*
abrasive, 1. *a.* raspante. 2. *n.* abrasivo *m.*
abreast, *adv.* de frente.
abridge, *v.* abreviar.
abridgment, *n.* abreviación *f.;* compendio *m.*
abroad, *adv.* en el extranjero, al extranjero.
abrogate, *v.* abrogar, revocar.
abrogation, *n.* abrogación, revocación *f.*
abrupt, *a.* repentino; brusco.
abruptly, *adv.* bruscamente, precipitadamente.
abruptness, *n.* precipitación; brusquedad *f.*
abscess, *n.* absceso *m.*
abscond, *v.* fugarse.
absence, *n.* ausencia, falta *f.*
absent, *a.* ausente.
absentee, *a. & n.* ausente *m.*
absent-minded, *a.* distraído.
absinthe, *n.* absenta *f.*
absolute, *a.* absoluto.
absolutely, *adv.* absolutamente.
absoluteness, *n.* absolutismo *m.*
absolution, *n.* absolución *f.*
absolutism, *n.* absolutismo, despotismo *m.*
absolve, *v.* absolver.
absorb, *v.* absorber; preocupar.
absorbed, *a.* absorbido; absorto.
absorbent, *a.* absorbente.
absorbing, *a.* interesante.
absorption, *n.* absorción; preocupación *f.*
abstain, *v.* abstenerse.
abstemious, *a.* abstemio, sobrio.
abstinence, *n.* abstinencia *f.*
abstract, 1. *n.* resumen *m.* 2. *v.* abstraer.
abstracted, *a.* distraído.
abstraction, *n.* abstracción *f.*
abstruse, *a.* abstruso.
absurd, *a.* absurdo, ridículo.
absurdity, *n.* absurdo *m.*
absurdly, *adv.* absurdamente.
abundance, *n.* abundancia *f.*
abundant, *a.* abundante.
abundantly, *adv.* abundantemente.

abuse, 1. *n.* abuso *m.* 2. *v.* abusar de; maltratar.
abusive, *a.* abusivo.
abusively, *adv.* abusivamente, ofensivamente.
abut (on), *v.* terminar (en); lindar (con).
abutment, *n.* (building) estribo, contrafuerte *m.*
abyss, *n.* abismo *m.*
Abyssinian, *a. & n.* abisinio - nia.
academic, *a.* académico.
academy, *n.* academia *f.*
acanthus, *n.* (bot.) acanto *m.*
accede, *v.* acceder; consentir.
accelerate, *v.* acelerar.
acceleration, *n.* aceleración *f.*
accelerator, *n.* (auto.) acelerador *m.*
accent, 1. *n.* acento *m.* 2. *v.* acentuar.
accentuate, *v.* acentuar.
accept, *v.* aceptar.
acceptability, *n.* aceptabilidad *f.*
acceptable, *a.* aceptable.
acceptably, *adv.* aceptablemente.
acceptance, *n.* aceptación *f.*
access, *n.* acceso *m.,* entrada *f.*
accessible, *a.* accesible.
accessory, 1. *a.* accesorio. 2. *n.* cómplice *m. & f.*
accident, *n.* accidente *m.* **by a.,** por casualidad.
accidental, *a.* accidental.
accidentally, *adv.* accidentalmente, casualmente.
acclaim, *v.* aclamar.
acclamation, *n.* aclamación *f.*
acclimate, *v.* aclimatar.
acclivity, *n.* subida *f.*
accolade, *n.* acolada *f.*
accommodate, *v.* acomodar.
accommodating, *a.* bondadoso, complaciente.
accommodation, *n.* servicio *m.; (pl.)* alojamiento *m.*
accompaniment, *n.* acompañamiento *m.*
accompanist, *n.* acompañador *m.*
accompany, *v.* acompañar.
accomplice, *n.* cómplice *m. & f.*
accomplish, *v.* llevar a cabo; realizar.
accomplished, *a.* acabado, cumplido; culto.
accomplishment, *n.* realización *f.;* logro *m.*
accord, 1. *n.* acuerdo *m.* 2. *v.* otorgar.
accordance, *n.:* **in a. with,** de acuerdo con.
accordingly, *adv.* en conformidad.
according to, *prep.* según.
accordion, *n.* (mus.) acordeón *m.*
accost, *v.* dirigirse a.
account, 1. *n.* relato *m.;* (com.) cuenta *f.* **on a. of,** a causa de.

on no a., de ninguna manera.
2. v. a. for, explicar.

accountable, a. responsable.

accountant, n. contador -ra.

accounting, n. contabilidad f.

accouter, v. equipar, ataviar.

accouterments, n. equipo, atavio m.

accredit, v. acreditar.

accretion, n. aumento m.

accrual, n. aumento, incremento m.

accrue, v. provenir; acumularse.

accumulate, v. acumular.

accumulation, n. acumulación f.

accumulative, a. acumulativo.

accumulator, n. acumulador m.

accuracy, n. exactitud, precisión f.

accurate, a. exacto.

accursed, a. maldito.

accusation, n. acusación f., cargo m.

accusative, a. & n. acusativo m.

accuse, v. acusar.

accused, a. & n. acusado, procesado m.

accuser, n. acusador -ra.

accustom, v. acostumbrar.

accustomed, a. acostumbrado.

ace, 1. a. sobresaliente. 2. n. as m.

acerbity, n. acerbidad, amargura f.

acetate, n. (chem.) acetato m.

acetic, a. acético.

acetylene, 1. a. acetilénico. 2. n. (chem.) acetileno m.

ache, 1. n. dolor m. 2. v. doler.

achieve, v. lograr, llevar a cabo.

achievement, n. realización f.; hecho notable.

acid, a. & n. ácido m.

acidify, v. acidificar.

acidity, n. acidez f.

acidosis, n. (med.) acidismo m.

acid test, prueba decisiva.

acidulous, a. agrio, acídulo.

acknowledge, v. admitir (receipt) acusar.

acme, n. apogeo, colmo m.

acne, n. (med.) acne m. & f.; barros m.pl.

acolyte, n. acólito m.

acorn, n. bellota f.

acoustics, n. acústica f.

acquaint, v. familiarizar. **to be acquainted with**, conocer.

acquaintance, n. conocimiento m. (person known) conocido -da. **to make the a. of**, conocer.

acquainted, be acquainted with, v. conocer.

acquiesce, v. consentir.

acquiescence, n. consentimiento m.

acquire, v. adquirir.

acquirement, n. adquisición f.; (pl.) conocimientos m.pl.

acquisition, n. adquisición f.

acquisitive, a. adquisitivo.

acquit, v. exonerar, absolver.

acquittal, n. absolución f.

acre, n. acre m.

acreage, número de acres.

acrid, a. acre, picante.

acrimonious, a. acrimonioso, mordaz.

acrimony, n. acrimonia, aspereza f.

acrobat, n. acróbata m.

across, 1. adv. a través, al otro lado. 2. prep. al otro lado de, a través de.

acrostic, n. acróstico m.

act, 1. n. acción f.; acto m. 2. v. actuar, portarse. **act as**, hacer de. **act on**, decidir sobre.

acting, 1. a. interino. 2. n. acción f.; (theat.) representación f.

actinism, n. actinismo m.

actinium, n. (chem.) actinio m.

action, n. acción f. **take a.**, tomar medidas.

activate, v. activar.

activation, n. activación f.

activator, n. (chem.) activador m.

active, a. activo.

activity, n. actividad f.

actor, n. actor m.

actress, n. actriz f.

actual, a. real, efectivo.

actuality, n. realidad, actualidad f.

actually, adv. en realidad.

actuary, n. actuario m.

actuate, v. impulsar, mover.

acumen, n. cacumen m., perspicacia f.

acupuncture, n. acupuntura f.

acute, a. agudo; perspicaz.

acutely, adv. agudamente.

acuteness, n. agudeza f.

adage, n. refrán, proverbio m.

adamant, a. firme.

Adam's apple, nuez de la garganta.

adapt, v. adaptar.

adaptable, a. adaptable.

adaptability, n. adaptabilidad f.

adaptation, n. adaptación f.

adapter, n. (tech.) adaptador m.; (mech.) ajustador m.

adaptive, a. adaptable, acomodable.

add, v. agregar, añadir. **a. up**, sumar.

adder, n. víbora f.; serpiente m.

addict, n. adicto; ('fan') aficionado m.

addition, n. adición f. **in a. to**, además de.

additional, a. adicional.

addle, v. confundir.

address, 1. n. dirección f.; señas f.pl. (speech) discurso. 2. v. dirigirse a.

addressee, n. destinatario -ia.

adduce, v. aducir.

adenoid, a. adenoideo.

adept, a. adepto.

adeptly, adv. diestramente.

adeptness, n. destreza f.

adequacy, n. suficiencia f.

adequate, a. adecuado.

adequately, adv. adecuadamente.

adhere, v. adherirse, pegarse.

adherence, n. adhesión f.; apego m.

adherent, n. adherente, partidario m.

adhesion, n. adhesión f.

adhesive, a. adhesivo. **a. tape**, esparadrapo m.

adhesiveness, n. adhesividad f.

adieu, 1. interj. adiós. 2. n. despedida f.

adjacent, a. adyacente.

adjective, n. adjetivo m.

adjoin, v. lindar (con).

adjoining, a. contiguo.

adjourn, v. suspender, levantar.

adjournment, n. suspensión f.; (leg.) espera f.

adjunct, n. adjunto m.; (gram.) atributo m.

adjust, v. ajustar, acomodar; arreglar.

adjuster, n. ajustador m.

adjustment, n. ajuste; arreglo m.

adjutant, n. (mil.) ayudante m.

administer, v. administrar.

administration, n. administración f.; gobierno m.

administrative, a. administrativo.

administrator, n. administrador m.

admirable, a. admirable.

admirably, adv. admirablemente.

admiral, n. almirante m.

admiralty, n. ministerio de marina.

admiration, n. admiración f.

admire, v. admirar.

admirer, n. admirador -ra; enamorado -da.

admiringly, adv. admirativamente.

admissible, a. admisible, aceptable.

admission, n. admisión; entrada f.

admit, v. admitir.

admittance, n. entrada f.

admittedly, adv. reconocidamente.

admixture, n. mezcla f.

admonish, v. amonestar.

admonition, n. admonición f.

adolescence, n. adolescencia f.

adolescent, n. & a. adolescente.

adopt, v. adoptar.

adoption, n. adopción f.

adorable, a. adorable.

adoration, n. adoración f.

adore, v. adorar.

adorn, v. adornar.

adornment, n. adorno m.

adrenalin, n. adrenalina f.

adrift, adv. a la ventura.

adroit, a. diestro.

adulate, v. adular.
adulation, n. adulación f.
adult, a. & n. adulto m.
adulterant, a. & n. adulterante m.
adulterate, v. adulterar.
adulterer, n. adúltero m.
adulteress, n. adúltera f.
adultery, n. adulterio m.
advance, 1. n. avance; adelanto m. **in a.,** de antemano, antes. **2.** v. avanzar, adelantar.
advanced, a. avanzado, adelantado.
advancement, n. adelantamiento m.; promoción f.
advantage, n. ventaja f. **take a. of,** aprovecharse de.
advantageous, a. provechoso, ventajoso.
advantageously, adv. ventajosamente.
advent, n. venida, llegada f.
adventitious, a. adventicio, espontáneo.
adventure, n. aventura f.
adventurer, n. aventurero m.
adventurous, a. aventurero, intrépido.
adventurously, adv. arriesgadamente.
adverb, n. adverbio m.
adverbial, a. adverbial.
adversary, n. adversario m.
adverse, a. adverso.
adversely, adv. adversamente.
adversity, n. adversidad f.
advert, v. hacer referencia a.
advertise, v. avisar, anunciar.
advertisement, n. aviso, anuncio m.
advertiser, n. anunciante, avisador m.
advertising, n. publicidad f.
advice, n. consejos m.pl.
advisability, n. prudencia, propiedad f.
advisable, a. aconsejable, prudente.
advisably, adv. prudentemente.
advise, v. aconsejar.
advisedly, adv. avisadamente, prudentemente.
advisement, n. consideración f.; **take under a.,** someter a estudio.
adviser, n. consejero m.
advocacy, n. abogacía; defensa f.
advocate, 1. n. abogado m. **2.** v. apoyar.
aegis, n. amparo m.
aerate, v. airear, ventilar.
aeration, n. aeración, ventilación f.
aerial, a. aéreo.
aerie, n. nido de águila.
aeronautics, n. aeronáutica f.
aerosol bomb, n. bomba insecticida.
afar, adv. lejos. **from a.,** de lejos, desde lejos.
affability, n. afabilidad, amabilidad f.

affable, a. afable.
affably, adv. afablemente.
affair, n. asunto m. **love a.,** aventura amorosa.
affect, v. afectar; (emotionally) conmover.
affectation, n. afectación f.
affected, a. artificioso.
affecting, a. conmovedor.
affection, n. cariño m.
affectionate, a. afectuoso, cariñoso.
affectionately, adv. afectuosamente, con cariño.
affiance, v. dar palabra de casamiento; **become affianced,** comprometerse.
affidavit, n. (leg.) declaración, deposición f.
affiliate, 1. n. afiliado m. **2.** v. afiliar.
affiliation, n. afiliación f.
affinity, n. afinidad f.
affirm, v. afirmar.
affirmation, n. afirmación, aserción f.
affirmative, 1. n. afirmativa f. **2.** a. afirmativo.
affirmatively, adv. afirmativamente, aseveradamente.
affix, 1. n. (gram.) afijo m. **2.** v. fijar, pegar, poner.
afflict, v. afligir.
affliction, n. aflicción f.; mal m.
affluence, n. abundancia, opulencia f.
affluent, a. opulento, afluente.
afford, v. proporcionar. **be able to a.,** tener con que comprar.
affront, 1. n. afrenta f. **2.** v. afrentar, insultar.
afield, adv. lejos de casa; lejos del camino; lejos del asunto.
afire, adv. ardiendo.
afloat, adv. (naut.) a flote.
aforementioned, aforesaid, a. dicho, susodicho.
afraid, to be a., tener miedo, temer.
African, n. & a. africano -na.
aft, adv. (naut.) a popa, en popa.
after, 1. prep. después de. **2.** conj. después que.
aftermath, n. resultados m.pl., consecuencias f.pl.
afternoon, n. tarde f. **good a.,** buenas tardes.
afterthought, n. idea tardía.
afterward(s), adv. después.
again, adv. otra vez, de nuevo. **to do a.,** volver a hacer.
against, prep. contra; en contra de.
agape, adv. con la boca abierta.
agate, n. ágata f.
age, 1. n. edad f. **of a.,** mayor de edad. **old a.,** vejez f. **2.** v. envejecer.
aged, a. viejo, anciano, añejo.
ageism, n. discriminación contra las personas de edad.
ageless, a. sempiterno.
agency, n. agencia f.

agenda, n. agenda f., orden m.
agent, n. agente; representante m.
agglutinate, v. aglutinar.
agglutination, n. aglutinación f.
aggrandize, v. agrandar; elevar.
aggrandizement, n. engrandecimiento m.
aggravate, v. agravar; irritar.
aggravation, n. agravamiento; empeoramiento m.
aggregate, a. & n. agregado m.
aggregation, n. agregación f.
aggression, n. agresión f.
aggressive, a. agresivo.
aggressively, adv. agresivamente.
aggressiveness, n. agresividad f.
aggressor, n. agresor m.
aghast, a. horrorizado.
agile, a. ágil.
agility, n. agilidad, ligereza, prontitud f.
agitate, v. agitar.
agitation, n. agitación f.
agitator, n. agitador m.
agnostic, a. & n. agnóstico m.
ago, adv. hace. **two days a.,** hace dos días.
agonized, a. angustioso.
agony, n. sufrimiento m.; angustia f.
agrarian, a. agrario.
agree, v. estar de acuerdo; convenir. **a. with one,** sentar bien.
agreeable, a. agradable.
agreeably, adv. agradablemente.
agreement, n. acuerdo m.
agriculture, n. agricultura f.
ahead, adv. adelante.
aid, 1. n. ayuda f. **2.** v. ayudar.
aide, n. ayudante m.
ailing, adj. enfermo.
ailment, n. enfermedad f.
aim, 1. n. puntería f.; (purpose) propósito m. **2.** v. apuntar.
aimless, a. sin objeto.
air, n. aire m. **by a.** por avión. **2.** v. ventilar, airear.
airbag, n. (in automobiles) saco de aire m.
air-conditioned, a. enfriado por aire.
air-conditioning, acondicionamiento del aire.
aircraft, n. máquina de volar.
aircraft carrier, n. portaaviones m.
airing, n. ventilación f.
airline, n. línea aérea.
airliner, n. avión de transporte.
airmail, n. correo aéreo.
airplane, n. avión, aeroplano m.
air pollution, contaminación atmosférica.
airport, n. aeropuerto m.

air pressure, presión atmosférica.

air raid, ataque aéreo.

airsick, a. mareado.

airtight, a. hermético.

aisle, n. pasillo m.

ajar, a. entreabierto.

akin, a. emparentado, semejante.

alacrity, n. alacridad, presteza f.

alarm, 1. n. alarma f. **2.** v. alarmar.

alarmist, n. alarmista m. & f.

albino, n. albino -na.

album, n. álbum m.

alcohol, n. alcohol m.

alcoholic, a. alcohólico.

alcove, n. alcoba f.

ale, n. cerveza inglesa.

alert, 1. n. alarma f. **on the a.,** alerta, sobre aviso. **2.** a. listo, vivo. **3.** v. poner sobre aviso.

alfalfa, n. alfalfa f.

algebra, n. álgebra f.

alias, n. alias m.

alibi, n. excusa f.; (leg.) coartada f.

alien, 1. a. ajeno, extranjero. **2.** n. extranjero -ra.

alienate, v. enajenar.

alight, v. bajar, apearse.

align, v. alinear.

alike, 1. a. semejante, igual. **2.** adv. del mismo modo, igualmente.

alimentary canal, tubo digestivo.

alive, a. vivo; animado.

alkali, n. (chem.) álcali, cali m.

alkaline, a. alcalino.

all, a. & pron. todo. **not at a.,** de ninguna manera, nada.

allay, v. aquietar.

allegation, n. alegación f.

allege, v. alegar; pretender.

allegiance, n. lealtad f.; (to country) homenaje m.

allegory, n. alegoría f.

allergy, n. alergia f.

alleviate, v. aliviar.

alley, n. callejón m. **bowling a.,** bolera f., boliche m.

alliance, n. alianza f.

allied, a. aliado.

alligator, n. caimán m.; (Mex.) lagarto m. **a. pear,** aguacate m.

allocate, v. colocar, asignar.

allot, v. asignar.

allotment, n. lote, porción f.

allow, v. permitir, dejar.

allowance, n. abono m.; dieta f. **make a. for,** tener en cuenta.

alloy, n. mezcla f. (metal) aleación f.

all right, está bien.

allude, v. aludir.

allure, 1. n. atracción f. **2.** v. atraer, tentar.

alluring, a. tentador, seductivo.

allusion, n. alusión f.

ally, 1. n. aliado m. **2.** v. aliar.

almanac, n. almanaque m.

almighty, a. todopoderoso.

almond, n. almendra f.

almost, adv. casi.

alms, n. limosna f.

aloft, adv. arriba, en alto.

alone, adv. solo, a solas. **to leave a.,** dejar en paz.

along, prep. por; a lo largo de. **a. with,** junto con.

alongside, 1. adv. al lado. **2.** prep. junto a.

aloof, a. apartado.

aloud, adv. en voz alta.

alpaca, n. alpaca f.

alphabet, n. alfabeto m.

alphabetical, a. alfabético.

alphabetize, v. alfabetizar.

already, adv. ya.

also, adv. también.

altar, n. altar m.

alter, v. alterar.

alteration, n. alteración f.

alternate, 1. a. alterno. **2.** n. substituto -ta. **3.** v. alternar.

alternative, 1. a. alternativo. **2.** n. alternativa f.

although, conj. aunque.

altitude, n. altura f.

alto, n. contralto m.

altogether, adv. en junto; enteramente.

altruism, n. altruismo m.

alum, n. alumbre m.

aluminum, n. aluminio m.

always, adv. siempre.

amalgam, n. amalgama f.

amalgamate, v. amalgamar.

amass, v. amontonar.

amateur, n. aficionado -da.

amaze, v. asombrar; sorprender.

amazement, n. asombro m.

amazing, a. asombroso, pasmoso.

ambassador, n. embajador m.

amber, 1. a. ambarino. **2.** n. ámbar m.

ambidextrous, a. ambidextro.

ambiguity, n. ambigüedad f.

ambiguous, a. ambiguo.

ambition, n. ambición f.

ambitious, a. ambicioso.

ambulance, n. ambulancia f.

ambush, 1. n. emboscada f. **2.** v. acechar.

ameliorate, v. mejorar.

amenable, a. tratable, dócil.

amend, v. enmendar.

amendment, n. enmienda f.

amenity, n. amenidad f.

American, a. & n. americano -na, norteamericano -na.

amethyst, n. amatista f.

amiable, a. amable.

amicable, a. amigable.

amid, prep. entre, en medio de.

amidships, adv. (naut.) en medio del navío.

amiss, adv. mal. **to take a.,** llevar a mal.

amity, n. amistad, armonía f.

ammonia, n. amoníaco m.

ammunition, n. munición f.

amnesia, n. (med.) amnesia f.

amnesty, n. amnistía f., indulto m.

amniocentesis, n. amniocéntesis m.

amoeba, n. amiba f.

among, prep. entre.

amoral, a. amoral.

amorous, a. amoroso.

amorphous, a. amorfo.

amortize, v. (com.) amortizar.

amount, 1. n. cantidad, suma f. **2.** v. a. to, subir a.

ampere, n. (elec.) amperio m.

amphibian, a. & n. anfibio m.

amphitheater, n. anfiteatro, circo m.

ample, a. amplio; suficiente.

amplify, v. amplificar.

amputate, v. amputar.

amuse, v. entretener, divertir.

amusement, n. diversión f.

an, art. un, una.

anachronism, n. anacronismo, m.

analogous, a. análogo, parecido.

analogy, n. analogía f.

analysis, n. análisis m. & f.

analyst, n. analizador m.

analytic, a. analítico.

analyze, v. analizar.

anarchy, n. anarquía f.

anatomy, n. anatomía f.

ancestor, n. antepasado m.

ancestral, a. de los antepasados, hereditario.

ancestry, n. linaje, abolengo m.

anchor, 1. n. ancla f. **to weigh a.,** levar el ancla. **2.** v. anclar.

anchorage, n. (naut.) ancladero, anclaje m.

anchovy, n. anchoa f.

ancient, a. & n. antiguo.

and, conj. y, (before i-, hi-) e.

anecdote, n. anécdota f.

anemia, n. (med.) anemia f.

anesthetic, n. anestesia f.

anew, adv. de nuevo.

angel, n. ángel m.

anger, 1. n. ira f., enojo m. **2.** v. enfadar, enojar.

angle, n. ángulo m.

angry, a. enojado, enfadado.

anguish, n. angustia f.

angular, a. angular.

aniline, n. (chem.) anilina f.

animal, a. & n. animal m.

animate, 1. adj. animado. **2.** v. animar.

animated, a. vivo, animado.

animation, n. animación, viveza f.

animosity, n. rencor m.

anise, n. anís m.

ankle, n. tobillo m.

annals, n.pl. anales m.pl.

annex, 1. n. anexo m., adición f. **2.** v. anexar.

annexation, n. anexión, adición f.

annihilate, v. aniquilar, destruir.

anniversary, n. aniversario m.

annotate, v. anotar.

annotation, n. anotación f., apunte m.

announce, v. anunciar.

announcement, n. anuncio, aviso m.

announcer, n. anunciador m.; (radio) anunciador, noticiador m.

annoy, v. molestar.

annoyance, n. molestia, incomodidad f.

annual, a. anual.

annuity, n. anualidad, pensión f.

annul, v. anular, invalidar.

anode, n. (elec.) ánodo m.

anoint, v. untar; (rel.) ungir.

anomalous, a. anómalo, irregular.

anonymous, a. anónimo.

another, a. & pron. otro.

answer, 1. n. contestación, respuesta f. 2. v. contestar, responder. **a. for,** ser responsable de.

answerable, a. discutible, refutable.

ant, n. hormiga f.

antacid, a. & n. antiácido m.

antagonism, n. antagonismo m.

antagonist, n. antagonista m.

antagonistic, a. antagónico, hostil.

antagonize, v. contrariar.

antarctic, a. & n. antártico m.

antecedent, a. & n. antecedente m.

antedate, v. antedatar.

antelope, n. antílope m., gacela f.

antenna, n. antena f.

anterior, a. anterior.

anteroom, n. antecámara f.

anthem, n. himno m.; (religious) antífona f.

anthology, n. antología f.

anthracite, n. antracita f.

anthrax, n. (med.) ántrax m.

anthropology, n. antropología f.

antiaircraft, a. antiaéreo.

antibody, n. anticuerpo m.

anticipate, v. esperar, anticipar.

anticipation, n. anticipación f.

anticlerical, a. anticlerical.

anticlimax, n. anticlímax m.

antidote, n. antídoto m.

antimony, n. antimonio m.

antinuclear, a. antinuclear.

antipathy, n. antipatía f.

antiquated, a. anticuado.

antique, 1. a. antiguo. 2. n. antigüedad f.

antiquity, n. antigüedad f.

antiseptic, a. & n. antiséptico m.

antisocial, a. antisocial.

antitoxin, n. (med.) antitoxina f.

antler, n. asta f.

anvil, n. yunque m.

anxiety, n. ansia, ansiedad f.

anxious, a. inquieto, ansioso.

any, a. alguno; (at all) cualquiera; (after not) ninguno.

anybody, pron. alguien; (at all) cualquiera; (after not) nadie.

anyhow, adv. de todos modos; en todo caso.

anyone, pron. = anybody.

anything, pron. algo; (at all) cualquier cosa; (after not) nada.

anyway, adv. = anyhow.

anywhere, adv. en alguna parte; (at all) dondequiera; (after not) en ninguna parte.

apart, adv. aparte. **to take a.,** deshacer.

apartheid, n. apartheid m.

apartment, n. apartamento, piso m.

apathetic, a. apático.

apathy, n. apatía f.

ape, 1. n. mono m. 2. v. imitar.

aperture, n. abertura f.

apex, n. ápice m.

aphorism, n. aforismo m.

apiary, n. apiario, abejar m.

apiece, adv. por persona; cada uno.

apologetic, a. apologético.

apologist, n. apologista m. & f.

apologize, v. excusarse, disculparse.

apology, n. excusa; apología f.

apoplectic, a. apoplético.

apoplexy, n. apoplejía f.

apostate, n. apóstata m. & f.

apostle, n. apóstol m.

apostolic, a. apostólico.

appall, v. espantar; desmayar.

apparatus, n. aparato m.

apparel, n. ropa f.

apparent, a. aparente; claro.

apparition, n. fantasma f.

appeal, 1. n. súplica f.; interés m.; (leg.) apelación f. 2. v. apelar, suplicar; interesar.

appear, v. aparecer, asomar; (seem) parecer; (leg.) comparecer.

appearance, n. apariencia f., aspecto m.

appease, v. aplacar, apaciguar.

appeasement, n. apaciguamiento m.

appeaser, n. apaciguador, pacificador m.

appellant, n. apelante, demandante m.

appellate, a. (leg.) de apelación.

appendage, n. pertenencia f.

appendectomy, n. (med.) apendectomía f.

appendicitis, n. (med.) apendicitis m.

appendix, n. apéndice m.

appetite, n. apetito m.

appetizer, n. apertivo m.

appetizing, a. apetitivo.

applaud, v. aplaudir.

applause, n. aplauso m.

apple, n. manzana f. **a. tree,** manzano m.

applesauce, n. compota de manzana.

appliance, n. utensilio, aparato m.

applicable, a. aplicable.

applicant, n. suplicante m. & f.; candidato -ta.

application, n. solicitud f.

applied, a. aplicado. **a. for,** pedido.

appliqué, n. (sewing) aplicación f.

apply, v. aplicar. **a. for,** solicitar, pedir.

appoint, v. nombrar.

appointment, n. nombramiento, puesto m.

apportion, v. repartir.

apposition, n. (gram.) aposición f.

appraisal, n. valoración f.; apremio m.

appraise, v. avaluar, tasar; estimar.

appreciable, a. apreciable; notable.

appreciate, v. apreciar, estimar.

appreciation, n. aprecio; reconocimiento m.

apprehend, v. prender, capturar.

apprehension, n. aprensión f.

apprehensive, a. aprensivo.

apprentice, n. aprendiz m.

apprise, v. informar.

approach, 1. n. acceso; método m. 2. v. acercarse.

approachable, a. accesible.

approbation, n. aprobación f.

appropriate, 1. a. apropiado. 2. v. apropiar.

appropriation, n. apropiación f.

approval, n. aprobación f.

approve, v. aprobar.

approximate, 1. a. aproximado. 2. v. aproximar.

approximately, adv. aproximadamente.

approximation, n. aproximación f.

appurtenance, n. pertenencia f.

apricot, n. albaricoque, damasco m.

April, n. abril m.

apron, n. delantal m.

apropos, adv. a propósito.

apt, a. apto; capaz.

aptitude, n. aptitud; facilidad f.

aquarium, n. acuario m., pecera f.

aquatic, a. acuático.

aqueduct, n. acueducto m.

aqueous, a. ácueo, acuoso, aguoso.

aquiline, a. aquilino, aguileño.

Arab, a. & n. árabe m. & f.

arable, a. cultivable.

arbitrary, a. arbitrario.

arbitrate, v. arbitrar.

arbitration, n. arbitraje m., arbitración f.

arbitrator, n. arbitrador -ra.

arbor, n. emparrado m.

arboreal, a. arbóreo.

arc, *n.* arco *m.*
arch, 1. *n.* arco *m.* **2.** *v.* arquear, encorvar.
archaeology, *n.* arqueología *f.*
archaic, *a.* arcaico.
archbishop, *n.* arzobispo *m.*
archdiocese, *n.* archidiócesis *m.*
archduke, *n.* archiduque *m.*
archer, *n.* arquero *m.*
archery, *n.* ballestería *f.*
archipelago, *n.* archipiélago *m.*
architect, *n.* arquitecto *m.*
architectural, *a.* arquitectural.
architecture, *n.* arquitectura *f.*
archive, *n.* archivo *m.*
archway, *n.* arcada *f.*
arctic, *a.* ártico.
ardent, *a.* ardiente.
ardor, *n.* ardor *m.,* pasión *f.*
arduous, *a.* arduo, difícil.
area, *n.* área; extensión *f.*
area code, prefijo *m.*
arena, *n.* arena *f.*
Argentine, *a.* & *n.* argentino -na.
argue, *v.* disputar; sostener.
argument, *n.* disputa *f.;* razonamiento *m.*
argumentative, *a.* argumentoso.
aria, *n.* (mus.) aria *f.*
arid, *a.* árido, seco.
arise, *v.* surgir.
aristocracy, *n.* aristocracia *f.*
aristocrat, *n.* aristócrata *m.*
aristocratic, *a.* aristocrático.
arithmetic, *n.* aritmética *f.*
ark, *n.* arca *f.*
arm, 1. *n.* brazo *m.;* (weapon) arma *f.* **2.** *v.* armar.
armament, *n.* armamento *m.*
armchair, *n.* sillón *m.,* butaca *f.*
armed forces, fuerzas militares.
armful, *n.* brazada *f.*
armhole, *n.* (sew.) sobaquera *f.*
armistice, *n.* armisticio *m.*
armor, *n.* armadura *f.,* blindaje *m.*
armored, *a.* blindado.
armory, *n.* armería *f.,* arsenal *m.*
armpit, *n.* sobaco *m.*
army, *n.* ejército *m.*
arnica, *n.* árnica *f.*
aroma, *n.* fragancia *f.*
aromatic, *a.* aromático.
around, *prep.* alrededor de, a la vuelta de; cerca de **a. here,** por aquí.
arouse, *v.* despertar; excitar.
arraign, *v.* (leg.) procesar criminalmente.
arrange, *v.* arreglar; concertar; (mus.) adaptar.
arrangement, *n.* arreglo; orden *m.*
array, 1. *n.* orden; adorno *m.* **2.** *v.* adornar.
arrears, *n.* atrasos *m.pl.*
arrest, 1. *n.* detención *f.* **2.** *v.* detener, arrestar.
arrival, *n.* llegada *f.*
arrive, *v.* llegar.

arrogance, *n.* arrogancia *f.*
arrogant, *a.* arrogante.
arrogate, *v.* arrogarse, usurpar.
arrow, *n.* flecha *f.*
arrowhead, *n.* punta de flecha.
arsenal, *n.* arsenal *m.*
arsenic, *n.* arsénico *m.*
arson, *n.* incendio premeditado.
art, *n.* arte *m.* (*f.* in *pl.*); (skill) maña *f.*
arterial, *a.* arterial.
arteriosclerosis, *n.* arteriosclerosis *m.*
artery, *n.* arteria *f.*
artesian well, pozo artesiano.
artful, *a.* astuto.
arthritis, *n.* artritis *m.*
artichoke, *n.* alcachofa *f.*
article, *n.* artículo *m.*
articulate, *v.* articular.
articulation, *n.* articulación *f.*
artifice, *n.* artificio *m.*
artificial, *a.* artificial.
artificially, *adv.* artificialmente.
artillery, *n.* artillería *f.*
artisan, *n.* artesano *m.*
artist, *n.* artista *m.* & *f.*
artistic, *a.* artístico.
artistry, *n.* arte *m.* & *f.*
artless, *a.* natural, cándido.
as, *adv.* & *conj.* como; **as . . . as . . .** tan . . . como.
asbestos, *n.* asbesto *m.*
ascend, *v.* ascender.
ascendancy, *n.* ascendiente *m.*
ascendant, *a.* ascendente.
ascent, *n.* subida *f.,* ascenso *m.*
ascertain, *v.* averiguar.
ascetic, 1. *a.* ascético. **2.** *n.* asceta *m.* & *f.*
ascribe, *v.* atribuir.
ash, *n.* ceniza *f.*
ashamed, *a.* avergonzado.
ashen, *a.* pálido.
ashore, *adv.* a tierra. **go a.,** desembarcar.
ashtray, *n.* cenicero *m.*
Asiatic, *a.* & *n.* asiático -ca.
aside, *adv.* al lado. **a. from.** aparte de.
ask, *v.* preguntar; invitar; (request) pedir. **a. for,** pedir. **a. a question,** hacer una pregunta.
askance, *adv.* de soslayo; con recelo.
asleep, *a.* dormido. **to fall a.,** dormirse.
asparagus, *n.* espárrago *m.*
aspect, *n.* aspecto *m.,* apariencia *f.*
asperity, *n.* aspereza *f.*
aspersion, *n.* calumnia *f.*
asphalt, *n.* asfalto *m.*
asphyxia, *n.* asfixia *f.*
asphyxiate, *v.* asfixiar, sofocar.
aspirant, *a.* & *n.* aspirante.
aspirate, *v.* aspirar.
aspiration, *n.* aspiración *f.*
aspirator, *n.* aspirador *m.*
aspire, *v.* aspirar. **a. to,** ambicionar.
aspirin, *n.* aspirina *f.*
ass, *n.* asno, burro *m.*

assail, *v.* asaltar, acometer.
assailant, *n.* asaltador *m.*
assassin, *n.* asesino *m.*
assassinate, *v.* asesinar.
assassination, *n.* asesinato *m.*
assault, 1. *n.* asalto *m.* **2.** *v.* asaltar, atacar.
assay, *v.* examinar; ensayar.
assemblage, *n.* asamblea *f.*
assemble, *v.* juntar, convocar; (mechanism) montar.
assembly, *n.* asamblea, concurrencia *f.*
assent, 1. *n.* asentimiento *m.* **2.** *v.* asentir, convenir.
assert, *v.* afirmar, aseverar. **a. oneself,** harcerse sentir.
assertion, *n.* aserción, aseveración *f.*
assertive, *a.* asertivo.
assess, *v.* tasar, avaluar.
assessor, *n.* asesor *m.*
asset, *n.* ventaja *f.* **assets,** (com.) capital *m.*
asseverate, *v.* aseverar, afirmar.
asseveration, *n.* aseveración *f.*
assiduous, *a.* asiduo.
assiduously, *adv.* asiduamente.
assign, *v.* asignar; destinar.
assignable, *a.* asignable, transferible.
assignation, *n.* asignación *f.*
assignment, *n.* misión; tarea *f.*
assimilate, *v.* asimilar.
assimilation, *n.* asimilación *f.*
assimilative, *a.* asimilativo.
assist, *v.* ayudar, auxiliar.
assistance, *n.* ayuda *f.,* auxilio *m.*
assistant, *n.* ayudante, asistente *m.*
associate, 1. *n.* socio *m.* **2.** *v.* asociar.
association, *n.* asociación; sociedad *f.*
assonance, *n.* asonancia *f.*
assort, *v.* surtir con variedad.
assorted, *a.* variado, surtido.
assortment, *n.* surtido *m.*
assuage, *v.* mitigar, aliviar.
assume, *v.* suponer; asumir.
assuming, *a.* presuntuoso. **a. that,** dado que.
assumption, *n.* suposición; (rel.) ásunción *f.*
assurance, *n.* seguridad, confianza *f.*
assure, *v.* asegurar; dar confianza.
assured, 1. *a.* seguro. **2.** *a.* & *n.* (com.) asegurado *m.*
assuredly, *adv.* ciertamente.
aster, *n.* (bot.) aster *m.*
asterisk, *n.* asterisco *m.*
astern, *adv.* (naut.) a popa.
asteroid, *n.* asteroide *m.*
asthma, *n.* (med.) asma *f.*
astigmatism, *n.* astigmatismo *m.*
astir, *adv.* en movimiento.
astonish, *v.* asombrar, pasmar.
astonishment, *n.* asombro *m.,* sorpresa *f.*

astound, v. pasmar, sorprender.

astral, a. astral, estelar.

astray, a. desviado.

astride, adv. a horcajadas.

astringent, a. & n. astringente m.

astrology, n. astrología f.

astronaut, n. astronauta m.

astronomy, n. astronomía f.

astute, a. astuto; agudo.

asunder, adv. en dos.

asylum, n. asilo, refugio m.

asymmetry, n. asimetría f.

at, prep. a, en; cerca de.

ataxia, n. (med.) ataxia f.

atheist, n. ateo m.

athlete, n. atleta m.

athletic, a. atlético.

athletics, n. atletismo m., deportes m.pl.

athwart, prep. á través de.

Atlantic, 1. a. atlántico. 2. n. Atlántico m.

Atlantic Ocean, el mar atlántico.

atlas, n. atlas m.

atmosphere, n. atmósfera f.; (fig.) ambiente m.

atmospheric, a. atmosférico.

atoll, n. atolón m.

atom, n. átomo m.

atomic, a. atómico.

atomic bomb, bomba atómica.

atomic energy, energía atómica.

atomic theory, teoría atómica.

atomic weight, peso atómico.

atonal, a. (mus.) atonal.

atone, v. expiar, compensar.

atonement, n. expiación; reparación f.

atrocious, a. atroz.

atrocity, n. atrocidad f.

atrophy, 1. n. (med.) atrofia f. 2. v. atrofiar.

atropine, n. (chem.) atropina f.

attach, v. juntar; prender; (hook) enganchar; (fig.) atribuir.

attaché, n. agregado m.

attachment, 1. enlace m.; accesorio m.; (emotional) afecto, cariño m.

attack, 1. n. ataque m. 2. v. atacar.

attacker, n. asaltador m.

attain, v. lograr, alcanzar.

attainable, a. accesible, realizable.

attainment, n. logro; (pl.) dotes f.pl.

attempt, 1. n. ensayo; esfuerzo m.; tentativa f. 2. v. ensayar, intentar.

attend, v. atender; (a meeting) asistir a.

attendance, n. asistencia; presencia f.

attendant, 1. a. concomitante. 2. n. servidor -ra.

attention, n. atención f.; obsequio m. **to pay a. to**, hacer caso a.

attentive, a. atento.

attentively, adv. atentamento.

attenuate, v. atenuar, adelgazar.

attest, v. confirmar, atestiguar.

attic, n. desván m., guardilla f.

attire, 1. n. traje m. 2. v. vestir.

attitude, n. actitud f., ademán m.

attorney, n. abogado, apoderado m.

attract, v. atraer. **a. attention**, llamar la atención.

attraction, n. atracción f., atractivo m.

attractive, a. atractivo; simpático.

attributable, a. atribuible, imputable.

attribute, 1. n. atributo m. 2. v. atribuir.

attrition, n. roce, desgaste m.; atrición f.

attune, v. armonizar.

auction, n. subasta f., (S.A.) venduta f.

auctioneer, n. subastador m., (S.A.) martillero m.

audacious, a. audaz.

audacity, n. audacia f.

audible, a. audible.

audience, n. auditorio, público m.; entrevista f.

audiovisual, a. audiovisual.

audit, v. revisar cuentas.

audition, n. audición f.

auditor, n. interventor, revisor m.

auditorium, n. sala f.; teatro m.

auditory, a. & n. auditorio m.

augment, v. aumentar.

augur, v. augurar, pronosticar.

August, n. agosto m.··

aunt, n. tía f.

auspice, n. auspicio m.

auspicious, a. favorable; propicio.

austere, a. austero.

austerity, n. austeridad, severidad f.

Austrian, a. & n. austríaco -ca.

authentic, a. auténtico.

authenticate, v. autenticar.

authenticity, n. autenticidad f.

author, n. autor, escritor m.

authoritarian, a. & n. autoritario m.

authoritative, a. autoritario; autorizado.

authoritatively, adv. autorizadamente.

authority, n. autoridad f.

authorization, n. autorización f.

authorize, v. autorizar.

auto, n. auto, automóvil m.

autobiography, n. autobiografía f.

autocracy, n. autocracia f.

autocrat, n. autócrata m. & f.

autograph, n. autógrafo m.

automatic, a. automático.

automatically, adv. automáticamente.

automobile, n. automóvil, coche m.

automotive, a. automotriz.

autonomy, n. autonomía f.

autopsy, n. autopsia f.

autumn, n. otoño m.

avail, 1. n. of no a., en vano. 2. v. a. oneself of, aprovechar.

available, a. disponible.

avalanche, n. alud m.

avarice, n. avaricia, codicia f.

avariciously, adv. avaramente.

avenge, v. vengar.

avenger, n. vengador -ra.

avenue, n. avenida f.

average, 1. a. medio; común. 2. n. promedio, término medio m. 3. v. calcular el promedio.

averse, a. adverso.

aversion, n. aversión f.

avert, v. desviar; impedir.

aviary, n. pajarera, avería f.

aviation, n. aviación f.

aviator, n. aviador -ra.

aviatrix, n. aviatriz f.

avid, a. ávido.

avocation, n. pasatiempo f.

avoid, v. evitar.

avoidable, a. evitable.

avoidance, n. evitación f.; (leg.) anulación f.

avow, v. declarar; admitir.

avowal, n. admisión f.

avowed, a. reconocido; admitido.

avowedly, adv. reconocidamente; confesadamente.

await, v. esperar, aguardar.

awake, a. despierto.

awaken, v. despertar.

award, 1. n. premio m. 2. v. otorgar.

aware, a. enterado, consciente.

awash, a. & adv. (naut.) a flor de agua.

away, adv. (see under verb: go away, put away, take away, etc.)

awe, n. pavor m.

awesome, a. pavoroso; aterrador.

awful, a. horrible, terrible, muy malo.

awhile, adv. por un rato.

awkward, a. torpe, desmañado; (fig.) delicado, embarazoso.

awning, n. toldo m.

awry, a. oblicuo, torcido.

ax, **axe**, n. hacha f.

axiom, n. axioma m.

axis, n. eje m.

axle, n. eje m.

ayatollah, n. ayatola m.

azure, a. azulado.

B

babble, 1. n. balbuceo, murmullo m. 2 v. balbucear.

babbler, n. hablador -ra, charlador -ra.

baboon, n. mandril m.

baby, n. nene, bebé m.

babyish, *a.* infantil.

bachelor, *n.* soltero *m.*

bacillus, *n.* bacilo, microbio *m.*

back, 1. *adv.* atrás. **to be b.**, estar de vuelta. **b. of,** detrás de. **2.** *n.* espalda *f.;* (of animal) lomo *m.*

backbone, *n.* espinazo *m.;* (fig.) firmeza *f.*

backer, *n.* sostenedor -ra.

background, *n.* fondo *m.* antecedentes *m.pl.*

backing, *n.* apoyo *m.,* garantía *f.*

backlash, *n.* repercusión negativa.

backlog, *n.* rezago *m.*

backpack, *n.* mochila *f.*

backstage, *n.* entre bastidores *m.*

backward, 1. *a.* atrasado. **2.** *adv.* hacia atrás.

backwardness, *n.* atraso *m.*

backwater, *n.* remolino *m.;* contracorriente *f.*

backwoods, *n.* monte *m.;* región apartada.

bacon, *n.* tocino *m.*

bacteria, *n.* bacterias *f.pl.*

bacteriologist, *n.* bacteriólogo *m.*

bacteriology, *n.* bacteriología *f.*

bad, *a.* malo.

badge, *n.* insignia, divisa *f.*

badger, 1. *n.* tejón *m.* **2.** *v.* atormentar.

badly, *adv.* mal.

badness, *n.* maldad *f.*

bad-tempered, *a.* de mal humor.

baffle, *v.* desconcertar.

bafflement, *n.* contrariedad; confusión *f.*

bag, 1. *n.* saco *m.;* bolsa *f.* **2.** *v.* ensacar, cazar.

baggage, *n.* equipaje *m.* **b. check,** talón *m.*

baggage cart (airport), carrillo para llevar equipaje.

baggy, *a.* abotagado; bolsudo; hinchado.

bagpipe, *n.* gaita *f.*

bail, 1. *n.* fianza *f.* **2.** *v.* desaguar.

bailiff, *n.* alguacil *m.*

bait, 1. *n.* cebo *m.* **2.** *v.* cebar.

bake, *v.* cocer en horno.

baker, *n.* panadero, hornero *m.*

bakery, *n.* panadería *f.*

baking, *n.* hornada *f.* **b. powder,** levadura *f.*

balance, *n.* balanza *f.;* equilibrio *m.;* (com.) saldo *m.*

balcony, *n.* balcón *m.;* (theat.) galería *f.*

bald, *a.* calvo.

baldness, *n.* calvicie *f.*

bale, 1. *n.* bala *f.* **2.** *v.* embalar.

balk, *v.* frustrar; rebelarse.

balky, *a.* rebelón.

ball, *n.* bola, pelota *f.;* (dance) baile *m.*

ballad, *n.* romance, *m.;* balada *f.*

ballast, 1. *n.* lastre *m.* **2.** *v.* lastrar.

ball bearing, *n.* cojinete de bolas *m.*

ballerina, *n.* bailarina *f.*

ballet, *n.* danza *f.;* ballet *m.*

ballistics, *n.* balística *f.*

balloon, *n.* globo *m.* **b. tire,** neumático de balón.

ballot, 1. *n.* balota *f.,* voto *m.* **2.** *v.* balotar, votar.

ballroom, *n.* salón de baile *m.*

balm, *n.* bálsamo; ungüento *m.*

balmy, *a.* fragante; reparador; calmante.

balsa, *n.* bálsamo *m.*

balsam, *n.* bálsamo *m.*

balustrade, *n.* barandilla *f.*

bamboo, *n.* bambú *m.,* caña *f.*

ban, 1. *n.* prohibición *f.* **2.** *v.* prohibir; proscribir.

banal, *a.* trivial; vulgar.

banana, *n.* banana *f.,* cambur *m.* **b. tree,** banano, plátano *m.*

band, 1. *n.* venda *f.;* (of men) banda, cuadrilla, partida *f.* **2.** *v.* asociarse.

bandage, 1. *n.* vendaje *m.* **2.** *v.* vendar.

bandanna, *n.* pañuelo (grande) *m.;* bandana *f.*

bandbox, *n.* caja de cartón.

bandit, *n.* bandido -da.

bandmaster, *n.* músico mayor *m.*

bandstand, *n.* kiosco de música *m.*

bang, 1. *interj.* ¡pum! **2.** *n.* ruido de un golpe. **3.** *v.* golpear ruidosamente.

banish, *v.* desterrar.

banishment, *n.* destierro *m.*

banister, *n.* pasamano *m.*

bank, 1. *n.* banco *m.;* (of a river) margen *m.* or *f.* **2.** *v.* depositar.

bankbook, *n.* libreta de depositos *f.*

banker, *n.* banquero *m.*

banking, 1. *a.* bancaria. **2.** *n.* banca *f.*

bank note, *n.* billete de banco *m.*

bankrupt, *a.* insolvente.

bankruptcy, *n.* bancarrota *f.*

banner, *n.* bandera *f.;* estandarte *m.*

banquet, *n.* banquete *m.*

banter, 1. *n.* choteo *m.;* zumba; burla *f.* **2.** *v.* chotear; zumbar; burlarse.

baptism, *n.* bautismo, bautizo *m.*

baptismal, *a.* bautismal.

Baptist, *n.* bautista *m.*

baptize, *v.* bautizar.

bar, 1. *n.* barra *f.;* obstáculo *m.;* (tavern) taberna *f.,* bar *m.* **2.** *v.* barrear; prohibir; excluir.

barbarian, 1. *a.* bárbaro. **2.** *n.* bárbaro -ra.

barbarism, *n.* barbarismo *m.,* barbarie *f.*

barbarous, *n.* bárbaro, cruel.

barbecue, *n.* animal asado entero; (Mex.) barbacoa *f.*

barber, *n.* barbero *m.* **b. shop,** barberéa *f.*

barbiturate, *n.* barbiturado *m.*

bare, 1. *a.* desnudo; descubierto. **2.** *v.* desnudar; descubrir.

bareback, *adv.* sin silla.

barefoot(ed), *a.* descalzo.

barely, *adv.* escasamente, apenas.

bareness, *n.* desnudez *f.;* pobreza *f.*

bargain, 1. *n.* ganga *f.,* compra ventajosa *f.;* contrato *m.* **2.** *v.* regatear; negociar.

barge, *n.* lanchón *m.,* barcaza *f.*

baritone, *n.* barítono *m.*

barium, *n.* bario *m.*

bark, 1. *n.* corteza *f.;* (of dog) ladra *f.* **2.** *v.* ladrar.

barley, *n.* cebada *f.*

barn, *n.* granero *m.*

barnacle, *n.* lapa *f.*

barnyard, *n.* corral *m.*

barometer, *n.* barómetro *m.*

barometric, *a.* barométrico.

baron, *n.* barón *m.*

baroness, *n.* baronesa *f.*

baronial, *a.* baronial.

baroque, *a.* barroco.

barracks, *n.* cuartel *m.*

barrage, *n.* cortina de fuego *f.*

barred, *a.* excluido; prohibido.

barrel, *n.* barril *m.;* (of gun) cañón *m.*

barren, *a.* estéril.

barrenness, *n.* esterilidad *f.*

barricade, *n.* barricada, barrera *f.*

barrier, *n.* barrera *f.;* obstáculo *m.*

barroom, *n.* cantina *f.*

bartender, *n.* tabernero; cantinero *m.*

barter, 1. *n.* cambio, trueque *m.* **2.** *v.* cambiar, trocar.

base, 1. *a.* bajo, vil. **2.** *n.* base *f.* **3.** *v.* basar.

baseball, *n.* beisbol *m.*

baseboard, *n.* tabla de resguardo.

basement, *n.* sótano *m.*

baseness, *n.* bajeza, vileza *f.*

bashful, *a.* vergonzoso, tímido.

bashfully, *adv.* timidamente; vergonzosamente.

bashfulness, *n.* vergüenza; timidez *f.*

basic, *a.* fundamental, básico.

basin, *n.* bacía *f.;* (of river) cuenca *f.*

basis, *n.* base *f.*

bask, *v.* tomar el sol.

basket, *n.* cesta, canasta *f.*

bass, *n.* (fish) lobina *f.;* (mus.) bajo profundo *m.* **b. viol.** violón *m.*

bassinet, *n.* bacinete *m.*

bassoon, *n.* bajón *m.*

bastard, *a.* & *n.* bastardo; hijo natural *m.*

baste, v. (sew) bastear; (cooking) pringar.

bat, 1. n. (animal) murciélago m.; (baseball) bate m. **2.** v. batear.

batch, n. cantidad de cosas.

bath, n. baño m.

bathe, v. bañar.

bather, n. bañista.

bathing resort, n. balneario m.

bathrobe, n. bata de baña f., peinador m.

bathroom, n. cuarto de baño.

bathtub, n. bañera f.

baton, n. bastón m.; (mus.) batuta f.

battalion, n. batallón m.

batter, 1. n. (cooking) batido m.; (baseball) voleador m. **2.** v. batir; derribar.

battery, n. batería f.; (elec.) pila f.

batting, n. agramaje, moldeaje m.

battle, 1. n. batalla f.; combate m. **2.** v. batallar.

battlefield, n. campo de batalla.

battleship, n. acorazado m.

bauxite, n. bauxita f.

bawl, v. gritar; vocear.

bay, 1. n. bahía f. **2.** v. aullar.

bayonet, n. bayoneta f.

bazaar, n. bazar m., feria f.

be, v. ser; estar. (See hacer; hay; tener in Sp.-Eng. section).

beach, n. playa f.

beacon, n. faro m.

bead, n. cuenta f.; pl. (rel.) rosario m.

beading, n. abalorio m.

beady, a. globuloso; burbujoso.

beak, n. pico m.

beaker, n. vaso con pico m.

beam, n. viga f.; (of wood) madero m.; (of light) rayo m.

beaming, a. radiante.

bean, n. haba, habichuela f., frijol m.

bear, 1. n. oso -sa. **2.** v. llevar; (endure) aguantar.

bearable, a. sufrible; suportable.

beard, n. barba f.

bearded, a. barbado; barbudo.

beardless, a. lampiño; imberbe.

bearer, n. portador -ra.

bearing, n. porte, aguante m.

bearskin, n. piel de oso f.

beast, n. bestia f.; bruto m.

beat, v. golpear; batir; pulsar; (in games) ganar, vencer.

beaten, a. vencido; batido.

beatify, v. beatificar.

beating, n. paliza f.

beau, n. novio m.

beautiful, a. hermoso, bello.

beautifully, adv. bellamente.

beautify, v. embellecer.

beauty, n. hermosura, belleza f.

beaver, n. castor m.

becalm, v. calmar; sosegar; encalmarse.

because, conj. porque. b. of, a causa de.

beckon, v. hacer señas.

become, v. hacerse; ponerse.

becoming, a. propio, correcto; be b., quedar bien, sentar bien.

bed, n. cama f.; lecho m.; (of river) cauce m.

bedbug, n. chinche m.

bedclothes, n. ropa de cama.

bedding, n. colchones m.pl.

bedfellow, n. compañero de cama m.

bedizen, v. adornar; aderezar.

bedridden, a. postrado (en cama).

bedrock, n. (mining) lecho de roca m.; (fig.) fundamento m.

bedroom, n. alcoba f.; (Mex.) recámara f.

bedside, n. lado de cama m.

bedspread, n. cubrecama, sobrecama f.

bedstead, n. armadura de cama f.

bedtime, n. hora de acostarse.

bee, n. abeja f.

beef, n. carne de vaca.

beefsteak, n. bistec, bisté m.

beehive, n. colmena f.

beer, n. cerveza f.

beeswax, n. cera de abejas.

beet, n. remolacha f.; (Mex.) betabel m.

beetle, n. escarabajo m.

befall, v. suceder, sobrevenir.

befitting, a. conveniente; propio; digno.

before, 1. adv. antes. **2.** prep. antes de; (in front of) delante de. **3.** conj. antes que.

beforehand, adv. de antemano.

befriend, v. amparar.

befuddle, v. confundir; aturdir.

beg, v. rogar, suplicar; (for alms) mendigar.

beget, v. engendrar; producir.

beggar, n. mendigo -ga; (Sp. Am.) limosnero -ra.

beggarly, a. pobre, miserable.

begin, v. empezar, comenzar, principiar.

beginner, n. principiante m.

beginning, n. principio, comienzo m.

begrudge, v. envidiar.

behalf: in, on b. of, a favor de, en pro de.

behave, v. portarse; comportarse.

behavior, n. conducta f.; comportamiento m.

behead, v. decapitar.

behind, 1. adv. atrás, detrás. **2.** prep. detrás de.

behold, v. contemplar.

beige, a. crema.

being, n. existencia f.; (person) ser m.

bejewel, v. adornar con joyas.

belated, a. atrasado, tardío.

belch, 1. n. eructo m. **2.** v. vomitar; eructar.

belfry, n. campanario m.

Belgian, 1. a. belga. **2.** n. belga m. & f.

Belgium, n. Bélgica f.

belie, v. desmentir.

belief, n. creencia f.; parecer m.

believable, a. creíble.

believe, v. creer.

believer, n. creyente m.

belittle, v. dar poca importancia a.

bell, n. campana f.; (of house) campanilla f.; (electric) timbre m.

bellboy, n. mozo, botones m.

bellicose, a. guerrero.

belligerence, n. beligerancia f.

belligerent, a. & n. beligerante.

belligerently, adv. belicosamente.

bellow, v. bramar, rugir.

bellows, n. fuelle m.

belly, n. vientre m.; panza, barriga f.

belong, v. pertenecer.

belongings, n. propiedad f.

beloved, a. querido, amado.

below, 1. adv. debajo, abajo. **2.** prep. debajo de.

belt, n. cinturón m.

bench, n. banco m.

bend, 1. n. vuelta; curva f. **2.** v. encorvar, doblar.

beneath, 1. adv. debajo, abajo. **2.** prep. debajo de.

benediction, n. bendición f.

benefactor, n. bienhechor -ra.

benefactress, n. bienhechora f.

beneficial, a. provechoso, beneficioso.

beneficiary, n. beneficiario, beneficiado m.

benefit, 1. n. provecho, beneficio m. **2.** v. beneficiar.

benevolence, n. benevolencia f.

benevolent, a. benévolo.

benevolently, adv. benignamente.

benign, a. benigno.

benignity, n. benignidad; bondad f.

bent, 1. a. encorvado. b. on, resuelto a. **2.** n. inclinación f.

benzene, n. bencina f.

bequeath, v. legar.

bequest, n. legado m.

berate, v. reñir, regañar.

bereave, v. despojar; desolar.

bereavement, n. privación f.; despojo m.

berry, n. baya f.

berth, n. camarote m.; (naut.) litera f.; (for vessel) amarradero m.

beseech, v. suplicar; implorar.

beseechingly, adv. suplicantemente.

beset, v. acosar; rodear.

beside, prep. al lado de.

besides, adv. además, por otra parte.

besiege, v. sitiar; asediar.

besieged, *a.* sitiado.

besieger, *n.* sitiador *m.*

besmirch, *v.* manchar; deshonrar.

best, *a. & adv.* mejor. **at b.,** a lo más.

bestial, *a.* bestial; brutal.

bestir, *v.* incitar; intrigar.

best man, *n.* padrino de boda.

bestow, *v.* conferir.

bestowal, *n.* dádiva; presentación *f.*

bet, 1. *n.* apuesta *f.* **2.** *v.* apostar.

betoken, *v.* denotar, significar.

betray, *v.* traicionar; revelar.

betrayal, *n.* traición *f.*

betroth, *v.* contraer esponsales; prometer.

betrothal, *n.* esponsales *m.pl.*

better, 1. *a. & adv.* mejor. **2.** *v.* mejorar.

between, *prep.* entre, en medio de.

bevel, 1. *n.* cartabón *m.* **2.** *v.* cortar al sesgo.

beverage, *n.* bebida *f.;* (cold) refresco *m.*

bewail, *v.* llorar; lamentar.

beware, *v.* guardarse, precaverse.

bewilder, *v.* aturdir.

bewildered, *a.* descarriado.

bewildering, *a.* aturdente.

bewilderment, *n.* aturdimiento *m.;* perplejidad *f.*

bewitch, *v.* hechizar; embrujar.

beyond, *prep.* más allá de.

biannual, *a.* semianual; semestral.

bias, 1. *n.* parcialidad *f.;* prejuicio *m.* **on the b.,** al sesgo. **2.** *v.* predisponer, influir.

bib, *n.* babador *m.*

Bible, *n.* Biblia *f.*

Biblical, *a.* bíblico.

bibliography, *n.* bibliografía *f.*

bicarbonate, *n.* bicarbonato *m.*

bicentennial, *a. & n.* bicentenario *m.*

biceps, *n.* bíceps *m.*

bicker, *v.* altercar.

bicycle, *n.* bicicleta *f.*

bicyclist, *n.* biciclista *m.*

bid, 1. *n.* proposición, oferta *f.* **2.** *v.* mandar; ofrecer.

bidder, *n.* postor *m.*

bide, *v.* aguardar; esperar.

bier, *n.* ataúd *m.*

bifocal, *a.* bifocal.

big, *a.* grande.

bigamist, *n.* bígamo -ma.

bigamy, *n.* bigamia *f.*

bigot, *n.* persona intolerante.

bigotry, *n.* intolerancia *f.*

bilateral, *a.* bilateral.

bile, *n.* bilis *f.*

bilingual, *a.* bilingüe.

bilious, *a.* bilioso.

bill, 1. *n.* cuenta, factura *f.;* (money) billete *m.;* (of bird) pico *m.* **2.** *v.* facturar.

billet, 1. *n.* billete *m.;* (mil.) boleta *f.* **2.** *v.* aposentar.

billfold, *n.* cartera *f.*

billiard balls, *n.* bolas de billar.

billiards, *n.* billar *m.*

billion, *n.* billón *m.*

bill of health, *n.* certificado de sanidad.

bill of lading, *n.* conocimiento de embarque.

bill of sale, *n.* escritura de venta.

billow, *n.* ola; oleada *f.*

bimetallic, *a.* bimetálico.

bimonthly, *a. & adv.* bimestral.

bin, *n.* hucha *f.;* depósito *m.*

bind, *v.* atar; obligar; (book) encuadernar.

bindery, *n.* taller de encuadernación *m.*

binding, *n.* encuadernación *f.*

binocular, 1. *a.* binocular. **2.** *n.pl.* gemelos *m.pl.*

biochemistry, *n.* bioquímica *f.*

biodegradable, *a.* biodegradable.

biofeedback, *n.* retroalimentación biológica.

biographer, *n.* biógrafo *m.*

biographical, *a.* biográfico.

biography, *n.* biografía *f.*

biological, *a.* biológico.

biologically, *adv.* biológicamente.

biology, *n.* biología *f.*

bipartisan, *a.* bipartito.

biped, *n.* bípedo *m.*

bird, *n.* pájaro *m.;* ave *f.*

bird of prey, *n.* ave de rapiña *m.*

birth, *n.* nacimiento *m.* **give b. to,** dar a luz.

birth control, *n.* contracepción *f.*

birthday, *n.* cumpleaños *m.*

birthmark, *n.* estigma *f.,* marca de nacimiento.

birthplace, *n.* natalicio *m.*

birth rate, *n.* natalidad *f.*

birthright, *n.* primogenitura *f.*

biscuit, *n.* bizcocho *m.*

bisect, *v.* bisecar.

bishop, *n.* obispo *m.;* (chess) alfil *m.*

bishopric, *n.* obispado *f.*

bismuth, *n.* bismuto *m.*

bison, *n.* bisonte *m.*

bit, *n.* pedacito *m.;* (mech.) taladro *m.;* (for horse) bocado *m.;* (computer) bit *m.*

bitch, *n.* perra *f.*

bite, 1. *n.* bocado *m.;* picada *f.* **2.** *v.* morder; picar.

biting, *a.* penetrante; mordaz.

bitter, *a.* amargo.

bitterly, *adv.* amargamente; agriamente.

bitterness, *n.* amargura *f.;* rencor *m.*

bivouac, 1. *n.* vivaque *m.* **2.** *v.* vivaquear.

biweekly, *a.* quincenal.

black, *a.* negro.

Black, *n.* (person) negro -gra; persona de color.

blackberry, *n.* mora *f.*

blackbird, *n.* mirlo *m.*

blackboard, *n.* pizarra *f.*

blacken, *v.* ennegrecer.

black eye, *n.* ojo amoratado.

blackguard, *n.* tunante; pillo *m.*

blackmail, 1. *n.* chantaje *m.* **2.** *v.* amenazar con chantaje.

black market, *n.* mercado negro.

blackout, *n.* oscurecimiento, apagamiento *m.*

blacksmith, *n.* herrero *m.*

bladder, *n.* vejiga *f.*

blade, *n.* (sword) hoja *f.;* (oar) pala *f.;* (grass) brizna *f.*

blame, *v.* culpar, echar la culpa *a.*

blameless, *a.* inculpable.

blanch, *v.* blanquear; escaldar.

bland, *a.* blando.

blank, *a. & n.* blanco.

blanket, *n.* manta *f.;* cobertor *m.*

blare, 1. *n.* sonido de trompeta. **2.** *v.* sonar como trompeta.

blaspheme, *v.* blasfemar.

blasphemer, *n.* blasfemo, blasfemador *m.*

blasphemous, *a.* blasfemo, impío.

blasphemy, *n.* blasfemia *f.*

blast, 1. *n.* barreno *m.;* (wind) ráfaga *f.* **2.** *v.* barrenar.

blatant, *a.* bramante.

blaze, 1. *n.* llama, hoguera *f.* **2.** *v.* encenderse en llama.

blazing, *a.* flameante.

bleach, *v.* blanquear.

bleachers, *n.* asientos al aire libre.

bleak, *a.* frío y sombrío.

bleakness, *n.* intemperie *f.*

bleed, *v.* sangrar.

blemish, 1. *n.* mancha *f.;* lunar *m.* **2.** *v.* manchar.

blend, 1. *n.* mezcla *f.* **2.** *v.* mezclar, combinar.

blended, *a.* mezclado.

bless, *v.* bendecir.

blessed, *a.* bendito.

blessing, *a.* bendición *f.*

blight, 1. *n.* plaga *f.;* tizón *m.* **2.** *v.* atizonar.

blind, *a.* ciego.

blindfold, *v.* vendar los ojos.

blinding, *a.* deslumbrante; ofuscante.

blindly, *adv.* ciegamente.

blindness, *n.* ceguedad, ceguera *f.*

blink, 1. *n.* guiñada *f.* **2.** *v.* guiñar.

bliss, *n.* felicidad *f.*

blissful, *a.* dichoso; bienaventurado.

blissfully, *adv.* felizmente.

blister, *n.* ampolla *f.*

blithe, *a.* alegre; jovial; gozoso.

blizzard, *n.* chubasco de nieve.

bloat, *v.* hinchar.

bloc, *n.* grupo (político); bloc.

block, 1. *n.* bloque *m.;* (street) manzana, cuadra *f.* **2.** *v.* bloquear.

blockade, 1. *n.* bloqueo *m.* **2.** *v.* bloquear.

blond, *a. & n.* rubio -ia.

blood, *n.* sangre *f.;* parentesco, linaje *m.*

bloodhound, *n.* sabueso *m.*

bloodless, *a.* exangüe; desangrado.

blood poisoning, *n.* envenenamiento de sangre.

blood pressure, *n.* presión arterial.

bloodshed, *n.* matanza *f.*

bloodthirsty, *a.* cruel, sanguinario.

bloody, *a.* ensangrentado, sangriento.

bloom, 1. *n.* flor *f.* **2.** *v.* florecer.

blooming, *a.* lozano; fresco.

blossom, 1. *n.* flor *f.* **2.** *v.* florecer.

blot, 1. *n.* mancha *f.* **2.** *v.* manchar.

blotch, 1. *n.* mancha, roncha *f.* **2.** *v.* manchar.

blotter, *n.* papel secante.

blouse, *n.* blusa *f.*

blow, 1. *n.* golpe *m.;* (fig.) chasco *m.* **2.** *v.* soplar.

blowout, *n.* reventón de neumático.

blubber, *n.* grasa de ballena.

bludgeon, *n.* porra *f.*

blue, *a.* azul; triste, melancólico.

bluebird, *n.* azulejo *m.*

blue jeans, *n.* jeans *m.pl.*

blueprint, *n.* heliografía *f.*

bluff, 1. *n.* risco *m.* **2.** *v.* alardear; baladronar.

bluing, *n.* añil *m.*

blunder, 1. *n.* desatino *m.* **2.** *v.* desatinar.

blunderer, *n.* desatinado *m.*

blunt, 1. *a.* embotado; descortés. **2.** *v.* embotar.

bluntly, *adv.* bruscamente.

bluntness, *n.* grosería *f.*

blur, 1. *n.* trazo confuso. **2.** *v.* hacer indistinto.

blush, 1. *n.* rubor, sonrojo *m.* **2.** *v.* sonrojarse.

bluster, 1. *n.* fanfarria *f.* **2.** *v.* fanfarrear.

boar, *n.* verraco *m.* **wild b.,** jabalí *m.*

board, 1. *n.* tabla; (govt.) consejo *m.;* junta *f.* **b. and room,** cuarto y comida, casa y comida. **2.** *v.* (ship) abordar.

boarder, *n.* pensionista *m. & f.*

boardinghouse, pensión *f.*, casa de huéspedes.

boast, 1. *n.* jactancia *f.* **2.** *v.* jactarse.

boaster, *n.* fanfarrón *m.*

boastful, *a.* jactancioso.

boastfulness, *n.* jactancia *f.*

boat, *n.* barco, buque, bote *m.*

boathouse, *n.* casilla de botes *f.*

boatswain, *n.* contramaestre *m.*

bob, *v.* menear.

bobbin, *n.* bobina *f.*

bobby pin, *n.* invisible *f.*, gancho *m.*

bodice, *n.* corpiño *m.*

bodily, *a.* corporal.

body, *n.* cuerpo *m.*

bodyguard, *n.* guardia de corps.

bog, *n.* pantano *m.*

Bohemian, *a. & n.* bohemio -mia.

boil, 1. *n.* (med.) divieso *m.* **2.** *v.* hervir.

boiler, *n.* marmita; caldera *f.*

boisterous, *a.* tumultuoso.

boisterously, *adv.* tumultuosamente.

bold, *a.* atrevido, audaz.

boldface, *n.* (type) letra negra.

boldly, *adv.* audazmente; descaradamente.

boldness, *n.* atrevimiento *m.;* osadía *f.*

Bolivian, *a. & n.* boliviano -na.

bologna, *n.* salchicha *f.*

bolster, 1. *n.* travesero, cojín *m.* **2.** *v.* apoyar, sostener.

bolt, 1. *n.* perno *m.;* (of door) cerrojo *m.;* (lightning) rayo *m.* **2.** *v.* acerrojar.

bomb, 1. *n.* bomba *f.* **2.** *v.* bombardear.

bombard, *v.* bombardear.

bombardier, *n.* bombardero *m.*

bombardment, *n.* bombardeo *m.*

bomber, *n.* avión de bombardeo.

bombproof, *a.* a prueba de granadas.

bombshell, *n.* bomba *f.*

bonbon, *n.* dulce, bombón *m.*

bond, *n.* lazo *m.;* (com.) bono *m.*

bondage, *n.* esclavitud, servidumbre *f.*

bonded, *a.* garantizado.

bone, *n.* hueso *m.*

boneless, *a.* sin huesos.

bonfire, *n.* hoguera, fogata *f.*

bonnet, *n.* gorra *f.*

bonus, *n.* bono *m.*

bony, *a.* huesudo.

book, *n.* libro *m.*

bookbinder, *n.* encuadernador *m.*

bookcase, *n.* armario para libros.

bookkeeper, *n.* tenedor de libros.

bookkeeping, *n.* contabilidad *f.*

booklet, *n.* folleto *m.*, libreta *f.*

bookseller, *n.* librero *m.*

bookstore, *n.* librería *f.*

boom, *n.* (naut.) botalón *m.;* prosperidad repentina.

boon, *n.* dádiva *f.*

boor, *n.* patán, rústico *m.*

boorish, *a.* villano.

boost, 1. *n.* alza; ayuda *f.* **2.** *v.* levantar, alzar; fomentar.

booster, *n.* fomentador *m.*

boot, *n.* bota *f.*

bootblack, *n.* limpiabotas *m.*

booth, *n.* cabaña; casilla *f.*

booty, *n.* botín *m.*

border, 1. *n.* borde *m.;* frontera *f.* **2.** *v.* **b. on,** lindar con.

borderline, 1. *a.* marginal. **2.** *n.* margen *m.*

bore, 1. *n.* lata *f.;* persona pesada. **2.** *v.* aburrir, fastidiar; (mech.) taladrar.

boredom, *n.* aburrimiento *m.*

boric acid, *n.* ácido bórico *m.*

boring, *a.* aburrido, pesado.

born, *a.* nacido. **be born,** nacer.

born-again, *a.* renacido.

borrow, *v.* pedir prestado.

bosom, *n.* seno, pecho *m.*

boss, *n.* jefe, patrón *m.*

botany, *n.* botánica *f.*

both, *pron. & a.* ambos, los dos.

bother, 1. *n.* molestia *f.* **2.** *v.* molestar, incomodar.

bothersome, *a.* molesto.

bottle, 1. *n.* botella *f.* **2.** *v.* embotellar.

bottom, *n.* fondo *m.*

boudoir, *n.* tocador *m.*

bough, *n.* rama *f.*

boulder, *n.* canto rodado.

boulevard, *n.* bulevar *m.*

bounce, 1. *n.* brinco *m.* **2.** *v.* brincar; hacer saltar.

bound, 1. *n.* salto *m.* **2.** *v.* limitar.

boundary, *n.* límite, lindero *m.*

bouquet, *n.* ramillete de flores.

bourgeois, *a. & n.* burgués.

bout, *n.* encuentro; combate *m.*

bow, 1. *n.* saludo *m.;* (of ship) proa *f.;* (archery) arco *m.;* (ribbon) lazo *m.* **2.** *v.* saludar, inclinar.

bowels, *n.* intestinos *m.pl.;* entrañas *f.pl.*

bowl, 1. *n.* vasija *f.;* platón *m.* **2.** *v.* jugar a los bolos. **b. over,** derribar.

bowlegged, *a.* perniabierto.

bowling, *n.* bolos *m.pl.*

box, 1. *n.* caja *f.;* (theat.) palco *m.* **2.** *v.* (sports) boxear.

boxcar, *n.* vagón *m.*

boxer, *n.* boxeador, pugilista *m.*

boxing, *n.* boxeo *m.*

box office, *n.* taquilla *f.*

boy, *n.* muchacho, chico *m.*

boycott, 1. *n.* boicoteo *m.* **2.** *v.* boicotear.

boyhood, *n.* muchachez *f.*

boyish, *a.* pueril.

boyishly, *adv.* puerilmente.

brace, 1. *n.* grapón *m.;* pl. tirantes *m.pl.* **2.** *v.* reforzar.

bracelet, *n.* brazalete *m.*, pulsera *f.*

bracket, *n.* ménsula *f.*

brag, *v.* jactarse.

braggart, 1. *a.* jactancioso. **2.** *n.* jaque *m.*

braid, 1. *n.* trenza *f.* **2.** *v.* trenzar.

brain, *n.* cerebro, seso *m.*

brainy, *a.* sesudo, inteligente.

brake, 1. *n.* freno *m.* **2.** *v.* frenar.

bran, *n.* salvado *m.*
branch, *n.* ramo *m.; (of tree)* rama *f.*
brand, *n.* marca *f.*
brandish, *v.* blandir.
brand-new, *a.* enteramente nuevo.
brandy, *n.* aguardiente, coñac *m.*
brash, *a.* impetuoso.
brass, *n.* bronce, latón *m.*
brassiere, *n.* corpiño, sostén *m.*
brat, *n.* mocoso *m.*
bravado, *n.* bravata *f.*
brave, *a.* valiente.
bravery, *n.* valor *m.*
brawl, 1. *n.* alboroto *m.* **2.** *v.* alborotar.
brawn, *n.* músculo *m.*
bray, *v.* rebuznar.
brazen, *a.* desvergonzado.
Brazil, *n.* Brasil *m.*
Brazilian, *a. & n.* brasileño -ña. —
breach, *n.* rotura, infracción *f.*
bread, *n.* pan *m.*
breadth, *n.* anchura *f.*
break, 1. *n.* rotura; pausa *f.* **2.** *v.* quebrar, romper.
breakable, *a.* rompible, frágil.
breakage, *n.* rotura *f.*, destrozo *m.*
breakfast, 1. *n.* desayuno, almuerzo *m.* **2.** *v.* desayunarse, almorzar.
breakneck, *a.* rápido, precipitado, atropellado.
breast, *n.* pecho, seno *m.*
breath, *n.* aliento; soplo *m.*
breathe, *v.* respirar.
breathless, *a.* desalentado.
breathlessly, *adv.* jadeantemente, intensamente.
bred, *a.* criado; educado.
breeches, *n.pl.* calzones; pantalones, *m.pl.*
breed, 1. *n.* raza *f.* **2.** *v.* engendrar; criar.
breeder, *n.* criador *m.*
breeding, *n.* cría *f.*
breeze, *n.* brisa *f.*
breezy, *a.: it is b.,* hace brisa.
brevity, *n.* brevedad *f.*
brew, *v.* fraguar, elaborar.
brewer, *n.* cervecero *m.*
brewery, *n.* cervecería *f.*
bribe, 1. *n.* soborno, cohecho *m.* **2.** *v.* sobornar, cohechar.
briber, *n.* sobornador *m.*
bribery, *n.* soborno, cohecho *m.*
brick, *n.* ladrillo *m.*
bricklayer, *n.* albañil *m.*
bridal, *a.* nupcial.
bride, *n.* novia *f.*
bridegroom, *n.* novio *m.*
bridesmaid, *n.* madrina de boda.
bridge, *n.* puente *m.*
bridged, *a.* conectado.
bridgehead, *n. (mil.)* cabeza de puente.
bridle, *n.* brida *f.*
brief, *a.* breve.
briefcase, *n.* maletín *m.*

briefly, *adv.* brevemente.
briefness, *n.* brevedad *f.*
brier, *n.* zarza *f.*
brig, *n.* bergantín *m.*
brigade, *n.* brigada *f.*
bright, *a.* claro, brillante.
brighten, *v.* abrillantar; alegrar.
brightness, *n.* resplandor *m.*
brilliance, *n.* brillantez *f.*
brilliant, *a.* brillante.
brim, *n.* borde *m.; (of hat)* ala *f.*
brine, *n.* salmuera *f.*
bring, *v.* traer. **b. about,** efectuar, llevar a cabo.
brink, *n.* borde *m.*
briny, *a.* salado.
brisk, *a.* vivo; enérgico.
briskly, *adv.* vivamente.
briskness, *n.* viveza *f.*
bristle, *n.* cerda *f.*
bristly, *a.* hirsuto.
Britain, *n.* **Great B.,** Gran Bretaña *f.*
British, *a.* británico.
British Empire, imperio británico.
British Isles, islas británicas.
Briton, *n.* inglés *m.*
brittle, *a.* quebradizo, frágil.
broad, *a.* ancho.
broadcast, 1. *n.* radiodifusión *m.* **2.** *v.* radiodifundir.
broadcaster, *n.* locutor *m.*
broadcloth, *n.* paño fino.
broaden, *v.* ensanchar.
broadly, *adv.* ampliamente.
broadminded, *a.* tolerante, liberal.
brocade, *n.* brocado *m.*
brocaded, *a.* espolinado.
broil, *v.* asar.
broiler, *n.* parilla *f.*
broken, *a.* roto, quebrado.
broken-hearted, *a.* angustiado.
broker, *n.* corredor, cambista *m.*
brokerage, *n.* corretaje *m.*
bronchial, *a.* bronquial.
bronchitis, *n.* bronquitis *f.*
bronze, *n.* bronce *m.*
brooch, *n.* broche *m.*
brood, 1. *n.* cría, progenie *f.* **2.** *v.* empollar; cobijar.
brook, *n.* arroyo *m.*, quebrada *f.*
broom, *n.* escoba *f.*
broomstick, *n.* palo de escoba.
broth, *n.* caldo *m.*
brothel, *n.* burdel *m.*
brother, *n.* hermano *m.*
brotherhood, *n.* fraternidad *f.*
brother-in-law, *n.* cuñado *m.*
brotherly, *a.* fraternal.
brow, *n.* ceja; frente *f.*
brown, *a.* pardo, moreno.
browse, *v.* ramonear.
bruise, 1. *n.* contusión *f.* **2.** *v.* magullar.
brunette, *a. & n.* moreno -na, trigueño -ña.
brush, 1. *n.* cepillo *m.; brocha *f.* **2.** *v.* cepillar.
brushwood, *n.* matorral *m.*

brusque, *a.* brusco.
brusquely, *adv.* bruscamente.
brutal, *a.* brutal.
brutality, *n.* brutalidad *f.*
brutalize, *v.* embrutecer.
brute, *n.* bruto *m.,* bestia *f.*
bubble, *n.* ampolla *f.*
bucket, *n.* cubo *m.*
buckle, *n.* hebilla *f.*
buckram, *n.* bucarán *m.*
bucksaw, *n.* sierra de bastidor.
buckshot, *n.* posta *f.*
buckwheat, *n.* trigo sarraceno.
bud, 1. *n.* brote *m.* **2.** *v.* brotar.
budding, *n.* en capullo.
budge, *v.* moverse.
budget, *n.* presupuesto *m.*
buffalo, *n.* búfalo *m.*
buffer, *n.* parachoques *m.*
buffet, *n.* bufet *m.; (furniture)* aparador *m.*
buffoon, *n.* bufón *m.*
bug, *n.* insecto *m.*
bugle, *n.* clarín *m.; corneta *f.*
build, *v.* construir.
builder, *n.* constructor *m.*
building, *n.* edificio *m.*
bulb, *n.* bulbo *m.; (of lamp)* bombilla, ampolla *f.*
bulge, 1. *n.* abultamiento *m.* **2.** *v.* abultar.
bulk, *n.* masa *f.,; grueso *m.;* mayoría *f.*
bulkhead, *n.* frontón *m.*
bulky, *a.* grueso, abultado.
bull, *n.* toro *m.*
bulldog, *n.* perro de presa.
bullet, *n.* bala *f.*
bulletin, *n.* boletín *m.*
bulletproof, *a.* a prueba de bala.
bullfight, *n.* corrida de toros.
bullfighter, *n.* torero *m.*
bullfinch, *n.* pinzón real *m.*
bully, 1. *n.* rufián *m.* **2.** *v.* bravear.
bulwark, *n.* baluarte *m.*
bum, *n.* holgazán *m.*
bump, 1. *n.* golpe, choque *m.* **2.** *v.* **b. into,** chocar contra.
bumper, *n.* parachoques *m.*
bun, *n.* bollo *m.*
bunch, *n.* racimo; montón *m.*
bundle, 1. *n.* bulto *m.* **2.** *v.* **b. up,** abrigar.
bungalow, *n.* casa de un solo piso.
bungle, *v.* estropear.
bunion, *n.* juanete *m.*
bunk, *n.* litera *f.*
bunny, *n.* conejito *m.*
bunting, *n.* lanilla, banderas *f.*
buoy, *n.* boya *f.*
buoyant, *a.* boyante; vivaz.
burden, 1. *n.* carga *f.* **2.** *v.* cargar.
burdensome, *a.* gravoso.
bureau, *n. (furniture)* cómoda *f.; departamento m.*
burglar, *n.* ladrón *m.*
burglarize, *v.* robar.
burglary, *n.* robo *m.*
burial, *n.* entierro *m.*
burlap, *n.* arpillera *f.*
burly, *a.* corpulento.

burn, v. quemar; arder.

burner, n. mechero m.

burning, a. ardiente.

burnish, v. pulir; acicalar.

burrow, v. minar; horadar.

burst, v. reventar.

bury, v. enterrar.

bus, n. autobús m.

bush, n. arbusto m.

bushy, a. matoso; peludo.

business, n. negocios m.pl.; comercio m.

businesslike, a. directo.

businessman, n. comerciante m.

businesswoman, n. mujer de negocios.

bust, n. busto; pecho m.

bustle, n. bullicio m.; animación f.

busy, a. ocupado, atareado.

busybody, n. entremetido m.

but, conj. pero; sino.

butcher, n. carnicero m.

butchery, n. carnicería; matanza f.

butler, n. mayordomo m.

butt, n. punta f.; cabo extremo m.

butter, n. manteca, mantequilla f.

buttercup, n. ranúnculo m.

butterfat, n. mantequilla f.

butterfly, n. mariposa f.

buttermilk, n. suero (de leche) m.

button, n. botón m.

buttonhole, n. ojal m.

buttress, n. sostén; refuerzo m.

buxom, a. regordete.

buy, v. comprar.

buyer, n. comprador -ra.

buzz, 1. n. zumbido m. **2.** v. zumbar.

buzzard, n. gallinazo m.

buzzer, n. zumbador m.

buzz saw, n. sierra circular f.

by, prep. por; (near) cerca de, al lado de; (time) para.

by-and-by, adv. pronto; luego.

bygone, a. pasado.

bylaw, n. estatuto, reglamento m.

bypass, n. desvío m.

byproduct, n. producto accesorio m.

bystander, n. espectador; mirón m.

byte, n. en teoría de la información: ocho bits.

byway, n. camino desviado m.

C

cab, n. coche de alquiler.

cabaret, n. cabaret m.

cabbage, n. repollo m.

cabin, n. cabaña f.

cabinet, n. gabinete; ministerio m.

cabinetmaker, n. ebanista m.

cable, n. cable m.

cablegram, n. cablegrama f.

cache, n. escondite m.

cackle, 1. n. charla f., cacareo m. **2.** v. cacarear.

cacophony, n. cacofonía f.

cactus, n. cacto m.

cad, n. persona vil.

cadaver, n. cadáver m.

cadaverous, a. cadavérico.

cadence, n. cadencia f.

cadet, n. cadete m.

cadmium, n. cadmio m.

cadre, n. núcleo; (mil.) cuadro m.

café, n. café, cantina f.

cafeteria, n. cafetería f.

caffeine, n. cafeína f.

cage, 1. n. jaula f. **2.** v. enjaular.

caged, a. enjaulado.

caisson, n. arcón m.; (mil.) furgón m.

cajole, v. lisonjear; adular.

cake, n. torta f.; bizcocho m.

calamitous, a. calamitoso.

calamity, n. calamidad f.

calcify, v. calcificar.

calcium, n. calcio m.

calculable, a. calculable.

calculate, v. calcular.

calculating, a. interesado.

calculation, n. calculación f.; cálculo m.

calculus, n. cálculo m.

caldron, n. caldera f.

calendar, n. calendario m.

calf, n. ternero m.

calfskin, n. piel de becerro.

caliber, n. calibre m.

calico, n. percal m.

caliper, n. calibrador m.

calisthenics, n. calistenia, gimnasia f.

calk, v. calafatear; rellenar.

calker, n. calafate m.

call, 1. n. llamada f. **2.** v. llamar.

calligraphy, n. caligrafía f.

calling, n. vocación f.

calling card, n. tarjeta (de visita) f.

callously, adv. insensiblemente.

callow, a. sin experiencia.

callus, n. callo m.

calm, 1. a. tranquilo, calmado. **2.** n. calma f. **3.** v. calmar.

calmly, adv. serenamente.

calmness, n. calma f.

caloric, a. calórico.

calorie, n. caloría f.

calorimeter, n. calorímetro m.

calumniate, v. calumniar.

calumny, n. calumnia f.

Calvary, n. Calvario m.

calve, v. parir (la vaca).

calyx, n. cáliz m.

camaraderie, n. compañerismo m., compadrería f.

cambric, n. batista f.

camel, n. camello m.

camellia, n. camelia f.

camel's hair, n. piel de camello.

cameo, n. camafeo m.

camera, n. cámara f.

camouflage, n. camuflaje m.

camouflaging, n. simulacro, disfraz m.

camp, 1. n. campamento m. **2.** v. acampar.

campaign, n. campaña f.

camper, n. acampado m.

campfire, n. fogata de campamento.

camphor, n. alcanfor m.

camphor ball, n. bola de alcanfor.

campus, n. campo de colegio (o universidad) m.

can, v. (be able) poder.

can, 1. n. lata f. **2.** v. conservar en latas.

Canada, n. Canadá m.

Canadian, a. & n. canadiense.

canal, n. canal m.

canalize, v. canalizar.

canard, n. embuste m.

canary, n. canario m.

cancel, v. cancelar.

cancellation, n. cancelación f.

cancer, n. cáncer m.

candelabrum, n. candelabro m.

candid, a. cándido, sincero.

candidacy, n. candidatura f.

candidate, n. candidato -ta.

candidly, adv. candidamente.

candidness, n. candidez; sinceridad f.

candied, a. garapiñado.

candle, n. vela f.

candlestick, n. candelero m.

candor, n. candor m.; sinceridad f.

candy, n. dulces m.pl.

cane, n. caña f.; (for walking) bastón m.

canine, a. canino.

canister, n. frasco m.; lata f.

canker, n. llaga; úlcera f.

cankerworm, n. oruga f.

canned, a. envasado.

canner, n. envasador m.

cannery, n. fábrica de conservas alimenticias f.

cannibal, n. caníbal m.

cannon, n. cañón m.

cannonade, n. cañoneo m.

cannoneer, n. cañonero m.

canny, a. sagaz; prudente.

canoe, n. canoa f.

canon, n. canon m.; (rel.) canónigo m.

canonical, a. canónico.

canonize, v. canonizar.

canopy, n. dosel m.

cant, n. hipocresía f.

cantaloupe, n. melón m.

canteen, n. cantina f.

canter, 1. n. medio galope m. **2.** v. galopar.

cantonment, n. (mil.) acuartelamiento m.

canvas, n. lona f.

canyon, n. cañón, desfiladero m.

cap, 1. n. tapa f.; (headwear) gorro m. **2.** v. tapar.

capability, n. capacidad f.

capable, a. capaz.

capably, adv. hábilmente.

capacious, a. espacioso.

capacity, *n.* capacidad *f.*

cape, *n.* capa *f.*, (geog.) cabo *m.*

caper, *n.* zapateta *f.*; (bot.) alcaparra *f.*

capillary, *a.* capilar.

capital, *n.* capital *m.*; (govt.) capital *f.*

capitalism, *n.* capitalismo *m.*

capitalist, *n.* capitalista *m.*

capitalistic, *a.* capitalista.

capitalization, *n.* capitalización *f.*

capitalize, *v.* capitalizar.

capitulate, *v.* capitular.

capon, *n.* capón *m.*

caprice, *n.* capricho *m.*

capricious, *a.* caprichoso.

capriciously, *adv.* caprichosamente.

capriciousness, *n.* capricho *m.*

capsize, *v.* zozobrar, volcar.

capsule, *n.* cápsula *f.*

captain, *n.* capitán *m.*

caption, *n.* título *m.*; (motion pictures) subtítulo *m.*

captious, *a.* capcioso.

captivate, *v.* cautivar.

captivating, *a.* encantador.

captive, *n.* cautivo -va, prisionero -ra.

captivity, *n.* cautividad *f.*

captor, *n.* apresador *m.*

capture, **1.** *n.* captura *f.* **2.** *v.* capturar.

car, *n.* coche, carro *m.*; (of train) vagón, coche *m.* **baggage c.**, vagón de equipajes. **parlor c.**, coche salón.

carafe, *n.* garrafa *f.*

caramel, *n.* caramelo *m.*

carat, *n.* quilate *m.*

caravan, *n.* caravana *f.*

caraway, *n.* alcaravea *f.*

carbide, *n.* carburo *m.*

carbine, *n.* carabina *f.*

carbohydrate, *n.* hidrato de carbono.

carbon, *n.* carbón *m.*

carbon dioxide, anhídrido carbónico.

carbon monoxide, monóxido de carbono.

carbon paper, *n.* papel carbón *m.*

carbuncle, *n.* carbunclo *m.*

carburetor, *n.* carburador *m.*

carcinogenic, *a.* carcinogénico.

card, *n.* tarjeta *f.* **playing c.**, naipe *m.*

cardboard, *n.* cartón *m.*

cardiac, *a.* cardíaco.

cardigan, *n.* chaqueta de punto.

cardinal, **1.** *a.* cardinal. **2.** *n.* cardenal *m.*

care, **1.** *n.* cuidado. **2.** *v.* **c. for**, cuidar.

careen, *v.* carenar; encharse de costado.

career, *n.* carrera *f.*

carefree, *a.* descuidado.

careful, *a.* cuidadoso. **be c.**, tener cuidado.

carefully, *adv.* cuidadosamente.

carefulness, *n.* esmero; cuidado *m.*; cautela *f.*

careless, *a.* descuidado.

carelessly, *adv.* descuidadamente; negligentemente.

carelessness, *n.* descuido *m.*

caress, **1.** *n.* caricia *f.* **2.** *v.* acariciar.

caretaker, *n.* guardián *m.*

cargo, *n.* carga *f.*

caricature, *n.* caricatura *f.*

caries, *n.* carias *f.*

carload, *a.* furgonada, vagonada.

carnal, *a.* carnal.

carnation, *n.* clavel *m.*

carnival, *n.* carnaval *m.*

carnivorous, *a.* carnívoro.

carol, *n.* villancico *m.*

carouse, *v.* parrandear.

carpenter, *n.* carpintero *m.*

carpet, *n.* alfombra *f.*

carpeting, *n.* alfombrado *m.*

car pool, *n.* uso habitual, por varias personas, de un automóvil perteneciente a una de ellas.

carriage, *n.* carruaje; (bearing) porte *m.*

carrier, *n.* portador -ra.

carrier pigeon, *n.* paloma mensajera.

carrot, *n.* zanahoria *f.*

carrousel, *n.* volantín *m.*

carry, *v.* llevar, cargar. **c. out**, cumplir, llevar a cabo.

cart, *n.* carreta *f.*

cartage, *n.* acarreo, carretaje *m.*

cartel, *n.* cartel *m.*

cartilage, *n.* cartílago *m.*

carton, *n.* caja de cartón.

cartoon, *n.* caricatura *f.*

cartoonist, *n.* caricaturista *m.*

cartridge, *n.* cartucho *m.*

carve, *v.* esculpir; (meat) trinchar.

carver, *n.* tallador; grabador *m.*

carving, *n.* entalladura *f.*; arte de trinchar. **c. knife**, trinchante *m.*

cascade, *n.* cascada *f.*

case, *n.* caso *m.*; (box) caja *f.* **in any c.**, sea como sea.

cash, **1.** *n.* dinero contante. **2.** *v.* efectuar, cambiar.

cashier, *n.* cajero -ra.

cashmere, *n.* casimir *m.*

casino, *n.* casino *m.*

cask, *n.* barril *m.*

casket, *n.* ataúd *m.*

casserole, *n.* cacerola *f.*

cassette, *n.* cassette *m.*, cartucho *m.*

cast, **1.** *n.* (theat.) reparto de papeles. **2.** *v.* echar; (theat.) repartir.

castanet, *n.* castañuela *f.*

castaway, *n.* náufrago *m.*

caste, *n.* casta *f.*

caster, *n.* tirador *m.*

castigate, *v.* castigar.

Castilian, *a.* castellano.

cast iron, *n.* hierro colado *m.*

castle, *n.* castillo *m.*

castoff, *a.* descartado.

casual, *a.* casual.

casually, *adv.* casualmente.

casualness, *n.* casualidad *f.*

casualty, *n.* víctima *f.*; (mil.) baja *f.*

cat, *n.* gato -ta.

cataclysm, *n.* cataclismo *m.*

catacomb, *n.* catacumba *f.*

catalogue, *n.* catálogo *m.*

catapult, *n.* catapulta *f.*

cataract, *n.* catarata *f.*

catarrh, *n.* catarro *m.*

catastrophe, *n.* catástrofe *m.*

catch, *v.* alcanzar, atrapar, coger.

catchy, *a.* contagioso.

catechism, *n.* catequismo *m.*

catechize, *v.* catequizar.

categorical, *a.* categórico.

category, *n.* categoría *f.*

cater, *v.* abastecer; proveer. **c. to**, complacer.

caterpillar, *n.* gusano *m.*

catgut, *n.* cuerda (de tripa).

catharsis, *n.* purga *f.*

cathartic, **1.** *a.* catártico; purgante. **2.** *n.* purgante *m.*

cathedral, *n.* catedral *f.*

cathode, *n.* cátodo *m.*

Catholic, **1.** *a.* católico. **2.** *n.* católico -ca.

Catholicism, *n.* catolicismo *m.*

catnap, *n.* siesta corta.

catsup, *n.* salsa de tomate.

cattle, *n.* ganado *m.*

cattleman, *n.* ganadero *m.*

cauliflower, *n.* coliflor *m.*

causation, *n.* causalidad *f.*

cause, *n.* causa *f.*

causeway, *n.* calzada *f.*; terraplén *m.*

caustic, *a.* cáustico.

cauterize, *v.* cauterizar.

cautery, *n.* cauterio *m.*

caution, *n.* cautela *f.*

cautious, *a.* cauteloso.

cavalcade, *n.* cabalgata *f.*

cavalier, *n.* caballero *m.*

cavalry, *n.* caballería *f.*

cave, cavern, *n.* caverna *f.*

cave-in, *n.* hundimiento *m.*

caviar, *n.* caviar *m.*

cavity, *n.* hueco *m.*

cayman, *n.* caimán *m.*

cease, *v.* cesar.

ceaseless, *a.* incesante.

cedar, *n.* cedro *m.*

cede, *v.* ceder.

ceiling, *n.* cielo *m.*

celebrant, *n.* celebrante *m.*

celebrate, *v.* celebrar.

celebration, *n.* celebración *f.*

celebrity, *n.* persona célebre.

celerity, *n.* celeridad; prontitud *f.*

celery, *n.* apio *m.*

celestial, *a.* celeste.

celibacy, *n.* celibato *m.*

celibate, *a.* & *n.* célibe *m.*

cell, *n.* celda *f.*; (biol.) célula *f.*

cellar, *n.* sótano *m.*

cellist, a. celista m.

cello, n. violoncelo m.

cellophane, n. celofán m.

cellular, a. celular.

celluloid, n. celuloide m.

cellulose, 1. a. celuloso. 2. n. celulosa f.

Celtic, a. céltico.

cement, n. cemento m.

cemetery, n. cementerio m.; campo santo m.

censor, n. censor m.

censorious, a. severo; crítico.

censorship, n. censura f.

censure, 1. n. censura f. 2. v. censurar.

census, n. censo m.

cent, n. centavo, céntimo m.

centenary, a. & n. centenario m.

centennial, a. & n. centenario m.

center, n. centro m.

centerfold, n. página central desplegable en una revista.

centerpiece, n. centro de mesa.

centigrade, a. centígrado.

centigrade thermometer, termómetro centígrado.

central, a. central.

Central American, a. & n. centroamericano -na.

centralize, v. centralizar.

century, n. siglo m.

century plant, n. maguey f.

ceramic, a. cerámico.

ceramics, n. cerámica f.

cereal, n. cereal m.

cerebral, a. cerebral.

ceremonial, a. ceremonial.

ceremonious, a. ceremonioso.

ceremony, n. ceremonia f.

certain, a. cierto, seguro.

certainly, adv. sin duda, seguramente.

certainty, n. certeza f.

certificate, n. certificado m.

certification, n. certificación f.

certified, a. certificado.

certify, v. certificar.

certitude, n. certeza f.

cessation, n. cesación f., discontinuación f.

cession, n. cesión f.

chafe, v. irritar.

chafing dish, n. escalfador m.

chagrin, n. disgusto m.

chain, 1. n. cadena f. 2. v. encadenar.

chair, n. silla f.

chairman, n. presidente m.

chairperson, n. presidente -ta; persona que preside.

chalk, n. tiza f.

challenge, 1. n. desafío m. 2. v. desafiar.

challenger, n. desafiador m.

chamber, n. cámara f.

chamberlain, n. camarero m.

chambermaid, n. camarera f.

chameleon, n. camaleón m.

chamois, n. gamuza f.

champagne, n. champán m., champaña f.

champion, 1. n. campeón m. 2. v. defender.

championship, n. campeonato m.

chance, 1. n. oportunidad, ocasión f. by c., por casualidad, por acaso. take a c., aventurarse.

chancel, n. antealtar m.

chancellery, n. cancillería f.

chancellor, n. canciller m.

chandelier, n. araña de luces.

change, 1. n. cambio f.; (from a bill) moneda f. 2. v. cambiar.

changeability, n. mutabilidad f.

changeable, a. variable, inconstante.

changer, n. cambiador m.

channel, 1. n. canal m. 2. v. encauzar.

chant, 1. n. canto llano m. 2. v. cantar.

chaos, n. caos m.

chaotic, a. caótico.

chap, 1. n. (coll.) tipo m. 2. v. rajar.

chapel, n. capilla f.

chaperon, n. dueña m.

chaplain, n. capellán m.

chapter, n. capítulo m.

char, v. carbonizar.

character, n. carácter m.

characteristic, 1. a. característico. 2. n. característica f.

characterization, n. caracterización f.

characterize, v. caracterizar.

charcoal, n. carbón leña.

charge, 1. n. acusación f.; ataque m. 2. v. cargar; acusar; atacar.

chariot, n. carroza f.

charisma, n. carisma m.

charitable, a. caritativo.

charitableness, n. caridad f.

charitably, adv. caritativamente.

charity, n. caridad f.; (alms) limosna f.

charlatan, n. charlatán -na.

charlatanism, n. charlatanería f.

charm, 1. n. encanto m.; (witchcraft) hechizo m. 2. v. encantar; hechizar.

charming, a. encantador.

charred, a. carbonizado.

chart, n. mapa m.

charter, 1. n. carta f. 2. v. alquilar.

charter flight, vuelo charter m.

chase, 1. n. caza f. 2. v. cazar; perseguir.

chaser, n. perseguidor m.

chasm, n. abismo m.

chassis, n. chasis m.

chaste, a. casto.

chasten, v. corregir, castigar.

chastise, v. castigar.

chastisement, n. castigo m.

chastity, n. castidad, pureza f.

chat, 1. n. plática, charla f. 2. v. platicar, charlar.

chateau, n. castillo m.

chattels, n.pl. bienes m.

chatter, 1. v. cotorrear; (teeth) rechinar. 2. n. cotorreo m.

chatterbox, n. charlador m.

chauffeur, n. chofer m.

cheap, a. barato.

cheapen, v. rebajar, menospreciar.

cheaply, adv. barato.

cheapness, n. baratura f.

cheat, v. engañar.

cheater, n. engañador m.

check, 1. n. verificación f.; (bank) cheque m.; (restaurant) cuenta f.; (chess) jaque m. 2. v. verificar.

checkers, n. juego de damas.

checkmate, v. dar mate.

cheek, n. mejilla f.

cheer, 1. n. alegría f.; aplauso m. 2. v. alegrar; aplaudir.

cheerful, a. alegre.

cheerfully, adv. alegremente.

cheerfulness, n. alegría f.

cheerless, a. triste.

cheery, a. alegre.

cheese, n. queso m. cottage c., requesón m.

chef, n. cocinero en jefe.

chemical, 1. a. químico. 2. n. reactivo m.

chemically, adv. químicamente.

chemist, n. químico m.

chemistry, n. química f.

chemotherapy, n. quimoterapía f.

chenille, n. felpilla f.

cherish, v. apreciar.

cherry, n. cereza f.

cherub, n. querubín m.

chess, n. ajedrez m.

chest, n. arca f.; (physiology) pecho m.

chestnut, n. castaña f.

chevron, n. sardineta f.

chew, v. mascar, masticar.

chewer, n. mascador m.

chic, a. elegante, paquete.

chicanery, n. trampería f.

chick, n. pollito m.

chicken, n. pollo m., gallina f.

chicken-hearted, a. cobarde.

chicken pox, n. viruelas locas f.

chicle, n. chicle m.

chicory, n. achicoria f.

chide, v. regañar, reprender.

chief, 1. a. principal. 2. n. jefe m.

chiefly, adv. principalmente, mayormente.

chieftain, n. caudillo m.; (Indian c.) cacique m.

chiffon, n. chifón m.

chilblain, n. sabañón m.

child, n. niño -ña; hijo -ja.

childbirth, n. parto m.

childhood, n. niñez f.

childish, a. pueril.

childishness, n. puerilidad f.

childless, a. sin hijos.

childlike, a. infantil.

Chilean, a. & n. chileno -na.

chili, n. chile ají m.

chill, 1. *n.* frío; escalofrío *m.* **2.** *v.* enfriar.

chilliness, *n.* frialdad *f.*

chilly, *a.* frío; friolento.

chimes, *n.* juego de campanas.

chimney, *n.* chimenea *f.*

chimpanzee, *n.* chimpancé *m.*

chin, *n.* barba *f.*

china, *n.* loza *f.*

chinchilla, *n.* chinchilla *f.*

Chinese, *a.* & *n.* chino -na.

chink, *n.* grieta *f.*

chintz, *n.* zaraza *f.*

chip, 1. *n.* astilla *f.* **2.** *v.* astillar.

chiropodist, *n.* pedicuro *m.*

chiropractor, *n.* quiroprático *m.*

chirp, 1. *n.* chirrido *m.* **2.** *v.* chirriar, piar.

chisel, 1. *n.* cincel *m.* **2.** *v.* cincelar, talar.

chivalrous, *a.* caballeroso.

chivalry, *n.* caballería *f.*

chive, *n.* cebollino *m.*

chloride, *n.* cloruro *m.*

chlorine, *n.* cloro *m.*

chloroform, *n.* cloroformo *m.*

chlorophyll, *n.* clorófila *f.*

chock-full, *a.* repleto, colmado.

chocolate, *n.* chocolate *m.*

choice, 1. *a.* selecto, escogido. **2.** *n.* selección *f.;* escogimiento *m.*

choir, *n.* coro *m.*

choke, *v.* sofocar, ahogar.

cholera, *n.* cólera *f.*

choleric, *a.* colérico, irascible.

choose, *v.* elegir, escoger.

chop, 1. *n.* chuleta, costilla *f.* **2.** *v.* tajar; cortar.

chopper, *n.* tajador *m.*

choppy, *a.* agitado.

choral, *a.* coral.

chord, *n.* cuerda *f.*

chore, *n.* tarea *f.,* quehacer *m.*

choreography, *n.* coreografía *f.*

chorister, *n.* corista *m.*

chorus, *n.* coro *m.*

christen, *v.* bautizar.

Christendom, *n.* cristiandad *f.*

Christian, *a.* & *n.* cristiano -na.

Christianity, *n.* cristianismo *m.*

Christmas, *n.* navidad, pascua *f.* Merry C., felices pascuas. C. Eve, nochebuena *f.*

chromatic, *a.* cromático.

chromium, *n.* cromo *m.*

chromosome, *n.* cromosoma *m.*

chronic, *a.* crónico.

chronicle, *n.* crónica *f.*

chronological, *a.* cronológico.

chronology, *n.* cronología *f.*

chrysalis, *n.* crisálida *f.*

chrysanthemum, *n.* crisantemo *m.*

chubby, *a.* regordete.

chuck, *v.* (cluck) cloquear; (throw) echar, tirar.

chuckle, *v.* reír entre dientes.

chum, *n.* amigo *m.;* compinche *m.*

chummy, *a.* íntimo.

chunk, *n.* trozo *m.*

chunky, *a.* fornido, trabado.

church, *n.* iglesia *f.*

churchman, *n.* eclesiástico *m.*

churchyard, *n.* cementerio *m.*

churn, 1. *n.* mantequera *f.* **2.** *v.* agitar, revolver.

chute, *n.* conducto *m.;* canal *f.*

cicada, *n.* cigarra, chicharra *f.*

cider, *n.* sidra *f.*

cigar, *n.* cigarro, puro *m.*

cigarette, *n.* cigarrillo, pitillo *m.* c. case, cigarrillera *f.*

cinchona, *n.* cinchona *f.*

cinder, *n.* ceniza *f.*

cinema, *n.* cine *m.*

cinnamon, *n.* canela *f.*

cipher, *n.* cifra *f.*

circle, *n.* círculo *m.*

circuit, *n.* circuito *m.*

circuitous, *a.* tortuoso.

circuitously, *adv.* tortuosamente.

circular, *a.* circular, redondo.

circularize, *v.* hacer circular.

circulate, *v.* circular.

circulation, *n.* circulación *f.*

circulator, *n.* diseminador *m.*

circulatory, *a.* circulatorio.

circumcise, *v.* circuncidar.

circumcision, *n.* circuncisión *f.*

circumference, *n.* circunferencia *f.*

circumlocution, *n.* circunlocución *f.*

circumscribe, *v.* circunscribir; limitar.

circumspect, *a.* discreto.

circumstance, *n.* circunstancia *f.*

circumstantial, *a.* circunstancial, indirecto.

circumstantially, *adv.* minuciosamente.

circumvent, *v.* evadir, evitar.

circumvention, *n.* trampa *f.;* estratagema *f.*

circus, *n.* circo *m.*

cirrhosis, *n.* cirrosis *f.*

cistern, *n.* cisterna *f.*

citadel, *n.* ciudadela *f.*

citation, *n.* citación *f.*

cite, *v.* citar.

citizen, *n.* ciudadano -na.

citizenship, *n.* ciudadanía *f.*

citric, *a.* cítrico.

city, *n.* ciudad *f.*

civic, *a.* cívico.

civics, *n.* ciencia del gobierno civil.

civil, *a.* civil; cortés.

civilian, *a.* & *n.* civil *m.*

civility, *n.* cortesía *f.*

civilization, *n.* civilización *f.*

civilize, *v.* civilizar.

civil service, *n.* servicio civil oficial *m.*

civil war, *n.* guerra civil *f.*

clabber, 1. *n.* cuajo *m.* **2.** *v.* cuajarse.

clad, *a.* vestido.

claim, 1. *n.* demanda; pretensión *f.* **2.** *v.* demandar, reclamar.

claimant, *n.* reclamante *m.*

clairvoyance, *n.* clarividencia *f.*

clairvoyant, *a.* clarividente.

clam, *n.* almeja *f.*

clamber, *v.* trepar.

clamor, 1. *n.* clamor *m.* **2.** *v.* clamar.

clamorous, *a.* clamoroso.

clamp, 1. *n.* prensa de sujeción *f.* **2.** *v.* asegurar, sujetar.

clan, *n.* tribu *f.*

clandestine, *a.* clandestino.

clandestinely, *adv.* clandestinamente.

clangor, *n.* estruendo *m.,* estrépito *m.*

clannish, *a.* unido; exclusivista.

clap, *v.* aplaudir.

clapboard, *n.* chilla *f.*

claque, *n.* claque *f.*

claret, *n.* clarete *m.*

clarification, *n.* clarificación *f.*

clarify, *v.* clarificar.

clarinet, *n.* clarinete *m.*

clarinetist, *n.* clarinero *m.*

clarity, *n.* claridad *f.*

clash, 1. *n.* choque *m.* **2.** *v.* chocar.

clasp, 1. *n.* broche *m.* **2.** *v.* abrochar.

class, *n.* clase *f.*

classic, classical, *a.* clásico.

classicism, *n.* clasicismo *m.*

classifiable, *a.* clasificable, calificable.

classification, *n.* clasificación *f.*

classify, *v.* clasificar.

classmate, *n.* compañero de clase.

classroom, *n.* sala de clase.

clatter, 1. *n.* alboroto *m.* **2.** *v.* alborotar.

clause, *n.* cláusula *f.*

claustrophobia, *n.* claustrofobia *f.*

claw, *n.* garra *f.*

clay, *n.* arcilla *f.;* barro *m.*

clean, 1. *a.* limpio. **2.** *v.* limpiar.

cleaner, *n.* limpiador -ra.

cleanliness, *n.* limpieza *f.*

cleanse, *v.* limpiar, purificar.

cleanser, *n.* limpiador *m.,* purificador *m.*

clear, *a.* claro.

clearance, *n.* espacio libre. c. sale, venta de liquidación.

clearing, *n.* despejo *m.;* desmonte *m.*

clearly, *adv.* claramente, evidentemente.

clearness, *n.* claridad *f.*

cleavage, *n.* resquebradura *f.*

cleaver, *n.* partidor *m.,* hacha *f.*

clef, *n.* clave, llave *f.*

clemency, *n.* clemencia *f.*

clench, *v.* agarrar.

clergy, *n.* clero *m.*

clergyman, *n.* clérigo *m.*

clerical, *a.* clerical. c. work, trabajo de dependientes.

clericalism, *n.* clericalismo *m.*

clerk, *n.* dependiente, escribiente *m.*

clerkship, *n.* escribanía *f.,* secretaría *f.*

clever, a. diestro, hábil.

cleverly, adv. diestramente, habilmente.

cleverness, n. destreza f.

cliché, n. cliché m.

client, n. cliente m.

clientele, n. clientela f.

cliff, n. precipicio, risco m.

climate, n. clima m.

climatic, a. climático.

climax, n. colmo m., culminación f.

climb, v. escalar; subir.

climber, n. trepador m., escalador m; (bot.) enredadera f.

clinch, v. afirmar.

cling, v. pegarse.

clinic, n. clínica f.

clinical, a. clínico.

clinically, adv. clinicalmente.

clip, 1. n. grapa f. **paper c.,** gancho m. **2.** v. prender; (shear) trasquilar.

clipper, n. recortador m; (aero.) clíper m.

clipping, n. recorte m.

clique, n. camarilla f., compadraje m.

cloak, n. capa f., manto m.

clock, n. reloj m. **alarm c.,** despertador m.

clod, n. terrón m; césped m.

clog, v. obstruir.

cloister, n. claustro m.

clone, m. ser viviente reproducido a base de las células de otro.

close, 1. a. cercano. **2.** adv. cerca. **c. to,** cerca de. **3.** v. cerrar; tapar.

closely, adv. (near) de cerca; (tight) estrechamente; (care) cuidadosamente.

closeness, n. contigüidad f., apretamiento m; (airless) falta de ventilación f.

closet, n. gabinete m. **clothes c.,** ropero m.

clot, 1. n. coagulación f. **2.** v. coagularse.

cloth, n. paño m; tela f.

clothe, v. vestir.

clothes, clothing, n. ropa f.

clothing, n. vestidos m., ropa f.

cloud, n. nube f.

cloudburst, n. chaparrón m.

cloudiness, n. nebulosidad f.; obscuridad f.

cloudless, a. despejado, sin nubes.

cloudy, a. nublado.

clove, n. clavo m.

clover, n. trébol m.

clown, n. bufón m.

clownish, a. grosero; bufonesco.

cloy, v. saciar.

club, 1. n. porra f.; (social) círculo, club m.; (cards) basto m. **2.** v. golpear con una porra.

clubfoot, n. pateta m., pie zambo m.

clue, n. seña, pista f.

clump, n. grupo m., masa f.

clumsiness, n. tosquedad f., desmaña f.

clumsy, a. torpe, desmañado.

cluster, 1. n. grupo m.; (fruit) racimo m. **2.** v. agrupar.

clutch, 1. n. (auto.) embrague m. **2.** v. agarrar.

clutter, 1. n. confusión f. **2.** v. poner en desorden.

coach, 1. n. coche, vagón m.; coche ordinario; (sports) entrenador m. **2.** v. entrenar.

coachman, n. cochero m.

coagulate, v. coagular.

coagulation, n. coagulación f.

coal, n. carbón m.

coalesce, v. unirse, soldarse.

coalition, n. coalición f.

coal oil, n. petróleo m.

coal tar, n. alquitrán m.

coarse, a. grosero, burdo; (material) tosco, grueso.

coarsen, v. vulgarizar.

coarseness, n. grosería; tosquedad f.

coast, 1. n. costa f., litoral m. **2.** v. deslizarse.

coastal, a. costanero.

coast guard, n. costanero f.

coat, 1. n. saco m., chaqueta f.; (paint) capa f. **2.** v. cubrir.

coat of arms, n. escudo m.

coax, v. instar.

cobalt, n. cobalto m.

cobbler, n. zapatero m.

cobblestone, n. guijarro m.

cobra, n. cobra f.

cobweb, n. telaraña f.

cocaine, n. cocaína f.

cock, n. (rooster) gallo m.; (water, etc.) llave f.; (gun) martillo m.

cockfight, n. riña de gallos f.

cockpit, n. gallera f.; reñidero de gallos m.

cockroach, n. cucaracha f.

cocktail, n. coctel m.

cocky, a. confiado, atrevido.

cocoa, n. cacao m.

coconut, n. coco m.

cocoon, n. capullo m.

cod, n. bacalao m.

code, n. código m.; clave f.

codeine, n. codeína f.

codfish, n. bacalao m.

codify, v. compilar.

coeducation, n. coeducación f.

coequal, a. mutuamente igual.

coerce, v. forzar.

coercion, n. coerción f.

coercive, a. coercitivo.

coexist, v. coexistir.

coffee, n. café m. **c. plantation,** cafetal m.

coffer, n. cofre m.

coffin, n. ataúd m.

cog, n. diente de rueda m.

cogent, a. convincente.

cogitate, v. pensar, reflexionar.

cognizance, n. conocimiento m., comprensión f.

cognizant, a. conocedor, informado.

cogwheel, n. rueda dentada f.

cohere, v. pegarse.

coherent, a. coherente.

cohesion, n. cohesión f.

cohesive, a. cohesivo.

cohort, n. cohorte f.

coiffure, n. peinado, tocado m.

coil, 1. n. rollo m.; (naut.) adujada f. **2.** v. enrollar.

coin, n. moneda f.

coinage, n. sistema monetario f.

coincide, v. coincidir.

coincidence, n. coincidencia; casualidad f.

coincident, a. coincidente.

coincidental, a. coincidental.

coincidentally, adv. coincidentalmente, al mismo tiempo.

colander, n. colador m.

cold, a. & n. frío m.; (med.) resfriado m. **to be c.,** tener frío; (weather) hacer frío.

coldly, adv. friamente.

coldness, n. frialdad f.

collaborate, v. colaborar.

collaboration, n. colaboración f.

collaborator, n. colaborador m.

collapse, 1. n. desplome m.; (med.) colapso m. **2.** v. desplomarse.

collar, n. cuello m.

collarbone, n. clavícula f.

collate, v. comparar.

collateral, 1. a. colateral. **2.** n. garantía f.

collation, n. comparación f.; (food) colación f., merienda f.

colleague, n. colega m. & f.

collect, v. cobrar; recoger; coleccionar.

collection, n. colección f.

collective, a. colectivo.

collectively, adv. colectivamente, en masa.

collector, n. colector -ra; coleccionista m. & f.

college, n. colegio m.; universidad f.

collegiate, a. colegiado m.

collide, v. chocar.

collision, n. choque m.

colloquial, a. familiar.

colloquially, adv. familiarmente.

colloquy, n. conversación f., coloquio m.

collusion, n. colusión f., connivencia f.

Colombian, a. & n. colombiano -na.

colon, n. colon m.; (punct.) dos puntos.

colonel, n. coronel m.

colonial, a. colonial.

colonist, n. colono m.

colonization, n. colonización f.

colonize, v. colonizar.

colony, n. colonia f.

color, 1. n. color; colorido m. **2.** v. colorar; colorir.

coloration, n. colorido m.

colored, a. de color.

colorful, a. vívido.

colorless, a. descolorido, sin color.

colossal, a. colosal.

colt, n. porto m.

column, n. columna f.

coma, n. coma m.

comb, 1. n. peine m. **2.** v. peinar.

combat, 1. n. combate m. **2.** v. combatir.

combatant, n. combatiente m.

combative, a. combativo.

combination, n. combinación f.

combine, v. combinar.

combustible, a. & n. combustible m.

combustion, n. combustión f.

come, v. venir. **c. back,** volver. **c. in,** entrar. **c. out,** salir. **c. up,** subir. **c. upon,** encontrarse con.

comedian, n. cómico -ca.

comedienne, n. cómica f., actriz f.

comedy, n. comedia f.

comet, n. cometa m.

comfort, 1. n. confort m.; solaz m. **2.** v. confortar; solazar.

comfortable, a. cómodo.

comfortably, adv. cómodamente.

comforter, n. colcha f.

comfortingly, adv. confortantemente.

comfortless, a. sin consuelo; sin comodidades.

comic, comical, a. cómico.

coming, 1. n. venida f., llegada f. **2.** a. próximo, que viene, entrante.

comma, n. coma f.

command, 1. n. mando m. **2.** v. mandar.

commandeer, v. reclutir forzosamente, expropiar.

commander, n. comandante m.

commander in chief, n. generalísimo, jefe supremo.

commandment, n. mandato; mandamiento m.

commemorate, v. conmemorar.

commemoration, n. conmemoración f.

commemorative, a. conmemorativo.

commence, v. comenzar, principiar.

commencement, n. comienzo m.; graduación f.

commend, v. encomendar.

commendable, a. recomendable.

commendably, adv. loablemente.

commendation, n. recomendación f.

commensurate, a. proporcionado.

comment, 1. n. comento m. **2.** v. comentar.

commentary, n. comentario m.

commentator, n. comentador -ra.

commerce, n. comercio m.

commercial, a. comercial.

commercialism, n. comercialismo m.

commercialize, v. mercantilizar, explotar.

commercially, a. & adv. comercial.

commiserate, v. compadecerse.

commissary, n. comisario m.

commission, 1. n. comisión f. **2.** v. comisionar.

commissioner, n. comisionista m. & f.

commit, v. cometer.

commitment, n. compromiso m.

committee, n. comité m.

commodious, a. cómodo.

commodity, n. mercadería f.

common, a. común; ordinario.

commonly, adv. comúnmente, vulgarmente.

commonplace, a. trivial, banal.

commonwealth, n. estado m.; nación f.

commotion, n. tumulto m.

communal, a. comunal, público.

commune, 1. n. distrito municipal m.; comuna f. **2.** v. conversar.

communicable, a. comunicativo.

communicate, v. comunicar.

communication, n. comunicación f.

communicative, a. comunicativo.

communion, n. comunión f. **take c.,** comulgar.

communiqué, n. comunicación f.

communism, n. comunismo m.

communist, n. comunista m. & f.

communistic, a. comunístico.

community, n. comunidad f.

commutation, n. conmutación f.

commuter, n. empleado que viaja diariamente desde su domicilio hasta la ciudad donde trabaja.

compact, 1. a. compacto. **2.** n. pacto m.; (lady's) polvera f.

companion, n. compañero -ra.

companionable, a. sociable.

companionship, n. compañerismo m.

company, n. compañía f.

comparable, a. comparable.

comparative, a. comparativo.

comparatively, a. relativamente.

compare, v. comparar.

comparison, n. comparación f.

compartment, n. compartimiento m.

compass, n. compás m.; (naut.) brújula f.

compassion, n. compasión f.

compassionate, a. compasivo.

compassionately, adv. compasivamente.

compatible, a. compatible.

compatriot, n. compatriota m. & f.

compel, v. obligar.

compensate, v. compensar.

compensation, n. compensación f.

compensatory, a. compensatorio.

compete, v. competir.

competence, n. competencia f.

competent, a. competente, capaz.

competently, adv. competentemente.

competition, n. concurrencia f.; concurso m.

competitive, a. competidor.

competitor, n. competidor -ra.

compile, v. compilar.

complacency, n. complacencia f.

complacent, a. complaciente.

complacently, adv. complacientemente.

complain, v. quejarse.

complaint, n. queja f.

complement, n. complemento m.

complete, 1. a. completo **2.** v. completar.

completely, adv. completamente, enteramente.

completeness, n. integridad f.

completion, n. terminación f.

complex, a. complejo.

complexion, n. tez f.

complexity, n. complejidad f.

compliance, n. consentimiento m. **in c. with,** de acuerdo con.

compliant, a. dócil; complaciente.

complicate, v. complicar.

complicated, a. complicado.

complication, n. complicación f.

complicity, n. complicidad f.

compliment, 1. n. flor f. **2.** v. felicitar; echar flores.

complimentary, a. galante, obsequioso, regaloso.

comply, v. cumplir.

component, a. & n. componente m.

comport, v. portarse.

compose, v. componer.

composed, a. tranquilo; (made up) compuesto.

composer, n. compositor -ra.

composite, a. compuesto.

composition, n. composición f.

composure, n. serenidad f.; calma f.

compote, n. compota f.

compound, a. & n. compuesto m.

comprehend, v. comprender.

comprehensible, a. comprensible.

comprehension, n. comprensión f.

comprehensive, a. comprensivo.

compress, 1. n. cabezal m. **2.** v. comprimir.

compressed, a. comprimido.

compression, n. compresión f.

compressor, n. compresor m.

comprise, *v.* comprender; abarcar.

compromise, 1. *n.* compromiso *m.* **2.** *v.* comprometer.

compromiser, *n.* compromisario *m.*

compulsion, *n.* compulsión *f.*

compulsive, *a.* compulsivo.

compulsory, *a.* obligatorio.

compunction, *n.* compunción *f.;* escrúpulo *m.*

computation, *n.* computación *f.*

compute, *v.* computar, calcular.

computer, *n.* computadora *f.,* ordenador *m.*

computerize, *v.* procesar en computadora.

comrade, *n.* camarada *m. & f.;* compañero -ra.

comradeship, *n.* camaradería *f.*

concave, *a.* cóncavo.

conceal, *v.* ocultar, esconder.

concealment, *n.* ocultación *f.*

concede, *v.* conceder.

conceit, *n.* amor propio; engreimiento *m.*

conceited, *a.* engreído.

conceivable, *a.* concebible.

conceive, *v.* concebir.

concentrate, *v.* concentrar.

concentration, *n.* concentración *f.*

concept, *n.* concepto *m.*

conception, *n.* concepción *f.;* concepto *m.*

concern, 1. *n.* interés *m.;* inquietud *f.;* (com.) negocio *m.* **2.** *v.* concernir.

concerning, *prep.* respecto a.

concert, *n.* concierto *m.*

concerted, *a.* convenido.

concession, *n.* concesión *f.*

conciliate, *v.* conciliar.

conciliation, *n.* conciliación *f.*

conciliator, *n.* conciliador *m.*

conciliatory, *a.* conciliatorio.

concise, *a.* conciso.

concisely, *adv.* concisamente.

conciseness, *n.* concisión *f.*

conclave, *n.* conclave *m.*

conclude, *v.* concluir.

conclusion, *n.* conclusión *f.*

conclusive, *a.* conclusivo, decisivo.

conclusively, *adv.* concluyentemente.

concoct, *v.* confeccionar.

concomitant, *n. & a.* concomitante.

concord, *n.* concordia *f.*

concordat, *n.* concordato *m.*

concourse, *n.* concurso *m.;* confluencia *f.*

concrete, *a.* concreto.

concretely, *adv.* concretamente.

concubine, *n.* concubina, amiga *f.*

concur, *v.* concurrir.

concurrence, *n.* concurrencia *f.;* casualidad *f.*

concurrent, *a.* concurrente.

concussion, *n.* concusión *f.;* (c.

of the brain) conmoción cerebral *f.*

condemn, *v.* condenar.

condemnable, *a.* culpable, condenable.

condemnation, *n.* condenación *f.*

condensation, *n.* condensación *f.*

condense, *v.* condensar.

condenser, *n.* condensador *m.*

condescend, *v.* condescender.

condescension, *n.* condescendencia *f.*

condiment, *n.* condimento *m.*

condition, 1. *n.* condición *f.;* estado *m.* **2.** *v.* acondicionar.

conditional, *a.* condicional.

conditionally, *adv.* condicionalmente.

condole, *v.* condolerse.

condolence, *n.* pésame *m.*

condominium, *n.* apartamento en propiedad *m.*

condone, *v.* condonar.

conducive, *a.* conducente.

conduct, 1. *n.* conducta *f.* **2.** *v.* conducir.

conductivity, *n.* conductividad *f.*

conductor, *n.* conductor *m.*

conduit, *n.* caño *m.,* canal *f.;* conducto *m.*

cone, *n.* cono *m.* **ice-cream c.,** barquillo de helado.

confection, *n.* confitura *f.*

confectioner, *n.* confitero *m.*

confectionery, *n.* dulcería *f.*

confederacy, *n.* federación *f.*

confederate, *a. & n.* confederado *m.*

confederation, *n.* confederación *f.*

confer, *v.* conferenciar; conferir.

conference, *n.* conferencia *f.;* congreso *m.*

confess, *v.* confesar.

confession, *n.* confesión *f.*

confessional, 1. *n.* confesionario *m.* **2.** *a.* confesional.

confessor, *n.* confesor *m.*

confetti, *n.* confetti *m.*

confidant, confidante, *n.* confidente *m. & f.*

confide, *v.* confiar.

confidence, *n.* confianza *f.*

confident, *a.* confiado; cierto.

confidential, *a.* confidencial.

confidentially, *adv.* confidencialmente, en secreto.

confidently, *adv.* confiadamente.

confine, 1. *n.* confín *m.* **2.** *v.* confinar; encerrar.

confirm, *v.* confirmar.

confirmation, *n.* confirmación *f.*

confiscate, *v.* confiscar.

confiscation, *n.* confiscación *f.*

conflagration, *n.* incendio *m.*

conflict, 1. *n.* conflicto *m.* **2.** *v.* oponerse; estar en conflicto.

conform, *v.* conformar.

conformation, *n.* conformación *f.*

conformer, *n.* conformista *m. & f.*

conformist, *n.* conformista *m. & f.*

conformity, *n.* conformidad *f.*

confound, *v.* confundir.

confront, *v.* confrontar.

confuse, *v.* confundir.

confusion, *n.* confusión *f.*

congeal, *v.* congelar, helar.

congealment, *n.* congelación *f.*

congenial, *a.* congenial.

congenital, *a.* congénito.

congenitally, *adv.* congenitalmente.

congestion, *n.* congestión *f.*

conglomerate, 1. *v.* conglomerar. **2.** *a.* conglomerado.

conglomeration, *n.* conglomeración *f.*

congratulate, *v.* felicitar.

congratulation, *n.* felicitación *f.*

congratulatory, *a.* congratulatorio.

congregate, *v.* congregar.

congregation, *n.* congregación *f.*

congress, *n.* congreso *m.*

conic, *n.* cónica *f.* **2.** *a.* cónico.

conjecture, 1. *n.* conjetura *f.* **2.** *v.* conjeturar.

conjugal, *a.* conyugal, matrimonial.

conjugate, *v.* conjugar.

conjugation, *n.* conjugación *f.*

conjunction, *n.* conjunción *f.*

conjunctive, 1. *n.* (gram.) conjunción *f.* **2.** *a.* conjuntivo.

conjunctivitis, *n.* conjuntivitis *f.*

conjure, *v.* conjurar.

connect, *v.* juntar; relacionar.

connection, *n.* conexión *f.*

connivance, *n.* consentimiento *m.*

connive, *v.* disimular.

connoisseur, *n.* perito -ta.

connotation, *n.* connotación *f.*

connote, *v.* connotar.

connubial, *a.* conyugal.

conquer, *v.* conquistar.

conquerable, *a.* conquistable, vencible.

conqueror, *n.* conquistador *m.*

conquest, *n.* conquista *f.*

conscience, *n.* conciencia *f.*

conscientious, *a.* concienzudo.

conscientiously, *adv.* escrupulosamente.

conscious, *a.* consciente.

consciously, *adv.* con conocimiento.

consciousness, *n.* consciencia *f.*

conscript, 1. *n.* conscripto *m.,* recluta *m.* **2.** *v.* reclutar, alistar.

conscription, *n.* conscripción *f.,* alistamiento *m.*

consecrate, *v.* consagrar.

consecration, n. consagración f.

consecutive, a. consecutivo, seguido.

consecutively, adv. consecutivamente, de seguida.

consensus, n. consenso m., acuerdo general m.

consent, 1. n. consentimiento m. 2. v. consentir.

consequence, n. consecuencia f.

consequent, a. consiguiente.

consequential, a. importante.

consequently, adv. por lo tanto, por consiguiente.

conservation, n. conservación f.

conservatism, n. conservatismo m.

conservative, a. conservador, conservativo.

conservatory, n. (plants) invernáculo m.; (school) conservatorio m.

conserve, v. conservar.

consider, v. considerar.

considerable, a. considerable.

considerably, adv. considerablemente.

considerate, a. considerado.

considerately, adv. consideradamente.

consideration, n. consideración f.

considering, prep. visto que, en vista de.

consign, v. consignar.

consignment, n. consignación f., envío m.

consist, v. consistir.

consistency, n. consistencia f.

consistent, a. consistente.

consolation, n. consolación f.

console, v. consolar.

consolidate, v. consolidar.

consommé, n. caldo m.

consonant, n. consonante f.

consort, 1. n. conyuge m. & f.; socio. 2. v. asociarse.

conspicuous, a. conspicuo.

conspicuously, adv. visiblemente, llamativamente.

conspicuousness, n. visibilidad f.; evidencia f.; fama f.

conspiracy, n. conspiración f.; complot m.

conspirator, n. conspirador -ra.

conspire, v. conspirar.

conspirer, n. conspirante m. & f.

constancy, n. constancia f., lealtad f.

constant, a. constante.

constantly, adv. constantemente, de continuo.

constellation, n. constelación f.

consternation, n. consternación f.

constipation, n. constipación f.

constituency, n. distrito electoral m.

constituent, 1. a. constituyente. 2. n. elector m.

constitute, v. constituir.

constitution, n. constitución f.

constitutional, a. constitucional.

constrain, v. constreñir.

constraint, n. constreñimiento m., compulsión f.

constrict, v. apretar, estrechar.

construct, v. construir.

construction, n. construcción f.

constructive, a. constructivo.

constructively, adv. constructivamente; por deducción.

constructor, n. constructor m.

construe, v. interpretar.

consul, n. cónsul m.

consular, a. consular.

consulate, n. consulado m.

consult, v. consultar.

consultant, n. consultante m. & f.

consultation, n. consulta f.

consume, v. consumir.

consumer, n. consumidor -ra.

consummation, n. consumación f.

consumption, n. consumo m.

consumptive, 1. n. tísico m. 2. a. consuntivo.

contact, 1. n. contacto m. 2. v. ponerse en contacto con.

contagion, n. contagio m.

contagious, a. contagioso.

contain, v. contener.

container, n. envase m.

contaminate, v. contaminar.

contemplate, v. contemplar.

contemplation, n. contemplación f.

contemplative, a. contemplativo.

contemporary, n. & a. contemporáneo -nea.

contempt, n. desprecio m.

contemptible, v. vil, despreciable.

contemptuous, a. desdeñoso.

contemptuously, adv. desdeñosamente.

contend, v. contender; competir.

contender, n. competidor m.

content, 1. a. contento. 2. n. contenido m. 3. v. contentar.

contented, a. contento.

contention, n. contención f.

contentment, n. contentamiento m.

contest, 1. n. concurso m. 2. v. disputar.

contestable, a. contestable.

context, n. contexto m.

contiguous, a. contiguo.

continence, n. continencia f., castidad f.

continent, n. continente m.

continental, a. continental.

contingency, n. eventualidad f., casualidad f.

contingent, a. contingente.

continual, a. continuo.

continuation, n. continuación f.

continue, v. continuar.

continuity, n. continuidad f.

continuous, a. continuo.

continuously, adv. continualmente.

contour, n. contorno m.

contraband, n. contrabando m.

contraception, n. contracepción f.

contract, 1. n. contrato m. 2. v. contraer.

contraction, n. contracción f.

contractor, n. contratista m.

contradict, v. contradecir.

contradiction, n. contradicción f.

contradictory, a. contradictorio, opuesto.

contralto, n. contralto m.

contrary, a. & n. contrario m.

contrast, 1. n. contraste m. 2. v. contrastar.

contribute, v. contribuir.

contribution, n. contribución f.

contributive, contributory, a. contribuyente.

contributor, n. contribuidor m.

contrite, a. contrito.

contrition, n. contrición f.

contrivance, n. aparato m.; estratagema f.

contrive, v. inventar, tramar; darse maña.

control, 1. n. control m. 2. v. controlar.

controllable, a. controlable, dominable.

controller, n. interventor m., contralor m.

controversial, a. contencioso.

controversy, n. controversia f.

contusion, n. contusión f.

convalesce, v. convalecer.

convalescence, n. convalecencia f.

convalescent, n. convaleciente m. & f.

convene, v. juntarse; convocar.

convenience, n. comodidad f.

convenient, a. cómodo. to be c., convenir.

conveniently, adv. cómodamente.

convent, n. convento m.

convention, n. convención f.

conventional, a. convencional.

conventionally, adv. convencionalmente.

converge, v. convergir.

convergence, n. convergencia f.

convergent, a. convergente.

conversant, a. versado; entendido (de).

conversation, n. conversación, plática f.

conversational, a. de conversación.

conversationalist, n. conversador m.

converse, v. conversar.

conversely, adv. a la inversa.

convert, 1. n. convertido m. 2. v. convertir.

converter, n. convertidor m.

convertible, a. convertible.

convex, a. convexo.

convey, *v.* transportar; comunicar.

conveyance, *n.* transporte; vehículo *m.*

conveyor, *n.* conductor *m.;* (mech.) transportador *m.*

convict, 1. *n.* reo *m.* 2. *v.* probar de culpa.

conviction, *n.* convicción *f.*

convince, *v.* convencer.

convincing, *a.* convincente.

convivial, *a.* cónvival.

convocation, *n.* convocación; asamblea *f.*

convoke, *v.* convocar, citar.

convoy, *n.* convoy *m.;* escolta *f.*

convulse, *v.* convulsionar; agitar violentamente.

convulsion, *n.* convulsión *f.*

convulsive, *a.* convulsivo.

cook, 1. *n.* cocinero -ra. 2. *v.* cocinar, cocer.

cookbook, *n.* libro de cocina *m.*

cooky, *n.* galleta dulce *f.*

cool, 1. *a.* fresco. 2. *v.* refrescar.

cooler, *n.* enfriadera *f.*

coolness, *n.* frescura *f.*

coop, 1. *n.* jaula *f.* **chicken c.,** gallinero *m.* 2. *v.* enjaular.

cooperate, *v.* cooperar.

cooperation, *n.* cooperación *f.*

cooperative, *a.* cooperativo.

cooperatively, *adv.* cooperativamente.

coordinate, *v.* coordinar.

coordination, *n.* coordinación *f.*

coordinator, *n.* coordinador *m.*

cope, *v.* contender. **c. with,** superar, hacer frente a.

copier, *n.* copiadora *f.*

copious, *a.* copioso, abundante.

copiously, *adv.* copiosamente.

copiousness, *n.* copia *f.,* abundancia *f.*

copper, *n.* cobre *m.*

copy, 1. *n.* copia *f.;* ejemplar *m.* 2. *v.* copiar.

copyist, *n.* copista *m.* & *f.*

copyright, *n.* derechos de propiedad literaria *m.pl.*

coquetry, *n.* coquetería *f.*

coquette, *n.* coqueta *f.*

coral, *n.* coral *m.*

cord, *n.* cuerda *f.*

cordial, *a.* cordial.

cordiality, *n.* cordialidad *f.*

cordially, *adv.* cordialmente.

cordovan, *n.* cordobán *m.*

corduroy, *n.* pana *f.*

core, *n.* corazón; centro *m.*

cork, *n.* corcho *m.*

corkscrew, *n.* tirabuzón *m.*

corn, *n.* maíz *m.*

cornea, *n.* córnea *f.*

corner, *n.* rincón *m.;* (of street) esquina *f.*

cornet, *n.* corneta *f.*

cornetist, *n.* cornetín *m.*

cornice, *n.* cornisa *f.*

cornstarch, *n.* maicena *f.*

corollary, *n.* corolario *m.*

coronary, *a.* coronario.

coronation, *n.* coronación *f.*

corporal, 1. *a.* corpóreo. 2. *n.* cabo *m.*

corporate, *a.* corporativo.

corporation, *n.* corporación *f.*

corps, *n.* cuerpo *m.*

corpse, *n.* cadáver *m.*

corpulent, *a.* corpulento.

corpuscle, *n.* corpúsculo *m.*

corral, 1. *n.* corral *m.* 2. *v.* acorralar.

correct, 1. *a.* correcto. 2. *v.* corregir.

correction, *n.* corrección; enmienda *f.*

corrective, *n.* & *a.* correctivo.

correctly, *adv.* correctamente.

correctness, *n.* exactitud *f.*

correlate, *v.* correlacionar.

correlation, *n.* correlación *f.*

correspond, *v.* corresponder.

correspondence, *n.* correspondencia *f.*

correspondent, *a.* correspondiente.

corresponding, *a.* correspondiente.

corridor, *n.* corredor, pasillo *m.*

corroborate, *v.* corroborar.

corroboration, *n.* corroboración *f.*

corroborative, *a.* corroborante.

corrode, *v.* corroer.

corrosion, *n.* corrosión *f.*

corrugate, *v.* arrugar; ondular.

corrupt, 1. *a.* corrompido. 2. *v.* corromper.

corruptible, *a.* corruptible.

corruption, *n.* corrupción *f.*

corruptive, *a.* corruptivo.

corset, *n.* corsé *m.,* (girdle) faja *f.*

cortege, *n.* comitiva *f.,* séquito *m.*

corvette, *n.* corbeta *f.*

cosmetic, *a.* & *n.* cosmético.

cosmic, *a.* cósmico.

cosmopolitan, *a.* & *n.* cosmopolita *m.* & *f.*

cosmos, *n.* cosmos *m.*

cost, 1. *n.* coste *m.;* costa *f.* 2. *v.* costar.

Costa Rican, *a.* & *n.* costarricense *m.* & *f.*

costly, *a.* costoso, caro.

costume, *n.* traje; disfraz *m.*

cot, *n.* catre *m.*

coterie, *n.* camarilla *f.*

cotillion, *n.* cotillón *m.*

cottage, *n.* casita *f.*

cottage cheese, *n.* requesón *m.*

cotton, *n.* algodón *m.*

cottonseed, *n.* semilla del algodón *f.*

couch, *n.* sofá *m.*

cougar, *n.* cuguar *m.*

cough, 1. *n.* tos *f.* 2. *v.* toser.

council, *n.* consejo, concilio *m.*

counsel, 1. *n.* consejo; (law) abogado *m.* 2. *v.* aconsejar. **to keep one's c.,** no decir nada.

counselor, *n.* consejero; (law) abogado *m.*

count, 1. *n.* cuenta *f.;* (title) conde *m.* 2. *v.* contar.

countenance, 1. *n.* aspecto *m.;* cara *f.* 2. *v.* aprobar.

counter, 1. *adv.* **c. to,** contra, en contra de. 2. *n.* mostrador *m.*

counteract, *v.* contrariar.

counteraction, *n.* oposición *f.*

counterbalance, 1. *n.* contrapeso *m.* 2. *v.* contrapesar.

counterfeit, 1. *a.* falsificado. 2. *v.* falsear.

countermand, *v.* contramandar.

counteroffensive, *n.* contraofensiva *f.*

counterpart, *n.* contraparte *f.*

countess, *n.* condesa *f.*

countless, *a.* innumerable.

country, *n.* campo *m.;* (pol.) país *m.;* (homeland) patria *f.*

countryman, *n.* paisano *m.* **fellow c.,** compatriota *m.*

countryside, *n.* campo, paisaje *m.*

county, *n.* condado *m.*

coupé, *n.* cupé *m.*

couple, 1. *n.* par *m.* 2. *v.* unir.

coupon, *n.* cupón, talón *m.*

courage, *n.* valor *m.*

courageous, *a.* valiente.

course, *n.* curso *m.* **of c.,** por supuesto, desde luego.

court, 1. *n.* corte *f.;* cortejo *m.;* (of law) tribunal *m.* 2. *v.* cortejar.

courteous, *a.* cortés.

courtesy, *n.* cortesía *f.*

courthouse, *n.* palacio de justicia *m.,* tribunal *m.*

courtier, *n.* cortesano *m.*

courtly, *a.* cortés, galante.

courtroom, *n.* sala de justicia *f.*

courtship, *n.* corte *f.*

courtyard, *n.* patio *m.*

cousin, *n.* primo -ma.

covenant, *n.* contrato, convenio *m.*

cover, 1. *n.* cubierta, tapa *f.* 2. *v.* cubrir, tapar.

covet, *v.* ambicionar, suspirar por.

covetous, *a.* codicioso.

cow, *n.* vaca *f.*

coward, *n.* cobarde *m.* & *f.*

cowardice, *n.* cobardía *f.*

cowardly, *a.* cobarde.

cowboy, *n.* vaquero, gaucho *m.*

cower, *v.* agacharse.

cowhide, *n.* cuero *m.*

coy, *a.* recatado, modesto.

coyote, *n.* coyote *m.*

cozy, *a.* cómodo y agradable.

crab, *n.* cangrejo *m.*

crab apple, *n.* manzana silvestre *f.*

crack, 1. *n.* hendedura *f.;* (noise) crujido *m.* 2. *v.* hender; crujir.

cracker, *n.* galleta *f.*

cradle, *n.* cuna *f.*

craft, *n.* arte *m.*

craftsman, *n.* artesano *m.*

craftsmanship, *n.* mano de obra *f.*

crafty, *a.* ladino.

crag, *n.* despeñadero *m.*

cram, *v.* rellenar, hartar.

cramp, *n.* calambre *m.*

cranberry, *n.* arándano *m.*

crane, 1. *n.* (bird) grulla *f.;* (mech.) grúa *f.*

cranium, *n.* cráneo *m.*

crank, *n.* (mech.) manivela *f.*

cranky, *a.* chiflado, caprichoso.

crash, 1. *n.* choque; estallido *m.* **2.** *v.* estallar.

crate, *n.* canasto *m.*

crater, *n.* cráter *m.*

crave, *v.* desear; anhelar.

craven, *a.* cobarde.

craving, *n.* sed *m.*, anhelo *m.*

crawl, *v.* andar a gatas, arrastrarse.

crayon, *n.* creyón; lápiz *m.*

crazy, *a.* loco.

creak, *v.* crujir.

creaky, *a.* crujidero.

cream, *n.* crema *f.*

creamery, *n.* lechería *f.*

crease, 1. *n.* pliegue *m.* **2.** *v.* plegar.

create, *v.* crear.

creation, *n.* creación *f.*

creative, *a.* creativo, creador.

creator, *n.* criador -ra.

creature, *n.* criatura *f.*

credence, *n.* creencia *f.*

credentials, *n.* credenciales *f.pl.*

credibility, *n.* credibilidad *f.*

credible, *a.* creíble.

credit, 1. *n.* crédito *m.* **on c.,** al fiado. **2.** *v.* (com.) abonar.

creditable, *a.* fidedigno.

credit card, *n.* tarjeta de crédito *f.*

creditor, *n.* acreedor -ra.

credo, *n.* credo *m.*

credulity, *n.* credulidad *f.*

credulous, *a.* crédulo.

creed, *n.* credo *m.*

creek, *n.* riachuelo *m.*

creep, *v.* gatear.

cremate, *v.* cremar.

crematory, *n.* crematorio *m.*

creosote, *n.* creosota *f.*

crepe, *n.* crespón *m.*

crescent, *a.* & *n.* creciente *f.*

crest, *n.* cresta; cima *f.;* (heraldry) timbre *m.*

cretonne, *n.* cretona *f.*

crevice, *n.* grieta *f.*

crew, *n.* tripulación *f.*

crib, *n.* pesebre *m.;* camita de niño.

cricket, *n.* grillo *m.*

crime, *n.* crimen *m.*

criminal, *a.* & *n.* criminal.

criminologist, *n.* criminologo *m.*

criminology, *n.* criminología *f.*

crimson, *a.* & *n.* carmesí *m.*

cringe, *v.* encogerse, temblar.

cripple, 1. *n.* lisiado -da. **2.** *v.* estropear, lisiar.

crisis, *n.* crisis *f.*

crisp, *a.* crespo, fresco.

crispness, *n.* encrespadura *f.*

crisscross, *a.* entrelazado.

criterion, *n.* criterio *m.*

critic, *n.* crítico *m.*

critical, *a.* crítico.

criticism, *n.* crítica; censura *f.*

criticize, *v.* criticar; censurar.

critique, *n.* crítica *f.*

croak, 1. *n.* graznido *m.* **2.** *v.* graznar.

crochet, 1. *n.* crochet *m.* **2.** *v.* hacer crochet.

crock, *n.* cazuela *f.;* olla de barro.

crockery, *n.* loza *f.*

crocodile, *n.* cocodrilo *m.*

crony, *n.* compinche *m.*

crooked, *a.* encorvado; deshonesto.

croon, *v.* canturrear.

crop, *n.* cosecha *f.*

croquet, *n.* juego de croquet *m.*

croquette, *n.* croqueta *f.*

cross, 1. *a.* enojado, mal humorado. **2.** *n.* cruz *f.* **3.** *v.* cruzar, atravesar.

crossbreed, 1. *n.* mestizo *m.* **2.** *v.* cruzar.

cross-examine, *v.* interrogar.

cross-eyed, *a.* bisco.

cross-fertilization, *n.* alogamia *f.*

crossing, crossroads, *n.* cruce *m.*

cross section, *n.* corte transversal *m.*

crotch, *n.* bifurcación *f.;* (anat.) bragadura *f.*

crouch, *v.* agacharse.

croup, *n.* (med.) crup *m.*

croupier, *n.* crupié *m.*

crow, *n.* cuervo *m.*

crowd, 1. *n.* muchedumbre *f.;* tropel *m.* **2.** *v.* apretar.

crowded, *a.* lleno de gente.

crown, 1. *n.* corona *f.* **2.** *v.* coronar.

crown prince, *n.* príncipe heredero *m.*

crucial, *a.* crucial.

crucible, *n.* crisol *m.*

crucifix, *n.* crucifijo *m.*

crucifixion, *n.* crucifixión *f.*

crucify, *v.* crucificar.

crude, *a.* crudo; (oil) bruto.

crudeness, *a.* crudeza.

cruel, *a.* cruel.

cruelty, *n.* crueldad *f.*

cruet, *n.* vinagrera *f.*

cruise, 1. *n.* viaje por mar. **2.** *v.* navegar.

cruiser, *n.* crucero *m.*

crumb, *n.* miga; migaja *f.*

crumble, *v.* desmigajar; desmoronar.

crumple, *v.* arrugar; encogerse.

crusade, *n.* cruzada *f.*

crusader, *n.* cruzado *m.*

crush, *v.* aplastar.

crust, *n.* costra *f.*

crustacean, *n.* crustáceo *m.*

crutch, *n.* muleta *f.*

cry, 1. *n.* grito *m.* **2.** *v.* gritar; (weep) llorar.

cryosurgery, *n.* criocirugía *f.*

crypt, *n.* gruta *f.,* cripta *f.*

cryptic, *a.* secreto.

cryptography, *n.* criptografía *f.*

crystal, *n.* cristal *m.*

crystalline, *a.* cristalino, transparente.

crystallize, *v.* cristalizar.

cub, *n.* cachorro *m.*

Cuban, *n.* & *a.* cubano -na.

cube, 1. *n.* cubo *m.*

cubic, *a.* cúbico.

cubicle, *n.* cubículo *m.*

cubic measure, *n.* medida de capacidad *f.*

cubism, *n.* cubismo *m.*

cuckoo, *n.* cuco *m.*

cucumber, *n.* pepino *m.*

cuddle, *v.* abrazar.

cudgel, *n.* palo *m.*

cue, *n.* apunte *m.;* (billiards) taco *m.*

cuff, *n.* puño de camisa. **c. links,** gemelos.

cuisine, *n.* arte culinario *f.*

culinary, *a.* culinario.

culminate, *v.* culminar.

culmination, *n.* culminación *f.*

culpable, *a.* culpable.

culprit, *n.* criminal; delincuente *m.*

cult, *n.* culto *m.*

cultivate, *v.* cultivar.

cultivated, *a.* cultivado.

cultivation, *n.* cultivo *m.;* cultivación *f.*

cultivator, *n.* cultivador *m.*

cultural, *a.* cultural.

culture, *n.* cultura *f.*

cultured, *a.* culto.

cumbersome, *a.* pesado, incómodo.

cumulative, *a.* acumulativo.

cunning, 1. *a.* astuto. **2.** *n.* astucia *f.*

cup, *n.* taza, jícara *f.*

cupboard, *n.* armario, aparador *m.*

cupidity, *n.* avaricia *f.*

curable, *a.* curable.

curator, *n.* guardián *m.*

curb, 1. *n.* freno *m.* **2.** *v.* refrenar.

curd, *n.* cuajada *f.*

curdle, *v.* cuajarse, coagularse.

cure, 1. *n.* remedio *m.* **2.** *v.* curar, sanar.

curfew, *n.* toque de queda *m.*

curio, *n.* objeto curioso.

curiosity, *n.* curiosidad *f.*

curious, *a.* curioso.

curl, 1. *n.* rizo *m.* **2.** *v.* rizar.

curly, *a.* rizado.

currant, *n.* grosella *f.*

currency, *n.* circulación *f.;* dinero *m.*

current, *a.* & *n.* corriente *f.*

currently, *adv.* corrientemente.

curriculum, *n.* plan de estudio *m.*

curse, 1. *n.* maldición *f.* **2.** *v.* maldecir.

cursory, *a.* sumario.

curt, a. brusco.
curtail, v. reducir; restringir.
curtain, n. cortina f.; (theat.) telón m.
curtsy, 1. n. reverencia f. **2.** v. hacer una reverencia.
curvature, n. curvatura f.
curve, 1. n. curva f. **2.** v. encorvar.
cushion, n. cojín m.; almohada f.
cuspidor, n. escupidera f.
custard, n. flan m.; natillas f.pl.
custodian, n. custodio m.
custody, n. custodia f.
custom, n. custumbre f.
customary, a. acostumbrado, usual.
customer, n. cliente m. & f.
customhouse, customs, n. aduana f.
cut, 1. n. corte m.; cortada f.; tajada f.; (printing) grabado m. **2.** v. cortar; tajar.
cute, a. mono, lindo.
cut glass, n. cristal tallado m.
cuticle, n. cutícula f.
cutlery, n. cuchillería f.
cutlet, n. coteleta, chuleta f.
cutter, n. cortador -ra; (naut.) cúter m.
cutthroat, n. asesino m.
cyclamate, n. ciclamato m.
cycle, n. ciclo m.
cyclist, n. ciclista m. & f.
cyclone, n. ciclón, huracán m.
cyclotron, n. ciclotrón m.
cylinder, n. cilindro m.
cylindrical, a. cilíndrico.
cymbal, n. címbalo m.
cynic, n. cínico m.
cynical, a. cínico.
cynicism, n. cinismo m.
cypress, n. ciprés m. **c. nut,** piñuela f.
cyst, n. quiste m.

D

dad, n. papa m., papito m.
daffodil, n. narciso m.
dagger, n. puñal m.
dahlia, n. dalia f.
daily, a. diario, cotidiano.
daintiness, n. delicadeza f.
dainty, a. delicado.
dairy, n. lechería, quesería f.
dais, n. tablado m.
daisy, n. margarita f.
dale, n. valle m.
dally, v. holgar; perder el tiempo.
dam, n. presa f.; dique m.
damage, 1. n. daño m. **2.** v. dañar.
damask, n. damasco m.
damn, v. condenar.
damnation, n. condenación f.
damp, a. húmedo.
dampen, v. humedecer.
dampness, n. humedad f.
damsel, n. doncella f.
dance, 1. n. baile m.; danza f. **2.** v. bailar.

dancer, n. bailador -ra; (professional) bailarín -na.
dancing, n. baile m.
dandruff, n. caspa f.
dandelion, n. amargón m.
dandy, n. petimetre m.
danger, n. peligro m.
dangerous, a. peligroso.
dangle, v. colgar.
Danish, a. & n. danés -sa; dinamarqués -sa.
dapper, a. gallardo.
dare, v. atreverse, osar.
daredevil, n. atrevido m., -da f.
daring, 1. a. atrevido. **2.** n. osadía f.
dark, 1. a. obscuro; moreno. **2.** n. obscuridad f.
darken, v. obscurecer.
darkness, n. obscuridad f.
darkroom, n. cámara obscura f.
darling, a. & n. querido, amado.
darn, v. zurcir.
darning needle, n. aguja de zurcir m.
dart, n. dardo m.
dash, n. arranque m.; (punct.) guión m.
data, n. datos m.
data processing, proceso de datos m.
date, n. fecha f.; (engagement) cita f.; (fruit) dátil m.
daughter, n. hija f.
daughter-in-law, n. nuera f.
daunt, v. intimidar.
dauntless, a. intrépido.
davenport, n. sofá m.
dawn, 1. n. alba, madrugada f. **2.** v. amanecer.
day, n. día m. **good d.,** buenos días.
daybreak, n. alba, madrugada f.
daydream, n. fantasía f.
daylight, n. luz del día.
daze, v. aturdir.
dazzle, v. deslumbrar.
deacon, n. diácono m.
dead, a. muerto.
deaden, v. amortecer.
deadline, n. límite absoluto m.
deadlock, n. paro m.
deadly, a. mortal.
deaf, a. sordo.
deafen, v. ensordecer.
deaf-mute, n. sordomudo m.
deafness, n. sordera f.
deal, 1. n. trato m.; negociación f. **a great d., a good d.,** mucho. **2.** v. tratar; negociar.
dealer, n. comerciante m., (at cards) tallador -ra.
dean, n. decano m.
dear, a. querido; caro.
dearth, n. escasez m.
death, n. muerte f.
deathless, a. inmortal.
debacle, n. desastre m.
debase, v. degradar.
debatable, a. discutible.
debate, 1. n. debate m. **2.** v. disputar, deliberar.

debauch, v. corromper.
debilitate, v. debilitar.
debit, n. débito m.
debonair, a. cortés; alegre; vivo.
debris, n. escombros m.pl.
debt, n. deuda f.
debtor, n. deudor -ra.
debunk, v. traer a la realidad.
debut, n. debut, estreno m.
debutante, n. debutante f.
decade, n. década f.
decadence, n. decadencia f.
decadent, a. decadente.
decaffeinated, a. descafeinado.
decalcomania, n. calcomanía f.
decanter, n. garrafa f.
decapitate, v. descabezar.
decay, 1. n. descaecimiento m.; (dental) caries f. **2.** v. decaer; (dental) cariarse.
deceased, a. muerto, difunto.
deceit, n. engaño m.
deceitful, a. engañoso.
deceive, v. engañar.
December, n. diciembre m.
decency, n. decencia f.; decoro m.
decent, a. decente.
decentralize, v. descentralizar.
deception, n. decepción f.
deceptive, a. deceptivo.
decibel, n. decibelio m.
decide, v. decidir.
decimal, a. decimal.
decipher, v. descifrar.
decision, n. decisión f.
decisive, a. decisivo.
deck, n. cubierta f.
declamation, n. declamación f.
declaration, n. declaración f.
declarative, a. declarativo.
declare, v. declarar.
declension, n. declinación f.
decline, 1. n. decadencia f. **2.** v. decaer; negarse; (gram.) declinar.
decompose, v. descomponer.
decongestant, n. descongestionante m.
decorate, v. decorar, adornar.
decoration, n. decoración f.
decorative, a. decorativo.
decorator, n. decorador m.
decorous, a. correcto.
decorum, n. decoro m.
decrease, v. disminuir.
decree, n. decreto m.
decrepit, a. decrépito.
decry, v. descreditar.
dedicate, v. dedicar; consagrar.
dedication, n. dedicación; dicatoria f.
deduce, deduct, v. deducir.
deduction, n. rebaja f.
deductive, a. deductivo.
deed, n. acción; hazaña f.
deem, v. estimar.
deep, a. hondo, profundo.
deepen, v. profundizar, ahondar.
deep freeze, n. congelación f.
deeply, adv. profundamente.
deer, n. venado, ciervo m.
deface, v. mutilar.

defamation, n. calumnia f.
defame, v. difamar.
default, 1. n. defecto m. **2.** v. faltar.
defeat, 1. n. derrota f. **2.** v. derrotar.
defect, n. defecto m.
defective, a. defectivo.
defend, v. defender.
defendant, n. acusado -da.
defender, n. defensor -ra.
defense, n. defensa f.
defensive, a. defensivo.
defer, v. aplazar; deferir.
deference, n. deferencia f.
defiance, n. desafío m.
defiant, a. desafiador.
deficiency, n. defecto m.
deficient, a. deficiente.
deficit, n. déficit, descubierto m.
defile, 1. n. desfiladero m. **2.** v. profanar.
define, v. definir.
definite, a. exacto; definitivo.
definitely, adv. definidamente.
definition, n. definición f.
definitive, a. definitivo.
deflation, n. desinflación f.
deflect, v. desviar.
deform, v. deformar.
deformity, n. deformidad f.
defraud, v. defraudar.
defray, v. costear.
deft, a. diestro.
defy, v. desafiar.
degenerate, 1. a. degenerado. **2.** v. degenerar.
degeneration, n. degeneración f.
degradation, n. degradación f.
degrade, v. degradar.
degree, n. grado m.
deign, v. condescender.
deity, n. deidad f.
dejected, a. abatido.
dejection, n. tristeza f.
delay, 1. n. retardo m., demora f. **2.** v. tardar, demorar.
delegate, 1. n. delegado -da. **2.** v. delegar.
delegation, n. delegación f.
delete, v. suprimir.
deliberate, 1. a. premeditado. **2.** v. deliberar.
deliberately, adv. deliberadamente.
deliberation, n. deliberación f.
deliberative, a. deliberativo.
delicacy, n. delicadeza f.
delicate, a. delicado.
delicious, a. delicioso.
delight, n. deleite m.
delightful, a. deleitoso.
delinquency, n. delincuencia f.
delinquent, a. & n. delincuente.
delirious, a. delirante.
deliver, v. entregar.
deliverance, n. liberación; salvación f.
delivery, n. entrega f.; (med.) parto m.
delude, v. engañar.
deluge, n. inundación f.

delusion, n. decepción f.; engaño m.
delve, v. cavar, sondear.
demagogue, n. demagogo m.
demand, 1. n. demanda f. **2.** v. demandar; exigir.
demarcation, n. demarcación f.
demeanor, n. conducta f.
demented, a. demente, loco.
demilitarize, v. desmilitarizar.
demobilize, v. desmovilizar.
democracy, n. democracia f.
democrat, n. demócrata m. & f.
democratic, a. democrático.
demolish, v. demoler.
demon, n. demonio m.
demonstrate, v. demostrar.
demonstration, n. demostración f.
demonstrative, a. demostrativo.
demoralize, v. desmoralizar.
demure, a. modesto, serio.
den, n. caverna f.; retrete m.
denature, v. alterar.
denial, n. negación f.
denim, n. tela para jeans, azul de Vergara.
Denmark, n. Dinamarca f.
denomination, n. denominación; secta f.
denote, v. denotar.
denounce, v. denunciar.
dense, a. denso, espeso; estúpido.
density, n. densidad f.
dent, 1. n. abolladura f. **2.** v. abollar.
dental, a. dental.
dentist, n. dentista m.
dentistry, n. odontología f.
denture, n. dentadura f.
denunciation, n. denunciación f.
deny, v. negar, rehusar.
deodorant, n. desodorante m.
depart, v. partir; irse, marcharse.
department, n. departamento m.
departmental, a. departamental.
departure, n. salida; desviación f.
depend, v. depender.
dependability, n. confiabilidad f.
dependable, a. confiable.
dependence, n. dependencia f.
dependent, a. & n. dependiente m.
depict, v. pintar; representar.
deplete, v. agotar.
deplorable, a. deplorable.
deplore, v. deplorar.
deport, v. deportar.
deportation, n. deportación f.
deportment, n. conducta f.
depose, v. deponer.
deposit, 1. n. depósito m. **2.** v. depositar.
depositor, n. depositante m. & f.
depot, n. depósito m.; (railway) estación f.

depravity, n. depravación f.
deprecate, v. deprecar.
depreciate, v. depreciar.
depreciation, n. depreciación f.
depredation, n. depredación f.
depress, v. deprimir; desanimar.
depression, n. depresión f.
deprive, v. privar.
depth, n. profundidad, hondura f.
depth charge, n. carga de profundidad f.
deputy, n. diputado m.
deride, v. burlar.
derision, n. burla f.
derivation, n. derivación f.
derivative, a. derivativo.
derive, v. derivar.
derogatory, a. derogatorio.
derrick, n. grúa f.
descend, v. descender, bajar.
descendant, n. descendiente m. & f.
descent, n. descenso m.; origen m.
describe, v. describir.
description, n. descripción f.
descriptive, a. descriptivo.
desecrate, v. profanar.
desert, 1. n. desierto m. **2.** v. abandonar.
deserter, n. desertor m.
desertion, n. deserción f.
deserve, v. merecer.
design, 1. n. diseño m. **2.** v. diseñar.
designate, v. señalar, apuntar.
designation, n. designación f.
designer, n. diseñador -ra; (technical) proyectista m. & f.
desirability, n. conveniencia f.
desirable, a. deseable.
desire, 1. n. deseo m. **2.** v. desear.
desirous, a. deseoso.
desist, v. desistir.
desk, n. escritorio m.
desolate, 1. a. desolado. **2.** v. desolar.
desolation, n. desolación, ruina f.
despair, 1. n. desesperación f. **2.** v. desesperar.
despatch, dispatch, 1. n. despacho m.; prontitud f. **2.** v. despachar.
desperado, n. bandido m.
desperate, a. desesperado.
desperation, n. desesperación f.
despicable, a. vil.
despise, v. despreciar.
despite, prep. a pesar de.
despondent, a. abatido; desanimado.
despot, n. déspota m.
despotic, a. despótico.
dessert, n. postre m.
destination, n. destinación f.
destine, v. destinar.
destiny, n. destino m.
destitute, a. destituido.
destitution, n. destitución f.
destroy, v. destrozar, destruir.

destroyer, *n.* destruidor *m.;* (naval) destróyer *m.*

destruction, *n.* destrucción *f.*

destructive, *a.* destructivo.

desultory, *a.* inconexo; casual.

detach, *v.* separar, desprender.

detachment, *n.* (mil.) destacamento *m.*

detail, 1. *n.* detalle *m.* **2.** *v.* detallar.

detain, *v.* detener.

detect, *v.* descubrir.

detection, *n.* detección *f.*

detective, *n.* detective *m.*

detente, *n.* détente *f.*

detention, *n.* detención; cautividad *f.*

deter, *v.* disuadir.

detergent, *n. & a.* detergente *m.*

deteriorate, *v.* deteriorar.

deterioration, *n.* deterioración *f.*

determination, *n.* determinación *f.*

determine, *v.* determinar.

deterrence, *n.* disuasión *f.*

detest, *v.* detestar.

detonate, *v.* detonar.

detour, *n.* desvío *m.*

detract, *v.* disminuir.

detriment, *n.* detrimento *m.,* daño *m.*

detrimental, *a.* dañoso.

devaluate, *v.* depreciar.

devastate, *v.* devastar.

develop, *v.* desarrollar; (phot.) revelar.

developing nation, nación en desarrollo.

development, *n.* desarrollo *m.*

deviate, *v.* desviar.

deviation, *n.* desviación *f.*

device, *n.* aparato; artificio *m.*

devil, *n.* diablo, demonio *m.*

devious, *a.* desviado.

devise, *v.* inventar.

devoid, *a.* desprovisto.

devote, *v.* dedicar, consagrar.

devoted, *a.* devoto.

devotee, *n.* aficionado *m.*

devotion, *n.* devoción *f.*

devour, *v.* devorar.

devout, *a.* devoto.

dew, *n.* rocío, sereno *m.*

dexterity, *n.* destreza *f.*

dexterous, *a.* diestro.

diabetes, *n.* diabetes *f.*

diabolic, *a.* diabólico.

diadem, *n.* diadema *f.*

diagnose, *v.* diagnosticar.

diagnosis, *n.* diagnóstico *m.*

diagonal, *n.* diagonal *f.*

diagram, *n.* diagrama *m.*

dial, *n.* cuadrante *m.,* carátula *f.*

dialect, *n.* dialecto *m.*

dialogue, *n.* diálogo *m.*

diameter, *n.* diámetro *m.*

diamond, *n.* diamante, brillante *m.*

diaper, *n.* pañal *m.*

diarrhea, *n.* diarrea *f.*

diary, *n.* diario *m.*

diathermy, *n.* diatermia *f.*

dice, *n.* dados *m.pl.*

dictate, 1. *n.* dictamen *m.* **2.** *v.* dictar.

dictation, *n.* dictado *m.*

dictator, *n.* dictador *m.*

dictatorship, *n.* dictadura *f.*

diction, *n.* dicción *f.*

dictionary, *n.* diccionario *m.*

die, 1. *n.* matriz *f.;* (game) dado *m.* **2.** *v.* morir.

diet, *n.* dieta *f.*

dietary, *a.* dietético.

dietitian, *n.* dietista *f. & m.*

differ, *v.* diferir.

difference, *n.* diferencia *f.* **to make no d.,** no importar.

different, *a.* diferente, distinto.

differential, *a.* diferencial *f.*

differentiate, *v.* diferenciar.

difficult, *a.* difícil.

difficulty, *n.* dificultad *f.*

diffident, *a.* tímido.

diffuse, *v.* difundir.

diffusion, *n.* difusión *f.*

dig, *v.* cavar.

digest, 1. *n.* extracto *m.* **2.** *v.* digerir.

digestible, *a.* digerible.

digestion, *n.* digestión *f.*

digestive, *a.* digestivo.

digital, *a.* digital.

digitalis, *n.* digital *f.*

dignified, *a.* digno.

dignify, *v.* dignificar.

dignitary, *n.* dignatario *m.*

dignity, *n.* dignidad *f.*

digress, *v.* divagar.

digression, *n.* digresión *f.*

dike, *n.* dique *m.*

dilapidated, *a.* dilapidado.

dilapidation, *n.* dilapidación *f.*

dilate, *v.* dilatar.

dilatory, *a.* dilatorio.

dilemma, *n.* dilema *m.*

dilettante, *n.* dilettante *m. & f.*

diligence, *n.* diligencia *f.*

diligent, *a.* diligente, aplicado.

dilute, *v.* diluir.

dim, 1. *a.* oscuro. **2.** *v.* oscurecer.

dimension, *n.* dimensión *f.*

diminish, *v.* disminuir.

diminution, *n.* disminución *f.*

diminutive, *a.* diminutivo.

dimness, *n.* oscuridad *f.*

dimple, *n.* hoyuelo *m.*

din, *n.* alboroto *m.*

dine, *v.* comer, cenar.

diner, *n.* coche comedor *m.*

dingy, *a.* deslucido, deslustrado.

dinner, *n.* comida, cena *f.*

dinosaur, *n.* dinosauro *m.*

diocese, *n.* diócesis *f.*

dip, *v.* sumergir, hundir.

diphtheria, *n.* difteria *f.*

diploma, *n.* diploma *m.*

diplomacy, *n.* diplomacia *f.*

diplomat, *n.* diplomático *m.*

diplomatic, *a.* diplomático.

dipper, *n.* cucharón *m.*

dire, *a.* horrendo.

direct, 1. *a.* directo. **2.** *v.* dirigir.

direction, *n.* dirección *f.*

directive, *n.* directivo *m.*

directly, *adv.* directamente.

director, *n.* director -ra.

directory, *n.* directorio *m.,* guía *f.*

dirigible, *n.* dirigible *m.*

dirt, *n.* basura *f.;* (earth) tierra *f.*

dirty, *a.* sucio.

disability, *n.* inhabilidad *f.;* invalidez *m.*

disable, *v.* incapacitar.

disabuse, *v.* desengañar.

disadvantage, *n.* desventaja *f.*

disagree, *v.* desconvenir; disentir.

disagreeable, *a.* desagradable.

disagreement, *n.* desacuerdo *m.*

disappear, *v.* desaparecer.

disappearance, *n.* desaparición *f.*

disappoint, *v.* disgustar, desilusionar.

disappointment, *n.* disgusto *m.,* desilusión *f.*

disapproval, *n.* desaprobación *f.*

disapprove, *v.* desaprobar.

disarm, *v.* desarmar.

disarmament, *n.* desarme *m.*

disarrange, *v.* desordenar; desarreglar.

disaster, *n.* desastre *m.*

disastrous, *a.* desastroso.

disavow, *v.* repudiar.

disavowal, *n.* repudiación *f.*

disband, *v.* dispersarse.

disbelieve, *v.* descreer.

disburse, *v.* desembolsar, pagar.

discard, *v.* descartar.

discern, *v.* discernir.

discerning, *a.* discernidor, perspicaz.

discernment, *n.* discernimiento *m.*

discharge, *v.* descargar; despedir.

disciple, *n.* discípulo *m.*

disciplinary, *a.* disciplinario.

discipline, *n.* disciplina *f.*

disclaim, *v.* repudiar.

disclaimer, *n.* negador *m.*

disclose, *v.* revelar.

disclosure, *n.* descubrimiento *m.*

disco, *n.* discoteca *f.*

discolor, *v.* descolorar.

discomfort, *n.* incomodidad *f.*

disconcert, *v.* desconcertar.

disconnect, *v.* desunir; desconectar.

disconnected, *a.* desunido.

disconsolate, *a.* desconsolado.

discontent, *n.* descontento *m.*

discontented, *a.* descontento.

discontinue, *v.* descontinuar.

discord, *n.* discordia *f.*

discordant, *a.* disonante.

discotheque, *n.* discoteca *f.*

discount, *n.* descuento *m.*

discourage, *v.* desalentar, desanimar.

discouragement, n. desaliento, desánimo m.
discourse, n. discurso m.
discourteous, a. descortés.
discourtesy, n. descortesía f.
discover, v. descubrir.
discoverer, n. descubridor -ra.
discovery, n. descubrimiento m.
discreet, a. discreto.
discrepancy, n. discrepancia f.
discretion, n. discreción f.
discriminate, v. distinguir; diferenciar parcialmente.
discrimination, n. discernimiento m.; discriminación f.
discuss, v. discutir.
discussion, n. discusión f.
disdain, 1. n. desdén m. 2. v. desdeñar.
disdainful, a. desdeñoso.
disease, n. enfermedad f., mal m.
disembark, v. desembarcar.
disentangle, v. desenredar.
disfigure, v. desfigurar.
disgrace, 1. n. vergüenza; deshonra f. 2. v. deshonrar.
disgraceful, a. vergonzoso.
disguise, 1. n. disfraz m. 2. v. disfrazar.
disgust, 1. n. fastidio m. 2. v. fastidiar.
dish, n. plato m.
dishearten, v. desanimar; descorazonar.
dishonest, a. deshonesto.
dishonesty, n. deshonestidad f.
dishonor, n. deshonra f. 2. v. deshonrar.
dishonorable, a. deshonroso.
disillusion, 1. n. desengaño m. 2. v. desengañar.
disinfect, v. desinfectar.
disinfectant, n. desinfectante m.
disinherit, v. desheredar.
disintegrate, v. desintegrar.
disinterested, a. desinteresado.
disk, n. disco m.
dislike, 1. n. antipatía f. 2. v. no gustar de.
dislocate, v. dislocar.
dislodge, v. desalojar.
disloyal, a. desleal; infiel.
disloyalty, n. deslealtad f.
dismal, a. lúgubre.
dismantle, v. desmantelar.
dismay, 1. n. consternación f. 2. v. consternar.
dismiss, v. despedir.
dismissal, n. despedida f.
dismount, v. apearse.
disobedience, n. desobediencia f.
disobedient, a. desobediente.
disobey, v. desobedecer.
disorder, n. desorden m.
disorderly, a. desarreglado, desordenado.
disown, v. repudiar.
dispassionate, a. desapasionado; templado.
dispatch, 1. n. despacho m. 2. v. despachar.

dispel, v. despersar.
dispensary, n. dispensario m.
dispensation, n. dispensación f.
dispense, v. dispensar.
dispersal, n. dispersión f.
disperse, v. dispersar.
displace, v. dislocar.
display, 1. despliegue m., exhibición f. 2. desplegar, exhibir.
displease, v. disgustar; ofender.
displeasure, n. disgusto, sinsabor m.
disposable, a. disponible.
disposal, n. disposición f.
dispose, v. disponer.
disposition, n. disposición f.; índole f., genio m.
dispossess, v. desposeer.
disproportionate, a. desproporcionado.
disprove, v. confutar.
dispute, 1. n. disputa f. 2. v. disputar.
disqualify, v. inhabilitar.
disregard, 1. n. desatención f. 2. v. desatender.
disrepair, n. descompostura f.
disreputable, a. desacreditado.
disrespect, n. falta de respeto.
disrespectful, a. irrespetuoso.
disrobe, v. desvestir.
disrupt, v. romper; desbaratar.
dissatisfaction, n. descontento m.
dissatisfy, v. descontentar.
dissect, v. disecar.
dissemble, v. disimular.
disseminate, v. diseminar.
dissension, n. disensión f.
dissent, 1. n. disensión f. 2. v. disentir.
dissertation, n. disertación f.
dissimilar, a. desemejante.
dissipate, v. disipar.
dissipation, n. disipación f.; libertinaje m.
dissolute, a. disoluto.
dissolution, n. disolución f.
dissolve, v. disolver; derretirse.
dissonant, a. disonante.
dissuade, v. disuadir.
distance, n. distancia f. at a d., in the d., a lo lejos.
distant, a. distante, lejano.
distaste, n. disgusto, sinsabor m.
distasteful, a. desagradable.
distill, v. destilar.
distillation, n. destilación f.
distillery, n. destilería f.
distinct, a. distinto.
distinctive, a. distintivo; característico.
distinctly, adv. distintamente.
distinction, n. distinción f.
distinguish, v. distinguir.
distinguished, a. distinguido.
distort, v. falsear; torcer.
distract, v. distraer.
distraction, n. distracción f.
distraught, a. aturrullado; demente.
distress, 1. n. dolor m. 2. v. afligir.

distribute, v. distribuir.
distribution, n. distribución f.; reparto m.
distributor, n. distribuidor -ra.
district, n. distrito m.
distrust, 1. n. desconfianza f. 2. v. desconfiar.
distrustful, a. desconfiado; sospechoso.
disturb, v. incomodar; inquietar.
disturbance, n. disturbio m.
ditch, n. zanja f.; foso m.
divan, n. diván m.
dive, 1. n. clavado m.; (coll.) leonera f. 2. v. echar un clavado; bucear.
diver, n. buzo m.
diverge, v. divergir.
divergence, n. divergencia f.
divergent, a. divergente.
diverse, a. diverso.
diversion, n. diversión f.; pasatiempo m.
diversity, n. diversidad f.
divert, v. desviar; divertir.
divest, v. desnudar, despojar.
divide, v. dividir.
dividend, n. dividendo m.
divine, a. divino.
divinity, n. divinidad f.
division, n. división f.
divorce, 1. n. divorcio m. 2. v. divorciar.
divorcee, n. divorciada f.
divulge, v. divulgar, revelar.
dizziness, n. vértigo, mareo m.
dizzy, a. mareado.
do, v. hacer.
docile, a. dócil.
dock, 1. n. muelle m. dry d., astillero m. 2. v. entrar en muelle.
doctor, n. médico m.; doctor -ra.
doctrine, n. doctrina f.
document, n. documento m.
documentary, a. documental.
documentation, n. documentación f.
dodge, 1. n. evasión f. 2. v. evadir.
doe, n. gama f.
dog, n. perro m.
dogma, n. dogma m.
dogmatic, a. dogmático.
dogmatism, n. dogmatismo m.
doily, n. servilletita f.
doleful, a. triste.
doll, n. muñeca f.
dollar, n. dólar m.
dolorous, a. lastimoso.
dolphin, n. delfín m.
domain, n. dominio m.
dome, n. domo m.
domestic, a. doméstico.
domesticate, v. domesticar.
domicile, n. domicilio m.
dominance, n. dominación f.
dominant, a. dominante.
dominate, v. dominar.
domination, n. dominación f.
domineer, v. dominar.
domineering, a. tiránico, mandón.

dominion, *n.* dominio; territorio *m.*

domino, *n.* dominó *m.*

donate, *v.* donar; contribuir.

donation, *n.* donación *f.*

donkey, *n.* asno, burro *m.*

doom, 1. *n.* perdición, ruina *f.* **2.** *v.* perder, ruinar.

door, *n.* puerta *f.*

doorman, *n.* portero *m.*

doorway, *n.* entrada *f.*

dope, *n.* narcótico *m.*

dormant, *a.* durmiente.

dormitory, *n.* dormitorio *m.*

dosage, *n.* dosificación *f.*

dose, *n.* dosis *f.*

dot, *n.* punto *m.*

double, 1. *a.* doble. **2.** *v.* duplicar.

double-breasted, *a.* cruzado.

double-cross, *v.* traicionar.

doubly, *adv.* doblemente.

doubt, 1. *n.* duda *f.* **2.** *v.* dudar.

doubtful, *a.* dudoso, incierto.

doubtless, 1. *a.* indudable. **2.** *adv.* sin duda.

dough, *n.* pasta, masa *f.*

doughnut, *n.* buñuelo *m.*

dove, *n.* paloma *f.*

dowager, *n.* viuda *f.*

down, 1. *a.* abajo. **2.** *prep.* **d. the street,** *etc.* calle abajo, *etc.*

downcast, *a.* cabizbajo.

downfall, *n.* ruina, perdición *f.*

downhearted, *a.* descorazonado.

downpour, *n.* chaparrón *m.*

downright, *a.* absoluto, completo.

downstairs, 1. *adv.* abajo. **2.** *n.* primer piso.

downtown, *adv.* al centro, en el centro.

downward, 1. *a.* descendente. **2.** *adv.* hacia abajo.

dowry, *n.* dote *f.*

doze, *v.* dormitar.

dozen, *n.* docena *f.*

draft, 1. *n.* dibujo *m.;* (com.) giro *m.;* (mil.) conscripción *f.* **2.** *v.* dibujar; (mil.) reclutar.

draftee, *n.* conscripto *m.*

drag, *v.* arrastrar.

dragon, *n.* dragón *m.*

drain, 1. *n.* desaguadero *m.* **2.** *v.* desaguar.

drainage, *n.* drenaje *m.*

drama, *n.* drama *m.*

dramatic, *a.* dramático.

dramatics, *n.* dramática *f.*

dramatist, *n.* dramaturgo *m.*

dramatize, *v.* dramatizar.

drape, *n.* cortina *f.*

drapery, *n.* colgaduras *f.pl.;* ropaje *m.*

drastic, *a.* drástico.

draw, *v.* dibujar; atraer. **d. up,** formular.

drawback, *n.* desventaja *f.*

drawer, *n.* cajón *m.*

drawing, *n.* dibujo *m.;* rifa *f.*

dread, 1. *n.* terror *m.* **2.** *v.* temer.

dreadful, *a.* terrible.

dreadfully, *adv.* horrendamente.

dream, 1. *n.* sueño, ensueño *m.* **2.** *v.* soñar.

dreamer, *n.* soñador -ra; visionario -ia.

dreamy, *a.* soñador, contemplativo.

dreary, *a.* monótono y pesado.

dredge, 1. *n.* rastra *f.* **2.** *v.* rastrear.

dregs, *n.* sedimento *m.*

drench, *v.* mojar.

dress, 1. *n.* vestido; traje *m.* **2.** *v.* vestir.

dresser, *n.* (furniture) tocador.

dressing, *n.* (med.) curación *f.;* (cookery) condimento, relleno *m.*

dressing gown, *n.* batá *f.*

dressmaker, *n.* modista *m. & f.*

drift, 1. *n.* tendencia *f.;* (naut.) deriva *f.* **2.** *v.* (naut.) derivar; (snow) amontonarse.

drill, 1. *n.* ejercicio *m.;* (mech.) taladro *m.* **2.** *v.* (mech.) taladrar.

drink, 1. *n.* bebida *f.* **2.** *v.* beber, tomar.

drinkable, *a.* potable, bebible.

drip, *v.* gotear.

drive, 1. *n.* paseo *m.* **2.** *v.* impeler; (auto.) guiar, conducir.

driver, *n.* chofer *m.*

driveway, *n.* entrada para coches.

drizzle, 1. *n.* llovizna *f.* **2.** *v.* lloviznar.

dromedary, *n.* dromedario *m.*

droop, *v.* inclinarse.

drop, 1. *n.* gota *f.* **2.** *v.* soltar; dejar, caer.

dropout, *n.* joven que abandona sus estudios.

dropper, *n.* cuentagotas *f.*

dropsy, *n.* hidropesía *f.*

drought, *n.* seca, sequía *f.*

drove, *n.* manada *f.*

drown, *v.* ahogar.

drowse, *v.* adormecer.

drowsiness, *n.* somnolencia *f.*

drowsy, *a.* soñoliento.

drudge, *n.* ganapán *m.*

drudgery, *n.* trabajo penoso.

drug, 1. *n.* droga *f.* **2.** *v.* narcotizar.

druggist, *n.* farmacéutico, boticario *m.*

drugstore, *n.* farmacia, botica, droguería *f.*

drum, *n.* tambor *m.*

drummer, *n.* tambor *m.*

drumstick, *n.* palillo *m.;* (leg) pierna *f.*

drunk, *a. & n.* borracho.

drunkard, *n.* borrachón *m.*

drunken, *a.* borracho; ebrio.

drunkenness, *n.* embriaguez *f.*

dry, 1. *a.* seco, árido. **2.** *v.* secar.

dry cell, *n.* pila seca *f.*

dry-cleaner, *n.* tintorero *m.*

dryness, *n.* sequedad *f.*

dual, *a.* doble.

dubious, *a.* dudoso.

duchess, *n.* duquesa *f.*

duck, 1. *n.* pato *m.* **2.** *v.* zabullir; (avoid) esquivar.

duct, *n.* canal *m.*

due, 1. *a.* debido; (com.) vencido. **2. dues,** *n.* cuota *f.*

duel, *n.* duelo *m.*

duelist, *n.* duelista *m.*

duet, *n.* dúo *m.*

duke, *n.* duque *m.*

dull, *a.* apagado, desteñido; sin punta; (fig.) pesado, soso.

dullness, *n.* estupidez; pesadez *f.;* deslustre *m.*

duly, *adv.* debidamente.

dumb, *a.* mudo; (coll.) estúpido.

dumbwaiter, *n.* montaplatos *m.*

dumfound, *v.* confundir.

dummy, *n.* figurón *m.*

dump, 1. *n.* depósito *m.* **2.** *v.* descargar.

dune, *n.* duna *f.*

dungeon, *n.* calabozo *m.*

dunk, *v.* mojar.

dupe, *v.* engañar.

duplicate, 1. *a. & n.* duplicado *m.* **2.** *v.* duplicar.

duplication, *n.* duplicación *f.*

duplicity, *n.* duplicidad *f.*

durability, *n.* durabilidad *f.*

durable, *a.* durable, duradero.

duration, *n.* duración *f.*

duress, *n.* compulsión *m.;* encierro *m.*

during, *prep.* durante.

dusk, *n.* crepúsculo *m.*

dusky, *a.* oscuro; moreno.

dust, 1. *n.* polvo *m.* **2.** *v.* polvorear; despolvorear.

dusty, *a.* empolvado.

Dutch, *a.* holandés -sa.

dutiful, *a.* respetuoso.

dutifully, *adv.* respetuosamente, obedientemente.

duty, *n.* deber *m.;* (com.) derechos *m.pl.*

duty-free, *a.* libre de derechos.

dwarf, 1. *n.* enano -na. **2.** *v.* achicar.

dwell, *v.* habitar, residir. **d. on,** espaciarse en.

dwelling, *n.* morada, casa *f.*

dwindle, *v.* disminuirse.

dye, 1. *n.* tintura *f.* **2.** *v.* teñir.

dyer, *n.* tintorero -ra.

dynamic, *a.* dinámico.

dynamite, *n.* dinamita *f.*

dynamo, *n.* dínamo *m.*

dynasty, *n.* dinastía *f.*

dysentery, *n.* disentería *f.*

dyslexia, *n.* dislexia *f.*

dyspepsia, *n.* dispepsia *f.*

E

each, 1. *a.* cada. **2.** *pron.* cada uno -na. **e. other,** el uno al otro.

eager, *a.* ansioso.

eagerly, *adv.* ansiosamente.

eagerness, *n.* ansia *f.*

eagle, *n.* águila *f.*

ear, n. oído m.; (outer) oreja f.; (of corn) mazorca f.
earache, n. dolor de oído m.
earl, n. conde m.
early, a. & adv. temprano.
earn, v. ganar.
earnest, a. serio.
earnestly, adv. seriamente.
earnings, n. ganancias f.pl.; (com.) ingresos m.pl.
earphone, n. auricular m.
earring, n. pendiente, arete m.
earth, n. tierra f.
earthquake, n. terremoto m.
ease, 1. n. reposo m.; facilidad f. 2. v. aliviar.
easel, n. caballete m.
easily, adv. fácilmente.
east, n. oriente, este m.
Easter, n. Pascua Florida.
eastern, a. oriental.
eastward, adv. hacia el este.
easy, a. fácil.
eat, v. comer.
eaves, n. socarrén m.
ebb, 1. n. menguante f. 2. v. menguar.
ebony, n. ébano m.
eccentric, a. excéntrico.
eccentricity, n. excentricidad f.
ecclesiastic, a. & n. eclesiástico. m.
ecclesiastical, a. eclasiástico.
echelon, n. escalón m.
echo, n. eco m.
eclipse, 1. n. eclipse m. 2. v. eclipsar.
ecological, a. ecológico.
ecology, n. ecología f.
economic, a. económico.
economical, a. económico.
economics, n. economía política.
economist, n. economista m.
economize, v. economizar.
economy, n. economía f.
ecstasy, n. éxtasis m.
Ecuadorian, a. & n. ecuatoriano -na.
ecumenical, a. ecuménico.
eczema, n. eczema f.
eddy, 1. n. remolino m. 2. v. remolinar.
edge, 1. n. filo; borde m. 2. v. e. one's way, abrirse paso.
edible, a. comestible.
edict, n. edicto m.
edifice, n. edificio m.
edify, v. edificar.
edition, n. edición f.
editor, n. redactor m.
editorial, n. editorial m. e. staff, redacción f.
educate, v. educar.
education, n. instrucción; enseñanza f.
educational, a. educativo.
educator, n. educador, pedagogo m.
eel, n. anguila f.
efface, v. tachar.
effect, 1. n. efecto m. in e., en vigor. 2. v. efectuar, realizar.
effective, a. eficaz; efectivo; en vigor.

effectively, adv. eficazmente.
effectiveness, n. efectividad f.
effectual, a. eficaz.
effeminate, a. afeminado.
efficacy, n. eficacia f.
efficiency, n. eficiencia f.
efficient, a. eficaz.
efficiently, adv. eficazmente.
effigy, n. efigie m.
effort, n. esfuerzo m.
effrontery, n. impudencia f.
effusive, a. expansivo.
egg, n. huevo m. fried e., huevo frito. soft-boiled e., h. pasado por agua. scrambled eggs, huevos revueltos.
eggplant, n. berenjena f.
egoism, egotism, n. egoísmo m.
egoist, egotist, n. egoísta m. & f.
egotism, n. egotismo m.
egotist, n. egotista m.
Egypt, n. Egipto m.
Egyptian, a. & n. egipcio -ia.
eight, a. & pron. ocho.
eighteen, a. & pron. dieciocho.
eighth, a. octavo.
eightieth, a. octogésimo m.
eighty, a. & pron. ochenta.
either, 1. a. & pron. cualquiera de los dos. 2. adv. tampoco. 3. conj. either . . . or, o . . . o.
ejaculate, v. exclamar.
eject, v. expeler.
ejection, n. expulsión f.
elaborate, 1. a. elaborado. 2. v. elaborar; ampliar.
elapse, v. transcurrir; pasar.
elastic, a. & n. elástico m.
elasticity, n. elasticidad f.
elate, v. exaltar.
elation, n. exaltación f.
elbow, n. codo m.
elder, 1. a. mayor. 2. n. anciano m.
elderly, a. de edad.
eldest, a. mayor.
elect, v. elegir.
election, n. elección f.
elective, a. electivo.
electorate, n. electorado m.
electric, electrical, a. eléctrico.
electrician, n. electricista m.
electricity, n. electricidad f.
electrocardiogram, n. electrocardiograma m.
electrocute, v. electrocutar.
electrode, n. electrodo m.
electrolysis, n. electrólisis f.
electron, n. electrón m.
electronics, n. electrónica f.
elegance, n. elegancia f.
elegant, a. elegante.
elegy, n. elegía f.
element, n. elemento m.
elemental, a. elemental.
elementary, a. elemental.
elephant, n. elefante m.
elevate, v. elevar.
elevation, n. elevación f.
elevator, n. ascensor m.
eleven, a. & pron. once.
eleventh, a. undécimo.
elf, n. duende m.
elicit, v. sacar; despertar.

eligibility, n. elegibilidad f.
eligible, a. elegible.
eliminate, v. eliminar.
elimination, n. eliminación f.
elixir, n. elixir m.
elk, n. alce m., anta f.
elm, n. olmo m.
elocution, n. elocución f.
elongate, v. alargar.
elope, v. fugarse.
eloquence, n. elocuencia f.
eloquent, a. elocuente.
eloquently, adv. elocuentemente.
else, adv. más. someone e., otra persona. something e., otra cosa. or e., de otro modo.
elsewhere, adv. en otra parte.
elucidate, v. elucidar.
elude, v. eludir.
elusive, a. evasivo.
emaciated, a. enflaquecido.
emanate, v. emanar.
emancipate, v. emancipar.
emancipation, n. emancipación f.
emancipator, n. libertador m.
embalm, v. embalsamar.
embankment, n. malecón, dique m.
embargo, n. embargo m.
embark, v. embarcar.
embarrass, v. avergonzar; turbar.
embarrassing, a. penoso, vergonzoso.
embarrassment, n. turbación; vergüenza f.
embassy, n. embajada f.
embellish, v. hermosear, embellecer.
embellishment, n. embellecimiento m.
embezzle, v. apropiarse dinero ilícitamente.
emblem, n. emblema m.
embody, v. incorporar.
embrace, 1. n. abrazo m. 2. v. abrazar.
embroider, v. bordar.
embroidery, n. bordado m.
embryo, n. embrión m.
embryonic, a. embrionario.
emerald, n. esmeralda f.
emerge, v. salir.
emergency, n. emergencia f.
emergent, a. emergente.
emery, n. esmeril m.
emetic, n. emético m.
emigrant, a. & n. emigrante m. & f.
emigrate, v. emigrar.
emigration, n. emigración f.
eminence, n. altura; eminencia f.
eminent, a. eminente.
emissary, n. emisario m.
emission, n. emisión f.
emit, v. emitir.
emolument, n. emolumento m.
emotion, n. emoción f.
emotional, a. sensible.
emperor, n. emperador m.
emphasis, n. énfasis m. or f.

emphasize, v. acentuar, recalcar.
emphatic, a. enfático.
empire, n. imperio m.
empirical, a. empírico.
employ, v. emplear.
employee, n. empleado -da.
employer, n. patrón -ona.
employment, n. empleo m.
empower, v. autorizar.
emptiness, n. vaciedad; futilidad f.
empty, 1. a. vacío. 2. v. vaciar.
emulate, v. emular.
emulsion, n. emulsión f.
enable, v. capacitar; permitir.
enact, v. promulgar, decretar.
enactment, n. ley f., estatuto m.
enamel, 1. n. esmalte m. 2. v. esmaltar.
enamored, a. enamorado.
enchant, v. encantar.
enchantment, n. encanto m.
encircle, v. circundar.
enclose, v. encerrar. **enclosed**, (in letter) adjunto.
enclosure, n. recinto m.; (in letter) incluso m.
encompass, v. circundar.
encounter, 1. n. encuentro m. 2. v. encontrar.
encourage, v. animar.
encouragement, n. estímulo m.
encroach, v. usurpar; meterse.
encyclical, n. encíclica f.
encyclopedia, n. enciclopedia f.
end, 1. n. fin, término, cabo; extremo; (aim) propósito m. 2. v. acabar; terminar.
endanger, v. poner en peligro.
endear, v. hacer querer.
endeavor, 1. n. esfuerzo m. 2. v. esforzarse.
ending, n. conclusión f.
endless, a. sin fin.
endorse, v. endosar; apoyar.
endorsement, n. endoso m.
endow, v. dotar, fundar.
endowment, n. dotación f., fundación f.
endurance, n. resistencia f.
endure, v. soportar, resistir, aguantar.
enema, n. enema; lavativa f.
enemy, n. enemigo -ga.
energetic, a. enérgico.
energy, n. energía f.
enervate, v. enervar.
enervation, n. enervación f.
enfold, v. envolver.
enforce, v. ejecutar.
enforcement, n. ejecución f.
engage, v. emplear; ocupar.
engaged, (to marry) comprometido.
engagement, n. combate; compromiso; contrato m.; cita f.
engine, n. máquina f. (railroad) locomotora f.
engineer, n. ingeniero; maquinista m.
engineering, n. ingeniería f.
England, n. Inglaterra f.
English, a. & n. inglés m.

Englishman, n. inglés m.
Englishwoman, n. inglesa f.
engrave, v. grabar.
engraver, n. grabador m.
engraving, n. grabado m.
engross, v. absorber.
enhance, v. aumentar en valor; realzar.
enigma, n. enigma m.
enigmatic, a. enigmático.
enjoy, v. gozar de; disfrutar de. **oneself**, divertirse.
enjoyable, a. agradable.
enjoyment, n. goce m.
enlarge, v. agrandar; ampliar.
enlargement, n. ensanchamiento m., ampliación f.
enlarger, n. amplificador m.
enlighten, v. informar.
enlightenment, n. esclarecimiento m.; cultura f.
enlist, v. reclutar; alistarse.
enlistment, n. alistamiento m.
enliven, v. avivar.
enmesh, v. entrampar.
enmity, n. enemistad f.
enormity, n. enormidad f.
enormous, a. enorme.
enough, a. & adv. bastante. **to be e.**, bastar.
enrage, v. enfurecer.
enrich, v. enriquecer.
enroll, v. registrar; matricularse.
enrollment, n. matriculación f.
ensign, n. bandera f.; (naval) sub-teniente m.
enslave, v. esclavizar.
ensue, v. seguir, resultar.
entail, v. envolver.
entangle, v. enredar.
enter, v. entrar.
enterprise, n. empresa f.
enterprising, a. emprendedor.
entertain, v. entretener; divertir.
entertainment, n. entretenimiento m.; diversión f.
enthrall, v. esclavizar.
enthusiasm, n. entusiasmo m.
enthusiast, n. entusiasta m. & f.
enthusiastic, a. entusiasmado.
entice, v. inducir.
entire, a. entero.
entirely, adv. enteramente.
entirety, n. totalidad f.
entitle, v. autorizar; (book) titular.
entity, n. entidad f.
entrails, n. entrañas f.pl.
entrance, n. entrada f.
entrant, n. competidor m.
entreat, v. rogar, suplicar.
entreaty, n. ruego m., súplica f.
entrench, v. atrincherar.
entrust, v. confiar.
entry, n. entrada f.; (com.) partida f.
enumerate, v. enumerar.
enumeration, n. enumeración f.
enunciate, v. enunciar.
enunciation, n. enunciación f.
envelop, v. envolver.

envelope, n. sobre m., cubierta f.
enviable, a. envidiable.
envious, a. envidioso.
environment, n. ambiente m.
environmentalist, n. activista ecológico, ecologista m.
environmental protection, protección del ambiente.
environs, n. alrededores m.
envoy, n. enviado m.
envy, 1. n. envidia f. 2. v. envidiar.
eon, n. eón m.
ephemeral, a. efímero.
epic, 1. a. épico. 2. n. epopeya f.
epicure, n. epicúreo m.
epidemic, 1. a. epidémico. 2. n. epidemia f.
epidermis, n. epidermis f.
epigram, n. epigrama m.
epilepsy, n. epilepsia f.
epilogue, n. epílogo m.
episode, n. episodio m.
epistle, n. epístola f.
epitaph, n. epitafio m.
epithet, n. epíteto m.
epitome, n. epítome m.
epoch, n. época, era f.
equal, 1. a. & n. igual m. 2. v. igualar; equivaler.
equality, n. igualdad f.
equalize, v. igualar.
equanimity, n. ecuanimidad f.
equate, v. igualar.
equation, n. ecuación f.
equator, n. ecuador m.
equatorial, a. & a. ecuatorial f.
equestrian, 1. n. jinete m. 2. a. ecuestre.
equilibrium, n. equilibrio m.
equinox, n. equinoccio m.
equip, v. equipar.
equipment, n. equipo m.
equitable, a. equitativo.
equity, n. equidad, justicia f.
equivalent, a. & n. equivalente m.
equivocal, a. equívoco, ambiguo.
era, n. era, época, edad f.
eradicate, v. extirpar.
erase, v. borrar.
eraser, n. borrador m.
erasure, n. borradura f.
erect, 1. a. derecho, erguido. 2. v. erigir.
erection, erectness, n. erección f.
ermine, n. armiño m.
erode, v. corroer.
erosion, n. erosión f.
erotic, a. erótico.
err, v. equivocarse.
errand, n. encargo, recado m.
errant, a. errante.
erratic, a. errático.
erroneous, a. erróneo.
error, n. error m.
erudite, a. erudito.
erudition, n. erudición f.
eruption, n. erupción, irrupción f.

escalate, v. realizar una escalada.

escalator, n. escalera mecánica f.

escapade, n. escapada; correría f.

escape, 1. n. fuga, huída f. **fire e.**, escalera de salvamento. 2. v. escapar; fugarse.

eschew, v. evadir.

escort, 1. n. escolta f. 2. v. escoltar.

escrow, n. plica f.

escutcheon, n. escudo de armas m.

esophagus, n. esófago m.

esoteric, a. esotérico.

especially, adv. especialmente.

espionage, n. espionaje m.

essay, n. ensayo m.

essayist, n. ensayista f.

essence, n. esencia f.; perfume m.

essential, a. esencial.

essentially, adv. esencialmente.

establish, v. establecer.

establishment, n. establecimiento m.

estate, n. estado m.; hacienda f.; bienes m.pl.

esteem, 1. n. estima f. 2. v. estimar.

estimable, a. estimable.

estimate, 1. n. cálculo; presupuesto m. 2. v. estimar.

estimation, n. estimación f.; cálculo m.

estrange, v. extrañar; enajenar.

estuary, n. estuario m.

etching, n. grabado al agua fuerte.

eternal, a. eterno.

eternity, n. eternidad f.

ether, n. éter m.

ethereal, a. etéreo.

ethical, a. ético.

ethics, n. ética f.

ethnic, a. étnico.

etiquette, n. etiqueta f.

etymology, n. etimología f.

eucalyptus, n. eucalipto m.

eugenic, a. eugenésico.

eugenics, n. eugenesia f.

eulogize, v. elogiar.

eulogy, n. elogio m.

eunuch, n. eunuco m.

euphonious, a. eufónico.

Europe, n. Europa f.

European, a. & n. europeo pea.

euthanasia, n. eutanasia f.

evacuate, v. evacuar.

evade, v. evadir.

evaluate, v. avaluar.

evaluation, n. valoración f.

evangelist, n. evangelista m.

evaporate, v. evaporarse.

evaporation, n. evaporación f.

evasion, n. evasión f.

evasive, a. evasivo.

eve, n. víspera f.

even, 1. a. llano; igual. 2. adv. aun; hasta. **not e.**, ni siquiera.

evening, n. noche, tarde f. **good e.**, buenas noches.

evenness, n. uniformidad f.

event, n. acontecimiento, suceso m.

eventful, a. memorable.

eventual, a. eventual.

ever, adv. alguna vez; (after not) nunca. **e. since**, desde que.

everlasting, a. eterno.

every, a. cada, todos los.

everybody, pron. todo el mundo; cada uno.

everyday, a. ordinario, de cada día.

everyone, pron. cada uno; cada cual; todos.

everything, pron. todo m.

everywhere, adv. por todas partes, en todas partes.

evict, v. expulsar.

eviction, n. evicción f.

evidence, n. evidencia f.

evident, a. evidente.

evidently, adv. evidentemente.

evil, 1. a. malo; maligno. 2. n. mal m.

evince, v. revelar.

evoke, v. evocar.

evolution, n. evolución f.

evolve, v. desenvolver; desarrollar.

ewe, v. oveja f.

exact, 1. a. exacto. 2. v. exigir.

exacting, a. exigente.

exactly, adv. exactamente.

exaggerate, v. exagerar.

exaggeration, n. exageración f.

exalt, v. exaltar.

exaltation, n. exaltación f.

examination, n. examen m.; (legal) interrogatorio m.

examine, v. examinar.

example, n. ejemplo m.

exasperate, v. exasperar.

exasperation, n. exasperación f.

excavate, v. excavar, cavar.

exceed, v. exceder.

exceedingly, adv. sumamente, extremadamente.

excel, v. sobresalir.

excellence, n. excelencia f.

Excellency, n. (title) Excelencia f.

excellent, a. excelente.

except, 1. prep. salvo, excepto. 2. v. exceptuar.

exception, n. excepción f.

exceptional, a. excepcional.

excerpt, n. extracto.

excess, n. exceso m.

excessive, a. excesivo.

exchange, 1. n. cambio; canje m. **stock e.**, bolsa f. **telephone e.**, central telefónica. 2. v. cambiar, canjear.

exchangeable, a. cambiable.

excise, 1. n. sisa f. 2. v. extirpar.

excite, v. agitar; provocar; emocionar.

excitement, n. agitación, conmoción f.

exciting, a. emocionante.

exclaim, v. exclamar.

exclamation, n. exclamación f.

exclamation point or mark, n. punto de admiración m.

exclude, v. excluir.

exclusion, n. exclusión f.

exclusive, a. exclusivo.

excommunicate, v. excomulgar, descomulgar.

excommunication, n. excomunión f.

excrement, n. excremento m.

excruciating, a. penosísimo.

exculpate, v. justificar.

excursion, n. excursión; jira f.

excuse, 1. n. excusa f. 2. v. excusar, perdonar; dispensar; disculpar.

execrable, a. execrable.

execute, v. ejecutar.

execution, n. ejecución f.

executioner, n. verdugo m.

executive, a. & n. ejecutivo m.

executor, n. testamentario m.

exemplary, a. ejemplar.

exemplify, v. ejemplificar.

exempt, 1. a. exento. 2. v. exentar.

exercise, 1. n. ejercicio m. 2. v. ejercitar.

exert, v. esforzar.

exertion, n. esfuerzo m.

exhale, v. exhalar.

exhaust, 1. n. (auto.) escape m. 2. v. agotar.

exhaustion, n. agotamiento m.

exhaustive, a. agotador.

exhibit, 1. n. exhibición, exposición f. 2. v. exhibir.

exhibition, n. exhibición f.

exhilarate, v. alegrar; estimular.

exhort, v. exhortar.

exhortation, n. exhortación f.

exhume, v. exhumar.

exigency, n. exigencia f., urgencia f.

exile, 1. n. destierro m., (person) desterrado m. 2. v. desterrar.

exist, v. existir.

existence, n. existencia f.

existent, a. existente.

exit, n. salida f.

exodus, n. éxodo m.

exonerate, v. exonerar.

exorbitant, a. exorbitante.

exorcise, v. exorcizar.

exotic, a. exótico.

expand, v. dilatar; ensanchar.

expanse, n. espacio m.; extensión f.

expansion, n. expansión f.

expansive, a. expansivo.

expatiate, v. espaciarse.

expatriate, 1. n. & a. expatriato m. 2. v. expatriar.

expect, v. esperar; contar con.

expectancy, n. esperanza f.

expectation, n. esperanza f.

expectorate, v. expectorar.

expediency, n. conveniencia f.

expedient, 1. a. oportuno. 2. n. expediente m.

expedite, v. acelerar, despachar.

expedition, n. expedición f.

expel, v. expeler, expulsar.

expend, v. desembolsar, expender.

expenditure, n. desembolso; gasto m.

expense, n. gasto m.; costa f.

expensive, a. caro, costoso.

expensively, adv. costosamente.

experience, 1. n. experiencia f. **2.** v. experimentar.

experienced, a. experimentado, perito.

experiment, 1. n. experimento m. **2.** v. experimentar.

experimental, a. experimental.

expert, a. & n. experto m.

expiate, v. expiar.

expiration, n. expiración f.

expire, v. expirar; (com.) vencerse.

explain, v. explicar.

explanation, n. explicación f.

explanatory, a. explicativo.

expletive, 1. n. interjección f. **2.** a. expletivo.

explicit, a. explícito, claro.

explode, v. estallar, volar; refutar.

exploit, 1. n. hazaña f. **2.** v. explotar.

exploitation, n. explotación f.

exploration, n. exploración f.

exploratory, a. exploratorio.

explore, v. explorar.

explorer, n. explorador m.

explosion, n. explosión f.

explosive, a. explosivo.

export, 1. n. exportación f. **2.** v. exportar.

exportation, n. exportación f.

expose, v. exponer; descubrir.

exposition, n. exposición f.

expository, a. expositivo.

expostulate, v. altercar.

exposure, n. exposición f.

expound, v. exponer, explicar.

express, 1. a. & n. expreso m. **e. company,** compañía de porteo. **2.** v. expresar.

expression, n. expresión f.

expressive, a. expresivo.

expressly, adv. expresamente.

expressman, n. empresario de expresos m.

expropriate, v. expropriar.

expulsion, n. expulsión f.

expunge, v. borrar, expurgar.

expurgate, v. expurgar.

exquisite, a. exquisito.

extant, a. existente.

extemporaneous, a. improvisado.

extend, v. extender.

extension, n. extensión f.

extensive, a. extenso.

extensively, adv. por extenso.

extent, n. extensión f.; grado m. **to a certain e.,** hasta cierto punto.

extenuate, v. extenuar.

exterior, a. & n. exterior m.

exterminate, v. exterminar.

extermination, n. exterminio m.

external, a. externo, exterior.

extinct, a. extinto.

extinction, n. extinción f.

extinguish, v. extinguir, apagar.

extol, v. alabar.

extort, v. exigir dinero sin derecho.

extortion, n. extorsión f.

extra, 1. a. extraordinario; adicional. **2.** n. (newspaper) extra m.

extract, 1. n. extracto m. **2.** v. extraer.

extraction, n. extracción f.

extraneous, a. extraño; ajeno.

extraordinary, a. extraordinario.

extravagance, n. extravagancia f.

extravagant, a. extravagante.

extreme, a. & n. extremo m.

extremity, n. extremidad f.

extricate, v. desenredar.

exuberant, a. exuberante.

exude, v. exudar.

exult, v. regocijarse.

exultant, a. triunfante.

eye, 1. n. ojo m. **2.** v. ojear.

eyeball, n. globo del ojo.

eyebrow, n. ceja f.

eyeglasses, n. lentes m.

eyelash, n. pestaña f.

eyelid, n. párpado m.

eyesight, n. vista f.

F

fable, n. fábula; ficción f.

fabric, n. tejido m., tela f.

fabricate, v. fabricar.

fabulous, a. fabuloso.

façade, n. fachada f.

face, 1. n. cara f. **to make faces,** hacer muecas. **2.** encararse con. **f. the street,** dar a la calle.

facet, n. faceta f.

facetious, a. chistoso.

facial, 1. n. masaje facial m. **2.** a. facial.

facile, a. fácil.

facilitate, v. facilitar.

facility, n. facilidad f.

facsimile, n. facsímile m.

fact, n. hecho m. **in f.,** en realidad.

faction, n. facción f.

factor, n. factor m.

factory, n. fábrica f.

factual, a. verdadero.

faculty, n. facultad f.

fad, n. boga; novedad f.

fade, v. desteñirse; (flowers) marchitarse.

fail, 1. n. **without f.,** sin falla. **2.** v. fallar; fracasar. **not to f. to,** no dejar de.

failure, n. fracaso m.

faint, 1. a. débil; vago; pálido. **2.** n. desmayo m. **3.** v. desmayarse.

faintly, adv. débilmente; indistintamente.

fair, 1. a. razonable, justo; (hair) rubio; (weather) bueno. **2.** n. feria f.

fairly, adv. imparcialmente; regularmente; claramente; bellamente.

fairness, n. justicia f.

fairy, n. hada f., duende m.

faith, n. fe; confianza f.

faithful, a. fiel.

fake, 1. a. falso; postizo. **2.** n. imitación; estafa f. **3.** v. imitar; fingir.

faker, n. imitador m.; farsante m.

falcon, n. halcón f.

fall, 1. n. caída; catarata f.; (season) otoño m.; (in price) baja f. **2.** v. caer; bajar. **f. asleep,** dormirse; **f. in love,** enamorarse.

fallacious, a. falaz.

fallacy, n. falacia f.

fallible, a. falible.

fallout, n. precipitación resultante de una explosión nuclear.

fallow, a. sin cultivar.

false, a. falso; postizo.

falsehood, n. falsedad; mentira f.

falseness, n. falsedad, perfidia f.

falsetto, n. falsete m.

falsification, n. falsificación f.

falsify, v. falsificar.

falter, v. vacilar; (in speech) tartamudear.

fame, n. fama f.

familiar, a. familiar; conocido. **to be f. with,** estar familiarizado con.

familiarity, n. familiaridad f.

familiarize, v. familiarizar.

family, n. familia; especie naje m.

famine, n. hambre; carestía f.

famished, a. muerto de hambre.

famous, a. famoso, célebre.

fan, n. abanico; ventilador m. (sports) aficionado -da.

fanatic, a. & n. fanático -ca.

fanatical, a. fanático.

fanaticism, n. fanatismo m.

fanciful, a. caprichoso; fantástico.

fancy, 1. a. fino, elegante. **f. foods,** novedades f.pl. **2.** n. fantasía f.; capricho m. **3.** v. imaginar.

fanfare, n. fanfarria f.

fang, n. colmillo m.

fantastic, a. fantástico.

fantasy, n. fantasía f.

far, 1. a. lejano, distante. **2.** adv. lejos. **how f.,** a qué distancia. **as f. as,** hasta. **so f.,** thus f., hasta aquí.

farce, n. farsa f.

fare, n. pasaje m.

farewell, 1. n. despedida f. **to**

say f. despedirse. 2. *interj.*
!adiós;

farfetched, *a.* forzado.

farm, 1. *n.* granja; hacienda *f.*
2. *v.* cultivar, labrar la tierra.

farmer, *n.* labrador, agricultor
m.

farmhouse, *n.* hacienda, alquería *f.*

farming, *n.* agricultura *f.;* cultivo *m.*

fascinate, *v.* fascinar, embelesar.

fascination, *n.* fascinación *f.*

fascism, *n.* fascismo *m.*

fashion, 1. *n.* moda; costumbre; guisa *f.* **2.** *v.* formar.

fashionable, *a.* de moda, en boga.

fast, 1. *a.* rápido, veloz;
(watch) adelantado; (color)
firme. **2.** *adv.* ligero, de prisa.
3. *n.* ayuno **4.** *v.* ayunar.

fasten, *v.* afirmar, atar; fijar.

fastener, *n.* asegurador *m.*

fastidious, *a.* melindroso.

fat, 1. *a.* gordo. **2.** *n.* grasa,
manteca *f.*

fatal, *a.* fatal.

fatality, *n.* fatalidad *f.*

fatally, *adv.* fatalmente.

fate, *n.* destino *m.;* suerte *f.*

fateful, *a.* fatal; ominoso.

father, *n.* padre *m.*

fatherhood, *n.* paternidad *f.*

father-in-law, *n.* suegro *m.*

fatherland, *n.* patria *f.*

fatherly, 1. *a.* paternal. **2.** *adv.*
paternalmente.

fathom, 1. *n.* braza *f.* **2.** *v.* sondar; (fig.) penetrar en.

fatigue, 1. *n.* fatiga *f.*, cansancio *m.* **2.** *v.* fatigar, cansar.

fatten, *v.* engordar, cebar.

faucet, *n.* grifo *m.*, llave *f.*

fault, *n.* culpa *f.;* defecto *m.* **at
f.,** culpable.

faultless, *a.* sin tacha, perfecto.

faultlessly, *adv.* perfectamente.

faulty, *a.* defectuoso, imperfecto.

favor, 1. *n.* favor *m.* **2.** *v.* favorecer.

favorable, *a.* favorable.

favorite, *a. & n.* favorito -ta.

favoritism, *n.* favoritismo *m.*

fawn, 1. *n.* cervato *m.* **2.** *v.* halagar, adular.

faze, *v.* desconcertar.

fear, 1. *n.* miedo, temor *m.* **2.** *v.*
temer.

fearful, *a.* temeroso, medroso.

fearless, *a.* intrépido; sin temor.

fearlessness, *n.* intrepidez *f.*

feasible, *a.* factible.

feast, *n.* banquete *m.;* fiesta *f.*

feat, *n.* hazaña *f.;* hecho *m.*

feather, *n.* pluma *f.*

feature, 1. *n.* facción *f.;* rasgo
m.; (movies) película principal. **2.** *v.* presentar como
atracción especial.

February, *n.* febrero *m.*

federal, *a.* federal.

federation, *n.* confederación,
federación *f.*

fee, *n.* honorarios *m.pl.*

feeble, *a.* débil.

feebleminded, *a.* imbécil.

feebleness, *n.* debilidad *f.*

feed, 1. *n.* pasto *m.* **2.** *v.* alimentar; dar de comer. **fed up
with,** harto de.

feedback, *n.* feedback *m.*, retroalimentación *f.*

feel, 1. *n.* sensación *f.* **2.** *v.* sentir; palpar. **f. like,** tener ganas
de.

feeling, *n.* sensación; sensibilidad *f.*

feign, *v.* fingir.

felicitate, *v.* felicitar.

felicitous, *a.* feliz.

felicity, *n.* felicidad *f.*, dicha *f.*

feline, *a.* felino.

fellow, *n.* compañero; socio
m.; (coll.) tipo *m.*

fellowship, *n.* compañía, (for
study) beca *f.*

felon, *n.* reo *m.*, felón *m.*

felony, *n.* felonía *f.*

felt, *n.* fieltro *m.*

female, *a. & n.* hembra *f.*

feminine, *a.* femenino.

fence, 1. *n.* cerca *f.* **2.** *v.* cercar.

fender, *n.* guardabarros *m.*

ferment, 1. *n.* fermento *m.;*
(fig.) agitación *f.* **2.** *v.* fermentar.

fermentation, *n.* fermentación
f.

fern, *n.* helecho *m.*

ferocious, *a.* feroz; fiero.

ferociously, *adv.* ferozmente.

ferocity, *n.* ferocidad, fiereza *f.*

ferry, *n.* transbordador *m.*,
barca de transporte.

fertile, *a.* fecundo; (land) fértil.

fertility, *n.* fertilidad *f.*

fertilization, *n.* fertilización *f.*

fertilize, *v.* fertilizar, abonar.

fertilizer, *n.* abono *m.*

fervency, *n.* ardor *m.*

fervent, *a.* ferviente.

fervently, *adv.* fervorosamente.

fervid, *a.* férvido.

fervor, *n.* fervor *m.*

fester, *v.* ulcerarse.

festival, *n.* fiesta *f.*

festive, *a.* festivo.

festivity, *n.* festividad *f.*

festoon, 1. *n.* festón *m.* **2.** *v.*
festonear.

fetch, *v.* ir por; traer.

fete, 1. *n.* fiesta *f.* **2.** *v.* festejar.

fetid, *a.* fétido.

fetish, *n.* fetiche *m.*

fetter, 1. *n.* grillete *m.* **2.** *v.* engrillar.

fetus, *n.* feto *m.*

feud, *n.* riña *f.;* feudo *m.*

feudal, *a.* feudal.

feudalism, *n.* feudalismo *m.*

fever, *n.* fiebre *f.*

feverish, *a.* febril.

feverishly, *adv.* febrilmente.

few, *a.* pocos. **a. f.,** algunos,
unos cuantos.

fiancé, fiancée, *n.* novio -via.

fiasco, *n.* fiasco *m.*

fiat, *n.* fiat *m.*, orden *f.*

fib, 1. *n.* mentira *f.* **2.** *v.* mentir.

fiber, *n.* fibra *f.*

fibrous, *a.* fibroso.

fickle, *a.* caprichoso.

fickleness, *n.* inconstancia *f.*

fiction, *n.* ficción *f.;* (literature) novelas *f.pl.*

fictitious, *a.* ficticio.

fidelity, *n.* fidelidad *f.*

fidget, *v.* inquietar.

field, *n.* campo *m.*

fiend, *n.* demonio *m.*

fiendish, *a.* diabólico, malvado.

fierce, *a.* fiero, feroz.

fiery, *a.* ardiente.

fiesta, *n.* fiesta *f.*

fife, *n.* pífano *m.*

fifteen, *a. & pron.* quince.

fifteenth, *n. & a.* décimoquinto.

fifth, *a.* quinto.

fifty, *a. & pron.* cincuenta.

fig, *n.* higo *m.* **f. tree,** higuera *f.*

fight, 1. *n.* lucha, pelea *f.* **2.** *v.*
luchar, pelear.

fighter, *n.* peleador -ra, luchador -ra.

figment, *n.* invención *f.*

figurative, *a.* metafórico.

figuratively, *adv.* figuradamente.

figure, 1. *n.* figura; cifra *f.* **2.** *v.*
figurar; calcular.

filament, *n.* filamento *m.*

file, 1. *n.* archivo *m.;* (instrument) lima *f.;* (row) fila *f.* **2.**
v. archivar; limar.

filial, *a.* filial.

filigree, *n.* filigrana *f.*

fill, *v.* llenar.

fillet, *n.* filete *m.*

filling, *n.* relleno *m.;* (dental)
empastadura *f.* **f. station,**
bomba *f.*

film, 1. *n.* película *f.*, film *m.* **2.**
v. filmar.

filter, 1. *n.* filtro *m.* **2.** *v.* filtrar.

filth, *n.* suciedad, mugre *f.*

filthy, *a.* sucio.

fin, *n.* aleta *f.*

final, 1. *a.* final, último. **2.** *n.*
examen final. **finals,** (sports)
final *f.*

finalist, *n.* finalista.

finally, *adv.* finalmente.

finances, *n.* recursos, fondos
m.pl.

financial, *a.* financiero.

financier, *n.* financiero *m.*

find, 1. *n.* hallazgo *m.* **2.** *v.* hallar; encontrar. **f. out,** averiguar, enterarse, saber.

fine, 1. *a.* fino; bueno. **2.** *adv.*
muy bien. **3.** *n.* multa *f.* **4.** *v.*
multar.

finery, *n.* gala *f.*, adorno *m.*

finesse, 1. *n.* artificio *m.* **2.** *v.*
valerse de artificio.

finger, *n.* dedo *m.*

finger bowl, *n.* enjuagatorio *m.*

fingernail, *n.* uña *f.*

fingerprint, 1. *n.* impresión digital *f.* **2.** *v.* tomar las impresiones digitales.

finicky, *a.* melindroso.

finish, 1. *n.* conclusión *f.* **2.** *v.* acabar, terminar.

finished, *a.* acabado.

finite, *a.* finito.

fir, *n.* abeto *m.*

fire, 1. *n.* fuego; incendio *m.* **2.** *v.* disparar, tirar; (coll.) despedir.

fire alarm, *n.* alarma de incendio *f.*

firearm, *n.* arma de fuego.

firecracker, *n.* triquitraque *m.*, buscapiés *m.*, petardo *m.*

fire engine, *n.* bomba de incendios *f.*

fire escape, *n.* escalera de incendios *f.*

fire extinguisher, *n.* matafuego *m.*

firefly, *n.* luciérnaga *f.*

fireman, *n.* bombero *m.*; (railway) fogonero *m.*

fireplace, *n.* hogar, fogón *m.*

fireproof, *a.* incombustible.

fireside, *n.* hogar *m.* fogón *m.*

fireworks, *n.* fuegos artificiales.

firm, 1. *a.* firme. **2.** *n.* casa de comercio.

firmness, *n.* firmeza *f.*

first, *a. & adv.* primero. **at f.,** al principio.

first aid, *n.* primeros auxilios *m.*

first-class, *a.* de primera clase.

fiscal, *a.* fiscal.

fish, 1. *n.* (food) pescado *m.*; (alive) pez *m.* **2.** *v.* pescar.

fisherman, *n.* pescador *m.*

fishhook, *n.* anzuelo *m.*

fishing, *n.* pesca *f.* **to go f.,** ir de pesca.

fishmonger, *n.* pescadero *m.*

fission, *n.* fisura *f.*

fissure, *n.* grieta *f.*, quebradura *f.*

fist, *n.* puño *m.*

fit, 1. *a.* capaz; justo. **2.** *n.* corte, talle *m.*; (med.) convulsión *f.* **3.** *v.* caber; quedar bien, sentar bien.

fitful, *a.* espasmódico; caprichoso.

fitness, *n.* aptitud; conveniencia *f.*

fitting, 1. *a.* conveniente. **to be f.,** convenir. **2.** *n.* ajuste *m.*

five, *a. & pron.* cinco.

fix, 1. *n.* apuro *m.* **2.** *v.* fijar; arreglar; componer, reparar.

fixation, *n.* fijación *f.*; fijeza *f.*

fixed, *a.* fijo.

fixture, *n.* instalación; guarnición *f.*

flabby, *a.* flojo.

flaccid, *a.* flojo; fláccido.

flag, *n.* bandera *f.*

flagellant, *n. & a.* flagelante *m.*

flagon, *n.* frasco *m.*

flagrant, *a.* flagrante.

flagrantly, *adv.* notoriamente.

flair, *n.* afición *f.*

flake, 1. *n.* lámina *f.*; copo de nieve. **2.** *v.* romperse en láminas.

flamboyant, *a.* flamante, llamativo.

flame, 1. *n.* llama *f.* **2.** *v.* llamear.

flaming, *a.* llameante, flamante.

flamingo, *n.* flamenco *m.*

flank, 1. *n.* ijada *f.*; (mil.) flanco *m.* **2.** *v.* flanquear.

flannel, *n.* franela *f.*

flap, 1. *n.* cartera *f.* **2.** *v.* aletear; sacudirse.

flare, 1. *n.* llamarada *f.* **2.** *v.* brillar; (fig.) enojarse.

flash, 1. *n.* resplandor *m.*; (lightning) rayo, relámpago *m.*; (fig.) instante *m.* **2.** *v.* brillar.

flashcube, *n.* cubo de flash *m.*

flashlight, *n.* linterna eléctrica.

flashy, *a.* resplandeciente; ostentoso.

flask, *n.* frasco *m.*

flat, 1. *a.* llano; (tire) desinflado. **2.** *n.* llanura *f.*; apartamiento *m.*

flatness, *n.* llanura *f.*

flatten, *v.* aplastar, allanar; abatir.

flatter, *v.* adular, lisonjear.

flatterer, *n.* lisonjero -ra. zalamero -ra.

flattery, *n.* adulación, lisonja *f.*

flaunt, *v.* ostentar.

flavor, 1. *n.* sabor *m.* **2.** *v.* sazonar.

flavoring, *n.* condimento *m.*

flaw, *n.* defecto *m.*

flax, *n.* lino *m.*

flay, *v.* despellejar; excoriar.

flea, *n.* pulga *f.*

fleck, 1. *n.* mancha *f.* **2.** *v.* varetear.

flee, *v.* huir.

fleece, 1. *n.* vellón *m.* **2.** *v.* esquilar.

fleet, 1. *a.* veloz. **2.** *n.* flota *f.*

fleeting, *a.* fugaz, pasajero.

flesh, *n.* carne *f.*

fleshy, *a.* gordo; carnoso.

flex, 1. *n.* doblez *m.* **2.** *v.* doblar.

flexibility, *n.* flexibilidad *f.*

flexible, *a.* flexible.

flier, *n.* aviador -ra.

flight, *n.* vuelo *m.*; fuga *f.*

flight attendant, *n.* azafata *f.*; ayudante de vuelo *m.*

flimsy, *a.* débil.

flinch, *v.* acobardarse.

fling, *v.* lanzar.

flint, *n.* pedernal *m.*

flip, *v.* lanzar.

flippant, *a.* impertinente.

flippantly, *adv.* impertinentemente.

flirt, 1. *n.* coqueta *f.* **2.** *v.* coquetear, flirtear.

flirtation, *n.* coqueteo *m.*

float, *v.* flotar.

flock, 1. *n.* rebaño *m.* **2.** *v.* congregarse.

flog, *v.* azotar.

flood, 1. *n.* inundación *f.* **2.** *v.* inundar.

floor, 1. *n.* suelo, piso *m.* **2.** *v.* derribar.

floral, *a.* floral.

florid, *a.* florido.

florist, *n.* florista *m. & f.*

flounce, 1. *n.* (sewing) volante *m.* **2.** *v.* pernear.

flounder, *n.* rodaballo *m.*

flour, *n.* harina *f.*

flourish, **1.** *n.* floreo *m.* **2.** *v.* florecer; prosperar; blandir.

flow, 1. *n.* flujo *m.* **2.** *v.* fluir.

flower, 1. *n.* flor *f.* **2.** *v.* florecer.

flowerpot, *n.* maceta de flores *f.*

flowery, *a.* florido.

fluctuate, *v.* fluctuar.

fluctuation, *n.* fluctuación *f.*

flue, *n.* humero *m.*

fluency, *n.* fluidez *f.*

fluent, *a.* fluente.

fluffy, *a.* velloso.

fluid, *a. & n.* fluído *m.*

fluidity, *n.* fluidez *f.*

fluoroscope, *n.* fluoroscopio *m.*

flurry, *n.* agitación *f.*

flush, 1. *a.* bien provisto. **2.** *n.* sonrojo *m.* **3.** *v.* limpiar con un chorro de agua; sonrojarse.

flute, *n.* flauta *f.*

flutter, 1. *n.* agitación *f.* **2.** *v.* agitarse.

flux, *n.* flujo *m.*

fly, 1. *n.* mosca *f.* **2.** *v.* volar.

foam, 1. *n.* espuma *f.* **2.** *v.* espumar.

focal, *a.* focal.

focus, 1. *n.* enfoque *m.* **2.** *v.* enfocar.

fodder, *n.* forraje *m.*

foe, *n.* adversario -ria, enemigo -ga.

fog, *n.* niebla *f.*

foggy, *a.* brumoso.

foil, *v.* frustrar.

foist, *v.* emponer.

fold, 1. *n.* pliegue *m.* **2.** *v.* doblar, plegar.

folder, *n.* circular *m.*; (for filing) carpeta *f.*

foliage, *n.* follaje *m.*

folio, *n.* infolio; folio *m.*

folklore, *n.* folklore *m.*

folks, *n.* gente, familia *f.*

follicle, *n.* folículo *m.*

follow, *v.* seguir.

follower, *n.* partidario -ria.

folly, *n.* locura *f.*

foment, *v.* fomentar.

fond, *a.* cariñoso, tierno. **be f. of,** ser aficionado a.

fondle, *v.* acariciar.

fondly, *adv.* tiernamente.

fondness, *n.* afición *f.*; cariño *m.*

food, *n.* alimento *m.*; comida *f.*

foodstuffs, *n.pl.* comestibles, víveres *m.pl.*

fool, 1. tonto -ta; bobo -ba; bufón -ona. **2.** v. engañar.

foolhardy, a. temerario.

foolish, a. bobo, tontó, majadero.

foolproof, a. seguro.

foot, n. pie m.

footage, n. longitud en pies.

football, n. fúbol, balompié m.

foothold, n. posición establecida.

footing, n. base f., fundamento m.

footlights, n.pl. luces del proscenio.

footnote, n. nota al pie de una página.

footprint, n. huella f.

footstep, n. paso m.

footstool, m. escañuelo m., banqueta f.

fop, n. petimetre m.

for, 1. prep. para; por. **as f., en cuanto a. what f.,** ¿para qué? **2.** conj. porque, pues.

forage, 1. n. forraje m. **2.** v. forrajear.

foray, n. correría f.

forbear, v. cesar; abstenerse.

forbearance, n. paciencia f.

forbid, v. prohibir.

forbidding, a. repugnante.

force, 1. n. fuerza f. **2.** v. forzar.

forceful, a. fuerte; enérgico.

forcible, a. fuerte; enérgico.

ford, 1. n. vado m. **2.** v. vadear.

fore, 1. a. delantero. **2.** n. delantera f.

fore and aft, de popa a proa.

forearm, n. antebrazo m.

forebears, n.pl. antepasados m.pl.

forebode, v. presagiar.

foreboding, n. presentimiento m.

forecast, 1. n. pronóstico m.; profecía f. **2.** v. pronosticar.

forecastle, n. (naut.) castillo de proa.

forefather, n. antepasado m.

forefinger, n. índice m.

forego, v. renunciar.

foregone, a. predeterminado.

foreground, n. primer plano.

forehead, n. frente f.

foreign, a. extranjero.

foreign aid, ayuda exterior.

foreigner, n. extranjero -ra; forastero -ra.

foreleg, n. pierna delantera.

foreman, n. capataz m.

foremost, 1. a. primero. **2.** adv. en primer lugar.

forenoon, n. mañana f.

forensic, a. forense.

forerunner, n. precursor -ra.

foresee, v. prever.

foreshadow, v. prefigurar, anunciar.

foresight, n. previsión f.

forest, n. bosque m.; selva f.

forestall, v. anticipar; prevenir.

forester, n. silvicultor; guardamonte m.

forestry, n. silvicultura f.

foretell, v. predecir.

forever, adv. por siempre, para siempre.

forevermore, adv. siempre.

forewarn, v. advertir, avisar.

foreword, n. prefacio m.

forfeit, 1. n. prenda, multa f. **2.** v. perder.

forfeiture, n. decomiso m., multa f.

forgather, v. reunirse.

forge, 1. n. fragua f. **2.** v. forjar; falsear.

forger, n. forjador; falsificador m.

forgery, n. falsificación f.

forget, v. olvidar.

forgetful, a. olvidadizo.

forgive, v. perdonar.

forgiveness, n. perdón m.

fork, 1. n. tenedor m.; bifurcación f. **2.** v. bifurcarse.

forlorn, a. triste.

form, 1. n. forma f.; (document) formulario m. **2.** v. formar.

formal, a. formal; ceremonioso. **f. dance,** baile de etiqueta. **f. dress,** traje de etiqueta.

formality, n. formalidad f.

formally, adv. formalmente.

format, n. formato m.

formation, n. formación f.

formative, a. formativo.

former, a. anterior; antiguo. **the f.,** aquél.

formerly, adv. antiguamente.

formidable, a. formidable.

formless, a. sin forma.

formula, n. fórmula f.

formulate, v. formular.

formulation, n. formulación f.; expresión f.

forsake, v. abandonar.

fort, n. fortaleza f.; fuerte m.

forte, a. & adv. (mus.) forte, fuerte.

forth, adv. adelante. **back and f.,** de aquí allá. **and so f.,** etcétera.

forthcoming, a. futuro, próximo.

forthright, a. franco.

forthwith, adv. inmediatamente.

fortification, n. fortificación f.

fortify, v. fortificar.

fortissimo, a. & adv. (mus.) fortísimo.

fortitude, n. fortaleza; fortitud f.

fortnight, n. quincena f.

fortress, n. fuerte m., fortaleza f.

fortuitous, a. fortuito.

fortunate, a. afortunado.

fortune, n. fortuna; suerte f.

fortune-teller, n. sortílego, adivino m.

forty, a. & pron. cuarenta.

forum, n. foro m.

forward, 1. a. delantero; atrevido. **2.** adv. adelante. **3.** v. trasmitir, reexpedir.

foster, 1. a. **f. child,** hijo adoptivo. **2.** v. fomentar, criar.

foul, a. sucio; impuro.

found, v. fundar.

foundation, n. fundación f.; (of building) cimientos m.pl.

founder, 1. n. fundador -ra. **2.** v. irse a pique.

foundry, n. fundición f.

fountain, n. fuente f.

four, a. & pron. cuatro.

fourteen, a. & pron. catorce.

fourth, a. & n. cuarto m.

fowl, n. ave f.

fox, n. zorro -rra.

fox trot, n. foxtrot m.

foxy, a. astuto.

foyer, n. salón de entrada.

fracas, n. riña f.

fraction, n. fracción f.

fracture, 1. n. fractura, rotura f. **2.** v. fracturar, romper.

fragile, a. frágil.

fragment, n. fragmento, trozo m.

fragmentary, a. fragmentario.

fragrance, n. fragancia f.

fragrant, a. fragante.

frail, a. débil, frágil.

frailty, n. debilidad, fragilidad f.

frame, 1. n. marco m.; armazón; cuadro, cuerpo m. **2.** v. fabricar; formar; encuadrar.

frame-up, n. (coll.) conspiración f.

framework, n. armazón m.

France, n. Francia f.

franchise, n. franquicia f.

frank, 1. a. franco. **2.** n. carta franca. **3.** v. franquear.

frankfurter, n. salchicha f.

frankly, adv. francamente.

frankness, n. franqueza f.

frantic, a. frenético.

fraternal, a. fraternal.

fraternity, n. fraternidad f.

fraternization, n. fraternización f.

fraternize, v. confraternizar.

fratricide, n. fratricida m. & f.

fraud, n. fraude m.

fraudulent, a. fraudulento.

fraudulently, adv. fraudulentamente.

fraught, a. cargado.

freak, n. rareza f.

freckle, n. peca f.

free, 1. a. libre; gratis. **2.** v. libertar, librar.

freedom, n. libertad f.

freeze, v. helar, congelar.

freezer, n. heladora f.

freight, 1. n. carga f.; flete m. **2.** v. cargar; fletar.

freighter, n. (naut.) fletador m.

French, a. & n. francés m.

Frenchman, n. francés m.

frenzied, a. frenético.

frenzy, n. frenesí m.

frequency, n. frecuencia f.

frequency modulation, modulación de frequencia.

frequent, a. frecuente.

frequently, *adv.* frecuentemente.

fresco, *n.* pintura al fresco.

fresh, *a.* fresco. **f. water,** agua dulce.

freshen, *v.* refrescar.

freshness, *n.* frescura *f.*

fret, *v.* quejarse, irritarse.

fretful, *a.* irritable.

fretfully, *adv.* de mala gana.

fretfulness, *n.* mal humor.

friar, *n.* fraile *m.*

fricassee, *n.* fricasé *m.*

friction, *n.* fricción *f.*

Friday, *n.* viernes *m.* **Good F.,** Viernes Santo.

fried, *a.* frito.

friend, *n.* amigo -ga.

friendless, *a.* sin amigos.

friendliness, *n.* amistad *f.*

friendly, *a.* amistoso.

friendship, *n.* amistad *f.*

fright, *n.* susto *m.*

frighten, *v.* asustar, espantar.

frightful, *a.* espantoso.

frigid, *a.* frígido, frío.

frill, *n.* (sewing) lechuga *f.*

fringe, *n.* fleco *m.;* borde *m.*

frisky, *a.* retozón.

fritter, *n.* fritura *f.*

frivolity, *n.* frivolidad *f.*

frivolous, *a.* frívolo.

frivolousness, *n.* frivolidad *f.*

frock, *n.* vestido de mujer. **f. coat,** levita *f.*

frog, *n.* rana *f.*

frolic, **1.** *n.* retozo *m.* **2.** *v.* retozar.

from, *prep.* de; desde.

front, *n.* frente; (of building) fachada *f.* **in f. of,** delante de.

frontal, *a.* frental.

frontier, *n.* frontera *f.*

frost, *n.* helada, escarcha *f.*

frosty, *a.* helado.

froth, *n.* espuma *f.*

frown, **1.** *n.* ceño *m.* **2.** *v.* fruncir el entrecejo.

frowzy, *a.* desaliñado.

frozen, *a.* helado; congelado.

fructify, *v.* fructificar.

frugal, *a.* frugal.

frugality, *n.* frugalidad *f.*

fruit, *n.* fruta *f.;* (benefits) frutos *m.pl.* **f. tree,** árbol frutal.

fruitful, *a.* productivo.

fruition, *n.* fruición *f.*

fruitless, *a.* inútil, vano.

frustrate, *v.* frustrar.

frustration, *n.* frustración *f.*

fry, *v.* freír.

fuel, *n.* combustible *m.*

fugitive, *a. & n.* fugitivo -va.

fugue, *n.* (mus.) fuga *f.*

fulcrum, *n.* fulcro *m.*

fulfill, *v.* cumplir.

fulfillment, *n.* cumplimiento *m.;* realización *f.*

full, *a.* lleno; completo; pleno.

fullness, *n.* plenitud *f.*

fulminate, *v.* volar; fulminar.

fulmination, *n.* fulminación, detonación *f.*

fumble, *v.* chapucear.

fume, **1.** *n.* humo *m.* **2.** *v.* humear.

fumigate, *v.* fumigar.

fumigator, *n.* fumigador *m.*

fun, *n.* diversión *f.* **to make f. of,** burlarse de. **to have f.,** divertirse.

function, **1.** *n.* función *f.* **2.** *v.* funcionar.

functional, *a.* funcional.

fund, *n.* fondo *m.*

fundamental, *a.* fundamental.

funeral, *n.* funeral *m.*

fungus, *n.* hongo *m.*

funnel, *n.* embudo *m.;* (of ship) chimenea *f.*

funny, *a.* divertido, gracioso. **to be f.,** tener gracia.

fur, *n.* piel *f.*

furious, *a.* furioso.

furlough, *n.* permiso *m.*

furnace, *n.* horno *m.*

furnish, *v.* surtir, proveer; (a house) amueblar.

furniture, *n.* muebles *m.pl.*

furrow, **1.** *n.* surco *m.* **2.** *v.* surcar.

further, **1.** *a. & adv.* más. **2.** *v.* adelantar, fomentar.

furthermore, *adv.* además.

fury, *n.* furor *m.;* furia *f.*

fuse, **1.** *n.* fusible *m.* **2.** *v.* fundir.

fuss, **1.** *n.* alboroto *m.* **2.** *v.* preocuparse por pequeñeces.

fussy, *a.* melindroso.

futile, *a.* fútil.

future, **1.** *a.* futuro. **2.** *n.* porvenir *m.*

futurology, *n.* futurología *f.*

G

gag, *n.* chiste *m.*

gaiety, *n.* alegría *f.*

gain, **1.** *n.* ganancia *f.* **2.** *v.* ganar.

gait, *n.* paso *m.*

gale, *n.* ventarrón *m.*

gall, *n.* hiel *f.;* (fig.) amargura *f.;* descaro *m.*

gallant, **1.** *a.* galante. **2.** *n.* galán *m.*

gallery, *n.* galería *f.;* (theat.) paraíso *m.*

gallon, *n.* galón *m.*

gallop, **1.** *n.* galope *m.* **2.** *v.* galopar.

gallows, *n.* horca *f.*

gamble, **1.** *n.* riesgo *m.* **2.** *v.* jugar; aventurar.

game, *n.* juego *m.;* (match) partida *f.;* (hunting) caza *f.*

gang, *n.* cuadrilla; pandilla *f.*

gangster, *n.* rufián *m.*

gap, *n.* raja *f.*

gape, *v.* boquear.

garage, *n.* garaje *m.*

garbage, *n.* basura *f.*

garden, *n.* jardín *m.;* (vegetable) huerta *f.*

gardener, *n.* jardinero -ra.

gargle, **1.** *n.* gárgara *f.* **2.** *v.* gargarizar.

garland, *n.* guirnalda *f.*

garlic, *n.* ajo *m.*

garment, *n.* prenda de vestir.

garrison, *n.* guarnición *f.*

garter, *n.* liga *f.;* ataderas *f.pl.*

gas, *n.* gas *m.*

gasohol, *n.* gasohol *m.*

gasoline, *n.* gasolina *f.*

gasp, **1.** *n.* boqueada *f.* **2.** *v.* boquear.

gate, *n.* puerta; entrada *f.*

gather, *v.* recoger; inferir; reunir.

gaudy, *a.* brillante; llamativo.

gauge, **1.** *n.* manómetro, indicador *m.* **2.** *v.* medir; estimar.

gaunt, *a.* flaco.

gauze, *n.* gasa *f.*

gay, **1.** *a.* alegre; homosexual. **2.** *n.* homosexual.

gaze, **1.** *n.* mirada *f.* **2.** *v.* mirar con fijeza.

gear, *n.* engranaje *m.* **in g.,** en juego.

gem, *n.* joya *f.*

gender, *n.* género *m.*

general, *a. & n.* general *m.*

generality, *n.* generalidad *f.*

generalize, *v.* generalizar.

generation, *n.* generación *f.*

generator, *n.* generador *m.*

generosity, *n.* generosidad *f.*

generous, *a.* generoso.

genial, *a.* genial.

genius, *n.* genio *m.*

gentle, *a.* suave; manso; benigno.

gentleman, *n.* señor, caballero *m.*

gentleness, *n.* suavidad *f.*

genuine, *a.* genuino.

genuineness, *n.* pureza *f.*

geographical, *a.* geográfico.

geography, *n.* geografía *f.*

geometric, *a.* geométrico.

geranium, *n.* geranio *m.*

germ, *n.* germen; microbio *m.*

German, *a. & n.* alemán mana.

Germany, *n.* Alemania *f.*

gesticulate, *v.* gesticular.

gesture, **1.** *n.* gesto *m.* **2.** *v.* gesticular, hacer gestos.

get, *v.* obtener; conseguir; (become) ponerse. **go and g.,** ir a buscar; **g. away,** irse; escaparse; **g. together,** reunirse; **g. on,** subir; **g. off,** bajar; **g. up,** levantarse; **g. there,** llegar.

ghastly, *a.* pálido; espantoso.

ghost, *n.* espectro, fantasma *m.*

giant, *n.* gigante *m.*

gift, *n.* regalo, don; talento *m.*

gild, *v.* dorar.

gin, *n.* ginebra *f.*

ginger, *n.* jengibre *m.*

gingerbread, *n.* pan de jengibre.

gingham, *n.* guinga *f.*

gird, *v.* ceñir.

girdle, *n.* faja *f.*

girl, *n.* muchacha, niña, chica *f.*

give, *v.* dar; regalar. **g. back,**

devolver. **g. up,** rendirse; renunciar.

giver, n. dador -ra; donador -ra.

glacier, n. ventisquero m.

glad, a. alegre, contento. **to be g.,** alegrarse.

gladly, adj. con mucho gusto.

gladness, n. alegría f.; placer m.

glamor, n. encanto m.; elegancia f.

glamorous, a. encantador, elegante.

glance, 1. n. vistazo m., ojeada f. **2.** v. ojear.

gland, n. glándula f.

glare, 1. n. reflejo; brillo m. **2.** v. deslumbrar; echar miradas indignadas.

glass, n. vidrio; vaso m.; (eye-glasses), lentes anteojos m.pl.

gleam, 1. n. fulgor m. **2.** v. fulgurar.

glee, n. alegría f.; júbilo m.

glide, v. deslizarse.

glimpse, 1. n. vistazo m. **2.** v. ojear.

glisten, 1. n. brillo m. **2.** v. brillar.

glitter, 1. n. resplandor m. **2.** v. brillar.

globe, n. globo; orbe m.

gloom, n. oscuridad; tristeza f.

gloomy, a. oscuro; sombrío, triste.

glorify, v. glorificar.

glorious, a. glorioso.

glory, n. gloria, fama f.

glossary, n. glosario m.

glove, n. guante m.

glow, 1. n. fulgor m. **2.** v. relucir; arder.

glue, 1. n. cola f. **2.** v. encolar, pegar.

glum, a. de mal humor.

glutton, n. glotón -ona.

gnaw, v. roer.

go, v. ir, irse. **g. away,** irse, marcharse. **g. back,** volver, regresar. **g. down,** bajar. **g. in,** entrar. **g. on,** seguir. **g. out,** salir. **g. up,** subir.

goal, n. meta f.; objeto m.

goat, n. cabra f.

goblet, n. copa f.

God, n. Dios m.

gold, n. oro m.

golden, a. áureo.

good, 1. a. bueno. **2.** n. bienes m.pl.; (com.) géneros m.pl.

good-bye, 1. n. adiós m. **2.** interj. ¡adiós!, ¡hasta la vista!, ¡hasta luego! **to say g. to,** despedirse de.

goodness, n. bondad f.

goose, n. ganso m.

gooseberry, n. uva crespa f.

gooseneck, 1. n. cuello de cisne m. **2.** a. curvo.

goose step, n. paso de ganso m.

gore, 1. n. sangre f. **2.** v. acornear.

gorge, 1. n. gorja f. **2.** v. engullir.

gorgeous, a. magnífico; precioso.

gorilla, n. gorila f.

gory, a. sangriento.

gosling, n. gansarón m.

gospel, n. evangelio m.

gossamer, 1. n. telaraña f. **2.** a. delgado.

gossip, 1. n. chisme m. **2.** v. chismear.

Gothic, a. gótico.

gouge, 1. n. gubia f. **2.** v. escoplear.

gourd, n. calabaza f.

gourmand, n. glotón m.

gourmet, a. gastrónomo -ma.

govern, v. gobernar.

governess, n. aya, institutriz f.

government, n. gobierno m.

governmental, a. gubernamental.

governor, n. gobernador m.

governorship, n. gobernatura f.

gown, n. vestido m. **dressing g.,** bata f.

grab, v. agarrar, arrebatar.

grace, n. gracia; gentileza; merced f.

graceful, a. agraciado.

graceless, a. réprobo.

gracious, a. gentil, cortés.

grackle, n. grajo m.

grade, 1. n. grado; nivel m.; pendiente; nota; calidad f. **2.** v. graduar.

grade crossing, n. paso a nivel m.

gradual, a. gradual.

gradually, adv. gradualmente.

graduate, 1. n. graduado -da, diplomado-da. **2.** v. graduar; diplomarse.

graft, 1. n. injerto m.; soborno público. **2.** v. injertar.

graham, a. centeno; acemita.

grail, n. grial m.

grain, n. grano; cereal m.

grain alcohol, n. alcohol de madera m.

gram, n. gramo m.

grammar, n. gramática f.

grammarian, n. gramático m.

grammar school, n. escuela elemental f.

grammatical, a. gramatical.

gramophone, n. gramófono m.

granary, n. granero m.

grand, a. grande, ilustre; estupendo.

grandchild, n. nieto -ta.

granddaughter, n. nieta f.

grandee, n. noble m.

grandeur, n. grandeza f.

grandfather, n. abuelo m.

grandiloquent, a. grandílocuo.

grandiose, a. grandioso.

grand jury, n. gran jurado m.

grandly, adv. grandiosamente.

grandmother, n. abuela f.

grand opera, n. ópera grande f.

grandparents, n. abuelos m.pl.

grandson, n. nieto m.

grandstand, n. andanada f., tribuna f.

grange, n. granja f.

granger, n. labriego m.

granite, n. granito m.

granny, n. abuelita f.

grant, 1. n. concesión; subvención f. **2.** v. otorgar; conceder; conferir. **take for granted,** tomar por cierto.

granular, a. granular.

granulate, v. granular.

granulation, n. granulación f.

granule, n. gránulo m.

grape, n. uva f.

grapefruit, n. toronja f.

grapeshot, n. metralla f.

grapevine, n. vid; parra f.

graph, n. gráfia f.

graphic, a. gráfico m.

graphite, n. grafito m.

graphology, n. grafología f.

grapple, v. agarrar.

grasp, 1. n. puño; poder; conocimiento m. **2.** v. empuñar agarrar; comprender.

grasping, a. codicioso.

grass, n. hierba f.; (marijuana) marijuana f.

grasshopper, n. saltamontes m.

grassy, a. herboso.

grate, n. reja f.

grateful, a. agradecido.

gratify, v. satisfacer.

grating, 1. n. enrejado m. **2.** a. discordante.

gratis, adv. & a. gratis.

gratitude, n. agradecimiento m.

gratuitous, adv. gratismente.

gratuity, n. propina f.

grave, 1. a. grave. **2.** n. sepultura; tumba f.

gravel, n. cascajo m.

gravely, adv. gravemente.

gravestone, n. lápida sepulcral f.

graveyard, n. cementerio m.

gravitate, v. gravitar.

gravitation, n. gravitación f.

gravity, n. gravedad; seriedad f.

gravure, n. grabado m.

gravy, n. salsa f.

gray, a. gris; (hair) cano.

grayish, a. pardusco.

gray matter, n. substancia gris f.

graze, v. rozar; (cattle) pastar.

grazing, a. pastando.

grease, 1. n. grasa f. **2.** v. engrasar.

greasy, a. grasiento.

great, a. grande, ilustre; estupendo.

Great Dane, n. mastín danés m.

greatness, n. grandeza f.

Greece, n. Grecia f.

greed, greediness, n. codicia, voracidad f.

greedy, a. voraz.

Greek, a. & n. griego -ga.

green, a. & n. verde m. **greens,** n. verduras f.pl.

greenery, *n.* verdor *m.*

greenhouse, *n.* invernáculo *m.*

greet, *v.* saludar.

greeting, *n.* saludo *m.*

gregarious, *a.* gregario.

grenade, *n.* granada *f.*; bomba *f.*

greyhound, *n.* galgo *m.*

grid, *n.* parrilla *f.*

griddle, *n.* tortera *f.*

griddlecake, *n.* tortita de harina *f.*

gridiron, *n.* parrilla *f.*, campo de fútbol *m.*

grief, *n.* dolor *m.*; pena *f.*

grievance, *n.* pesar; agravio *m.*

grieve, *v.* afligir.

grievous, *a.* penoso.

grill, 1. *n.* parrilla *f.* 2. *v.* asar a la parrilla.

grillroom, *n.* restaurante de servicio rápido *m.*

grim, *a.* ceñudo.

grimace, 1. *n.* mueca *f.* 2. *v.* hacer muecas.

grime, *n.* mugre *f.*

grimy, *a.* sucio; mugroso.

grin, 1. *n.* sonrisa *f.* 2. *v.* sonreír.

grind, *v.* moler; afilar.

grindstone, *n.* esmeriladora *f.*

gringo, *n.* gringo; yanqui *m.*

grip, 1. *n.* maleta *f.* 2. *v.* agarrar.

gripe, 1. *v.* agarrar. 2. *n.* asimiento *m.*, opresión *f.*

grippe, *n.* gripe *f.*

grisly, *a.* espantoso.

grist, *n.* molienda *f.*

gristle, *n.* cartílago *m.*

grit, *n.* arena *f.*, entereza *f.*

grizzled, *a.* tordillo.

groan, 1. *n.* gemido *m.* 2. *v.* gemir.

grocer, *n.* abacero *m.*

grocery, *n.* tienda de comestibles, bodega *f.*

grog, *n.* brebaje *m.*

groggy, *a.* medio borracho; vacilante.

groin, *n.* ingle *f.*

groom, *n.* (of horses) establero; (at wedding) novio *m.*

groove, 1. *n.* estría *f.* 2. *v.* acanalar.

grope, *v.* tentar; andar a tientas.

gross, 1. *a.* grueso; grosero. 2. *n.* gruesa *f.*

grossly, *adv.* groseramente.

grossness, *n.* grosería *f.*

grotesque, *a.* grotesco.

grotto, *n.* gruta *f.*

grouch, *n.* gruñón; descontento *m.*

ground, *n.* tierra *f.*; terreno; suelo; campo; fundamento *m.*

groundhog, *n.* marmota *f.*

groundless, *a.* infundado.

groundwork, *n.* base *f.*, fundamento *m.*

group, 1. *n.* grupo *m.* 2. *v.* agrupar.

groupie, *n.* muchacha que

acompaña a un grupo de música moderna.

grouse, *n.* chachalaca *f.*

grove, *n.* arboleda *f.*

grovel, *v.* rebajarse; envilecerse.

grow, *v.* crecer; cultivar.

growl, 1. *n.* gruñido *m.* 2. *v.* gruñir.

grown, *a.* crecido; desarrollado.

grownup, *n.* adulto *m.*

growth, *n.* crecimiento; vegetación *f.*; (med.) tumor *m.*

grub, *n.* gorgojo *m.*, larva *f.*

grubby, *a.* guasarapiento.

grudge, *n.* rencor *m.* **bear a g.,** guardar rencor.

gruel, 1. *n.* atole *m.* 2. *v.* estropear.

gruesome, *a.* horripilante.

gruff, *a.* ceñudo.

grumble, *v.* quejarse.

grumpy, *a.* gruñón; quejoso.

grunt, *v.* gruñir.

guarantee, 1. *n.* garantía *f.* 2. *v.* garantizar.

guarantor, *n.* fiador *m.*

guaranty, *n.* garantía *f.*

guard, 1. *n.* guardia *m.* or *f.* 2. *v.* vigilar.

guarded, *a.* cauteloso.

guardhouse, *n.* prisión militar *f.*

guardian, *n.* guardián *m.*

guardianship, *n.* tutela *f.*

guardsman, *n.* centinela *m.*

guava, *n.* guayaba *f.*

gubernatorial, *a.* gubernativo.

guerrilla, *n.* guerrillero *m.*

guess, 1. *n.* conjetura *f.* 2. *v.* adivinar; (coll.) creer.

guesswork, *n.* conjetura *f.*

guest, *n.* huésped *m.* & *f.*

guffaw, *n.* risotada *f.*

guidance, *n.* dirección *f.*

guide, 1. *n.* guía *m.* & *f.* 2. *v.* guiar.

guidebook, *n.* guía *f.*

guidepost, *n.* poste indicador *m.*

guild, *n.* gremio *m.*

guile, *n.* engaño *m.*

guillotine, 1. *n.* guillotina *f.* 2. *v.* guillotinar.

guilt, *n.* culpa *f.*

guiltily, *adv.* culpablemente.

guiltless, *a.* inocente.

guilty, *a.* culpable.

guinea fowl, *n.* gallina de Guinea *f.*

guinea pig, *n.* cobayo *m.*

guise, *n.* modo *m.*

guitar, *n.* guitarra *f.*

gulch, *n.* quebrada *f.*

gulf, *n.* golfo *m.*

gull, *n.* gaviota *f.*

gullet, *n.* esófago *m.*, zanja *f.*

gullible, *a.* crédulo.

gully, *n.* barranca *f.*

gulp, 1. *n.* trago *m.* 2. *v.* tragar.

gum, 1. *n.* goma *f.*; (anat.) encía *f.* **chewing g.,** chicle *m.* 2. *v.* engomar.

gumbo, *n.* quimbombó *m.*

gummy, *a.* gomoso.

gun, *n.* fusil; cañón *m.*

gunboat, *n.* cañonero *m.*

gunman, *n.* bandido *m.*

gunner, *n.* artillero *m.*

gunpowder, *n.* pólvora *f.*

gunshot, *n.* escopetazo *m.*

gunwale, *n.* borda *f.*

gurgle, 1. *n.* gorgoteo *m.* 2. *v.* gorgotear.

guru, *n.* gurú *m.*

gush, 1. *n.* chorro *m.* 2. *v.* brotar, chorrear.

gusher, *n.* pozo de chorro de petróleo *m.*

gust, *n.* soplo *m.*; ráfaga *f.*

gustatory, *a.* del sentido del gusto.

gusto, *n.* gusto; placer *m.*

gusty, *a.* borrascoso.

gut, *n.* intestino *m.*, tripa *f.*

gutter, *n.* canal; zanja *f.*

guttural, *a.* gutural.

guy, *n.* tipo *m.*

guzzle, *v.* engullir; tragar.

gym, *n.* gimnasio *m.*

gymnasium, *n.* gimnasio *m.*

gymnast, *n.* gimnasta *m.*

gymnastic, *a.* gimnástico.

gymnastics, *n.* gimnasia *f.*

gynecology, *n.* ginecología *f.*

gypsum, *n.* yeso *m.*

Gypsy, *a.* & *n.* gitano -na.

gyrate, *v.* girar.

gyroscope, *n.* giroscopio *m.*

H

habeas corpus, *n.* habeas corpus *m.*

haberdasher, *n.* camisero *m.*

haberdashery, *n.* camisería *f.*

habiliment, *n.* vestuario *m.*

habit, *n.* costumbre *f.*, hábito *m.* **be in the h. of,** estar acostumbrado a; soler.

habitable, *a.* habitable.

habitat, *n.* habitación *f.*, ambiente *m.*

habitation, *n.* habitación *f.*

habitual, *a.* habitual.

habituate, *v.* habituar.

habitué, *n.* parroquiano *m.*

hack, 1. *n.* coche de alquiler. 2. *v.* tajar.

hackneyed, *a.* trillado.

hacksaw, *n.* sierra para cortar metal *f.*

haddock, *n.* merluza *f.*

haft, *n.* mango *m.*

hag, *n.* bruja *f.*

haggard, *a.* trasnochado.

haggle, *v.* regatear.

hail, 1. *n.* granizo; (greeting) saludo *m.* 2. *v.* granizar; saludar.

Hail Mary, *n.* Ave María *m.*

hailstone, *n.* piedra de granizo *f.*

hailstorm, *n.* granizada *f.*

hair, *n.* pelo; cabello *m.*

haircut, *n.* corte de pelo.

hairdo, *n.* peinado *m.*

hairdresser, *n.* peluquero *m.*

hairpin, n. horquilla f.; gancho m.

hair's-breadth, n. ancho de un pelo m.

hairspray, n. aerosol para cabello.

hairy, a. peludo.

halcyon, 1. n. alcedón m. 2. a. tranquilo.

hale, a. sano.

half, 1. a. medio. 2. n. mitad f.

half-and-half, a. mitad y mitad.

half-baked, a. medio crudo.

half-breed, n. mestizo m.

half brother, n. medio hermano m.

half-hearted, a. sin entusiasmo.

half-mast, a. & n. media asta m.

halfpenny, n. media penique m.

halfway, adv. a medio camino.

half-wit, n. bobo m.

halibut, n. hipogloso m.

hall, n. corredor m.; (for assembling) sala f. **city h.**, ayuntamiento m.

hallmark, n. marca del contraste f.

hallow, v. consagrar.

Halloween, n. víspera de Todos los Santos f.

hallucination, n. alucinación f.

hallway, n. pasadizo m.

halo, n. halo m.; corona f.

halt, 1. a. cojo. 2. n. parada f. 3. v. parar. 4. interj. ¡alto!

halter, n. cabestro m.

halve, v. dividir en dos partes.

halyard, n. driza f.

ham, n. jamón m.

hamburger, n. albóndiga f.

hamlet, n. aldea f.

hammer, 1. n. martillo m. 2. v. martillar.

hammock, n. hamaca f.

hamper, n. canasta f., cesto m.

hamstring, 1. n. tendón de la corva m. 2. v. desjarretar.

hand, 1. mano f. **on the other h.**, en cambio. 2. v. pasar. **h. over**, entregar.

handbag, n. cartera f.

handball, n. pelota f.

handbook, n. manual m.

handcuff, n. esposas f.

handful, n. puñado m.

handicap, n. desventaja f.

handicraft, n. artífice m.

handiwork, n. artefacto m.

handkerchief, n. pañuelo m.

handle, 1. n. mango m. 2. v. manejar.

handmade, a. hecho a mano m.

handmaid, n. criada de mano f.

hand organ, n. organillo m.

handsome, a. guapo; hermoso.

hand-to-hand, adv. de mano a mano.

handwriting, n. escritura f.

handy, a. diestro; útil; a la mano.

hang, v. colgar; ahorcar.

hangar, n. hangar m.

hangdog, a. & n. camastrón m.

hanger, n. colgador, gancho m.

hanger-on, n. dependiente; mogollón m.

hang glider, n. aparato para vuelo libre.

hanging, 1. n. ahorcadura f. 2. a. colgante.

hangman, n. verdugo m.

hangnail, n. padrastro m.

hang out, v. enarbolar.

hangup, n. tara (psicológica) f.

hank, n. madeja f.

hanker, v. ansiar; apetecer.

haphazard, a. casual.

happen, v. acontecer, suceder, pasar.

happening, n. acontecimiento m.

happiness, n. felicidad; dicha f.

happy, a. feliz; contento; dichoso.

happy-go-lucky, a. & n. descuidado m.

harakiri, n. harakiri (suicidio japonés) m.

harangue, 1. n. arenga f. 2. v. arengar.

harass, v. acosar; atormentar.

harbinger, n. presagio m.

harbor, 1. n. puerto; albergue m. 2. v. abrigar.

hard, 1. a. duro; difícil. 2. adv. mucho.

hard coal, antracita m.

harden, v. endurecer.

hard-headed, a. terco.

hard-hearted, a. empedernido.

hardiness, n. vigor m.

hardly, adv. apenas.

hardness, n. dureza; dificultad f.

hardship, n. penalidad f.; trabajo m.

hardware, n. ferretería f.

hardwood, n. madera dura f.

hardy, a. fuerte, robusto.

hare, n. liebre f.

harebrained, a. tolondro.

harelip, 1. n. labio leporino m. 2. a. labihendido.

harem, n. harén m.

hark, v. escuchar; atender.

Harlequin, n. arlequín m.

harlot, n. ramera f.

harm, 1. n. mal, daño; perjuicio m. 2. v. dañar.

harmful, a. dañoso.

harmless, a. inocente.

harmonic, n. armónico m.

harmonica, n. armónica f.

harmonious, a. armonioso.

harmonize, v. armonizar.

harmony, n. armonía f.

harness, n. arnés m.

harp, n. arpa f.

harpoon, n. arpón m.

harridan, n. vieja regañona f.

harrow, 1. n. rastro m.; grada f. 2. v. gradar.

harry, v. acosar.

harsh, a. áspero.

harshness, n. aspereza f.

harvest, 1. n. cosecha f. 2. v. cosechar.

hash, n. picadillo m.

hashish, n. haxis m.

hasn't, v. no tiene (neg. + tener).

hassle, n. lío m., molestia f.; controversia f.

hassock, n. cojín m.

haste, n. prisa f.

hasten, v. apresurarse, darse prisa.

hasty, a. apresurado.

hat, n. sombrero m.

hatch, 1. n. (naut.) cuartel m. 2. v. incubar; (fig.) tramar.

hatchery, n. criadero m.

hatchet, n. hacha pequeña.

hate, 1. n. odio m. 2. v. odiar, detestar.

hateful, a. detestable.

hatred, n. odio m.

haughtiness, n. arrogancia f.

haughty, a. altivo.

haul, 1. n. (fishery) redada f. 2. v. tirar, halar.

haunch, n. anca f.

haunt, 1. n. lugar frecuentado. 2. v. frecuentar, andar por.

have, v. tener; haber.

haven, n. puerto; asilo m.

haven't, v. no tiene (neg. + tener).

havoc, n. ruina f.

hawk, n. halcón m.

hawker, n. buhonero m.

hawser, n. cable m.

hawthorn, n. espino m.

hay, n. heno m.

hay fever, n. catarro anual de la nariz m.; alergia nasal.

hayfield, n. henar m.

hayloft, n. henil m.

haystack, n. hacina de heno f.

hazard, 1. n. azar m. 2. v. aventurar.

hazardous, a. peligroso.

haze, n. niebla f.

hazel, n. avellano m.

hazy, a. brumoso.

he, pron. él m.

head, 1. n. cabeza f.; jefe m. 2. v. dirigir; encabezar.

headache, n. dolor de cabeza.

headband, n. venda para cabeza f.

headfirst, adv. de cabeza.

headgear, n. tocado m.

headlight, n. linterna delantera f., farol de tope m.

headline, n. encabezado m.

headlong, a. precipitoso.

head-on, adv. de frente.

headquarters, n. jefatura f.; (mil.) cuartel general.

headstone, n. lápida mortuoria f.

headstrong, a. terco.

headwaters, n. cabeceras f.

headway, n. avance m., progreso m.

headwork, n. trabajo mental m.

heady, a. impetuoso.

heal, v. curar, sanar.

health, n. salud f.

healthful, a. saludable.

healthy, a. sano; salubre.

heap, n. montón m.

hear, v. oír. **h. from,** tener noticias de. **h. about,** h. **of,** oír hablar de.

hearing, n. oído m.

hearsay, n. rumor m.

hearse, n. ataúd m.

heart, n. corazón m.; ánimo m. **by h.,** de memoria.

heartache, n. angustia f.

heartbreak, n. angustia f.; pesar m.

heartbroken, a. acongojado.

heartburn, n. acedía f.

heartfelt, a. sentido.

hearth, n. hogar m., chimenea f.

heartless, a. empedernido.

heartsick, a. desconsolado.

heart-stricken, a. afligido.

heart-to-heart, adv. franco; sincero.

hearty, a. cordial; vigoroso.

heat, 1. n. calor; ardor m.; calefacción f. 2. v. calentar.

heated, a. acalorado.

heater, n. calentador m.

heath, n. matorral m.

heathen, a. & n. pagano -na.

heather, n. brezo m.

heatstroke, n. insolación f.

heat wave, n. onda de calor f.

heave, v. tirar.

heaven, n. cielo m.

heavenly, a. divino.

heavy, a. pesado; oneroso.

Hebrew, a. & n. hebreo -ea.

hectic, a. turbulento.

hedge, n. seto m.

hedgehog, n. erizo m.

hedonism, n. hedonismo m.

heed, 1. n. cuidado m. 2. v. atender.

heedless, a. desatento; incauto.

heel, n. talón m.; (of shoe) tacón m.

heifer, n. novilla f.

height, n. altura f.

heighten, v. elevar; exaltar.

heinous, a. nefando.

heir, heiress, n. heredero -ra.

helicopter, n. helicóptero m.

heliotrope, n. heliotropo m.

helium, n. helio m.

hell, n. infierno m.

Hellenism, n. helenismo m.

hellish, a. infernal.

hello, interj. ¡hola!; (on telephone) aló; bueno.

helm, n. timón m.

helmet, n. yelmo, casco m.

helmsman, n. limonero m.

help, 1. n. ayuda f. **help!** ¡socorro! 2. v. ayudar. **h. oneself,** servirse. **can't help (but),** no poder menos de.

helper, n. ayudante m.

helpful, a. útil; servicial.

helpfulness, n. utilidad f.

helpless, a. imposibilitado.

hem, 1. n. ribete m. 2. v. ribetear.

hemisphere, n. hemisferio m.

hemlock, n. abeto m.

hemoglobin, n. hemoglobina f.

hemophilia, n. hemofilia f.

hemorrhage, n. hemorragia f.

hemorrhoid, n. hemorriodes f.pl.

hemp, n. cáñamo m.

hemstitch, 1. n. vainica f. 2. v. hacer una vainica.

hen, n. gallina f.

hence, adv. por lo tanto.

henceforth, adv. de aquí en adelante.

henchman, n. paniaguado m.

henna, n. alheña f.

her, 1. a. su. 2. pron. ella; la; le.

herald, n. heraldo m.

heraldic, a. heráldico.

heraldry, n. heráldica f.

herb, n. yerba, hierba f.

herbaceous, a. herbáceo.

herbarium, n. herbario m.

herd, 1. n. hato, rebaño m. 2. v. reunir en hatos.

here, adv. aquí; acá.

hereafter, adv. en lo futuro.

hereby, adv. por éstas, por la presente.

hereditary, a. hereditario.

heredity, n. herencia f.

herein, adv. aquí dentro; incluso.

heresy, n. herejía f.

heretic, 1. a. herético. 2. n. hereje m. & f.

heretical, a. herético.

heretofore, adv. hasta ahora.

herewith, adv. con esto, adjunto.

heritage, n. herencia f.

hermetic, a. hermético.

hermit, n. ermitaño m.

hernia, n. hernia f.

hero, n. héroe m.

heroic, a. heroico.

heroically, adv. heroicamente.

heroin, n. heroína f.

heroine, n. heroína f.

heroism, n. heroísmo m.

heron, n. garza f.

herring, n. arenque m.

hers, pron. suyo, de ella.

herself, pron. sí, sí misma, se. **she h.,** ella misma. **with h.,** consigo.

hertz, n. hertzio m.

hesitancy, n. hesitación f.

hesitant, a. indeciso.

hesitate, v. vacilar.

hesitation, n. duda; vacilación f.

heterogeneous, a. heterogéneo.

heterosexual, a. heterosexual.

hexagon, n. hexágono m.

hibernate, v. invernar.

hibernation, n. invernada f.

hibiscus, n. hibisco m.

hiccup, 1. n. hipo m. 2. v. tener hipo.

hickory, n. nogal americano m.

hidden, a. oculto; escondido.

hide, 1. n. cuero m.; piel f. 2. v. esconder; ocultar.

hideous, a. horrible.

hide-out, n. escondite m.

hierarchy, n. jerarquía f.

high, a. alto, elevado; (in price) caro.

highbrow, n. erudito m.

high fidelity, de alta fidelidad.

highly, adv. altamente; sumamente.

high school, n. escuela secundaria f.

highway, n. carretera f.; camino real m.

hijacker, n. secuestrador, pirata de aviones m.

hike, n. caminata f.

hilarious, a. alegre, bullicioso.

hilariousness, hilarity, n. hilaridad f.

hill, n. colina f.; cerro m.; **down h.,** cuesta abajo. **up h.,** cuesta arriba.

hilt, n. puño m. **up to the h.,** a fondo.

him, pron. él; lo; le.

himself, pron. sí, sí mismo; se. **he h.,** él mismo. **with h.,** consigo.

hinder, v. impedir.

hindmost, a. último.

hindquarter, n. cuarto trasero m.

hindrance, n. obstáculo m.

hinge, 1. n. gozne m. 2. v. engoznar. **h. on,** depender de.

hint, 1. n. insinuación f.; indicio m. 2. v. insinuar.

hip, n. cadera f.

hippopotamus, n. hipopótamo m.

hire, v. alquilar.

his, 1. a. su. 2. pron. suyo, de él.

Hispanic, a. hispano.

hiss, v. silbar, sisear.

historian, n. historiador m.

historic, historical, a. histórico.

history, n. historia f.

histrionic, a. histriónico.

hit, 1. n. golpe m.; (coll.) éxito m. 2. v. golpear, dar.

hitch, v. amarrar; enganchar.

hither, adv. acá, hacia acá.

hitherto, adv. hasta ahora.

hive, n. colmena f.

hives, n. urticaria f.

hoard, 1. n. acumulación f. 2. v. acaparar; atesorar.

hoarse, a. ronco.

hoax, 1. n. engaño m. 2. v. engañar.

hobby, n. afición f., pasatiempo m.

hobgoblin, n. trasgo m.

hobnob, v. tener intimidad.

hobo, n. vagabundo m.

hockey, n. hockey m. **ice-h.,** hockey sobre hielo.

hod, n. esparavel m.

hodgepodge, n. baturillo m.; mezcolanza f.

hoe, 1. n. azada f. 2. v. cultivar con azada.

hog, n. cerdo, puerco m.

hoist, 1. n. grúa f., elevador m. 2. v. elevar, enarbolar.

hold, 1. n. presa f.; agarro m.;

(naut.) bodega f. **to get h. of,** conseguir, apoderarse de. **2.** v. tener; detener; sujetar; celebrar.

holder, n. tenedor m. **cigarette h.,** boquilla f.

holdup, n. salteamiento m.

hole, n. agujero; hoyo; hueco m.

holiday, n. día de fiesta.

holiness, n. santidad f.

Holland, n. Holanda f.

hollow, 1. a. hueco. **2.** n. cavidad f. **3.** v. ahuecar; excavar.

holly, n. acebo m.

hollyhock, n. malva real f.

holocaust, n. holocausto m.

hologram, n. holograma m.

holography, n. holografía f.

holster, n. pistolera f.

holy, a. santo.

holy day, n. disanto m.

Holy See, n. Santa Sede f.

Holy Spirit, n. Espíritu Santo m.

Holy Week, n. Semana Santa f.

homage, n. homenaje m.

home, n. casa, morada f; hogar m. **at h.,** en casa. **to go h.,** ir a casa.

homeland, n. patria f.

homely, a. feo; casero.

home rule, n. autonomía f.

homesick, a. nostálgico.

homespun, a. casero; tocho.

homeward, adv. hacia casa.

homicide, n. homicida m. & f.

homily, n. homilía f.

homogeneous, a. homogéneo.

homogenize, v. homogenizar.

homosexual, n. & a. homosexual m.

Honduras, n. Honduras f.

hone, 1. n. piedra de afilar f. **2.** v. afilar.

honest, a. honrado, honesto; sincero.

honestly, adv. honradamente; de veras.

honesty, n. honradez, honestidad f.

honey, n. miel f.

honeybee, n. abeja obrera f.

honeymoon, n. luna de miel.

honeysuckle, n. madreselva f.

honor, 1. n. honra f.; honor m. **2.** v. honrar.

honorable, a. honorable; ilustre.

honorary, a. honorario.

hood, n. capota; capucha f.; (auto.) cubierta del motor.

hoodlum, n. pillo m., rufián m.

hoof, n. pezuña f.

hook, 1. n. gancho m. **2.** v. enganchar.

hoop, n. cerco m.

hop, 1. n. salto m. **2.** v. saltar.

hope, 1. n. esperanza f. **2.** v. esperar.

hopeful, a. lleno de esperanzas.

hopeless, a. desesperado; sin remedio.

horde, n. horda f.

horehound, n. marrubio m.

horizon, n. horizonte m.

horizontal, a. horizontal.

hormone, n. hormón m.

horn, n. cuerno m.; (music) trompa f.; (auto.) bocina f.

hornet, n. avispón m.

horny, a. córneo; calloso.

horoscope, n. horóscopo m.

horrendous, a. horrendo.

horrible, a. horrible.

horrid, a. horrible.

horrify, v. horrorizar.

horror, n. horror m.

horse, n. caballo m. **to ride a h.,** cabalgar.

horseback, n. **on h.,** a caballo. **to ride h.,** montar a caballo.

horsefly, n. tábano m.

horsehair, n. pelo de caballo m.; tela de crin f.

horseman, n. jinete m.

horsemanship, n. manejo m., equitación f.

horsepower, n. caballo de fuerza m.

horseradish, n. rábano picante m.

horseshoe, n. herradura f.

hortatory, a. exhortatorio.

horticulture, n. horticultura f.

hose, n. medias f.pl; (garden) manguera f.

hosiery, n. calcetería f.

hospitable, a. hospitalario.

hospital, n. hospital m.

hospitality, n. hospitalidad f.

hospitalization, n. hospitalización f.

hospitalize, v. hispitalizar.

host, n. anfitrión m., dueño de la casa; (rel.) hostia f.

hostage, n. rehén m.

hostel, n. hostería f.

hostelry, n. fonda f., parador m.

hostess, n. anfitriona f., dueña de la casa.

hostile, a. hostil.

hostility, n. hostilidad f.

hot, a. caliente; (sauce) picante. **to be h.,** tener calor; (weather) hacer calor.

hotbed, n. estercolero m. (fig.) foco m.

hotel, n. hotel m.

hot-headed, a. turbulente, alborotadizo.

hothouse, n. invernáculo m.

hound, 1. n. sabueso m. **2.** v. perseguir; seguir la pista.

hour, n. hora f.

hourglass, n. reloj de arena m.

hourly, 1. a. por horas. **2.** adv. a cada hora.

house, 1. n. casa f.; (theat.) público m. **2.** v. alojar, albergar.

housefly, n. mosca ordinaria f.

household, n. familia; casa f.

housekeeper, n. ama de llaves.

housemaid, n. criada f., sirvienta f.

housewife, n. ama de casa.

housework, n. tareas domésticas f.

hovel, n. choza f.

hover, v. revolotear.

hovercraft, n. hovercraft m.

how, adv. cómo. **h. much,** cuánto. **h. many,** cuántos. **h. far,** a qué distancia.

however, adv. como quiera; sin embargo.

howl, 1. n. aullido m. **2.** v. aullar.

hub, n. centro m.; eje m. **h. of a wheel,** cubo de la rueda m.

hubbub, n. alborota f., bulla f.

hue, n. matiz; color m.

hug, 1. n. abrazo m. **2.** v. abrazar.

huge, a. enorme.

hulk, n. casco de buque m.

hull, 1. n. cáscara f.; (naval) casco m. **2.** v. decascarar.

hum, 1. n. zumbido m. **2.** v. tararear; zumbar.

human, a. & n. humano -na.

humane, a. humano, humanitario.

humanism, n. humanidad f.; benevolencia f.

humanitarian, a. humanitario.

humanity, n. humanidad f.

humanly, adv. humanamente.

humble, a. humilde.

humbug, n. farsa f., embaucador m.

humdrum, a. monótono.

humid, a. húmedo.

humidity, n. humedad f.

humiliate, v. humillar.

humiliation, n. mortificación f.; bochorno m.

humility, n. humildad f.

humor, 1. n. humor; capricho m. **2.** v. complacer.

humorist, n. humorista m.

humorous, a. divertido.

hump, n. joroba f.

humpback, n. jorobado m.

humus, n. humus m.

hunch, n. giba f.; (idea) corazonada f.

hunchback, n. jorobado m.

hundred, 1. a. & pron. cien, ciento. **200,** doscientos. **300,** trescientos. **400,** cuatrocientos. **500,** quinientos. **600,** seiscientos. **700,** setecientos. **800,** ochocientos. **900,** novecientos. **2.** n. centenar m.

hundredth, n. & a. centésimo m.

Hungarian, a. & n. húngaro - ra.

Hungary, Hungría f.

hunger, n. hambre f.

hungry, a. hambriento. **to be h.,** tener hambre.

hunt, 1. n. caza f. **2.** v. cazar. **h. up,** buscar.

hunter, n. cazador m.

hunting, n. caza f. **to go h.,** ir de caza.

hurdle, n. zarzo m., valla f.; dificultad f.

hurl, v. arrojar.

hurricane, *n.* huracán *m.*
hurry, 1. *n.* prisa *f.* **to be in a h.**, tener prisa. 2. *v.* apresurar; darse prisa.
hurt, 1. *n.* daño, perjuicio *m.* 2. *v.* dañar; lastimar; doler; ofender.
hurtful, *a.* perjudicial, dañino.
hurtle, *v.* lanzar.
husband, *n.* marido, esposo *m.*
husk, 1. *n.* cáscara *f.* 2. *v.* descascarar.
husky, *a.* fornido.
hustle, *v.* empujar.
hut, *n.* choza *f.*
hyacinth, *n.* jacinto *m.*
hybrid, *a.* híbrido.
hydrangea, *n.* hortensia *f.*
hydraulic, *a.* hidráulico.
hydroelectric, *a.* hidroeléctrico.
hydrogen, *n.* hidrógeno *m.*
hydrophobia, *n.* hidrofobia. *f.*
hydroplane, *n.* hidroavión *m.*
hydrotherapy, *n.* hidroterapia *f.*
hyena, *n.* hiena *f.*
hygiene, *n.* higiene *f.*
hygienic, *a.* higiénico.
hymn, *n.* himno *m.*
hymnal, *n.* himnario *m.*
hypercritical, *a.* hipercrítico.
hyphen, *n.* guión *m.*
hyphenate, *v.* separar con guión.
hypnosis, *n.* hipnosis *f.*
hypnotic, *a.* hipnótico.
hypnotism, *n.* hipnotismo *m.*
hypnotize, *v.* hipnotizar.
hypochondria, *n.* hipocondría *f.*
hypochondriac, *n. & a.* hipocondríaco *m.*
hypocrisy, *n.* hipocresía *f.*
hypocrite, *n.* hipócrita *m. & f.*
hypocritical, *a.* hipócrita.
hypodermic, *a.* hipodérmico.
hypotenuse, *n.* hipotenusa *f.*
hypothesis, *n.* hipótesis *f.*
hypothetical, *a.* hipotético.
hysterectomy, *n.* histerectomía *f.*
hysteria, hysterics, *n.* histeria *f.*
hysterical, *a.* histérico.

I

I, *pron.* yo.
iambic, *a.* yámbico.
ice, *n.* hielo *m.*
iceberg, *n.* iceberg *m.*
icebox, *n.* refrigerador *m.*
ice cream, *n.* helado, mantecado *m.;* **i.-c. cone**, barquillo de helado.
ice skate, *n.* patín de cuchilla *m.*
icon, *n.* icón *m.*
icy, *a.* helado; indiferente.
idea. *n.* idea *f.*
ideal, *a.* ideal.
idealism, *n.* idealismo *m.*
idealist, *n.* idealista *m. & f.*
idealistic, *a.* idealista.

idealize, *v.* idealizar.
ideally, *adv.* idealmente.
identical, *a.* idéntico.
identifiable, *a.* identificable.
identification, *n.* identificación *f.* **i. papers**, cédula de identidad *f.*
identify, *v.* identificar.
identity, *n.* identidad *f.*
ideology, *n.* ideología *f.*
idiocy, *n.* idiotez *f.*
idiom, *n.* modismo *m.;* idioma *m.*
idiot, *n.* idiota *m. & f.*
idiotic, *a.* idiota, tonto.
idle, *a.* desocupado; perezoso.
idleness, *n.* ociosidad, pereza *f.*
idol, *n.* ídolo *m.*
idolatry, *n.* idolatría *f.*
idolize, *v.* idolatrar.
idyl, *n.* idilio *m.*
idyllic, *a.* idílico.
if, *conj.* si. **even if**, aunque.
ignite, *v.* encender.
ignition, *n.* ignición *f.*
ignoble, *a.* innoble, indigno.
ignominious, *a.* ignominioso.
ignoramus, *n.* ignorante *m.*
ignorance, *n.* ignorancia *f.*
ignorant, *a.* ignorante. **to be i. of**, ignorar.
ignore, *v.* desconocer, pasar por alto.
ill, *a.* enfermo, malo.
illegal, *a.* ilegal.
illegible, *a.* ilegible.
illegibly, *a.* ilegiblemente.
illegitimacy, *n.* ilegitimidad *f.*
illegitimate, *a.* ilegítimo; desautorizado.
illicit, *a.* ilícito.
illiteracy, *n.* analfabetismo *m.*
illiterate, *a. & n.* analfabeto - ta.
illness, *n.* enfermedad, maldad *f.*
illogical, *a.* ilógico.
illuminate, *v.* iluminar.
illumination, *n.* iluminación *f.*
illusion, *n.* ilusión *f.;* ensueño *m.*
illusive, *a.* ilusivo.
illustrate, *v.* ilustrar; ejemplificar.
illustration, *n.* ilustración *f.;* ejemplo; grabado *m.*
illustrative, *a.* ilustrativo.
illustrious, *a.* ilustre.
ill will, *n.* malevolencia *f.*
image, *n.* imagen, estatua *f.*
imagery, *n.* imaginación *f.*
imaginable, *a.* imaginable.
imaginary, *a.* imaginario.
imagination, *n.* imaginación *f.*
imaginative, *a.* imaginativo.
imagine, *v.* imaginarse, figurarse.
imam, *n.* imán *m.*
imbecile, *n. & a.* imbécil *m.*
imitate, *v.* imitar.
imitation, *n.* imitación *f.*
imitative, *a.* imitativo.
immaculate, *a.* inmaculado.
immanent, *a.* inmanente.

immaterial, *a.* inmaterial; sin importancia.
immature, *a.* inmaturo.
immediate, *a.* inmediato.
immediately, *adv.* inmediatamente.
immense, *a.* inmenso.
immerse, *v.* sumergir.
immigrant, *n. & a.* inmigrante *m.*
immigrate, *v.* inmigrar.
imminent, *a.* inminente.
immobile, *a.* inmóvil.
immoderate, *a.* inmoderado.
immodest, *a.* inmodesto; atrevido.
immoral, *a.* inmoral.
immorality, *n.* inmoralidad *f.*
immorally, *adv.* licenciosamente.
immortal, *a.* inmortal.
immortality, *n.* inmortalidad *f.*
immortalize, *v.* inmortalizar.
immune, *a.* inmune.
immunity, *n.* inmunidad *f.*
immunize, *v.* inmunizar.
impact, *n.* impacto *m.*
impair, *v.* empeorar, perjudicar.
impale, *v.* empalar.
impart, *v.* impartir, comunicar.
impartial, *a.* imparcial.
impatience, *n.* impaciencia *f.*
impatient, *a.* impaciente.
impede, *v.* impedir, estorbar.
impediment, *n.* impedimento *m.*
impel, *v.* impeler.
impenetrable, *a.* impenetrable.
impenitent, *n. & a.* impenitente *m.*
imperative, *a.* imperativo.
imperceptible, *a.* imperceptible.
imperfect, *a.* imperfecto.
imperfection, *n.* imperfección *f.*
imperial, *a.* imperial.
imperialism, *n.* imperialismo *m.*
imperious, *a.* imperioso.
impersonal, *a.* impersonal.
impersonate, *v.* personificar; imitar.
impersonation, *n.* personificación *f.;* imitación *f.*
impertinence, *n.* impertinencia *f.*
impervious, *a.* impermeable.
impetuous, *a.* impetuoso.
impetus, *n.* impetú *m.,* impulso *m.*
impinge, *v.* tropezar; infringir.
implacable, *a.* implacable.
implant, *v.* implantar; inculcar.
implement, *n.* herramienta *f.*
implicate, *v.* implicar; embrollar.
implication, *n.* inferencia *f.;* complicidad *f.*
implicit, *a.* implícito.
implied, *a.* implícito.
implore, *v.* implorar.
imply, *v.* significar; dar a entender.

impolite, *a.* descortés.
import, 1. *n.* importación *f.* **2.** *v.* importar.
importance, *n.* importancia *f.*
important, *a.* importante.
importation, *n.* importación *f.*
importune, *v.* importunar.
impose, *v.* imponer.
imposition, *n.* imposición *f.*
impossibility, *n.* imposibilidad *f.*
impossible, *a.* imposible.
impotence, *n.* impotencia *f.*
impotent, *a.* impotente.
impregnable, *a.* impregnable.
impregnate, *v.* impregnar; fecundizar.
impresario, *n.* empresario *m.*
impress, *v.* impresionar.
impression, *n.* impresión *f.*
impressive, *a.* imponente.
imprison, *v.* encarcelar.
imprisonment, *n.* prisión, encarcelación *f.*
improbable, *a.* improbable.
impromptu, *a.* extemporáneo.
improper, *a.* impropio.
improve, *v.* mejorar; progresar.
improvement, *n.* mejoramiento; progreso *m.*
improvise, *v.* improvisar.
impudent, *a.* descarada.
impugn, *v.* impugnar.
impulse, *n.* impulso *m.*
impulsive, *a.* impulsivo.
impunity, *n.* impunidad *f.*
impure, *a.* impuro.
impurity, *n.* impureza *f.*; deshonestidad *f.*
impute, *v.* imputar.
in, 1. *prep.* en; dentro de. **2.** *adv.* adentro.
inadvertent, *a.* inadvertido.
inalienable, *a.* inalienable.
inane, *a.* mentecato.
inaugural, *a.* inaugural.
inaugurate, *v.* inaugurar.
inauguration, *n.* inauguración *f.*
Inca, *n.* inca *m.*
incandescent, *a.* incandescente.
incantation, *n.* encantación *f.*, conjuro *m.*
incapacitate, *v.* incapacitar.
incarcerate, *v.* encarcelar.
incarnate, *a.* encarnado; personificado.
incarnation, *n.* encarnación *f.*
incendiary, *a.* incendiario.
incense, 1. *n.* incienso *m.* **2.** *v.* indignar.
incentive, *n.* incentivo *m.*
inception, *n.* cimienzo *m.*
incessant, *a.* incesante.
incest, *n.* incesto *m.*
inch, *n.* pulgada *f.*
incidence, *n.* incidencia *f.*
incident, *n.* incidente *m.*
incidental, *a.* incidental.
incidentally, *adv.* incidentalmente; entre paréntesis.
incinerator, *n.* incinerador *m.*
incipient, *a.* incipiente.

incision, *n.* incisión *f.*; cortadura *f.*
incisive, *a.* incisivo; mordaz.
incisor, *n.* incisivo *m.*
incite, *v.* incitar, instigar.
inclination, *n.* inclinación *f.*; declive *m.*
incline, 1. *n.* pendiente *m.* **2.** *v.* inclinar.
inclose, *v.* incluir.
include, *v.* incluir.
including, *prep.* incluso.
inclusive, *a.* inclusivo.
incognito, *n.* & *adv.* incógnito *m.*
income, *n.* renta *f.*; ingresos *m.pl.*
incomparable, *a.* incomparable.
inconvenience, 1. *n.* incomodidad *f.* **2.** *v.* incomodar.
inconvenient, *a.* incómodo.
incorporate, *v.* incoporar; dar cuerpo.
incorrigible, *a.* incorregible.
increase, *v.* crecer; aumentar.
incredible, *a.* increíble.
incredulity, *n.* incredulidad *f.*
incredulous, *a.* incrédulo.
increment, *n.* incremento *m.*, aumento *m.*
incriminate, *v.* incriminar.
incrimination, *n.* incriminación *f.*
incrust, *v.* incrustar.
incubator, *n.* incubadora *f.*
inculcate, *v.* inculcar.
incumbency, *n.* incumbencia *f.*
incumbent, *a.* obligatorio; colocado sobre.
incur, *v.* incurrir.
incurable, *a.* incurable.
indebted, *a.* obligado; adeudado.
indeed, *adv.* verdaderamente, de veras. **no i.**, de ninguna manera.
indefatigable, *a.* incansable.
indefinite, *a.* indefinido.
indefinitely, *adv.* indefinidamente.
indelible, *a.* indeleble.
indemnify, *v.* indemnizar.
indemnity, *n.* indemnificación *f.*
indent, 1. *n.* diente *f.*, mella *f.* **2.** *v.* indentar, mellar.
indentation, *n.* indentación *f.*
independence, *n.* independencia *f.*
independent, *a.* independiente.
in-depth, *adj.* en profundidad.
index, *n.* índice *m.*; (of book) tabla *f.*
India, *n.* India *f.*
Indian, *a.* & *n.* indio -dia.
indicate, *v.* indicar.
indication, *n.* indicación *f.*
indicative, *a.* & *n.* indicativo *m.*
indict, *v.* encausar.
indictment, *n.* (law) sumaria *m.*; denuncia *f.*
indifference, *n.* indiferencia *f.*
indifferent, *a.* indiferente.
indigenous, *a.* indígena.

indigent, *a.* indigente, pobre.
indigestion, *n.* indigestión *f.*
indignant, *a.* indignado.
indignation, *n.* indignación *f.*
indignity, *n.* indignidad *f.*
indirect, *a.* indirecto.
indiscreet, *a.* indiscreto.
indiscretion, *n.* indiscreción *f.*
indiscriminate, *a.* promiscuo.
indispensable, *a.* indispensable.
indisposed, *a.* indispuesto.
individual, *a.* & *n.* individuo *m.*
individuality, *n.* individualidad *f.*
individually, *adv.* individualmente.
indivisible, *a.* indivisible.
indoctrinate, *v.* doctrinar, enseñar.
indolent, *a.* indolente.
indoor, *a.* interior. **indoors**, *adv.* en casa; bajo techo.
indorse, *v.* endosar.
induce, *v.* inducir, persuadir.
induct, *v.* instalar, iniciar.
induction, *n.* introducción *f.*; instalación *f.*
inductive, *a.* inductivo; introductor.
indulge, *v.* favorecer. **i. in**, entregarse a.
indulgence, *n.* indulgencia *f.*
indulgent, *a.* indulgente.
industrial, *a.* industrial.
industrialist, *n.* industrial *m.*
industrious, *a.* industrioso, trabajador.
industry, *n.* industria *f.*
ineligible, *a.* inelegible.
inept, *a.* inepto.
inert, *a.* inerte.
inertia, *n.* inercia *f.*
inevitable, *a.* inevitable.
inexplicable, *a.* inexplicable.
infallible, *a.* infalible.
infamous, *a.* infame.
infamy, *n.* infamia *f.*
infancy, *n.* infancia *f.*
infant, *n.* nene *m.*; criatura *f.*
infantile, *a.* infantil.
infantry, *n.* infantería *f.*
infatuated, *a.* infatuado.
infect, *v.* infectar.
infection, *n.* infección *f.*
infectious, *a.* infeccioso.
infer, *v.* inferir.
inference, *n.* inferencia *f.*
inferior, *a.* inferior.
infernal, *a.* infernal.
inferno, *n.* infierno *m.*
infest, *v.* infestar.
infidel, 1. *n.* infiel *m.*; pagano *m.* **2.** *a.* infiel.
infidelity, *n.* infidelidad *f.*
infiltrate, *v.* infiltrar.
infinite, *a.* infinito.
infinitesimal, *a.* infinitesimal.
infinitive, *n.* & *a.* infinitivo *m.*
infinity, *n.* infinidad *f.*
infirm, *a.* enfermizo.
infirmary, *n.* hospital *m.*, enfermería *f.*
infirmity, *n.* enfermedad *f.*
inflame, *v.* inflamar.

inflammable, a. inflamable.
inflammation, n. inflamación f.
inflammatory, a. inflamante; (med.) inflamatorio.
inflate, v. inflar.
inflation, n. inflación f.
inflection, n. inflexión f.; (of the voice) modulación de la voz f.
inflict, v. infligir.
infliction, n. imposición f.
influence, 1. n. influencia f. 2. v. influir en.
influential, a. influyente.
influenza, n. gripe f.
inform, v. informar. **i. oneself**, enterarse.
informal, a. informal.
information, n. informaciones f.pl.
infringe, v. infringir.
infuriate, v. enfurecer.
ingenious, a. ingenioso.
ingenuity, n. ingeniosidad; destreza f.
ingredient, n. ingrediente m.
inhabit, v. habitar.
inhabitant, n. habitante m. & f.
inhale, v. inhalar.
inherent, a. inherente.
inherit, v. heredar.
inheritance, n. herencia f.
inhibit, v. inhibir.
inhibition, n. inhibición f.
inhuman, a. inhumano.
inimical, a. hostil.
inimitable, a. inimitable.
iniquity, n. iniquidad f.
initial, a. & n. inicial f.
initiate, v. iniciar.
initiation, n. iniciación f.
initiative, n. iniciativa f.
inject, v. inyectar.
injection, n. inyección f.
injunction, n. mandato m.; (law) embargo m.
injure, v. herir; lastimar; ofender.
injurious, a. perjudicial.
injury, n. herida; afrenta f perjuicio m.
injustice, n. injusticia f.
ink, n. tinta f.
inland, 1. a. interior. 2. adv. tierra adentro.
inlet, n. entrada f.; ensenada f.; estuario m.
inmate, n. residente m.; (of a prison) preso m.
inn, n. posada f.; mesón m.
inner, a. interior. **i. tube**, cámara de aire.
innocence, n. inocencia f.
innocent, a. inocente.
innocuous, a. innocuo.
innovation, n. innovación f.
innuendo, n. insinuación f.
innumerable, a. innumerable.
inoculate, v. inocular.
inoculation, n. inoculación f.
input, n. aducto m.
inquest, n. indagación f.
inquire, v. preguntar; inquirir.
inquiry, n. pregunta; investigación f.

inquisition, n. escudriñamiento m.; (church) Inquisición f.
insane, a. loco. **to go i.**, perder la razón; volverse loco.
insanity, n. locura f.; demencia f.
inscribe, v. inscribir.
inscription, n. inscripción; dedicatoria f.
insect, n. insecto m.
insecticide, n. & a. insecticida f.
inseparable, a. inseparable.
insert, v. insertar, meter.
insertion, n. cosa insertada f.
inside, 1. a. & n. interior m. 2. adv. adentro, por dentro. **i. out**, al revés. 3. prep. dentro de.
insidious, a. insidioso.
insight, n. perspicacia f.; comprensión f.
insignia, n. insignias f.pl.
insignificance, n. insignificancia f.
insignificant, a. insignificante.
insinuate, v. insinuar.
insinuation, n. insinuación f.
insipid, a. insípido.
insist, v. insistir.
insistence, n. insistencia f.
insistent, a. insistente.
insolence, n. insolencia f.
insolent, a. insolente.
insomnia, n. insomnio m.
inspect, v. inspeccionar, examinar.
inspection, n. inspección f.
inspector, n. inspector m.
inspiration, n. inspiración f.
inspire, v. inspirar.
install, v. instalar.
installation, n. instalación f.
installment, n. plazo m.
instance, n. ocasión f. **for i.**, por ejemplo.
instant, a. & n. instante m.
instantaneous, a. instantáneo.
instantly, adv. al instante.
instead, adv. en lugar de eso. **i. of**, en vez de, en lugar de.
instigate, v. instigar.
instill, v. instilar.
instinct, n. instinto m.
instinctive, a. instintivo.
institute, 1. n. instituto m. 2. v. instituir.
institution, n. institución f.
instruct, v. instruir.
instruction, n. instrucción f.
instructive, a. instructivo.
instructor, n. instructor m.
instrument, n. instrumento m.
instrumental, a. instrumental.
insufficient, a. insuficiente.
insular, a. insular; estrecho de miras.
insulate, v. aislar.
insulation, n. aislamiento m.
insulator, n. aislador m.
insulin, n. insulina f.
insult, 1. n. insulto m. 2. v. insultar.
insuperable, a. insuperable.
insurance, n. seguro m.

insure, v. asegurar.
insurgent, a. & n. insurgente m.
insurrection, n. insurrección f.
intact, a. intacto.
intangible, a. intangible, impalpable.
integral, a. íntegro.
integrate, v. integrar.
integrity, n. integridad f.
intellect, n. intelecto m.
intellectual, a. & n. intelectual m. & f.
intelligence, n. inteligencia f.
intelligent, a. inteligente.
intelligible, a. inteligible.
intend, v. pensar; intentar; destinar.
intense, a. intenso.
intensify, v. intensificar.
intensity, n. intensidad f.
intensive, a. intensivo.
intent, n. intento m.
intention, n. intención f.
intentional, a. intencional.
intercede, v. interceder.
intercept, v. interceptar; detener.
intercourse, n. tráfico m.; comunicación f.; coito m.
interest, 1. n. interés m. 2. v. interesar.
interesting, a. interesante.
interface, n. aparato o zona de contacto.
interfere, v. meterse; intervenir. **i. with**, estorbar.
interference, n. intervención f.; obstáculo m.
interior, a. interior.
interject, v. interponer; intervenir.
interjection, n. interjección f.; interposición f.
interlude, n. intervalo m.; (theat.) intermedio m.; (music) interludio m.
intermediary, n. intermediario m.
intermediate, a. intermedio.
interment, n. entierro m.
intermission, n. intermisión f.; (theat.) entreacto m.
intermittent, a. intermitente.
intern, 1. n. interno m. 2. v. internar.
internal, a. interno.
international, a. internacional.
internationalism, n. internacionalismo m.
interne, n. practicante de hospital m.
interpose, v. interponer.
interpret, v. interpretar.
interpretation, n. interpretación f.
interpreter, n. intérprete m. & f.
interrogate, v. interrogar.
interrogation, n. interrogación; pregunta f.
interrogative, a. interrogativo.
interrupt, v. interrumpir.
interruption, n. interrupción f.
intersect, v. cortar.

intersection, *n.* intersección *f.;* (street) bocacalle *f.*
intersperse, *v.* entremezclar.
interval, *n.* intervalo *m.*
intervene, *v.* intervenir.
intervention, *n.* intervención *f.*
interview, **1.** *n.* entrevista *f.* **2.** *v.* entrevistar.
intestine, *n.* intestino *m.*
intimacy, *n.* intimidad; familiaridad *f.*
intimate, **1.** *a.* íntimo, familiar. **2.** *n.* amigo íntimo. **3.** *v.* insinuar.
intimidate, *v.* intimidar.
intimidation, *n.* intimidación *f.*
into, *prep.* en, dentro de.
intonation, *n.* entonación *f.*
intone, *v.* entonar.
intoxicate, *v.* embriagar.
intoxication, *n.* embriaguez *f.*
intravenous, *a.* intravenoso.
intrepid, *a.* intrépido.
intricacy, *n.* intrincación *f.;* enredo *m.*
intricate, *a.* intrincado; complejo.
intrigue, **1.** *n.* intriga *f.* **2.** *v.* intrigar.
intrinsic, *a.* intrínseco.
introduce, *v.* introducir; (a person) presentar.
introduction, *n.* presentación; introducción *f.*
introductory, *a.* introductivo.
introvert, *n.* & *a.* introverso *m.*
intrude, *v.* entremeterse.
intruder, *n.* intruso -sa.
intuition, *n.* intuición *f.*
intuitive, *a.* intuitivo.
inundate, *v.* inundar.
invade, *v.* invadir.
invader, *n.* invasor *m.*
invalid, *a.* & *n.* inválido -da.
invariable, *a.* invariable.
invasion, *n.* invasión *f.*
invective, **1.** *n.* invectiva *f.* **2.** *a.* ultrajante.
inveigle, *v.* seducir.
invent, *v.* inventar.
invention, *n.* invención *f.*
inventive, *a.* inventivo.
inventor, *n.* inventor *m.*
inventory, *n.* inventario *m.*
invertebrate, *n.* & *a.* invertebrado *m.*
invest, *v.* investir; (com.) invertir.
investigate, *v.* investigar.
investigation, *n.* investigación *f.*
investment, *n.* inversión *f.*
inveterate, *a.* inveterado.
invidious, *a.* difamatorio.
invigorate, *v.* vigorizar, fortificar.
invincible, *a.* invencible.
invisible, *a.* invisible.
invitation, *n.* invitación *f.*
invite, *v.* invitar, convidar.
invocation, *n.* invocación *f.*
invoice, *n.* factura *f.*
invoke, *v.* invocar.
involuntary, *a.* involuntario.

involve, *v.* envolver; implicar.
involved, *a.* complicado.
invulnerable, *a.* invulnerable.
inward, *adv.* hacia adentro.
inwardly, *adv.* interiormente.
iodine, *n.* iodo *m.*
irate, *a.* encolerizado.
Ireland, *n.* Irlanda *f.*
iris, *n.* (anat.) iris *m.;* (botany) flor de lis *f.*
Irish, *a.* irlandés.
irk, *v.* fastidiar.
iron, **1.** *n.* hierro *m.;* (appliance) plancha *f.* **2.** *v.* planchar.
ironical, *a.* irónico.
irony, *n.* ironía *f.*
irrational, *a.* irracional; ilógico.
irregular, *a.* irregular.
irregularity, *n.* irregularidad *f.*
irrelevant, *a.* ajeno.
irresistible, *a.* irresistible.
irresponsible, *a.* irresponsable.
irreverent, *a.* irreverente.
irrevocable, *a.* irrevocable.
irrigate, *v.* regar; (med.) irrigar.
irrigation, *n.* riego *m.*
irritability, *n.* irritabilidad *f.*
irritable, *a.* irritable.
irritant, *n.* & *a.* irritante *m.*
irritate, *v.* irritar.
irritation, *n.* irritación *f.*
island, *n.* isla *f.*
isolate, *v.* aislar.
isolation, *n.* aislamiento *m.*
isosceles, *a.* isósceles.
issuance, *n.* emisión *f.;* publicación *f.*
issue, **1.** *n.* emisión; edición; progenie *f.;* número *m.;* punto en disputa. **2.** *v.* emitir; publicar.
isthmus, *n.* istmo *m.*
it, *pron.* ello; él, ella; lo, la.
Italian, *a.* & *n.* italiano -na.
Italy, *n.* Italia *f.*
itch, **1.** *n.* picazón *f.* **2.** *v.* picar.
item, *n.* artículo; detalle *m.;* inserción *f.;* (com.) renglón *m.*
itemize, *v.* detallar.
itinerant, **1.** *n.* viandante *m.* **2.** *a.* ambulante.
itinerary, *n.* itinerario *m.*
its, *a.* su.
itself, *pron.* sí; se.
ivory, *n.* marfil *m.*
ivy, *n.* hiedra *f.*

J

jab, **1.** *n.* pinchazo *m.* **2.** *v.* pinchar.
jack, *n.* (for lifting) gato *m.;* (cards) sota *f.*
jackal, *n.* chacal *m.*
jackass, *n.* asno *m.*
jacket, *n.* chaqueta *f.;* saco *m.*
jack-of-all-trades, *n.* estuche *m.*
jade, *n.* (horse) rocín *m.;*

(woman) picarona *f.;* (mineral) jade *m.*
jaded, *a.* rendido.
jagged, *a.* mellado.
jaguar, *n.* jaguar *m.*
jail, *n.* cárcel *f.*
jailer, *n.* carcelero *m.*
jam, **1.** *n.* conserva *f.;* apretura *f.* **2.** *v.* apiñar, apretar; trabar.
janitor, *n.* portero *m.*
January, *n.* enero *m.*
Japan, *n.* Japón *m.*
Japanese, *a.* & *n.* japonés -esa.
jar, **1.** *n.* jarro *m.* **2.** *v.* chocar; agitar.
jargon, *n.* jerga *f.*
jasmine, *n.* jazmín *m.*
jaundice, *n.* ictericia *f.*
jaunt, *n.* paseata *f.*
javelin, *n.* jabalina *f.*
jaw, *n.* quijada *f.*
jay, *n.* grajo *m.*
jazz, *n.* jazz *m.*
jealous, *a.* celoso. **to be j.,** tener celos.
jealousy, *n.* celos *m.pl.*
jeans, *n.* jeans *m.pl.*
jeer, **1.** *n.* burla *f.,* mofa *f.* **2.** *v.* burlar, mofar.
jelly, *n.* jalea *f.*
jellyfish, *n.* aguamar *m.*
jeopardize, *v.* arriesgar.
jeopardy, *n.* riesgo *m.*
jerk, **1.** *n.* sacudida *f.* **2.** *v.* sacudir.
jerky, *a.* espasmódico.
Jerusalem, *n.* Jerusalén *m.*
jest, **1.** *n.* broma *f.* **2.** *v.* bromear.
jester, *n.* bufón *m.;* burlón *m.*
Jesuit, **1.** *n.* jesuita *m.* **2.** *a.* jesuítico.
Jesus Christ, *n.* Jesucristo *m.*
jet, *n.* chorro *m.;* (gas) mechero *m.*
jet lag, *n.* fatiga que sufre un viajero en avión, por causa del cambio de horas.
jetsam, *n.* echazón *f.*
jettison, *v.* echar mercancías al mar.
jetty, *n.* muelle *m.*
Jew, *n.* judío -día.
jewel, *n.* joya *f.*
jeweler, *n.* joyero *m.*
jewelry, *n.* joyería *f.* **j. store,** joyería *f.*
Jewish, *a.* judío.
jib, *n.* (naut.) foque *m.*
jiffy, *n.* instante *m.*
jig, *n.* jiga *f.* **j-saw,** sierra de vaivén *f.*
jilt, *v.* dar calabazas.
jingle, **1.** *n.* retintín *m.;* rima pueril *f.* **2.** *v.* retiñir.
jinx, **1.** *n.* aojo *m.* **2.** *v.* aojar.
jittery, *a.* nervioso.
job, *n.* empleo *m.*
jobber, *n.* destajista *m.,* remendero *m.*
jockey, *n.* jockey *m.*
jocular, *a.* jocoso.
jog, **1.** *n.* empujoncito *m.* **2.** *v.* empujar; estimular. **to j. along,** ir a un trote corto.

join, v. juntar; unir.
joiner, n. ebanista m.
joint, n. juntura f.
jointly, adv. conjuntamente.
joke, 1. n. broma, chanza f.; chiste m. 2. v. bromear.
joker, n. bromista m. & f.
jolly, a. alegre, jovial.
jolt, 1. n. sacudido m. 2. v. sacudir.
jonquil, n. junquillo m.
jostle, v. rempujar.
journal, n. diario m.; revista f.
journalism, n. periodismo m.
journalist, n. periodista m. & f.
journey, 1. n. viaje m.; jornada f. 2. v. viajar.
journeyman, n. jornalero m., oficial m.
jovial, a. jovial.
jowl, n. carrillo m.
joy, n. alegría f.
joyful, joyous, a. alegre, gozoso.
jubilant, a. jubiloso.
jubilee, n. jubileo m.
Judaism, n. judaísmo m.
judge, 1. n. juez m. 2. v. juzgar.
judgment, n. juicio m.
judicial, a. judicial.
judiciary, a. judiciario.
judicious, a. juicioso.
jug, n. jarro m.
juggle, v. escamotear.
juice, n. jugo, zumo m.
juicy, a. jugoso.
July, n. julio m.
jumble, 1. n. revoltillo m. 2. v. arrebujar, revolver.
jump, 1. n. salto m. 2. v. saltar, brincar.
junction, n. confluencia f.; (railway) empalme m.
juncture, n. junta f.
June, n. junio m.
jungle, n. selva f.
junior, a. menor; más joven. Jr., hijo.
juniper, n. enebro m.
junk, n. basura f.
junket, 1. n. leche cuajada f. 2. v. festejar.
jurisdiction, n. jurisdicción f.
jurisprudence, n. jurisprudencia f.
jurist, n. jurista m.
juror, n. jurado m.
jury, n. jurado m.
just, 1. a. justo; exacto. 2. adv. exactamente; (only) sólo. j. now, ahora mismo. to have j., acabar de.
justice, n. justicia f.; (person) juez m.
justifiable, a. justificable.
justification, n. justificación f.
justify, v. justificar.
jut, v. sobresalir.
jute, n. yute m.
juvenile, a. juvenil.

K

kaleidoscope, n. calidoscopio m.

kangaroo, n. canguro m.
karakul, n. caracul m.
karat, n. quilate m.
karate, n. karate m.
keel, 1. n. quilla f. 2. v. to k. over, volcarse.
keen, a. agudo; penetrante.
keep, v. mantener, retener; guardar; preservar. k. on, seguir, continuar.
keeper, n. guardián m.
keepsake, n. recuerdo m.
keg, n. barrilito m.
kennel, n. perrera f.
kerchief, n. pañuelo m.
kernel, n. pepita f.; grano m.
kerosene, n. kerosén m.
ketchup, n. salsa de tomate f.
kettle, n. caldera, olla f.
kettledrum, n. tímpano m.
key, n. llave f.; (music) clave f.; (piano) tecla f.
keyhole, n. bocallave f.
khaki, a. caqui.
kick, 1. n. patada f. 2. v. patear; (coll.) quejarse.
kid, 1. n. cabrito m.; (coll.) niño -ña, chico, -ca. 2. v. (coll.) bromear.
kidnap, v. secuestrar.
kidnaper, n. secuestrador m.
kidney, n. riñón m.
kidney bean, n. frijol m.
kill, v. matar.
killer, n. matador m.
kiln, n. horno m.
kilogram, n. kilogramo m.
kilohertz, n. kilohertzio m.
kilometer, n. kilómetro m.
kilowatt, n. kilovatio m.
kin, n. parentesco m.; parientes m.pl.
kind, 1. a. bondadoso, amable. 2. n. género m.; clase f. k. of, algo, un poco.
kindergarten, n. kindergarten m.
kindle, v. encender.
kindling, n. encendimiento m. k.-wood, leña menuda f.
kindly, a. bondadoso.
kindness, n. bondad f.
kindred, n. parentesco m.
kinetic, a. cinético.
king, n. rey m.
kingdom, n. reino m.
kink, n. retorcimiento m.
kiosk, n. kiosco m.
kiss, 1. n. beso m. 2. v. besar.
kitchen, n. cocina f.
kite, n. cometa f.
kitten, n. gatito -ta.
kleptomania, n. cleptomanía f.
kleptomaniac, n. cleptómano m.
knack, n. don m., destreza f.
knapsack, n. alforja f.
knead, v. amasar.
knee, n. rodilla f.
kneecap, n. rodillera f.
kneel, v. arrodillarse.
knickers, n. calzón corto m., pantalones m.

knife, n. cuchillo m.
knight, n. caballero m.; (chess) caballo m.
knit, v. tejer.
knob, n. tirador m.
knock, 1. n. golpe m.; llamada f. 2. v. golpear; tocar, llamar.
knot, 1. n. nudo; lazo m. 2. v. anudar.
knotty, a. nudoso.
know, v. saber; (a person) conocer.
knowledge, n. conocimiento, saber m.
knuckle, n. nudillo m. k. bone, jarrete m. to k. under, ceder a.
Korea, n. Corea f.

L

label, 1. n. rótulo m. 2. v. rotular; designar.
labor, 1. n. trabajo m.; la clase obrera. 2. v. trabajar.
laboratory, n. laboratorio m.
laborer, n. trabajador, obrero m.
laborious, a. laborioso, difícil.
labor union, n. gremio obrero m.
labyrinth, n. laberinto m.
lace, 1. n. encaje m.; (of shoe) lazo m. 2. v. amarrar.
lacerate, v. lacerar, lastimar.
laceration, n. laceración f., desgarro m.
lack, 1. n. falta f. 2. faltar, carecer.
lackadaisical, a. indiferente; soñador.
laconic, a. lacónico.
lacquer, 1. n. laca f., barniz m. 2. v. laquear, barnizar.
lactic, a. láctico.
lactose, n. lactosa f.
ladder, n. escalera f.
ladle, 1. n. cucharón m. 2. v. servir con cucharón.
lady, n. señora, dama f.
ladybug, n. mariquita f.
lag, 1. n. retraso m. 2. v. quedarse atrás.
lagoon, n. laguna f.
laid-back, a. de buen talante.
laity, n. laicidad f.
lake, n. lago m.
lamb, n. cordero m.
lame, 1. a. cojo; estropeado. 2. v. estropear.
lament, 1. n. lamento m. 2. v. lamentar.
lamentable, a. lamentable.
lamentation, n. lamento m.; lamentación f.
laminate, a. laminado.
lamp, n. lámpara f.
lampoon, 1. n. pasquín m. 2. v. pasquinar.
lance, 1. n. lanza f. 2. v. (med.) abrir.
land, 1. n. país m.; tierra f. native l., patria f. 2. v. desembarcar; (plane) aterrizar.

landholder, n. hacendado m.

landing, n. (of stairs) descanso m.; (ship) desembarcadero m.; (airplane) aterrizaje m.

landlady, landlord, n. propietario -ria.

landmark, n. mojón m., señal f.; rasgo sobresaliente m.

landscape, n. paisaje m.

landslide, n. derrumbe m.

lane, n. senda f.

language, n. lengua f., idioma; lenguaje m.

languid, a. lánguido.

languish, v. languidecer.

languor, n. languidez f.

lanolin, n. lanolina f.

lantern, n. linterna f.; farol m.

lap, 1. n. regazo m.; falda f. 2. v. lamer.

lapel, n. solapa f.

lapse, 1. n. lapso m. 2. v. pasar; decaer; caer en error.

larceny, n. ratería f.

lard, n. manteca f.

large, a. grande.

largely, v. ampliamente; mayormente; muy.

largo, n. & a. (mus.) largo m.

lariat, n. lazo m.

lark, n. (bird) alondra f.

larva, n. larva f.

laryngitis, n. laringitis f.

larynx, n. laringe f.

lascivious, a. lascivo.

laser, n. láser m.

lash, 1. n. azote, latigazo m. 2. v. azotar.

lass, n. doncella f.

lassitude, n. lasitud f.

lasso, 1. n. lazo m. 2. v. enlazar.

last, 1. a. pasado; (final) último. at l., por fin. 2. v. durar.

lasting, a. duradero.

latch, n. aldaba f.

late, 1. a. tardío; (deceased) difunto. to be l., llegar tarde. 2. adv. tarde.

lately, adv. recientemente.

latent, a. latente.

lateral, a. lateral.

lather, 1. n. espuma de jabón. 2. v. enjabonar.

Latin, n. latín m.

Latin America, n. Hispanoamérica, América Latina f.

Latin American, a. & n. hispanoamericano -na.

latitude, n. latitud f.

latrine, n. letrina f.

latter, a. posterior. the l., éste.

lattice, n. celosía f.

laud, v. loar.

laudable, a. laudable.

laudanum, n. láudano m.

laudatory, a. laudatorio.

laugh, 1. n. risa, risotada f. 2. v. reír. l. at, reírse de.

laughable, a. risible.

laughter, n. risa f.

launch, 1. n. (naut.) lancha f. 2. v. lanzar.

launder, v. lavar y planchar la ropa.

laundry, n. lavandería f.

laundryman, n. lavandero m.

laureate, n. & a. laureado.

laurel, a. laureado.

lava, n. lava f.

lavatory, n. lavatorio m.

lavender, n. lavándula f.

lavish, 1. a. pródigo. 2. v. prodigar.

law, n. ley f.; derecho m.

lawful, a. legal.

lawless, a. sin ley.

lawn, n. césped; prado m.

lawsuit, n. pleito m.

lawyer, n. abogado m.

lax, a. flojo, laxo.

laxative, n. purgante m.

laxity, n. laxidad f.; flojedad f.

lay, 1. a. secular. 2. v. poner.

layer, n. capa f.

layman, n. lego, seglar m.

lazy, a. perezoso.

lead, 1. n. plomo m.; (theat.) papel principal. to take the l., tomar la delantera. 2. v. conducir; dirigir.

leaden, a. plomizo; pesado; abatido.

leader, n. líder; jefe; director m.

leadership, n. dirección f.

leaf, n. hoja f.

leaflet, n. (bot.) hojilla f.; folleto m.

league, n. liga; (measure) legua f.

leak, 1. n. escape; goteo m. 2. v. gotear; (naut.) hacer agua.

leakage, n. goteo m., escape m., pérdida f.

leaky, a. llovedizo, resquebrajado.

lean, 1. a. flaco, magro. 2. v. apoyarse, arrimarse.

leap, 1. n. salto m. 2. v. saltar.

leap year, n. año bisiesto m.

learn, v. aprender; saber.

learned, a. erudito.

learning, n. erudición f., instrucción f.

lease, 1. n. arriendo m. 2. v. arrendar.

leash, 1. n. correa f. 2. v. atraillar.

least, a. menor; mínimo. the l., lo menos. at l., por lo menos.

leather, n. cuero m.

leathery, a. coriáceo.

leave, 1. n. licencia f. to take l., despedirse. 2. v. dejar; (depart) salir, irse. l. out, omitir.

leaven, 1. n. levadura f. 2. v. fermentar, imbuir.

lecherous, a. lujurioso.

lecture, n. conferencia f.

lecturer, n. conferencista m.; catedrático m.

ledge, n. borde m.; capa f.

ledger, n. libro mayor m.

lee, n. sotavento m.

leech, n. sanguijuela f.

leek, n. porro m.

leer, v. mirar de soslayo.

leeward, a. sotavento.

left, a. izquierdo. the l., la iz-

quierda. to be left, quedarse.

leftist, n. izquierdista m. & f.

leg, n. pierna f.

legacy, n. legado m., herencia f.

legal, a. legal.

legalize, v. legalizar.

legation, n. legación, embajada f.

legend, n. leyenda f.

legendary, a. legendario.

legible, a. legible.

legion, n. legión f.

legislate, v. legislar.

legislation, n. legislación f.

legislator, n. legislador m.

legislature, n. legislatura f.

legitimate, a. legítimo.

legume, n. legumbre f.

leisure, n. desocupación f.; horas libres.

leisurely, 1. a. deliberado. 2. adv. despacio.

lemon, n. limón m.

lemonade, n. limonada f.

lend, v. prestar.

length, n. largo m.; duración f.

lengthen, v. alargar.

lengthwise, adv. a lo largo.

lengthy, a. largo.

lenient, a. indulgente.

lens, n. lente m. or f.

Lent, n. cuaresma f.

Lenten, a. cuaresmal.

lentil, n. lenteja f.

leopard, n. leopardo m.

leper, n. leproso m.

leprosy, n. lepra.

lesbian, n. lesbiana f.

lesion, n. lesión f.

less, a. & adv. menos.

lessen, v. disminuir.

lesser, a. menor; más pequeño.

lesson, n. lección f.

lest, conj. para que no.

let, v. dejar; permitir; arrendar.

lethal, a. letal.

lethargic, a. letárgico.

lethargy, n. letargo m.

letter, n. carta f.; (of alphabet) letra f.

letterhead, n. membrete m.

lettuce, n. lechuga f.

leukemia, n. leucemia f.

levee, n. recepción f.

level, 1. a. llano, nivelado. 2. n. nivel m.; llanura f. 3. v. allanar; nivelar.

lever, n. palanca f.

levity, n. levedad f.

levy, 1. n. leva f. 2. v. imponer.

lewd, a. lascivo.

lexicon, n. léxico m.

liability, n. riesgo m.; obligación f.

liable, a. sujeto; responsable.

liaison, n. vinculación f., enlace m.; concubinaje m.

liar, n. embustero -ra.

libel, 1. n. libelo m. 2. v. difamar.

libelous, a. difamatorio.

liberal, a. liberal; generoso.

liberalism, *n.* liberalismo *m.*

liberality, *n.* liberalidad *f.*

liberate, *v.* libertar.

liberty, *n.* libertad *f.*

libidinous, *a.* libidinoso.

librarian, *n.* bibliotecario *m.*

library, *n.* biblioteca *f.*

libretto, *n.* libreto *m.*

license, *n.* licencia *f.;* permiso *m.*

licentious, *a.* licencioso.

lick, *v.* lamer.

licorice, *n.* regaliz *m.*

lid, *n.* tapa *f.*

lie, 1. *n.* mentira *f.* **2.** *v.* mentir. **l. down,** acostarse, echarse.

lieutenant, *n.* teniente *m.*

life, *n.* vida *f.*

lifeboat, *n.* bote salvavidas *m.*

life buoy, *n.* buya *f.*

life insurance, *n.* seguro de vida *m.*

lifeless, *a.* sin vida.

life preserver, *n.* salvavidas *m.*

life style, *n.* modo de vida *m.*

lift, *v.* levantar, alzar, elevar.

ligament, *n.* ligamento *m.*

ligature, *n.* ligadura *f.*

light, 1. *a.* ligero; liviano; (in color) claro. **2.** *n.* luz; candela *f.* **3.** *v.* encender; iluminar.

lighten, *v.* aligerar; aclarar; iluminar.

lighter, *n.* encendedor *m.*

lighthouse, *n.* faro *m.*

lightness, *n.* ligereza *f.*; agilidad *f.*

lightning, *n.* relámpago *m.*

like, 1. *a.* semejante. **2.** *prep.* como. **3.** *v.* **I like . . . me gusta, me gustan . . . I should like,** quisiera.

likeable, *a.* simpático, agradable.

likelihood, *n.* probabilidad *f.*

likely, *a.* probable; verosímil.

liken, *v.* comparar; asemejar.

likeness, *n.* semejanza *f.*

likewise, *adv.* igualmente.

lilac, *n.* lila *f.*

lilt, 1. *n.* cadencia alegre *f.* **2.** *v.* cantar alegremente.

lily, *n.* lirio *m.*

lily of the valley, *n.* muguete *m.*

limb, *n.* rama *f.*

limber, *a.* flexible. **to l. up,** ponerse flexible.

limbo, *n.* limbo *m.*

lime, *n.* cal *f.;* (fruit) limoncito *m.,* lima *f.*

limestone, *n.* piedra caliza *f.*

limewater, *n.* agua de cal *f.*

limit, 1. *n.* límite *m.* **2.** *v.* limitar.

limitation, *n.* limitación *f.*

limitless, *a.* ilimitado.

limousine, *n.* limousine *f.*

limp, 1. *n.* cojera *f.* **2.** *a.* flojo. **3.** *v.* cojear.

limpid, *a.* límpido.

line, 1. *n.* línea; fila; raya *f.;* (of print) renglón *m.* **2.** *v.* forrar; rayar.

lineage, *n.* linaje *m.*

lineal, *a.* lineal.

linear, *a.* linear, longitudinal.

linen, *n.* lienzo, lino *m.;* ropa blanca.

liner, *n.* vapor *m.*

linger, *v.* demorarse.

lingerie, *n.* ropa blanca *f.*

linguist, *n.* lingüista *m. & f.*

linguistic, *a.* lingüístico.

liniment, *n.* linimento *m.*

link, 1. *n.* eslabón; vínculo *m.* **2.** *v.* vincular.

linoleum, *n.* linóleo *m.*

linseed, *n.* linaza *f.;* simiente de lino *f.*

lint, *n.* hilacha *f.*

lion, *n.* león *m.*

lip, *n.* labio *m.*

lipstick, *n.* lápiz de labios.

liqueur, *n.* cordial *m.*

liquid, *a. & n.* líquido *m.*

liquidate, *v.* liquidar.

liquidation, *n.* liquidación *f.*

liquor, *n.* licor *m.*

lisp, 1. *n.* ceceo *m.* **2.** *v.* cecear.

list, 1. *n.* lista *f.* **2.** *v.* registrar.

listen (to), *v.* escuchar.

listless, *a.* indiferente.

litany, *n.* letanía *f.*

liter, *n.* litro *m.*

literal, *a.* literal.

literary, *a.* literario.

literate, *a.* literato.

literature, *n.* literatura *f.*

litigant, *n. & a.* litigante *m.*

litigation, *n.* litigio, pleito *m.*

litter, 1. *n.* litera *f.;* cama de paja. **2.** *v.* poner en desorden.

little, *a.* pequeño; (quantity) poco.

liturgical, *a.* litúrgico.

liturgy, *n.* liturgia *f.*

live, *1. a.* vivo. **2.** *v.* vivir.

livelihood, *n.* subsistencia *f.*

lively, *a.* vivo; rápido; animado.

liver, *n.* hígado *m.*

livery, *n.* librea *f.*

livestock, *n.* ganadería *f.*

livid, *a.* lívido.

living, *1. a.* vivo. **2.** *n.* sustento *m.* **to earn (make) a living,** ganarse la vida.

lizard, *n.* lagarto *m.,* lagartija *f.*

llama, *n.* llama *f.*

load, 1. *n.* carga *f.* **2.** *v.* cargar.

loaf, 1. *n.* pan *m.* **2.** *v.* holgazanear.

loam, *n.* marga *f.*

loan, 1. *n.* préstamo *m.* **2.** *v.* prestar.

loathe, *v.* aborrecer, detestar.

lobby, *n.* vestíbulo *m.*

lobe, *n.* lóbulo *m.*

lobster, *n.* langosta *f.*

local, *a.* local.

locale, *n.* localidad *f.*

locality, *n.* localidad *f.,* lugar *m.*

localize, *v.* localizar.

locate, *v.* situar; hallar.

location, *n.* sitio *m.;* posición *f.*

lock, 1. *n.* cerradura *f.;* (pl.) cabellos *m.pl.* **2.** *v.* cerrar con llave.

locker, *n.* cajón *m.;* ropero *m.*

locket, *n.* guardapelo *m.,* medallón *m.*

lockjaw, *n.* trismo *m.*

locksmith, *n.* cerrajero *m.*

locomotive, *n.* locomotora *f.*

locust, *n.* cigarra *f.,* saltamontes *m.*

locution, *n.* locución *f.*

lode, *n.* filón *m.,* vena *f.*

lodge, 1. *n.* logia; (inn) posada *f.* **2.** *v.* fijar; alojar, morar.

lodger, *n.* inquilino *m.*

lodging, *n.* posada *f.*

loft, *n.* piso *m.,* sobrado *m.*

lofty, *a.* alto; altivo.

log, *n.* tronco de árbol; (naut.) barquilla *f.*

loge, *n.* palco *m.*

logic, *n.* lógica *f.*

logical, *a.* lógico.

loin, *n.* lomo *m.*

loiter, *v.* haraganear.

lone, *a.* solitario.

loneliness, *n.* soledad *f.;* tristeza *f.*

lonely, lonesome, *a.* solo y triste.

lonesome, *a.* solitario; triste.

long, 1. *a.* largo. **a l. time,** mucho tiempo. **2.** *adv.* mucho tiempo. **how l.,** cuánto tiempo. **no longer,** ya no. **3.** *v.* **l. for,** anhelar.

longevity, *n.* longevidad *f.*

longing, *n.* anhelo *m.*

longitude, *n.* longitud *m.*

look, 1. *n.* mirada *f.;* aspecto *m.* **2.** *v.* parecer; mirar. **l. at,** mirar. **l. for,** buscar. **l. like,** parecerse a. **l. out!,** ¡cuidado! **l. up,** buscar; ir a ver, venir a ver.

looking glass, *n.* espejo *m.*

loom, 1. *n.* telar *m.* **2.** *v.* asomar.

loop, *n.* vuelta *f.*

loophole, *n.* abertura *f.,* mirador *m.*

loose, *a.* suelto; flojo.

loosen, *v.* soltar; aflojar.

loot, 1. *n.* botín *m.,* saqueo *m.* **2.** *v.* saquear.

lopsided, *a.* desequilibrado.

loquacious, *a.* locuaz.

lord, *n.* señor *m.;* (Brit. title) lord *m.*

lordship, *n.* señorío *m.*

lose, *v.* perder.

loss, *n.* pérdida *f.*

lost, *a.* perdido.

lot, *n.* suerte *f.* **building l.,** solar *m.* **a lot (of), lots of,** mucho.

lotion, *n.* loción *f.*

lottery, *n.* lotería *f.*

loud, *1. a.* fuerte; ruidoso. **2.** *adv.* alto.

loudspeaker, *n.* altavoz *m.*

lounge, *n.* sofá *m.;* salón de fumar *m.*

louse, *n.* piojo *m.*

love, 1. *n.* amor *m.* **in l.,** enamorado. **to fall in l.,** enamorarse. **2.** *v.* querer; amar; adorar.

lovely, *a.* hermoso.
lover, *n.* amante *m.*
low, *a.* bajo; vil.
lower, *v.* bajar; (in price) rebajar.
lowly, *a.* humilde.
loyal, *a.* leal, fiel.
loyalist, *n.* lealista *m. & f.*
loyalty, *n.* lealtad *f.*
lozenge, *n.* pastilla *f.*
lubricant, *n.* lubricante *m.*
lubricate, *v.* engrasar, lubricar.
lucid, *a.* claro, lúcido.
luck, *n.* suerte; fortuna *f.*
lucky, *a.* afortunado. **to be l.,** tener suerte.
lucrative, *a.* lucrativo.
ludicrous, *a.* ridículo.
luggage, *n.* equipaje *m.*
lukewarm, *a.* tibio.
lull, 1. *n.* momento de calma. 2. *v.* calmar.
lullaby, *n.* arrullo *m.*
lumbago, *n.* lumbago *m.*
lumber, *n.* madera *f.*
luminous, *a.* luminoso.
lump, *n.* protuberancia *f.;* (of sugar) terrón *m.*
lunacy, *n.* locura *f.*
lunar, *a.* lunar.
lunatic, *a. & n.* loco -ca.
lunch, luncheon, 1. *n.* merienda *f.,* almuerzo *m.* 2. *v.* merendar, almorzar.
lung, *n.* pulmón *m.*
lunge, 1. *n.* estocada *f.* 2. *v.* dar un estocada.
lure, *v.* atraer.
lurid, *a.* rojizo; fantástico.
lurk, *v.* esconderse; espiar.
luscious, *a.* sabroso, delicioso.
lust, *n.* sensualidad; codicia *f.*
luster, *n.* lustre *m.*
lustful, *a.* sensual, lascivo.
lusty, *a.* vigoroso.
lute, *n.* laúd *m.*
Lutheran, *n. & a.* luterano *m.*
luxuriant, *a.* exuberante, frondoso.
luxurious, *a.* lujoso.
luxury, *n.* lujo *m.*
lying, *a.* mentiroso.
lymph, *n.* linfa *f.*
lynch, *v.* linchar.
lyre, *n.* lira *f.*
lyric, *a.* lírico.
lyricism, *n.* lirismo *m.*

M

macabre, *a.* macabre.
macaroni, *n.* macarrones *m.*
machine, *n.* máquina *f.*
machine gun, *n.* ametralladora *f.*
machinery, *n.* maquinaria *f.*
machinist, *n.* maquinista, mecánico *m.*
macho, *a.* machista.
mackerel, *n.* escombro *m.*
mad, *a.* loco; furioso.
madam, *n.* señora *f.*
mafia, *n.* mafia *f.*
magazine, *n.* revista *f.*

magic, 1. *a.* mágico. 2. *n.* magia *f.*
magician, *n.* mágico *m.*
magistrate, *n.* magistrado *m.*
magnanimous, *a.* magnánimo.
magnate, *n.* magnate *m.*
magnesium, *n.* magnesio *m.*
magnet, *n.* imán *m.*
magnetic, *a.* magnético.
magnificence, *n.* magnificencia *f.*
magnificent, *a.* magnífico.
magnify, *v.* magnificar.
magnitude, *n.* magnitud *f.*
mahogany, *n.* caoba *f.*
maid, *n.* criada *f.* **old m.,** soltera *f.*
maiden, *a.* soltero.
mail, 1. *n.* correo *m.* **air m.,** correo aéreo. **by return m.,** a vuelta de correo. 2. *v.* echar al correo.
mailbox, *n.* buzón *m.*
mailman, *n.* cartero *m.*
maim, *v.* multilar.
main, *a.* principal.
mainframe, *n.* componente central de una computadora.
mainland, *n.* continente *m.*
maintain, *v.* mantener; sostener.
maintenance, *n.* mantenimiento; sustento *m.;* conservación *f.*
maize, *n.* maíz *m.*
majestic, *a.* majestuoso.
majesty, *n.* majestad *f.*
major, 1. *a.* mayor. 2. *n.* (mil.) comandante *m.;* (study) especialidad *f.*
majority, *n.* mayoría *f.*
make, 1. *n.* marca *f.* 2. *v.* hacer; fabricar; (earn) ganar.
maker, *n.* fabricante *m.*
makeshift, *a.* provisional.
make-up, *n.* cosméticos *m.pl.*
malady, *n.* mal *m.,* enfermedad *f.*
mals.ia, *n.* paludismo *m.*
male, *a. & n.* macho *m.*
malevolent, *a.* malévolo.
malice, *n.* malicia *f.*
malicious, *a.* malicioso.
malign, 1. *v.* difamar. 2. *a.* maligno.
malignant, *a.* maligno.
malnutrition, *n.* desnutrición *f.*
malt, *n.* malta *m. & f.*
mammal, *n.* mamífero *m.*
man, *n.* hombre; varón *m.*
manage, *v.* manejar; dirigir; administrar; arreglárselas. **m. to,** lograr.
management, *n.* dirección, administración *f.*
manager, *n.* director *m.*
mandate, *n.* mandato *m.*
mandatory, *a.* obligatorio.
mandolin, *n.* mandolina *f.*
mane, *n.* crines *f.*
maneuver, 1. *n.* maniobra *f.* 2. *v.* maniobrar.
manganese, *n.* manganeso *m.*
manger, *n.* pesebre *m.*

mangle, 1. *n.* planchadora mecánica. 2. *v.* mutilar.
manhood, *n.* virilidad *f.*
mania, *n.* manía *f.*
maniac, *a. & n.* maniático *m.*
manicure, *n.* manicuro *m.*
manifest, 1. *a. & n.* manifiesto *m.* 2. *v.* manifestar.
manifesto, *n.* manifesto *m.*
manifold, 1. *a.* muchos. 2. *n.* (auto.) tubo múltiple.
manipulate, *v.* manipular.
mankind, *n.* humanidad *f.*
manly, *a.* varonil.
manner, *n.* manera *f.,* modo *m.* **manners,** modales *m.pl.*
mannerism, *n.* manerismo *m.*
mansion, *n.* mansión *f.*
mantel, *n.* manto de chimenea.
mantle, *n.* manto *m.*
manual, *a. & n.* manual *m.*
manufacture, *v.* fabricar.
manufacturer, *n.* fabricante *m.*
manufacturing, *n.* fabricación *f.*
manure, *n.* abono, estiércol *m.*
manuscript, *n.* manuscrito *m.*
many, *a.* muchos. **how m.,** so m., tantos. **too m.,** demasiados, cuántos. **as m. as,** tantos como.
map, *n.* mapa *m.*
maple, *n.* arce *m.*
mar, *v.* estropear; desfigurar.
marble, *n.* mármol *m.*
march, 1. *n.* marcha *f.* 2. *v.* marchar.
mare, *n.* yegua *f.*
margarine, *n.* margarina *f.*
margin, *n.* margen *m. or f.*
marijuana, *n.* marijuana *f.*
marine, 1. *a.* marino. 2. *n.* soldado de marina.
mariner, *n.* marinero *m.*
marionette, *n.* marioneta *f.*
marital, *a.* marital.
maritime, *a.* marítimo.
mark, 1. *n.* marca *f.* 2. *v.* marcar.
market, *n.* mercado *m.* **meat m.,** carnicería *f.* **stock m.,** bolsa *f.*
marmalade, *n.* mermelada *f.*
maroon, *a. & n.* color rojo oscuro.
marquis, *n.* marqués *m.*
marriage, *n.* matrimonio *m.*
married, *a.* casado. **to get m.,** casarse.
marrow, *n.* medula *f.;* substancia *f.*
marry, *v.* casarse con; casar.
marsh, *n.* pantano *m.*
marshal, *n.* mariscal *m.*
marshmallow, *n.* malvarisco *m.;* bombón de altea *m.*
martial, *a.* marcial. **m. law,** gobierno militar.
martyr, *n.* mártir *m. & f.*
martyrdom, *n.* martirio *m.*
marvel, 1. *n.* maravilla *f.* 2. *v.* maravillarse.
marvelous, *a.* maravilloso.
mascot, *n.* mascota *f.*
masculine, *a.* masculino.

mash, v. majar. mashed pota-toes, puré de papas m.

mask, n. máscara f.

mason, n. albañil m.

masquerade, n. mascarada f.

mass, n. masa f.; (rel.) misa f. to say m., cantar misa. m. production, producción en serie.

massacre, 1. n. carnicería, matanza f. 2. v. matar atrozmente, destrozar.

massage, n. masaje m.; soba f. 2. v. sobar.

masseur, n. masajista m. & f.

massive, a. macizo, sólido.

mast, n. palo, árbol m.

master, 1. n. amo; maestro m. 2. v. domar, dominar.

masterpiece, n. obra maestra.

mastery, n. maestría f.

mat, 1. n. estera; palleta f. 2. v. enredar.

match, 1. n. igual m; fósforo m.; (sport) partida, contienda f.; (marriage) noviazgo; casamiento. 2. v. ser igual a; igualar.

mate, 1. n. consorte m. & f.; compañero -ra. 2. v. igualar; casar.

material, a. & n. material m. raw materials, materias primas.

materialism, n. materialismo m.

materialize, v. materializar.

maternal, a. materno.

maternity, n. maternidad f.

mathematical, a. matemático.

mathematics, n. matemáticas f.pl.

matinee, n. matiné m.

matrimony, n. matrimonio m.

matron, n. matrona; directora f.

matter, 1. n. materia f.; asunto m. what's the m.?, ¿qué pasa? 2. v. importar.

mattress, n. colchón m.

mature, 1. a. maduro. 2. v. madurar.

maturity, n. madurez f.

maudlin, a. sentimental en exceso; peneque.

maul, v. maltratar a golpes.

maxim, n. máxima f.

maximum, a. & n. máximo.

may, v. poder.

May, n. mayo m.

maybe, adv. quizá, quizás, tal vez.

mayonnaise, n. mayonesa f.

mayor, n. alcalde m.

maze, n. laberinto m.

me, pron. mí; me. with me, conmigo.

meadow, n. prado m.; vega f.

meager, a. magro; pobre.

meal, n. comida; (flour) harina f.

mean, 1. a. bajo; malo. 2. n. medio (see also means). 3. v. significar; querer decir.

meaning, n. sentido, significado m.

means, n.pl. medios, recursos. by all m., sin falta. by no m., de ningún modo. by m. of, por medio de.

meanwhile, adv. mientras tanto.

measles, n. sarampión m.

measure, 1. n. medida f.; (music) compás m. 2. v. medir.

measurement, n. medida, dimensión f.

meat, n. carne f.

mechanic, n. mecánico m.

mechanical, a. mecánico.

mechanism, n. mecanismo m.

mechanize, v. mecanizar.

medal, n. medalla f.

meddle, v. meterse, entremeterse.

mediate, v. mediar.

medical, a. médico.

medicine, n. medicina f.

medieval, a. medioeval.

mediocre, a. mediocre.

mediocrity, n. mediocridad f.

meditate, v. meditar.

meditation, n. meditación f.

Mediterranean, n. Mediterráneo m.

medium, 1. a. mediano, medio. 2. n. medio m.

medley, n. mezcla f., ensalada f.

meek, a. manso; humilde.

meekness, n. modestia; humildad f.

meet, 1. a. propio. 2. n. concurso m. 3. v. encontrar; reunirse; conocer.

meeting, n. reunión f.; mitin m.

megahertz, n. megahertzio m.

megaphone, n. megáfono m.

melancholy, 1. a. melancólico. 2. n. melancolía f.

mellow, a. suave; blando; maduro.

melodious, a. melodioso.

melodrama, n. melodrama f.

melody, n. melodía f.

melon, n. melón m.

melt, v. derretir.

meltdown, n. fundición resultante de un accidente en un reactor nuclear.

member, n. socio -ia; miembro m.

membership, n. membrecía f.

membrane, n. membrana f.

memento, n. recuerdo m.

memoir, n. memoria f.

memorable, a. memorable.

memorandum, n. memorándum, volante m.

memorial, 1. a. conmemorativo. 2. n. memorial m.

memorize, v. aprender de memoria.

memory, n. memoria f.; recuerdo m.

menace, 1. n. amenaza f. 2. v. amenazar.

mend, v. reparar, remendar.

menial, 1. a. servil. 2. n. sirviente m.

menopause, n. menopausia f.

menstruation, n. menstruación f.

menswear, n. ropa de caballeros f.

mental, a. mental.

mentality, n. mentalidad f.

menthol, n. mentol m.

mention, 1. n. mención f. 2. v. mencionar.

menu, n. menú m., lista f.

mercantile, a. mercantil.

mercenary, a. & n. mercenario -ria.

merchandise, n. mercancía f.

merchant, 1. a. mercante. 2. n. comerciante m.

merciful, a. misericordioso, compasivo.

merciless, a. cruel, inhumano.

mercury, n. mercurio m.

mercy, n. misericordia; merced f.

mere, a. mero, puro.

merely, adv. solamente; simplemente.

merge, v. unir, combinar.

merger, n. consolidación, fusión.

meringue, n. merengue m.

merit, 1. n. mérito m. 2. v. merecer.

meritorious, a. meritorio.

mermaid, n. sirena f.

merriment, n. regocijo m.

merry, a. alegre, festivo.

merry-go-round, n. caballitos m.

mesh, n. malla f.

mess, 1. n. lío m.; confusión f.; (mil.) salón comedor, rancho m. 2. v. m. up, ensuciar; enredar.

message, n. mensaje, recado m.

messenger, n. mensajero -ra.

messy, a. confuso, desarreglado.

metabolism, n. metabolismo m.

metal, n. metal m.

metallic, a. metálico.

metaphysics, n. metafísica f.

meteor, n. meteoro m.

meteorology, n. meteorología f.

meter, n. medidor; (measure) metro m.

method, n. método m.

meticulous, a. meticuloso.

metric, a. métrico.

metropolis, n. metrópoli f.

metropolitan, a. metropolitano.

Mexican, a. & n. mexicano -.

Mexico, n. México m.

mezzanine, n. entresuelo m.

microbe, n. microbio m.

microfiche, n. microficha f.

microfilm, n. microfilm m.

microform, n. microforma f.

microphone, n. micrófono m.

microscope, n. microscopio m.
microscopic, a. microscópico.
mid, a. medio.
middle, a. & n. medio m. **in the m. of,** en medio de, a mediados de.
middle-aged, a. de edad madura.
Middle East, n. Medio Oriente m.
midget, n. enano -na.
midnight, n. medianoche f.
midwife, n. partera f.
might, n. poder m., fuerza f.
mighty, a. poderoso.
migraine, n. migraña f.; jaqueca f.
migrate, v. emigrar.
migration, n. emigración f.
migratory, a. migratorio.
mild, a. moderado, suave; templado.
mildew, n. añublo m., moho m.
mile, n. milla f.
militant, a. militante.
militarism, n. militarismo m.
military, a. militar.
militia, n. milicia f.
milk, 1. n. leche f. **2.** v. ordeñar.
milkman, n. lechero m.
milky, a. lácteo; lechoso.
mill, 1. n. molino m.; fábrica f. **2.** v. moler.
miller, n. molinero m.
millimeter, n. milímetro m.
milliner, n. modista m. & f.
millinery, n. sombrerería f.
million, n. millón m.
millionaire, n. millonario -ria.
mimic, 1. n. mimo m. **2.** v. imitar.
mind, 1. n. mente; opinión f. **2.** v. obedecer. **never m.,** no se ocupe.
mindful, a. atento.
mine, 1. pron. mío. **2.** n. mina f. **3.** v. minar.
miner, n. minero m.
mineral, n. & a. mineral m.
mine sweeper, n. dragaminas f.
mingle, v. mezclar.
miniature, n. miniatura f.
miniaturize, v. miniaturizar.
minimize, v. menospreciar.
minimum, a. & n. mínimo m.
mining, n. minería f.
minister, 1. n. ministro; (rel.) pastor m. **2.** v. ministrar.
ministry, n. ministerio m.
mink, n. visón m.; (fur) piel de visón m.
minor, 1. a. menor. **2.** n. menor de edad.
minority, n. minoría f.
minstrel, n. juglar m.
mint, 1. n. menta f.; casa de moneda. **2.** v. acuñar.
minus, prep. menos.
minute, 1. a. minucioso. **2.** n. minuto, momento m.
miracle, n. milagro m.
miraculous, a. milagroso.
mirage, n. miraje m.
mire, n. lodo m.

mirror, n. espejo m.
mirth, n. alegría; risa f.
misbehave, v. portarse mal.
miscellaneous, a. misceláneo.
mischief, n. travesura, diablura f.
mischievous, a. travieso, dañino.
miser, n. avaro -ra.
miserable, a. miserable; infeliz.
miserly, a. avariento, tacaño.
misfortune, n. desgracia f., infortunio, revés m.
misgiving, n. recelo m., desconfianza f.
mishap, n. desgracia f., contratiempo m.
mislead, v. extraviar, despistar; pervertir.
misplaced, a. extraviado.
mispronounce, v. pronunciar mal.
miss, 1. n. señorita f. **2.** v. perder; echar de menos, extrañar. **be missing,** faltar.
missile, n. proyectil m.
mission, n. misión; comisión f.
missionary, n. misionero -ra.
mist, n. niebla, bruma f.
mistake, 1. n. equivocación f.; error m. **to make a m.,** equivocarse.
mistaken, a. equivocado.
mister, n. señor m.
mistletoe, n. muérdago m.
mistreat, v. maltratar.
mistress, n. ama; señora; concubina f.
mistrust, v. desconfiar; sospechar.
misty, a. nebuloso, brumoso.
misunderstand, v. entender mal.
misuse, v. maltratar; abusar.
mite, n. pizca f., blanca f.
mitten, n. mitón, confortante m.
mix, v. mezclar. **m. up,** confundir.
mixture, n. mezcla, mixtura f.
mix-up, n. confusión f.
moan, 1. n. quejido, gemido m. **2.** v. gemir.
mob, n. muchedumbre f.; gentío m.
mobilization, n. movilización f.
mobilize, v. movilizar.
mock, v. burlar.
mockery, n. burla f.
mod, a. a la última; en boga.
mode, n. modo m.
model, 1. n. modelo m. **2.** v. modelar.
moderate, 1. a. moderado. **2.** v. moderar.
moderation, n. moderación; sobriedad f.
modern, a. moderno.
modernize, v. modernizar.
modest, a. modesto.
modesty, n. modestia f.
modify, v. modificar.
modulate, v. modular.
moist, a. húmedo.

moisten, v. humedecer.
moisture, n. humedad f.
molar, n. molar m.
molasses, n. molaza f.
mold, 1. n. molde; moho m. **2.** v. moldar, formar; enmohecerse.
moldy, a. mohoso.
mole, n. lunar m.; (animal) topo m.
molecule, n. molécula f.
molest, v. molestar.
mollify, v. molificar.
moment, n. momento m.
momentary, a. momentáneo.
momentous, a. importante.
monarch, n. monarca m.
monarchy, n. monarquía f.
monastery, n. monasterio m.
Monday, n. lunes m.
monetary, a. monetario.
money, n. dinero m. **m. order,** giro postal.
mongrel, 1. n. mestizo m. **2.** a. mestizo, cruzado.
monitor, n. amonestador m.
monk, n. monje m.
monkey, n. mono -na.
monocle, n. monóculo m.
monologue, n. monólogo m.
monopolize, v. monopolizar.
monopoly, n. monopolio m.
monosyllable, n. monosílabo m.
monotone, n. monotonía f.
monotonous, a. monótono.
monotony, n. monotonía f.
monsoon, n. monzón m.
monster, n. monstruo m.
monstrosity, n. monstruosidad f.
monstrous, a. monstruoso.
month, n. mes m.
monthly, a. mensual.
monument, n. momumento m.
monumental, a. monumental.
mood, n. humor m.; (gram.) modo m.
moody, a. caprichoso, taciturno.
moon, n. luna f.
moonlight, n. luz de la luna.
moor, 1. n. párano m. **2.** v. anclar.
mop, 1. n. estropajo m. **2.** v. fregar.
moped (vehicle), n. velomotor m.
moral, 1. a. moral. **2.** n. moraleja f. **morals,** moralidad f.
morale, n. espíritu m.
moralist, n. moralista m. & f.
morality, n. moralidad, ética f.
morbid, a. mórbido.
more, a. & adv. más. **m. and m.,** cada vez más.
moreover, adv. además.
morgue, n. necrocomio m.
morning, n. mañana f. **good m.,** buenos días.
morose, a. malhumorado.
morphine, n. morfina f.
morsel, n. bocado m.
mortal, a. & n. mortal m.
mortality, n. mortalidad f.

mortar, n. mortero m.
mortgage, 1. n. hipoteca f. **2.** v. hipotecar.
mortify, v. mortificar.
mosaic, n. & a. mosaico m.
mosquito, n. mosquito m.
moss, n. musgo m.
most, 1. a. más. **2.** adv. más; sumamente. **3.** pron. **m. of,** la mayor parte de.
mostly, adv. principalmente; en su mayor parte.
moth, n. polilla f.
mother, n. madre f.
mother-in-law, n. suegra f.
motif, n. tema m.
motion, 1. n. moción f.; movimiento m. **2.** v. hacer señas.
motionless, a. inmóvil.
motion picture, n. película f.
motivate, v. motivar.
motive, n. motivo m.
motor, n. motor m.
motorboat, n. bote de gasolina.
motorcycle, n. motocicleta f.
motorist, n. motorista m. & f.
motto, n. lema m.
mound, n. terrón; montón m.
mount, 1. n. monte m.; (horse) montura f. **2.** v. montar; subir.
mountain, n. montaña f.
mountaineer, n. montañés m.
mountainous, a. montañoso.
mourn, v. lamentar, llorar; llevar luto.
mournful, a. triste.
mourning, n. luto; lamento m.
mouse, n. ratón, ratoncito m.
mouth, n. boca f.; (of river) desembocadura f.
movable, a. movible, movedizo.
move, 1. n. movimiento m.; mudanza f. **2.** v. mover; mudarse; emocionar conmover. **m. away,** quitar; alejarse; mudarse.
movement, n. movimiento m.
movie, n. película f. **m. theater, movies,** cine m.
moving, a. conmovedor; persuasivo.
mow, v. guadañar, segar.
Mr., title. Señor (Sr.).
Mrs., title. Señora (Sra.).
much, a. & adv. mucho. **how m.,** cuánto. **so m.,** tanto. **too m.,** demasiado. **as m. as,** tanto como.
mucilage, n. mucílago m.
mucous, a. mucoso.
mucous membrane, n. mucosa f.
mud, n. fango, lodo m.
muddy, 1. a. lodoso; turbio. **2.** v. ensuciar; enturbiar.
muff, n. manguito m.
muffin, n. panecillo m.
mug, n. cubilete m.
mulatto, n. mulato m.
mule, n. mula f.
mullah, n. mullah m.
multinational, a. multinacional.

multiple, a. múltiple.
multiplication, n. multiplicación f.
multiplicity, n. multiplicidad f.
multiply, v. multiplicar.
multitude, n. multitud f.
mummy, n. momia f.
mumps, n. poperas f.pl.
municipal, a. municipal.
munificent, a. munífico.
munition, n. municiones m.
mural, a. & n. mural m.
murder, 1. n. asesinato; homicidio m. **2.** v. asesinar.
murderer, n. asesino -na.
murmur, 1. n. murmullo m. **2.** v. murmurar.
muscle, n. músculo m.
muscular, a. muscular.
muse, 1. n. musa f. **2.** v. meditar.
museum, n. museo m.
mushroom, n. seta f., hongo m.
music, n. música f.
musical, a. musical; melodioso.
musician, n. músico m.
muslin, n. muselina f., percal m.
must, v. deber; tener que.
mustache, n. bigotes m.pl.
mustard, n. mostaza f.
muster, 1. n. (mil.) revista f. **2.** v. agregar.
mute, a. & n. mudo m.
mutilate, v. mutilar.
mutiny, 1. n. motín f. **2.** amotinarse.
mutter, v. refunfuñar, gruñir.
mutton, n. carnero m.
mutual, a. mutuo.
muzzle, 1. n. hocico m.; bozal m. **2.** v. embozar.
my, a. mi.
myriad, n. miríada f.
myrtle, n. mirto m.
myself, pron. mí, mí mismo; me. **I m.,** yo mismo.
mysterious, a. misterioso.
mystery, n. misterio m.
mystic, a. místico.
mystify, v. confundir.
myth, n. mito m.
mythical, a. mítico.
mythology, n. mitología f.

N

nag, 1. n. jaca f. **2.** v. regañar; sermonear.
nail, 1. n. clavo m.; (finger) uña f. **2.** v. clavar.
naïve, a. ingenuo.
naked, a. desnudo.
name, 1. n. nombre m.; reputación f. **2.** v. nombrar, mencionar.
namely, adv. a saber; es decir.
namesake, n. tocayo m.
nap, n. siesta f. **to take a n.,** echar una siesta.
naphtha, n. nafta f.
napkin, n. servilleta f.
narcissus, n. narciso m.

narcotic, a. & n. narcótico m.
narrate, v. narrar.
narrative, 1. a. narrativo. **2.** n. cuento, relato m.
narrow, a. estrecho, angosto. **n.-minded,** intolerante.
nasal, a. nasal.
nasty, a. desagradable; antipático.
nation, n. nación f.
national, a. nacional.
nationalism, n. nacionalismo m.
nationality, n. nacionalidad f.
nationalization, n. nacionalización f.
nationalize, v. nacionalizar.
native, 1. a. nativo. **2.** n. natural; indígena m. & f.
nativity, n. natividad f.
natural, a. natural.
naturalist, n. naturalista m.
naturalize, v. naturalizar.
naturalness, n. naturalidad f.
nature, n. naturaleza f.; índole f.; humor m.
naughty, a. travieso, desobediente.
nausea, n. náusea f.
nauseous, a. nauseoso.
nautical, a. náutico.
naval, a. naval.
nave, n. nave f.
navel, n. ombligo m.
navigable, a. navegable.
navigate, v. navegar.
navigation, n. navegación f.
navigator, n. navegante m.
navy, n. marina f.
near, 1. a. cercano, próximo. **2.** adv. cerca. **3.** prep. cerca de.
nearby, 1. a. cercano. **2.** adv. cerca.
nearly, adv. casi.
nearsighted, a. corto de vista.
neat, a. aseado; ordenado.
neatness, n. aseo m.
nebulous, a. nebuloso.
necessary, a. necesario.
necessity, n. necesidad f.
neck, n. cuello m.
necklace, n. collar m.
necktie, n. corbata f.
nectar, n. néctar m.
need, 1. n. necesidad; (poverty) pobreza f. **2.** v. necesitar.
needle, n. aguja f.
needless, a. innecesario, inútil.
needy, a. indigente, necesitado, pobre.
nefarious, a. nefario.
negative, 1. a. negativo. **2.** n. negativa f.
neglect, 1. n. negligencia f.; descuido m. **2.** v. descuidar.
negligee, n. negligee m., bata de casa f.
negligent, a. negligente, descuidado.
negligible, a. insignificante.
negotiate, v. negociar.
negotiation, n. negociación f.
Negro, n. negro -ra.
neighbor, n. vecino -na.

neighborhood, n. vecindad f.
neither, 1. a. & pron. ninguno de los dos. **2.** adv. tampoco. **3.** conj. **neither . . . nor,** ni . . . ni.
neon, n. neón m. **n. light,** tubo neón m.
nephew, n. sobrino m.
nerve, n. nervio m.; (coll.) audacia f.
nervous, a. nervioso.
nest, n. nido m.
net, 1. a. neto. **2.** n. red f. **hair n.,** albanega f. **3.** redar; (com.) ganar.
netting, n. red m.; obra de malla f.
network, n. (radio) red radio-difusora.
neuralgia, n. neuralgia f.
neurology, n. neurología f.
neurotic, a. neurótico.
neutral, a. neutral.
neutrality, n. neutralidad f.
neutron, n. neutrón m.
neutron bomb, bomba de neutrones f.
never, adv. nunca, jamás; **n. mind,** no importa.
nevertheless, adv. no obstante, sin embargo.
new, a. nuevo.
news, n. noticias f.pl.
newsboy, n. vendedor de periódicos.
newspaper, n. periódico m.
New Testament, n. Nuevo Testamento m.
new year, n. año nuevo m.
next, 1. a. próximo; siguiente; contiguo. **2.** adv. luego, después. **n. door,** al lado. **n. to,** al lado de.
nibble, v. picar.
nice, a. simpático, agradable; amable; hermoso; exacto.
nick, n. muesca f., picadura f. **in the n. of time,** apunto.
nickel, n. níquel m.
nickname, 1. n. apodo, mote m. **2.** v. apodar.
nicotine, n. nicotina f.
niece, n. sobrina f.
niggardly, a. mezquino.
night, n. noche f. **good n.,** buenas noches. **last n.,** anoche. **n. club,** cabaret m.
nightclub, n. cabaret m.
nightgown, n. camisa de dormir.
nightingale, n. ruiseñor m.
nightly, adv. todas las noches.
nightmare, n. pesadilla f.
nimble, a. ágil.
nine, a. & pron. nueve.
nineteen, a. & pron. diecinueve.
ninety, a. & pron. noventa.
ninth, a. noveno.
nipple, n. teta f.; pezón m.
nitrogen, n. nitrógeno m.
no, 1. a. ninguno. **no one,** nadie. **2.** adv. no.
nobility, n. nobleza f.
noble, a. & n. noble m.

nobleman, n. noble m.
nobody, pron. nadie.
nocturnal, a. nocturno.
nocturne, n. nocturno f.
nod, 1. n. seña con la cabeza. **2.** v. inclinar la cabeza; (doze) dormitar.
no-frills, a. sin extras.
noise, n. ruido m.
noiseless, a. silencioso.
noisy, a. ruidoso.
nominal, a. nominal.
nominate, v. nombrar.
nomination, n. nombramiento m., nominación f.
nominee, n. nombrado m.
nonaligned (in political sense), a. no alineado.
nonchalant, a. indiferente.
noncombatant, n. no combatiente m.
noncommittal, a. evasivo; reservado.
nondescript, a. difícil de describir.
none, pron. ninguno.
nonentity, n. nulidad f.
nonpartisan, a. sin afiliación.
non-proliferation, n. no proliferación m.
nonsense, n. tontería f.
noodle, n. fideo m.
noon, n. mediodía m.
noose, n. lazo corredizo m.; dogal m.
nor, conj. ni.
normal, a. normal.
north, n. norte m.
North America, n. Norte América f.
North American, a. & n. norteamericano -na.
northeast, n. nordeste m.
northern, a. septentrional.
North Pole, n. polo norte m.
northwest, n. noroeste m.
Norway, n. Noruega f.
Norwegian, a. & n. noruego -ga.
nose, n. nariz f.
nostalgia, n. nostalgia f.
nostril, n. ventana de la nariz; (pl.) narices.
not, adv. no. **no. at all,** de ninguna manera. **n. even,** ni siquiera.
notable, a. notable.
notary, n. notario m.
notation, a. notación f.
notch, n. muesca f.; corte m.
note, 1. n. nota f.; apunte m. **2.** v. notar.
notebook, n. libreta f., cuaderno m.
noted, a. célebre.
notepaper, n. papel de notas m.
noteworthy, a. notable.
nothing, pron. nada.
notice, 1. n. aviso m.; noticia f. **2.** v. observar, fijarse en.
noticeable, a. notable.
notification, n. notificación f.
notify, v. notificar.

notion, n. noción f.; idea f.; (p) novedades f.pl.
notoriety, n. notoriedad f.
notorious, a. notorio.
noun, n. nombre, sustantivo
nourish, v. nutrir, alimentar.
nourishment, n. nutrimen alimento m.
novel, 1. a. nuevo, original. n. novela f.
novelist, n. novelista m. & f.
novelty, n. novedad f.
November, n. noviembre m.
novena, n. novena f.
novice, n. novicio -cia, nova -ta.
Novocaine, n. novocaína f.
now, adv. ahora. **n. and the** de vez en cuando. **by n., y** **from n. on,** de ahora en ad lante. **just n.,** ahorita. **right** ahora mismo.
nowhere, adv. en ningu parte.
nozzle, n. boquilla f.
nuance, n. matiz m.
nuclear, a. nuclear.
nuclear warhead, cabeza n clear f.
nuclear waste, desechos n cleares m.pl.
nucleus, n. núcleo m.
nude, a. desnudo.
nuisance, n. molestia f.
nuke, n. armamento o react nuclear.
nullify, v. anular.
number, 1. n. número m.; cif f. **license n.,** matrícula f. **2.** numerar, contar.
numerical, a. numérico.
numerous, a. numeroso.
nun, n. monja f.
nuptial, a. nupcial.
nurse, 1. n. enfermera (child's) ama, niñera f. **2.** criar, alimentar, amamant cuidar.
nursery, n. cuarto destinad los niños; (agr.) plantel, cr dero m.
nurture, v. nutrir.
nut, n. nuez f.; (mech.) tuen f.
nutrition, n. nutrición f.
nutritious, a. nutritivo.
nylon, n. nilón m.
nymph, n. ninfa f.

O

oak, n. roble m.
oar, n. remo m.
oasis, n. oasis m.
oat, n. avena f.
oath, n. juramento m.
oatmeal, n. harina de avena
obedience, n. obediencia f.
obedient, a. obediente.
obese, a. obeso, gordo.
obey, v. obedecer.
obituary, n. obituario m.
object, 1. n. objeto m.; (gra

complemento m. 2. v. oponerse; objectar.

objection, n. objección f.

objectionable, a. censurable.

objective, a. & n. objetivo m.

obligation, n. obligación f.

obligatory, a. obligatorio.

oblige, v. obligar; complacer.

oblique, a. oblicuo.

obliterate, v. borrar; destruir.

oblivion, n. olvido m.

oblong, a. oblongo.

obnoxious, a. ofensivo, odioso.

obscene, a. obsceno, indecente.

obscure, 1. a. obscuro. 2. v. obscurecer.

observance, n. observancia; ceremonia f.

observation, n. observación f.

observatory, n. observatorio m.

observe, v. observar; celebrar.

observer, n. observador -ra.

obsession, n. obsesión f.

obsolete, a. anticuado.

obstacle, n. obstáculo m.

obstetrician, n. obstétrico m.

obstinate, a. obstinado, terco.

obstruct, v. obstruir, impedir.

obstruction, n. obstrucción f.

obtain, v. obtener, conseguir.

obtuse, a. obtuso.

obviate, v. obviar.

obvious, a. evidente, obvio.

occasion, 1. n. ocasión f. 2. v. ocasionar.

occasional, a. ocasional.

occult, a. oculto.

occupant, n. ocupante m.; inquilino -na.

occupation, n. ocupación f.; empleo m.

occupy, v. ocupar; emplear.

occur, v. ocurrir.

occurrence, n. ocurrencia f.

ocean, n. océano m.

o'clock: it's one o., es la una. it's two o., son las dos, etc. at . . . o., a las . . .

octagon, n. octágono m.

octave, n. octava f.

October, n. octubre m.

octopus, n. pulpo m.

oculist, n. oculista m.

odd, a. impar; suelto; raro.

odious, a. odioso.

odor, n. olor m.; fragancia f.

of, prep. de.

off, adv. (see under verb: stop off, take off, etc.)

offend, v. ofender.

offender, n. ofensor -ra; delincuente m.

offense, n. ofensa f.; crimen m.

offensive, 1. a. ofensivo. 2. n. ofensiva f.

offer, 1. n. oferta f. 2. v. ofrecer.

offering, n. oferta f.

office, n. oficina f.; despacho m.; oficio, cargo m.

officer, n. oficial m. police o., agente de policía.

official, 1. a. oficial. 2. n. oficial, funcionario m.

officiate, v. oficiar.

officious, a. oficioso.

offspring, n. hijos m.pl.; progenie f.

often, adv. muchas veces, a menudo. how o., con qué frecuencia.

oil, 1. n. aceite m.; óleo; petróleo m. 2. v. aceitar; engrasar.

oily, a. aceitoso.

ointment, n. ungüento m.

okay, adv. bien; de acuerdo.

old, a. viejo; antiguo. o. man, o. woman, viejo -ja.

old-fashioned, a. fuera de moda.

Old Testament, n. Antiguo Testamento m.

olive, n. aceituna, oliva f.

ombudsman, n. ombudsman m.

omelet, n. tortilla de huevos.

omen, n. agüero m.

ominous, a. ominoso, siniestro.

omission, n. omisión f.; olvido m.

omit, v. omitir.

omnibus, n. ómnibus m.

omnipotent, a. omnipotente.

on, prep. en, sobre, encima de. 2. adv. adelante.

once, adv. una vez. at o., en seguida. o. in a while, de vez en cuando.

one, a. & pron. uno.

oneself, pron. sí mismo; se. with o., consigo.

onion, n. cebolla f.

only, 1. a. único, solo. 2. adv. sólo, solamente.

onward, adv. adelante.

opal, n. ópalo m.

opaque, a. opaco.

open, 1. a. abierto; franco. o. air, aire libre. 2. v. abrir.

opening, n. abertura f.

opera, n. ópera f. o. glasses, anteojos de ópera; gemelos m.pl.

operate, v. operar.

operation, n. operación f. to have an o., operarse, ser operado.

operative, a. eficaz, operativo.

operator, n. operario -ria. elevator o., ascensorista m. & f. telephone o., telefonista m. & f.

operetta, n. opereta f.

ophthalmic, a. oftálmico.

opinion, n. opinión f.

opponent, n. antagonista m. & f.

opportunism, n. oportunismo m.

opportunity, n. ocasión, oportunidad f.

oppose, v. oponer.

opposite, 1. a. opuesto, contrario. 2. prep. al frente de. 3. n. contrario m.

opposition, n. oposición f.

oppress, v. oprimir.

oppression, n. opresión f.

oppressive, a. opresivo.

optic, a. óptico.

optician, n. óptico m.

optics, n. óptica f.

optimism, n. optimismo.

optimistic, a. optimista.

option, n. opción, elección f.

optional, a. discrecional, facultativo.

optometry, n. optometría f.

opulent, a. opulento.

or, conj. o, (before o-, ho-) u.

oracle, n. oráculo m.

oral, a. oral, vocal.

orange, n. naranja f.

oration, n. discurso m.; oración f.

orator, n. orador m.

oratory, n. elocuencia f.; (church) oratorio m.

orbit, n. órbita f.

orchard, n. huerto m.

orchestra, n. orquesta f. o. seat, butaca f.

orchid, n. orquídea f.

ordain, v. ordenar.

ordeal, n. prueba f.

order, 1. n. orden, m. or f.; clase f.; (com.) pedido m. in o. that, para que. 2. v. ordenar; mandar; pedir.

orderly, a. ordenado.

ordinance, n. ordenanza f.

ordinary, a. ordinario.

ordination, n. ordenación f.

ore, n. mineral m.

organ, n. órgano m.

organdy, n. organdí m.

organic, a. orgánico.

organism, n. organismo m.

organist, n. organista m. & f.

organization, n. organización f.

organize, v. organizar.

orgy, n. orgía f.

orient, 1. n. oriente m. 2. v. orientar.

Oriental, a. oriental.

orientation, n. orientación f.

origin, n. origen m.

original, a. & n. original m.

originality, n. originalidad f.

ornament, 1. n. ornamento m. 2. v. ornamentar.

ornamental, a. ornamental, decorativo.

ornate, a. ornado.

ornithology, n. ornitología f.

orphan, n. & a. huérfano -na.

orphanage, n. orfanato m.

orthodox, a. ortodoxo.

ostentation, n. ostentación f.

ostentatious, a. ostentoso.

ostrich, n. avestruz m.

other, a. & pron. otro. every o. day, un día sí y otro no.

otherwise, adv. de otra manera.

ought, v. deber.

ounce, n. onza f.

our, ours, a. & pron. nuestro.

ourselves, pron. nosotros mismos; nos.

oust, v. desalojar.

ouster, n. desahuco m.

out, 1. adv. fuera, afuera. out of, fuera de. 2. prep. por.

outbreak, *n.* erupción *f.*
outcast, *n.* paria *m.* & *f.*
outcome, *n.* resultado *m.*
outdoors, *adv.* fuera de casa; al aire libre.
outer, *a.* exterior, externo.
outfit, **1.** *n.* equipo; traje *m.* **2.** *v.* equipar.
outgrowth, *n.* resultado *m.*
outing, *n.* paseo *m.*
outlaw, **1.** *n.* bandido *m.* **2.** *v.* proscribir.
outlet, *n.* salida *f.*
outline, **1.** *n.* contorno; esbozo *m.;* silueta *f.* **2.** *v.* esbozar.
outlive, *v.* sobrevivir.
out-of-date, *a.* pasado.
outpost, *n.* puesto avanzado.
output, *n.* capacidad *f.;* educto *m.*
outrage, **1.** *n.* ultraje *m.;* atrocidad *f.* **2.** *v.* ultrajar.
outrageous, *a.* atroz.
outrun, *v.* exceder.
outside, **1.** *a.* & *n.* exterior *m.* **2.** *adv.* afuera, por fuera. **3.** *prep.* fuera de.
outskirt, *n.* borde *m.*
outward, *adv.* hacia afuera.
outwardly, *adv.* exteriormente.
oval, **1.** *a.* oval, ovalado. **2.** *n.* óvalo *m.*
ovary, *n.* ovario *m.*
ovation, *n.* ovación *f.*
oven, *n.* horno *m.*
over, **1.** *prep.* sobre, encima de; por. **2.** *adv.* **o. here,** aquí. **o. there,** allí, por allí. **to be o.,** estar terminado.
overcoat, *n.* abrigo, sobretodo *m.*
overcome, *v.* superar, vencer.
overdue, *a.* restrasado.
overflow, **1.** *n.* inundación *f.* **2.** *v.* inundar.
overhaul, *v.* repasar.
overhead, *adv.* arriba, en lo alto.
overkill, *n.* efecto mayor que el pretendido.
overlook, *v.* pasar por alto.
overnight, *adv.* **to stay or stop o.,** pasar la noche.
overpower, *v.* vencer.
overrule, *v.* predominar.
overrun, *v.* invadir.
oversee, *v.* superentender.
oversight, *n.* equivocación *f.*
overt, *a.* abierto.
overtake, *v.* alcanzar.
overthrow, **1.** *n.* trastorno *m.* **2.** *v.* trastornar.
overture, *n.* obertura *f.*
overturn, *v.* trastornar.
overview, *n.* visión de conjunto *f.*
overweight, *a.* demasiado pesado.
overwhelm, *v.* abrumar.
overwork, *v.* trabajar demasiado.
owe, *v.* deber. **owing to,** debido a.
owl, *n.* lechuza *f.*

own, **1.** *a.* propio. **2.** *v.* poseer.
owner, *n.* dueño -ña.
ox, *n.* buey *m.*
oxygen, *n.* oxígeno *m.*
oxygen tent, *n.* tienda de oxígeno *f.*
oyster, *n.* ostra *f.*

P

pace, **1.** *n.* paso *m.* **2.** *v.* pasearse. **p. off,** medir a pasos.
pacific, *a.* pacífico.
pacifier, *n.* pacificador *m.;* (baby p.) chupete *m.*
pacifism, *n.* pacifismo *m.*
pacifist, *n.* pacifista *m.* & *f.*
pacify, *v.* pacificar.
pack, **1.** *n.* fardo; paquete *m.;* (animals) muta *f.* **p. of cards,** baraja *f.* **2.** *v.* empaquetar; (baggage) empacar.
package, *n.* paquete, bulto *m.*
pact, *n.* pacto *m.*
pad, **1.** *n.* colchoncillo *m.* **p. of paper,** bloc de papel. **2.** *v.* rellenar.
paddle, **1.** *n.* canalete *m.* **2.** *v.* remar.
padlock, *n.* candado *m.*
pagan, *a.* & *n.* pagano -na.
page, *n.* página *f.;* (boy) paje *m.*
pageant, *n.* espectáculo *m.;* procesión *f.*
pail, *n.* cubo *m.*
pain, **1.** *n.* dolor *m.* **to take pains,** esmerarse.
painful, *a.* doloroso; penoso.
paint, **1.** *n.* pintura *f.* **2.** *v.* pintar.
painter, *n.* pintor -ra.
painting, *n.* pintura *f.;* cuadro *m.*
pair, **1.** *n.* par *m.;* pareja *f.* **2.** *v.* parear. **p. off,** emparejarse.
pajamas, *n.* pijama *m.*
palace, *n.* palacio *m.*
palatable, *a.* sabroso, agradable.
palate, *n.* paladar *m.*
palatial, *a.* palaciego, suntuoso.
pale, *a.* pálido. **to turn pale,** palidecer.
paleness, *n.* palidez *f.*
palette, *n.* paleta *f.*
pallbearer, *n.* andero *m.*
pallid, *a.* pálido.
palm, *n.* palma *f.* **p. tree,** palmera *f.*
palpitate, *v.* palpitar.
paltry, *a.* miserable.
pamper, *v.* mimar.
pamphlet, *n.* folleto *m.*
pan, *n.* cacerola *f.*
panacea, *n.* panacea *f.*
Pan-American, *a.* panamericano.
pane, *n.* hoja *f.,* cuadro *m.*
panel, *n.* tablero *m.*
pang, *n.* dolor; remordimiento *m.*
panic, *n.* pánico *m.*

panorama, *n.* panorama *m.*
pant, *v.* jadear.
panther, *n.* pantera *f.*
pantomine, *n.* pantomima *f.;* mímica *f.*
pantry, *n.* despensa *f.*
pants, *n.* pantalones, *m.pl.*
panty hose, *n.* pantyhose *m.* (medias hasta la cintura).
papal, *a.* papal.
paper, *n.* papel; periódico; artículo *m.*
paperback, *n.* libro en rústica *m.*
paper hanger, *n.* empapelador *m.*
par, *n.* paridad *f.;* (com.) par *f.*
parable, *n.* parábola *f.*
parachute, *n.* paracaídas *m.*
parade, **1.** *n.* desfile *m.,* procesión *f.* **2.** *v.* desfilar.
paradise, *n.* paraíso *m.*
paradox, *n.* paradoja *f.*
paraffin, *n.* parafina *f.*
paragraph, *n.* párrafo *m.*
parakeet, *n.* perico *m.*
parallel, **1.** *n.* paralelo. **2.** *v.* correr parejas con.
paralysis, *n.* parálisis *f.*
paralyze, *v.* paralizar.
paramedic, *n.* paramédico *m.*
parameter, *n.* parámetro *m.*
paramount, *a.* supremo.
paraphrase, **1.** *n.* paráfrasis *f.* **2.** *v.* parafrasear.
parasite, *n.* parásito *m.*
parcel, *n.* paquete *m.* **p. of land,** lote de terreno.
parchment, *n.* pergamino *m.*
pardon, **1.** *n.* perdón *m.* **2.** *v.* perdonar.
pare, *v.* pelar.
parentage, *n.* origen *m.;* extracción *f.*
parenthesis, *n.* paréntesis *f.*
parents, *n.* padres *m.pl.*
parish, *n.* parroquia *f.*
Parisian, *a.* & *n.* parisiense *m.* & *f.*
park, **1.** *n.* parque *m.* **2.** *v.* estacionar.
parkway, *n.* bulevar *m.*
parley, *n.* conferencia *f.;* (mil.) parlamento *m.*
parliament, *n.* parlamento *m.*
parliamentary, *a.* parlamentario.
parlor, *n.* sala *f.,* salón *m.*
parochial, *a.* parroquial.
parody, **1.** *n.* parodia *f.* **2.** *v.* parodiar.
parole, **1.** *n.* palabra *f.;* (mil.) santo y seña. **2.** *v.* poner en libertad bajo palabra.
paroxysm, *n.* paroxismo *m.*
parrot, *n.* loro, papagayo *m.*
parsimony, *n.* parsimonia *f.*
parsley, *n.* perejil *m.*
parson, *n.* párroco *m.*
part, **1.** *n.* parte *f.,* (theat.) papel *m.* **2.** *v.* separarse; partirse. **p. with,** desprenderse de.
partake, *v.* tomar parte.
partial, *a.* parcial.

participant, n. participante m. & f.

participate, v. participar.

participation, n. participación f.

participle, n. participio m.

particle, n. partícula f.

particular, a. & n. particular m.

parting, n. despedida f.

partisan, a. & n. partidario -ria.

partition, n. tabique m.

partly, adv. en parte.

partner, n. socio -cia; compañero -ra.

partridge, n. perdiz f.

party, n. tertulia, fiesta f.; grupo m.; (political) partido m.

pass, 1. n. pase; (mountain) paso m. 2. v. pasar. **p. away,** fallecer.

passable, a. transitable; regular.

passage, n. pasaje; (corridor) pasillo m.

passé, a. anticuado.

passenger, n. pasajero -ra.

passerby, n. transeúnte m. & f.

passion, n. pasión f.

passionate, a. apasionado.

passive, a. pasivo.

passport, n. pasaporte m.

past, 1. a. & n. pasado m. 2. prep. más allá de; después de.

paste, 1. n. pasta f. 2. v. empastar; pegar.

pasteurize, v. pasteurizar.

pastime, n. pasatiempo m.; diversión f.

pastor, n. pastor m.

pastry, n. pastelería f.

pasture, 1. n. pasto m.; pradera f. 2. v. pastar.

pat, 1. n. golpecillo m. **to stand p.,** mantenerse firme. 2. v. dar golpecillos.

patch, 1. n. remiendo m. 2. v. remendar.

patent, 1. a. & n. patente m. 2. v. patentar.

patent leather, n. charol m.

paternal, a. paterno, paternal.

paternity, n. paternidad f.

path, n. senda f.

pathetic, a. patético.

pathology, n. patología f.

pathos, n. rasgo conmovedor m.

patience, n. paciencia f.

patient, 1. a. paciente. 2. n. enfermo, paciente m.

patio, n. patio m.

patriarch, n. patriarca m.

patriot, n. patriota m.

patriotic, a. patriótico.

patriotism, n. patriotismo m.

patrol, 1. n. patrulla f. 2. v. patrullar.

patrolman, n. vigilante m.; patrullador m.

patron, n. patrón m.

patronize, v. condescender; patrocinar; ser cliente de.

pattern, n. modelo m.

pauper, n. indigent m. & f.

pause, 1. n. pausa f. 2. v. pausar.

pave, v. pavimentar. **p. the way,** preparar el camino.

pavement, n. pavimento m.

pavilion, n. pabellón m.

paw, 1. n. pata f. 2. v. patear.

pawn, 1. n. prenda f.; (chess) peón de ajedrez m. 2. v. empeñar.

pay, 1. n. pago; sueldo, salario m.; 2. v. pagar. **p. back,** pagar; vengarse de.

payment, n. pago m.; recompensa f.

pea, n. guisante m.

peace, n. paz f.

peaceable, a. pacífico.

peaceful, a. tranquilo.

peach, n. durazno, melocotón m.

peacock, n. pavo real m.

peak, n. pico, cumbre; máximo m.

peal, n. repique; estruendo m. **p. of laughter,** risotada f.

peanut, n. maní, cacahuete m.

pear, n. pera f.

pearl, n. perla f.

peasant, n. campesino -na.

pebble, n. guija f.

peck, 1. n. picotazo m. 2. v. picotear.

peculiar, a. peculiar.

pecuniary, a. pecuniario.

pedagog, n. pedagogo m.

pedagogy, n. pedagogía f.

pedal, n. pedal m.

pedant, n. pedante m.

peddler, n. buhonero m.

pedestal, n. pedestal m.

pedestrian, n. peatón -na.

pediatrician, n. pediatra m. & f.

pedigree, n. genealogía f.

peek, 1. n. atisbo m. 2. v. atisbar.

peel, 1. n. corteza f.; (fruit) pellejo m. 2. v. descortezar; pelar.

peep, n. ojeada f.

peer, 1. n. par m. 2. v. mirar fijamente.

peg, n. clavija; estaquilla f.; gancho m.

pelt, 1. n. pellejo m. 2. v. apedrear; (rain) caer con fuerza.

pelvis, n. pelvis f.

pen, n. pluma f.; corral m. **fountain p.,** pluma fuente.

penalty, n. pena; multa f.; castigo m.

penance, n. penitencia f. **to do p.,** penar.

penchant, n. propensión f.

pencil, n. lápiz m.

pending, a. pendiente. **to be p.,** pender.

penetrate, v. penetrar.

penetration, n. penetración f.

penicillin, n. penicilina f.

peninsula, n. península f.

penitent, n. & a. penitente m.

penknife, n. cortaplumas f.

penniless, a. indigente.

penny, n. penique m.

pension, n. pensión f.

pensive, a. pensativo.

penury, n. penuria f.

people, 1. n. gente f.; (of a nation) pueblo m. 2. v. poblar.

pepper, n. pimienta f.; (plant) pimiento m.

per, prep. por.

perambulator, n. cochecillo de niño m.

perceive, v. percibir.

percent, adv. por ciento.

percentage, n. porcentaje m.

perceptible, a. perceptible.

perception, n. percepción f.

perch, n. percha f.; (fish) perca f.

perdition, n. perdición f.

peremptory, a. perentorio, terminante.

perennial, a. perenne.

perfect, 1. a. perfecto. 2. v. perfeccionar.

perfection, n. perfección f.

perforation, n. perforación f.

perform, v. hacer; ejecutar; (theat.) representar.

performance, n. ejecución f.; (theat.) representación f.

perfume, 1. n. perfume m.; fragancia f. 2. v. perfumar.

perfunctory, a. perfunctorio, superficial.

perhaps, adv. quizá, quizás, tal vez.

peril, n. peligro m.

perilous, a. peligroso.

perimeter, n. perímetro m.

period, n. período m.; (punct.) punto m.

periodic, a. periódico.

periodical, n. revista f.

periphery, n. periferia f.

perish, v. perecer.

perishable, a. perecedero.

perjury, n. perjurio m.

permanent, a. permanente. **p. wave,** ondulado permanente.

permeate, v. penetrar.

permissible, a. permisible.

permission, n. permiso m.

permit, 1. n. permiso m. 2. v. permitir.

pernicious, a. pernicioso.

perpendicular, n. & a. perpendicular m.

perpetrate, v. perpetrar.

perpetual, a. perpetuo.

perplex, v. confundir.

perplexity, n. perplejidad f.

persecute, v. perseguir.

persecution, n. persecución f.

perseverance, n. perseverancia f.

persevere, v. perseverar.

persist, v. persistir.

persistent, a. persistente.

person, n. persona f.

personage, n. personaje m.

personal, a. personal.

personality, n. personalidad f.

personnel, n. personal m.

perspective, n. perspectiva f.

perspiration, n. sudor m.

perspire, v. sudar.

persuade, *v.* persuadir.

persuasive, *a.* persuasivo.

pertain, *v.* pertenecer.

pertinent, *a.* pertinente.

perturb, *v.* perturbar.

peruse, *v.* leer con cuidado.

pervade, *v.* penetrar; llenar.

perverse, *a.* perverso.

perversion, *n.* perversión *f.*

pessimism, *n.* pesimismo *m.*

pestilence, *n.* pestilencia *f.*

pet, 1. *n.* favorito -ta. **2.** *v.* mimar.

petal, *n.* pétalo *m.*

petition, 1. *n.* petición, súplica *f.* **2.** *v.* pedir, suplicar.

petrify, *v.* petrificar.

petroleum, *n.* petróleo *m.*

petticoat, *n.* enagua *f.*

petty, *a.* mezquino, insignificante.

petulant, *a.* quisquilloso.

pew, *n.* banco de iglesia *m.*

pewter, *n.* peltre *m.*

phantom, *n.* espectro, fantasma *m.*

pharmacist, *n.* farmacéutico, boticario *m.*

pharmacy, *n.* farmacia, botica *f.*

phase, *n.* fase *f.*

pheasant, *n.* faisán *m.*

phenomenal, *a.* fenomenal.

phenomenon, *n.* fenómeno *f.*

philanthropy, *n.* filantropía *f.*

philately, *n.* filatelia *f.*

philosopher, *n.* filósofo *m.*

philosophical, *a.* filosófico.

philosophy, *n.* filosofía *f.*

phlegm, *n.* flema *f.*; frialdad de ánimo *f.*

phobia, *n.* fobia *f.*

phonetic, *a.* fonético.

phonograph, *n.* fonógrafo *m.*

phosphorus, *n.* fósforo *m.*

photocopier, *n.* fotocopiadora *f.*

photocopy, 1. *n.* fotocopia *f.* **2.** *v.* fotocopiar.

photoelectric, *a.* fotoeléctrico.

photogenic, *a.* fotogénico.

photograph, 1. *n.* fotografía *f.* **2.** *v.* fotografiar; retratar.

photography, *n.* fotografía *f.*

Photostat, *n.* fotocopia *f.*

phrase, 1. *n.* frase *f.* **2.** *v.* expresar.

physical, *a.* físico.

physician, *n.* médico *m.*

physics, *n.* física *f.*

physiology, *n.* fisiología *f.*

physiotherapy, *n.* fisioterapia *f.*

physique, *n.* físico *m.*

pianist, *n.* pianista *m. & f.*

piano, *n.* piano *m.*

picayune, *a.* insignificante.

piccolo, *n.* flautín *m.*

pick, 1. *n.* pico *m.* **2.** *v.* escoger. **p. up,** recoger.

picket, *n.* piquete *m.*

pickle, 1. *n.* salmuera *f.*; encurtido *m.* **2.** *v.* escabechar.

pickpocket, *n.* cortabolsas *m. & f.*

picnic, *n.* picnic *m.*

picture, 1. *n.* cuadro; retrato *m.*; fotografía *f.*; (movie) película *f.* **2.** *v.* imaginarse.

picturesque, *a.* pintoresco.

pie, *n.* pastel *m.*

piece, *n.* pedazo *m.*; pieza *f.*

pier, *n.* muelle *m.*

pierce, *v.* perforar; pinchar; traspasar.

piety, *n.* piedad *f.*

pig, *n.* puerco, cerdo, lechón *m.*

pigeon, *n.* paloma *f.*

pigeonhole, *n.* casilla *f.*

pigment, *n.* pigmento *m.*

pile, 1. *n.* pila *f.*; montón *m.pl.*; (med.) hemorroides *f.pl.* **2.** *v.* amontonar.

pilfer, *v.* ratear.

pilgrim, *n.* peregrino -na, romero -ra.

pilgrimage, *n.* romería *f.*

pill, *n.* píldora *f.*

pillage, 1. *n.* pillaje *m.* **2.** *v.* pillar.

pillar, *n.* columna *f.*

pillow, *n.* almohada *f.*

pillowcase, *n.* funda de almohada *f.*

pilot, 1. *n.* piloto *m.* **2.** *v.* pilotear.

pimple, *n.* grano *m.*

pin, 1. *n.* alfiler; broche *m.*; (mech.) clavija *f.* **2.** *v.* prender. **p. up,** fijar.

pinch, 1. *n.* pellizco *m.* **2.** *v.* pellizcar.

pine, 1. *n.* pino *m.* **2.** *v.* **p. away,** languidecer. **p. for,** anhelar.

pineapple, *n.* piña *f.*, ananá *m.*

pink, *a.* rosado.

pinnacle, *n.* pináculo *m.*; cumbre *f.*

pint, *n.* pinta *f.*

pioneer, *n.* pionero -ra.

pious, *a.* piadoso.

pipe, *n.* pipa *f.*; tubo; (of organ) cañón *m.*

piper, *n.* flautista *m. & f.*

piquant, *a.* picante.

pirate, *n.* pirata *m.*

pistol, *n.* pistola *f.*

piston, *n.* pistón *m.*

pit, *n.* hoyo *m.*; (fruit) hueso *m.*

pitch, 1. *n.* brea *f.*; grado de inclinación; (music) tono *m.*; **2.** *v.* lanzar; (ship) cabecear.

pitchblende, *n.* pechblenda *f.*

pitcher, *n.* cántaro *m.*; (baseball) lanzador *m.*

pitchfork, *n.* horca *f.*; tridente *m.*

pitfall, *n.* trampa *f.*, hoya cubierta *f.*

pitiful, *a.* lastimoso.

pitiless, *a.* cruel.

pity, 1. *n.* compasión, piedad *f.* **to be a p.,** ser lástima. **2.** *v.* compadecer.

pivot, *n.* espiga *f.*, pivote *m.*; punto de partido *m.* **2.** *v.* girar sobre un pivote.

pizza, *n.* pizza *f.*

placard, 1. *n.* cartel *m.* **2.** *v.* fijar carteles.

placate, *v.* aplacar.

place, 1. *n.* lugar, sitio, puesto *m.* **2.** *v.* colocar, poner.

placid, *a.* plácido.

plagiarism, *n.* plagio *m.*

plague, 1. *n.* plaga, peste *f.* **2.** *v.* atormentar.

plain, 1. *a.* sencillo; puro; evidente. **2.** *n.* llano *m.*

plaintiff, *n.* demandador -ra.

plan, 1. *n.* plan, propósito *m.* **2.** *v.* planear; pensar. **p. on,** contar con.

plane, 1. *n.* plano; (tool) cepillo *m.* **2.** *v.* allanar; acepillar.

planet, *n.* planeta *m.*

planetarium, *n.* planetario *m.*

plank, *n.* tablón *m.*

plant, 1. *n.* mata, planta *f.* **2.** *v.* sembrar, plantar.

plantation, *n.* plantación *f.* **coffee p.,** cafetal *m.*

planter, *n.* plantador; hacendado *m.*

plasma, *n.* plasma *m.*

plaster, 1. *n.* yeso; emplasto *m.* **2.** *v.* enyesar; emplastar.

plastic, *a.* plástico.

plate, 1. *n.* plato *m.*; plancha de metal *f.* **2.** *v.* planchear.

plateau, *n.* meseta *f.*

platform, *n.* plataforma *f.*

platinum, *n.* platino *m.*

platitude, *n.* perogrullada *f.*

platter, *n.* fuente *f.*; platel *m.*

plaudit, *n.* aplauso *m.*

plausible, *a.* plausible.

play, 1. *n.* juego *m.*; (theat.) pieza *f.* **2.** *v.* jugar; (music) tocar; (theat.) representar. **p. a part,** hacer un papel.

player, *n.* jugador -ra; (music) músico *m.*; (theat.) actor *m.*, actriz *f.*

playful, *a.* juguetón.

playground, *n.* campo de deportes; patio de recreo.

playmate, *n.* compañero -ra de juego.

playwright, *n.* dramaturgo *m.*

plea, *n.* ruego *m.*; súplica *f.*; (legal) declaración *f.*

plead, *v.* suplicar; declararse. **p. a case,** defender un pleito.

pleasant, *a.* agradable.

please, 1. *v.* gustar, agradar. **Pleased to meet you,** Mucho gusto en conocer a Vd. **2.** *adv.* por favor. **Please . . .** Haga el favor de . . ., Tenga la bondad de . . ., Sírvase . . .

pleasure, *n.* gusto, placer *m.*

pleat, 1. *n.* pliegue *m.* **2.** *v.* plegar.

plebiscite, *n.* plebiscito *m.*

pledge, 1. *n.* empeño *m.* **2.** *v.* empeñar.

plentiful, *a.* abundante.

plenty, *n.* abundancia *f.* **p. of,** bastante. **p. more,** mucho más.

pleurisy, *n.* pleuritis *f.*

pliable, pliant, *a.* flexible.

pliers, *n.pl.* alicates *m.pl.*

plight, *n.* apuro, aprieto *m.*

plot, 1. *n.* conspiración; (of a story) trama; (of land) parcela *f.* **2.** *v.* conspirar; tramar.

plow, 1. *n.* arado *m.* **2.** *v.* arar.

pluck, 1. *n.* valor *m.* **2.** *v.* arrancar; desplumar.

plug, 1. *n.* tapón; (elec.) enchufe *m.* **spark p.,** bujía *f.* **2.** *v.* tapar.

plum, *n.* ciruela *f.*

plumage, *n.* plumaje *m.*

plumber, *n.* plomero *m.*

plume, *n.* pluma *f.*

plump, *a.* regordete.

plunder, 1. *n.* botín *m.;* despojos *m.pl.* **2.** *v.* saquear.

plunge, *v.* zambullir; precipitar.

plural, *a.* & *n.* plural *m.*

plus, *prep.* más.

plutocrat, *n.* plutócrata *m.* & *f.*

pneumatic, *a.* neumático.

pneumonia *n.* pulmonía *f.*

poach, *v.* (eggs) escalfar; invadir; cazar en vedadado.

pocket, 1. *n.* bolsillo *m.* **2.** *v.* embolsar.

pocketbook, *n.* cartera *f.*

podiatry, *n.* podiatría *f.*

poem, *n.* poema *m.*

poet, *n.* poeta *m.*

poetic, *a.* poético.

poetry, *n.* poesía *f.*

poignant, *a.* conmovedor.

point, 1. *n.* punta *f.;* punto *m.* **2.** *v.* apuntar. **p. out,** señalar.

pointed, *a.* puntiagudo; directo.

pointless, *a.* inútil.

poise, 1. *n.* equilibrio *m.;* serenidad *f.* **2.** *v.* equilibrar; estar suspendido.

poison, 1. *n.* veneno *m.* **2.** *v.* envenenar.

poisonous, *a.* venenoso.

poke, 1. *n.* empuje *m.,* hurgonada *f.* **2.** *v.* picar; haronear.

Poland, *n.* Polonia *f.*

polar, *a.* polar.

pole, *n.* palo; (geog.) polo *m.*

police, *n.* policía *f.*

policeman, *n.* policía *m.*

policy, *n.* política *f.* **insurance p.,** póliza de seguro.

Polish, *a.* & *n.* polaco *m.*

polish, 1. *n.* lustre *m.* **2.** *v.* pulir, lustrar.

polite, *a.* cortés.

politic, political, *a.* político.

politician, *n.* político *m.*

politics, *n.* política *f.*

poll, *n.* encuesta *f.;* (pl.) urnas *f.pl.*

pollen, *n.* polen *m.*

pollute, *v.* contaminar.

polo, *n.* polo *m.*

polygamy, *n.* poligamia *f.*

polygon, *n.* polígono *m.*

pomp, *n.* pompa *f.*

pompous, *a.* pomposo.

poncho, *n.* poncho *m.*

pond, *n.* charca *f.*

ponder, *v.* ponderar, meditar.

ponderous, *a.* ponderoso, pesado.

pontiff, *n.* pontífice *m.*

pontoon, *n.* pontón *m.*

pony, *n.* caballito *m.*

pool, *n.* charco *m.* **swimming p.,** piscina *f.*

poor, *a.* pobre; (not good) malo.

pop, *n.* chasquido *m.*

popcorn, *n.* maíz tostado *m.*

pope, *n.* papa *m.*

popular, *a.* popular.

popularity, *n.* popularidad *f.*

population, *n.* población *f.*

porcelain, *n.* porcelana *f.*

porch, *n.* pórtico *m.;* galería *f.*

pore, *n.* poro *m.*

pork, *n.* carne de puerco.

pornography, *n.* pornografía *f.*

porous, *a.* poroso, esponjoso.

port, *n.* puerto; (naut.) babor *m.* **p. wine,** oporto *m.*

portable, *a.* portátil.

portal, *n.* portal *m.*

portend, *v.* pronosticar.

portent, *n.* presagio *m.,* portento *m.*

porter, *n.* portero *m.*

portfolio, *n.* cartera *f.*

porthole, *n.* porta *f.*

portion, *n.* porción *f.*

portly, *a.* corpulento.

portrait, *n.* retrato *m.*

portray, *v.* pintar.

Portugal, *n.* Portugal *m.*

Portuguese, *a.* & *n.* portugués-sa.

pose, 1. *n.* postura; actitud *f.* **2.** *v.* posar. **p. as,** pretender ser.

position, *n.* posición *f.*

positive, *a.* positivo.

possess, *v.* poseer.

possession, *n.* posesión *f.*

possessive, *a.* posesorio.

possibility, *n.* posibilidad *f.*

possible, *a.* posible.

post, 1. *n.* poste; puesto *m.* **2.** *v.* fijar; situar; echar al correo.

postage, *n.* porte de correo. **p. stamp,** sello *m.*

postal, *a.* postal.

post card, tarjeta postal.

poster, *n.* cartel, letrero *m.*

posterior, *a.* posterior.

posterity, *n.* posteridad *f.*

postgraduate, *a.* postgraduado.

postmark, *n.* matasellos *m.*

post office, casa de correos.

postpone, *v.* posponer, aplazar.

postscript, *n.* posdata *f.*

posture, *n.* postura *f.*

pot, *n.* olla, marmita; (marijuana) marijuana, hierba *f.* **flower p.,** tiesto *m.*

potassium, *n.* potasio *m.*

potato, *n.* patata, papa *f.* **sweet p.,** batata *f.*

potent, *a.* potente, poderoso.

potential, *a.* & *n.* potencial *f.*

potion, *n.* poción *f.,* pócima *f.*

pottery, *n.* alfarería *f.*

pouch, *n.* saco *m.;* bolsa *f.*

poultry, *n.* aves de corral.

pound, 1. *n.* libra *f.* **2.** *v.* golpear.

pour, *v.* echar; verter; llover a cántaros.

poverty, *n.* pobreza *f.*

powder, 1. *n.* polvo *m.;* (gun) pólvora *f.* **2.** *v.* empolvar; pulverizar.

power, *n.* poder *m.;* potencia *f.*

powerful, *a.* poderoso, fuerte.

powerless, *a.* impotente.

practical, *a.* prático.

practically, *adv.* casi; práticamente.

practice, 1. *n.* prática; costumbre; clientela *f.* **2.** *v.* practicar; ejercer.

practiced, *a.* experto.

practitioner, *n.* practicante *m.*

pragmatic, *a.* pragmática.

prairie, *n.* llanura; (So. Amer.) pampa *f.*

praise, 1. *n.* alabanza *f.* **2.** *v.* alabar.

prank, *n.* travesura *f.*

pray, *v.* rezar; (beg) rogar.

prayer, *n.* oración; súplica *f.;* ruego *m.*

preach, *v.* predicar; sermonear.

preacher, *n.* predicador *m.*

preamble, *n.* preámbulo *m.*

precarious, *a.* precario.

precaution, *n.* precaución *f.*

precede, *v.* preceder, anteceder.

precedent, *a.* & *n.* precedente *m.*

precept, *n.* precepto *m.*

precinct, *n.* recinto *m.*

precious, *a.* precioso.

precipice, *n.* precipicio *m.*

precipitate, *v.* precipitar.

precise, *a.* preciso, exacto.

precision, *n.* precisión *f.*

preclude, *v.* evitar.

precocious, *a.* precoz.

predatory, *a.* de rapiña, rapaz.

predecessor, *n.* predecesor, antecesor *m.*

predicament, *n.* dificultad *f.;* apuro *m.*

predict, *v.* pronosticar, predecir,

predilection, *n.* predilección *f.*

predispose, *v.* predisponer.

predominant, *a.* predominante.

prefabricate, *v.* fabricar de antemano.

preface, *n.* prefacio *m.*

prefer, *v.* preferir.

preferable, *a.* preferible.

preference, *n.* preferencia *f.*

prefix, 1. *n.* prefijo *m.* **2.** *v.* prefijar.

pregnant, *a.* preñada.

prehistoric, *a.* prehistórico.

prejudice, *n.* prejuicio *m.*

prejudiced, *a.* prejuiciado.

preliminary, *a.* preliminar.

prelude, *n.* preludio *m.*

premature, *a.* prematuro.

premeditate, *v.* premeditar.

premier, *n.* premier ministro.

première, *n.* estreno *m.*

premise, *n.* premisa *f.*

premium, n. premio m.

premonition, n. presentimiento m.

prenatal, a. prenatal.

preparation, n. preparativo m.; preparación f.

preparatory, a. preparatorio. p. to, antes de.

prepare, v. preparar.

preponderant, a. preponderante.

preposition, n. preposición f.

preposterous, a. prepóstero, absurdo.

prerequisite, n. requisito previo.

prerogative, n. prerrogativa f.

prescribe, v. prescribir; (med.) recetar.

prescription, n. prescripción; (med.) receta f.

presence, n. presencia f.; porte m.

present, 1. a. presente. **to be present at,** asistir a. **2.** n. presente; (gift) regalo m. **at p.,** ahora. **for the p.,** por ahora. **3.** v. presentar.

presentable, a. presentable.

presentation, n. presentación; introducción f.; (theat.) representación f.

presently, adv. luego; dentro de poco.

preservative, a. & n. preservativo m.

preserve, 1. n. conserva f.; (hunting) vedado m. **2.** v. preservar.

preside, v. presidir.

presidency, n. presidencia f.

president, n. presidente -ta.

press, 1. n. prensa f. **2.** v. apretar; urgir; (clothes) planchar.

pressing, a. urgente.

pressure, n. presión f.

pressure cooker, n. cocina de presión f.

prestige, n. prestigio m.

presume, v. presumir; suponer.

presumptuous, a. presumtuoso.

presuppose, v. presuponer.

pretend, v. fingir. **p. to the throne,** aspirar al trono.

pretense, n. pretensión f.; fingimiento m.

pretension, n. pretensión f.

pretentious, a. presumido.

pretext, n. pretexto m.

pretty, 1. a. bonito, lindo. **2.** adv. bastante.

prevail, v. prevalecer.

prevailing, prevalent, a. predominante.

prevent, v. impedir; evitar.

prevention, n. prevención f.

preventive, a. preventivo.

preview, n. vista previa f.

previous, a. anterior, previo.

prey, n. presa f.

price, n. precio m.

priceless, a. sin precio.

prick, 1. n. punzada f. **2.** v. punzar.

pride, n. orgullo m.

priest, n. sacerdote, cura m.

prim, a. severamente modesto.

primary, a. primario, principal.

prime, 1. a. primero. **2.** n. flor f. **3.** v. alistar.

prime minister, n. primer ministro m.

primitive, a. primitivo.

prince, n. príncipe m.

princess, n. princesa f.

principal, 1. a. principal. **2.** n. principal; director m.

principle, n. principio m.

print, 1. n. letra f.; (art) grabado m. **2.** v. imprimir, estampar.

printing, n. imprenta f.

printing press, n. prensa f.

printout, n. impreso producido por una computadora.

priority, n. prioridad, precedencia f.

prism, n. prisma m.

prison, n. prisión, cárcel f.

prisoner, n. prisionero, preso m.

privacy, n. soledad f.

private, 1. a. particular. **2.** n. soldado raso. **in p.,** en particular.

privation, n. privación f.

privet, n. ligustro m.

privilege, n. privilegio m.

privy, n. letrina f.

prize, 1. n. premio m. **2.** v. apreciar, estimar.

probability, n. probabilidad f.

probable, a. probable.

probate, n. testamentario.

probation, n. prueba f.; probación f.; libertad condicional f.

probe, 1. n. indagación f. **2.** v. indagar; tentar.

probity, n. probidad f.

problem, n. problema m.

procedure, n. procedimiento m.

proceed, v. proceder; proseguir.

process, n. proceso m.

procession, n. procesión f.

proclaim, v. proclamar, anunciar.

proclamation, n. proclamación f.; decreto m.

procrastinate, v. dilatar.

procure, v. obtener, procurar.

prodigal, n. & a. pródigo m.

prodigy, n. prodigio m.

produce, v. producir.

product, n. producto m.

production, n. producción f.

productive, a. productivo.

profane, 1. a. profano. **2.** v. profanar.

profanity, n. profanidad f.

profess, v. profesar; declarar.

profession, n. profesión f.

professional, a. & n. profesional m.

professor, n. profesor -ra; catedrático m.

proficient, a. experto, proficiente.

profile, n. perfil m.

profit, 1. n. provecho m.; ventaja f.; (com.) ganancia f. **2.** v. aprovechar; beneficiar.

profitable, a. provechoso, ventajoso, lucrativo.

profiteer, 1. n. explotador m. **2.** v. explotar.

profound, a. profundo, hondo.

profuse, a. pródigo, profuso.

prognosis, n. pronóstico m.

program, n. programa m.

progress, 1. n. progresos m.pl. **in p.,** en marcha. **2.** v. progresar; marchar.

progressive, a. progresivo; progresista.

prohibit, v. prohibir.

prohibition, n. prohibición f.

prohibitive, a. prohibitivo.

project, 1. n. proyecto m. **2.** v. proyectar.

projectile, n. proyectil m.

projection, n. proyección f.

projector, n. proyector m.

proliferation, n. proliferación f.

prolific, a. prolífico.

prologue, n. prólogo m.

prolong, v. prolongar.

prominent, a. prominente; eminente.

promiscuous, a. promiscuo.

promise, 1. n. promesa f. **2.** v. prometer.

promote, v. fomentar; estimular; adelantar.

promotion, n. promoción f.; adelanto m.

prompt, 1. a. pronto; puntual. **2.** v. impulsar; (theat.) apuntar.

promulgate, v. promulgar.

pronoun, n. pronombre m.

pronounce, v. pronunciar.

pronunciation, n. pronunciación f.

proof, n. prueba f.

proofread, v. corregir pruebas.

prop, 1. n. apoyo m. **2.** v. sostener.

propaganda, n. propaganda f.

propagate, v. propagar.

propel, v. propulsar.

propeller, n. hélice f.

propensity, n. tendencia f.

proper, a. propio; correcto.

property, n. propiedad f.

prophecy, n. profecía f.

prophesy, v. predecir, profetizar.

prophet, n. profeta m.

prophetic, a. profético.

propitious, a. propicio.

proponent, n. & a. proponente f.

proportion, n. proporción f.

proportionate, a. proporcionado.

proposal, n. propuesta; oferta f.; (marriage) declaración f.

propose, v. proponer; pensar; declararse.

proposition, n. proposición f.

proprietor, n. propietario, dueño m.

propriety, n. corrección f., decoro m.

prosaic, a. prosaico.

proscribe, v. proscribir.

prose, n. prosa f.

prosecute, v. acusar, procesar.

prospect, n. perspectiva; esperanza f.

prospective, a. anticipado, presunto.

prosper, v. prosperar.

prosperity, n. prosperidad f.

prosperous, a. próspero.

prostitute, 1. n. prostituta f. **2.** v. prostituir. **3.** a. prostituido.

prostrate, 1. a. postrado. **2.** v. postrar.

protect, v. proteger; amparar.

protection, n. protección f.; amparo m.

protective, a. protector.

protector, n. protector m.

protégé, n. protegido -da.

protein, n. proteína f.

protest, 1. n. protesta f. **2.** v. protestar.

Protestant, a. & n. protestante m.

protocol, n. protocolo m.

proton, n. protón m.

protract, v. alargar, demorar.

protrude, v. salir fuera.

protuberance, n. protuberancia f.

proud, a. orgulloso.

prove, v. comprobar.

proverb, n. proverbio, refrán m.

provide, v. proporcionar; proveer.

provided, conj. con tal que.

providence, n. providencia f.

province, n. provincia f.

provincial, 1. a. provincial. **2.** n. provinciano -na.

provision, 1. n. provisión f.; (pl.) comestibles m.pl. **2.** v. abastecer.

provocation, n. provocación f.

provoke, v. provocar.

prowess, n. proeza f.

prowl, v. rondar.

proximity, n. proximidad f.

proxy, n. delegado m. by p., mediante apoderado.

prudence, n. prudencia f.

prudent, a. prudente, cauteloso.

prune, n. ciruela pasa.

pry, v. atisbar; curiosear; (mech.) alzaprimar.

psalm, n. salmo m.

pseudonym, n. seudónimo m.

psychedelic, a. psiquedélico.

psychiatrist, n. psiquiatra m.

psychiatry, n. psiquiatría f.

psychoanalysis, n. psicoanálisis m. or f.

psychological, a. psicológico.

psychology, n. psicología f.

psychosis, n. psicosis f.

ptomaine, n. tomaína f.

public, a. & n. público m.

publication, n. publicación; revista f.

publicity, n. publicidad f.

publish, v. publicar.

publisher, n. editor m.

pudding, n. pudín m.

puddle, n. charco, lodazal m.

Puerto Rico, n. Puerto Rico m.

Puerto Rican, a. & n. puertorriqueño -ña.

puff, 1. n. soplo m.; (of smoke) bocanada f. powder p., polvera f. **2.** v. jadear; echar bocanadas. p. up, hinchar; (fig.) engreír.

pugnacious, a. pugnaz.

pull, 1. n. tirón m.; (coll.) influencia f. **2.** v. tirar; halar.

pulley, n. polla f., motón m.

pulmonary, a. pulmonar.

pulp, n. pulpa f.; (of fruit) carne f.

pulpit, n. púlpito m.

pulsar, n. pulsar m.

pulsate, v. pulsar.

pulse, n. pulso m.

pump, 1. n. bomba f. **2.** v. bombear. p. up, inflar.

pumpkin, n. calabaza f.

pun, n. juego de palabras.

punch, 1. n. puñetazo; (mech.) punzón; (beverage) ponche m. **2.** v. dar puñetazos; punzar.

punctual, a. puntual.

punctuate, v. puntuar.

puncture, 1. n. pinchazo m., perforación f. **2.** v. pinchar, perforar.

pungent, a. picante, pungente.

punish, v. castigar.

punishment, n. castigo m.

punitive, a. punitivo.

puny, a. encanijado.

pupil, n. alumno -na; (anat.) pupila f.

puppet, n. muñeco m.

puppy, n. perrito m.

purchase, 1. n. compra f. **2.** v. comprar.

pure, a. puro.

purée, n. puré m.

purge, v. purgar.

purify, v. purificar.

puritanical, a. puritano.

purity, n. pureza f.

purple, 1. a. purpúreo. **2.** n. púrpura f.

purport, 1. n. significación f. **2.** v. significar.

purpose, n. propósito m. on p., de propósito.

purse, n. bolsa f.

pursue, v. perseguir.

pursuit, n. caza; busca; ocupación f. p. plane, caza m.

push, 1. n. empuje; impulso m. **2.** v. empujar.

put, v. poner, colocar. p. away, guardar. p. in, meter. p. off, dejar. p. on, ponerse. p. out, apagar. p. up with, aguantar.

putrid, a. podrido.

puzzle, 1. enigma; rompecabezas m. **2.** v. dejar perplejo. p. out, descifrar.

pyramid, n. pirámide f.

pyromania, n. piromanía f.

Q

quadrangle, n. cuadrángulo m.

quadraphonic, a. cuadrafónico.

quadruped, a. & n. cuadrúpedo m.

quail, 1. n. codorniz f. **2.** v. descorazonarse.

quaint, a. arcaico y curioso.

quake, 1. n. temblor m. **2.** v. temblar.

qualification, n. requisito m.; (pl.) preparaciones.

qualified, a. calificado, competente; preparado.

qualify, v. calificar, modificar; llenar los requisitos.

quality, n. calidad f.

quandary, n. incertidumbre f.

quantity, n. cantidad f.

quarantine, n. cuarentena f.

quarrel, 1. n. riña, disputa f. **2.** v. reñir, disputar.

quarry, n. cantera; (hunting) presa f.

quarter, n. cuarto m.; (pl.) vivienda f.

quarterly, 1. a. trimestral. **2.** adv. por cuartos.

quartet, n. cuarteto m.

quartz, n. cuarzo m.

quasar, n. quasar m.

quaver, v. temblar.

queen, n. reina f.; (chess) dama f.

queer, a. extraño, raro.

quell, v. reprimir.

quench, v. apagar.

query, 1. n. pregunta f. **2.** v. preguntar.

quest, n. busca f.

question, 1. n. pregunta; cuestión f. q. mark, signo de interrogación. **2.** v. preguntar; interrogar; dudar.

questionable, a. dudoso.

questionnaire, n. cuestionario m.

quick, a. rápido.

quicken, v. acelerar.

quicksand, n. arena movediza.

quiet, 1. a. quieto, tranquilo; callado. to be q., keep q., callarse. **2.** n. calma; quietud f. **3.** v. tranquilizar. q. down, callarse; calmarse.

quilt, n. colcha f.

quinine, n. quinina f.

quintet, n. (mus.) quinteto m.

quip, n. pulla f. **2.** v. echar pullas.

quit, v. dejar; renunciar a. q. doing (etc.) dejar de hacer (etc.).

quite, adv. bastante; completamente. not q., no precisamente; no completamente.

quiver, 1. *n.* aljabe *f.;* temblor *m.* **2.** *v.* temblar.

quixotic, *a.* quijotesco.

quorum, *n.* quórum *m.*

quota, *n.* cuota *f.*

quotation, *n.* citación; (com.) cotización *f.* **q. marks,** comillas *f.pl.*

quote, *v.* citar; (com.) cotizar.

R

rabbi, *n.* rabí, rabino *m.*

rabbit, *n.* conejo *m.*

rabble, *n.* canalla *f.*

rabid, *a.* rabioso.

rabies, *n.* hidrofobia *f.*

race, 1. *n.* raza; carrera *f.* **2.** *v.* echar una carrera; correr de prisa.

rack, 1. *n.* (cooking) pesebre *m.;* (clothing) colgador *m.* **2.** *v.* atormentar.

racket, *n.* (noise) ruido *m.;* (tennis) raqueta *f.;* (graft) fraude organizado.

radar, *n.* radar *m.*

radiance, *n.* brillo *m.*

radiant, *a.* radiante.

radiate, *v.* irradiar.

radiation, *n.* irradiación *f.*

radiator, *n.* colorífero *m.;* (auto.) radiador *m.*

radical, *a. & n.* radical *m.*

radio, *n.* radio *m. or f.* **r. station,** estación radiodifusora.

radioactive, *a.* radioactivo.

radish, *n.* rábano *m.*

radium, *n.* radio *m.*

radius, *n.* radio *m.*

raffle, 1. *n.* rifa, lotería *f.* **2.** *v.* rifar.

raft, *n.* balsa *f.*

rafter, *n.* viga *f.*

rag, *n.* trapo *m.*

ragamuffin, *n.* galopín *m.*

rage, 1. *n.* rabia *f.* **2.** *v.* rabiar.

ragged, *a.* andrajoso; desigual.

raid, *n.* (mil.) correría *f.*

rail, *n.* baranda *f.;* carril *m.* **by r.,** por ferrocarril.

railroad, *n.* ferrocarril *m.*

rain, 1. *n.* lluvia *f.* **2.** *v.* llover.

rainbow, *n.* arco iris *m.*

raincoat, *n.* impermeable *m.*

rainfall, *n.* precipitación *f.*

rainy, *a.* lluvioso.

raise, 1. *n.* aumento *m.* **2.** *v.* levantar, alzar; criar.

raisin, *n.* pasa *f.*

rake, 1. *n.* rastro *m.* **2.** *v.* rastrillar.

rally, 1. *n.* reunión *f.* **2.** *v.* reunirse.

ram, *n.* carnero *m.*

ramble, *v.* vagar.

ramp, *n.* rampa *f.*

rampart, *n.* terraplén *m.*

ranch, *n.* rancho *m.*

rancid, *a.* rancio.

rancor, *n.* rencor *m.*

random, *a.* fortuito. **at r.,** a la ventura.

range, 1. *n.* extensión *f.;* alcance *m.;* estufa; sierra *f.;* terreno de pasto. **2.** *v.* recorrer; extenderse.

rank, 1. *a.* espeso; rancio. **2.** *n.* fila *f.;* grado, rango *m.* **3.** *v.* clasificar.

ransack, *v.* saquear.

ransom, 1. *n.* rescate *m.* **2.** *v.* rescatar.

rap, 1. *n.* golpecito *m.* **2.** *v.* golpear.

rapid, *a.* rápido.

rapport, *n.* armonía *f.*

rapture, *n.* éxtasis *m.*

rare, *a.* raro.

rascal, *n.* pícaro, bribón *m.*

rash, 1. *a.* temerario. **2.** *n.* erupción *f.*

raspberry, *n.* frambuesa *f.*

rat, *n.* rata *f.*

rate, 1. *n.* velocidad; tasa *f.;* precio *m.;* (of exchange; of interest) tipo *m.* **at any r.,** de todos modos. **2.** *v.* valuar.

rather, *adv.* bastante; más bien, mejor dicho.

ratify, *v.* ratificar.

ratio, *n.* razón; proporción *f.*

ration, 1. *n.* ración *f.* **2.** *v.* racionar.

rational, *a.* racional.

rattle, 1. *n.* ruido *m.;* matraca *f.* **r. snake,** culebra de cascabel. **2.** *v.* matraquear; rechinar.

raucous, *a.* ronco.

ravage, *v.* pillar; destruir; asolar.

rave, *v.* delirar; entusiasmarse.

ravel, *v.* deshilar.

raven, *n.* cuervo *m.*

ravenous, *a.* voraz.

raw, *a.* crudo; verde.

ray, *n.* rayo *m.*

rayon, *n.* rayón *m.*

razor, *n.* navaja de afeitar. **r. blade,** hoja de afeitar.

reach, 1. *n.* alcance *m.* **2.** *v.* alcanzar.

react, *v.* reaccionar.

reaction, *n.* reacción *f.*

reactionary, 1. *a.* reaccionario. **2.** *n.* (pol.) retrógrado *m.*

read, *v.* leer.

reader, *n.* lector *m.;* libro de lectura.

readily, *adv.* fácilmente.

reading, *n.* lectura *f.*

ready, *a.* listo, preparado; dispuesto.

real, *a.* verdadero; real.

realist, *n.* realista *m. & f.*

reality, *n.* realidad *f.*

realization, *n.* comprensión; realización *f.*

realize, *v.* darse cuenta de; realizar.

really, *adv.* de veras; en realidad.

realm, *n.* reino; dominio *m.*

reap, *v.* segar, cosechar.

rear, 1. *a.* posterior. **2.** *n.* parte posterior. **3.** *v.* criar; levantar.

reason, 1. *n.* razón; causa *f.;* motivo *m.* **2.** *v.* razonar.

reasonable, *a.* razonable.

reassure, *v.* calmar, tranquilizar.

rebate, *n.* rebaja *f.*

rebel, 1. *n.* rebelde *m. & f.* **2.** *v.* rebelarse.

rebellion, *n.* rebelión *f.*

rebellious, *a.* rebelde.

rebirth, *n.* renacimiento *m.*

rebound, 1. *v.* repercutir; resaltar.

rebuff, 1. *n.* repulsa *f.* **2.** *v.* rechazar.

rebuke, 1. *n.* reprensión *f.* **2.** *v.* reprender.

rebuttal, *n.* refutación *f.*

recalcitrant, *a.* recalcitrante.

recall, *v.* recordar; acordarse de; hacer volver.

recapitulate, *v.* recapitular.

recede, *v.* retroceder.

receipt, *n.* recibo *m.;* (com., pl.) ingresos *m.pl.*

receive, *v.* recibir.

receiver, *n.* receptor *m.*

recent, *a.* reciente.

recently, *adv.* recién.

receptacle, *n.* receptáculo *m.*

reception, *n.* acogida; recepción *f.*

receptionist, *n.* recepcionista *m. & f.*

receptive, *a.* receptivo.

recess, *n.* nicho; retiro; recreo *m.*

recipe, *n.* receta *f.*

recipient, *n.* receptor, recipiente *m.*

reciprocate, *v.* corresponder; reciprocar.

recite, *v.* recitar.

reckless, *a.* descuidado; imprudente.

reckon, *v.* contar; calcular.

reclaim, *v.* reformar; (leg.) reclamar.

recline, *v.* reclinar; recostar.

recognition, *n.* reconocimiento *m.*

recognize, *v.* reconocer.

recoil, 1. *n.* culatada *f.* **2.** *v.* recular.

recollect, *v.* recordar, acordarse de.

recommend, *v.* recomendar.

recommendation, *n.* recomendación *f.*

recompense, 1. *n.* recompensa *f.* **2.** *v.* recompensar.

reconcile, *v.* reconciliar.

recondition, *v.* reacondicionar.

reconsider, *v.* considerar de nuevo.

reconstruct, *v.* reconstruir.

record, 1. *n.* registro; (sports) record *m.* **phonograph r.,** disco *m.* **2.** *v.* registrar.

record player, *n.* tocadiscos *m.*

recount, *v.* relatar; contar.

recover, *v.* recobrar; restablecerse.

recovery, *n.* recobro *m.;* recuperación *f.*

recruit, 1. *n.* recluta *m.* **2.** *v.* reclutar.

rectangle, *n.* rectángulo *m.*

rectify, *v.* rectificar.

recuperate, *v.* recuperar.

recur, *v.* recurrir.

recycle, *v.* reciclar.

red, *a.* rojo; colorado.

redeem, *v.* redimir, rescatar.

redemption, *n.* redención *f.*

reduce, *v.* reducir.

reduction, *n.* reducción *f.*

reed, *n.* caña *f.,* (S.A.) bejuco *m.*

reef, *n.* arrecife, escollo *m.*

reel, 1. *n.* aspa *f.,* carrete *m.* 2. *v.* aspar.

refer, *v.* referir.

referee, *n.* árbitro *m.*

reference, *n.* referencia *f.*

refill, 1. *n.* relleno *m.* 2. *v.* rellenar.

refine, *n.* refinar.

refinement, *n.* refinamiento *m.;* cultura *f.*

reflect, *v.* reflejar; reflexionar.

reflection, *n.* reflejo *m.;* reflexión *f.*

reflex, *a.* reflejo.

reform, 1. *n.* reforma *f.* 2. *v.* reformar.

reformation, *n.* reformación *f.*

refractory, *a.* refractorio.

refrain, 1. *n.* estribillo *m.* 2. *v.* abstenerse.

refresh, *v.* refrescar.

refreshment, *n.* refresco *m.*

refrigerator, *n.* refrigerador *m.*

refuge, *n.* refugio *m.*

refugee, *n.* refugiado -da.

refund, 1. *n.* reembolso *m.* 2. *v.* reembolsar.

refusal, *n.* negativa *f.*

refuse, 1. *n.* basura *f.* 2. *v.* negarse, rehusar.

refute, *v.* refutar.

regain, *v.* recobrar.

regal, *a.* real.

regard, 1. *n.* aprecio; respeto *m.* **with r. to,** con respecto a. 2. *v.* considerar; estimar.

regarding, *prep.* en cuanto a, acerca de.

regardless (of), a pesar de.

regent, *n.* regente *m.*

regime, *n.* régimen *m.*

regiment, 1. *n.* regimiento *m.* 2. *v.* regimentar.

region, *n.* región *f.*

register, 1. *n.* registro *m.* **cash r.,** caja registradora. 2. *v.* registrar; matricularse; (a letter) certificar.

registration, *n.* registro *m.;* matrícula *f.*

regret, 1. *n.* pena *f.* 2. *v.* sentir, lamentar.

regular, *a.* regular; ordinario.

regularity, *n.* regularidad *f.*

regulate, *v.* regular.

regulation, *n.* regulación *f.*

regulator, *n.* regulador *m.*

rehabilitate, *v.* rehabilitar.

rehearse, *v.* repasar; (theat.) ensayar.

reign, 1. *n.* reino, reinado *m.* 2. *v.* reinar.

reimburse, *v.* reembolsar.

rein, 1. *n.* rienda *f.* 2. *v.* refrenar.

reincarnation, *n.* reencarnación *f.*

reindeer, *n.* reno *m.*

reinforce, *v.* reforzar.

reinforcement, *n.* refuerzo *m.;* armadura *f.*

reiterate, *v.* reiterar.

reject, *v.* rechazar.

rejoice, *v.* regocijarse.

rejoin, *v.* reunirse con; replicar.

rejuvenate, *v.* rejuvenecer.

relapse, 1. *n.* recaída *f.* 2. *v.* recaer.

relate, *v.* relatar, contar; relacionar. **r. to,** llevarse bien con.

relation, *n.* relación *f.;* pariente *m. & f.*

relative, 1. *a.* relativo. 2. *n.* pariente *m. & f.*

relativity, *n.* relatividad *f.*

relax, *v.* descansar; relajar.

relay, 1. *n.* relevo *m.* 2. *v.* retransmitir.

release, 1. *n.* liberación *f.* 2. *v.* soltar.

relent, *v.* ceder.

relevant, *a.* pertinente.

reliability, *n.* veracidad *f.*

reliable, *a.* responsable; digno de confianza.

relic, *n.* reliquia *f.*

relief, *n.* alivio; (sculpture) relieve *m.*

relieve, *v.* aliviar.

religion, *n.* religión *f.*

religious, *a.* religioso.

relinquish, *v.* abandonar.

relish, 1. *n.* sabor; condimento *m.* 2. *v.* saborear.

reluctant, *a.* renuente.

rely, *v. r.* **on,** confiar en; contar con; depender de.

remain, 1. *n.* (pl.) restos *m.pl.* 2. *v.* quedar, permanecer.

remainder, *n.* resto *m.*

remark, 1. *n.* observación *f.* 2. *v.* observar.

remarkable, *a.* notable.

remedial, *a.* reparador.

remedy, 1. *n.* remedio *m.* 2. *v.* remediar.

remember, *v.* acordarse de, recordar.

remembrance, *n.* recuerdo *m.*

remind, *v. r.* **of,** recordar.

reminisce, *v.* pensar en o hablar de cosas pasadas.

remiss, *a.* remiso; flojo.

remit, *v.* remitir.

remorse, *n.* remordimiento *m.*

remote, *a.* remoto.

removal, *n.* alejamiento *m.;* eliminación *f.*

remove, *v.* quitar; remover.

renaissance, *n.* renacimiento *m.*

rend, *v.* hacer pedazos; separar.

render, *v.* dar; rendir; (theat.) interpretar.

rendezvous, *n.* cita *f.*

rendition, *n.* interpretación, rendición *f.*

renege, *v.* renunciar.

renew, *v.* renovar.

renewal, *n.* renovación; (com.) prórroga *f.*

renounce, *v.* renunciar a.

renovate, *v.* renovar.

renown, *n.* renombre *m.,* fama *f.*

rent, 1. *n.* alquiler *m.* 2. *v.* arrendar, alquilar.

repair, 1. *n.* reparo *m.* 2. *v.* reparar.

repatriate, *v.* repatriar.

repay, *v.* pagar; devolver.

repeat, *v.* repetir.

repel, *v.* repeler, repulsar.

repent, *v.* arrepentirse.

repentance, *n.* arrepentimiento *m.*

repercussion, *n.* repercusión *f.*

repertoire, *n.* repertorio *m.*

repetition, *n.* repetición *f.*

replace, *v.* reemplazar.

replenish, *v.* rellenar; surtir de nuevo.

reply, 1. *n.* respuesta *f.* 2. *v.* replicar; contestar.

report, 1. *n.* informe *m.* 2. *v.* informar, contar; denunciar; presentarse.

reporter, *n.* repórter, reportero *m.*

repose, 1. *n.* reposo *m.* 2. *v.* reposar; reclinar.

reprehensible, *a.* reprensible.

represent, *v.* representar.

representation, *n.* representación *f.*

representative, 1. *a.* representativo. 2. *n.* representante *m.*

repress, *v.* reprimir.

reprimand, 1. *n.* regaño *m.* 2. *v.* regañar.

reprisal, *n.* represalia *f.*

reproach, 1. *n.* reproche *m.* 2. *v.* reprochar.

reproduce, *v.* reproducir.

reproduction, *n.* reproducción *f.*

reproof, *n.* censura *f.*

reprove, *v.* censurar, regañar.

reptile, *n.* reptil *m.*

republic, *n.* república *f.*

republican, *a. & n.* republicano -na.

repudiate, *v.* repudiar.

repulsive, *a.* repulsivo, repugnante.

reputation, *n.* reputación; fama *f.*

repute, 1. *n.* reputación *f.* 2. *v.* reputar.

request, 1. *n.* súplica *f.,* ruego *m.* 2. *v.* pedir; rogar, suplicar.

require, *v.* requerir; exigir.

requirement, *n.* requisito *m.*

requisite, 1. *a.* necesario. 2. *n.* requisito *m.*

requisition, *n.* requisición *f.*

rescind, *v.* rescindir, anular.

rescue, 1. *n.* rescate *m.* 2. *v.* rescatar.

research, n. investigación f.
resemble, v. parecerse a, asemejarse a.
resent, v. resentirse de.
reservation, n. reservación f.
reserve, 1. n. reserva f. **2.** v. reservar.
reservoir, n depósito; tanque m.
reside, v. residir, morar.
residence, n. residencia, morada f.
resident, n. residente m. & f.
residue, n. residuo m.
resign, v. dimitir; resignar.
resignation, n. dimisión, resignación f.
resist, v. resistir.
resistance, n. resistencia f.
resolute, a. resuelto.
resolution, n. resolución f.
resolve, v. resolver.
resonant, a. resonante.
resort, 1. n. recurso m.; expediente m. **summer r.,** lugar de veraneo. **2.** v. acudir, recurrir.
resound, v. resonar.
resource, n. recurso m.
respect, 1. n. respeto m. **with r. to,** con respecto a. **2.** v. respetar.
respectable, a. respetable.
respectful, a. respetuoso.
respective, a. respectivo.
respiration, n. respiración f.
respite, n. pausa, tregua f.
respond, v. responder.
response, n. respuesta f.
responsibility, n. responsabilidad f.
responsible, a. responsable.
responsive, a. respondiente, sensible.
rest, 1. n. descanso; reposo m.; (music) pausa f. **the r.,** el resto, lo demás; los demás. **2.** v. descansar; rocostar.
restaurant, n. restaurante m.
restful, a. tranquilo.
restitution, n. restitución f.
restless, a. inquieto.
restoration, n. restauración f.
restore, v. restaurar.
restrain, v. refrenar.
restraint, n. limitación, restricción f.
restrict, v. restringir, limitar.
result, 1. n. resultado m. **2.** v. resultar.
resume, v. reasumir; empezar de nuevo.
resurgent, a. resurgente.
resurrect, v. resucitar.
retail, n. at r., al por menor.
retain, v. retener.
retaliate, v. vengarse.
retard, v. retardar.
retention, n. retención f.
reticent, a. reticente.
retire, v. retirar.
retort, 1. n. réplica; (chem.) retorta f. **2.** v. replicar.
retreat, 1. n. retiro m.; (mil.) retirada, retreta f. **2.** v. retirarse.

retribution, n. retribución f.
retrieve, v. recobrar.
return, 1. n. vuelta f., regreso; retorno m. **by r. mail,** a vuelta de correo. **2.** v. volver, regresar; devolver.
reunion, n. reunión f.
reveal, v. revelar.
revelation, n. revelación f.
revenge, n. venganza f. **to get r.,** vengarse.
revenue, n. renta f.
revere, v. reverenciar, venerar.
reverence, 1. n. reverencia f. **2.** v. reverenciar.
reverend, 1. a. reverendo. **2.** n. pastor m.
reverent, a. reverente.
reverse, 1. a. inverso. **2.** n. revés, inverso m. **3.** v. invertir; revocar.
revert, v. revertir.
review, 1. n. repaso m.; revista f. **2.** v. repasar; revistar.
revise, v. revisar.
revision, n. revisión f.
revival, n. reavivamiento m.
revive, v. avivar; revivir.
revoke, v. revocar.
revolt, 1. n. rebelión f. **2.** v. rebelarse.
revolution, n. revolución f.
revolutionary, a. & n. revolucionario -ria.
revolve, v. girar; dar vueltas.
revolver, n. revólver m.
reward, 1. n. pago m.; recompensa f. **2.** v. recompensar.
rhetoric, n. retórica f.
rheumatism, n. reumatismo m.
rhinoceros, n. rinoceronte m.
rhyme, 1. n. rima f. **2.** v. rimar.
rhythm, n. ritmo m.
rhythmical, a. rítmico.
rib, n. costilla f.
ribbon, n. cinta f.
rice, n. arroz m.
rich, a. rico.
rid, v. librar. **get r. of,** deshacerse de, quitarse.
riddle, n. enigma; rompecabezas m.
ride, 1. n. paseo (a caballo o en coche) m. **2.** v. cabalgar; ir en coche.
ridge, n. cerro m.; arruga f.; (of a roof) caballete m.
ridicule, 1. n. ridículo m. **2.** v. ridiculizar.
ridiculous, a. ridículo.
rifle, 1. n. fusil m. **2.** v. robar.
rig, 1. n. aparejo m. **2.** v. aparejar.
right, 1. a. derecho; correcto. **to be r.,** tener razón. **2.** adv. bien, correctamente. **r. here,** etc., aquí mismo, etc. **all r.,** está bien, muy bien. **3.** n. derecho m.; justicia f. **to the r.,** a la derecha. **4.** v. corregir; enderezar.
righteous, a. justo.
rigid, a. rígido.
rigor, n. rigor m.
rigorous, a. riguroso.

rim, n. margen m. or f.; borde m.
ring, 1. n. anillo m.; sortija f.; círculo; campaneo m. **2.** v. cercar; sonar; tocar.
rinse, v. enjuagar, lavar.
riot, n. motín; alboroto m.
rip, 1. n. rasgadura f. **2.** v. rasgar; descoser.
ripe, a. maduro.
ripen, v. madurar.
ripoff, n. robo, atraco m.
ripple, 1. n. onda f. **2.** v. ondear.
rise, 1. n. subida f. **2.** v. ascender; levantarse; (moon) salir.
risk, 1. n. riesgo m. **2.** v. arriesgar.
rite, n. rito m.
ritual, a. & n. ritual m.
rival, n. rival m. & f.
rivalry, n. rivalidad f.
river, n. río m.
rivet, 1. n. remache, roblón f. **2.** v. remachar, roblar.
road, n. camino m.; carretera f.
roam, v. vagar.
roar, 1. n. rugido, bramido m. **2.** v. rugir, bramar.
roast, 1. n. asado m. **2.** v. asar.
rob, v. robar.
robber, n. ladrón -na.
robbery, n. robo m.
robe, n. manto m.
robin, n. petirrojo m.
robust, a. robusto.
rock, 1. n. roca f.; (music) rock m., musica (de) rock f. **2.** v. mecer; oscilar.
rocker, n. mecedora f.
rocket, n. cohete m.
rocky, a. pedregoso.
rod, n. varilla f.
rodent, n. roedor m.
rogue, n. bribón, pícaro m.
roguish, a. pícaro.
role, n. papel m.
roll, 1. n. rollo m.; lista f.; panecillo m. **to call the r.,** pasar lista. **2.** v. rodar. **r. up,** enrollar.
roller, n. rodillo, cilindro m.
Roman, a. & n. romano -na.
romance, 1. a. románico. **2.** n. romance m.; amorío m.
romantic, a. romántico.
romp, v. retozar; jugar.
roof, 1. n. techo m. **2.** v. techar.
room, n. cuarto m., habitación f.; lugar m. **2.** v. alojarse.
roommate, n. compañero -ra de cuarto.
rooster, n. gallo m.
root, n. raíz f. **to take r.,** arraigar.
rope, n. cuerda, soga f.
rose, n. rosa f.
rosy, a. róseo, rosado.
rot, 1. n. putrefacción f. **2.** v. pudrirse.
rotary, a. giratorio; rotativo.
rotate, v. girar; alternar.
rotation, n. rotación f.
rotten, a. podrido.
rouge, n. colorete m.

rough, *a.* áspero; rudo; grosero; aproximado.

round, 1. *a.* rodondo. **r. trip,** viaje de ida y vuelta. 2. *n.* ronda *f.;* (boxing) asalto *m.*

rouse, *v.* despertar.

rout, 1. *n.* derrota *f.* 2. *v.* derrotar.

route, *n.* ruta, vía *f.*

routine, 1. *a.* rutinario. 2. *n.* rutina *f.pl.*

rove, *v.* vagar.

rover, *n.* vagabundo -da.

row, 1. *n.* fila; pelea *f.* 2. *v.* (naut.) remar.

rowboat, *n.* bote de remos.

rowdy, *a.* alborotoso.

royal, *a.* real.

royalty, *n.* realeza *f.;* (pl.) regalías *f.pl.*

rub, *v.* frotar. **r. against,** rozar. **r. out,** borrar.

rubber, *n.* goma *f.;* caucho *m.;* (pl.) chanclos *m.pl.,* zapatos de goma.

rubbish, *n.* basura *f.;* (nonsense) tonterías *f.pl.*

ruby, *n.* rubí *m.*

rudder, *n.* timón *m.*

ruddy, *a.* colorado.

rude, *a.* rudo; grosero; descortés.

rudiment, *n.* rudimento *m.*

rue, *v.* deplorar; lamentar.

ruffian, *n.* rufián, bandolero *m.*

ruffle, 1. *n.* volante fruncido. 2. *v.* fruncir; irritar.

rug, *n.* alfombra *f.*

rugged, *a.* áspero; robusto.

ruin, 1. *n.* ruina *f.* 2. *v.* arruinar.

ruinous, *a.* ruinoso.

rule, 1. *n.* regla *f.* **as a r.,** por regla general. 2. *v.* gobernar; mandar; rayar.

ruler, *n.* gobernante; soberano *m.;* regla *f.*

rum, *n.* ron *m.*

rumble, *v.* retumbar.

rumor, *n.* rumor *m.*

run, *v.* correr; hacer correr. **r. away,** escaparse. **r. into,** chocar con.

runner, *n.* corredor -ra; mensajero -ra.

rupture, 1. *n.* rotura; hernia *f.* 2. *v.* reventar.

rural, *a.* rural, campestre.

rush, 1. *n.* prisa *f.;* (bot.) junco *m.* 2. *v.* ir de prisa.

Russia, *n.* Rusia *f.*

Russian, *a.* & *n.* ruso -sa.

rust, 1. *n.* herrumbre *f.* 2. *v.* aherrumbrarse.

rustic, *a.* rústico.

rustle, 1. *n.* susurro *m.* 2. *v.* susurrar.

rusty, *a.* mohoso.

rut, *n.* surco *m.*

ruthless, *a.* cruel, inhumano.

rye, *n.* centeno *m.*

S

saber, *n.* sable *m.*

saber, *n.* sable *m.*

sable, *n.* cebellina *f.*

sabotage, *n.* sabotaje *m.*

sachet, *n.* perfumador *m.*

sack, 1. *n.* saco *m.* 2. *v.* (mil.) saquear.

sacred, *a.* sagrado, santo.

sacrifice, 1. *n.* sacrificio *m.* 2. *v.* sacrificar.

sacrilege, *n.* sacrilegio *m.*

sad, *a.* triste.

saddle, 1. *n.* silla de montar. 2. *v.* ensillar.

safe, 1. *a.* seguro; salvo. 2. *n.* caja de caudales.

safeguard, 1. *n.* salvaguardia *m.* 2. *v.* proteger, poner a salvo.

safety, *n.* seguridad, protección *f.*

safety pin, *n.* imperdible *m.*

sage, 1. *a.* sabio, sagaz. 2. *n.* sabio *m.;* (bot.) salvia *f.*

sail, 1. *n.* vela *f.;* paseo por mar. 2. *v.* navegar; embarcarse.

sailboat, *n.* barco de vela.

sailor, *n.* marinero *m.*

saint, *n.* santo -ta.

sake, *n.* **for the s. of,** por; por el bien de.

salad, *n.* ensalada *f.* **s. bowl,** ensaladera *f.*

salary, *n.* sueldo, salario *m.*

sale, *n.* venta *f.*

salesman, *n.* vendedor *m.;* viajante de comercio.

sales tax, impuesto sobre la venta.

saliva, *n.* saliva *f.*

salmon, *n.* salmón *m.*

salt, 1. *a.* salado. 2. *n.* sal *f.* 3. *v.* salar.

salute, 1. *n.* saludo *m.* 2. *v.* saludar.

salvage, *v.* salvar; recobrar.

salvation, *n.* salvación; redención *f.*

salve, *n.* emplasto, ungüento *m.*

same, *a.* & *pron.* mismo. **it's all the s.,** lo mismo da.

sample, 1. *n.* muestra *f.* 2. *v.* probar.

sanatorium, *n.* sanatorio *m.*

sanctify, *v.* santificar.

sanction, 1. *n.* sanción *f.* 2. *v.* sancionar.

sanctity, *n.* santidad *f.*

sanctuary, *n.* santuario, asilo *m.*

sand, *n.* arena *f.*

sandal, *n.* sandalia *f.*

sandwich, *n.* sandwich *m.*

sandy, *a.* arenoso; (color) rufo.

sane, *a.* cuerdo; sano.

sanitary, *a.* higiénico, sanitario.

sanitation, *n.* saneamiento *m.*

sanity, *n.* cordura *f.*

sap, 1. *n.* savia *f.;* (coll.) estúpido, bobo *m.* 2. *v.* agotar.

sapphire, *n.* zafiro *m.*

sarcasm, *n.* sarcasmo *m.*

sardine, *n.* sardina *f.*

sash, *n.* cinta *f.*

satellite, *n.* satélite *m.*

satin, *n.* raso *m.*

satire, *n.* sátira *f.*

satisfaction, *n.* satisfacción; recompensa *f.*

satisfactory, *a.* satisfactorio.

satisfy, *v.* satisfacer. **be satisfied that . . . ,** estar convencido de que.

saturate, *v.* saturar.

Saturday, *n.* sábado *m.*

sauce, *n.* salsa; compota *f.*

saucer, *n.* platillo *m.*

saucy, *a.* descarado, insolente.

sausage, *n.* salchicha *f.*

savage, *a.* & *n.* salvaje *m.*

save, 1. *v.* salvar; guardar; ahorrar, economizar. 2. *prep.* salvo, excepto.

savings, *n.* ahorros *m.pl.*

savior, *n.* salvador *m.*

savor, 1. *n.* sabor *m.* 2. *v.* saborear.

savory, *a.* sabroso.

saw, 1. *n.* sierra *f.* 2. *v.* aserrar.

say, *v.* decir; recitar.

saying, *n.* dicho, refrán *m.*

scaffold, *n.* andamio; (gallows) patíbulo *m.*

scald, *v.* escaldar.

scale, 1. *n.* escala; (of fish) escama *f.;* (pl.) balanza *f.* 2. *v.* escalar; escamar.

scalp, 1. *n.* pericráneo *m.* 2. *v.* escalpar.

scan, *v.* hojear, repasar; (poetry) escandir.

scandal, *n.* escándalo *m.*

scant, *a.* escaso.

scar, *n.* cicatriz *f.*

scarce, *a.* escaso; raro.

scarcely, *adv.* & *conj.* apenas.

scare, 1. *n.* susto *m.* 2. *v.* asustar. **s. away,** espantar.

scarf, *n.* pañueleta, bufanda *f.*

scarlet, *n.* escarlata *f.*

scatter, *v.* esparcir; dispersar.

scavenger, *n.* basurero *m.*

scenario, *n.* escenario *m.*

scene, *n.* vista *f.,* paisaje *m.;* (theat.) escena *f.* **behind the scenes,** bajo cuerda.

scenery, *n.* paisaje *m.;* (theat.) decorado *m.*

scent, 1. *n.* olor, perfume; (sense) olfato *m.* 2. *v.* perfumar; (fig.) sospechar.

schedule, 1. *n.* programa, horario *m.* 2. *v.* fijar la hora para.

scheme, 1. *n.* proyecto; esquema *m.* 2. *v.* intrigar.

scholar, *n.* erudito; becado -da.

scholarship, *n.* beca; erudición *f.*

school, 1. *n.* escuela *f.;* colegio *m.;* (of fish) banco *m.* 2. *v.* enseñar.

sciatica, *n.* ciática *f.*

science, *n.* ciencia *f.*

science fiction, *n.* ciencia ficción *f.*

scientific, *a.* científico.

scientist, *n.* científico -ca.

scissors, *n.* tijeras *f.pl.*
scoff, *v.* mofarse, burlarse.
scold, *v.* regañar.
scoop, 1. *n.* cucharón *m.;* cucharada *f.* 2. *v.* **s. out**, recoger, sacar.
scope, *n.* alcance; campo *m.*
scorch, 1. *n.* tantos *m.pl.;* (music) partitura *f.* 2. *v.* marcar, hacer tantos.
scorn, 1. *n.* desprecio *m.* 2. *v.* despreciar.
scornful, *a.* desdeñoso.
Scotch, *a.* escocés.
Scotland, *n.* Escocia *f.*
scour, *v.* fregar, estregar.
scourge, *n.* azote *m.;* plaga *f.*
scout, 1. *n.* explorador *m.* 2. *v.* explorar, reconocer.
scramble, 1. *n.* ribatiña *f.* 2. *v.* bregar. **scrambled eggs**, huevos revueltos.
scrap, 1. *n.* migaja *f.;* pedacito *m.;* (coll.) riña *f.* **s. metal**, hierro viejo. **s. paper**, papel borrador. 2. *v.* desechar; (coll.) reñir.
scrape, 1. *n.* lío, apuro *m.* 2. *v.* rascar; (feet) restregar.
scratch, 1. *n.* rasguño *m.* 2. *v.* rasguñar; rayar.
scream, 1. *n.* grito, chillido *m.* 2. *v.* gritar, chillar.
screen, *n.* biombo *m.;* (for window) tela metálica; (movie) pantalla *f.*
screw, 1. *n.* tornillo *m.* 2. *v.* atornillar.
screwdriver, *n.* destornillador *m.*
scribble, *v.* hacer garabatos.
scroll, *n.* rúbrica *f.;* rollo de papel.
scrub, *v.* gregar, estregar.
scruple, *n.* escrúpulo *m.*
scrupulous, *a.* escrupuloso.
sculptor, *n.* escultor *m.*
sculpture, 1. *n.* escultura *f.* 2. *v.* esculpir.
scythe, *n.* guadaña *f.*
sea, *n.* mar *m. or f.*
seabed, *n.* lecho marino *m.*
seal, 1. *n.* sello *m.;* (animal) foca *f.* 2. *v.* sellar.
seam, *n.* costura *f.*
seaport, *n.* puerto de mar.
search, 1. *n.* registro *m.* **in s. of**, en busca de. 2. *v.* registrar. **s. for**, buscar.
seasick, *a.* mareado. **to get s.**, marearse.
season, *n.* estación; sazón, temporada *f.* 2. *v.* sazonar.
seasoning, *n.* condimento *m.*
seat, 1. *n.* asiento *m.;* residencia, sede *f.;* (theat.) localidad *f.* 2. *v.* sentar. **be seated**, sentarse.
second, 1. *a. & n.* segundo *m.* 2. *v.* apoyar, segundar.
secondary, *a.* secundario.
secret, *a. & n.* secreto *m.*
secretary, *n.* secretario -ria; (govt.) ministro *m.;* (furniture) papelera *f.*

sect, *n.* secta *f.;* partido *m.*
section, *n.* sección, parte *f.*
sectional, *a.* regional, local.
secular, *a.* secular.
secure, 1. *a.* seguro. 2. *v.* asegurar; obtener, conseguir; (fin.) garantizar.
security, *n.* seguridad; garantía *f.*
sedative, *a. & n.* sedativo *m.*
seduce, *v.* seducir.
see, *v.* ver; comprender. **s. off**, despedirse de. **s. to**, encargarse de.
seed, 1. *n.* semilla *f.* 2. *v.* sembrar.
seek, *v.* buscar. **s. to**, tratar de.
seem, *v.* parecer.
seep, *v.* colarse.
segment, *n.* segmento *m.*
segregate, *v.* segregar.
seize, *v.* agarrar; apoderarse de.
seldom, *adv.* rara vez.
select, 1. *a.* escogido, selecto. 2. *v.* elegir, seleccionar.
selection, *n.* selección *f.*
selective, *a.* escogedor.
selfish, *a.* egoísta.
selfishness, *n.* egoísmo *m.*
sell, *v.* vender.
semester, *n.* semestre *m.*
semicircle, *n.* semicírculo *m.*
senate, *n.* senado *m.*
senator, *n.* senador -ra.
send, *v.* mandar, enviar; (a wire) poner. **s. away**, despedir. **s. back**, devolver. **s. for**, mandar buscar. **s. off**, expedir. **s. word**, mandar recado.
senile, *a.* senil.
senior, *a.* mayor; más viejo. **Sr.**, padre.
senior citizen, persona de edad.
sensation, *n.* sensación *f.*
sensational, *a.* sensacional.
sense, 1. *n.* sentido; juicio *m.* 2. *v.* percibir; sospechar.
sensible, *a.* sensato, razonable.
sensitive, *a.* sensible; sensitivo.
sensual, *a.* sensual.
sentence, 1. *n.* frase; (gram.) oración; (leg.) sentencia *f.* 2. *v.* condenar.
sentiment, *n.* sentimiento *m.*
sentimental, *a.* sentimental.
separate, 1. *a.* separado; suelto. 2. *v.* separar, dividir.
separation, *n.* separación *f.*
September, *n.* septiembre *m.*
sequence, *n.* serie *f.* **in s.**, seguidos.
serenade, 1. *n.* serenata *f.* 2. *v.* dar serenata a.
serene, *a.* sereno; tranquilo.
sergeant, *n.* sargento *m.*
serial, *a.* en serie, de serie.
series, *n.* serie *f.*
serious, *a.* serio; grave.
sermon, *n.* sermón *m.*
serpent, *n.* serpiente *f.*
servant, *n.* criado -da; servidor -ra.
serve, *v.* servir.

service, 1. *n.* servicio *m.* **at the s. of**, a las órdenes de. **to be of s.**, servir; ser útil. 2. *v.* (auto.) reparar.
session, *n.* sesión *f.*
set, 1. *a.* fijo. 2. *n.* colección *f.;* (of a game) juego; (mech.) aparato; (theat.) decorado *m.* 3. *v.* poner, colocar; fijar; (sun) ponerse. **s. forth**, exponer. **s. off, s. out**, salir. **s. up**, instalar; establecer.
settle, *v.* solucionar; arreglar; establecerse.
settlement, *n.* caserío; arreglo; acuerdo *m.*
settler, *n.* poblador -ra.
seven, *a. & pron.* siete.
seventeen, *a. & pron.* diecisiete.
seventh, *a.* séptimo.
seventy, *a. & pron.* setenta.
sever, *v.* desunir; romper.
several, *a. & pron.* varios.
severe, *a.* severo; grave.
severity, *n.* severidad *f.*
sew, *v.* coser.
sewer, *n.* cloaca *f.*
sex, *n.* sexo *m.*
sexism, *n.* sexismo *m.*
sexist, *a. & n.* sexista.
sexton, *n.* sacristán *m.*
sexual, *a.* sexual.
shabby, *a.* haraposo, desaliñeado.
shade, 1. *n.* sombra *f.;* tinte *m.;* (window) transparente *m.* 2. *v.* sombrear.
shadow, *n.* sombra *f.*
shady, *a.* sombroso; sospechoso.
shaft, *n.* columna; (mech.) asta *f.*
shake, *v.* sacudir; agitar; temblar. **s. hands with**, dar la mano a.
shallow, *a.* poco hondo; superficial.
shame, 1. *n.* vergüenza *f.* **to be a s.**, ser una lástima. 2. *v.* avergonzar.
shameful, *a.* vergonzoso.
shampoo, *n.* champú *m.*
shape, 1. *n.* forma *f.;* estado *m.* 2. *v.* formar.
share, 1. *n.* parte; (stock) acción *f.* 2 *v.* compartir.
shark, *n.* tiburón *m.*
sharp, *a.* agudo; (blade) afilado.
sharpen, *v.* aguzar; afilar.
shatter, *v.* estrellar; hacer pedazos.
shave, 1. *n.* afeitada *f.* 2. *v.* afeitarse.
shawl, *n.* rebozo, chal *m.*
she, *pron.* ella *f.*
sheaf, *n.* gavilla *f.*
shear, *v.* cizallar.
shears, *n.* cizallas *f.pl.*
sheath, *n.* vaina *f.*
shed, 1. *n.* cobertizo *m.* 2. *v.* arrojar, quitarse.
sheep, *n.* oveja *f.*

sheet, *n.* sábana; (of paper) hoja *f.*

shelf, *n.* estante, *m.,* repisa *f.*

shell, 1. *n.* cáscara; (sea) concha *f.;* (mil.) proyectil *m.* 2. *v.* desgranar; bombardear.

shellac, *n.* laca *f.*

shelter, 1. *n.* albergue; refugio *m.* 2. *v.* albergar; amparar.

shepherd, *n.* pastor *m.*

sherry, *n.* jerez *m.*

shield, 1. *n.* escudo *m.* 2. *v.* amparar.

shift, 1. *n.* cambio; (work) turno *m.* 2. *v.* cambiar, mudar. **s. for oneself,** arreglárselas.

shine, 1. *n.* brillo, lustre *m.* 2. *v.* brillar; (shoes) lustrar.

shiny, *a.* brillante, lustroso.

ship, 1. *n.* barco *m.,* nave *f.* 2. *v.* embarcar; (com.) enviar.

shipment, *n.* envío, embarque *m.*

shirk, *v.* faltar a.

shirt, *n.* camisa *f.*

shiver, 1. *n.* temblor *m.* 2. *v.* temblar.

shock, 1. *n.* choque *m.* 2. *v.* chocar.

shoe, *n.* zapato *m.*

shoelace, *n.* lazo *m.;* cordón de zapato.

shoemaker, *n.* zapatero *m.*

shoot, *v.* tirar; (gun) disparar. **s. away, s. off,** salir disparado.

shop, *n.* tienda *f.*

shopping, *n.* **to go s.,** hacer compras, ir de compras.

shore, *n.* orilla; playa *f.*

short, *a.* corto; breve; (in stature) pequeño, bajo. **a s. time,** poco tiempo. **in s.,** en suma.

shortage, *n.* escasez; falta *f.*

shorten, *v.* acortar, abreviar.

shortly, *adv.* en breve, dentro de poco.

shorts, *n.* calzoncillos *m.pl.*

shot, *n.* tiro, disparo *m.*

shoulder, 1. *n.* hombro *m.* 2. *v.* asumir; cargar con.

shout, 1. *n.* grito *m.* 2. *v.* gritar.

shove, 1. *n.* empujón *m.* 2. *v.* empujar.

shovel, 1. *n.* pala *f.* 2. *v.* traspalar.

show, 1. *n.* ostentación *f.;* (theat.) función *f.;* espectáculo *m.* 2. *v.* enseñar, mostrar; verse. **s. up,** destacarse; (coll.) asomar.

shower, *n.* chubasco *m.;* (bath) ducha *f.*

shrapnel, *n.* metralla *f.*

shrewd, *a.* astuto.

shriek, 1. *n.* chillido *m.* 2. *v.* chillar.

shrill, *a.* chillón, agudo.

shrimp, *n.* camarón *m.*

shrine, *n.* santuario *f.*

shrink, *v.* encogerse, contraerse. **s. from,** huir de.

shroud, 1. *n.* mortaja *f.* 2. *v.* (fig.) ocultar.

shrub, *n.* arbusto *m.*

shudder, 1. *n.* estremecimiento *m.* 2. *v.* estremecerse.

shun, *v.* evitar, huir de.

shut, *v.* cerrar. **s. in,** encerrar. **s. up,** (coll.) callarse.

shutter, *n.* persiana *f.*

shy, *a.* tímido, vergonzoso.

sick, *a.* enfermo. **s. of,** aburrido de, cansado de.

sickness, *n.* enfermedad *f.*

side, 1. *n.* lado; partido *m.;* parte *f.;* (anat.) costado *m.* 2. *v.* **s. with,** ponerse del lado de.

sidewalk, *n.* acera, vereda *f.*

siege, *n.* asedio *m.*

sieve, *n.* cedazo *m.*

sift, *v.* cerner.

sigh, 1. *n.* suspiro *m.* 2. *v.* suspirar.

sight, 1. *n.* vista *f.;* punto de interés. **to lose s. of,** perder de vista. 2. *v.* divisar.

sign, 1. *n.* letrero; señal, seña *f.* 2. *v.* firmar. **s. up,** inscribirse.

signal, 1. *n.* señal *f.* 2. *v.* hacer señales.

signature, *n.* firma *f.*

significance, *n.* significación *f.*

significant, *a.* significativo.

signify, *v.* significar.

silence, 1. *n.* silencio *m.* 2. *v.* hacer callar.

silent, *a.* silencioso; callado.

silk, *n.* seda *f.*

silken, silky, *a.* sedoso.

sill, *n.* umbral de puerta *m.,* solera *f.*

silly, *a.* necio, tonto.

silo, *n.* silo *m.*

silver, *n.* plata *f.*

silverware, *n.* artículos de plata.

similar, *a.* semejante, parecido.

similarity, *n.* semejanza *f.*

simple, *a.* sencillo, simple.

simplicity, *n.* sencillez *f.*

simplify, *v.* simplificar.

simulate, *v.* simular.

simultaneous, *a.* simultáneo.

sin, 1. *n.* pecado *m.* 2. *v.* pecar.

since, 1. *adv.* desde entonces. 2. *prep.* desde. 3. *conj.* desde que; puesto que.

sincere, *a.* sincero.

sincerely, *adv.* sinceramente.

sincerity, *n.* sinceridad *f.*

sinew, *n.* tendón *m.*

sinful, *a.* pecador.

sing, *v.* cantar.

singe, *v.* chamuscar.

singer, *n.* cantante *m. & f.*

single, *a.* solo; (room) sencillo; (unmarried) soltero.

singular, *a. & n.* singular *m.*

sinister, *a.* siniestro.

sink, 1. *n.* fregadero *m.* 2. *v.* hundir; (fig.) abatir.

sinner, *n.* pecador -ra.

sinuous, *a.* sinuoso.

sinus, *n.* seno; hueco *m.*

sip, 1. *n.* sorbo *m.* 2. *v.* sorber.

siphon, *n.* sifón *m.*

sir, *title.* señor.

siren, *n.* sirena *f.*

sirloin, *n.* solomillo *m.*

sisal, *n.* henequén *m.*

sister, *n.* hermana *f.*

sister-in-law, *n.* cuñada *f.*

sit, *v.* sentarse; posar. **be sitting,** estar sentado. **s. down,** sentarse. **s. up,** incorporarse; quedar levantado.

site, *n.* sitio, local *m.*

sitting, *n.* sesión *f.*

situate, *v.* situar.

situation, *n.* situación *f.*

six, *a. & pron.* seis.

sixteen, *a. & pron.* dieciseis.

sixth, *a.* sexto.

sixty, *a. & pron.* sesenta.

size, 1. *n.* tamaño *f.;* (of shoe, etc.) número *m.*

sizing, *n.* aderezo *m.*

skate, 1. *n.* patín *m.* 2. *v.* patinar.

skateboard, *n.* monopatín *m.*

skein, *n.* madeja *f.*

skeleton, *n.* esqueleto *m.*

skeptic, *n.* escéptico -ca.

skeptical, *a.* escéptico.

sketch, 1. *n.* esbozo *m.* 2. *v.* esbozar.

ski, 1. *n.* esquí *m.* 2. *v.* esquiar.

skid, 1. *v.* resbalar. 2. *n.* varadera *f.*

skill, *n.* destreza, habilidad *f.*

skillful, *a.* diestro, hábil.

skim, *v.* rasar; (milk) desnatar. **s. over, s. through,** hojear.

skin, 1. *n.* piel; (of fruit) corteza *f.* 2. *v.* desollar.

skip, 1. *n.* brinco *m.* 2. *v.* brincar. **s. over,** pasar por alto.

skirmish, 1. *n.* escaramuza *f.*

skirt, *n.* falda *f.*

skull, *n.* cráneo *m.*

skunk, *n.* zorrillo *m.*

sky, *n.* cielo *m.*

skylight, *n.* tragaluz *m.*

skyscraper, *n.* rascacielos *m.*

slab, *n.* tabla *f.*

slack, *a.* flojo; descuidado.

slacken, *v.* relajar.

slacks, *n.* pantalones flojos.

slam, 1. *n.* portazo *m.* 2. *v.* cerrar de golpe.

slander, 1. *n.* calumnia *f.* 2. *v.* calumniar.

slang, *n.* jerga *f.*

slant, 1. *n.* sesgo *m.* 2. *v.* sesgar.

slap, 1. *n.* bofetada, palmada *f.* 2. *v.* dar una bofetada.

slash, 1. *n.* cuchillada *f.* 2. *v.* acuchillar.

slat, *n.* tablilla *f.* 2. *v.* lanzar.

slate, 1. *n.* pizarra *f.;* lista de candidatos. 2. *n.* destinar.

slaughter, 1. *n.* matanza *f.* 2. *v.* matar.

slave, *n.* esclavo -va.

slavery, *n.* esclavitud *f.*

Slavic, *a.* eslavo.

slay, *v.* matar, asesinar.

sled, *n.* trineo *m.*

sleek, *a.* liso.

sleep, 1. *n.* sueño *m.* **to get much s.,** dormir mucho. 2. *v.* dormir.

sleeper, sleeping car, *n.* coche cama.

sleepy, *a.* soñoliento. **to be s.,** tener sueño.

sleet, 1. *n.* cellisca *f.* **2.** *v.* cellisquear.

sleeve, *n.* manga *f.*

sleigh, *n.* trineo *m.*

slender, *a.* delgado.

slice, 1. *n.* rebanada *f.;* (of meat) tajada *f.* **2.** *v.* rebanar; tajar.

slide, *v.* resbalar, deslizarse.

slide rule, *n.* regla de cálculo *f.*

slight, 1. *n.* desaire *m.* **2.** *a.* pequeño; leve. **3.** *v.* desairar.

slim, *a.* delgado.

slime, *n.* lama *f.*

sling, 1. *n.* honda *f.;* (med.) cabestrillo *m.* **2.** *v.* tirar.

slink, *v.* escabullirse.

slip, 1. *n.* imprudencia; (garment) combinación *f.;* (of paper) trozo *m.;* ficha *f.* **2.** *v.* resbalar; deslizar. **s. up,** equivocarse.

slipper, *n.* chinela *f.*

slippery, *a.* resbaloso.

slit, 1. *n.* abertura *f.* **2.** *v.* cortar.

slogan, *n.* lema *m.*

slope, 1. *n.* declive *m.* **2.** *v.* inclinarse.

sloppy, *a.* desaliñado, chapucero.

slot, *n.* ranura *f.*

slot machine, *n.* máquina de servicio automático *f.*

slouch, 1. *n.* patán *m.* **2.** *v.* estar gacho.

slovenly, *a.* desaliñado.

slow, 1. *a.* lento; (watch) atrasado. **2.** *v.* **s. down, s. up,** retardar; ir más despacio.

slowly, *adv.* despacio.

slowness, *n.* lentitud *f.*

sluggish, *a.* perezoso, inactivo.

slum, *n.* barrio bajo *m.*

slumber, *v.* dormitar.

slur, 1. *n.* estigma *m.* **2.** *v.* menospreciar.

slush, *n.* fango *m.*

sly, *a.* taimado. **on the s.** a hurtadillas.

smack, 1. *n.* manotada *f.* **2.** *v.* manotear.

small, *a.* pequeño.

smallpox, *n.* viruela *f.*

smart, 1. *a.* listo; elegante. **2.** *v.* escocer.

smash, *v.* aplastar; hacer pedazos.

smear, 1. *n.* mancha; difamación *f.* **2.** *v.* manchar; difamar.

smell, 1. *n.* olor; (sense) olfato *m.* **2.** *v.* oler.

smelt, 1. *n.* eperlano *m.* **2.** *v.* fundir.

smile, 1. *n.* sonrisa *f.* **2.** *v.* sonreír.

smite, *v.* afligir; apenar.

smock, *n.* camisa de mujer *f.*

smoke, 1. *n.* humo *m.* **2.** *v.* fumar; (food) ahumar.

smokestack, *n.* chimenea *f.*

smolder, *v.* arder sin llama.

smooth, 1. *a.* liso; suave; tranquilo. **2.** *v.* alisar.

smother, *v.* sofocar.

smug, *a.* presumido.

smuggle, *v.* pasar de contrabando.

snack, *n.* bocadillo *m.*

snag, *n.* nudo *m.,* obstáculo *m.*

snail, *n.* caracol *m.*

snake, *n.* culebra, serpiente *f.*

snap, 1. *n.* trueno *m.* **2.** *v.* tronar, romper.

snapshot, *n.* instantánea *f.*

snare, *n.* trampa *f.*

snarl, 1. *n.* gruñido *m.* **2.** *v.* gruñir; (hair) enredar.

snatch, *v.* arrebatar.

sneak, *v.* ir, entrar, salir (etc.) a hurtadillas.

sneaker, *n.* sujeto ruín *m.*

sneer, 1. *n.* mofa *f.* **2.** *v.* mofarse.

sneeze, 1. *n.* estornudo *m.* **2.** *v.* estornudar.

snicker, *n.* risita *m.*

snob, *n.* esnob *m.*

snore, 1. *n.* ronquido *m.* **2.** *v.* roncar.

snow, 1. *n.* nieve *f.* **2.** *v.* nevar.

snowdrift, *n.* ventisquero *m.*

snub, *v.* desairar.

snug, *a.* abrigado y cómodo.

so, 1. *adv.* así; (also) también. **so as to,** para. **so that,** para que. **so . . . as,** tan . . . como. **so . . . that,** tan . . . que. **2.** *conj.* así es que.

soak, *v.* empapar.

soap, 1. *n.* jabón *m.* **2.** *v.* enjabonar.

soar, *v.* remontarse.

sob, 1. *n.* sollozo *m.* **2.** *v.* sollozar.

sober, *a.* sobrio; pensativo.

sociable, *a.* sociable.

social, 1. *a.* social. **2.** *n.* tertulia *f.*

socialism, *n.* socialismo *m.*

socialist, *a.* & *n.* socialista *m.*

society, *n.* sociedad; compañía *f.*

sociology, *n.* sociología *f.*

sock, 1. *n.* calcetín; puñetazo *m.* **2.** *v.* dar un puñetazo a.

socket, *n.* cuenca *f.;* (elec.) enchufe *m.*

sod, *n.* césped *m.*

soda, *n.* soda; (chem.) sosa *f.*

sodium, *n.* sodio *m.*

sofa, *n.* sofá *m.*

soft, *a.* blando; fino; suave.

soft drink, *n.* bebida no alcohólica *m.*

soften, *v.* ablandar; suavizar.

soil, 1. *n.* suelo *m.;* tierra *f.* **2.** *v.* ensuciar.

sojourn, *n.* morada *f.,* estandia *f.*

solace, 1. *n.* solaz *m.* **2.** *v.* solazar.

solar, *a.* solar.

solar system, *n.* sistema solar *m.*

solder, 1. *v.* soldar. **2.** *n.* soldadura *f.*

soldier, *n.* soldado *m.*

sole, 1. *n.* suela; (of foot) planta *f.;* (fish) lenguado *m.* **2.** *a.* único.

solemn, *a.* solemne.

solemnity, *n.* solemnidad *f.*

solicit, *v.* solicitar.

solicitous, *a.* solícito.

solid, *a.* & *n.* sólido *m.*

solidify, *v.* solidificar.

solidity, *n.* solidez *f.*

solitary, *a.* solitario.

solitude, *n.* soledad *f.*

solo, *n.* solo *m.*

soloist, *n.* solista *m.*

soluble, *a.* soluble.

solution, *n.* solución *f.*

solve, *v.* solucionar; resolver.

solvent, *a.* solvente.

somber, *a.* sombrío.

some, *a.* & *pron.* algo (de), un poco (de); alguno; (pl.) algunos, unos.

somebody, someone, *pron.* alguien.

somehow, *adv.* de algún modo.

someone, *n.* alguien o alguno.

somersault, *n.* salto mortal *m.*

something, *pron.* algo, alguna cosa.

sometime, *adv.* alguna vez.

sometimes, *adv.* a veces, algunas veces.

somewhat, *adv.* algo, un poco.

somewhere, *adv.* en (*or a*) alguna parte.

son, *n.* hijo *m.*

song, *n.* canción *f.*

son-in-law, *n.* yerno *m.*

soon, *adv.* pronto. **as s. as possible,** cuanto antes. **sooner or later,** tarde o temprano. **no sooner . . . than,** apenas . . . cuando.

soot, *n.* hollín *m.*

soothe, *v.* calmar.

soothingly, *adv.* tiernamente.

sophisticated, *a.* sofisticado.

sophomore, *n.* estudiante de segundo año *m.*

soprano, *n.* soprano *m.* & *f.*

sorcery, *n.* encantamiento *m.*

sordid, *a.* sórdido.

sore, 1. *n.* llaga *f.* **2.** *a.* lastimado; (coll.) enojado. **to be s.,** doler.

sorority, *n.* hermandad de mujeres *f.*

sorrow, *n.* pesar, dolor *m.,* aflicción *f.*

sorrowful, *a.* doloroso; afligido.

sorry, *a.* **to be s.,** sentir, lamentar. **to be s. for,** compadecer.

sort, 1. *n.* tipo *m.;* clase, especie *f.* **s. of,** algo, un poco. **2.** *v.* clasificar.

soul, *n.* alma *f.*

sound, 1. *a.* sano; razonable; firme. **2.** *n.* sonido *m.* **3.** *v.* sonar; parecer.

soup, *n.* sopa *f.*

sour, *a.* agrio; ácido; rancio.

source, *n.* fuente; causa *f.*

south, *n.* sur *m.*

South America, *n.* Sud América, América del Sur.

South American, *a.* & *n.* sudamericano -na.

southeast, *n.* sudeste *m.*

southern, *a.* meridional.

South Pole, *n.* polo sur *m.*

southwest, *n.* sudoeste *m.*

souvenir, *n.* recuerdo *m.*

sovereign, *n.* soberano *m.*

sovereignty, *n.* soberanía *f.*

Soviet Russia, *n.* Rusia Soviética *f.*

sow, 1. *n.* puerca *f.* **2.** *v.* sembrar.

space, 1. *n.* espacio *m.* **2.** *v.* espaciar.

space shuttle, *n.* vehículo que comunica a dos naves espaciales.

spacious, *a.* espacioso.

spade, 1. *n.* laya; (cards) espada *f.* **2.** *v.* layar.

spaghetti, *n.* fideo *m.*

Spain, *n.* España *f.*

span, 1. *n.* tramo *m.* **2.** *v.* extenderse sobre.

Spaniard, *n.* español -la.

Spanish, *a.* & *n.* español *m.*

spank, *v.* pegar.

spanking, *n.* tunda, zumba *f.*

spar, *v.* altercar.

spare, 1. *a.* de respuesto. **2.** *v.* perdonar; ahorrar; prestar. **have . . . to s.,** tener . . . de sobra.

spark, *n.* chispa *f.*

sparkle, 1. *n.* destello *m.* **2.** *v.* chispear. **sparkling wine,** vino espumoso.

spark plug, *n.* bujía *f.*

sparrow, *n.* gorrión *m.*

sparse, *a.* esparcido.

spasm, *n.* espasmo *m.*

spasmodic, *a.* espasmódico.

spatter, *v.* salpicar; manchar.

speak, *v.* hablar.

speaker, *n.* conferencista *m.* & *f.*

spear, *n.* lanza *f.*

special, *a.* especial. **s. delivery,** entrega inmediata, entrega urgente.

specialist, *n.* especialista *m.* & *f.*

specialty, *n.* especialidad *f.*

species, *n.* especie *f.*

specific, *a.* específico.

specify, *v.* especificar.

specimen, *n.* espécimen *m.;* muestra *f.*

spectacle, *n.* espectáculo *m.;* (pl.) lentes, anteojos *m.pl.*

spectacular, *a.* espectacular, aparatoso.

spectator, *n.* espectador -ra.

spectrum, *n.* espectro *m.*

speculate, *v.* especular.

speculation, *n.* especulación *f.*

speech, *n.* habla *f.;* lenguaje; discurso *m.* **part of s.,** parte de la oración.

speechless, *a.* mudo.

speed, 1. *n.* velocidad; rapidez

f. **2.** *v.* **s. up,** acelerar, apresurar.

speedometer, *n.* velocímetro *m.*

speedy, *a.* veloz, rápido.

spell, 1. *n.* hechizo; rato; (med.) ataque *m.* **2.** *v.* escribir; relevar.

spelling, *n.* ortografía *f.*

spend, *v.* gastar; (time) pasar.

spendthrift, *n.* pródigo; manirroto *m.*

sphere, *n.* esfera *f.*

spice, 1. *n.* especia *f.* **2.** *v.* especiar.

spider, *n.* araña *f.*

spike, *n.* alcayata *f.*

spill, *v.* derramar.

spillway, *n.* vertedero *m.*

spin, *v.* hilar; girar.

spinach, *n.* espinaca *f.*

spine, *n.* espinazo *m.*

spinet, *n.* espineta *f.*

spinster, *n.* solterona *f.*

spiral, *a.* & *n.* espiral *m.*

spire, *n.* caracol *m.,* espira *f.*

spirit, *n.* espíritu; ánimo *m.*

spiritual, *a.* espiritual.

spiritualism, *n.* espiritismo *m.*

spit, *v.* escupir.

spite, *n.* despecho *m.* **in s. of,** a pesar de.

splash, 1. *n.* salpicadura *f.* **2.** *v.* salpicar.

splendid, *a.* espléndido.

splendor, *n.* esplendor *m.*

splice, 1. *v.* empalmar. **2.** *n.* empalme *m.*

splint, *n.* tablilla *f.*

splinter, 1. *n.* astilla *f.* **2.** *v.* astillar.

split, 1. *n.* división *f.* **2.** *v.* dividir, romper en dos.

splurge, 1. *v.* fachendear. **2.** *n.* fachenda *f.*

spoil, 1. *n.* (pl.) botín *m.* **2.** *v.* echar a perder; (a child) mimar.

spoke, *n.* rayo (de rueda) *m.*

spokesman, *n.* interlocutor *m.*

sponge, *n.* esponja *f.*

sponsor, 1. *n.* patrocinador *m.* **2.** *v.* patrocinar; costear.

spontaneity, *n.* espontaneidad *f.*

spontaneous, *a.* espontáneo.

spool, *n.* carrete *m.*

spoon, *n.* cuchara *f.*

spoonful, *n.* cucharada *f.*

sporadic, *a.* esporádico.

sport, *n.* deporte *m.*

sportsman, 1. *a.* deportivo. **2.** *n.* deportista *f.*

spot, 1. *n.* mancha *f.;* lugar, punto *m.* **2.** *v.* distinguir.

spouse, *n.* esposo (o esposa) *m. or f.*

spout, 1. *n.* chorro; (of teapot) pico *m.* **2.** *v.* correr a chorro.

sprain, 1. *n.* torcedura *f.* **2.** *v.* torcerse.

sprawl, *v.* tenderse.

spray, 1. *n.* rociada *f.* **2.** *v.* rociar.

spread, 1. *n.* propagación; ex-

tensión; (for bed) colcha *f.* **2.** *v.* propagar; extender.

spree, *n.* parranda *f.*

sprig, *n.* ramita *f.*

sprightly, *a.* garboso.

spring, 1. *n.* resorte, muelle *m.;* (season) primavera *f.;* (of water) manantial *m.*

springboard, *n.* trampolín *m.*

sprinkle, *v.* rociar; (rain) lloviznar.

sprint, *n.* carrera *f.*

sprout, *n.* retoño *m.*

spry, *a.* ágil.

spun, *a.* hilado.

spur, 1. *n.* espuela *f.* **on the s. of the moment,** sin pensarlo. **2.** *v.* espolear.

spurious, *a.* espurio.

spurn, *v.* rechazar, despreciar.

spurt, 1. *n.* chorro *m.;* esfuerzo supremo. **2.** *v.* salir en chorro.

spy, 1. *n.* espía *m.* & *f.* **2.** *v.* espiar.

squabble, 1. *n.* riña *f.* **2.** *v.* reñir.

squad, *n.* escuadra *f.*

squadron, *n.* escuadrón *m.*

squalid, *a.* escuálido.

squall, *n.* borrasca *f.*

squalor, *n.* escualidez *f.*

squander, *v.* malgastar.

square, 1. *a.* cuadrado. **2.** *n.* cuadrado *m.;* plaza *f.*

square dance, *n.* contradanza *f.*

squat, *v.* agacharse.

squeak, 1. *n.* chirrido *m.* **2.** *v.* chirriar.

squeamish, *a.* escrupuloso.

squeeze, 1. *n.* apretón *m.* **2.** *v.* apretar; (fruit) exprimir.

squirrel, *n.* ardilla *f.*

squirt, 1. *n.* chisguete *m.* **2.** *v.* jeringar.

stab, 1. *n.* puñalada *f.* **2.** *v.* apuñalar.

stability, *n.* estabilidad *f.*

stabilize, *v.* estabilizar.

stable, 1. *a.* estable, equilibrado. **2.** *n.* caballeriza *f.*

stack, 1. *n.* pila *f.* **2.** *v.* apilar.

stadium, *n.* estadio *m.*

staff, *n.* personal *m.* **editorial s.,** cuerpo de redacción. **general s.,** estado mayor.

stag, *n.* ciervo *m.*

stage, 1. *n.* etapa; (theat.) escena *f.* **2.** *v.* representar.

stagflation, *n.* estagnación e inflación a la vez.

stagger, *v.* tambalear.

stagnant, *a.* estancado.

stagnate, *v.* estancarse.

stain, 1. *n.* mancha *f.* **2.** *v.* manchar.

staircase, stairs, *n.* escalera *f.*

stake, *n.* estaca; (bet) apuesta *f.* **at s.,** en juego; en peligro.

stale, *a.* rancio.

stalemate, *n.* estancación *f.,* tablas.

stalk, *n.* caña *f.;* (of flower) tallo *m.*

stall, 1. *n.* tenderete; (for

horse) pesebre *m.* 2. *v.* demorar; (motor) atascar.
stallion, *n.* garañón *m.*
stalwart, *a.* fornido.
stamina, *n.* vigor *m.*
stammer, *v.* tartamudear.
stamp, 1. *n.* sello *m.,* estampilla *f.* 2. *v.* sellar.
stampede, *n.* estampida *f.*
stand, 1. *n.* puesto *m.;* posición; (speaker's) tribuna; (furniture) mesita *f.* 2. *v.* estar; estar de pie; aguantar. **s. up,** pararse, levantarse.
standard, 1. *a.* normal, corriente. 2. *n.* norma *f.* **s. of living,** nivel de vida.
standardize, *v.* uniformar.
standing, *a.* fijo; establecido.
standpoint, *n.* punto de vista *m.*
staple, *n.* materia prima *f.*
star, *n.* estrella *f.*
starboard, *n.* estribor *m.*
starch, 1. *n.* almidón *m.;* (in diet) fécula *f.* 2. *v.* almidonar.
stare, *v.* mirar fijamente.
stark, 1. *a.* severo. 2. *adv.* completamente.
start, 1. *n.* susto; principio *m.* 2. *v.* comenzar, empezar; salir; poner en marcha; causar.
startle, *v.* asustar.
starvation, *n.* hambre *f.*
starve, *v.* morir de hambre.
state, 1. *n.* estado *m.* 2. *v.* declarar, decir.
statement, *n.* declaración *f.*
stateroom, *n.* camarote *m.*
statesman, *n.* estadista *m.*
static, 1. *a.* estático. 2. *n.* estática *f.*
station, *n.* estación *f.*
stationary, *a.* estacionario, fijo.
stationery, *n.* papel de escribir.
statistics, *n.* estadística *f.*
statue, *n.* estatua *f.*
stature, *n.* estatura *f.*
status, *n.* estado legal *m.*
statute, *n.* ley *f.*
staunch, *a.* fiel; constante.
stay, 1. *n.* estancia; vista *f.* 2. *v.* quedar, permanecer; parar; alojarse. **s. away,** ausentarse. **s. up,** velar.
steadfast, *a.* inmutable.
steady, 1. *a.* firme; permanente; regular. 2. *v.* sostener.
steak, *n.* biftec, bistec *m.*
steal, 1. *n.* plagio *m.* 2. *v.* robar. **s. away,** escabullirse.
stealth, *n.* cautela *f.*
steam, *n.* vapor *m.*
steamboat, steamer, steamship, *n.* vapor *m.*
steel, 1. *n.* acero *m.* 2. *v.* **s. oneself,** fortalecerse.
steep, *a.* escarpado, empinado.
steeple, *n.* campanario *m.*
steer, 1. *n.* buey *m.* 2. *v.* guiar, manejar.
stellar, *a.* astral.
stem, 1. *n.* tallo *m.* 2. *v.* parar. **s. from,** emanar de.

stencil, 1. *n.* estarcidor. 2. *v.* estarcir.
stenographer, *n.* estenógrafo-fa.
stenography, *n.* taquigrafía *f.*
step, 1. *n.* paso *m.;* medida *f.;* (stairs) escalón *m.* 2. *v.* pisar. **s. back,** retirarse.
stepladder, *n.* escalera de mano *f.*
stereophonic, *a.* estereofónico.
stereotype, 1. *n.* estereotipo. 2 *v.* estereotipar.
sterile, *a.* estéril.
sterilize, *v.* esterilizar.
sterling, *a.* esterlina, genuino.
stern, 1. *n.* popa *f.* 2. *a.* duro, severo.
stethoscope, *n.* estetoscopio *m.*
stevedore, *n.* estibador *m.*
stew, 1. *n.* guisado *m.* 2. *v.* estofar.
steward, *n.* camarero.
stewardess, *n.* azafata *f.,* aeromoza *f.*
stick, 1. *n.* palo, bastón *m.* 2. *v.* pegar; (put) poner, meter.
sticky, *a.* pegajoso.
stiff, *a.* tieso; duro.
stiffness, *n.* tiesura *f.*
stifle, *v.* sofocar; (fig.) suprimir.
stigma, *n.* estigma *m.*
still, 1. *a.* quieto; silencioso. **to keep s.,** callarse. 2. *adv.* todavía, aún; no obstante. 3. *n.* alambique *m.*
stillborn, *a. & a.* nacido muerto *m.*
still life, *n.* naturaleza muerta *f.*
stillness, *n.* silencio *m.*
stilted, *a.* altisonante.
stimulant, *a. & n.* estimulante *m.*
stimulate, *v.* estimular.
stimulus, *n.* estímulo *m.*
sting, 1. *n.* picadura *f.* 2. *v.* picar.
stingy, *a.* tacaño.
stipulate, *v.* estipular.
stir, 1. *n.* conmoción *f.* 2. *v.* mover. **s. up,** conmover; suscitar.
stitch, 1. *n.* puntada *f.* 2. *v.* coser.
stock, *n.* surtido *f.;* raza *f.;* (finance) acciones. *f.pl.* **in s.,** en existencia. **to take s. in,** tener fe en
stock exchange, *n.* bolsa *f.*
stockholder, *n.* corredor de bolsa *m.*
stocking, *n.* media *f.*
stockyard, *n.* corral de ganado *m.*
stodgy, *a.* pesado.
stoical, *a.* estoico.
stole, *n.* estola *f.*
stolid, *a.* impasible.
stomach, *n.* estómago *m.*
stone, *n.* piedra *f.*
stool, *n.* banquillo *m.*
stoop, *v.* encorvarse; (fig.) rebajarse.

stop, 1. *n.* parada *f.* 2. *v.* to, poner fin a. 2. *v.* parar; suspender; detener; impedir. **s. doing** (etc.), dejar de hacer (etc.).
stopgap, *n.* subterfugio *m.*
storage, *n.* almacenaje *m.*
store, 1. *n.* tienda; provisión *f.* **department s.,** almacén *m.* 2. *v.* guardar; almacenar.
storm, *n.* tempestad, tormenta *f.*
stormy, *a.* tempestuoso.
story, *n.* cuento; relato *m.;* historia *f.* **short s.,** cuento.
stout, *a.* corpulento.
stove, *n.* hornilla; estufa *f.*
straight, 1. *a.* recto; derecho. 2. *adv.* directamente.
straighten, *v.* enderezar. **s. out,** poner en orden.
straightforward, *a.* recto, sincero.
strain, 1. *n.* tensión *f.* 2. *v.* colar.
strainer, *n.* colador *m.*
strait, *n.* estrecho *m.*
strand, 1. *n.* hilo *m.* 2. *v.* **be stranded,** encallarse.
strange, *a.* extraño; raro.
stranger, *n.* extranjero -ra. forastero -ra; desconocido -da.
strangle, *v.* estrangular.
strap, *n.* correa *f.*
stratagem, *n.* estratagema *f.*
strategic, *a.* estratégico.
strategy, *n.* estrategia *f.*
stratosphere, *n.* estratosfera *f.*
straw, *n.* paja *f.*
strawberry, *n.* fresa *f.*
stray, 1. *a.* vagabundo. 2. *v.* extraviarse.
streak, 1. *n.* racha; raya *f.;* lado *m.* 2. *v.* rayar.
stream, *n.* corriente *f.*
street, *n.* calle *f.*
streetcar, *n.* tranvía *m.*
strength, *n.* fuerza *m.*
strengthen, *v.* reforzar.
strenuous, *a.* estrenuo.
streptococcus, *n.* estreptococo *m.*
stress, 1. *n.* tensión *f.;* énfasis *m.* 2. *v.* recalcar; acentuar.
stretch, 1. *n.* trecho *m.* **at one s.,** de un tirón. 2. *v.* tender; extender; estirarse.
stretcher, *n.* camilla *f.*
strew, *v.* esparcir.
stricken, *a.* agobiado.
strict, *a.* estricto; severo.
stride, 1. *n.* tranco *m.;* (fig., pl.) progresos. 2. *v.* andar a trancos.
strife, *n.* contienda *f.*
strike, 1. *n.* huelga *f.* 2. *v.* pegar; chocar con; (clock) dar.
string, *n.* cuerda *f.;* cordel *m.*
string bean, *n.* habichuela *f.*
stringent, *a.* estricto.
strip, 1. *n.* tira *f.* 2. despojar; desnudarse.
stripe, *n.* raya *f.;* (mil.) galón *m.*
strive, *v.* esforzarse.

stroke, n. golpe m.; (swimming) brazada f.; (med.) ataque m. **s. of luck,** suerte f.

stroll, 1. n. paseo m. 2. v. pasearse.

stroller, n. vagabundo m.

strong, a. fuerte.

stronghold, n. fortificación f.

structure, n. estructura f.

struggle, 1. n. lucha f. 2. v. luchar.

strut, 1. n. pavonada f. 2. v. pavonear.

stub, 1. n. cabo; (ticket) talón m. 2. v. **s. one's toe on,** tropezar con.

stubborn, a. testarudo.

stucco, 1. n. estuco. 2. v. estucar.

student, n. alumno -na, estudiante -ta.

studio, n. estudio m.

studious, a. aplicado; estudioso.

study, 1. n. estudio m. 2. v. estudiar.

stuff, 1. n. cosas f.pl. 2. v. llenar; rellenar.

stuffing, n. relleno m.

stumble, v. tropezar.

stump, n. tronco m.

stun, v. aturdir.

stunt, 1. n. suerte f. 2. v. impedir crecimiento.

stupendous, a. estupendo.

stupid, a. estúpido.

stupidity, n. estupidez f.

stupor, n. estupor m.

sturdy, a. robusto.

stutter, 1. v. tartamudear. 2. n. tartamudeo m.

sty, n. pocilga f.

style, n. estilo m.; moda f.

stylish, a. elegante; a la moda.

suave, a. afable, suave.

subconscious, a. subconsciente.

subdue, v. dominar.

subject, 1. a. sujeto. 2. n. tema m.; (of study) materia f.; (pol.) súbdito -ta; (gram.) sujeto m. 3. v. someter.

subjugate, v. sojuzgar, subjugar.

subjunctive, a. & n. subjuntivo m.

sublimate, v. sublimar.

sublime, a. sublime.

submarine, a. & n. submarino m.

submerge, v. sumergir.

submission, n. sumisión f.

submit, v. someter.

subnormal, a. subnormal.

subordinate, 1. a. & n. subordinado -na. 2. v. subordinar.

subscribe, v. aprobar; abonarse.

subscription, n. abono m.

subsequent, a. subsiguiente.

subservient, a. servicial.

subside, v. apaciguarse.

subsidy, n. subvención f.

substance, n. substancia f.

substantial, a. substancial; considerable.

substitute, 1. a. substitutivo. 2. n. substituto m. 3. v. substituir.

substitution, n. substitución f.

subterfuge, n. subterfugio m.

subtle, a. sutil.

subtract, v. substraer.

suburb, n. suburbio m.; (pl.) afueras f.pl.

subway, n. metro m.

succeed, v. lograr, tener éxito; (in office) suceder a.

success, n. éxito m.

successful, a. próspero; afortunado.

succession, n. sucesión f.

successive, a. sucesivo.

successor, n. sucesor -ra; heredero -ra.

succor, 1. n. socorro m. 2. v. socorrer.

succumb, v. sucumbir.

such, a. tal.

suck, v. chupar.

suction, n. succión f.

sudden, a. repentino, súbito. **all of a s.,** de repente.

suds, n. jabonaduras f.

sue, v. demandar.

suffer, v. sufrir; padecer.

suffice, v. bastar.

sufficient, a. suficiente.

suffocate, v. sofocar.

sugar, n. azúcar m.

suggest, v. sugerir.

suggestion, n. sugerencia f.

suicide, n. suicidio m.; (person) suicida m. & f. **to commit s.,** suicidarse.

suit, 1. n. traje; (cards) palo; (law) pleito m. 2. v. convenir a.

suitable, a. apropiado; que conviene.

suitcase, n. maleta f.

suite, n. serie f., séquito m.

suitor, n. pretendiente m.

sullen, a. hosco.

sum, 1. n. suma f. 2. v. **s. up,** resumir.

summarize, v. resumir.

summary, n. resumen m.

summer, n. verano m.

summon, v. llamar; (law) citar.

summons, n. citación f.

sumptuous, a. suntuoso.

sun, 1. n. sol m. 2. v. tomar el sol.

sunburn, n. quemadura de sol.

sunburned, a. quemado por el sol.

Sunday, n. domingo m.

sunken, a. hundido.

sunny, a. asoleado. **s. day,** día de sol. **to be s.,** (weather) hacer sol.

sunshine, n. luz del sol.

superb, a. soberbio.

superficial, a. superficial.

superfluous, a. superfluo.

superhuman, a. sobrehumano.

superintendent, n. superinten-

dente m.; (of building) conserje m.; (of school) director general.

superior, a. & n. superior m.

superiority, n. superioridad f.

superlative, a. superlativo.

supernatural, a. sobrenatural.

supersede, v. reemplazar.

superstar, n. superstar m.

superstition, n. superstición f.

superstitious, a. supersticioso.

supervise, v. supervisar.

supper, n. cena f.

supplement, 1. n. suplemento m. 2. v. suplementar.

supply, 1. n. provisión f.; (com.) surtido m.; (econ.) existencia f. 2. v. suplir; proporcionar.

support, 1. n. sustento; apoyo m. 2. v. mantener; apoyar.

suppose, v. suponer. **be supposed to,** deber.

suppress, v. suprimir.

suppression, n. supresión f.

supreme, a. supremo.

sure, a. seguro, cierto. **for s.,** con seguridad. **to make s.,** asegurarse.

surety, n. garantía f.

surf, n. marejada f.

surface, n. superficie f.

surge, v. surgir.

surgeon, n. cirujano m.

surgery, n. cirujía f.

surmise, 1. n. conjetura f. 2. v. suponer.

surmount, v. vencer.

surname, n. apellido m.

surpass, v. superar.

surplus, a. & n. sobrante m.

surprise, 1. n. sorpresa 2. v. sorprender. **I am surprised . . . ,** me extraña . . .

surrender, 1. n. rendición f. 2. v. rendir.

surround, v. rodear, circundar.

surveillance, n. vigilancia f.

survey, 1. n. examen estudio m. 2. v. examinar, estudiar; (land) medir.

survival, n. supervivencia f.

survive, v. sobrevivir.

susceptible, a. susceptible.

suspect, v. sospechar.

suspend, v. suspender.

suspense, n. incertidumbre f. **in s.,** en suspenso.

suspension, n. suspensión f.

suspension bridge, n. puente colgante m.

suspicion, n. sospecha f.

suspicious, a. sospechoso.

sustain, v. sustentar; mantener.

swallow, 1. n. trago m.; (bird) golondrina f. 2. v. tragar.

swamp, 1. n. pantano m. 2. v. (fig.) abrumar.

swan, n. cisne m.

swap, 1. n. trueque m. 2. v. cambalachear.

swarm, n. enjambre m.

sway, 1. n. predominio m. 2. v. bambolearse; (fig.) influir en.

swear, v. jurar. **s. off,** renunciar a.

sweat, 1. sudor m. **2.** v. sudar.

sweater, n. suéter m.

Swede, n. sueco -ca.

Sweden, n. Suecia f.

Swedish, a. sueco.

sweep, v. barrer.

sweet, 1. a. dulce; amable, simpático. **2.** n. (pl.) dulces m.pl.

sweetheart, n. amante m.

sweetness, n. dulzura f.

swell, 1. a. (coll.) estupendo, excelente. **2.** n. (mar.) oleada f. **3.** v. hincharse; aumentar.

swelter, v. sofacar.

swift, a. rápido, veloz.

swim, 1. n. nadada f. **2.** v. nadar.

swindle, 1. n. estafa. **2.** v. estafar.

swine, n. puercos m.pl.

swing, 1. n. columpio m. **in full s.,** en plana actividad. **2.** v. mecer; balancear.

swirl, 1. n. remolino m. **2.** v. arremolinar.

Swiss, a. & n. suizo -za.

switch, 1. n. varilla f.; (elec.) llave f., conmutador m.; (railway) cambiavia m. **2.** v. cambiar; trocar.

switchboard, n. cuadro conmutador m.

Switzerland, n. Suiza f.

sword, n. espada f.

syllable, n. sílaba f.

symbol, n. símbolo m.

sympathetic, a. compasivo. **to be s.,** tener simpatía.

sympathy, n. lástima; condolencia f.

symphony, n. sinfonía f.

symptom, n. síntoma m.

synchronize, v. sincronizar.

syndicate, n. sindicato m.

syndrome, n. sindroma m.

synonym, n. sinónimo m.

synthetic, a. sintético.

syringe, n. jeringa f.

syrup, n. almíbar f.; (cough) jarabe m.

system, n. sistema m.

systematic, a. sistemático.

T

tabernacle, n. tabernáculo m.

table, n. mesa; (list) tabla f.

tablespoon, n. cuchara f.

tablespoonful, n. cucharada f.

tablet, n. tableta; (med.) pastilla f.

tack, n. tachuela f.

tact, n. tacto m.

tag, n. etiqueta f., rótulo m.

tail, n. cola f., rabo m.

tailor, n. sastre m.

take, v. tomar; llevar. **t. away,** quitar. **t. off,** quitarse. **t. out,** sacar. **t. long,** tardar mucho.

tale, n. cuento m.

talent, n. talento m.

talk, 1. n. plática, habla f.; discurso m. **2.** v. hablar.

talkative, a. locuaz.

tall, a. alto.

tame, 1. a. manso, domesticado. **2.** v. domesticar.

tamper, v. **t. with,** entremeterse en.

tan, 1. a. color de arena. **2.** v. curtir; tostar.

tangible, a. tangible.

tangle, 1. n. enredo m. **2.** v. enredar.

tank, n. tanque m.

tap, 1. n. golpe ligero. **2.** v. golpear ligeramente; decantar.

tape, n. cinta f.

tape recorder, n. magnetófono m.

tapestry, n. tapiz m.; tapicería f.

tar, 1. n. brea f. **2.** v. embrear.

target, n. blanco m.

tarnish, 1. n. deslustre m. **2.** v. deslustrar.

task, n. tarea f.

taste, 1. n. gusto; sabor m. **2.** v. gustar; progar. **t. of,** saber a.

tasty, a. sabroso.

taut, a. tieso.

tavern, n. taberna f.

tax, 1. n. impuesto m. **2.** v. imponer impuestos.

taxi, n. taxi, taxímetro m.

tea, n. té m.

teach, v. enseñar.

teacher, n. maestro -tra, profesor -ra.

team, n. equipo m.; pareja f.

tear, 1. n. rasgón m.; lágrima f. **2.** v. rasgar, lacerar; separar.

tease, v. atormentar; embromar.

teaspoon, n. cucharita f.

technical, a. técnico.

technique, n. técnica f.

tedious, a. tedioso.

telegram, n. telegrama m.

telegraph, 1. telégrafo m. **2.** v. telegrafiar.

telephone, 1. teléfono m. **t. book,** directorio telefónico. **2.** v. telefonear; llamar por teléfono.

telescope, 1. n. telescopio m. **2.** v. enchufar.

television, n. televisión f.

tell, v. decir; contar; distinguir.

temper, 1. n. temperamento, genio m. **2.** v. templar.

temperament, n. temperamento m.

temperamental, a. sensible, emocional.

temperance, n. moderación; sobriedad f.

temperate, a. templado.

temperature, n. temperatura f.

tempest, n. tempestad f.

tempestuous, a. tempestuoso.

temple, n. templo m.

temporary, a. temporal, temporario.

tempt, v. tentar.

temptation, n. tentación f.

ten, a. & pron. diez.

tenant, n. inquilino -na.

tend, v. tender. **t. to,** atender.

tendency, n. tendencia f.

tender, 1. a. tierno. **2.** v. ofrecer.

tenderness, n. ternura f.

tennis, n. tenis m.

tenor, n. tenor m.

tense, 1. a. tenso. **2.** n. tiempo m.

tent, n. tienda, carpa f.

tenth, a. décimo.

term, 1. n. término; plazo m. **2.** v. llamar.

terrace, n. terraza f.

terrible, a. terrible, espantoso.

territory, n. territorio m.

terror, n. terror, espanto m.

test, 1. n. prueba f.; examen m. **2.** v. probar, examinar.

testament, n. testamento m.

testify, v. atestiguar, testificar.

testimony, n. testimonio m.

text, n. texto; tema m.

textile, 1. a. textil. **2.** n. tejido m.

texture, n. textura f.; tejido m.

than, conj. que; de.

thank, v. agradecer, dar gracias; **thanks, th. you,** gracias.

thankful, a. agradecido; grato.

that, 1. a. ese, aquel. **2.** dem. pron. ése, aquél; eso, aquello. **3.** rel. pron. & conj. que.

the, art. el, la, los, las; lo.

theater, n. teatro m.

theft, n. robo m.

their, a. su.

theirs, pron. suyo, de ellos.

them, pron. ellos, ellas; los, las; les.

theme, n. tema m.; (mus.) motivo m.

themselves, pron. sí, sí mismos -as. **they th.,** ellos mismos, ellas mismas. **with th.,** consigo.

then, adv. entonces, después; pues.

thence, adv. de allí.

theology, n. teología f.

theory, n. teoría f.

there, adv. allí, allá, ahí. **there is, there are,** hay.

therefore, adv. por lo tanto, por consiguiente.

thermometer, n. termómetro m.

they, pron. ellos, ellas.

thick, a. espeso, grueso, denso; torpe.

thicken, v. espesar, condensar.

thief, n. ladrón -na.

thigh, n. muslo m.

thimble, n. dedal m.

thin, 1. a. delgado; raro; claro; escaso. **2.** v. enrarecer; adelgazar.

thing, n. cosa f.

think, v. pensar; creer.

thinker, n. pensador -ra.

third, a. tercero.

Third World, *n.* Tercer Mundo *m.*

thirst, *n.* sed *f.*

thirsty, *a.* sediento. **to be th.,** tener sed.

thirteen, *a. & pron.* trece.

thirty, *a. & pron.* treinta.

this, 1. *a.* este. 2. *pron.* éste; esto.

thorough, *a.* completo; cuidadoso.

though, 1. *adv.* sin embargo. 2. *conj.* aunque. **as th.,** como si.

thought, *n.* pensamiento *m.*

thoughtful, *a.* pensativo; considerado.

thousand, *a. & pron.* mil.

thread, *n.* hilo *m.;* (of screw) rosca *f.*

threat, *n.* amenaza *f.*

threaten, *v.* amenazar.

three, *a. & pron.* tres.

thrift, *n.* economía, frugalidad *f.*

thrill, 1. *n.* emoción *f.* 2. *v.* emocionar.

thrive, *v.* prosperar.

throat, *n.* garganta *f.*

throne, *n.* trono *m.*

through, 1. *prep.* por; a través de; por medio de. 2. *a.* continuo. **th. train,** tren directo. **to be th.,** haber terminado.

throughout, 1. *prep.* por todo, durante todo. 2. *adv.* en todas partes; completamente.

throw, 1. *n.* tiro *m.* 2. *v.* tirar, lanzar. **th. away,** arrojar. **th. out,** echar.

thrust, 1. *n.* lanzada *f.* 2. *v.* empujar.

thumb, *n.* pulgar *m.*

thunder, 1. *n.* trueno *m.* 2. *v.* tronar.

Thursday, *n.* jueves *m.*

thus, *adv.* así, de este modo.

thwart, *v.* frustrar.

ticket, 1. *n.* billete, boleto *m.* **t. window,** taquilla *f.* **round trip t.,** billete de ida y vuelta.

tickle, 1. *n.* cosquilla *f.* 2. *v.* hacer cosquillas a.

ticklish, *a.* cosquilloso.

tide, *n.* marea *f.*

tidy, 1. *a.* limpio, ordenado. 2. *v.* poner en orden.

tie, 1. *n.* corbata *f.;* lazo; (game) empate *m.* 2. *v.* atar; anudar.

tier, *n.* hilera *f.*

tiger, *n.* tigre *m.*

tight, *a.* apretado; tacaño.

tighten, *v.* estrechar, apretar.

tile, *n.* teja *f.,* azulejo *m.*

till, 1. *prep.* hasta. 2. *conj.* hasta que. 3. *n.* cajón *m.* 4. *v.* cultivar, labrar.

tilt, 1. *n.* inclinación; justa *f.* 2. *v.* inclinar; justar.

timber, *n.* madera *f.;* (beam) madero *m.*

time, *n.* tiempo *m.;* vez *f.;* (of day) hora *f.*

timetable, *n.* horario, itinerario *m.*

timid, *a.* tímido.

timidity, *n.* timidez *f.*

tin, *n.* estaño *m.;* hojalata *f.* **t. can,** lata *f.*

tint, 1. *n.* tinte *m.* 2. *v.* teñir.

tiny, *a.* chiquito, pequeñito.

tip, 1. *n.* punta; propina *f.* 2. *v.* inclinar; dar propina a.

tire, 1. *n.* llanta, goma *f.,* neumático *m.* 2. *v.* cansar.

tired, *a.* cansado.

tissue, *n.* tejido *m.* **t. paper,** papel de seda.

title, 1. *n.* título *m.* 2. *v.* titular.

to, *prep.* a; para.

toast, 1. *n.* tostada *f.;* (drink) brindis *m.* 2. *v.* tostar; brindar por.

tobacco, *n.* tabaco *m.*

today, *adv.* hoy.

toe, *n.* dedo del pie.

together, 1. *a.* juntos. 2. *adv.* juntamente.

toil, 1. *n.* trabajo *m.* 2. *v.* afanarse.

toilet, *n.* tocado; excusado, retrete *m.* **t. paper,** papel higiénico.

token, *n.* señal *f.*

tolerance, *n.* tolerancia *f.*

tolerate, *v.* tolerar.

tomato, *n.* tomate *m.*

tomb, *n.* tumba *f.*

tomorrow, *adv.* mañana. **day after t.,** pasado mañana.

ton, *n.* tonelada *f.*

tone, *n.* tono *m.*

tongue, *n.* lengua *f.*

tonic, *n.* tónico *m.*

tonight, *adv.* esta noche.

tonsil, *n.* amígdala *f.*

too, *adv.* también; demasiado. **t. much,** demasiado. **t. many,** demasiados.

tool, *n.* herramienta *f.*

tooth, *n.* diente *m.;* (back) muela *f.*

toothache, *n.* dolor de muela.

toothbrush, *n.* cepillo de dientes.

top, 1. *n.* parte de arriba. 2. *v.* cubrir; sobrepasar.

topic, *n.* tópico *m.*

topical, *a.* tópico.

torch, *n.* antorcha *f.*

torment, 1. *n.* tormento *m.* 2. *v.* atormentar.

torrent, *n.* torrente *m.*

torture, 1. *n.* tortura *f.* 2. *v.* torturar.

toss, *v.* tirar; agitar.

total, 1. *a.* total, entero. 2. *n.* total *m.*

totalitarian, *a.* totalitario.

touch, 1. *n.* tacto *m.* **in t.,** en comunicación. 2. *v.* tocar; conmover.

tough, *a.* tosco; tieso; fuerte.

tour, 1. *n.* viaje *m.,* jira *f.* 2. *v.* viajar.

tourist, *n.* turista *m. & f.*

tournament, *n.* torneo *m.*

tow, 1. *n.* remolque *m.* 2. *v.* remolcar.

toward, *prep.* hacia.

towel, *n.* toalla *f.*

tower, *n.* torre *f.*

town, *n.* pueblo *m.*

toy, 1. *n.* juguete *m.* 2. *v.* jugar.

trace, 1. *n.* vestigio; rastro *m.* 2. *v.* trazar; rastrear; investigar.

track, 1. *n.* huella, pista *f.* **race t.,** hipódromo *m.* 2. *v.* rastrear.

tract, *n.* trecho, tracto; tratado *m.*

tractor, *n.* tractor *m.*

trade, 1. *n.* comercio, negocio; oficio; canje *m.* 2. *v.* comerciar, negociar; cambiar.

trader, *n.* comerciante *m.*

tradition, *n.* tradición *f.*

traditional, *a.* tradicional.

traffic, 1. *n.* tráfico *m.* 2. *v.* traficar.

tragedy, *n.* tragedia *f.*

tragic, *a.* trágico.

trail, 1. *n.* sendero; rastro *m.* 2. *v.* rastrear; arrastrar.

train, 1. *n.* tren *m.* 2. *v.* enseñar; disciplinar; (sport) entrenarse.

traitor, *n.* traidor *m.*

tramp, 1. *n.* caminata *f.;* vagabundo *m.* 2. *v.* patear.

tranquil, *a.* tranquilo.

tranquillity, *n.* tranquilidad *f.*

transaction, *n.* transacción *f.*

transfer, 1. *n.* traslado *m.;* boleto de transbordo. 2. *v.* trasladar, transferir.

transform, *v.* transformar.

transfusion, *n.* transfusión *f.*

transition, *n.* transición *f.*

translate, *v.* traducir.

translation, *n.* traducción *f.*

transmit, *v.* transmitir.

transparent, *a.* transparente.

transport, 1. *n.* transporte *m.,* transportación *f.* 2. *v.* transportar.

transportation, *n.* transporte *m.*

transsexual, *a.* transexual.

transvestite, *n.* travesti *m.*

trap, 1. *n.* trampa *f.* 2. *v.* atrapar.

trash, *n.* desecho *m.;* basura *f.*

travel, 1. *n.* tráfico *m.;* (pl.) viajes *m.pl.* 2. *v.* viajar.

traveler, *n.* viajero -ra.

traveler's check, *n.* cheque de viaje *m.*

tray, *n.* bandeja *f.*

tread, 1. *n.* pisada *f.;* (of a tire) cubierta *f.* 2. *v.* pisar.

treason, *n.* traición *f.*

treasure, *n.* tesoro *m.*

treasurer, *n.* tesorero -ra.

treasury, *n.* tesorería *f.*

treat, *v.* tratar; convidar.

treatment, *n.* trato, tratamiento *m.*

treaty, *n.* tratado, pacto *m.*

tree, *n.* árbol *m.*

tremble, *v.* temblar.

tremendous, *a.* tremendo.

trench, *n.* foso *m.;* (mil.) trinchera *f.*

trend, 1. *n.* tendencia *f.* **2.** *v.* tender.

trespass, *v.* traspasar; violar.

triage, *n.* clasificación de los heridos después del combate.

trial, *n.* prueba *f.;* (leg.) proceso, juicio *m.*

triangle, *n.* triangulo *m.*

tribulation, *n.* tribulación *f.*

tributary, *a. & n.* tributario *m.*

tribute, *n.* tributo *m.*

trick, 1. *n.* engaño *m.;* maña *f.;* (cards) baza *f.* **2.** *v.* engañar.

trifle, 1. *n.* pequeñez *f.* **2.** *v.* juguetear.

trigger, *n.* gatillo *m.*

trim, 1. *a.* ajustado, acicalado. **2.** *n.* adorno *m.* **3.** *v.* adornar; ajustar; cortar un poco.

trinket, *n.* bagatela, chuchería *f.*

trip, 1. *n.* viaje *m.* **2.** *v.* tropezar.

triple, 1. *a.* triple **2.** *v.* triplicar.

trite, *a.* banal.

triumph, 1. *n.* triunfo *m.* **2.** *v.* triunfar.

triumphant, *a.* triunfante.

trivial, *a.* trivial.

trolley, *n.* tranvía *m.*

troop, *n.* tropa *f.*

trophy, *n.* trofeo *m.*

tropical, *a.* trópico.

tropics, *n.* trópico *m.*

trot, 1. *n.* trote *m.* **2.** *v.* trotar.

trouble, 1. *n.* apuro *m.;* congoja; aflicción *f.* **2.** *v.* molestar; afligir.

troublesome, *a.* penoso, molesto.

trough, *n.* artesa *f.*

trousers, *n.* pantalones, calzones *m.pl.*

trout, *n.* trucha *f.*

truce, *n.* tregua *f.*

truck, *n.* camión *m.*

true, *a.* verdadero; cierto, verdad.

trumpet, *n.* trompeta, trompa *f.*

trunk, *n.* baúl *m.;* (of a tree) tronco *m.*

trust, 1. *n.* confianza *f.* **2.** *v.* confiar.

trustworthy, *a.* digno de confianza.

truth, *n.* verdad *f.*

truthful, *a.* veraz.

try, 1. *n.* prueba *f.;* ensayo *m.* **2.** *v.* tratar; probar; ensayar; (leg.) juzgar. **t. on,** probarse.

T-shirt, *n.* camiseta *f.*

tub, *n.* tina *f.*

tube, *n.* tubo *m.*

tuberculosis, *n.* tuberculosis, tisis *f.*

tuck, 1. *n.* recogido *m.* **2.** *v.* recoger.

Tuesday, *n.* martes *m.*

tug, 1. *n.* tirada *f.;* (boat) remolcador *m.* **2.** *v.* tirar.

tuition, *n.* matrícula, colegiatura *f.*

tumble, 1. caída *f.* **2.** *v.* caer, tumbar; voltear.

tumult, *n.* tumulto, alboroto *m.*

tune, 1. *n.* tono *m.;* melodía, canción *f.* **2.** *v.* templar.

tunnel, *n.* túnel *m.*

turf, *n.* césped *m.*

Turkey, *n.* Turquía *f.*

Turkish, *a.* turco.

turmoil, *n.* disturbio *m.*

turn, 1. *n.* vuelta *f.;* giro; turno *m.* **2.** *v.* volver, tornear, girar; transformar. **t. around,** volverse. **t. on,** encender; abrir. **t. off, t. out,** apagar.

turnip, *n.* nabo *m.*

turret, *n.* torrecilla *f.*

turtle, *n.* tortuga *f.*

tutor, 1. *n.* tutor *m.* **2.** *v.* enseñar.

twelve, *a. & pron.* doce.

twenty, *a. & pron.* veinte.

twice, *adv.* dos veces.

twig, *n.* varita, ramita *f.;* vástago *m.*

twilight, *n.* crepúsculo *m.*

twin, *n.* gemelo -la.

twine, 1. *n.* guita *f.* **2.** *v.* torcer.

twinkle, *v.* centellear.

twist, *v.* torcer.

two, *a. & pron.* dos.

type, 1. *n.* tipo *m.* **2.** *v.* escribir a máquina.

typewriter, *n.* máquina de escribir.

typhoid fever, fiebre tifoidea.

typical, *a.* típico.

typist, *n.* mecanógrafo -fa.

tyranny, *n.* tiranía *f.*

tyrant, *n.* tirano *m.*

U

udder, *n.* ubre *f.*

ugly, *a.* feo.

ulcer, *n.* úlcera *f.*

ulterior, *a.* ulterior.

ultimate, *a.* último.

umbrella, *n.* paraguas *m.* **sun u.,** quitasol *m.*

umpire, *n.* árbitro *m.*

unable, *a.* incapaz. **to be u.,** no poder.

unanimous, *a.* unánime.

uncertain, *a.* incierto, inseguro.

uncle, *n.* tío *m.*

unconscious, *a.* inconsciente; desmayado.

uncover, *v.* descubrir.

under, 1. *adv.* debajo, abajo. **2.** *prep.* bajo, debajo de.

underestimate, *v.* menospreciar, subestimar.

undergo, *v.* sufrir.

underground, *a.* subterráneo.

underline, *v.* subrayar.

underneath, 1. *adv.* por debajo. **2.** *prep.* debajo de.

undershirt, *n.* camiseta *f.*

understand, *v.* entender, comprender.

undertake, *v.* emprender.

underwear, *n.* ropa interior.

undo, *v.* deshacer; desatar.

undress, *v.* desnudar, desvestir.

uneasy, *a.* inquieto.

uneven, *a.* desigual.

unexpected, *a.* inesperado.

unfair, *a.* injusto.

unfit, *a.* incapaz; inadecuado.

unfold, *v.* desplegar; revelar.

unforgettable, *a.* inolvidable.

unfortunate, *a.* desafortunado, desgraciado.

unhappy, *a.* infeliz.

uniform, *a. & n.* uniforme *m.*

unify, *v.* unificar.

union, *n.* unión *f.* **labor u.,** sindicato de obreros.

unique, *a.* único.

unisex, *a.* unisex.

unit, *n.* unidad *f.*

unite, *v.* unir.

unity, *n.* unidad *f.*

universal, *a.* universal.

universe, *n.* universo *m.*

university, *n.* universidad *f.*

unleaded, *a.* sin plomo.

unless, *conj.* a menos que, si no es que.

unlike, *a.* disímil.

unload, *v.* descargar.

unlock, *v.* abrir.

untie, *v.* desatar, soltar.

until, 1. *prep.* hasta. **2.** *conj.* hasta que.

unusual, *a.* raro, inusitado.

up, 1. *adv.* arriba. **2.** *prep.* **u. the street,** *etc.* calle arriba, etc.

uphold, *v.* apoyar, defender.

upholster, *v.* entapizar.

upon, *prep.* sobre, encima de.

upper, *a.* superior.

upright, *a.* derecho, recto.

uproar, *n.* alboroto, tumulto *m.*

upset, 1. *n.* trastorno *m.* **2.** *v.* trastornar.

uptight, *a.* (psicológicamente) tenso, tieso.

upward, *adv.* hacia arriba.

urge, 1. *n.* deseo *m.* **2.** *v.* instar.

urgency, *n.* urgencia *f.*

urgent, *a.* urgente. **to be u.,** urgir.

us, *pron.* nosotros -as; nos.

use, 1. *n.* uso *m.* **2.** *v.* usar, emplear. **u. up,** gastar, agotar. **be used to,** ser acostumbrado a.

useful, *a.* útil.

useless, *a.* inútil.

usher, 1. *n.* acomodador *m.* **2.** *v.* introducir.

usual, *a.* usual.

utensil, *n.* utensilio *m.*

utmost, *a.* sumo, extremo.

utter, 1. *a.* completo. **2.** *v.* proferir; dar.

utterance, *n.* expresión *f.*

V

vacancy, *n.* vacante *f.*

vacant, *a.* desocupado, libre.

vacation, *n.* vacaciones *f.pl.*

vaccinate, *v.* vacunar.

vacuum, n. vacuo, vacío m. **v. cleaner,** aspirador m.

vagrant, n. vagabundo.

vague, a. vago.

vain, a. vano; vanidoso. **in v.,** en vano.

valiant, a. valiente.

valid, a. válido.

valley, n. valle m.

valor, n. valor m., valentía f.

valuable, a. precioso. **to be v.,** valer mucho.

value, 1. n. valor, importe m. **2.** v. valorar; estimar.

vandal, n. vándalo m.

vanish, v. desaparecer.

vanity, n. vanidad f. **v. case,** polvera f.

vanquish, v. vencer.

vapor, n. vapor m.

variation, n. variación f.

variety, n. variedad f.

various, a. varios, diversos.

varnish, 1. n. barniz m. **2.** v. barnizar.

vary, v. variar; cambiar.

vase, n. vaso, jarrón m.

vasectomy, n. vasectomía f.

vassal, n. vasallo m.

vast, a. vasto.

vat, n. tina f., tanque m.

vault, n. bóveda f.

vegetable, 1. a. & n. vegetal m.; (pl.) legumbres, verderas f.pl.

vehement, a. vehemente.

vehicle, n. vehículo m.

veil, 1. n. velo m. **2.** v. velar.

vein, n. vena f.

velocity, n. velocidad f.

velvet, n. terciopelo m.

vengeance, n. venganza f.

vent, n. apertura f.

ventilate, v. ventilar.

venture, n. ventura f.

verb, n. verbo m.

verbose, a. verboso.

verdict, n. veredicto, fallo m.

verge, n. borde m.

verify, v. verificar.

versatile, a. versátil.

verse, n. verso m.

version, n. versión f.

vertical, a. vertical.

very, 1. a. mismo. **2.** adv. muy.

vessel, n. vasija f.; barco m.

vest, n. chaleco m.

veteran, a. & n. veterano -na.

veto, n. veto m.

vex, v. molestar.

via, prep. por la vía de; por.

viaduct, n. viaducto m.

vibrate, v. vibrar.

vibration, n. vibración f.

vice, n. vicio m.

vicinity, n. vecindad f.

vicious, a. vicioso.

victim, n. víctima f.

victor, n. vencedor m.

victorious, a. victorioso.

victory, n. victoria f.

videodisc, n. videodisco m.

videotape, n. video m., magnetoscopio m.

view, 1. n. vista f. **2.** v. ver.

vigil, n. vigilia, vela f.

vigilant, a. vigilante.

vigor, n. vigor m.

vile, a. vil, bajo.

village, n. aldea f.

villain, n. malvado m.

vine, n. parra, vid f.

vinegar, n. vinagre m.

vintage, n. vendimia f.

violate, v. violar.

violation, n. violación f.

violence, n. violencia f.

violent, a. violento.

violin, n. violín m.

virgin, n. virgen f.

virile, a. viril.

virtual, a. virtual.

virtue, n. virtud f.

virtuous, a. virtuoso.

virus, n. virus m.

visa, n. visa f.

visible, a. visible.

vision, n. visión f.

visit, 1. n. visita f. **2.** v. visitar.

visitor, n. visitante m. & f.

visual, a. visual.

vital, a. vital.

vitality, n. vitalidad f.

vitamin, n. vitamina f.

vivacious, a. vivaz.

vivid, a. vivo; gráfico.

vocabulary, n. vocabulario m.

vocal, a. vocal.

vogue, n. boga; moda f.

voice, 1. n. voz f. **2.** v. expresar.

void, 1. a. vacío. **2.** n. vacío m. **3.** v. invalidar.

volume, n. volumen, tomo m.

voluntary, a. voluntario.

volunteer, 1. n. voluntario m. **2.** v. ofrecerse.

vomit, v. vomitar.

vote, 1. n. voto m. **2.** v. votar.

voter, n. votante m. & f.

vouch, v. **v. for,** garantizar.

vow, 1. n. voto m. **2.** v. jurar.

vowel, n. vocal f.

voyage, n. viaje m.

vulgar, a. vulgar; común.

vulnerable, a. vulnerable.

W

wade, v. vadear.

wag, v. menear.

wage, 1. n. (pl.) sueldo, salario m. **2.** v. **w. war,** hacer guerra.

wagon, n. carreta f.

wail, 1. n. lamento, gemido m. **2.** v. lamentar, gemir.

waist, n. cintura f.

wait, 1. n. espera f. **2.** v. esperar. **w. for,** esperar. **w. on,** atender.

waiter, waitress, n. camarero -ra.

wake, v. **w. up,** despertar.

walk, 1. n. paseo m.; vuelta; caminata f.; modo de andar. **2.** v. andar; caminar; ir a pie.

wall, n. pared; (outdoor) tapia; muralla f.

wallcovering, n. tapizado de pared m.

wallet, n. cartera f.

wallpaper, n. empapelado m.

walnut, n. nuez f.

waltz, n. vals m.

wander, v. vagar.

want, 1. n. necesidad f. **2.** v. querer.

war, n. guerra f.

ward, 1. n. (pol.) barrio m.; (hospital) cuadra f. **2.** v. **w. off,** parar.

wares, n. mercancías f.pl.

warlike, a. belicoso.

warm, 1. a. caliente; (fig.) caluroso. **to be w.,** tener calor; (weather) hacer calor. **2.** v. calentar.

warmth, n. calor m.

warn, v. advertir.

warp, v. alabear.

warrant, v. justificar.

warrior, n. guerrero m.

warship, n. navío de guerra.

wash, v. lavar.

wasp, n. avispa f.

waste, 1. n. gasto m.; desechos m.pl. **2.** v. gastar, perder.

watch, 1. n. reloj m.; (mil.) guardia f. **2.** v. observar, mirar. **w. for,** esperar. **w. out for,** tener cuidado con. **w. over,** guardar; velar por.

watchful, a. desvelado.

watchmaker, n. relojero m.

watchman, n. sereno m.

water, 1. n. agua f. **w. color,** acuarela f. **2.** v. aguar.

waterbed, n. cama de agua f.

waterfall, n. catarata f.

waterproof, a. impermeable.

wave, 1. n. onda; ola f. **2.** v. ondear; agitar; hacer señas.

waver, v. vacilar.

wax, 1. n. cera f. **2.** v. encerar.

way, n. camino; modo m., manera f. **in a w.,** hasta cierto punto. **a long w.,** muy lejos. **by the w.,** a propósito. **this w.,** por aquí. **that w.,** por allí. **which w.,** por dónde.

we, pron. nosotros -as.

weak, a. débil.

weaken, v. debilitar.

weakness, n. debilidad f.

wealth, n. riqueza f.

wealthy, a. rico.

weapon, n. arma f.

wear, 1. n. uso, desgaste m.; (clothes) ropa f. **2.** v. usar, llevar. **w. out,** gastar; cansar.

weary, a. cansado, rendido.

weather, n. tiempo m.

weave, v. tejer.

weaver, n. tejedor -ra.

web, n. tela f.

wedding, n. boda f.

wedge, n. cuña f.

Wednesday, n. miércoles m.

weed, n. maleza f.

week, n. semana f. **w. end,** fin de semana.

weekday, n. día de trabajo.

weekly, a. semanal.

weep, v. llorar.

weigh, v. pesar.

weight, *n.* peso *m.*

weird, *a.* misterioso, sobrenatural.

welcome, 1. *a.* bienvenido. **you're w.,** de nada, no hay de qué. **2.** *n.* acogida, bienvenida *f.* **3.** *v.* acoger, recibir bien.

welfare, *n.* bienestar *m.*

well, 1. *a.* sano, bueno. **2.** *adv.* bien; pues. **3.** *n.* pozo *m.*

well-known, *a.* bien conocido.

west, *n.* oeste, occidente *m.*

western, *a.* occidental.

westward, *adv.* hacia el oeste.

wet, 1. *a.* mojado. **to get w.,** mojarse. **2.** *v.* mojar.

whale, *n.* ballena *f.*

what, 1. *a.* qué; cuál. **2.** *interrog. pron.* qué. **3.** *rel. pron.* lo que.

whatever, 1. *a.* cualquier. **2.** *pron.* lo que; todo lo que.

wheat, *n.* trigo *m.*

wheel, *n.* rueda *f.* **steering w.,** volante *m.*

when, 1. *adv.* cuándo. **2.** *conj.* cuando.

whenever, *conj.* siempre que, cuando quiera que.

where, 1. *adv.* dónde, adónde. **2.** *conj.* donde.

wherever, *conj.* dondequiera que, adondequiera que.

whether, *conj.* si.

which, 1. *a.* qué. **2.** *interrog. pron.* cuál. **3.** *rel. pron.* que; el cual; lo cual.

whichever, *a. & pron.* cualquiera que.

while, 1. *conj.* mientras; mientras que. **2.** *n.* rato *m.* **to be worth w.,** valer la pena.

whip, 1. *n.* látigo *m.* **2.** *v.* azotar.

whirl, *v.* girar.

whirlpool, *n.* vórtice *m.*

whirlwind, *n.* torbellino *m.*

whisk broom, *n.* escobilla *f.*

whisker, *n.* bigote *m.*

whiskey, *n.* whisky *m.*

whisper, 1. *n.* cuchicheo *m.* **2.** *v.* cuchichear.

whistle, 1. *n.* pito; silbido *m.* **2.** *v.* silbar.

white, 1. *a.* blanco. **2.** *n.* (of egg) clara *f.*

who, whom, 1. *interrog. pron.* quién. **2.** *rel. pron.* que; quien.

whoever, whomever, *pron.* quienquiera que.

whole, 1. *a.* entero. **the wh.,** todo el. **2.** *n.* totalidad *f.* **on the wh.,** por lo general.

wholesale, 1. *a.* **at wh.,** al por mayor.

wholesome, *a.* sano, saludable.

wholly, *adv.* enteramente.

whose, 1. *interrog. adj.* de quién. **2.** *rel. adj.* cuyo.

why, *adv.* por qué; para qué.

wicked, *a.* malo, malvado.

wickedness, *n.* maldad *f.*

wide, 1. *a.* ancho; extenso. **2.**

widen, *v.* ensanchar; extender.

widespread, *a.* extenso.

widow, *n.* viuda *f.*

widower, *n.* viudo *m.*

width, *n.* anchura *f.*

wield, *v.* manejar, empuñar.

wife, *n.* esposa, señora, mujer *f.*

wig, *n.* peluca *f.*

wild, *a.* salvaje; bárbaro.

wilderness, *n.* desierto *m.*

wildlife, *n.* fauna silvestre *f.*

will, 1. *n.* voluntad *f.;* testamento *m.* **2.** *v.* querer; determinar; (leg.) legar.

willful, *a.* voluntarioso; premeditado.

willing, *a.* **to be w.,** estar dispuesto.

willingly, *adv.* de buena gana.

wilt, *v.* marchitar.

win, *v.* ganar.

wind, 1. *n.* viento *m.* **2.** *v.* torcer; dar cuerda a.

window, *n.* ventana; (of car) ventanilla *f.*

windy, *a.* ventoso. **to be w.,** (weather) hacer viento.

wine, *n.* vino *m.*

wing, *n.* ala *f.;* (theat.) bastidor *m.*

wink, 1. *n.* guiño *m.* **2.** *v.* guiñar.

winner, *n.* ganador -ra.

winter, *n.* invierno *m.*

wipe, *v.* limpiar; (dry) secar. **w. out,** destruir.

wire, 1. *n.* alambre; hilo; telegrama *m.* **2.** *v.* telegrafiar.

wireless, *n.* telégrafo sin hilos.

wisdom, *n.* juicio *m.;* sabiduría *f.*

wise, *a.* sensato, juicioso; sabio.

wish, 1. *n.* deseo; voto *m.* **2.** *v.* desear; querer.

wit, *n.* ingenio *m.,* sal *f.*

witch, *n.* bruja *f.*

with, *prep.* con.

withdraw, *v.* retirar.

wither, *v.* marchitar.

withhold, *v.* retener, suspender.

within, 1. *adv.* dentro, por dentro. **2.** *prep.* dentro de; en.

without, 1. *adv.* fuera, por fuera. **2.** *prep.* sin.

witness, 1. *n.* testigo; testimonio *m.* **2.** *v.* presenciar; atestar.

witty, *a.* ingenioso, gracioso.

wizard, *n.* hechicero *m.*

woe, *n.* dolor *m.;* pena *f.*

wolf, *n.* lobo *m.*

woman, *n.* mujer *f.*

womb, *n.* entrañas *f.pl.,* matriz *f.*

wonder, 1. *n.* maravilla; admiración *f.* **for a w.,** por milagro. **no w.,** no es extraño. **2.** *v.* preguntarse; maravillarse.

wonderful, *a.* maravilloso; estupendo.

woo, *v.* cortejar.

wood, *n.* madera; (for fire) leña *f.*

wooden, *a.* de madera.

wool, *n.* lana *f.*

word, *n.* palabra *f.* **the words** (of a song), la letra. **2.** *v.* expresar.

work, 1. *n.* trabajo *m.;* (of art) obra *f.* **2.** *v.* trabajar; obrar; funcionar.

worker, *n.* trabajador -ra; obrero -ra.

workman, *n.* obrero *m.*

world, *n.* mundo *m.* **w. war,** guerra mundial.

worldly, *a.* mundano.

worldwide, *a.* mundial.

worm, *n.* gusano *m.*

worn, *a.* usado. **w. out,** gastado, cansado, rendido.

worry, 1. *n.* preocupación *f.* **2.** *v.* preocupar.

worse, *a.* peor. **to get w.,** empeorar.

worship, 1. *n.* adoración *f.* **2.** *v.* adorar.

worst, *a.* peor.

worth, 1. *a.* **to be w.,** valer. **2.** *n.* valor *m.*

worthless, *a.* sin valor.

worthy, *a.* digno.

wound, 1. *n.* herida *f.* **2.** *v.* herir.

wrap, 1. *n.* (pl.) abrigos *m.pl.* **2.** *n.* envolver.

wrapping, *n.* cubierta *f.*

wrath, *n.* ira, cólera *f.*

wreath, *n.* guirnalda; corona *f.*

wreck, 1. *n.* ruina *f.;* accidente *m.* **2.** *v.* destrozar, arruinar.

wrench, *n.* llave *f.* **monkey w.,** llave inglesa.

wrestle, *v.* luchar.

wretched, *a.* miserable.

wring, *v.* retorcer.

wrinkle, 1. *n.* arruga *f.* **2.** *v.* arrugar.

wrist, *n.* muñeca *f.* **w. watch,** reloj de pulsera.

write, *v.* escribir. **w. down,** apuntar.

writer, *n.* escritor -ra.

writhe, *v.* contorcerse.

wrong, 1. *a.* equivocado; incorrecto. **to be w.,** equivocarse; no tener razón. **2.** *adv.* mal, incorrectamente. **3.** *n.* agravio *m.* **right and w.,** el bien y el mal. **4.** *v.* agraviar, ofender.

X, Y, Z

x-ray, *n.* rayo X *m.*

xylophone, *n.* xilófono *m.*

yacht, *n.* yate *m.*

yard, *n.* patio, corral *m.;* (measure) yarda *f.*

yarn, *n.* hilo.

yawn, 1. *n.* bostezo *m.* **2.** *v.* bostezar.

year, *n.* año *m.*

yearly, *a.* anual.

yearn, v. anhelar.
yell, 1. n. grito m. **2.** v. gritar.
yellow, a. amarillo.
yes, adv. sí.
yesterday, adv. ayer.
yet, adv. todavía, aún.
yield, v. producir; ceder.
yoke, n. yugo m.
yolk, n. yema f.
you, pron. usted, (pl.) ustedes; lo, la, los, las; le, les; (familiar) tú, (pl.) vosotros -as; ti; te, (pl.) os. **with y.,** contigo.
young, a. joven.
your, a. su; (familiar) tu; (pl.) vuestro.
yours, pron. suyo; (familiar) tuyo; (pl.) vuestro.
yourself, -selves, pron. sí; se; (familiar) ti; te. **with y.,** consigo; contigo. **you y.,** usted mismo, ustedes mismos; tú mismo, vosotros mismos.

youth, n. juventud f.; (person) joven m.
youthful, a. juvenil.
zap, v. desintegrar, aniquilar.
zeal, n. celo, fervor m.
zealous, a. celoso, fervoroso.
zero, n. cero m.
zest, n. gusto m.
zip code, n. número de distrito postal.
zone, n. zona f.
zoo, n. jardín zoológico.